S0-BDG-727

The American Vision

Individual and Collective Modes

The American Vision

Individual and Collective Modes

Rhoda B. Nathan and Judith S. Neaman
Hofstra University

Scott, Foresman and Company
Glenview, Illinois   London

Library of Congress Catalog Card Number: 72–82720
ISBN: 0–673–07714–4

Copyright © 1973 by Scott, Foresman and Company, Glenview, Illinois 60025.
Philippines Copyright 1973 by Scott, Foresman and Company.
All Rights Reserved.
Printed in the United States of America.

Regional offices of Scott, Foresman and Company are located in Dallas, Oakland,
N.J., Palo Alto, and Tucker, Ga.

Cover photo: Detail of the Mosaic or Honeycomb Quilt, ca. 1840, from the American Quilts Collection of The Art Institute of Chicago. The unfinished 68 x 75 inch quilt was a gift of Robert G. Robinson to The Art Institute of Chicago and is reproduced here in its original colors with the permission of The Art Institute of Chicago.

Acknowledgments

"The Theory of Democratic Collectivism" by Walter Lippmann from *The Good Society.* Copyright 1936, 1937, 1943 by Walter Lippmann. Reprinted by permission of Atlantic-Little, Brown and Company.

"Solidarity" by Herbert Marcuse from *An Essay on Liberation.* Copyright © 1969 by Herbert Marcuse. Reprinted by permission of Beacon Press.

The selection on pp. 36–42 is from *Elmer Gantry* by Sinclair Lewis, copyright 1927, by Harcourt Brace Jovanovich, Inc.; renewed, 1955, by Michael Lewis. Reprinted by permission of the publishers.

"Religion and Culture in Present-Day America" by Will Herberg from *Roman Catholicism and the American Way of Life,* ed. by T. T. McAvoy, copyright 1959. Reprinted by permission of the University of Notre Dame Press.

The material on pp. 59–64 is from *The Basic Writings of Sigmund Freud,* trans. and ed. by Dr. A. A. Brill. Copyright 1938 by Random House, Inc. Copyright renewed 1965 by Gioia Bernheim and Edmund R. Brill. Reprinted by permission.

"Instinct and the Unconscious" by Carl Jung from *The Collected Works of C. G. Jung,* ed. by G. Adler, M. Fordham, H. Read, trans. by R. F. C. Hull, volume 8, *The Structure and Dynamics of the Psyche* (copyright © 1960 and 1969 by Princeton University Press), pp. 129–138. Reprinted by permission of Princeton University Press.

The selection on pp. 70–73 is from *I Never Promised You a Rose Garden* by Hannah Green. Copyright © 1964 by Hannah Green. Reprinted by permission of Holt, Rinehart and Winston, Inc.

"The Hero and the God" by Joseph Campbell from *The Hero with a Thousand Faces* by Joseph Campbell, Bollingen Series XVII (copyright 1949 by Princeton University Press), pp. 30–40. Reprinted by permission of Princeton University Press.

"Joy Is the Prize: The Esalen Foundation" by Leo Litwak from *The New York Times Magazine*, 1967. Reprinted by permission of The Author and his agent, James Brown Associates, Inc. Copyright © 1967 by Leo Litwak.

"The War Between the Redskins and the Feds" by Vine Deloria, Jr. from *The New York Times Magazine*, Dec. 7, 1969. © 1969 by The New York Times Company. Reprinted by permission.

"Simplicio: 'I'd Rather Be in Puerto Rico' " by Oscar Lewis from *La Vida* by Oscar Lewis. Copyright © 1965, 1966 by Oscar Lewis. Reprinted by permission of Random House, Inc.

"Black Power: Its Need and Substance" by Stokely Carmichael from *Black Power* by Stokely Carmichael and Charles V. Hamilton. Copyright © 1967 by Stokely Carmichael and Charles V. Hamilton. Reprinted by permission of Random House, Inc.

"What Is the Battle?" by E. Merrill Root from *Collectivism on the Campus* by E. Merrill Root. Copyright 1955 by E. Merrill Root. Reprinted by permission of Devin-Adair Company, Publishers.

"What College Did to Me" by Robert Benchley from *Inside Benchley* by Robert Benchley. Copyright 1927 by Harper & Row, Publishers, Inc. Reprinted by permission of the publishers.

"What Business Is a University In?" by Irving Kristol from *The New York Times Magazine*, March 22, 1970. © 1970/'69/'71 by The New York Times Company. Reprinted by permission.

"Beyond New Leftism" by Steven Kelman reprinted from *Commentary* by permission; copyright © 1969 by the American Jewish Committee.

The selection on pp. 166–181 is from "Youth Revolt, the Future is Now," copyright © 1970 by Margaret Mead, as adapted by *The Saturday Review* taken from the chapter entitled "The Future: Prefigurative Cultures and Unknown Children" from *Culture and Commitment* by Margaret Mead. Reprinted by permission of Doubleday & Company, Inc.

"The Pump House Gang" by Tom Wolfe reprinted with the permission of Farrar, Straus & Giroux, Inc. from *The Pump House Gang* by Tom Wolfe, copyright © 1968 by Tom Wolfe, copyright © 1966 by the World Journal Tribune Corp.

"Rock Style: Defying the American Dream" by Sara Davidson from *Harper's Magazine*, July 1969. Reprinted by permission of Curtis Brown, Ltd. Copyright © 1969 by Harper's Magazine, Inc.

"On And On Mick's Orgy Rolls" by Albert Goldman from *The New York Times Magazine*, November 23, 1969. Copyright © 1969 by Albert Goldman. Reprinted by permission of The Sterling Lord Agency, Inc.

". . . Or 'A Whitewash of Jagger?' " by Albert Goldman from *New York Times Magazine*, January 3, 1971. Copyright © 1971 by Albert Goldman. Reprinted by permission of The Sterling Lord Agency, Inc.

"Oneida" by Mark Holloway from *Heavens on Earth* by Mark Holloway. Reprinted by permission of Howard Moorepark, Literary Agent.

"Open Land: Getting Back to the Communal Garden" by Sara Davidson from *Harper's Magazine*, June 1970. Reprinted by permission of Curtis Brown, Ltd. Copyright © 1970 by Harper's Magazine, Inc.

The selection on pp. 255–267 is from *Puritanism and the Wilderness: The Intellectual Significance of the New England Frontier, 1629–1700* by Peter Carroll (New York: Columbia University Press, 1969), pp. 1–25. Reprinted by permission of Columbia University Press.

"The Human Surplus" by Joseph Wood Krutch from *Human Nature and the Human Condition* by Joseph Wood Krutch. Copyright © 1959 by Joseph Wood Krutch. Reprinted by permission of Random House, Inc.

"Eco-Catastrophe!" by Paul R. Ehrlich. Copyright 1969 by Paul R. Ehrlich. Reprinted by permission.

The selection on pp. 314–323 is from *The Grapes of Wrath* by John Steinbeck. Copyright 1939, copyright © renewed 1967 by John Steinbeck. Reprinted by permission of The Viking Press, Inc.

"The Interior Castle" by Jean Stafford Reprinted with the permission of Farrar, Straus & Giroux, Inc. from *Children Are Bored on Sunday* by Jean Stafford, copyright 1946, 1953 by Jean Stafford. First published in *The Partisan Review*.

"Flammonde" by Edwin Arlington Robinson reprinted with permission of The Macmillan Company from *Collected Poems* by Edwin Arlington Robinson. Copyright 1916 by Edwin Arlington Robinson, renewed 1944 by Ruth Nivison.

"Mr. Flood's Party" by Edwin Arlington Robinson reprinted with permission of The Macmillan Company from *Collected Poems* by Edwin Arlington Robinson. Copyright 1921 by Edwin Arlington Robinson, renewed 1949 by Ruth Nivison.

"Desert Places" by Robert Frost from *The Poetry of Robert Frost* edited by Edward Connery Lathem. Copyright 1936 by Robert Frost. Copyright ©1964 by Lesley Frost Ballantine. Copyright ©1969 by Holt, Rinehart and Winston, Inc. Reprinted by permission of Holt, Rinehart and Winston, Inc.

"The Hollow Men" by T. S. Eliot from *Collected Poems 1909–1962* by T. S. Eliot, copyright 1936, by Harcourt Brace Jovanovich, Inc., copyright ©1963, 1964 by T. S. Eliot. Reprinted by permission of the publishers and Faber and Faber Ltd.

"Mind" by Richard Wilbur from *Things of This World,* ©1956, by Richard Wilbur. Reprinted by permission of Harcourt Brace Jovanovich, Inc.

The selection on pp. 356–361 is from the Introduction by James Chillman, Jr., in *Frederic Remington, Artist of the Old West* by Harold McCracken. Copyright 1947, by Harold McCracken. Reprinted by permission of J. B. Lippincott Company.

"Loren MacIver" by John I. H. Baur from *Loren MacIver/I. Rice Perreria* by John I. H. Baur. Published by the Whitney Museum of American Art, 1953.

The selection on pp. 372–377 is from *Jasper Johns: Prints Nineteen Sixty to Nineteen Seventy* by Richard S. Field, copyright 1970. Reprinted by permission of Praeger Publishers, Inc.

"American Self-Portrait" by Oliver W. Larkin from *Art and Life in America,* revised and enlarged edition, by Oliver W. Larkin. Copyright 1949, ©1960 by Oliver W. Larkin. Reprinted by permission of Holt, Rinehart and Winston, Inc.

Preface

The American Vision: Individual and Collective Modes explores the concepts of individual and collective action as they have been manifested in political and social movements, in literature, and in the arts in America. Although the ideologies of individualism and collectivism have always coexisted, there seems to be a growing trend toward collective action. The selections in this anthology, chosen from both fiction and nonfiction, from writings of the past and of the present, enable students to understand the development of these two major ideologies and to judge future trends.

The approach of this text makes it especially useful for American studies courses and their interdisciplinary majors in literature, history, and sociology. It is also appropriate for freshman composition courses; the selections in each section illustrate particular skills in composition or rhetoric, such as argumentation, documentation, description, and organization. Each part, consisting of introductory essays, readings, writing exercises, and questions for discussion, is a "package" of teaching materials for discussion and writing. In addition, students may use any of the sections as a nucleus for further reading in that subject area.

The text is divided into three parts. The first part, The Formation of the American Consciousness, concentrates on the areas of political theory, religion, and psychology. The second part, Diversity and Community, is more sociological in nature and focuses on ethnic groups, the campus, the young, communal living, and the environment. The third part, The Expression of the Self, includes fiction, poetry, and painting. Each part is followed by a number of suggested topics for student essays and a set of discussion questions based on programmed learning theory, graduated in difficulty and progressing from a limited topic to broad, interdisciplinary subjects. The writing topics are related to the readings and cover the major types of essays: the familiar, or expository, essay, the formal essay or critique, the descriptive essay, and the research paper. (A list of suggested research-paper subjects, with short bibliographies, is also provided.) The discussion questions concentrate on one particular section in each part and examine the ideas and themes in that section.

The readings within each section were chosen not only because they represent the concepts of individualism and collectivism, but also for their intrinsic interest. Each section includes both earlier and later writings, providing a clear understanding of the continuity of American thought and of the obvious relevance of the past to our present concerns. Introductory essays to each section discuss the historical development of the themes of the section, and, we hope, increase the students' awareness of the relations between the history, politics, literature, and culture of America.

Rhoda B. Nathan
Judith S. Neaman

Contents

Diversity and Community

The Expression of the Self: Literature and the Arts

The Arts: Sight and Insight   352

Photographs

Introduction

In an article in a recent issue of the *New York Times,* Dr. Rollo May, examining the myths of America, the ideals which a country creates for itself, noted that they are changing from myths of individualism to myths of collectivism. In order to understand the change that is taking place, we must examine both the past and the present of the American image. In the past, the impressions of Americans, based upon our early history, have not been those of surging crowds or of people with joined hands. Rather, they have been images of a single explorer in the wilderness, overwhelmed by the magnitude of Niagara, or of Caleb Bingham's trappers on the loneliness of the Missouri, or of the solitary pioneer woman recalling in her diary a dangerous "remove" to a desolate tract of land. Even in war memorials, those pieces of art most often commemorating group activity, George Washington stands at the head of his troops, or a single officer leads his men, his head and shoulders projecting just beyond their mass. The American activist, the pioneer, the principled individual, were all exceptional people, hence eccentrics, because they distinguished themselves from the mass. tinguished themselves from the mass.

The tendency to envision the hero as a loner, whether representative of an intellectual, political, or physical ideal, is not, of course, specifically American. The hero is an epic figure, and as such, both represents and surpasses the social ideal. Epics belong to periods of upheaval and formation; hence, they are found whenever and wherever a nation is undergoing a process of dynamic development and change. This was true of the classical heroes Achilles, Odysseus, and Aeneas, who epitomized Greek and Roman ideals, as well as of the medieval European heroes Roland, Charlemagne, and Siegfried, who embodied the national ethic of their countries. America was unique in the sense that it seemed to the first settlers a new wilderness utterly devoid of civilization. For this reason, the formative stages of American development seem more dramatic, since its early civilization arose from no internal centers. America has its epic heroes, and they represent both varied regional and national ideals. Our heroes are often mythic personifications of archetypes: Pecos Bill is the Hispano-American arch-cowboy; Davy Crockett the Anglo-Scottish frontiersman; and Jay Gatsby the Midwesterner's dream of the East Coast millionaire. Paul Bunyan is the lumberjack conqueror of the north woods, and the quintessential figure of the "noble scout" is Natty Bumppo, who, in Cooper's own words, "stands as a protest, on behalf of simplicity and perfect freedom, against encroaching law and order." Like Natty Bumppo, all of these heroes, literary and legendary, symbolize the triumph of the rugged but representative individual in a many-faceted society.

When a country becomes more settled geographically and legally, the nature of the epic changes as the underlying ideals change. There is less need for and less admiration of the rugged eccentric who lives by physical strength. The more civilized and apparently less threatening virtues of sharp wit and political skill are seen to be better suited to a crowded and formalized society. It was inevitable, therefore, that the New England Yankee should emerge as a focal figure, embodying American shrewdness, canniness, and know-how. Yankee aptitude was not merely a regional trait: it came to epitomize to all the world the intelligence of the low-keyed individualist, who was not flamboyant in personality as earlier heroes had been, but obviously capable and masterful. The archetypal Yankee, frequently an itinerant who lived by his wits, was to appear first as Yankee Hill, then as Seba Smith's Jack Downing, and finally, somewhat transformed but still recognizable, as Mark Twain's early folk heroes. The familiar elements of homespun frontier courage and independence were thus linked with a new element of wry humor to create still another heroic type.

It should be pointed out, however, that even epics, celebrating as they do the single effort or achievement in terms of skill, wit, or courage, offer a sense of mass collective action. Neither the concept of the exceptional individual—the hero—nor the concept of the mass stands alone, for one cannot exist without the other. The hero is only great by comparison with the masses. The people are only important because they are the base upon which the ideal of an emerging hero is built. Hence, although Americans cherish heroes, they also identify great events with mass movements, because fundamental to the American ideal is an unwavering faith in mass opportunity. The history of America bears endless evidence of the energy of its people in the many vigorous group thrusts dating from its earliest days: the westward expansion, the gold rush, the labor movement, to enumerate but a few. That the myth of the rugged individual was to emerge earlier than the myth of the mass was owing to the character of our earliest society. The first American settlers, having no tradition, no heritage, no status assigned to them by their past on these shores, had to achieve everything they did by themselves. At the same time, constituting the sole legal binding framework for their existence, was the knowledge they bore that they were from the very first committed to uphold the Mayflower Compact, which linked together collectively all individuals into a "civil body politic." In the strictest sense the American colonial was heir to two almost simultaneous sets of values transplanted from the Old World: the egalitarian and democratic way of life of the early Pilgrim settlers, with their congregational structure; and the aristocratic and enterprising attitudes of the somewhat later Puritan immigrants, with their strict dependence upon the individual Calvinist conscience.

The adopted American, St. John de Crèvecoeur, identified clearly both the heroic and popular tendencies when he wrote that "we are all animated with the spirit of industry which is unfettered and unrestrained, because each person works for himself." He illustrated this social theory by describing the manner in which the poor of Europe seem to regenerate themselves in America. The poor labor individually but the laws protect the fruits of their labor. "From whence proceed these laws? From our government. Whence the government? It is derived from the original genius and strong desire of the people, ratified and confirmed by the crown. This is the great chain which links us all. . . ." So the individual laborer reaps the reward of personal effort by grace of a collective law—a social contract promulgated by the mass.

Given the pluralism of American life and the great variety of groups which comprise the nation, collectivism is bound to constitute an intrinsic force in the history of the country. It is not surprising to find that groups themselves and apologists for group movements should count collectivism as one of the great positive forces in the formation of American life. The democratic ideal is founded upon a concept of mass opportunity and the equality of all individuals within the mass. From the beginning, the recognizable goals have been mass education, government for the people, and a system of mobile economic opportunity, all of which tend to perpetuate the potential for equality. In America, individual enterprise, public philanthropy, and centrally organized welfare systems live side by side. Out of the public approval of mass literacy, a concept imported by the Puritans and first implemented in their Dame Schools, arises the emphasis upon the equality of understanding and the expectation of economic melioration. Thus, each person, regardless of social status, starts out the educational equal of every other person.

In the political realm, there have been times in our nation's history when collectivism and individualism have worked together. Today, however, American youth tend to see the predominance of a single authority as an infringement upon the collective power of Americans. If this is true, it is certainly partly because they are proclaiming a new age of participatory democracy; hence they may be termed anti-aristocratic and anti-individualist. They speak for the power of the mass, not for the ascendancy of the individual. They proclaim: "We have no princes for whom we toil, starve, and bleed; we [could be] the most perfect society in the world." (Crèvecoeur) We may then conclude that in ages of rebellion when efforts are being made to restore or cede power to the people, the movements will be collective in nature and the myths will match them. In times of crisis, however, when the welfare of the nation itself is at stake, the people may cry out for strong personalities, for clearly identifiable individuals to lead them. Perhaps we shall discover that the myths will also change then.

The selections in this volume, chosen from various genres, represent a number of fields of interest in American life. Whenever possible, both individualist and collectivist positions appear, and whenever both trends have appeared from the inceptions of various disciplines in this country, they are represented so that the long tradition of both tendencies becomes apparent to the reader. We are often too present-minded, asserting the novelty of present-day thought out of mere ignorance of the past. From this collection should emerge a series of questions: What effect have individualist or collectivist modes of thought had upon each discipline? How have these two trends influenced the history of the nation? What are the historical, psychological, political, economic, and aesthetic bases of these two trends?

We hope that thoughtful readers will be stimulated to add their own questions and draw their own conclusions about the causes, the values, and the future of these underlying philosophical currents in American life and the part they play in forming the character of each individual American and of the collective nation.

Discussion-Instruction Exercises

The object of this anthology is to make students more aware of the identifying traits of collectivism and individualism and to encourage them to reflect independently upon the ramifications of the growing emphasis on collectivism in contemporary American society. For this reason, we are appending to each section a new type of apparatus based upon self-instruction techniques.

The instruction mirrors the organization of the book; it is both collective and individual. It may be used by the individual student as a guide to the development of large historical concepts or by the group as a background for both discussion and speculation. We hope that these sections will elicit from the students new ideas and will establish in their minds the complexity of relations between historical periods, philosophical persuasions, and the literatures which developed them and developed from them.

This instruction is a form of teaching in which students work by reasoning which is, at its best, inductive, to build from facts to concepts. The students first learn a fact and are immediately asked to employ this information by responding to a question which is based upon the integration of the material they have just learned. Whereas the learning in this type of instruction can often be tested by a single answer, the nature of the information imparted by the selections in this text is not best utilized by the stimulation of a single correct answer but, instead, by the encouragement of students to think in many ways about the reading matter and to reach certain independent conclusions.

We have felt that students will be able to think more productively if they focus attention on certain passages in the selections which will, in turn, direct attention to major issues in the section. Therefore, each section is preceded by a broad philosophical and social background sketch which touches upon the origins of the material included in the section. Each of the three parts of the book is followed by an inductive discussion which is based upon the material the student has learned from both the introductory essays and the selections.

Obviously, the students' ability to observe and to think profitably about the information and issues which appear in the selections will depend upon how acute they have been in observing the relevant information and upon how imaginative and ingenious they have been in selecting subtle and varied points of view.

To obtain the most benefit from the exercises, students should cover the answers with a sheet of paper, then read the question, answer it, and check their answers against the correct one given. Students can align their paper with the line above each answer, moving the paper down as they finish that question.

The Formation of the American Consciousness

Political Theory: One and Indivisible

The politics of this nation are firmly rooted in the protection and encouragement of the individual as well as the recognition of the collective will. Although the American version of the European Enlightenment was late in developing and suffered a lag in the transplanting, it absorbed a number of principles of that rational movement, principally a preference for a secular government which guaranteed the right of dissent, the right of free speech to reasonable men, and the imposition of restraints upon arbitrary rule. The founders of our republic were familiar with John Locke's position that political institutions arose as a result of social contracts among people. They adapted to their own government Montesquieu's theory, expressed in *The Spirit of the Laws,* that the government which works best to insure liberty is one whose powers are separated into the three branches of the executive, the legislative, and the judicial. Along with these guarantees of the rights of the individual, America took from the European Enlightenment the seed of collective egalitarianism, and, nourished by the democratic climate of the New World, it developed into the deep concern for the united will of the majority expressed in our Constitution.

In the second half of the twentieth century, we have arrived at a crisis of polarization between two political units, the individual and the people. The new mode of political thought appears to be entirely based on collective power, not on the traditional power of the majority but rather on the collectively asserted powers of separately constituted minority groups who claim to constitute a real majority in terms of shared numbers and goals and common aspirations. Hence the revitalized Jeffersonianism in today's politics, which is construed as the power of any group to will a change in government through popular action when that government is no longer responsive to the mandate of its constituents. The new collectivists constitute an articulate and activist force in American political life. They are more interested in changing this society collectively than living within it as individuals. They have a real revulsion toward liberalism, which they consider to be ineffective and archaic. They are not averse to violence in the service of change. They share an ideological anti-Americanism which derives from their conviction that American society has conspired in their oppression. They identify with the "third world" of authoritarian Communism. They flirt with the notion of a "fourth party" since the existing three parties do not represent the collective will of all the minority groups, among which are numbered women's liberation, the New Left, student power groups, homosexual political societies, as well as the various ethnic minorities.

What of the individual and his or her role in American political life today? The American Revolution did not after all produce a level, homogenized mass as did the later Marxist revolutions. In the political writing of the founding fathers, all the stipulations provide for the maintenance of individual opportunity and the protection of individual differences. Although, in the words of the Revolutionary writer Jonathan Boucher, "it is laid down that the end of government is the common good of mankind" under the mandate of a "compact of the people," this philosophical basis was never intended to be construed as an infringement upon the rights of the individual. In the nineteenth century Emerson celebrated the "new importance given to the individual" as a sign of his time, "also marked by an analogous political movement." He deplored the fact that for the most part the men of his world were "bugs" and "spawn," were called "the mass and the herd," but placed his confidence in the handful of individuals who would attain full stature and leave their imprint upon the political and social times in which they lived.

The politics of today have undergone a profound change from the optimistic individualism so characteristic of the nineteenth century in general. One may seriously question the individual's right to the pursuit of happiness in the face of the overriding welfare of the mass. If the concerted will of the group can bring about a change in the economic and political fortunes of that group, then increasingly the rights of the lone citizen are considered to be more and more expendable in the face of the total good. Much of the current political change is the direct result of the politics of confrontation with its collective power slogans preempting the more leisurely processes of change with their built-in guarantees for the protection of the individual. From this new political style there derives a new conformity, a reaching out to the extremes of the interpretation of democratization, a system in which large sweeping social gains must necessarily be callous to the plight of the single citizen.

An interesting realignment of political party organization in terms of the collective and the individual has occurred within recent years. If any one party in our political history could have been identified with the collective, it has been the Democratic party, which numbered among its loyal membership the unions and the large blocs of the working classes in general. The Republican party has always been the party of the individual, the entrepreneur, the person of property. In terms of the new collectivism, which has occurred on the right as well as the left, the working classes, the union organizations, the collective "hard hats," have now lent their support to the former party of the privileged individual. On the other hand, the Democratic party is now the last bastion of the lone left-over liberal of the thirties, clinging to a wan belief in the ability of the person of good will and conscience to effect a gradual liberalizing change in the political climate of this country, in the manner of an Adlai Stevenson of a decade ago. It is difficult to believe at this moment that in 1949 Lionel Trilling wrote in *The Liberal Imagination:* "In the United States at this time liberalism is not only the dominant, but even the sole intellectual tradition. For it is the plain fact that nowadays there are no conservative or reactionary ideas in circulation." Since that time we have seen in America a gradual emergence of both the radical and the conservative in politics, accompanied by a proportionate diminution of the liberal as the other two create a polarization of the extremes.

For the most part, the newly formed groups coming out of the inner cities, the campuses, the sexual minorities, are engaged in a "coalition politics" outside of the formal party structures; these groups count on "participatory democracy" to effect radical change. The utopian concepts which permeate Herbert Marcuse's visions of the political future point toward the well-being of the group in a semi-welfare state to be created through revolutionary measures. Demonstrations, direct action, and combative confrontation are the tools that will be utilized in urgent reform movements for which the ordinary democratic process is too slow and unwieldy. To effect this kind of radical change, the individual is powerless. Buildings cannot be seized by individuals, nor can institutions be "liberated" by the individual activist. The individual act of conscience in the flouting of the law is morally uplifting but politically impotent. The groups who favor collective action today believe that only the unified action of masses of people who are politically intent upon change can effect that change in a time of political revolution.

The tension in American politics brings thoughtful observers to a recognition of the impasse created by our native character and our heritage of individualism. Philip Slater, a sociologist at Brandeis University, has written a book called *American Culture at the Breaking Point*. In it he examines our untrammeled tradition of individualism, which prevents our dealing with the necessary processes inherent to social change. His major thesis is the exploration of the pull between the "ambivalent individualism, which prevents our dealing with the necessary processes inherent in social change. His major thesis is the exploration of the pull between the "ambivalent indithe need for the "new politics" of apocalypse but cannot bring himself to yield to the collective will because of its commitment to radical activism. Instead, he sees a solution in an alliance between the liberal and radical, the individual and the collective, to bring about social change and still keep control over the political process. Increasingly, this point of view seems to be the acceptable compromise, the attempt, in the best idealistic, even Emersonian, tradition, to reconcile the New Left with the Old Liberal, to produce a framework for social change through a politically viable structure, from which a "fourth party" might emerge as a fusion of traditional liberal individualism and the new mass politics.

Thomas Jefferson

First Inaugural Address

MARCH 4, 1801

Friends and Fellow Citizens: Called upon to undertake the duties of the first executive office of our country, I avail myself of the presence of that portion of my fellow citizens which is here assembled, to express my grateful thanks for the favor with which they have been pleased to look toward me, to declare a sincere consciousness that the task is above my talents, and that I approach it with those anxious and awful presentiments which the greatness of the charge and the weakness of my powers so justly inspire. A rising nation, spread over a wide and fruitful land, traversing all the seas with the rich productions of their industry, engaged in commerce with nations who feel power and forget right, advancing rapidly to destinies beyond the reach of mortal eye—when I contemplate these transcendent objects, and see the honor, the happiness, and the hopes of this beloved country committed to the issue and the auspices of this day, I shrink from the contemplation, and humble myself before the magnitude of the undertaking. Utterly indeed, should I despair, did not the presence of many whom I here see remind me, that in the other high authorities provided by our constitution, I shall find resources of wisdom, of virtue, and of zeal, on which to rely under all difficulties. To you, then, gentlemen, who are charged with the sovereign functions of legislation, and to those associated with you, I look with encouragement for that guidance and support which may enable us to steer with safety the vessel in which we are all embarked amid the conflicting elements of a troubled world.

During the contest of opinion through which we have passed, the animation of discussion and of exertions has sometimes worn an aspect which might impose on strangers unused to think freely and to speak and to write what they think; but this being now decided by the voice of the nation, announced according to the rules of the constitution, all will, of course, arrange themselves under the will of the law, and unite in common efforts for the common good. All, too, will bear in mind this sacred principle, that though the will of the majority is in all cases to prevail, that will, to be rightful, must be reasonable; that the minority possess their equal rights, which equal laws must protect, and to violate which would be oppression. Let us, then, fellowcitizens, unite with one heart and one mind. Let us restore to social intercourse that harmony and affection without which liberty and even life itself are but dreary things. And let us reflect that having banished from our land that religious intolerance under which mankind so long bled and suffered, we have yet gained little if we countenance a political intolerance as despotic, as wicked, and capable of as bitter and bloody persecutions. During the throes and convulsions of the ancient world, during the agonizing spasms of infuriated man, seeking through blood and slaughter his long-lost liberty, it was not wonderful that the agitation of the billows should reach even this distant and peaceful shore; that this should be more felt and feared by some and less by others; that this should divide opinions as to measures of safety. But every difference of opinion is not a difference of principle. We have called by different names brethren of the same principle. We are all republicans—we are federalists. If there be any among us who would wish to dissolve this Union or to change its republican form, let them stand undisturbed as monuments of the safety with which error of opinion may be tolerated where reason is left free to combat it. I know, indeed, that some honest men fear that a republican government cannot be strong; that this government is not strong enough. But would the honest patriot, in the full tide of successful experiment, abandon a government which has so far kept us free and firm, on the theoretic and visionary fear that this government, the world's best hope, may by possibility want energy to preserve itself? I trust not. I believe this, on the contrary, the strongest government on earth. I believe it is the only one where every man, at the call of the laws, would fly to the standard of the law, and would meet invasions of the public order as his own personal concern. Sometimes it is said that man cannot be trusted with the government of himself. Can he, then, be trusted with the government of others? Or have we found angels in the forms of kings to govern him? Let history answer this question.

Let us, then, with courage and confidence pursue our own federal and republican principles, our attachment to our union and representative government. Kindly separated by nature and a wide ocean from the exterminating havoc of one quarter of the globe; too high-minded to endure the degradations of the others; possessing a chosen country, with room enough for our descendants to the hundredth and thousandth generation; entertaining a due sense of our equal right to the use of our own faculties, to the acquisitions of our industry, to honor and confidence from our fellow citizens, resulting not from birth but from our actions and their sense of them; enlightened by a benign religion, professed, indeed, and practiced in various forms, yet all of them including honesty, truth, temperance, gratitude, and the love of man; acknowledging and adoring an overruling Providence, which by all its dispensations proves that it delights in the happiness of man here and his greater happiness hereafter; with all these blessings, what more is necessary to make us a happy and prosperous people? Still one thing more, fellow citizens—a wise and frugal government, which shall restrain men from injuring one another, which shall leave them otherwise free to regulate their own pursuits of industry and improvement, and shall not take from the mouth of labor the bread it has earned. This is the sum of good government, and this is necessary to close the circle of our felicities.

About to enter, fellow citizens, on the exercise of duties which comprehend everything dear and valuable to you, it is proper that you should understand what I deem the essential principles of our government, and consequently those which ought to shape its administration. I will compress them within the narrowest compass they will bear, stating the general principle, but not all its limitations. Equal and exact justice to all men, of whatever state or persuasion, religious or political; peace, commerce, and honest friendship with all nations—entangling alliances with none; the support of the State governments in all their rights, as the most competent administrations for our domestic concerns and the surest bulwarks against antirepublican tendencies; the preservation of the general government in its whole constitutional vigor, as the sheet anchor of our peace at home and safety abroad; a jealous care of the right of election by the people—a mild and safe corrective of abuses which are lopped by the sword of the revolution where peaceable remedies are unprovided; absolute acquiescence in the decisions of the majority—the vital principle of republics, from which there is no appeal but to force, the vital principle and immediate parent of despotism; a well-disciplined militia—our best reliance in peace and for the first moments of war, till regulars may relieve them; the supremacy of the civil over the military authority; economy in the public expense, that labor may be lightly burdened; the honest payment of our debts and sacred preservation of the public faith; encouragement of agriculture, and of commerce as its handmaid; the diffusion of information and the arraignment of all abuses at the bar of public reason; freedom of religion; freedom of the press; freedom of person under the protection of the *habeas corpus;* and trial by juries impartially selected—these principles form the bright constellation which has gone before us, and guided our steps through an age of revolution and reformation. The wisdom of our sages and the blood of our heroes have been devoted to their attainment. They should be the creed of our political faith—the text of civil instruction—the touchstone by which to try the services of those we trust; and should we wander from them in moments of error or alarm, let us hasten to retrace our steps and to regain the road which alone leads to peace, liberty, and safety.

I repair, then, fellow citizens, to the post you have assigned me. With experience enough in subordinate offices to have seen the difficulties of this, the greatest of all, I have learned to expect that it will rarely fall to the lot of imperfect man to retire from this station with the reputation and the favor which bring him into it. Without pretensions to that high confidence reposed in our first and great revolutionary character, whose preëminent services had entitled him to the first place in his country's love, and destined for him the fairest page in the volume of faithful history, I ask so much confidence only as may give firmness and effect to the legal administration of your affairs. I shall often go wrong through defect of judgment. When right, I shall often be thought wrong by those whose positions will not command a view of the whole ground. I ask your indulgence for my own errors, which will never be intentional; and your support against the errors of others, who may condemn what they would not if seen in all its parts. The approbation implied by your suffrage is a consolation to me for the past; and my future solicitude will be to retain the good opinion of those who have bestowed it in advance, to conciliate that of others by doing them all the good in my power, and to be instrumental to the happiness and freedom of all.

Relying, then, on the patronage of your good will, I advance with obedience to the work, ready to retire from it whenever you become sensible how much better choice it is in your power to make. And may that Infinite Power which rules the destinies of the universe, lead our councils to what is best, and give them a favorable issue for your peace and prosperity.

Fisher Ames
The Dangers of American Liberty

The political sphere, like the globe we tread upon, never stands still, but with a silent swiftness accomplishes the revolutions which, we are too ready to believe, are effected by our wisdom, or might have been controlled by our efforts. There is a kind of fatality in the affairs of republics that eludes the foresight of the wise as much as it frustrates the toils and sacrifices of the patriot and the hero. Events proceed, not as they were expected or intended, but as they are impelled by the irresistible laws of our political existence. Things inevitable happen, and we are astonished, as if they were miracles, and the course of nature had been overpowered or suspended to produce them. Hence it is that, till lately, more than half our countrymen believed our public tranquillity was firmly established, and that our liberty did not merely rest upon dry land, but was wedged, or rather rooted high above the flood in the rocks of granite, as immovably as the pillars that prop the universe. They, or at least the discerning of them, are at length no less disappointed than terrified to perceive that we have all the time floated, with a fearless and unregarded course, down the stream of events, till we are now visibly drawn within the revolutionary suction of Niagara, and every thing that is liberty will be dashed to pieces in the descent.

We have been accustomed to consider the pretension of Englishmen to be free as a proof how completely they were broken to subjection, or hardened in imposture. We have insisted, that they had no constitution, because they never made one; and that their boasted government, which is just what time and accident have made it, was palsied with age, and blue with the plague-sores of corruption. We have believed that it derived its stability, not from reason, but from prejudice; that it is supported, not because it is favorable to liberty, but as it is dear to national pride; that it is reverenced, not for its excellence, but because ignorance is naturally the idolater of antiquity; that it is not sound and healthful, but derives a morbid energy from disease, and an unaccountable aliment from the canker that corrodes its vitals.

But we maintained that the federal Constitution, with all the bloom of youth and splendor of innocence, was gifted with immortality. For if time should impair its force, or faction tarnish its charms, the people, ever vigilant to discern its wants, ever powerful to provide for them, would miraculously restore it to the field, like some wounded hero of the epic, to take a signal vengeance on its enemies, or like Antæus, invigorated by touching his mother earth, to rise the stronger for a fall.

There is of course a large portion of our citizens who will not believe, even on the evidence of facts, that any public evils exist, or are impending. They deride the apprehensions of those who foresee that licentiousness will prove, as it ever has proved, fatal to liberty. They consider her as a nymph, who need not be coy to keep herself pure, but that on the contrary, her chastity will grow robust by frequent scuffles with her seducers. They say, while a faction is a minority it will remain harmless by being outvoted; and if it should become a majority, all its acts, however profligate or violent, are then legitimate. For with the democrats the people is a sovereign who can do no wrong, even when he respects and spares no existing right, and whose voice, however obtained or however counterfeited, bears all the sanctity and all the force of a living divinity. . . .

They are certainly blind who do not see that we are descending from a supposed orderly and stable republican government into a licentious democracy, with a progress that baffles all means to resist, and scarcely leaves leisure to deplore its celerity. The institutions and the hopes that Washington raised are nearly prostrate; and his name and memory would perish, if the rage of his enemies had any power over history. But they have not—history will give scope to her vengeance, and posterity will not be defrauded.

But if our experience had not clearly given warning of our approaching catastrophe, the very nature of democracy would inevitably produce it.

A government by the passions of the multitude, or, no less correctly, according to the vices and ambition of their leaders, is a democracy. We have heard so long of the indefeasible sovereignty of the people, and have admitted so many specious theories of the rights of man, which are contradicted by his nature and experience, that few will dread at all, and fewer still will dread as they ought, the evils of an

American democracy. They will not believe them near, or they will think them tolerable or temporary. Fatal delusion!

When it is said, there may be a tyranny of the *many* as well as of the *few,* every democrat will yield at least a cold and speculative assent; but he will at all times act, as if it were a thing incomprehensible, that there should be any evil to be apprehended in the uncontrolled power of the people. He will say arbitrary power may make a tyrant, but how can it make its possessor a slave?

In the first place, let it be remarked, the power of individuals is a very different thing from their liberty. When I vote for the man I prefer, he may happen not to be chosen; or he may disappoint my expectations if he is; or he may be outvoted by others in the public body to which he is elected. I may then hold and exercise all the power that a citizen can have or enjoy, and yet such laws may be made and such abuses allowed as shall deprive me of all liberty. I may be tried by a jury, and that jury may be culled and picked out from my political enemies by a federal marshal. Of course, my life and liberty may depend on the good pleasure of the man who appoints that marshal. I may be assessed arbitrarily for my faculty, or upon conjectural estimation of my property, so that all I have shall be at the control of the government, whenever its displeasure shall exact the sacrifice. I may be told that I am a federalist, and as such bound to submit, in all cases whatsoever, to the will of the majority, as the ruling faction ever pretend to be. My submission may be tested by my resisting or obeying commands that will involve me in disgrace, or drive me to despair. I may become a fugitive, because the ruling party have made me afraid to stay at home; or, perhaps, while I remain at home, they may, nevertheless, think fit to inscribe my name on the list of emigrants and proscribed persons.

All this was done in France, and many of the admirers of French examples are impatient to imitate them. . . .

The people, as a body, cannot deliberate. Nevertheless, they will feel an irresistible impulse to act, and their resolutions will be dictated to them by their demagogues. The consciousness, or the opinion, that they possess the supreme power, will inspire inordinate passions; and the violent men, who are the most forward to gratify those passions, will be their favorites. What is called the government of the people is in fact too often the arbitrary power of such men. Here, then, we have the faithful portrait of democracy. What avails the boasted power of individual citizens? or of what value is the will of the majority, if that will is dictated by a committee of demagogues, and law and right are in fact at the mercy of a victorious faction? To make a nation free, the crafty must be kept in awe, and the violent in restraint. The weak and the simple find their liberty arise not from their own individual sovereignty, but from the power of law and justice over all. It is only by the due restraint of others, that I am free.

Popular sovereignty is scarcely less beneficent than awful, when it resides in their courts of justice; there its office, like a sort of human providence, is to warn, enlighten, and protect; when the people are inflamed to seize and exercise it in their assemblies, it is competent only to kill and destroy. Temperate liberty is like the dew, as it falls unseen from its own heaven; constant without excess, it finds vegetation thirsting for its refreshment, and imparts to it the vigor to take more. All nature, moistened with blessings, sparkles in the morning ray. But democracy is a water-spout that bursts from the clouds, and lays the ravaged earth bare to its rocky foundations. The labors of man lie whelmed with his hopes beneath masses of ruin, that bury not only the dead but their monuments.

It is the almost universal mistake of our country men, that democracy would be mild and safe in America. They charge the horrid excesses of France not so much to human nature, which will never act better, when the restraints of government, morals, and religion are thrown off, but to the characteristic cruelty and wickedness of Frenchmen.

The truth is, and let it humble our pride, the most ferocious of all animals, when his passions are roused to fury and are uncontrolled, is man; and of all governments, the worst is that which never fails to excite, but was never found to restrain those passions, that is, democracy. It is an illuminated hell, that in the midst of remorse, horror, and torture, rings with festivity; for experience shows, that one joy remains to this most malignant description of the damned, the power to make others wretched. When a man looks round and sees his neighbors mild and merciful, he cannot feel afraid of the abuse of their power over him; and surely if they oppress me, he will say, they will spare their own liberty, for that is dear to all mankind. It is so. The human heart is so constituted, that a man loves liberty as naturally as himself. Yet liberty is a rare thing in the world, though the love of it is so universal.

Walter Lippmann

The Theory of Democratic Collectivism

In countries like Great Britain or the United States there is no manifest disposition to establish a totalitarian order with a regimented population under a militarized autocracy, but for some sixty years these democracies have tended increasingly to seek relief from poverty and disorder by the use of collectivist measures.[1] In fact it may be said that contemporary progressives are gradual collectivists and that they hope by the gradualness of their methods to avoid the violence of dictatorship.

Those who hold this view are at present the overwhelming majority of public-spirited and well-disposed persons in the democratic countries. They are not fanatics who, in order to achieve a planned society, would be willing to sweep away the guaranties of liberty and the responsibility of rulers to the people. Their goal is the public administration of the economy, but they believe that no step must be taken to that goal without popular consent obtained by persuasion in open debate. They hold that in this way the advance into collectivism can be made without class struggle, dictatorship, or the militarization of society.

1. A. V. Dicey . . . says that "English legislative opinion has from about 1870 onwards given a doubtful, if not a negative reply" to the question whether "the evils which bring ruin on a commonwealth" can be cured by "the systematic extension of individual freedom and the removal of every kind of oppression."

For approximately three generations a gradual democratic advance into collectivism has been under way. This movement also has its ideology. But here again, as with the fascists and the communists, the theory is very different from the practice and the results are very different from the promises.

The theory of gradual collectivism rests upon the assumption that majorities express the will and represent the interests of society, and that they have inherited from the king the prerogatives of his sovereignty. The gradual collectivist believes in the absolutism of the majority, having by a fiction identified the mandates of transient majorities with the enduring and diverse purposes of the members of a community. He thinks it absurd that a few oligarchs in the Kremlin or demagogic dictators in Berlin or Rome should pretend that their personal decisions are the comprehensive purposes of great nations. Yet the gradual collectivist, under the banner of popular sovereignty, believes in the dictatorship of random aggregations of voters. In this theory the individual has no rights as against the majority, for constitutional checks and bills of rights exist only by consent of the majority. Even the right of the majority to rule is at the mercy of any passing majority. For there is nothing in the doctrine of the sovereignty of the majority to preclude the abolition of majority rule by vote of a majority. In fact it was under the aegis of this doctrine that Napoleon III and Hitler came to power.

Thus by one fiction the gradual collectivist identifies passing majorities with the nation. By another fiction he treats the legislators as representative of the majorities which elected them. And finally, by a third fiction he pretends that the executive and administrative machine represents the will of a majority of the legislators. The nation is supposed to have delegated its unlimited authority to a majority of the enfranchised voters. They are supposed to have delegated their unlimited authority to a majority in the legislative assembly. The assembly is supposed to have delegated its unlimited authority to the executive and the bureaucracy. To this central authority the gradual collectivist then proposes to entrust increasingly the administration of the social system.

It is evident that a regime of this sort is afflicted with an insoluble contradiction. In so far as it seeks to administer the economy under a rational and coherent plan, it must somehow prevent one majority from overriding the decisions of a previous majority. For if a plan is to be carried out, it must be adopted and the people must thereafter conform. If they do not conform, if they are free at any time to agitate for amendments, the plan ceases to be a plan. It would not be a plan if its parts were not closely interrelated; if it is subject to continual change at vital points, the whole design has to be remade continually. Suppose, for example, that the Russian people had had a democratic control over the Five-Year Plan, and that, having assented at the outset to the proposal that they manufacture steel before they manufactured clothing, they had changed their minds. They would not have amended the plan: they would have abolished it. It would have been necessary to draft a wholly different plan, and two years after the new plan had been put into effect the people might again have changed their minds. This would have called for still a different plan. But a series of different plans would be no plan at all.

The very essence of the democratic process is that the rulers are continually responsible to popular opinion, and unless that opinion is free to change, and in changing to alter the policy of the state, there is no democracy. The very essence of the conception of planning is that a design can be adopted to which the people will thereafter conform. That is equivalent to saying that a democratic people cannot have a planned economy, and that in so far as they desire a planned economy they must suspend responsible government.

Yet men of unimpeachable loyalty to democratic ideals are currently expounding the idea that the plan of an ordered society can be drawn up, that the people can be converted to it by agitation and propaganda, and that after the people have ratified it, the plan can be executed. Here, for example, is Professor Beard's idea of how, with "the approval, consent, acquiescence, knowledge and coöperation"[2] of the people, a planned and administered society can be established in the United States. He would create "a single national authority with two divisions: (1) a division charged with the responsibility of fixing a national standard-of-life budget with quantities, qualities, and specifications expressed in the most exact and scientific terms; (2) a division of production specialists empowered to show in how far, and by what methods, the resources and industrial arts of the United States can supply the requisite goods and materials." This national authority would produce a report, "with maps, pictures and other forms of graphic presentation," which would be "the most stupendous and superb presentation of accomplishments, possibilities and projects ever made in the whole history of civilization." Representatives of interests opposed to the plan would be invited to state their objections. "Thus would be disclosed the chief interests and methods standing in the path of realization" and "in this open way would be made clearer the measures and practical steps necessary to proceed with the program." The President would then present the report to the nation by messages, addresses, and radio. There would be an intensive campaign of propaganda. After that the report "would be made the prime document of policy to which all partial measures would be referred for consideration and testing." This "program for America would give direction to public education, now so rudderless."

Thus by unremitting government propaganda a way of life worked out by a government bureau would be inculcated upon the people. Once converted, they would presumably grant to the government all power necessary to carry out the plan. The report, says Mr. Beard, "would be made the prime document of policy." It is not clear who is to establish the primacy of the document. It is not clear what is to happen if the people change their minds about the national standard-of-life budget as drawn up by the national authority. It is not clear whether they would have the right to give up the plan or are supposed to surrender their right to change it. This is the insoluble contradiction of the gradual collectivist. For unless we are to suppose that the initial ballyhoo is to settle the issue, either the national authority will be in a perpetual state of confusion, like a man who might lay down the keel for a boat and is then told he must make it into a wagon, or the people, having once accepted the report, will have to be drilled unceasingly by a stupendous propaganda to keep them from changing their minds, and, the government having become deeply committed to the report, vested interests having been created, the dissenter would have to be treated as antisocial and unpatriotic.

2. Charles A. Beard, *The Open Door at Home*, pp. 311-13.

Herbert Marcuse
Solidarity

The preceding attempt to analyze the present opposition to the society organized by corporate capitalism was focused on the striking contrast between the radical and total character of the rebellion on the one hand, and the absence of a class basis for this radicalism on the other. This situation gives all efforts to evaluate and even discuss the prospects for radical change in the domain of corporate capitalism their abstract, academic, unreal character. The search for specific historical agents of revolutionary change in the advanced capitalist countries is indeed meaningless. Revolutionary forces emerge in the process of change itself; the translation of the potential into the actual is the work of political practice. And just as little as critical theory can political practice orient itself on a concept of revolution which belongs to the nineteenth and early twentieth century, and which is still valid in large areas of the Third World. This concept envisages the "seizure of power" in the course of a mass upheaval, led by a revolutionary party acting as the avant-garde of a revolutionary class and setting up a new central power which would initiate the basic social changes. Even in industrial countries where a strong Marxist party has organized the exploited masses, strategy is no longer guided by this notion—witness the long-range Communist policy of "popular fronts." And the concept is altogether inapplicable to those countries in which the integration of the working class is the result of structural economic-political processes (sustained high productivity; large markets; neo-colonialism; administered democracy) and where the masses themselves are forces of conservatism and stabilization. It is the very power of this society which contains new modes and dimensions of radical change.

The dynamic of this society has long since passed the stage where it could grow on its own resources, its own market, and on normal trade with other areas. It has grown into an imperialist power which, through economic and technical penetration and outright military intervention, has transformed large parts of the Third World into dependencies. Its policy is distinguished from classical imperialism of the preceding period by effective use of economic and technical conquests on the one hand, and by the political-strategic character of intervention on the other: the requirements of the global fight against communism supersede those of profitable investments. In any case, by virtue of the evolution of imperialism, the developments in the Third World pertain to the dynamic of the First World, and the forces of change in the former are not extraneous to the latter; the "external proletariat" is a basic factor of potential change within the dominion of corporate capitalism. Here is the coincidence of the historical factors of revolution: this predominantly agrarian proletariat endures the dual oppression exercised by the indigenous ruling classes and those of the foreign metropoles. A liberal bourgeoisie which would ally itself with the poor and lead their struggle does not exist. Kept in abject material and mental privation, they depend on a militant leadership. Since the vast majority outside the cities is unable to mount any concerted economic and political action which would threaten the existing society, the struggle for liberation will be a predominantly military one, carried out with the support of the local population, and exploiting the advantages of a terrain which impedes traditional methods of suppression. These circumstances, of necessity, make for guerrilla warfare. It is the great chance, and at the same time the terrible danger, for the forces of liberation. The powers that be will not tolerate a repetition of the Cuban example; they will employ ever more effective means and weapons of suppression, and the indigenous dictatorships will be strengthened with the ever more active aid from the imperialist metropoles. It would be romanticism to underrate the strength of this deadly alliance and its resolution to contain subversion. It seems that not the features of the terrain, nor the unimaginable resistance of the men and women of Vietnam, nor considerations of "world opinion," but fear of the other nuclear powers has so far prevented the use of nuclear or semi-nuclear weapons against a whole people and a whole country.

Under these circumstances, the preconditions for the liberation and development of the Third World must emerge in the advanced capitalist countries. Only the internal weakening of the superpower can finally stop the financing and equipping of suppression in the backward countries. The National Liberation Fronts threaten the life line of imperialism; they are not only a material but also an ideological catalyst of change. The Cuban revolution and the Viet Cong have demonstrated: it can be done; there is a morality, a humanity, a will, and a faith which can resist and deter the gigantic technical and economic force of capitalist expansion. More than the "socialist humanism" of the early Marx, this violent solidarity in defense, this elemental socialism in action, has given form and substance to the radicalism of the New Left; in this ideological respect too, the external revolution has become an essential part of the opposition within the capitalist metropoles. However, the exemplary force, the ideological power of the external revolution, can come to fruition only if the internal structure and cohesion of the capitalist system begin to disintegrate. The chain of exploitation must break at its strongest link.

Corporate capitalism is not immune against economic crisis. The huge "defense" sector of the economy not only places an increasingly heavy burden on the taxpayer, it also is largely responsible for the narrowing margin of profit. The growing opposition against the war in Vietnam points up the necessity of a thorough conversion of the economy, risking the danger of rising unemployment, which is a by-product of technical progress in automation. The "peaceful" creation of additional outlets for the productivity of the metropoles would meet with the intensified resistance in the Third World, and with the contesting and competitive strength of the Soviet orbit. The absorption of unemployment and the maintenance of an adequate rate of profit would thus require the stimulation of demand on an ever larger scale, thereby stimulating the rat race of the competitive struggle for existence through the multiplication of waste, planned obsolescence, parasitic and stupid jobs and services. The higher standard of living, propelled by the growing parasitic sector of the economy, would drive wage demands toward capital's point of no return. But the structural tendencies which determine the development of corporate capitalism do not justify the assumption that aggravated class struggles would terminate in a socialist revolution through organized political action. To be sure, even the most advanced capitalist welfare state remains a class society and therefore a state of conflicting class interests. However, prior to the disintegration of the state power, the apparatus and the suppressive force of the system would keep the class struggle within the capitalist framework. The translation of the economic into the radical political struggle would be the consequence rather than the cause of change. The change itself could then occur in a general, unstructured, unorganized, and diffused process of disintegration. This process may be sparked by a crisis of the system which would activate the resistance not only against the political but also against the mental repression imposed by the society. Its insane features, expression of the ever more blatant contradiction between the available resources for liberation and their use for the perpetuation of servitude, would undermine the daily routine, the repressive conformity, and rationality required for the continued functioning of the society.

The dissolution of social morality may manifest itself in a collapse of work discipline, slowdown, spread of disobedience to rules and regulations, wildcat strikes, boycotts, sabotage, gratuitous acts of noncompliance. The violence built into the system of repression may get out of control, or necessitate ever more totalitarian controls.

Even the most totalitarian technocratic-political administration depends, for its functioning, on what is usually called the "moral fiber": a (relatively) "positive" attitude among the underlying population toward the usefulness of their work and toward the necessity of the repressions exacted by the social organization of work. A society depends on the relatively stable and calculable sanity of the people, sanity defined as the regular, socially coordinated functioning of mind and body—especially at work, in the shops and offices, but also at leisure and fun. Moreover, a society also demands to a considerable extent, belief in one's beliefs (which is part of the required sanity); belief in the operative value of society's values. Operationalism is indeed an indispensable supplement to want and fear as forces of cohesion.

Now it is the strength of this moral fiber, of the operational values (quite apart from their ideational validity), which is likely to wear off under the impact of the growing contradictions within the society. The result would be a spread, not only of discontent and mental sickness, but also of inefficiency, resistance to work, refusal to perform, negligence, indifference—factors of dysfunction which would hit a highly centralized and coordinated apparatus, where breakdown at one point may easily affect large sections of the whole. To be sure, these are subjective factors, but they may assume material force in conjunction with the objective economic and political strains to which the system will be exposed on a global scale. Then, and only then, that political climate would prevail which could provide a mass basis for the new forms of organization required for directing the struggle.

We have indicated the tendencies which threaten the stability of the imperialist society and emphasized the extent to which the liberation movements in the Third World affect the prospective development of this society. It is to an even greater extent affected by the dynamic of "peaceful coexistence" with the old socialist societies, the Soviet orbit. In important aspects, this coexistence has contributed to the stabilization of capitalism: "world communism" has been the Enemy who would have to be invented if he did not exist—the Enemy whose strength justified the "defense economy" and the mobilization of the people in the national interest. Moreover, as the common Enemy of *all* capitalism, communism promoted the organization of a common interest superseding the intercapitalist differences and conflicts. Last but not least, the opposition within the advanced capitalist countries has been seriously weakened by the repressive Stalinist development of socialism, which made socialism not exactly an attractive alternative to capitalism.

More recently, the break in the unity of the communist orbit, the triumph of the Cuban revolution, Vietnam, and the "cultural revolution" in China have changed this picture. The possibility of constructing socialism on a truly popular base, without the Stalinist bureaucratization and the danger of a nuclear war as the imperialist answer to the emergence of this kind of socialist power, has led to some sort of common interest between the Soviet Union on the one side and the United States on the other.

In a sense, this is indeed the community of interests of the "haves" against the "have nots," of the Old against the New. The "collaborationist" policy of the Soviet Union necessitates the pursuance of power politics which increasingly reduces the prospect that Soviet society, by virtue of its basic institutions alone (abolition of private ownership and control of the means of production: planned economy) is still capable of making the transition to a free society. And yet, the very dynamic of imperialist expansion places the Soviet Union in the other camp: would the effective resistance in Vietnam, and the protection of Cuba be possible without Soviet aid?

However, while we reject the unqualified convergence thesis, according to which—at least at present—the assimilation of interests prevails upon the conflict between capitalism and Soviet socialism, we cannot minimize the essential difference between the latter and the new historical efforts to construct socialism by developing and creating a genuine solidarity between the leadership and the liberated victims of exploitation. The actual may considerably deviate from the ideal, the fact remains that, for a whole generation, "freedom," "socialism," and "liberation" are inseparable from Fidel and Ché and the guerrillas—not because their revolutionary struggle could furnish the model for the struggle in the metropoles, but because they have recaptured the truth of these ideas, in the day-to-day fight of men and women for a life as human beings: for a new life.

What kind of life? We are still confronted with the demand to state the "concrete alternative." The demand is meaningless if it asks for a blueprint of the specific institutions and relationships which would be those of the new society: they cannot be determined a priori; they will develop, in trial and error, as the new society develops. If we could form a concrete concept of the alternative today, it would not be that of an alternative; the possibilities of the new society are sufficiently "abstract," i.e., removed from and incongruous with the established universe to defy any attempt to identify them in terms of this universe. However, the question cannot be brushed aside by saying that what matters today is the destruction of the old, of the powers that be, making way for the emergence of the new. Such an answer neglects the essential fact that the old is not simply bad, that it delivers the goods, and that people have a real stake in it. There can be societies which are much worse—there are such societies today. The system of corporate capitalism has the right to insist that those who work for its replacement justify their action.

But the demand to state the concrete alternatives is justified for yet another reason. Negative thinking draws whatever force it may have from its empirical basis: the actual human condition in the given society, and the "given" possibilities to transcend this condition, to enlarge the realm of freedom. In this sense, negative thinking is by virtue of its own internal concepts "positive": oriented toward, and comprehending a future which is "contained" in the present. And in this containment (which is an important aspect of the general containment policy pursued by the established societies), the future appears as possible liberation. It is not the only alternative: the advent of a long period of "civilized" barbarism, with or without the nuclear destruction, is equally contained in the present. Negative thinking , and the praxis guided by it, is the positive and positing effort to prevent this utter negativity.

The concept of the primary, initial institutions of liberation is familiar enough and concrete enough: collective ownership, collective control and planning of the means of production and distribution. This is the foundation, a necessary but not sufficient condition for the alternative: it would make possible the usage of all available resources for the abolition of poverty, which is the prerequisite for the turn from quantity into quality: the creation of a reality in accordance with the new sensitivity and the new consciousness. This goal implies rejection of those policies of reconstruction, no matter how revolutionary, which are bound to perpetuate (or to introduce) the pattern of the unfree societies and their needs. Such false policy is perhaps best summed up in the formula "to catch up with, and to overtake the productivity level of the advanced capitalist countries." What is wrong with this formula is not the emphasis on the rapid improvement of the material conditions but on the model guiding their improvement. The model denies the alternative, the qualitative difference. The latter is not, and cannot be, the result of the fastest possible attainment of capitalist productivity, but rather the development of new modes and ends of production—"new" not only (and perhaps not at all) with respect to technical innovations and production relations, but with respect to the different human needs and the different human relationships in working for the satisfaction of these needs. These new relationships would be the result of a "biological" *solidarity* in work and purpose, expressive of a true harmony between social and individual needs and goals, between recognized necessity and free development—the exact opposite of the administered and enforced harmony organized in the advanced capitalist (and socialist?) countries. It is the image of this solidarity as elemental, instinctual, creative force which the young radicals see in Cuba, in the guerrillas, in the Chinese cultural revolution.

Solidarity and cooperation: not all their forms are liberating. Fascism and militarism have developed a deadly efficient solidarity. Socialist solidarity is autonomy: self-determination begins at home—and that is with every I, and the We whom the I chooses. And this end must indeed appear in the means to attain it, that is to say, in the strategy of those who, within the existing society, work for the new one. If the socialist relationships of production are to be a new way of life, a new Form of life, then their existential quality must show forth, anticipated and demonstrated, in the fight for their realization. Exploitation in all its forms must have disappeared from this fight: from the work relationships among the fighters as well as from their

individual relationships. Understanding, tenderness toward each other, the instinctual consciousness of that which is evil, false, the heritage of oppression, would then
testify to the authenticity of the rebellion. In short, the economic, political, and cultural features of a classless society must have become the basic needs of those who
fight for it. This ingression of the future into the present, this depth dimension of
the rebellion accounts, in the last analysis, for the incompatibility with the traditional
forms of the political struggle. The new radicalism militates against the centralized
bureaucratic communist as well as against the semi-democratic liberal organization.
There is a strong element of spontaneity, even anarchism, in this rebellion, expression
of the new sensibility, sensitivity against domination: the feeling, the awareness, that
the joy of freedom and the need to be free must precede liberation. Therefore the
aversion against preestablished Leaders, apparatchiks of all sorts, politicians no matter how leftist. The initiative shifts to small groups, widely diffused, with a high degree of autonomy, mobility, flexibility.

To be sure, within the repressive society, and against its ubiquitous apparatus,
spontaneity by itself cannot possibly be a radical and revolutionary force. It can become such a force only as the result of enlightenment, education, political practice—
in this sense indeed, as a result of organization. The anarchic element is an essential
factor in the struggle against domination: preserved but disciplined in the prepara-
tory political action, it will be freed and *aufgehoben* in the goals of the struggle.
Released for the construction of the initial revolutionary institutions, the antirepres-
sive sensibility, allergic to domination, would militate against the prolongation of
the "First Phase," that is, the authoritarian bureaucratic development of the productive forces. The new society could then reach relatively fast the level at which poverty could be abolished (this level could be considerably lower than that of advanced
capitalist productivity, which is geared to obscene affluence and waste). Then the
development could tend toward a sensuous culture, tangibly contrasting with the
gray-on-gray culture of the socialist societies of Eastern Europe. Production would
be redirected in defiance of all the rationality of the Performance Principle; socially
necessary labor would be diverted to the construction of an aesthetic rather than
repressive environment, to parks and gardens rather than highways and parking lots,
to the creation of areas of withdrawal rather than massive fun and relaxation. Such
redistribution of socially necessary labor (time), incompatible with any society governed by the Profit and Performance Principle, would gradually alter society in all
its dimensions—it would mean the ascent of the Aesthetic Principle as Form of the
Reality Principle: a culture of receptivity based on the achievements of industrial
civilization and initiating the end of its self-propelling productivity.

Not regression to a previous stage of civilization, but return to an imaginary
temps perdu in the real life of mankind: progress to a stage of civilization where
man has learned to ask for the sake of whom or of what he organizes his society;
the stage where he checks and perhaps even halts his incessant struggle for existence
on an enlarged scale, surveys what has been achieved through centuries of misery
and hecatombs of victims, and decides that it is enough, and that it is time to enjoy
what he has and what can be reproduced and refined with a minimum of alienated
labor: not the arrest or reduction of technical progress, but the elimination of those

of its features which perpetuate man's subjection to the apparatus and the intensification of the struggle for existence—to work harder in order to get more of the merchandise that has to be sold. In other words, electrification indeed, and all technical devices which alleviate and protect life, all the mechanization which frees human energy and time, all the standardization which does away with spurious and parasitarian "personalized" services rather than multiplying them and the gadgets and tokens of exploitative affluence. In terms of the latter (and only in terms of the latter), this would certainly be a regression—but freedom from the rule of merchandise over man is a precondition of freedom.

The construction of a free society would create new incentives for work. In the exploitative societies, the so-called work instinct is mainly the (more or less effectively) introjected necessity to perform productively in order to earn a living. But the life instincts themselves strive for the unification and enhancement of life; in nonrepressive sublimation they would provide the libidinal energy for work on the development of a reality which no longer demands the exploitative repression of the Pleasure Principle. The "incentives" would then be built into the instinctual structure of men. Their sensibility would register, as biological reactions, the difference between the ugly and the beautiful, between calm and noise, tenderness and brutality, intelligence and stupidity, joy and fun, and it would correlate this distinction with that between freedom and servitude. Freud's last theoretical conception recognizes the erotic instincts as work instincts—work for the creation of a sensuous environment. The social expression of the liberated work instinct is *cooperation,* which, grounded in solidarity, directs the organization of the realm of necessity and the development of the realm of freedom. And there is an answer to the question which troubles the minds of so many men of good will: what are the people in a free society going to do? The answer which, I believe, strikes at the heart of the matter was given by a young black girl. She said: for the first time in our life, we shall be free to think about what we are going to do.

Religion: The Inworking of the All

Although the phrase "under God" is a comparatively recent addition to the Pledge of Allegiance, there has never been any doubt that religion has been one of the most important bases of all American settlements. Freedom of conscience and obligation of conscience have gone hand in hand from the ordering of the first Puritan communities, founded firmly on the solid rock of theocratic law. Not only the lives of Puritans, perhaps unjustly rendered notorious by virtue of their Calvinist underpinnings, but the souls of all the early colonists were bound by Christian doctrine, with the understanding that all were obliged to spend their days in a manner that would fit them for salvation, should God have marked them for that blessed destiny. Even a man as urbane and sophisticated as the Anglican William Byrd, no Puritan but a Virginia gentleman and plantation owner, recorded in his diary an account of his rigid schedule of daily prayer and the "good thoughts" which prepared him for God's approbation. These early colonists, who saw themselves as chosen and covenanted Christians in the new Canaan, interpreted their mission as acts of individual conscience in the wilderness. Influenced by the prophets of the Old Testament to search their lives for imperfection and root it out and by the New Testament to vigilantly counteract their natural depravity, seventeenth-century Americans fashioned a religious climate of depth and privacy. There are an inordinate number of "meditations" and "contemplations," both in prose and poetry, by Jonathan Edwards, Anne Bradstreet, Edward Taylor, and Edward Johnson, attesting to the inwardness of the spiritual nature of this young country. For, although punishment for transgression was done in public, the religious life itself was a highly individual and subjective matter.

In the first half of the nineteenth century, the period of westward expansion, Christianity turned from the inwardness of Puritan religious practice to public or group "witness." The flourishing populist political movements in the South and Midwest had their impetus in a mobile society which encouraged group participation for the purpose of establishing communities of relatively rootless people. In this setting, political conservatism often accompanied religious fundamentalism. Group manifestations of faith were common in the camp meetings, which were often gatherings of homesteaders who came to hear sermons and experience mass conversions. Declarations for Christ, group baptisms, and frenzied tent revivalist campaigns became popular forms of religious expression. Masses of people were whipped into loud public commitment by the inflammatory oratory of gospel preachers in the tradition of Billy Sunday and William Jennings Bryant. The tradition still has a faithful and vocal following among the members of Billy Graham's Christian Crusade, the devotees of many faith healers, and the radio audiences of the weekly Sunday evening preachers of the airwaves. The orality of the populist religious groups, fostered by orators whose great virtue was, and still is, the skillful weaving of plain talk and hellfire theatrics, is pure gospel. The thrust is social, and in spite of the very real spectre of Hell conjured up by the rhetoric, comforting and optimistic. God is very near and familiar and accessible. One need only to approach Him openly and in the company of one's fellows, and there is every certainty that He will respond and show the way. Nowhere is there evident the lonely agony of the Puritan or the remoteness and majesty of the awesome God of the Mather family and Michael Wigglesworth. Democratization and proliferating sectarianism, resulting from the waves of immigration, have stripped the mystery and severity as well as the singleness of interpretation from the judging Deity whose origins were in New England. Religion, which began in this nation as the most compelling drive for the fulfillment of personal spiritual imperatives, has in large measure been transformed by the Elmer Gantrys of middle America into public spectacles of religiosity.

The growth of American sectarianism may be laid to yet another particularly American phenomenon: orthodoxy and dissent. In America, dissent rarely implies atheism or freethinking. The most passionate of vocal dissenters in America, George Fox, the Quaker, Anne Hutchinson, the Antinomian, and Ellery Channing, the Unitarian, were apt to be more deeply religious than the adherents of the traditional church from which they were breaking. They were likely to call down God's providence to foster their own religious innovations in the hopes of securing a more perfect kingdom of God here on earth. It was the hospitable climate of American tolerance which caused the inordinate proliferation of sects in American life. Shakers, Quakers, Mormons, Jehovah's Witnesses, Seventh Day Adventists, and a host of other branches from the original tree of Christianity attest to the plurality of American religious frameworks as they correspond with the enormous plurality of ethnic and cultural origins and preconditioning.

In the twentieth century, dissent has taken another subtler form: secularism. Although a recent Harris poll taken in 1968 indicates that 96 percent of the American people say they believe in God, the processes of urbanization and mechanization have weakened the profound religious beliefs which immigrants carried to the New World along with their dialects and native customs. Eighteenth-century rational deism, which seems to have skipped an entire century, has reemerged in the twentieth century to contribute to the growing secularism among America's large college-educated classes. A profound skepticism accompanies much of the secular spirit, oddly enough articulated by a group of American theologians, principally those originators of the "Is God Dead?" theory. The three most prominent voices of this particular secularist investigation are Thomas Altizer, William Hamilton, and Paul Van Buren—theologians who appear to be rewriting the traditional theological creed with the "theos" removed to suit the current secular theology so well defined in Harvey Cox's *The Secular City*. It is their observation that religion today provides, for fewer and fewer people, profound spiritual guidelines to personal behavior and codes of ethics. In some cases traditional Protestant morality is expressed in the Civil Rights movement; in other cases it is translated into egalitarian political crusading or mass supportive movements for the urban disadvantaged and the rural poor. The domestic Peace Corps and Vista may be cited as two secular equivalents of religious institutions in America.

Secularization has produced a palpable ambiguity in American religious life. Never has the institution of the church, whichever its denomination, boasted a healthier membership or more accelerated program of building. More than 125,000,000 Americans claim church affiliation, and 45 percent report that they attend denominational services regularly. Yet today the once commanding system of moral values does not emanate solely from the religious institutions as it once did. Wide experimentation in the rituals and disciplines of Oriental religions, principally Zen, have introduced to American youth a new source of spiritual guidelines. The Esalen Institute and other organizations specializing in sensitivity training offer a sensual release which promises spiritual fulfillment. Psychedelic or mind-expanding drug experimentation, often accompanied by religious ritual borrowed from ancient American Indian cultures, constitutes still another avenue to religious experience. The new morality, while it sometimes simulates a primitive form of Christianity, has very little to do with the established community-oriented ethic emanating from traditional church teaching. The generation of Young Americans served by this new morality are seen as paradoxically alienated and deeply religious. They give evidence of striving for faith in the sacraments accompanying hallucinogenic drug rituals, Far Eastern liturgies, and the sacramental use of lights and flowers. Religious needs, however, are fulfilled in an eclectic gathering of rituals from diverse sources, none of which is rooted in the theology of the Judeo-Christian civilization. Thus while there is an inordinate hunger for spiritual fulfillment, there is an alienation from its traditional Western source, the church and scripture. The restless search for affirmation darts from one alien source to another, from saffron robe to mandala to begging bowl to mushroom ritual.

The church, then, flourishes as an institution to serve the social and leisure needs within American community life, while more and more people look elsewhere for an authentic font of spiritual guidance. It is an oversimplification to conclude that now that the Virgin Mary has given way, or at least merged, in Cox's estimate, with Miss Teen-Age America, Americans will just have to look elsewhere for a religion to replace our secularized church. Most Americans are too deeply steeped in Judeo-Christian traditions to believe that Hindu mantras will work for them, no matter the fervor with which Allen Ginsberg chants them. Thus Americans face a peculiar dilemma in their religious life. The church as edifice prospers, supported by the community seeking to conserve traditional Christianity along with the whole of the political and social establishment. On the one hand, it gives significance to lives which have been depleted and rendered anonymous through the processes of automation characteristic of a sophisticated technological society. On the other hand, increasingly more people, despairing for the very same reasons, see in the church's conventional postures no relevance to their particular individual needs, which they feel the church has long neglected in pursuit of its denominational interests. In some cases, the institution has begun to meet the challenge. These instances have been mostly in the form of increased liturgical participation: rock and folk masses and changes in the service to include more of the congregation in the sacraments. In other cases religion remains a lonely challenge for the individual still engaging in the accepted American tradition of dissent.

Jonathan Edwards
Personal Narrative

I had a variety of concerns and exercises about my soul from my childhood; but had two more remarkable seasons of awakening, before I met with that change, by which I was brought to those new dispositions, and that new sense of things, that I have since had. The first time was when I was a boy, some years before I went to college, at a time of remarkable awakening in my father's congregation. I was then very much affected for many months, and concerned about the things of religion, and my soul's salvation; and was abundant in duties. I used to pray five times a day in secret, and to spend much time in religious talk with other boys; and used to meet with them to pray together. I experienced I know not what kind of delight in religion. My mind was much engaged in it, and had much self-righteous pleasure; and it was my delight to abound in religious duties. I with some of my school-mates joined together, and built a booth in a swamp, in a very retired spot, for a place of prayer. And besides, I had particular secret places of my own in the woods, where I used to retire by myself; and was from time to time much affected. My affections seemed to be lively and easily moved, and I seemed to be in my element when engaged in religious duties. And I am ready to think, many are deceived with such affections, and such a kind of delight as I then had in religion, and mistake it for grace.

But in process of time, my convictions and affections wore off; and I entirely lost all those affections and delights, and left off secret prayer, at least as to any constant performance of it; and returned like a dog to his vomit, and went on in the ways of sin. Indeed I was at times very uneasy, especially towards the latter part of my time at college; when it pleased God, to seize me with a pleurisy; in which he brought me nigh to the grave, and shook me over the pit of hell. And yet, it was not long after my recovery, before I fell again into my old ways of sin. But God would not suffer me to go on with any quietness; I had great and violent inward struggles, till, after many conflicts with wicked inclinations, repeated resolutions, and bonds that I laid myself under by a kind of vows to God, I was brought wholly to break off all former wicked ways and all ways of known outward sin; and to apply myself to seek salvation, and practice many religious duties; but without that kind of affection and delight which I had formerly experienced. My concern now wrought more by inward struggles, and conflicts, and self-reflections. I made seeking my salvation the main business of my life. But yet, it seems to me, I sought after a miserable manner; which has made me sometimes since to question, whether ever it issued in that which was saving; being ready to doubt, whether such miserable seeking ever succeeded. I was indeed brought to seek salvation in a manner that I never was before; I felt a spirit to part with all things in the world, for an interest in Christ. My concern continued and prevailed, with many exercising thoughts and inward struggles; but yet it never seemed to be proper, to express that concern by the name of terror.

From my childhood up, my mind had been full of objections against the doctrine of God's sovereignty, in choosing whom He would to eternal life, and rejecting whom He pleased; leaving them eternally to perish, and be everlastingly tormented in hell. It used to appear like a horrible doctrine to me. But I remember the time very well, when I seemed to be convinced, and fully satisfied, as to this sovereignty of God, and His justice in thus eternally disposing of men, according to His sovereign pleasure. But never could give an account, how, or by what means, I was thus convinced, not in the least imagining at the time, nor a long time after, that there was any extraordinary influence of God's Spirit in it; but only that now I saw further, and my reason apprehended the justice and reasonableness of it. However, my mind rested in it; and it put an end to all those cavils and objections. And there has been a wonderful alteration in my mind, with respect to the doctrine of God's sovereignty, from that day to this; so that I scarce ever have found so much as the rising of an objection against it, in the most absolute sense, in God's shewing mercy to whom He will shew mercy, and hardening whom he will. God's absolute sovereignty and justice, with respect to salvation and damnation, is what my mind seems to rest assured of, as much as of any thing that I see with my eyes; at least it is so at times. But I have often, since that first conviction, had quite another kind of sense of God's sovereignty than I had then. I have often since had not only a conviction, but a delightful conviction. The doctrine has very often appeared exceeding pleasant, bright and sweet. Absolute sovereignty is what I love to ascribe to God. But my first conviction was not so.

The first instance that I remember of that sort of inward, sweet delight in God and divine things that I have lived much in since, was on reading those words, 1 Tim. i:17, *Now unto the King eternal, immortal, invisible, the only wise God, be honor and glory for ever and ever, Amen.* As I read the words, there came into my soul, and was as it were diffused through it, a sense of the glory of the Divine Being; a new sense, quite different from anything I ever experienced before. Never any words of scripture seemed to me as these words did. I thought with myself, how excellent a Being that was, and how happy I should be, if I might enjoy that God, and be rapt up to Him in heaven, and be as it were swallowed up in Him for ever! I kept saying, and as it were singing, over these words of scripture to myself; and went to pray to God that I might enjoy Him, and prayed in a manner quite different from what I used to do; with a new sort of affection. But it never came into my thought, that there was anything spiritual, or of a saving nature in this.

From about that time, I began to have a new kind of apprehensions and ideas of Christ, and the work of redemption and the glorious way of salvation by Him. An inward, sweet sense of these things, at times, came into my heart; and my soul was led away in pleasant views and contemplations of them. And my mind was greatly engaged to spend my time in reading and meditating on Christ, on the beauty and excellency of His person, and the lovely way of salvation by free grace in Him. I found no books so delightful to me, as those that treated of these subjects. Those words Cant. ii:1 used to be abundantly with me, *I am the rose of Sharon, and the lily of the valleys.* The words seemed to me, sweetly to represent the loveliness and beauty of Jesus Christ. The whole book of Canticles used to be pleasant to me, and I used to be much in reading it, about that time; and found, from time to time, an inward sweetness, that would carry me away, in my contemplations. This I know not how to express otherwise, than by a calm, sweet abstraction of soul from all the concerns of this world; and sometimes a kind of vision, or fixed ideas and imaginations, of being alone in the mountains, or some solitary wilderness, far from all mankind, sweetly conversing with Christ, and wrapt and swallowed up in God. The sense I had of divine things, would often of a sudden kindle up, as it were, a sweet burning in my heart; an ardor of soul, that I know not how to express.

Not long after I first began to experience these things, I gave an account to my father of some things that had passed in my mind. I was pretty much affected by the discourse we had together; and when the discourse was ended, I walked abroad alone, in a solitary place in my father's pasture, for contemplation. And as I was walking there, and looking upon the sky and clouds, there came into my mind so sweet a sense of the glorious *majesty* and *grace* of God, as I know not how to express. I seemed to see them both in a sweet conjunction; majesty and meekness joined together; it was a sweet, and gentle, and holy majesty; and also a majestic meekness; an awful sweetness; a high, and great, and holy gentleness.

After this my sense of divine things gradually increased, and became more and more lively, and had more of that inward sweetness. The appearance of everything was altered; there seemed to be, as it were, a calm, sweet cast, or appearance of divine glory, in almost everything. God's excellency, His wisdom, His purity and love, seemed to appear in everything; in the sun, moon, and stars; in the clouds, and blue sky; in the grass, flowers, trees; in the water, and all nature; which used greatly to fix my mind. I often used to sit and view the moon for continuance; and in the day, spent much time in viewing the clouds and sky, to behold the sweet glory of God in these things; in the meantime, singing forth, with a low voice, my contemplations of the Creator and Redeemer. And scarce anything, among all the works of nature, was so sweet to me as thunder and lightning; formerly nothing had been so terrible to me. Before, I used to be uncommonly terrified with thunder, and to be struck with terror when I saw a thunder storm rising; but now, on the contrary, it rejoiced me. I felt God, so to speak, at the first appearance of a thunder storm; and used to take the opportunity, at such times, to fix myself in order to view the clouds, and see the lightnings play, and hear the majestic and awful voice of God's thunder, which oftentimes was exceedingly entertaining, leading me to sweet contemplations of my great and glorious God. While thus engaged, it always seemed natural for me to sing, or chant for my meditations; or, to speak my thoughts in soliloquies with a singing voice.

I felt then great satisfaction, as to my good state, but that did not content me. I had vehement longings of soul after God and Christ, and after more holiness, wherewith my heart seemed to be full, and ready to break; which often brought to my mind the words of the Psalmist, Psal. cxix:28: *My soul breaketh for the longing it hath.* I often felt a mourning and lamenting in my heart, that I had not turned to God sooner, that I might have had more time to grow in grace. My mind was greatly fixed on divine things; almost perpetually in the contemplation of them. I spent most of my time in thinking of divine things, year after year; often walking alone in the woods, and solitary places, for meditation, soliloquy, and prayer, and converse with God; and it was always my manner, at such times, to sing forth my contemplations. I was almost constantly in ejaculatory prayer, wherever I was. Prayer seemed to be natural to me, as the breath by which the inward burnings of my heart had vent. The delights which I now felt in the things of religion, were of an exceeding different kind from those before mentioned, that I had when a boy; and what I then had no more notion of, than one born blind has of pleasant and beautiful colors. They were of a more inward, pure, soul-animating and refreshing nature. Those former delights never reached the heart; and did not arise from any sight of the divine excellency of the things of God; or any taste of the soul-satisfying and life-giving good there is in them.

My sense of divine things seemed gradually to increase, till I went to preach at New York, which was about a year and a half after they began; and while I was there, I felt them, very sensibly, in a much higher degree than I had done before. My longings after God, and holiness, were much increased. Pure and humble, holy and heavenly Christianity appeared exceeding amiable to me. I felt a burning desire to be, in everything, a complete Christian; and conformed to the blessed image of Christ; and that I might live, in all things, according to the pure, sweet, and blessed rules of the gospel. I had an eager thirsting after progress in these things; which put me upon pursuing and pressing after them. It was my continual strife day and night, and constant inquiry, how I should *be* more holy and *live* more holily, and more becoming a child of God, and a disciple of Christ. I now sought an increase of grace and holiness, and a holy life, with much more earnestness, than ever I sought grace before I had it. I used to be continually examining myself, and studying and contriving for likely ways and means, how I should live holily, with far greater diligence and earnestness, than ever I pursued anything in my life; but yet with too great a dependence on my own strength; which afterwards proved a great damage to me. My experience had not then taught me, as it has done since, my extreme feebleness and impotence, every manner of way; and the bottomless depths of secret corruption and deceit there was in my heart. However, I went on with my eager pursuit after more holiness, and conformity to Christ.

The heaven I desired was a heaven of holiness; to be with God, and to spend my eternity in divine love and holy communion with Christ. My mind was very much taken up with contemplations on heaven, and the enjoyments there; and living there in perfect holiness, humility, and love: and it used at that time to appear a great part of the happiness of heaven, that there the saints could express their love to Christ. It appeared to me a great clog and burden, that what I felt within, I could not express as I desired. The inward ardor of my soul, seemed to be hindered and pent up, and could not freely flame out as it would. I used often to think, how in heaven this principle should freely and fully vent and express itself. Heaven appeared exceedingly delightful, as a world of love; and that all happiness consisted in living in pure, humble, heavenly, divine love.

I remember the thoughts I used then to have of holiness; and said sometimes to myself, "I do certainly know that I love holiness, such as the gospel prescribes." It appeared to me, that there was nothing in it but what was ravishingly lovely; the highest beauty and amiableness—a *divine* beauty; far purer than anything here upon earth; and that everything else was like mire and defilement, in comparison of it.

Holiness, as I then wrote down some of my contemplations on it, appeared to me to be of a sweet, pleasant, charming, serene, calm nature; which brought an inexpressible purity, brightness, peacefulness and ravishment to the soul. In other words, that it made the soul like a field or garden of God, with all manner of pleasant flowers; all pleasant, delightful, and undisturbed; enjoying a sweet calm, and the gently vivifying beams of the sun. The soul of a true Christian, as I then wrote my meditations, appeared like such a little white flower as we see in the spring of the year; low and humble on the ground, opening its bosom to receive the pleasant beams of the sun's glory; rejoicing as it were in a calm rapture; diffusing around a sweet fragrancy; standing peacefully and lovingly, in the midst of other flowers round about; all in like manner opening their bosoms, to drink in the light of the sun. There was no part of creature-holiness, that I had so great a sense of its loveliness, as humility, brokenness of heart, and poverty of spirit; and there was nothing that I so earnestly longed for. My heart panted after this—to lie low before God, as in the dust; that I might be nothing, and that God, might be ALL, that I might become as a little child.

While at New York, I was sometimes much affected with reflections on my past life, considering how late it was before I began to be truly religious; and how wickedly I had lived till then: and once so as to weep abundantly, and for a considerable time together.

On January 12, 1723, I made a solemn dedication of myself to God, and wrote it down; giving up myself, and all that I had to God; to be for the future in no respect my own; to act as one that had no right to himself, in any respect. And solemnly vowed, to take God for my whole portion and felicity; looking on nothing else as any part of my happiness, nor acting as if it were; and His law for the constant rule of my obedience; engaging to fight with all my might, against the world, the flesh, and the Devil, to the end of my life. But I have reason to be infinitely humbled, when I consider, how much I have failed, of answering my obligation.

I had then abundance of sweet religious conversation in the family where I lived, with Mr. John Smith and his pious mother. My heart was knit in affection to those in whom were appearances of true piety; and I could bear the thoughts of no other companions, but such as were holy, and the disciples of the blessed Jesus. I had great longings for the advancement of Christ's kingdom in the world; and my secret prayer used to be, in great part, taken up in praying for it. If I heard the least hint of any thing that happened, in any part of the world, that appeared, in some respect or other, to have a favorable aspect on the interest of Christ's kingdom, my soul eagerly catched at it; and it would much animate and refresh me. I used to be eager to read public news letters, mainly for that end; to see if I could not find some news favorable to the interest of religion in the world.

I very frequently used to retire into a solitary place, on the banks of Hudson's river, at some distance from the city, for contemplation on divine things, and secret converse with God; and had many sweet hours there. Sometimes Mr. Smith and I walked there together, to converse on the things of God; and our conversation used to turn much on the advancement of Christ's kingdom in the world, and the glorious things that God would accomplish for his church in the latter days. I had then, and at other times, the greatest delight in the holy scriptures, of any book whatsoever. Oftentimes in reading it, every word seemed to touch my heart. I felt a harmony between something in my heart, and those sweet and powerful words. I seemed often to see so much light exhibited by every sentence, and such a refreshing food communicated, that I could not get along in reading; often dwelling long on one sentence, to see the wonders contained in it; and yet almost every sentence seemed to be full of wonders.

I came away from New York in the month of April, 1723, and had a most bitter parting with Madam Smith and her son. My heart seemed to sink within me at leaving the family and city, where I had enjoyed so many sweet and pleasant days. I went from New York to Weathersfield, by water, and as I sailed away, I kept sight of the city as long as I could. However, that night, after this sorrowful parting, I was greatly comforted in God at Westchester, where we went ashore to lodge; and had a pleasant time of it all the voyage to Saybrook. It was sweet to me to think of meeting dear Christians in heaven, where we should never part more. At Saybrook we went ashore to lodge, on Saturday, and there kept the Sabbath; where I had a sweet and refreshing season, walking alone in the fields.

After I came home to Windsor, I remained much in a like frame of mind, as when at New York; only sometimes I felt my heart ready to sink with the thoughts of my friends at New York. My support was in contemplations on the heavenly state; as I find in my Diary of May 1, 1723. It was a comfort to think of that state, where there is fulness of joy; where reigns heavenly, calm, and delightful love, without alloy; where there are continually the dearest expressions of this love; where is the enjoyment of the persons loved, without ever parting; where those persons who appear so lovely in this world, will really be inexpressibly more lovely and full of love to us. And how sweetly will the mutual lovers join together to sing the praises of God and the Lamb! How will it fill us with joy to think, that this enjoyment, these sweet exercises will never cease, but will last to all eternity! I continued much in the same frame, in the general, as when at New York, till I went to New Haven as tutor to the college; particularly once at Bolton, on a journey from Boston, while walking out alone in the fields. After I went to New Haven I sunk in religion; my mind being diverted from my eager pursuits after holiness, by some affairs that greatly perplexed and distracted my thoughts.

In September, 1725, I was taken ill at New Haven, and while endeavoring to go home to Windsor, was so ill at the North Village, that I could go no further; where I lay sick for about a quarter of a year. In this sickness God was pleased to visit me again with the sweet influences of his Spirit. My mind was greatly engaged there in divine, pleasant contemplations, and longings of soul. I observed that those who watched with me, would often be looking out wishfully for the morning; which brought to my mind those words of the Psalmist, and which my soul with delight made its own language, *My soul waiteth for the Lord, more than they that watch for the morning, I say, more than they that watch for the morning;* and when the light of day came in at the windows, it refreshed my soul from one morning to another. It seemed to be some image of the light of God's glory.

I remember, about that time, I used greatly to long for the conversion of some that I was concerned with; I could gladly honor them, and with delight be a servant to them, and lie at their feet, if they were but truly holy. But, some time after this, I was again greatly diverted in my mind with some temporal concerns that exceedingly took up my thoughts, greatly to the wounding of my soul; and went on through various exercises, that it would be tedious to relate, which gave me much more experience of my own heart, than ever I had before.

Since I came to this town, I have often had sweet complacency in God, in views of his glorious perfections and the excellency of Jesus Christ. God has appeared to me a glorious and lovely being, chiefly on the account of his holiness. The holiness of God has always appeared to me the most lovely of all his attributes. The doctrines of God's absolute sovereignty, and free grace, in shewing mercy to whom he would shew mercy; and man's absolute dependence on the operations of God's Holy Spirit, have very often appeared to me as sweet and glorious doctrines. These doctrines have been much my delight. God's sovereignty has ever appeared to me, great part of his glory. It has often been my delight to approach God, and adore him as a sovereign God, and ask sovereign mercy of him.

I have loved the doctrines of the gospel; they have been to my soul like green pastures. The gospel has seemed to me the richest treasure; the treasure that I have most desired, and longed that it might dwell richly in me. The way of salvation by Christ has appeared, in a general way, glorious and excellent, most pleasant and most beautiful. It has often seemed to me, that it would in a great measure spoil heaven, to receive it in any other way. That text has often been affecting and delightful to me, Isa. xxxii:2. *A man shall be an hiding place from the wind, and a covert from the tempest, etc.*

It has often appeared to me delightful, to be united to Christ; to have him for my head, and to be a member of his body; also to have Christ for my teacher and prophet. I very often think with sweetness, and longings, and pantings of soul, of being a little child, taking hold of Christ, to be led by him through the wilderness of this world. That text, Matth. xviii:3, has often been sweet to me, *except ye be converted and become as little children, etc.* I love to think of coming to Christ, to receive salvation of him, poor in spirit, and quite empty of self, humbly exalting him alone; cut off entirely from my own root, in order to grow into, and out of Christ; to have God in Christ to be all in all; and to live by faith on the Son of God, a life of humble unfeigned confidence in him. That scripture has often been sweet to me, Psal. cxv:1. *Not unto us, O Lord, not unto us, but to thy name give glory, for thy mercy and for thy truth's sake.* And those words of Christ, Luke x:21. *In that hour Jesus rejoiced in spirit, and said, I thank thee, O Father, Lord of heaven and earth, that thou hast hid these things from the wise and prudent, and hast revealed them unto babes; even so, Father, for so it seemed good in thy sight.* That sovereignty of God which Christ rejoiced in, seemed to me worthy of such joy; and that rejoicing seemed to show the excellency of Christ, and of what spirit he was.

Sometimes, only mentioning a single word caused my heart to burn within me; or only seeing the name of Christ, or the name of some attribute of God. And God has appeared glorious to me, on account of the Trinity. It has made me have exalting thoughts of God, that he subsists in three persons; Father, Son and Holy Ghost. The sweetest joys and delights I have experienced, have not been those that have arisen from a hope of my own good state; but in a direct view of the glorious things of the gospel. When I enjoy this sweetness, it seems to carry me above the thoughts of my own estate; it seems at such times a loss that I cannot bear, to take off my eye from the glorious pleasant object I behold without me, to turn my eye in upon myself and my own good estate.

My heart has been much on the advancement of Christ's kingdom in the world. The histories of the least advancement of Christ's kingdom have been sweet to me. When I have read histories of past ages, the pleasantest thing in all my reading has been, to read of the kingdom of Christ being promoted. And when I have expected, in my reading, to come to any such thing, I have rejoiced in the prospect, all the way as I read. And my mind has been much entertained and delighted with the scripture promises and prophecies, which relate to the future glorious advancement of Christ's kingdom upon earth.

I have sometimes had a sense of the excellent fulness of Christ, and his meetness and suitableness as a Saviour; whereby he has appeared to me, far above all, the chief of ten thousands. His blood and atonement have appeared sweet, and his righteousness sweet; which was always accompanied with ardency of spirit; and inward strugglings and breathings, and groanings that cannot be uttered, to be emptied of myself, and swallowed up in Christ.

Once as I rode out into the woods for my health, in 1737, having alighted from my horse in a retired place, as my manner commonly has been, to walk for divine contemplation and prayer, I had a view that for me was extraordinary, of the glory of the Son of God, as Mediator between God and man, and His wonderful, great, full, pure, and sweet grace and love, and meek and gentle condescension. This grace that appeared so calm and sweet, appeared also great above the heavens. The person of Christ appeared ineffably excellent with an excellency great enough to swallow up all thought and conception—which continued, as near as I can judge, about an hour, which kept me the greater part of the time in a flood of tears, and weeping aloud. I felt an ardency of soul to be, what I know not otherwise how to express, emptied and annihilated; to lie in the dust, and to be full of Christ alone; to love Him with a holy and pure love; to trust in Him; to live upon Him; to serve and follow Him; and to be perfectly sanctified and made pure, with a divine and heavenly purity. I have, several other times, had views very much of the same nature, and which have had the same effects.

I have many times had a sense of the glory of the third person in the Trinity, in His office of Sanctifier, in His holy operations, communicating divine light and life to the soul. God, in the communications of His Holy Spirit, has appeared as an infinite fountain of divine glory and sweetness; being full, and sufficient to fill and satisfy the soul; pouring forth itself in sweet communications; like the sun in its glory, sweetly and pleasantly diffusing light and life. And I have sometimes had an affecting sense of the excellency of the Word of God as a Word of life; as the light of life; a sweet, excellent, life-giving Word; accompanied with a thirsting after that Word, that it might dwell richly in my heart.

Often, since I lived in this town, I have had very affecting views of my own sinfulness and vileness; very frequently to such a degree as to hold me in a kind of loud weeping, sometimes for a considerable time together; so that I have often been forced to shut myself up. I have had a vastly greater sense of my own wickedness, and the badness of my own heart, than ever I had before my conversion. It has often appeared to me, that if God should mark iniquity against me, I should appear the very worst of all mankind; of all that have been, since the beginning of the world to this time; and that I should have by far the lowest place in hell. When others, that have come to talk with me about their soul concerns, have expressed the sense they have had of their own wickedness, by saying that it seemed to them, that they were as bad as the Devil himself; I thought their expressions seemed exceeding faint and feeble, to represent my wickedness.

My wickedness, as I am in myself, has long appeared to me perfectly ineffable, and swallowing up all thought and imagination; like an infinite deluge, or mountains over my head. I know not how to express better what my sins appear to me to be, than by heaping infinite upon infinite, and multiplying infinite by infinite. Very often, for these many years, these expressions are in my mind, and in my mouth, "Infinite upon infinite—Infinite upon infinite!" When I look into my heart, and take a view of my wickedness, it looks like an abyss infinitely deeper than hell. And it appears to me, that were it not for free grace, exalted and raised up to the infinite height of all the fulness and glory of the great Jehovah, and the arm of His power and grace stretched forth in all the majesty of His power, and in all the glory of His sovereignty, I should appear sunk down in my sins below hell itself; far beyond the sight of everything but the eye of sovereign grace, that can pierce even down to such a depth. And yet it seems to me, that my conviction of sin is exceeding small, and faint; it is enough to amaze me, that I have no more sense of my sin. I know certainly, that I have very little sense of my sinfulness. When I have had turns of weeping and crying for my sins, I thought I knew at the time, that my repentance was nothing to my sin.

I have greatly longed of late, for a broken heart, and to lie low before God; and, when I ask for humility, I cannot bear the thoughts of being no more humble than other Christians. It seems to me, that though their degrees of humility may be suitable for them, yet it would be a vile self-exaltation in me, not to be the lowest in humility of all mankind. Others speak of their longing to be "humbled to the dust"; that may be a proper expression for them, but I always think of myself, that I ought, and it is an expression that has long been natural for me to use in prayer, "to lie infinitely low before God." And it is affecting to think, how ignorant I was, when a young Christian, of the bottomless, infinite depths of wickedness, pride, hypocrisy, and deceit, left in my heart.

I have a much greater sense of my universal, exceeding dependence on God's grace and strength, and mere good pleasure, of late, than I used formerly to have; and have experienced more of an abhorrence of my own righteousness. The very thought of any joy arising in me, on any consideration of my own amiableness, performances, or experiences, or any goodness of heart or life, is nauseous and detestable to me. And yet I am greatly afflicted with a proud and self-righteous spirit, much more sensibly than I used to be formerly. I see that serpent rising and putting forth its head continually, everywhere, all around me. Though it seems to me, that, in some respects, I was a far better Christian, for two or three years after my first conversion, than I am now; and lived in a more constant delight and pleasure; yet, of late years, I have had a more full and constant sense of the absolute sovereignty of God, and a delight in that sovereignty; and have had more of a sense of the glory of Christ, as a Mediator revealed in the gospel. On one Saturday night, in particular, I had such a discovery of the excellency of the gospel above all other doctrines, that I could not but say to myself, "This is my chosen light, my chosen doctrine"; and of Christ, "This is my chosen prophet." It appeared sweet, beyond all expression, to follow Christ, and to be taught, and enlightened, and instructed by Him; to learn of Him, and live to Him. Another Saturday night (January, 1739), I had such a sense, how sweet and blessed a thing it was to walk in the way of duty; to do that which was right and meet to be done, and agreeable to the holy mind of God; that it caused me to break forth into a kind of loud weeping, which held me some time, so that I was forced to shut myself up, and fasten the doors. I could not but, as it were, cry out, "How happy are they which do that which is right in the sight of God! They are blessed indeed; they are the happy ones!" I had, at the same time, a very affecting sense, how meet and suitable it was that God should govern the world, and order all things according to His own pleasure; and I rejoiced in it, that God reigned and that His will was done.

Sinclair Lewis

from **Elmer Gantry**

The climactic meeting of the Annual Prayer Week, to be addressed by President Quarles, four ministers, and a rich trustee who was in the pearl-button business, with Judson Roberts as star soloist, was not held at the Y.M.C.A. but at the largest auditorium in town, the Baptist Church, with hundreds of town-people joining the collegians.

The church was a welter of brownstone, with Moorish arches and an immense star-shaped window not yet filled with stained glass.

Elmer hoped to be late enough to creep in inconspicuously, but as his mother and he straggled up to the Romanesque portico, students were still outside, chattering. He was certain they were whispering, "There he is—Hell-cat Gantry. Say, is it really true he's under conviction of sin? I thought he cussed out the church more'n anybody in college."

Meek though Elmer had been under instruction by Jim and threats by Eddie and yearning by his mother, he was not normally given to humility, and he looked at his critics defiantly. "I'll show 'em! If they think I'm going to sneak in—"

He swaggered down almost to the front pews, to the joy of his mother, who had been afraid that as usual he would hide in the rear, handy to the door if the preacher should become personal.

There was a great deal of decoration in the church which had been endowed by a zealous alumnus after making his strike in Alaskan boarding-houses during the gold-rush. There were Egyptian pillars with gilded capitals, on the ceiling were gilt stars and clouds more woolen than woolly, and the walls were painted cheerily in three strata—green, watery blue, and khaki. It was an echoing and gaping church, and presently it was packed, the aisles full. Professors with string mustaches and dog-eared Bibles, men students in sweaters or flannel shirts, earnest young women students in homemade muslin with modest ribbons, over-smiling old maids of the town, venerable saints from the back-country with beards which partly hid the fact that they wore collars without ties, old women with billowing shoulders, irritated young married couples with broods of babies who crawled, slid, bellowed, and stared with embarrassing wonder at bachelors.

Five minutes later Elmer would not have had a seat down front. Now he could not escape. He was packed in between his mother and a wheezing fat man, and in the aisle beside his pew stood evangelical tailors and ardent school-teachers.

The congregation swung into "When the Roll Is Called Up Yonder" and Elmer gave up his frenzied but impractical plans for escape. His mother nestled happily beside him, her hand proudly touching his sleeve, and he was stirred by the march and battle of the hymn:

> When the trumpet of the Lord shall sound, and time shall
> be no more,
> And the morning breaks eternal, bright and far. . . .

They stood for the singing of "Shall We Gather at the River?" Elmer inarticulately began to feel his community with these humble, aspiring people—his own prairie tribe: this gaunt carpenter, a good fellow, full of friendly greetings; this farm-wife, so courageous, channeled by pioneer labor; this classmate, an admirable basketball player, yet now chanting beatifically, his head back, his eyes closed, his voice ringing. Elmer's own people. Could he be a traitor to them, could he resist the current of their united belief and longing?

> Yes, we'll gather at the river,
> The beautiful, the beautiful river,
> Gather with the saints at the river
> That flows by the throne of God.

Could he endure it to be away from them, in the chill void of Jim Lefferts' rationalizing, on that day when they should be rejoicing in the warm morning sunshine by the river rolling to the imperishable Throne?

And his voice—he had merely muttered the words of the first hymn—boomed out ungrudgingly:

> Soon our pilgrimage will cease;
> Soon our happy hearts will quiver
> With the melody of peace.

His mother stroked his sleeve. He remembered that she had maintained he was the best singer she had ever heard; that Jim Lefferts had admitted, "You certainly can make that hymn dope sound as if it meant something." He noted that people near by looked about with pleasure when they heard his Big Ben dominate the cracked jangling.

The preliminaries merely warmed up the audience for Judson Roberts. Old Jud was in form. He laughed, he shouted, he knelt and wept with real tears, he loved everybody, he raced down into the audience and patted shoulders, and for the moment everybody felt that he was closer to them than their closest friends.

"Rejoiceth as a strong man to run a race," was his text.

Roberts was really a competent athlete, and he really had skill in evoking pictures. He described the Chicago-Michigan game, and Elmer was lost in him, with him lived the moments of the scrimmage, the long run with the ball, the bleachers rising to him.

Roberts voice softened. He was pleading. He was not talking, he said, to weak men who needed coddling into the Kingdom, but to strong men, to rejoicing men, to men brave in armor. There was another sort of race more exhilarating than any game, and it led not merely to a score on a big board but to the making of a new world—it led not to newspaper paragraphs but to glory eternal. Dangerous—calling for strong men! Ecstatic—brimming with thrills! The team captained by Christ! No timid Jesus did he preach, but the adventurer who had joyed to associate with common men, with reckless fishermen, with captains and rulers, who had dared to face the soldiers in the garden, who had dared the myrmidons of Rome and death itself! Come! Who was gallant? Who had nerve? Who longed to live abundantly? Let them come!

They must confess their sins, they must repent, they must know their own weakness save as they were reborn in Christ. But they must confess not in heaven-pilfering weakness, but in training for the battle under the wind-torn banners of the Mighty Captain. Who would come? Who would come? Who was for vision and the great adventure?

He was among them, Judson Roberts, with his arms held out, his voice a bugle. Young men sobbed and knelt; a woman shrieked; people were elbowing the standers in the aisles and pushing forward to kneel in agonized happiness, and suddenly they were setting relentlessly on a bewildered Elmer Gantry, who had been betrayed into forgetting himself, into longing to be one with Judson Roberts.

His mother was wringing his hand, begging, "Oh, won't you come? Won't you make your old mother happy? Let yourself know the joy of surrender to Jesus!" She was weeping, old eyes puckered, and in her weeping was his every recollection of winter dawns when she had let him stay in bed and brought porridge to him across the icy floor; winter evenings when he had awakened to find her still stitching; and that confusing intimidating hour, in the abyss of his first memories, when he had seen her shaken beside a coffin that contained a cold monster in the shape of his father.

The basket-ball player was patting his other arm, begging, "Dear old Hell-cat, you've never let yourself be happy! You've been lonely! Let yourself be happy with us! You know I'm no mollycoddle. Won't you know the happiness of salvation with us?"

A thread-thin old man, very dignified, a man with secret eyes that had known battles, and mountain-valleys, was holding out his hands to Elmer, imploring with a humility utterly disconcerting, "Oh, come, come with us—don't stand there making Jesus beg and beg—don't leave the Christ that died for us standing out in the cold, begging!"

And, somehow, flashing through the crowd, Judson Roberts was with Elmer, honoring him beyond all the multitude, appealing for his friendship—Judson Roberts the gorgeous, beseeching:

"Are you going to hurt me, Elmer? Are you going to let me go away miserable and beaten, old man? Are you going to betray me like Judas, when I've offered you my Jesus as the most precious gift I can bring you? Are you going to slap me and defile me and hurt me? Come! Think of the joy of being rid of all those nasty little sins that you've felt so ashamed of! Won't you come kneel with me, won't you?"

His mother shrieked, "Won't you, Elmer? With him and me? Won't you make us happy? Won't you be big enough to not be afraid? See how we're all longing for you, praying for you!"

"Yes!" from around him, from strangers; and "Help *me* to follow you, Brother —I'll go if you will!" Voices woven, thick, dove-white and terrifying black of mourning and lightning-colored, flung around him, binding him— His mother's pleading, Judson Roberts' tribute—

An instant he saw Jim Lefferts, and heard him insist: "Why, sure, course they believe it. They hypnotize themselves. But don't let 'em hypnotize you!"

He saw Jim's eyes, that for him alone veiled their bright harshness and became lonely, asking for comradeship. He struggled; with all the blubbering confusion of a small boy set on by his elders, frightened and overwhelmed, he longed to be honest, to be true to Jim—to be true to himself and his own good honest sins and whatsoever penalties they might carry. Then the visions were driven away by voices that closed over him like surf above an exhausted swimmer. Volitionless, marveling at the sight of himself as a pinioned giant, he was being urged forward, forced forward, his mother on one arm and Judson on the other, a rhapsodic mob following.

Bewildered. Miserable. . . . False to Jim.

But as he came to the row kneeling in front of the first pew, he had a thought that made everything all right. Yes! He could have both! He could keep Judson and his mother, yet retain Jim's respect. He had only to bring Jim also to Jesus, then all of them would be together in beatitude!

Freed from misery by that revelation, he knelt, and suddenly his voice was noisy in confession, while the shouts of the audience, the ejaculations of Judson and his mother, exalted him to hot self-approval and made it seem splendidly right to yield to the mystic fervor.

He had but little to do with what he said. The willing was not his but the mob's; the phrases were not his but those of the emotional preachers and hysterical worshipers whom he had heard since babyhood:

"O God, oh, I have sinned! My sins are heavy on me! I am unworthy of compassion! O Jesus, intercede for me! Oh, let thy blood that was shed for me be my salvation! O God, I do truly repent of my great sinning and I do long for the everlasting peace of thy bosom!"

"Oh, praise God," from the multitude, and "Praise his holy name! Thank God, thank God, thank God! Oh, hallelujah, Brother, thank the dear loving God!"

He was certain that he would never again want to guzzle, to follow loose women, to blaspheme; he knew the rapture of salvation—yes, and of being the center of interest in the crowd.

Others about him were beating their foreheads, others were shrieking, "Lord, be merciful," and one woman—he remembered her as a strange, repressed, mad-eyed special student who was not known to have any friends—was stretched out, oblivious of the crowd, jerking, her limbs twitching, her hands clenched, panting rhythmically.

But it was Elmer, tallest of the converts, tall as Judson Roberts, whom all the students and most of the townpeople found important, who found himself important.

His mother was crying, "Oh, this is the happiest hour of my life, dear! This makes up for everything!"

To be able to give her such delight!

Judson was clawing Elmer's hand, whooping, "Liked to had you on the team at Chicago, but I'm a lot gladder to have you with me on Christ's team! If you knew how proud I am!"

To be thus linked forever with Judson!

Elmer's embarrassment was gliding into a robust self-satisfaction.

Then the others were crowding on him, shaking his hand, congratulating him: the football center, the Latin professor, the town grocer. President Quarles, his chin whisker vibrant and his shaven upper lip wiggling from side to side, was insisting, "Come, Brother Elmer, stand up on the platform and say a few words to us—you must—we all need it—we're thrilled by your splendid example!"

Elmer was not quite sure how he got through the converts, up the steps to the platform. He suspected afterward that Judson Roberts had done a good deal of trained pushing.

He looked down, something of his panic returning. But they were sobbing with affection for him. The Elmer Gantry who had for years pretended that he relished defying the whole college had for those same years desired popularity. He had it now—popularity, almost love, almost reverence, and he felt overpoweringly his rôle as leading man.

He was stirred to more flamboyant confession:

"Oh, for the first time I know the peace of God! Nothing I have ever done has been right, because it didn't lead to the way and the truth! Here I thought I was a good church-member, but all the time I hadn't seen the real light. I'd never been willing to kneel down and confess myself a miserable sinner. But I'm kneeling now, and, oh, the blessedness of humility!"

He wasn't, to be quite accurate, kneeling at all; he was standing up, very tall and broad, waving his hands; and though what he was experiencing may have been the blessedness of humility, it sounded like his announcements of an ability to lick anybody in any given saloon. But he was greeted with flaming hallelujahs, and he shouted on till he was rapturous and very sweaty:

"Come! Come to him now! Oh, it's funny that I who've been so great a sinner could dare to give you his invitation, but he's almighty and shall prevail, and he giveth his sweet tidings through the mouths of babes and sucklings and the most unworthy, and lo, the strong shall be confounded and the weak exalted in his sight!"

It was all, the Mithraic phrasing, as familiar as "Good morning" or "How are you?" to the audience, yet he must have put new violence into it, for instead of smiling at the recency of his ardor they looked at him gravely, and suddenly a miracle was beheld.

Ten minutes after his own experience, Elmer made his first conversion.

A pimply youth, long known as a pool-room tout, leaped up, his greasy face working, shrieked, "O God, forgive me!" butted in frenzy through the crowd, ran to the mourner's bench, lay with his mouth frothing in convulsion.

Then the hallelujahs rose till they drowned Elmer's accelerated pleading, then Judson Roberts stood with his arm about Elmer's shoulder, then Elmer's mother knelt with a light of paradise on her face, and they closed the meeting in a maniac pealing of

Draw me nearer, blessed Lord,
To thy precious bleeding side.

Elmer felt himself victorious over life and king of righteousness.

But it had been only the devoted, the people who had come early and taken front seats, of whom he had been conscious in his transports. The students who had remained at the back of the church now loitered outside the door in murmurous knots, and as Elmer and his mother passed them, they stared, they even chuckled, and he was suddenly cold. . . .

It was hard to give heed to his mother's wails of joy all the way to her boarding-house.

"Now don't you dare think of getting up early to see me off on the train," she insisted. "All I have to do is just to carry my little valise across the street. You'll need your sleep, after all this stirrin' up you've had tonight—I was so proud—I've never known anybody to really wrestle with the Lord like you did. Oh, Elmy, you'll stay true? You've made your old mother so happy! All my life I've sorrowed, I've waited, I've prayed and now I shan't ever sorrow again! Oh, you will stay true?"

He threw the last of his emotional reserve into a ringing, "You bet I will, Ma!" and kissed her good-night.

He had no emotion left with which to face walking alone, in a cold and realistic night, down a street not of shining columns but of cottages dumpy amid the bleak snow and unfriendly under the bitter stars.

His plan of saving Jim Lefferts, his vision of Jim with reverent and beatific eyes, turned into a vision of Jim with extremely irate eyes and a lot to say. With that vanishment his own glory vanished.

"Was I," he wondered, "just a plain damn' fool?"

"Jim warned me they'd nab me if I lost my head."

"Now I suppose I can't ever even smoke again without going to hell."

But he wanted a smoke. Right now!

He had a smoke.

It comforted him but little as he fretted on:

"There *wasn't* any fake about it! I really did repent all these darn' fool sins. Even smoking—I'm going to cut it out. I did feel the—the peace of God.

"But can I keep up this speed? Christ! I can't *do* it! Never take a drink or any-thing—

"I wonder if the Holy Ghost really was there and getting after me? I did feel different! I did! Or was it just because Judson and Ma and all those Christers were there whooping it up—

"Jud Roberts kidded me into it. With all his Big Brother stuff. Prob'ly pulls it everywhere he goes. Jim'll claim I— Oh, damn Jim, too! I got some rights! None of his business if I come out and do the fair square thing! And they *did* look up to me when I gave them the invitation! It went off fine and dandy! And that kid coming right up and getting saved. Mighty few fellows ever've pulled off a conversion as soon after their own conversion as I did! Moody or none of 'em. I'll bet it busts the records! Yes, sir, maybe they're right. Maybe the Lord has got some great use for me, even if I ain't always been all I might of been . . . someways . . . but I was never mean or tough or anything like that . . . just had a good time.

"Jim—what right's he got telling me where I head in? Trouble with him is, he thinks he knows it all. I guess these wise old coots that've written all these books about the Bible, I guess they know more'n one smart-aleck Kansas agnostic!

"Yes, sir! The whole crowd! Turned to me like I was an All-American preacher!

"Wouldn't be so bad to be a preacher if you had a big church and— Lot easier than digging out law-cases and having to put it over a jury and another lawyer maybe smarter'n you are.

"The crowd have to swallow what you tell 'em in a pulpit, and no back-talk or cross-examination allowed!"

For a second he snickered, but:

"Not nice to talk that way. Even if a fellow don't do what's right himself, no excuse for his sneering at fellows that do, like preachers. . . . There's where Jim makes his mistake.

"Not worthy to be a preacher. But if Jim Lefferts thinks for one single solitary second that I'm afraid to be a preacher because *he* pulls a lot of guff— I guess *I* know how I felt when I stood up and had all them folks hollering and rejoicing— I guess *I* know whether I experienced salvation or not! And I don't require any James Blaine Lefferts to tell me, neither!"

Thus for an hour of dizzy tramping; now colder with doubt than with the prairie wind, now winning back some of the exaltation of his spiritual adventure, but always knowing that he had to confess to an inexorable Jim.

Will Herberg

Religion and Culture in Present-Day America

I

Whatever may be true about the religious situation, it certainly cannot be doubted
that religion is enjoying a boom of unprecedented proportions in America today.
Well over 95 per cent of the American people identify themselves religiously, as
Protestants, Catholics, or Jews—an incredibly high figure by all available standards
of comparison. The proportion of Americans who are church members—that is, actually on the rolls of the churches—has nearly doubled in the past half century; in
the last twenty years indeed, church membership has been increasing twice as fast
as population. Church and synagogue attendance is rising rapidly, Sunday school en-
rollment is rising even more rapidly, and religious giving has reached a formidable
figure, even allowing for the inflationary devaluation of the dollar. Interest in religion and religious thinking is widespread on all cultural levels. Whatever the criterion
of religiousness we take—and by religiousness I mean the "externals" of religion,
using this term in a neutral sense, without prejudice—we cannot escape the conclusion that we are today witnessing an upsurge of religion without precedent in recent
times.

But it is a curious kind of religion. The very same people who are so unanimous in identifying themselves religiously, who are joining churches at an accelerating rate, and who take it for granted that religion is a "very important" thing, do
not hesitate to acknowledge that religion is quite peripheral to their everyday lives:
more than half of them quite frankly admit that their religious beliefs have no influence whatever on their ideas in economics and politics, and a good proportion of
the remainder are obviously uncertain. The very same people who distribute the
Bible in vast quantities, largely by voluntary effort, are unable in their majority to
give the name of one single book of the New Testament, and the showing is not very
different when you take the Bible as a whole. The very same people who, four out
of five, say they regard Jesus as divine, when asked to name the most important
event in all universal history, place the Christ-event—the birth or crucifixion of
Christ—fourteenth on the list, tied with the Wright brothers' invention of the airplane: the Number 1 event, almost without exception, is given as Columbus' discovery of America.[1]

This is the problem: America is in the grip of a great religious boom, that is
obvious; yet equally obvious, though not so easy to establish by facts and figures,
is the continuing "trend toward secularism in ideas," to use Professor Handlin's
phrase[2]—it is really a trend toward secularism not only in ideas, but in attitudes
and values as well. This is the problem: the religiousness of a secularist society, the

---

1. Data illustrating both sides of the contemporary religious situation will be found in Will Herberg, *Protestant-Catholic-Jew: An Essay in American Religious Sociology* (Doubleday, 1955),
esp. chaps. I, IV, and V.
2. Oscar Handlin, *The American People in the Twentieth Century* (Harvard, 1954), p. 222.

"strengthening of the religious structure in spite of increasing secularization."[3]
Thinking through this paradox will take us a long way toward understanding the
present religious situation in this country.

II

The best approach to the problem, I think, is to try to understand something of the
role that religious belonging plays in the social structure and functioning of contemporary America. I well recognize that religion has its transcendent dimension, which
escapes all external scrutiny and analysis; but I am deliberately limiting my inquiry
at this point to those aspects that are subject to such scrutiny and analysis, and I
think that these aspects are significant in the total picture. What, then, is it that
strikes one about the new function of religion in the life of the American people
today? It is, I think, that religion, in its tripartite form of Protestant-Catholic-Jew,
is rapidly becoming the primary context of self-identification and social location in
present-day America. Let us see what this really means.

By and large, since the latter part of the nineteenth century at any rate, Americans have tended to identify and locate themselves in terms of race, ethnicity, and
religion. "When asked the simple question, 'What are you?'," Gordon W. Allport has
noted, referring to certain recent researches, "only ten per cent of four-year-olds
answer in terms of racial, ethnic, or religious membership, but 75 per cent of nine-
year-olds do so"[4] —and the percentage is even higher for adults. "Race" in America
today means color, white vs. nonwhite, and racial stigmatization has introduced an
element of caste-like stratification into American life. For white Americans, ethnicity
(immigrant origin) and religion have been, and remain, the major sources of pluralistic
diversity, and therefore the major forms of self-identification and social location. But
the relation between the two has changed drastically in the course of the past generation, and it is this change that provides a clue to the new role of religion in American
life.

As long as large-scale immigration continued, and America was predominantly
a land of immigrants, in the days when "the immigrants were American history," as
Handlin puts it,[5] the dominant form of diversity, and therefore the dominant form
of self-identification, was immigrant ethnicity. The always interesting question about
a new family moving into the neighborhood—"What are they?"—was regularly answered in terms of ethnic-immigrant origin. Religion was felt to be an aspect of ethnicity, a part of the ethnic heritage, recent or remote. The enthusiasts of the "melting
pot" were eager to eliminate these diverse heritages as quickly as possible; the "cultural pluralists" were determined to perpetuate them; but both alike moved within
a pluralism based substantially on ethnicity, ethnic culture, and ethnic religion.

3. Marshall Sklare, *Conservative Judaism: An American Religious Movement* (Free Press, 1955),
p. 39.
4. Gordon W. Allport, *The Resolution of Intergroup Tensions*, p. 7.
5. Oscar Handlin, *The Uprooted: The Epic Story of the Great Migrations That Made the American People* (Little Brown, 1951), p. 3.

Within the past generation, the picture has been radically transformed. The stoppage of mass immigration during the first World War, followed by the anti-immigration legislation of the 1920's, undermined the foundations of immigrant ethnicity and the immigrant ethnic group with amazing rapidity; what it did was to facilitate the emergence of third and postthird generations, with their characteristic responses and attitudes, as a decisive influence on American life, no longer threatened with submergence by the next new wave of immigration. Within the threefold American scheme of race, ethnicity, and religion, a shift took place, a shift is taking place, from ethnicity to religion as the dominant form of self-identification—as the dominant way of answering the question, "What am I? how do I differ from 'one man's family'? where do I fit in in the totality of American society?" Ethnic identifications and traditions have not disappeared; on the contrary, with the third generation, they are enjoying a lively popularity as symbols of "heritage." But now the relation between ethnicity and religion has been reversed: religion is no longer an aspect of ethnicity; it is ethnicity, or rather what remains of it, that is taken up, redefined, and expressed through religious identifications and institutions. Religion, or at least the tripartite differentiation of Protestant, Catholic, and Jew has (aside from race) become the prevailing form of defining one's identity as an American in contemporary American society.

Keeping this in mind, we can begin to understand one of the most striking facts in the religious history of this country during the past half century—the transformation of America from a *Protestant* country into a *three-religion* country.

Writing just thirty years ago, André Siegfried described Protestantism as America's "national religion,"[6] and he was largely right, despite the ban on religious establishment in the Constitution. Normally, to be born an American meant to be a Protestant; this was the religious identification that in the American mind quite naturally went along with being an American. Non-Protestants felt the force of this conviction almost as strongly as did the Protestants; Catholics and Jews, despite their vastly increasing numbers, experienced their non-Protestant religion as a problem, even as an obstacle, to their becoming full-fledged Americans: it was a mark of their foreignness. (This was true despite the much esteemed colonial heritage of both Jews and Catholics, since it was not the "old American" elements in these two groups that influenced American attitudes, but the newer immigrant masses.) In the familiar Troeltschean sense, Protestantism—not any one of the multiplying denominations, but Protestantism as a whole—constituted America's "established church."

This is no longer the case. Today, to be born an American is no longer taken to mean that one is necessarily a Protestant; Protestantism is no longer the obvious and "natural" religious identification of the American. Today, the evidence strongly indicates, America has become a three-religion country: the normal religious implication of being an American today is that one is either a Protestant, a Catholic, or a Jew. These three are felt to be, by and large, three different forms of being religious in the American way; they are the three "religions of democracy," the "three great faiths" of America. Today, unlike fifty years ago, not only Protestants, but increas-

6. André Siegfried, *America Comes of Age* (Harcourt Brace Jovanovich, 1927), p. 33.

ingly Catholics and Jews as well, feel themselves, and are recognized to be, Americans not apart from, or in spite of, their religion, but because of it. If America today possesses a "church" in the Troeltschean sense—that is, a form of religious belonging which is felt to be involved in one's belonging to the national community—it is the tripartite religious system of Protestant-Catholic-Jew.

This transformation of America from a Protestant into a three-religion country has come about not because of any marked increase in Catholics or Jews—the Protestant-Catholic ratio has remained pretty well the same for the past thirty years, and the proportion of Jews in the general population has probably been declining. It has come about, as I have suggested, through the emergence of a stabilized American third generation, which is able to set its mark on American life because it is no longer threatened with dissolution by recurrent waves of mass immigration.

The immigrant generation, and this is true of all immigrant nationalities, established itself in America as an ethnic group with an ethnic culture, of which the ethnic language and the ethnic religion were generally the most significant elements. For the first, the immigrant generation, religion was part of ethnicity; for the Italian immigrant, in other words, his Catholicness was part of his Italianness; for the Jewish immigrant, his Judaism, his Jewish religion, was part of his *Yiddishkait,* his ethnic culture. You remember the movie "Marty." You remember how Marty brings home the girl Clara to introduce her to his mother. His mother is a good churchgoing Catholic, but what is the question she asks about Clara? Not "Is she Catholic?," but "Is she Italian?" Why? Because to the mother, the first-generation immigrant, if she's Italian, then she's Catholic, and if she's Catholic without being Italian, it doesn't do any good anyway! This is the outlook on ethnicity and religion characteristic of the immigrant generation.

The second generation is in a very different position. The second generation is marginal—"too American for the home and too foreign for the school," in Marcus Hansen's celebrated phrase. It is doubly alienated, belonging to two communities but at home in neither, torn away from the old moorings and not yet anchored in the new reality. The second generation responds to its marginality in a number of ways, but by and large it may be said that what the second generation wants most of all is to get rid of its foreignness and become American. This obviously influences its attitude to religion. Just because in the immigrant home, in which the second generation grows up, religion is understood to be a part of ethnicity, to be a part of the immigrant foreignness, the second generation takes a negative view of religion, sometimes breaking with it entirely, usually retaining an uneasy connection, mixed with hostility and embarrassment. The second generation—and that holds true for every immigrant group in America—is characteristically the least religious of American generations.

But now comes the third generation. The third generation—and with it we must include the postthird generations that have arisen on American soil—is again in a very different position. It is at last American, securely American, secure as any American is in his Americanness. But it is faced with a new problem, the problem of defining its identity. Ethnic identifications will no longer serve, as in one way or another they served the first and second generations. What then?—how is the third generation to answer the question, "What am I? how do I differ from 'one man's family'? where do I fit in the totality of American society?" In an effort to define its social identity—without which no tolerable life is possible—the American third generation goes in search of a "heritage." In a sensational reversal of earlier attitudes, the third generation seeks a "return." Some two decades ago, Marcus Lee Hansen, studying not Italians or Jews on the east coast, but Scandinavian Lutherans in the Midwest in the twenties and thirties, expressed this reversal in a classic formula: "What the son wishes to forget, the grandson wishes to remember."[7] The "son," constituting the second generation, wishes to "forget" because he wants so passionately to get rid of his foreignness; the "grandson," belonging to the third generation, wishes to "remember" because he needs a "heritage." But what of the grandfather can the grandson "remember"?—what of his grandfather's legacy can he take over and use for the purpose of giving himself a "heritage" and defining his identity? Not his grandfather's nationality, language, or culture; the American pattern of assimilative acculturation obviously makes that impossible. But the grandfather's religion is a very different thing: America not only permits, it even encourages, the perpetuation of one's religious diversity and distinctiveness without danger to one's Americanness. Of course, it is not the grandfather's religion as the grandfather would have recognized it; it is the grandfather's religion brought up to date and Americanized. But it serves; and so religion becomes the characteristic symbol of "heritage" for the third generation, and its return to its heritage becomes a return to religion. With Catholics and Jews, the process, however complex, is relatively unambiguous. With Protestants, however, there is a double movement: on the one side, a return to ethnically associated religion, as among Lutherans; on the other side, because of the confusion, blurring, and growing meaninglessness of denominational lines, a "return" to Protestantism rather than to any particular group within it as a form of religious identification. William H. Whyte's account, in *The Organization Man,* of the emergence of the United Protestant Church in Park Forest, Ill., a story which could be duplicated in so many other suburban communities, well illustrates this pattern of development; but even where denominational affiliations are still maintained, the basic identification is still Protestant, especially among the younger people. And so a three-religion America has emerged, an America in which being a Protestant, being a Catholic, and being a Jew are the three recognized alternative ways of being an American.

A word of caution is necessary. It should not be imagined that just because America has become, or is becoming, a three-religion country, all ethnic or religious group tensions are at an end. Anti-Semitism runs deeper than any merely sociological analysis can penetrate, and even on the sociological level, the new tripartite system would, for the time being at least, seem to make almost as much for the exacerbation as for the alleviation of intergroup tensions. Anti-Jewish manifestations are, for the moment, at a low ebb, but Protestant-Catholic antagonisms appear to be growing sharper. This accentuation of Protestant-Catholic tensions seems to me to be very largely a reflection of the painful transition period through which we

7. M. L. Hansen, *The Problem of the Third Generation Immigrant* (Augustana Historical Society, 1938), p. 9.

are passing; there is every reason to hope that with the stabilization of the new situation, these hostilities too will abate. Yet we should not overlook the fact that the new system of tripartite coexistence is bound to raise its own problems and breed its own tensions with which we will have to cope in the time to come.

III

What has the transformation of America from an ethnic into a religious pluralism, and concomitantly from a Protestant into a three-religion country, meant so far as the status and character of religion in this country are concerned?

Very obviously, it has made for a boom in religious belonging. To have a "name" in American society today—to have an identity, to be able to answer the question "What am I? where do I belong?"—means increasingly to identify oneself in religious terms, as Protestant, Catholic, or Jew. These are three alternative ways of being an American. This is eminently true of the burgeoning suburban sector of American society, least true in the rural areas, and measurably true in the older urban centers. It is certainly the over-all pattern of American life. Obviously, such self-identification in religious terms engenders a new sense of belonging to one's religious community; obviously, too, it impells to institutional affiliation, characteristically expressed in terms of concern for the children: "We have to join a church (or a temple) for the sake of the children." There is profound sociological wisdom in this remark, though its theological implications may be dubious. "The church," Oscar Handlin points out, "supplies a place where the children come to learn what they are"[8]—what kind of Americans they are. The mechanisms of other-directed conformity to which David Riesman has called attention serve to give religious belonging the compelling power it is acquiring in the pattern of suburban "sociability," but the new role of religion in this process is the result of the more basic factors I have tried to indicate in my remarks on the third generation and the transformation of America into a three-religion country.

Just as Americans are coming more and more to think of being a Protestant, being a Catholic, and being a Jew as three alternative ways of being an American, so they are coming to regard Protestantism, Catholicism, and Judaism, the "three great faiths," as three alternative (though not necessarily equal) expressions of a great overarching commitment which they all share by virtue of being Americans. This commitment is, of course, democracy or the American Way of Life. It is the common allegiance which (to use Professor Williams' phrase) provides Americans with the "common set of ideas, rituals, and symbols" through which an "overarching sense of unity" is achieved amidst diversity and conflict.[9] It is, in a sense far more real than John Dewey ever dreamed of, the "common religion" of Americans.

Let me illustrate this point with two texts borrowed from President Eisenhower, who may, I think, be taken as a representative American really serious about

8. Oscar Handlin, *The American People in the Twentieth Century,* p. 222.
9. Robin M. Williams, Jr., *American Society: A Sociological Interpretation* (Knopf, 1951), p. 312.

religion. "Our government," Mr. Eisenhower declared shortly after his election in 1952, "makes no sense unless it is founded in a deeply felt religious faith, *and I don't care what it is*."[10] It is the last phrase which I have emphasized—"and I don't care what it is"—to which I want to call your attention. Of course, President Eisenhower did not mean that literally; he would have been much disturbed had any sizable proportion of Americans become Buddhists, or Shintoists, or Confucianists—but of course that never entered his mind. When he said "I don't care what it is," he obviously meant "I don't care which of the three it is—Protestantism, Catholicism, or Judaism." And why didn't he care which it was? Because, in his view, as in the view of all normal Americans, they "all say the same thing." And what is the "same thing" which they all say? The answer is given to us from the current vocabulary: "the moral and spiritual values of democracy." These, for the typical American, are in a real sense final and ultimate; the three conventional religions are approved of and validated primarily because they embody and express these "moral and spiritual values of democracy."

Let me drive this home with the second text from President Eisenhower. In 1948, four years before his election, just before he became president of Columbia, Mr. Eisenhower made another important pronouncement on religion. "I am the most intensely religious man I know," he declared. "Nobody goes through six years of war without faith. That does not mean that I adhere to any sect. (Incidentally, following the way of all flesh, he was soon to join a "sect," the Presbyterian.) A democracy cannot exist without a religious base. I believe in democracy."[11] Here we have the entire story in a single phrase: I believe in religion because I believe in democracy! Precisely the same conviction, though expressed in a rather more sophisticated manner, was affirmed by an eminent New York rabbi not long ago. "The spiritual meaning of American democracy," he declared, "is realized in its three great faiths."[12] Similar statements, I assure you, could be found in the pronouncements of spokesmen of the other two religious groups.

What I am describing is essentially the "Americanization" of religion in America, and therefore also its thorough-going secularization. This process is not a recent one. It began for Protestantism some time after the Civil War and proceeded apace in the latter decades of the nineteenth century. Sidney Mead's brilliant description of this trend is particularly relevant.

> *What was not so obvious at the time (he writes) was that the United States, in effect, had two religions, or at least two different forms of the same religion, and that the prevailing Protestant ideology represented a syncretistic mingling of the two. The first was the religion of the (Protestant) denominations which was commonly articulated in terms of scholastic Protestant orthodoxy and almost universally practised in terms of the experimental religion of pietistic revivalism. . . . The second was the religion of the democratic society and nation.*

10. *New York Times,* December 23, 1952.
11. *New York Times,* May 4, 1948.
12. Rabbi David J. Seligson, quoted in *New York Times,* March 25, 1956.

*This . . . was articulated in terms of the destiny of America, under God, to be
fulfilled by perfecting the democratic way of life for the example and better-
ment of mankind.*[13]

With remarkably little change—something would have to be said about the
waning of scholastic orthodoxy and the new forms of pietistic revivalism—these
words could stand as a description of the current situation. What is new, what is
crucially new, is that this is no longer true merely of Protestantism; it is becoming
more and more true of Catholicism and Judaism as well, precisely because Catholicism and Judaism have become American, integral parts of the three-religion America.
In this, as in so many other respects, their Americanization has meant their "Protes-
tantization," using this term to describe the American Protestant ethos, so at vari-
ance with classical Protestant Christian faith. With the loss of their foreignness, of
their immigrant marginality, these two religious groups seem to be losing their capacity to resist dissolution in the culture. In becoming American, they have apparently
become American all the way.

We are now, I think, in a position to penetrate the apparent paradox with
which we initiated this discussion, the paradox of the religiousness of a secularist
society. How can Americans be so religious and so secularistic at the same time?
The answer is that for increasing numbers of Americans religion serves a function
largely unrelated to the content of faith, the function of defining their identity and
providing them with a context of belonging in the great wilderness of a mobile American society. Indeed, for such a purpose, the authentic content of faith may even
prove a serious handicap, for if it is Jewish or Christian faith, it carries a prophetic
impact which serves rather to unadjust than to adjust, to emphasize the ambiguity
of every earthly form of belonging rather than to let the individual rest secure in his
"sociability." For this reason, the typical American has developed a remarkable
capacity for being serious about religion without taking religion seriously—in which
respect he is not unlike sinful human beings of all ages. His ideas, values, and standards he takes from what is so often really his ultimate commitment, the American
Way of Life. He combines the two—his religion and his culture—by making the former an expression of the latter, his religion an expression of the "moral and spiritual
values of democracy." Hence his puzzling proreligious secularism, his secularistic re-
ligionism, which, looked at more closely, does not seem so puzzling after all.

IV

From the standpoint of the man of faith, of the man who takes his religious tradition
seriously, what does the picture of religion in contemporary America add up to? No
simple or unequivocal answer can be given.

On the one hand, the emergence of religion as a vehicle of American belonging
has made for a breakdown of antireligious prejudice. One of the most striking features

<hr>

13. Sidney E. Mead, "American Protestantism Since the Civil War. I. From Denominationalism
to Americanism," *The Journal of Religion,* vol. xxxvi, No. 1, January, 1956, p. 2.

of present-day American culture is the complete absence of an Ingersoll or a Darrow, of the "village atheist" on a national scale, or for that matter, except here and there, even on a village scale. Contemporary Americans, especially the younger generation, simply cannot understand the militant atheist of yesterday; he is so remote from their mentality as to be hardly credible. The breakdown of antireligion has contributed toward the new openness to religion that is so obvious today. Yet the religion that emerges is only too often a religiousness, or perhaps a proreligiousness, without religion, without serious religious content, conviction, or commitment. There is great danger, as one Jewish leader recently put it, that our church or synagogue cards may hide from us the basically secularistic character of our religion. There is even danger that with the rapid spread of a contentless religiousness, the very meaning of religion in its authentic sense may be lost for increasing numbers.

There is also a positive side to the "Americanization" of religion, which sees in Protestantism, Catholicism, and Judaism three forms of being religious in the American way. To the degree that this is felt to be true, the stigma of foreignness is lifted from Catholicism and Judaism, and from such ethnic forms of Protestantism as the Lutheran. There is a new freedom and tolerance, and at least the public equality of the "three great faiths" in American life. No one who remembers what misery the taint of foreignness once brought, and what a formidable obstacle it constituted to the preservation and communication of the "non-American" faiths, will fail to be grateful for this development. But it has been purchased at a heavy price, the price of embracing an idolatrous civic religion of Americanism.

I want to express myself here very clearly, and I will do so by speaking to you as Catholics. I recently lectured to the entire student body of a well-known Catholic girls' college. In the course of my remarks, I confronted them—not in such a way as to put them on their guard, of course—with Christopher Dawson's celebrated questions: "Are you Americans who happen to be Catholics, or Catholics who happen to be Americans?" Almost with one voice the girls answered, "Americans who happen to be Catholics . . ." You appreciate the significance of the question and the answer. The question really means: "Is your ultimate allegiance and your ultimate community the Universal Church, or is it the American nation?" The answer of the girls indicated that they normally thought of themselves as primarily Americans, but of course as Americans of the "Catholic kind," just as some of their friends were Americans of the "Protestant kind," and still others Americans of the "Jewish kind." Let me assure you that I have received the same kind of response from other Catholic groups—lay groups, that is—and from Protestant and Jewish audiences as well, when the question was put to them in their own terms.

What does that mean? It means that we have in America an invisible, formally unacknowledged, but very potent religion—the religion of democracy, the religion of the American Way of Life—of which the conventional religions are felt to be more or less adequate expressions. Americans do not put it that way, in just so many words, but that is how they feel and behave. In effect, this means that they participate in an actual civic religion, very much like the civic religion of the Roman Empire in early Christian times. The authentic relation between religion and culture is subverted, of which the civic religion is the sanctification, is idolatrized by being made ultimate, which means divine. Judaism, and Christianity in its two forms, become subordinated to the culture and tend to lose all sense of uniqueness, universality, and special vocation. To the man of Jewish or Christian faith, this divinization of the American Way—even if he acknowledges, as I do, the American Way to be one of the best ways of life yet devised for a mass society—must appear as abhorrent as the ancient civic religions appeared to the Jew or Christian of those days, in spite of the fact that our own civic religion is not officially established, overtly promulgated, or enforced through persecution.

It is not without significance that this conversion of democracy, or the American Way of Life, into the "common religion" of Americans has been given explicit formulation by a number of secularist-minded philosophers, such as Horace M. Kallen, who proclaims the "democratic faith" to be, for its "communicants"—the words are Kallen's—"the religion *of* and *for* religions, . . . all may freely come together in it."[14] What Kallen here states explicitly—the title of his article is "Democracy's True Religion"—is implicit in the ethos of American life and finds expression in many of its social and cultural, as well as religious, patterns. No wonder that Dean Sperry introduced his survey of religion in America with the words: "The honest critic of American affairs must therefore face the possibility that the true religion of his is not that of Protestant, Catholic, or Jew, but is rather a secular idolatry."[15]

The American conviction that "religion is a very good thing"—this may be taken as the second article in the American religious creed; the first is belief in God, and the third, and last, is that all really American religion is either Protestant, Catholic, or Jewish—the American conviction that religion is a very good thing, I say, means that religion is taken seriously and is endowed with a vigor and vitality that amazes foreign observers. But it also means that religion is thoroughly "functionalized," that is, converted into a tool for secular purposes. It is made to serve the sociological function of providing a form of identification and a context of belonging in a world of other-directed "sociability"; of this we have already spoken. But it is also made to serve the psychological function of conferring, on the one side, reassurance and "peace of mind," and on the other, a sense of power and achievement through "positive thinking." It is not our purpose to examine this aspect in any detail, but one thing should be noted. Just as religion on its sociological side seems to function best if it is unembarrassed with content, so religion on its psychological side easily comes to mean a contentless faith. In the one case, it may be said that Americans are religious about religion; in the other, that they have faith in faith. I appeal to you to take this description with the utmost seriousness. So eminent a religious leader as Daniel Poling quite simply describes his own conviction about faith in these words: "It was back in those days that I formed a habit which I have never broken. I began saying in the morning two words, 'I believe.' Those two words, with nothing added, . . . give me a running start for my day, for every day."[16] Another religious leader, not a Protestant, puts it this way: "The storehouse of

14. Horace M. Kallen, "Democracy's True Religion," *Saturday Review,* July 28, 1951.
15. W. S. Sperry, *Religion in America* (Macmillan, 1946), p. 19.
16. Daniel Poling, "A Running Start for Every Day," *Parade: The Sunday Picture Magazine,* September 19, 1954.

dynamic power on which you may draw, is *Faith*. Not religion, . . . not God, but *FAITH*."[17] And an advertisement in a New York paper of three eminently respectable churches is headed: "When Faith Alone Protects." In the entire ad neither God nor Christ is so much as mentioned. Church-going is recommended with the argument: "There are times in your life when faith alone protects. We all reach these times in hours of crisis which dot life's span. Regular church attendance helps you build your own personal reserve of faith."[18] What is this but picturing God as a great cosmic public utility, and religion or church-going as a way of charging one's storage battery of faith for use in emergencies? It is hardly necessary to point out that this faith in faith, this religion of religion, is just as idolatrous as faith in a stock or stone or the religion of magical self-salvation.

　　Americans crave security; they are bewildered and uneasy even in their prosperity. Americans crave personal power and achievement; they are frightened at the great heteronomous forces of a mass society which threaten to grind them into nothingness. Americans crave sociability; they are terrified at the prospect of being lost in the crowd. But most of all they crave reassurance about their goals and values, which they feel called into question and threatened on every side. And so they have fashioned their religion to serve these purposes by turning it into a man-centered cult of "peace of mind," "positive thinking," and American belonging. The religion that has emerged was bitingly described by Richard Niebuhr, speaking of latter-day Protestantism, two decades ago: "A God without wrath (brings) men without sin into a kingdom without judgment through the ministrations of a Christ without a cross."[19]

V

This is a picture of the religious situation in the United States today, but it is only a partial picture. There are other and more authentic stirrings of faith abroad, especially among the younger people on the campuses and their somewhat elder contemporaries in the suburban communities. These stirrings, fed from deeper sources, express themselves in different degrees on the various levels of interest, concern, and commitment, but everywhere the signs are unmistakable. Recent surveys have documented it,[20] and the report of the Student Council of Harvard University issued in February 1956 under the title of "Religion at Harvard," along with like expressions of student opinion on other campuses, may be taken as significant manifestations. This type of religious revival is very different, in its origins and in its expressions, from the religiousness we have been describing; it looks to religion not for "peace of mind," the "power of positive thinking," or the comfort of adjustment and be-

17. Louis Binstock, *The Power of Faith* (Prentice-Hall, 1952), p. 4.
18. Advertisement of three Episcopal churches, *New York Herald-Tribune,* April 15, 1955.
19. H. Richard Niebuhr, *The Kingdom of God in America* (Willett Clark, 1937), p. 193.
20. See esp. the report of the study of campus attitudes toward religion conducted by the Rev. James L. Stoner, director of the University Christian Mission of the National Council of Churches of Christ in the U.S.A., *New York Times,* October 22 and 24, 1956; cp. also Will Herberg, "The Religious Stirring on the Campus," *Commentary,* March, 1952.

longing, but for some outlook, perhaps even commitment, that will illumine the meaning of existence and give one the resources to preserve authenticity of being in a world poised at the brink of nothingness and trying to save itself by an increasingly rigid conformism. This deeper kind of faith combines with the mass religiousness of the American people in various ways, but the distinctive thing about it is that it fights shy of institutional embodiment and involvement. This constitutes a very real problem, for a religiousness without a firm institutional framework of tradition and doctrine is bound to degenerate into eccentricity, sentimentalism, or intellectual dilettantism. And in fact something of the sort seems to be occurring here and there, although usually what happens is that the stirrings of faith aroused in the "open" period of campus and immediate postcampus life are overwhelmed and dissipated by the overpowering force of American mass religiousness. What the final outcome will be, as these two very different types of religious revival meet and confront each other, it is still too soon to say. Only the future can tell what the deeper stirrings of faith, wherever they may arise, will amount to and what consequences they will hold for the American religion of tomorrow.

But even the more dubious forms of American religion should not be written off entirely. Even in this ambiguous structure, there may be elements and aspects— not always those, incidentally, that seem most promising to us today—which could in the longer view transform the character of American religion and bring it closer to the traditions of faith it claims to represent. Nothing is too unpromising or re- fractory to serve the divine will. After all, the God who is able to make the "wrath of men" to praise Him, is surely capable of turning even the superficialities, inade- quacies, and perversities of contemporary religion into an instrument of His redemp- tive purpose.

Judith S. Neaman

Zen Poems

One religious current in contemporary America is not represented by a lengthy selection, but it is so manifest and so influential that the editors feel that it must be mentioned. This is the growing movement toward and interest in oriental religions. Taoism and Zen are the two religions which are of special interest to the young who, turning away from the alienation and materialism of their parents' "establishment," seek peace in meditation, in philosophy, in the use of the ancient Chinese prophetic book of the *I Ching*.

Like their transcendentalist forebears, the young look to the natural world for consolation and to the internal world of psychic exploration for a sense of self-containment and a balm for the wounds caused by a society in which material achievement seems to them to have destroyed a sense of harmony and wholeness. Their literature is the *Book of Tao,* the works of Alan Watts, D. T. Suzuki, books of Zen riddles, and the Haiku of the Japanese. Their solution is not a new one. Emily Dickinson felt the same needs but reconciled her world and her needs in a slightly different manner when she wrote

> When Orient has been outgrown,
> And Occident becomes unknown,
> His name remain.

Below, we have offered a few short poems, Oriental in type, occidental in cast, which we hope will illustrate the need for and the interest in the religions of the Orient.

> America's body
> severed in zones
> Whole them in one
> warm flesh, zen bones.

> When every altar's empty
> There is no
> Light within—
> The tapers gutter.

KOAN
Where is three in one less than one?

Psychology: The Chrysalis
of All People

In considerations of psychology and psychiatry one must realize that, although they are relatively recent sciences, they have more distant roots in the works of experimental psychologists like Ribot and Charcot. The editors, therefore, have had to break precedent and refer to the works of two Europeans in a book specifically devoted to American studies. Freud and Jung were the indisputable fathers of modern psychiatry, and despite the fact that their theories were conceived and recorded in Europe, their greatest influence has been felt in American psychology and psychiatry. For this reason the section which follows includes a selection from the works of Freud—the representative of individualism in psychotherapy—and a selection from the works of Carl Jung—the representative of the collectivist theory of psychotherapy. Because the neo-Jungians are less well known than the neo-Freudians and because Jung's greatest influence in America has been in the disciplines of art and literary criticism and in studies of myth, a selection from the works of Joseph Campbell, an American mythologist, is also included.

When we speak of individualism and collectivism in psychology and psychiatry, we are referring to the *a priori* assumptions which underlie the therapeutic methods discovered by Freud and Jung respectively. Freud, although recognizing universal developmental stages in human psychic growth, was most concerned with the highly varied responses and accommodations of individual psyches to these stages. Jung tended to emphasize the view that all psyches are similar to one another since they all partake of the nature of a single "over-psyche"—the collective unconscious or "objective psyche," as Jungians are wont to call it.

Psychoanalytic method—as opposed to theory—is now undergoing a radical change. Current psychiatry utilizes two vastly different therapeutic processes: psychoanalysis of the individual as practiced by Jung and Freud and group therapy, which, although it may apply either Jungian or Freudian theories, treats groups of people in an external social or collective setting rather than individuals in a private internal milieu. "The Esalen Foundation: 'Joy Is the Prize' " presents this group therapy form of psychiatric collectivism.

Both Freud and Jung marked and changed modern society. The father figure of the infant study of psychiatry changed the emphasis of the older psychiatry, which had been devoted to the premise that physical causes and somatic cures were of prime importance in the diagnosis and treatment of psychic disorders. Freud revolutionized psychiatry in several ways. First, he introduced the conviction that psychic origins and treatments of emotional problems were quintessential to a successful understanding of mental illness. Second, he proposed that neurosis and tension arose from an interaction or a conflict between elements or parts of the psyche. These psychic components he named the *ego* (the socialized and cultural self which defines the individual being), the *superego* (what we may call the conscience), and the *id* (the primitive drive for fulfillment of desires, largely sexual in nature). Third, he distinguished certain stages of normal human development, the oral stage, the anal stage, and the genital stage. The child, frustrated in his attempts to fulfill or satisfy the instincts and desires associated with each stage, might be psychically arrested throughout his life because he would remain fixed in that particular stage which he could not satisfy. Last, but most important, Freud associated all psychic phenomena with sexual drives. Sexual fears, needs, and proclivities were, for Freud, both indices and causes of character traits and of health or neurosis. Erik Erikson extended Freud's studies into the larger arena of social psychology. He varied the names and the diagnoses of the psychic stages, but he too found that the nature of a society was determined by the psychic forces which war within the individual who has not developed into that maturity which enables him to perceive a unity of milieu and being. He might be called an inheritor of the legacy of Freud's work, *Civilization and Its Discontents.*

Jung, as student and assistant to Freud, broke with his mentor over the primarily sexual interpretation of all psychic motivation. Instead of searching for the materials of the individual and personal unconscious in the individual, Jung, examining the history of various cultures, reached the conclusion that all people share an "archaic heritage of archetypal forms."

The individual psyche is a force born of two types of experience, the internal experience of the unconscious world which lies within man, and the external experience of the universal environment of space, time, life, death, cause and effect. He described the psychic source as a structure, the units of which were archetypes or patterns endemic to all cultures. These archetypes of creation, birth, death, and knowledge appear in different forms but play identical roles in the myths of every society. He believed that the archetypal patterns which rule people's lives were not so much created as recognized, and though he believed that people were born with archetypal patterns imprinted on their minds, he was unwilling to maintain that they were biologically inherited. In myth, the plot structure of archetypal symbol, lay the racial memory or collective unconscious. Freud, on the other hand, felt that psycho-sexual forces which developed by stages in each individual were converted into various myths. For him, the motivation arose not from racial memory but from development of the individual. It is often difficult to see the differences between the two writers when we consider such works as Freud's late *Moses and Monotheism,* for both recognized the fundamental psychic symbolism of myth and the shared experience of all peoples, but we may say of Jung that he studied individuals by studying myth, and of Freud that he studied myth by studying individuals.

In a sense, Jung may be considered the more flexible of the two, since he recognized a greater variety of psychic drives than did Freud, who adhered more or less strictly to his several chief categories of psychic motivation: the Oedipus complex, the death wish, the sexual drives, wish fulfillment, and so on. Yet, Freud foresaw the fate and the flexibility of his own work as Jung did not, when he said in a letter to Jung that after his death his work would certainly not be sacrosanct. It would be varied, twisted, reinterpreted. The followers of Jung have generally adhered more closely to Jung than have the Freudians to Freud.

In our own age we see a greater search for the universal in the individual. Our literary critics, profoundly influenced by Jung, seek the mythic sources of literary motifs. Our new experiments in psychic studies are often directed toward the common elements of love, hate, fear, and joy, which lie in all human beings. An almost mystical certainty that, once tapped or touched by another, each person will yield up a secret self that is comprehensible because it lies in all of us, dominates such self-discovery groups as the Esalen Institute. Perhaps because we seek unity or community or brotherhood, we search for the single self we would like to believe we all share. Whether or not the source of these beliefs is entirely Jungian is difficult to say. Do we all share similar stages of mental growth, similar bodies, similar myths, similar parental conflicts? No one has yet been able to answer these questions to the universal satisfaction.

Thus, in the archetypes of myth study and motif study in art and the mystical faith in our own oneness, we are all Jungians. In our sensitivity to sexual symbolism and our desire to free ourselves of physical inhibition, we are all Freudians. Both theories have molded our society and our literature. Eugene O'Neill was perhaps the earliest of our writers to apply Freudian insight to a dramatic study of sexual drive in the life of an American woman, Nina Leeds, in "Strange Interlude." In a psycho-drama which reveals the inner life as well as the outer events of the characters' struggles, O'Neill experiments with an "interior monologue" device, a Freudian technique which permits the protagonists to reveal both the conscious and subconscious layers of their thoughts. T. S. Eliot's "Wasteland" reveals Jungian elements in its universal symbols. Robert Lowell's later poetry is frankly Freudian; Wallace Stevens' is Jungian. The poet Babette Deutsch's *Archetypal Patterns in American Poetry* is a critical work which grows out of the Jungian mode. In fiction, there is an increased awareness and use of the themes and preoccupations of psychoanalysis. Ken Kesey's *One Flew Over the Cuckoo's Nest* and Hannah Green's remarkable portrayal of the labyrinths of the schizophrenic personality in *I Never Promised You a Rose Garden* are two contemporary novelistic incursions into the psyche. In popular entertainment we have a current Freudian transcription of *Alice in Wonderland* playing to a receptive theater audience.

Today, whether we celebrate or scorn the influence of psychiatry, we are increasingly aware of psychic motivations, of a force called the unconscious, with which we must reckon forever. Perception and experience have been irrevocably altered. The realm of the unconscious, which had for so long remained dark and unexplored before the advent of Freudian and Jungian psychoanalysis, has now been illuminated and opened for all time. Its impact upon Western life is incalculable. We know only that it has transformed immeasurably the way in which we regard the dynamics of personality arising from the inner sources of psychic experience.

Sigmund Freud

Childhood and Concealing Memories

In a second essay,[1] I was able to demonstrate the purposive nature of our memories in an unexpected field. I started with the remarkable fact that the earliest recollections of a person often seemed to preserve the unimportant and accidental, whereas (frequently though not universally!) not a trace is found in the adult memory of the weighty and affective impressions of this period. As it is known that the memory exercises a certain selection among the impressions at its disposal, it would seem logical to suppose that this selection follows entirely different principles in childhood than at the time of intellectual maturity. However, close investigation points to the fact that such an assumption is superfluous. The indifferent childhood memories owe their existence to a process of displacement. It may be shown by psychoanalysis that in the reproduction they represent the substitute for other really significant impressions, whose direct reproduction is hindered by some resistance. As they do not owe their existence to their own contents, but to an associative relation of their contents to another repressed thought, they deserve the title of "concealing memories," by which I have designated them.

In the aforementioned essay I only touched upon, but in no way exhausted, the varieties in the relations and meanings of concealed memories. In the given example fully analyzed, I particularly emphasized a peculiarity in the temporal relation between the concealing memory and the contents of the memory concealed by it. The content of the concealing memory in that example belonged to one of the first years of childhood, while the thoughts represented by it, which remained practically unconscious, belonged to a later period of the individual in question. I called this form of displacement a retro-active or *regressive* one. Perhaps more often, one finds the reversed relation—that is, an indifferent impression of the most remote period becomes a concealing memory in consciousness, which simply owes its existence to an association with an earlier experience, against whose direct reproduction there are resistances. We would call these *encroaching* or *interposing* concealing memories. What most concerns the memory lies here chronologically beyond the concealing memory. Finally, there may be a third possible case, namely, the concealing memory may be connected with the impression it conceals, not only through its contents, but also through contiguity of time; this is the *contemporaneous* or *contiguous* concealing memory.

How large a portion of the sum total of our memory belongs to the category of concealing memories, and what part it plays in various neurotic hidden processes, these are problems into the value of which I have neither inquired, nor shall I enter here. I am concerned only with emphasizing the sameness between the forgetting of proper names with faulty recollection and the formation of concealing memories.

At first sight, it would seem that the diversities of both phenomena are far more striking than their exact analogies. There we deal with proper names, here

1. Published in the *Monatschrift f. Psychiatrie u. Neurologie*, 1899.

with complete impressions experienced either in reality or in thought; there we deal with a manifest failure of the memory function, here with a memory act which appears strange to us. Again, there we are concerned with a momentary disturbance— for the name just forgotten could have been reproduced correctly a hundred times before, and will be so again from tomorrow on; here we deal with lasting possession without a failure, for the indifferent childhood memories seem to be able to accompany us through a great part of life. In both these cases, the riddle seems to be solved in an entirely different way. There it is the forgetting, while here it is the remembering which excites our scientific curiosity.

After deeper reflection, one realizes that, although there is a diversity in the psychic material and in the duration of time of the two phenomena, yet these are by far outweighed by the conformities between the two. In both cases we deal with the failure of remembering; what should be correctly reproduced by the memory fails to appear, and instead something else comes as a substitute. In the case of forgetting a name, there is no lack of memory function in the form of name substitution. The formation of a concealing memory depends on the forgetting of other important impressions. In both cases, we are reminded by an intellectual feeling of the intervention of a disturbance, which in each case takes a different form. In the case of forgetting of names, *we are aware* that the substitutive names are *incorrect,* while in concealing memories, we are surprised that we have them at all. Hence, if psychologic analysis demonstrates that the substitutive formation in each case is brought about in the same manner—that is, through displacement along a superficial association—we are justified in saying that the diversities in material, in duration of time, and in the centering of both phenomena serve to enhance our expectation, that we have discovered something that is important and of general value. This generality purports that the stopping and straying of the reproducing function indicates more often than we suppose that there is an intervention of a prejudicial factor, a tendency which favors one memory and, at the same time, works against another.

The subject of childhood memories appears to me so important and interesting that I would like to devote to it a few additional remarks which go beyond the views expressed so far.

How far back into childhood do our memories reach? I am familiar with some investigations on this question by V. and C. Henri[2] and Potwin.[3] They assert that such examinations show wide individual variations, inasmuch as some trace their first reminiscences to the sixth month of life, while others can recall nothing of their lives before the end of the sixth or even the eighth year. But what connection is there between these variations in the behavior of childhood reminiscences, and what significance may be ascribed to them? It seems that it is not enough to procure the material for this question by simple inquiry, but it must later be subjected to a study in which the person furnishing the information must participate.

I believe we accept too indifferently the fact of infantile amnesia—that is, the failure of memory for the first years of our lives—and fail to find in it a strange riddle. We forget of what great intellectual accomplishments and of what complicated

2. "Enquête sur les premiers souvenirs de l'enfance," *L'Année psychologique,* iii, 1897.
3. "Study of Early Memories," *Psychological Review,* 1901.

emotions a child of four years is capable. We really ought to wonder why the memory of later years has, as a rule, retained so little of these psychic processes, especially as we have every reason for assuming that these same forgotten childhood activities have not glided off without leaving a trace in the development of the person, but that they have left a definite influence for all future time. Yet, in spite of this unparalleled effectiveness they were forgotten! This would suggest that there are particularly formed conditions of memory (in the sense of conscious reproduction) which have thus far eluded our knowledge. It is quite possible that the forgetting of childhood may give us the key to the understanding of those amnesias which, according to our newer studies, lie at the basis of the formation of all neurotic symptoms.

Of these retained childhood reminiscences, some appear to us readily comprehensible, while others seem strange or unintelligible. It is not difficult to correct certain errors in regard to both kinds. If the retained reminiscences of a person are subjected to an analytic test, it can be readily ascertained that a guarantee for their correctness does not exist. Some of the memory pictures are surely falsified and incomplete, or displaced in point of time and place. The assertions of persons examined, that their first memories reach back perhaps to their second year, are evidently unreliable. Motives can soon be discovered which explain the disfigurement and the displacement of these experiences, but they also demonstrate that these memory lapses are not the result of a mere unreliable memory. Powerful forces from a later period have moulded the memory capacity of our infantile experiences, and it is probably due to these same forces that the understanding of our childhood is generally so very strange to us.

The recollection of adults, as is known, proceeds through different psychic material. Some recall by means of visual pictures—their memories are of a visual character; other individuals can scarcely reproduce in memory the most paltry sketch of an experience; we call such persons *"auditifs"* and *"moteurs"* in contrast to the *"visuels,"* terms proposed by Charcot. These differences vanish in dreams; all our dreams are preponderantly visual. But this development is also found in the childhood memories; the latter are plastic and visual, even in those people whose later memory lacks the visual element. The visual memory, therefore, preserves the type of the infantile recollections. Only my earliest childhood memories are of a visual character; they represent plastically depicted scenes, comparable only to stage settings.

In these scenes of childhood, whether they prove true or false, one usually sees his own childish person both in contour and dress. This circumstance must excite our wonder, for adults do not see their own persons in their recollections of later experiences.[4] It is, moreover, against our experiences to assume that the child's attention during his experiences is centered on himself rather than exclusively on outside impressions. Various sources force us to assume that the so-called earliest childhood recollections are not true memory traces but later elaborations of the same, elaborations which might have been subjected to the influences of many later psychic forces. Thus, the "childhood reminiscences" of individuals altogether advance to the signification of "concealing memories," and thereby form a noteworthy

4. I assert this as a result of certain investigations made by myself.

analogy to the childhood reminiscences as laid down in the legends and myths of nations.

Whoever has examined mentally a number of persons by the method of psychoanalysis must have gathered in this work numerous examples of concealing memories of every description. However, owing to the previously discussed nature of the relations of the childhood reminiscences to later life, it becomes extraordinarily difficult to report such examples. For, in order to attach the value of the concealing memory to an infantile reminiscence, it would be often necessary to present the entire life-history of the person concerned. Only seldom is it possible, as in the following good example, to take out from its context and report a single childhood memory.

A twenty-four-year-old man preserved the following picture from the fifth year of his life: In the garden of a summer-house, he sat on a stool next to his aunt, who was engaged in teaching him the alphabet. He found difficulty in distinguishing the letter *m* from *n,* and he begged his aunt to tell him how to tell one from the other. His aunt called his attention to the fact that the letter *m* had one whole portion (a stroke) more than the letter *n.* There was no reason to dispute the reliability of this childhood recollection; its meaning, however, was discovered only later, when it showed itself to be the symbolic representation of another boyish inquisitiveness. For just as he wanted to know the difference between *m* and *n* at that time, so he concerned himself later about the difference between boy and girl, and he would have been willing that just this aunt should be his teacher. He also discovered that the difference was a similar one; that the boy again had one whole portion more than the girl, and at the time of this recognition, his memory awoke to the corresponding childish inquisitiveness.

The following interesting example is given by Brill:

"One of my patients informed me once that his memory went back to the time of his baptism, when he was about a week old. He maintained that he distinctly remembered the house and the stairway leading up to the first floor where he was supposed to have been baptized. He particularly recalled a lamp standing at the foot of the stairs and the minister who performed the baptism, a tall man in a black frock coat. He remembered vividly how his head was totally submerged in a basin of water. I was naturally skeptical and explained to him that I thought it was a concealing memory which probably hid something else of a much later date. He then informed me that he had entertained this memory for many years, but that when he imparted it to his mother, a few years ago, she laughed, declaring that there was no truth in it, that in the first place, he was not born in this particular house, but that he had merely lived there from the age of four to six, that she could not recall this particular lamp, that the minister who really baptized him was not tall, and what was more, that the baby's head is not submerged in a basin of water during baptism. Notwithstanding his mother's absolute denial, the patient continued to entertain this memory; he strongly felt that it was true despite all facts to the contrary.

"We then proceeded to analyze it. He stated that the most vivid element in the memory was the lamp, and so I asked him to concentrate his attention on it and give me his associations. He could see the lamp at the foot of the stairs, the stairway, and the room on the first floor. He then recalled that at the age of about five years, he was standing one afternoon in that room watching a Swedish servant who was either on a high chair or a step-ladder cleaning the chandelier. He became very inquisitive sexually and made a great effort to look under her clothes. She noticed it and gave him a very strong rebuke. He then recalled that a few years later, he watched through a keyhole to see his mother dress, and somehow she caught him and punished him very severely for it. He was very much humiliated, for she took him downstairs to the dining room and told his father and brother what he had done. At about the same age, probably a little before this episode with his mother, he was on the roof one evening and spied a woman undressing in a house across the street. In his great excitement, he ran down to call his brother, but when he returned, the woman had already slipped a nightgown on and was now pulling down the shades. He told me that for years he regretted that he went to call his brother. He kept on reproducing more scenes, all of which dealt with frustrated sexual looking.

"The lamp, therefore, represented a contrast association of darkness which stood in the way of his sexual inquisitiveness. That is why the lamp element was so accentuated in his memory.

"The question now presents itself, 'Why did he remember the fact of his baptism so vividly?' This young man is a good Christian; his parents are Christians, but his paternal grandfather was a Jew. He himself shows no traces of Semitism; the only thing he retains from his grandfather is the name. It is a German name which is often mistaken for a Jewish one, and for this reason, it has given him considerable trouble. He was refused, for instance, admission to a certain school because of his name. At college it was suspected that he was Jewish, and on that account he failed to be elected to a fraternity that admitted only Gentiles. The concealing memory of his baptims is thus a compensation for his suspected Judaism and that is why it retained its vividness, his mother's denial to the contrary. He had to be assured that he was baptized and, therefore, was a Christian. On the whole, the memory represents a religious scene in order to hide an immoral scene of marked affective content."

I would like to show by one more example the sense that may be gained by a childhood reminiscence through analytic work, although it may seem to contain no sense before. In my forty-third year, when I began to interest myself in what remained in my memory of my own childhood, a scene struck me which for a long time, as I afterwards believed, had repeatedly come to consciousness, and which through reliable identification could be traced to a period before the completion of my third year. I saw myself in front of a chest, the door of which was held open by my half-brother, twenty years my senior. I stood there demanding something and screaming; my mother, pretty and slender, then suddenly entered the room, as if returning from the street.

In these words I formulated this scene so vividly seen, which, however, furnished no other clue. Whether my brother wished to open or lock the chest (in the first explanation it was a "cupboard"), why I cried, and what bearing the arrival of my mother had, all these questions were dim to me; I was tempted to explain to myself that it dealt with the memory of a hoax by my older brother, which was interrupted by my mother. Such misunderstandings of childhood scenes retained in memory are not uncommon; we recall a situation, but it is not centralized; we do not know on which of the elements to place the psychic accent. Analytic effort led me to an entirely unexpected solution of the picture. I missed my mother and began to suspect that she was locked in this cupboard or chest, and therefore demanded that my brother should unlock it. As he obliged me and I became convinced that she was not in the chest, I began to cry; this is the moment firmly retained in the memory, which was directly followed by the appearance of my mother, who appeased my worry and anxiety.

But how did the child get the idea of looking for the absent mother in the chest? Dreams which occurred at the same time pointed dimly to a nurse, concerning whom other reminiscences were retained; as, for example, that she conscientiously urged me to deliver to her the small coins which I received as gifts, a detail which in itself may lay claim to the value of a concealing memory for later things. I then concluded to facilitate for myself this time the task of interpretation, and asked my now aged mother about that nurse. I found out all sorts of things, among others the fact that this shrewd but dishonest person had committed extensive robberies during the confinement of my mother, and that my half-brother was instrumental in bringing her to justice.

This information gave me the key to the scene from childhood, as through a sort of inspiration. The sudden disappearance of the nurse was not a matter of indifference to me; I had just asked this brother where she was, probably because I had noticed that he had played a part in her disappearance, and he, evasive and witty as he is to this day, answered that she was "boxed in." I understood this answer in the childish way, but asked no more, as there was nothing else to be discovered. When my mother left me shortly thereafter, I suspected that the naughty brother had treated her in the same way as he did the nurse, and therefore pressed him to open the chest.

I also understand now why in the translation of the visual childhood scene, my mother's slenderness was accentuated; she must have struck me as being newly restored. I am two-and-a-half years older than the sister born at that time, and when I was three years of age, I was separated from my half-brother.

Carl Jung

Instinct and the Unconscious[1]

The theme of this symposium concerns a problem that is of great importance for biology as well as for psychology and philosophy. But if we are to discuss the relation between instinct and the unconscious, it is essential that we start out with a clear definition of our terms.

1. All footnotes have been omitted, except note 7, here renumbered 2.

With regard to the definition of instinct, I would like to stress the significance of the "all-or-none" reaction formulated by Rivers; indeed, it seems to me that this peculiarity of instinctive activity is of special importance for the psychological side of the problem. I must naturally confine myself to this aspect of the question, because I do not feel competent to treat the problem of instinct under its biological aspect. But when I attempt to give a psychological definition of instinctive activity, I find I cannot rely solely on Rivers' criterion of the "all-or-none" reaction, and for the following reason: Rivers defines this reaction as a process that shows no gradation of intensity in respect of the circumstances which provoke it. It is a reaction that takes place with its own specific intensity under all circumstances and is not proportional to the precipitating stimulus. But when we examine the psychological processes of consciousness in order to determine whether there are any whose intensity is out of all proportion to the stimulus, we can easily find a great many of them in everybody, for instance disproportionate affects, impressions, exaggerated impulses, intentions that go too far, and others of the kind. It follows that all these processes cannot possibly be classed as instinctive processes, and we must therefore look round for another criterion.

We use the word "instinct" very frequently in ordinary speech. We speak of "instinctive actions," meaning by that a mode of behaviour of which neither the motive nor the aim is fully conscious and which is prompted only by obscure inner necessity. This peculiarity has already been stressed by an older English writer, Thomas Reid, who says: "By instinct, I mean a natural impulse to certain actions, without having any end in view, without deliberation and without any conception of what we do." Thus instinctive action is characterized by an *unconsciousness* of the psychological motive behind it, in contrast to the strictly conscious processes which are distinguished by the conscious continuity of their motives. Instinctive action appears to be a more or less abrupt psychic occurrence, a sort of interruption of the continuity of consciousness. On this account, it is felt as an inner necessity—which is, in fact, the definition of instinct given by Kant.

Accordingly, instinctive activity would have to be included among the specifically unconscious processes, which are accessible to consciousness only through their results. But were we to rest content with this conception of instinct, we should soon discover its insufficiency: it merely marks off instinct from the conscious processes and characterizes it as unconscious. If, on the other hand, we survey the unconscious processes as a whole, we find it impossible to class them all as instinctive, even though no differentiation is made between them in ordinary speech. If you suddenly meet a snake and get a violent fright, you can legitimately call this impulse instinctive because it is no different from the instinctive fear of snakes in monkeys. It is just the uniformity of the phenomenon and the regularity of its recurrence which are the most characteristic qualities of instinctive action. As Lloyd Morgan aptly remarks, it would be as uninteresting to bet on an instinctive reaction as on the rising of the sun tomorrow. On the other hand, it may also happen that someone is regularly seized with fright whenever he meets a perfectly harmless hen. Although the mechanism of fright in this case is just as much an unconscious impulse as the instinct, we must nevertheless distinguish between the two processes. In the former case the fear of snakes is a purposive process of general occurrence; the latter, when habitual, is a phobia and not an instinct, since it occurs only in isolation and is not a general peculiarity. There are many other unconscious compulsions of this kind—for instance, obsessive thoughts, musical obsessions, sudden ideas and moods, impulsive affects, depressions, anxiety states, etc. These phenomena are met with in normal as well as abnormal individuals. In so far as they occur only in isolation and are not repeated regularly they must be distinguished from instinctive processes, even though their psychological mechanism seems to correspond to that of an instinct. They may even be characterized by the all-or-none reaction, as can easily be observed in pathological cases. In psychopathology there are many such cases where a given stimulus is followed by a definite and relatively disproportionate reaction comparable to an instinctive reaction.

All these processes must be distinguished from instinctive ones. Only those unconscious processes which are inherited, and occur uniformly and regularly, can be called instinctive. At the same time they must show the mark of compelling necessity, a reflex character of the kind pointed out by Herbert Spencer. Such a process differs from a mere sensory-motor reflex only because it is more complicated. William James therefore calls instinct, not unjustly, "a mere excito-motor impulse, due to the preexistence of a certain 'reflex-arc' in the nerve-centres." Instincts share with reflexes their uniformity and regularity as well as the unconsciousness of their motivations.

The question of where instincts come from and how they were acquired is extraordinarily complicated. The fact that they are invariably inherited does nothing to explain their origin; it merely shifts the problem back to our ancestors. The view is widely held that instincts originated in individual, and then general, acts of will that were frequently repeated. This explanation is plausible in so far as we can observe every day how certain laboriously learnt activities gradually become automatic through constant practice. But if we consider the marvellous instincts to be found in the animal world, we must admit that the element of learning is sometimes totally absent. In certain cases it is impossible to conceive how any learning and practice could ever have come about. Let us take as an example the incredibly refined instinct of propagation in the yucca moth (*Pronuba yuccasella*). The flowers of the yucca plant open for one night only. The moth takes the pollen from one of the flowers and kneads it into a little pellet. Then it visits a second flower, cuts open the pistil, lays its eggs between the ovules and then stuffs the pellet into the funnel-shaped opening of the pistil. Only once in its life does the moth carry out this complicated operation.

Such cases are difficult to explain on the hypothesis of learning and practice. Hence other ways of explanation, deriving from Bergson's philosophy, have recently been put forward, laying stress on the factor of intuition. Intuition is an unconscious process in that its result is the irruption into consciousness of an unconscious content, a sudden idea or "hunch." It resembles a process of perception, but unlike the conscious activity of the senses and introspection the perception is unconscious. That is why we speak of intuition as an "instinctive" act of comprehension. It is a process analogous to instinct, with the difference that whereas instinct is a purposive impulse to carry out some highly complicated action, intuition is the unconscious, purposive apprehension of a highly complicated situation. In a sense, therefore, intuition is the reverse of instinct, neither more nor less wonderful than it. But we should never forget that what we call complicated or even wonderful is not at all wonderful for Nature, but quite ordinary. We always tend to project into things our own difficulties of understanding and to call them complicated, when in reality they are very simple and know nothing of our intellectual problems.

A discussion of the problem of instinct without reference to the concept of the unconscious would be incomplete, because it is just the instinctive processes which make the supplementary concept of the unconscious necessary. I define the unconscious as the totality of all psychic phenomena that lack the quality of consciousness. These psychic contents might fittingly be called "subliminal," on the assumption that every psychic content must possess a certain energy value in order to become conscious at all. The lower the value of a conscious content falls, the more easily it disappears below the threshold. From this it follows that the unconscious is the receptacle of all lost memories and of all contents that are still too weak to become conscious. These contents are products of an unconscious associative activity which also gives rise to dreams. Besides these we must include all more or less intentional repressions of painful thoughts and feelings. I call the sum of all these contents the "personal unconscious." But, over and above that, we also find in the unconscious qualities that are not individually acquired but are inherited, e.g., instincts as impulses to carry out actions from necessity, without conscious motivation. In this "deeper" stratum we also find the *a priori,* inborn forms of "intuition," namely the *archetypes*[2] of perception and apprehension, which are the necessary *a priori* determinants of all psychic processes. Just as his instincts compel man to a specifically human mode of existence, so the archetypes force his ways of perception and apprehension into specifically human patterns. The instincts and the archetypes together form the "collective unconscious." I call it "collective" because, unlike the personal unconscious, it is not made up of individual and more or less unique contents but of those which are universal and of regular occurrence. Instinct is an essentially collective, i.e., universal and regularly occurring phenomenon which has nothing to do with individuality. Archetypes have this quality in common with the instincts and are likewise collective phenomena.

In my view the question of instinct cannot be dealt with psychologically without considering the archetypes, because at bottom they determine one another. It is, however, extremely difficult to discuss this problem, as opinions about the role of instinct in human psychology are extraordinarily divided. Thus William James is of the opinion that man is swarming with instincts, while others restrict them to a very few processes barely distinguishable from reflexes, namely to certain movements

2. [This is the first occasion on which Jung uses the term "archetype" *(Archetypus).* Previously, in his publications, he had discussed the same concept under the term "primordial image" *(Urbild),* which he derived from Burckhardt (cf. *Symbols of Transformation,* par. 45, n. 45; *Two Essays,* par. 101). The primordial image, be it observed, is here and elsewhere used as the equivalent of the archetype; this has given rise to some confusion and to the belief that Jung's theory of hereditary elements involves the inheritance of representations (ideas or images), a view against which Jung repeatedly protests. The primordial image is, however, in the present text, clearly understood as a more graphic term for the archetype, an essentially unconscious entity which, as Jung points out, is an *a priori* form—the inherited component of the representational image perceived in consciousness.—Editors.]

executed by the infant, to particular reactions of its arms and legs, of the larynx, the use of the right hand, and the formation of syllabized sounds. In my opinion, this restriction goes too far, though it is very characteristic of human psychology in general. Above all, we should always remember that in discussing human instincts we are speaking of ourselves and, therefore, are doubtless prejudiced.

We are in a far better position to observe instincts in animals or in primitives than in ourselves. This is due to the fact that we have grown accustomed to scrutinizing our own actions and to seeking rational explanations for them. But it is by no means certain that our explanations will hold water, indeed it is highly unlikely. No superhuman intellect is needed to see through the shallowness of many of our rationalizations and to detect the real motive, the compelling instinct behind them. As a result of our artificial rationalizations it may seem to us that we were actuated not by instinct but by conscious motives. Naturally I do not mean to say that by careful training man has not succeeded in partially converting his instincts into acts of the will. Instinct has been domesticated, but the basic motive still remains instinct. There is no doubt that we have succeeded in enveloping a large number of instincts in rational explanations to the point where we can no longer recognize the original motive behind so many veils. In this way it seems as though we possessed practically no instincts any more. But if we apply the Rivers criterion of the disproportionate all-or-none reaction to human behaviour, we find innumerable cases where exaggerated reactions occur. Exaggeration, indeed, is a universal human peculiarity, although everybody carefully tries to explain his reactions in terms of rational motives. There is never any lack of good arguments, but the fact of exaggeration remains. And why is it that a man does not do or say, give or take, just as much as is needed, or reasonable, or justifiable in a given situation, but frequently so much more or less? Precisely because an unconscious process is released in him that runs its course without the aid of reason and therefore falls short of, or exceeds, the degree of rational motivation. This phenomenon is so uniform and so regular that we can only call it instinctive, though no one in this situation likes to admit the instinctive nature of his behaviour. I am therefore inclined to believe that human behaviour is influenced by instinct to a far higher degree than is generally supposed, and that we are prone to a great many falsifications of judgment in this respect, again as a result of an instinctive exaggeration of the rationalistic standpoint.

Instincts are typical modes of action, and wherever we meet with uniform and regularly recurring modes of action and reaction we are dealing with instinct, no matter whether it is associated with a conscious motive or not.

Just as it may be asked whether man possesses many instincts or only a few, so we must also raise the still unbroached question of whether he possesses many or few primordial forms, or archetypes, of psychic reaction. Here we are faced with the same difficulty I mentioned above: we are so accustomed to operating with conventional and self-evident concepts that we are no longer conscious of the extent to which they are based on archetypal modes of perception. Like the instincts, the primordial images have been obscured by the extraordinary differentiation of our thinking. Just as certain biological views attribute only a few instincts to man, so the theory of cognition reduces the archetypes to a few, logically limited categories of understanding.

In Plato, however, an extraordinarily high value is set on the archetypes as metaphysical ideas, as "paradigms" or models, while real things are held to be only the copies of these model ideas. Medieval philosophy, from the time of St. Augustine —from whom I have borrowed the idea of the archetype—down to Malebranche and Bacon, still stands on a Platonic footing in this respect. But in scholasticism we find the notion that archetypes are natural images engraved on the human mind, helping it to form its judgments. Thus Herbert of Cherbury says: "Natural instincts are expressions of those faculties which are found in every normal man, through which the Common Notions touching the internal conformity of things, such as the cause, means and purpose of things, the good, bad, beautiful, pleasing, etc. . . . are brought into conformity independently of discursive thought."

From Descartes and Malebranche onward, the metaphysical value of the "idea" or archetype steadily deteriorated. It became a "thought," an internal condition of cognition, as clearly formulated by Spinoza: "By 'idea' I understand a conception of the mind which the mind forms by reason of its being a thinking thing." Finally Kant reduced the archetypes to a limited number of categories of understanding. Schopenhauer carried the process of simplification still further, while at the same time endowing the archetypes with an almost Platonic significance.

In this all-too-summary sketch we can see once again that same psychological process at work which disguises the instincts under the cloak of rational motivations and transforms the archetypes into rational concepts. It is hardly possible to recognize the archetype under this guise. And yet the way in which man inwardly pictures the world is still, despite all differences of detail, as uniform and as regular as his instinctive actions. Just as we have been compelled to postulate the concept of an instinct determining or regulating our conscious actions, so, in order to account for the uniformity and regularity of our perceptions, we must have recourse to the correlated concept of a factor determining the mode of apprehension. It is this factor which I call the archetype or primordial image. The primordial image might suitably be described as the *instinct's perception of itself,* or as the self-portrait of the instinct, in exactly the same way as consciousness is an inward perception of the objective life-process. Just as conscious apprehension gives our actions form and direction, so unconscious apprehension through the archetype determines the form and direction of instinct. If we call instinct "refined," then the "intuition" which brings the instinct into play, in other words the apprehension by means of the archetype, must be something incredibly precise. Thus the yucca moth must carry within it an image, as it were, of the situation that "triggers off" its instinct. This image enables it to "recognize" the yucca flower and its structure.

The criterion of the all-or-none reaction proposed by Rivers has helped us to discover the operation of instinct everywhere in human psychology, and it may be that the concept of the primordial image will perform a similar service with regard to acts of intuitive apprehension. Intuitional activity can be observed most easily among primitives. There we constantly meet with certain typical images and motifs which are the foundations of their mythologies. These images are autochthonous and occur with great regularity; everywhere we find the idea of a magic power or substance, of spirits and their doings, of heroes and gods and their legends. In the great religions of the world we see the perfection of those images and at the same time their progressive incrustation with rational forms. They even appear in the exact sciences, as the foundation of certain indispensable auxiliary concepts such as energy, ether, and the atom. In philosophy, Bergson affords an example of the revival of a primordial image with his conception of "durée créatrice," which can be found in Proclus and, in its original form, in Heraclitus.

Analytical psychology is daily concerned, in the normal and sick alike, with disturbances of conscious apprehension caused by the admixture of archetypal images. The exaggerated actions due to the interference of instinct are caused by intuitive modes of apprehension actuated by archetypes and all too likely to lead to overintense and often distorted impressions.

Archetypes are typical modes of apprehension, and wherever we meet with uniform and regularly recurring modes of apprehension we are dealing with an archetype, no matter whether its mythological character is recognized or not.

The collective unconscious consists of the sum of the instincts and their correlates, the archetypes. Just as everybody possesses instincts, so he also possesses a stock of archetypal images. The most striking proof of this is the psychopathology of mental disturbances that are characterized by an irruption of the collective unconscious. Such is the case in schizophrenia; here we can often observe the emergence of archaic impulses in conjunction with unmistakable mythological images.

In my view it is impossible to say which comes first—apprehension of the situation, or the impulse to act. It seems to me that both are aspects of the same vital activity, which we have to think of as two distinct processes simply for the purpose of better understanding.

Hannah Green

from I Never Promised You a Rose Garden

"Something in a session not long ago keeps coming back to me," Dr. Fried said. "You were discussing being sick as if it were a volcano and you said of your sister that she would have to decorate her slopes herself. Do you know what you tell us now? Can you really not see that the gods and the devils and the whole Yr of yours is your own creation?"

"I didn't mean that at all!" Deborah said, backing away, and still hearing the Collect chanting years of people: *Snap out of it; it's all in your mind.* "Yr is real!"

"I have no doubt that it is real to you, but there is also something else that you seem to be saying—that the sickness stands apart from the symptoms which are often mistaken for it. Are you not saying that, although the symptoms bear on the sickness and are related to it, the two are not the same?"

"That's right."

"Then I want you to take me back into that past of yours again, before the slopes were decorated, and share with me a look at the volcano itself." She saw the look of terror, and added, "Not all at once; a little at a time."

They had gone over the Great Deceits, and also the many little ones that are inevitable in life, but which, because of Deborah's feelings and beliefs, seemed to be pointing the way to doom as meaningfully as if they had been arranged as part of a plan, a secret joke that everyone knew, but no one admitted knowing. After months of therapy, Deborah began to learn that there were many reasons why the world was horrifying to her. The shadow of the grandfather dynast was still dark over all the houses of the family. She went back often again, hearing grandfather's familiar voice saying, "Second in the class is not enough; you must be the first." "If you are hurt, never cry, but laugh. You must never let them know that they are hurting you." It was all directed against the smiling sharers of the secret joke. Pride must be the ability to die in agony as if you did it every day, gracefully. Even his pride in her was anger. "You're smart—you'll show them all!" He had sharpened her word-wit on his own, cheered the cutting edge of it, called women cows and brood-bitches, and slapped her half-roughly because she would grow up wasted, a woman. She would have to take on the whole world of fools and ingrates, and, even though she was a woman, win his battle: the ancient, mystical battle between a crippled immigrant and a long-dead Latvian Count.

In the place and time where Deborah was growing up, American Jews still fought the old battles that they had fled from in Europe only a few years earlier. And then there were the newer battles, pitched as the Nazis walked through Europe and screamed hatred in America. There were Bund marches in the larger cities, and flare-ups against synagogues and neighborhood Jews who had ventured out of the ghettos. Deborah remembered having seen the Blau house splashed with paint and the dead rats stinking beside the morning paper that told of Czech Jews running for the Polish border only to be shot by the "freedom-loving" Poles. She knew much of the hate and had been attacked once or twice by the neighborhood bullies, but the grandfather would say triumphantly, as if he saw in this an obscure kind of proof, "It's envy! The best and the smartest are always envied. Walk straight and don't let them know if they touch you." And then, as if the hate were peering through the joke, he would say "You'll show them! You're like me. They're all fools, the rest of them—you'll show them someday!"

What she had to "show them" was a harbinger, a deceiver, a seducer: her own precocity. The hint that she would someday be "someone" seemed to make the old man right. For a long time she used her bitter wit as a weapon to startle and amaze the adults in her armed truce with the world, but it never fooled the people of her own age for a single moment. The young knew her, and wise in their own fear, set out to destroy her.

"It was a willing soil then, to which this seed of Yr came," the doctor said. "The deceits of the grown-up world, the great gap between Grandfather's pretensions and the world you saw more clearly, the lies told by your own precocity, that you were special and the hard fact that you couldn't get to first base with your own contemporaries no matter how impressive your specialness was."

"The gap between the carefully brought up little rich girl with maids and imported dresses and the—and the—"

"And the what? Where are you now?"

"I don't know," she said, but she was speaking from a place in which she had been before. "There are no colors, only shades of gray. She is big and white. I am small and there are bars between. She gives food. Gray. I don't eat. Where is my . . . my . . ."

"Your what?"

"Salvation!" Deborah blurted.

"Go on," the doctor said.

"My . . . self, my love."

Dr. Fried peered at her intently for a while and then said, "I have a hunch—do you want to try it with me?"

"Do you trust me with it?"

"Certainly, or there wouldn't be this science at all, where the two of us work together. Your own basic knowledge of yourself and truth is sound. Believe in it."

"Go ahead then, or psychiatry will disappear." (Laughter.)

"Your mother had trouble with a pregnancy when you were very small, did she not?"

"Yes, she miscarried. Twins."

"And afterward went away to rest for a while?"

The light struck the past and there was a seeming sound of good, strong truth, like the pop of a hard-thrown ball into a catcher's glove. Connect. Deborah listened to the sound and then began to tumble over her words, filling the missing features of the ancient nightmare that was no more otherworldly than the simple experience of being left alone.

"The white thing must have been a nurse. I felt that everything warm had left. The feeling comes often, but I thought it could never have been true that I ever really *was* in such a place. The bars were crib bars. They must have been on my own crib. . . . The nurse was distant and cold . . . Hey! Hey!" The now-friendly light struck something else and its suddenness made the small, prosaic connection seem like a revelation full of greatness and wonder. "The bars . . . the bars of the crib and the cold and losing the ability to see colors . . . it's what happens *now!* It's part of the Pit—it's what happens *now, now!* When I am waiting to fall, those bands of dark across my eyes are the old crib bars and the cold is that old one—I always wondered why it meant more than just something you could end by putting on a coat."

The rush of words ended and Dr. Fried smiled. "It is as big, then, as abandonment and the going away of all love."

"I thought I was going to die, but at last they came back." She paused in the flight and another sudden question took her, as if it had been there forever. "Why doesn't everybody have black bands? Surely everyone is left alone sometimes, maybe for a week or two. Parents die, even, but the children don't go nuts and have mourning bands going up and down their retinas." It had come to her as another deeper proof that she was mismade somehow, that the fault was as elemental as her genes, a bad seed. She expected the doctor's sympathetic demur, a familiar and comforting lie with which she could light her own way back to Yr. Instead the words were strong.

"The memory may not change in form, but years of underlining give it a weight that can become tremendous. Each of the many many times you are called to remember the cold of abandonment, the bars, and the loneliness, this experience says deep inside you, 'You see? That's the way life is, after all.' "

The doctor rose to mark the session's end. "We have done very well this time, seeing where some of the ghosts of the past still clutch at you in the present."

Deborah murmured, "I wonder what the price will be."

The doctor touched her arm, "You set the price yourself. Tell all of Yr that it dare not compromise you in this search of ours."

Deborah pulled her arm away from the doctor's hand because of some obscure fear of touching. She was right, for the place where the hand had paused on her arm began to smoke and the flesh under the sweater sleeve seared and bubbled with the burning.

"I'm sorry," the doctor said, seeing Deborah's face go pale. "I didn't mean to touch you before you were ready."

"Lightning rods," Deborah answered, looking through the sweater arm to the charred flesh, and seeing how terrible it must be when one was the grounding path for such power.

The doctor, lost under the leap of the logic, could only look past the shaking body of the patient before her to where the hunted spirit had flashed for a moment in gladness and now was gone. "We will work hard, together, and we will understand."

"As long as we can stand at all," Deborah said.

Joseph Campbell

The Hero and the God

The standard path of the mythological adventure of the hero is a magnification of the formula represented in the rites of passage: *separation—initiation—return:* which might be named the nuclear unit of the monomyth.[1]

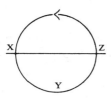

A hero ventures forth from the world of common day into a region of supernatural wonder: fabulous forces are there encountered and a decisive victory is won: the hero comes back from this mysterious adventure with the power to bestow boons on his fellow man.

1. The word *monomyth* is from James Joyce, *Finnegans Wake* (New York: Viking Press, Inc., 1939), p. 581.

Prometheus ascended to the heavens, stole fire from the gods, and descended. Jason sailed through the Clashing Rocks into a sea of marvels, circumvented the dragon that guarded the Golden Fleece, and returned with the fleece and the power to wrest his rightful throne from a usurper. Aeneas went down into the underworld, crossed the dreadful river of the dead, threw a sop to the three-headed watchdog Cerberus, and conversed, at last, with the shade of his dead father. All things were unfolded to him: the destiny of souls, the destiny of Rome, which he was about to found, "and in what wise he might avoid or endure every burden."[2] He returned through the ivory gate to his work in the world.

A majestic representation of the difficulties of the hero-task, and of its sublime import when it is profoundly conceived and solemnly undertaken, is presented in the traditional legend of the Great Struggle of the Buddha. The young prince Gautama Sakyamuni set forth secretly from his father's palace on the princely steed Kanthaka, passed miraculously through the guarded gate, rode through the night attended by the torches of four times sixty thousand divinities, lightly hurdled a majestic river eleven hundred and twenty-eight cubits wide, and then with a single sword-stroke sheared his own royal locks—whereupon the remaining hair, two finger-breadths in length, curled to the right and lay close to his head. Assuming the garments of a monk, he moved as a beggar through the world, and during these years of apparently aimless wandering acquired and transcended the eight stages of meditation. He retired to a hermitage, bent his powers six more years to the great struggle, carried austerity to the uttermost, and collapsed in seeming death, but presently recovered. Then he returned to the less rigorous life of the ascetic wanderer.

One day he sat beneath a tree, contemplating the eastern quarter of the world, and the tree was illuminated with his radiance. A young girl named Sujata came and presented milk-rice to him in a golden bowl, and when he tossed the empty bowl into a river it floated upstream. This was the signal that the moment of his triumph was at hand. He arose and proceeded along a road which the gods had decked and which was eleven hundred and twenty-eight cubits wide. The snakes and birds and the divinities of the woods and fields did him homage with flowers and celestial perfumes, heavenly choirs poured forth music, the ten thousand worlds were filled with perfumes, garlands, harmonies, and shouts of acclaim; for he was on his way to the great Tree of Enlightenment, the Bo Tree, under which he was to redeem the universe. He placed himself, with a firm resolve, beneath the Bo Tree, on the Immovable Spot, and straightway was approached by Kama-Mara, the god of love and death.

The dangerous god appeared mounted on an elephant and carrying weapons in his thousand hands. He was surrounded by his army, which extended twelve leagues before him, twelve to the right, twelve to the left, and in the rear as far as to the confines of the world; it was nine leagues high. The protecting deities of the universe took flight, but the Future Buddha remained unmoved beneath the Tree. And the god then assailed him, seeking to break his concentration.

Whirlwind, rocks, thunder and flame, smoking weapons with keen edges, burning coals, hot ashes, boiling mud, blistering sands and fourfold darkness, the Antago-

2. Virgil, *Aeneid*, VI, 892.

nist hurled against the Savior, but the missiles were all transformed into celestial flowers and ointments by the power of Gautama's ten perfections. Mara then deployed his daughters, Desire, Pining, and Lust, surrounded by voluptuous attendants, but the mind of the Great Being was not distracted. The god finally challenged his right to be sitting on the Immovable Spot, flung his razor-sharp discus angrily, and bid the towering host of the army to let fly at him with mountain crags. But the Future Buddha only moved his hand to touch the ground with his fingertips, and thus bid the goddess Earth bear witness to his right to be sitting where he was. She did so with a hundred, a thousand, a hundred thousand roars, so that the elephant of the Antagonist fell upon its knees in obeisance to the Future Buddha. The army was immediately dispersed, and the gods of all the worlds scattered garlands.

Having won that preliminary victory before sunset, the conqueror acquired in the first watch of the night knowledge of his previous existences, in the second watch the divine eye of omniscient vision, and in the last watch understanding of the chain of causation. He experienced perfect enlightenment at the break of day.[3]

Then for seven days Gautama—now the Buddha, the Enlightened—sat motionless in bliss; for seven days he stood apart and regarded the spot on which he had received enlightenment; for seven days he paced between the place of the sitting and the place of the standing; for seven days he abode in a pavilion furnished by the gods and reviewed the whole doctrine of causality and release; for seven days he sat beneath the tree where the girl Sujata had brought him milk-rice in a golden bowl, and there meditated on the doctrine of the sweetness of Nirvana; he removed to another tree and a great storm raged for seven days, but the King of Serpents emerged from the roots and protected the Buddha with his expanded hood; finally, the Buddha sat for seven days beneath a fourth tree enjoying still the sweetness of liberation. Then he doubted whether his message could be communicated, and he thought to retain the wisdom for himself; but the god Brahma descended from the zenith to implore that he should become the teacher of gods and men. The Buddha was thus persuaded to proclaim the path.[4] And he went back into the cities of men

3. This is the most important single moment in Oriental mythology, a counterpart of the Crucifixion of the West. The Buddha beneath the Tree of Enlightenment (the Bo Tree) and Christ on Holy Rood (the Tree of Redemption) are analogous figures, incorporating an archetypal World Savior, World Tree motif, which is of immemorial antiquity. Many other variants of the theme will be found among the episodes to come. The Immovable Spot and Mount Calvary are images of the World Navel, or World Axis. . . .

The calling of the Earth to witness is represented in traditional Buddhist art by images of the Buddha, sitting in the classic Buddha posture, with the right hand resting on the right knee and its fingers lightly touching the ground.

4. The point is that Buddhahood, Enlightenment, cannot be communicated, but only the *way* to Enlightenment. This doctrine of the incommunicability of the Truth which is beyond names and forms is basic to the great Oriental, as well as to the Platonic, traditions. Whereas the truths of science are communicable, being demonstrable hypotheses rationally founded on observable facts, ritual, mythology, and metaphysics are but guides to the brink of a transcendent illumination, the final step to which must be taken by each in his own silent experience. Hence one of the Sanskrit terms for sage is *muni*, "the silent one." *Sākyamuni* (one of the titles of Gautama Buddha) means "the silent one or sage (*muni*) of the Sakya clan." Though he is the founder of a widely taught world religion, the ultimate core of his doctrine remains concealed, necessarily, in silence.

where he moved among the citizens of the world, bestowing the inestimable boon of the knowledge of the Way.[5]

The Old Testament records a comparable deed in its legend of Moses, who, in the third month of the departure of Israel out of the land of Egypt, came with his people into the wilderness of Sinai; and there Israel pitched their tents over against the mountain. And Moses went up to God, and the Lord called unto him from the mountain. The Lord gave to him the Tables of the Law and commanded Moses to return with these to Israel, the people of the Lord.[6]

Jewish folk legend declares that during the day of the revelation diverse rumblings sounded from Mount Sinai. "Flashes of lightning, accompanied by an ever swelling peal of horns, moved the people with mighty fear and trembling. God bent the heavens, moved the earth, and shook the bounds of the world, so that the depths trembled, and the heavens grew frightened. His splendor passed through the four portals of fire, earthquake, storm, and hail. The kings of the earth trembled in their palaces. The earth herself thought the resurrection of the dead was about to take place, and that she would have to account for the blood of the slain she had absorbed, and for the bodies of the murdered whom she covered. The earth was not calmed until she heard the first words of the Decalogue.

"The heavens opened and Mount Sinai, freed from the earth, rose into the air, so that its summit towered into the heavens, while a thick cloud covered the sides of it, and touched the feet of the Divine Throne. Accompanying God on one side, appeared twenty-two thousand angels with crowns for the Levites, the only tribe that remained true to God while the rest worshiped the Golden Calf. On the second side were sixty myriads, three thousand five hundred and fifty angels, each bearing a crown of fire for each individual Israelite. Double this number of angels was on the third side; whereas on the fourth side they were simply innumerable. For God did not appear from one direction, but from all simultaneously, which, however, did not prevent His glory from filling the heaven as well as the earth. In spite of these innumerable hosts there was no crowding on Mount Sinai, no mob, there was room for all."[7]

. . . Whether presented in the vast, almost oceanic images of the Orient, in the vigorous narratives of the Greeks, or in the majestic legends of the Bible, the adventure of the hero normally follows the pattern of the nuclear unit above described: a separation from the world, a penetration to some source of power, and a life-enhancing return. The whole of the Orient has been blessed by the boon brought back by Gautama Buddha—his wonderful teaching of the Good Law—just as the Occident has been by the Decalogue of Moses. The Greeks referred fire, the first support of all human culture, to the world-transcending deed of their Prometheus, and the Romans the founding of their world-supporting city to Aeneas, following his departure from fallen Troy and his visit to the eerie underworld of the dead.

5. Greatly abridged from *Jataka*, Introduction, i, 58-75 (translated by Henry Clarke Warren, *Buddhism in Translations* (Harvard Oriental Series, 3) Cambridge, Mass.: Harvard University Press, 1896, pp. 56-87), and the *Lalitavistara* as rendered by Ananda K. Coomaraswamy, *Buddha and the Gospel of Buddhism* (New York: G. P. Putnam's Sons, 1916), pp. 24-38.
6. Exodus, 19:3-5.
7. Louis Ginzberg, *The Legends of the Jews* (Philadelphia: The Jewish Publication Society of America, 1911), Vol. III, pp. 90-94.

Everywhere, no matter what the sphere of interest (whether religious, political, or personal), the really creative acts are represented as those deriving from some sort of dying to the world; and what happens in the interval of the hero's nonentity, so that he comes back as one reborn, made great and filled with creative power, mankind is also unanimous in declaring. We shall have only to follow, therefore, a multitude of heroic figures through the classic stages of the universal adventure in order to see again what has always been revealed. This will help us to understand not only the meaning of those images for contemporary life, but also the singleness of the human spirit in its aspirations, powers, vicissitudes, and wisdom.

The following pages[8] will present in the form of one composite adventure the tales of a number of the world's symbolic carriers of the destiny of Everyman. The first great stage, that of the *separation* or *departure,* will be shown in Part I, Chapter I, in five subsections: (1) "The Call to Adventure," or the signs of the vocation of the hero; (2) "Refusal of the Call," or the folly of the flight from the god; (3) "Supernatural Aid," the unsuspected assistance that comes to one who has undertaken his proper adventure; (4) "The Crossing of the First Threshold"; and (5) "The Belly of the Whale," or the passage into the realm of night. The stage of *the trials and victories of initiation* will appear in Chapter II in six subsections: (1) "The Road of Trials," or the dangerous aspect of the gods; (2) "The Meeting with the Goddess" (*Magna Mater*), or the bliss of infancy regained; (3) "Woman as the Temptress," the realization and agony of Oedipus; (4) "Atonement with the Father"; (5) "Apotheosis"; and (6) "The Ultimate Boon."

The return and reintegration with society, which is indispensable to the continuous circulation of spiritual energy into the world, and which, from the standpoint of the community, is the justification of the long retreat, the hero himself may find the most difficult requirement of all. For if he has won through, like the Buddha, to the profound repose of complete enlightenment, there is danger that the bliss of this experience may annihilate all recollection of, interest in, or hope for, the sorrows of the world; or else the problem of making known the way of illumination to people wrapped in economic problems may seem too great to solve. And on the other hand, if the hero, instead of submitting to all of the initiatory tests, has, like Prometheus, simply darted to his goal (by violence, quick device, or luck) and plucked the boon for the world that he intended, then the powers that he has unbalanced may react so sharply that he will be blasted from within and without— crucified, like Prometheus, on the rock of his own violated unconscious. Or if the hero, in the third place, makes his safe and willing return, he may meet with such a blank misunderstanding and disregard from those whom he has come to help that his career will collapse. The third of the following chapters will conclude the discussion of these prospects under six subheadings: (1) "Refusal of the Return," or the world denied; (2) "The Magic Flight," or the escape of Prometheus; (3) "Rescue from Without"; (4) "The Crossing of the Return Threshold," or the return to the

---

8. [The pages referred to are not included in this excerpt, but this description of their contents is retained because it is an outline of the archetypal journey—Editors.]

world of common day; (5) "Master of the Two Worlds"; and (6) "Freedom to Live," the nature and function of the ultimate boon.[9]

The composite hero of the monomyth is a personage of exceptional gifts. Frequently he is honored by his society, frequently unrecognized or disdained. He and/or the world in which he finds himself suffers from a symbolical deficiency. In fairy tales this may be as slight as the lack of certain golden ring, whereas in apocalyptic vision the physical and spiritual life of the whole earth can be represented as fallen, or on the point of falling, into ruin.

Typically, the hero of the fairy tale achieves a domestic, microcosmic triumph, and the hero of myth a world-historical, macrocosmic triumph. Whereas the former —the youngest or despised child who becomes the master of extraordinary powers— prevails over his personal oppressors, the latter brings back from his adventure the means for the regeneration of his society as a whole. Tribal or local heroes, such as the emperor Huang Ti, Moses, or the Aztec Tezcatlipoca, commit their boons to a single folk; universal heroes—Mohammed, Jesus, Gautama Buddha—bring a message for the entire world.

Whether the hero be ridiculous or sublime, Greek or barbarian, gentile or Jew, his journey varies little in essential plan. Popular tales represent the heroic action as physical; the higher religions show the deed to be moral; nevertheless, there will be found astonishingly little variation in the morphology of the adventure, the character roles involved, the victories gained. If one or another of the basic elements of the archetypal pattern is omitted from a given fairy tale, legend, ritual, or myth, it is bound to be somehow or other implied—and the omission itself can speak volumes for the history and pathology of the example. . . .

Part II, "The Cosmogonic Cycle," unrolls the great vision of the creation and destruction of the world which is vouchsafed as revelation to the successful hero. Chapter I, *Emanations,* treats of the coming of the forms of the universe out of the void. Chapter II, *The Virgin Birth,* is a review of the creative and redemptive roles of the female power, first on a cosmic scale as the Mother of the Universe, then again on the human plane as the Mother of the Hero. Chapter III, *Transformations of the Hero,* traces the course of the legendary history of the human race through its typical stages, the hero appearing on the scene in various forms according to the changing needs of the race. And Chapter IV, *Dissolutions,* tells of the foretold end, first of the hero, then of the manifested world.

The cosmogonic cycle is presented with astonishing consistency in the sacred writings of all the continents,[10] and it gives to the adventure of the hero a new and interesting turn; for now it appears that the perilous journey was a labor not of

9. This circular adventure of the hero appears in a negative form in stories of the deluge type, where it is not the hero who goes to the power, but the power that rises against the hero, and again subsides. Deluge stories occur in every quarter of the earth. They form an integral portion of the archetypal myth of the history of the world, and so belong properly to Part II of the present discussion: "The Cosmogonic Cycle." The deluge hero is a symbol of the germinal vitality of man surviving even the worst tides of catastrophe and sin.

10. The present volume is not concerned with the historical discussion of this circumstance. That task is reserved for a work now under preparation. The present volume is a comparative, not genetic, study. Its purpose is to show that essential parallels exist in the myths themselves as well as in the interpretations and applications that the sages have announced for them.

attainment but of reattainment, not discovery but rediscovery. The godly powers sought and dangerously won are revealed to have been within the heart of the hero all the time. He is "the king's son" who has come to know who he is and therewith has entered into the exercise of his proper power—"God's son," who has learned to know how much that title means. From this point of view the hero is symbolical of that divine creative and redemptive image which is hidden within us all, only waiting to be known and rendered into life.

"For the One who has become many, remains the One undivided, but each part is all of Christ," we read in the writings of Saint Symeon the younger (949-1022 A.D.). "I saw Him in my house," the saint goes on. "Among all those everyday things He appeared unexpectedly and became unutterably united and merged with me, and leaped over to me without anything in between, as fire to iron, as the light to glass. And He made me like fire and like light. And I became that which I saw before and beheld from afar. I do not know how to relate this miracle to you. . . . I am man by nature, and God by the grace of God."[11]

A comparable vision is described in the apocryphal Gospel of Eve. "I stood on a lofty mountain and saw a gigantic man and another a dwarf; and I heard as it were a voice of thunder, and drew nigh for to hear; and He spake unto me and said: I am thou and thou art I; and wheresoever thou mayest be I am there. In all am I scattered, and whensoever thou willest, thou gatherest Me; and gathering Me, thou gatherest Thyself."[12]

The two—the hero and his ultimate god, the seeker and the found—are thus understood as the outside and inside of a single, self-mirrored mystery, which is identical with the mystery of the manifest world. The great deed of the supreme hero is to come to the knowledge of this unity in multiplicity and then to make it known.

Leo Litwak

The Esalen Foundation: "Joy Is the Prize"

Big Sur is an eighty-mile stretch of California coast below the Monterey Peninsula. It is approximately midway between Los Angeles and San Francisco and difficult of access from either direction. Before the coastal highway was completed in 1936, the shore was accessible only by foot. The Los Padres National Forest, one of the largest preserves in the country, extends thirty miles inland and is two hundred miles long; it occupies most of the area. Not much land is available for private ownership. There are only three hundred residents. The rugged terrain of Los Padres includes redwood canyons, barren mountain ranges, desert flora, thick forests. It is the province of mountain lions and wild boar.

11. Translated by Dom Ansgar Nelson. O.S.B. in *The Soul Afire* (New York: Pantheon Books, 1944), p. 303.
12. Quoted by Epiphanius, *Haeresses,* xxvi, 3.

Stone cliffs rise two thousand feet above the ocean. Beyond a wedge of meadow, the steeply inclined hillside begins. For great distances there is no meadow at all and the serpentine coastal highway hangs on the cliffside. It is a two-lane road, sometimes impassable after heavy rains. The fog bank wavers off shore. When it sweeps in, the traveler faces an uncanny trip, guided entirely by the few white dashes of the center line that are visible. With hairpin turns, sharp rises and declines, the road can be dangerous in bad weather. On clear days when the setting sun ignites dust particles on your windshield you are forced to drive blind for dangerous seconds.

Nonetheless, four thousand people traveled this road last year, in disregard of weather, aimed toward the Esalen Institute, famous until a few years ago under a different name, Big Sur Hot Springs. These are unlikely adventurers. They are doctors, social workers, clinical psychologists, teachers, students, business executives, engineers, housewives—or just fun lovers who have come to take the baths.

Big Sur Hot Springs was originally renowned as the Eden discovered by Henry Miller and Jack Kerouac. Joan Baez once lived there. The springs were purchased in 1910 from a man named Slade by Dr. Henry C. Murphy of Salinas. It was Dr. Murphy's intention to establish a health spa. In order to use the mineral waters he brought in two bathtubs by fishing sloop. They were hauled up the cliff and placed on a ledge at the source of the springs. But because of their inaccessibility, the springs did not flourish as a spa. Not until Dr. Murphy's grandson, Michael, assumed operation of the property in the mid-nineteen-fifties did the baths begin to receive attention— attention that has grown with the development of Esalen Institute.

Michael Murphy at thirty-seven appears to be in his early twenties. He is slender and boyish and has a marvelous smile. I took part in a panel discussion at Hot Springs some years ago and I was not impressed either by the topic, my performance or the audience. I did enjoy the baths. I had misgivings about Murphy's program, yet none about him. He seemed to me generous, charming, innocent, credulous, enthusiastic, and enormously sympathetic. A Stanford alumnus who had done some graduate work in psychology and philosophy, he had recently returned from an eighteen-month study of the art of meditation at the Aurobindo Ashram in Pondicherry, India, and he devoted a considerable part of each day to meditation. I believe he had—and still has—in mind some great mission, based on his Indian experience. I am not quite sure what the scope of his mission is. A friend of his told me: "Mike wants to turn on the world." Esalen Institute is his instrument for doing so. It has come a long way from the shoddy panels of a few years ago. Its spreading impact may seriously affect our methods of therapy and education.

In the course of a year, almost one thousand professional persons—social workers, psychiatrists, clinical psychologists—enroll in Esalen workshops. Close to seven hundred psychotherapists have been trained to administer techniques devised by staff members—Frederick Perls, Virginia Satir, Bernard Gunther, and William Schutz. These techniques have been demonstrated at hospitals, universities, and medical schools. This year Esalen has opened a San Francisco extension which in the first two months of operation has attracted an attendance in excess of ten thousand, offering the same workshops and seminars that are available at Big Sur. Esalen-type communities have begun to appear throughout the country, in Atlanta, Chicago, Los Angeles, Cleveland, La Jolla. One has even appeared in Vancouver, Canada. Murphy offers advice and help, and permits use of his mailing list.

Consider some offerings of the Esalen winter brochure. Seminars led by Alan Watts, the Zen interpreter, and Susan Sontag, the camp interpreter. Workshops for professional therapists conducted by Frederick Perls, an early associate of Freud and Wilhelm Reich and a founder of Gestalt therapy. A lecture panel including the psychologist Carl Rogers and Herman Kahn, the "thinking about the unthinkable" man. Some of the titles are "Kinetic Theater," "Psycotechnics," "Do You Do It? Or Does It Do You?", "Dante's Way to the Stars," "Creativity and the Daimonic," "On Deepening the Marriage Encounter," "Tibetan Book of the Dead," "Anxiety and Tension Control," "Racial Confrontation as a Transcendental Experience."

What principle guides a mélange that consists of dance workshops, therapy workshops, sensory-awareness experiments, the Tibetan Book of the Dead, Herman Kahn, Carl Rogers, Frederick Perls, and Susan Sontag?

Esalen's vice president, George B. Leonard, has written a general statement of purpose. He says: "We believe that all men somehow possess a divine potentiality; that ways may be worked out—specific, systematic ways—to help, not the few, but the many toward a vastly expanded capacity to learn, to love, to feel deeply, to create. We reject the tired dualism that seeks God and human potentialities by denying the joys of the senses, the immediacy of unpostponed life." The programs, he says, are aimed toward "the joys of the senses."

I had signed up for a workshop led by Dr. William Schutz, a group therapist who has taught at Harvard and the Albert Einstein College of Medicine, among other institutions, and has served on the staff of the National Training Laboratories Interne Training Program at Bethel, Me. His latest book, *Joy,* was published in 1967 by Grove Press.

In the brochure description of Dr. Schutz's workshop I read a warning that the experience would be more than verbal: "An encounter workshop with body movements, sensory awareness, fastasy experiments, psychodrama. Developing the ability to experience joy is the workshop's guiding theme."

Joy as the prize of a five-day workshop?

"How can we speak of joy," Leonard has written, "on this dark and suffering planet? How can we speak of anything else? We have heard enough of despair."

It was easy enough to dismiss the language. It seemed naive to promise so great a reward for so small an investment. Joy for $175 seemed cheap at the price, especially since the *New York Times* was paying. I did have considerable anxieties that some of those "body movements" might be humiliating. And what precisely was meant by "sensory awareness"?

Esalen has changed considerably since my previous visit. Rows of new cabins are ranged along terraces on the hillside. The lodge is located at the bottom of a steep incline, in a meadow. The meadow is perhaps 200 yards deep and ends at the cliff edge. The Pacific Ocean is 150 feet below. A staff of fifty operates the kitchen, supervises the baths, cleans the cabins and garden, and works on construction.

I passed hippy laborers, stripped to the waist, long hair flowing, operating with pick and shovel. Dreamy girls in long gowns played flutes near the pool.

I was somewhat put off by what I considered to be an excessive show of affection. Men hugged men. Men hugged women. Women hugged women. These were not hippies, but older folks, like myself, who had come for the workshop. People flew into one another's arms, and it wasn't my style at all.

After dinner, thirty of us met in the gallery for our first session. We began our excursion toward joy at 9 P.M. of a Sunday in a woodsy room on a balmy, starry night.

William Schutz, solidly built, with bald head and muzzle beard, began by telling us that in the course of the workshop we would come to dangerous ground. At such times we ought not to resist entering, for in this area lay our greatest prospect for self-transcendence. He told us to avoid verbal manipulations and to concentrate on our feelings.

We began with exercises. A fat lady in leotards directed us to be absurd. We touched our noses with our tongues. We jumped. We ran. We clutched one another, made faces at one another. Afterward, we gathered in groups of five and were given an ambiguous instruction to discover one another by touching in any way we found agreeable. I crouched in front of a strange-looking young man with an underslung jaw and powerful shoulders. I tried unlocking his legs and he glared at me.

When Schutz asked each group of five to select one couple that seemed least close, the young man with the underslung jaw selected me. The hostile pairs were then requested to stand at opposite diagonals of the room and approach each other. They were to do whatever they felt like doing when they met in the center of the room. A burly middle-aged man marched toward a petite lady. They met, they paused, stared, then suddenly embraced. The next couple, two husky men, both frozen rigid, confronted each other, stared, then also embraced. The young man and I came next. We started at opposite diagonals. We met in the center of the room. I found myself looking into the meanest, coldest eyes I had ever seen. He pressed his hands to his sides, and it was clear to me that we were not going to embrace. I reached for his hand to shake it. He jerked free. I put my hand on his shoulder; he shrugged me off. We continued staring and finally returned to our group.

There was a general discussion of this encounter. Some feared we might start fighting. Nothing, of course, was farther from my mind. I had gone out, intending to play their game and suddenly found myself staring at a lunatic. He had very mean, cold eyes, a crazy shape to his jaw, lips so grim that his ill-feeling was unmistakable. Back in our group he said to me, in a raspy, shrill voice: "You thought I was going to bat you in the face; that's why you turned away." There was a slurred quality to his speech, and it occurred to me that I might have triggered off a madman. I denied that I had turned away and I was challenged to stare him down. I was annoyed that I had been forced into something so silly.

We proceeded, on the basis of our first impressions, to give one another names, which we kept for the duration of the workshop. My nemesis accepted the name of Rebel. There was a plump, lovely girl we called Kate. A silent, powerful man with spectacles we named Clark. Our fat group leader received the name of Brigitte. A lumpy, solemn man with thick spectacles we named Gary. An elegant, trim middle-aged woman we named Sheba. A buxom, mournful woman with long hair became Joan. A jovial middle-aged pipe smoker with a Jean Hersholt manner we named Hans. A fierce, mustached swaggerer in Bermuda shorts was Daniel. A quiet man with a little boy's face we named Victor. I was named Lionel. We were addressed by these names at all times.

I considered this renaming of ourselves a naive attempt to create an atmosphere free of any outside reference. Many of the techniques impressed me as naive. It seemed tactless and obvious to ask so blunt and vague a question as: "What are you feeling?" Yet what happened in the course of five days was that the obvious became clarified. Clichés became significant.

I found myself discovering what had always been under my nose. I had not known how my body felt under conditions of tension or fear or grief. I discovered that I was numb. I had all sorts of tricks for avoiding encounter. I didn't particularly like to be touched. I avoided looking strangers in the eye. I took pride in my coolness and trickery. I didn't believe one should give oneself away. It seemed to me a virtue to appear cool, to be relatively immune to feeling, so that I could receive shocks without appearing to. I considered it important to keep up appearances. I'm no longer proud of what I now believe to be an incapacity rather than a talent.

I thought my group rather dull. I saw no great beauty and a great deal of weakness. I felt somewhat superior, since I was there on assignment, not by choice. I hated and feared Reb.

But in the next five days, I became enormously fond of these apparently uninteresting strangers. We encountered one another in violent and intimate ways, and I could no longer dismiss them.

I was convinced that Rebel was insane. He opened our second meeting with gratuitous insults. He referred to me as "Charley Goodguy." When Brigitte, the leader of our group, told him not to think in stereotypes, he sneered at her: "Why don't you shut up, Fats?" It is difficult to convey the nastiness of his tone—an abrasive, jeering quality.

Daniel exploded. He called Rebel a shark and a rattlesnake. He said he wanted to quit the group because he despised this frightening, violent kid. "You scare me," he told Reb. "It's people like you who are responsible for Vietnam and Auschwitz. You're a monster and you're going to suck up all the energy of this group and it's not worth it. I want to get out."

I told Daniel his response seemed excessive. Vietnam and Auschwitz? "He's a little hostile," I said.

Reb didn't want any favors from me. "Hostile?" he sneered. "Say, I bet I know what you are. You sound to me like a professor. Or a pawnbroker. Which are you, a professor or a pawnbroker?"

Schutz intervened. He said to me and Rebel: "I feel you have something going. Why don't you have it out?" He suggested that we arm wrestle, an innocuous contest, but, under the circumstances, there seemed to be a great deal invested in winning or losing. My arm felt numb, and there was some trembling in my thighs. I feared I might not have all my strength, and Rebel appeared to be a powerful kid.

I pinned him so easily, however, that the group accused him of having quit. Daniel was jubilant: "You're a loser. You're trying to get clobbered."

Rebel was teased into trying again. On the second trial, he pressed my left arm down and demanded a rematch with the right hand. We remained locked together for close to twenty minutes. It was unbearable. I lost all sensation in my hand and arm. I willed my hand not to yield. Finally, I hoped he would press me down and get it over with. It ended when Rebel squirmed around and braced his foot against the wall and the contest was called.

Daniel was delighted by the outcome. He felt as though I had won something for him. Schutz asked: "Why don't *you* wrestle Reb?" Daniel despised violence. He probably would lose and he didn't want to give that monster the satisfaction of a victory. Violence was right up that shark's alley. He refused to play his games. Nonetheless, Daniel was on the ground with Rebel a moment later, beet red with strain, trembling down to his calves. Rebel raised his elbow, pressed Daniel down, and the match was called off. Daniel leaped to his feet, circled the room. He suddenly charged Rebel, who was seated, and knocked him from his chair. He then rushed at Schutz, yelling: "It's you I hate, you bastard, for making me do this." Schutz did not flinch, and Daniel backed off. I could see that his impulse was histrionic. I felt sorry for Reb, who mumbled: "I copped out. I should have hit him."

Reb later presented a different guise. Far from being an idiot, he was an extremely precocious twenty-year-old computer engineer, self-taught in the humanities. His father had abandoned the family when he was a child. His mother was a cold customer—never a sign of feeling. He didn't know where he stood with her. She taunted him in the same abrasive style which he tried with us.

Reb suffered sexual agonies that had brought him several hundred miles in search of a solution. He considered himself perverse and contemptible, the only impotent twenty-year-old kid in the world. He admitted he found women repugnant as sexual objects, and it was hardly surprising that his crude advances were rebuffed. He admitted that his strategy had been to strike out in hope that someone would strike back so that he might *feel.* He was boyish and affectionate outside the group.

My feeling for him underwent a complete reversal. He began to impress me as an intelligent kid, trying with great courage to repair terrible injuries. The monster I had seen simply vanished.

I never anticipated the effect of these revelations, as one after another of these strangers expressed his grief and was eased. I woke up one night and felt as if everything were changed. I felt as if I were about to weep. The following morning the feeling was even more intense.

Brigitte and I walked down to the cliff edge. We lay beneath a tree. She could see that I was close to weeping. I told her that I'd been thinking about my numbness, which I had traced to the war. I tried to keep the tears down. I felt vulnerable and unguarded. I felt that I was about to lose all my secrets and I was ready to let them go. Not being guarded, I had no need to put anyone down, and I felt what it was to be unarmed. I could look anyone in the eyes and my eyes were open.

That night I said to Daniel: "Why do you keep diverting us with intellectual arguments? I see suffering in your eyes. You give me a glimpse of it, then you turn it off. Your eyes go dead and the intellectual stuff bores me. I feel that's part of your strategy."

Schutz suggested that the two of us sit in the center of the room and talk to each other. I told Daniel that I was close to surrender. I wanted to let go. I felt near to my grief. I wanted to release it and be purged. Daniel asked about my marriage and my work. Just when he hit a nerve, bringing me near the release I wanted, he began to speculate on the tragedy of the human condition. I told him: "You're letting me off and I don't want to be let off."

Schutz asked if I would be willing to take a fantasy trip.

It was late afternoon and the room was already dark. I lay down, Schutz beside me, and the group gathered around. I closed my eyes. Schutz asked me to imagine myself very tiny and to imagine that tiny self entering my own body. He wanted me to describe the trip.

I saw an enormous statue of myself, lying in a desert, mouth open as if I were dead. I entered my mouth. I climbed down my gullet, entering it as if it were a manhole. I climbed into my chest cavity. Schutz asked me what I saw. "It's empty," I said. "There's nothing here." I was totally absorbed by the effort to visualize entering myself and lost all sense of the group. I told Schutz there was no heart in my body. Suddenly, I felt tremendous pressure in my chest, as if tears were going to explode. He told me to go to the vicinity of the heart and report what I saw. There, on a ledge of the chest wall, near where the heart should have been, I saw a baby buggy. He asked me to look into it. I didn't want to, because I feared I might weep, but I looked, and I saw a doll. He asked me to touch it. I was relieved to discover that it was only a doll. Schutz asked me if I could bring a heart into my body. And suddenly there it was, a heart sheathed in slime, hung with blood vessels. And that heart broke me up. I felt my chest convulse. I exploded. I *burst* into tears.

I recognized the heart. The incident had occurred more than twenty years before and had left me cold. I had written about it in a story published long ago in *Esquire*. The point of the story was that such events should have affected me but never did. The war in Germany was about over. We had just taken a German village without resistance. We had fine billets in German houses. The cellars were loaded with jams and sausages and wine. I was the aid man with the outfit, and was usually summoned by the call of "Aid man!" When I heard that call I became numb, and when I was numb I could go anywhere and do anything. I figured the battles were over. It came as a shock when I heard the call this time. There were rifle shots, then: "Aid man!" I ran to the guards and they pointed to bushes ten yards from where they had been posted. They had spotted a German soldier and called for him to surrender. He didn't answer and they fired. I went to the bushes and turned him over. He was a kid about sixteen, blond, his hair strung out in the bushes, still alive. The .30-caliber bullets had scooped out his chest and I saw his heart. It was the same heart I put in my chest twenty-three years later. He was still alive, gray with shock, going fast. He stared up at me—a mournful, little boy's face. He asked: "Why did you shoot? I wanted to surrender." I told him we didn't know.

Now, twenty-three years later, I wailed for that German boy who had never mattered to me and I heaved up my numbness. The trip through my body lasted more than an hour. I found wounds everywhere. I remembered a wounded friend whimpering: "Help me, Leo," which I did—a close friend, yet after he was hit no friend at all, not missed a second after I heard of his death, numb to him as I was to everyone else, preparing for losses by anesthetizing myself. And in the course of that trip through my body I started to feel again, and discovered what I'd missed. I felt wide open, lightened, ready to meet others simply and directly. No need for lies, no need to fear humiliation. I was ready to be a fool. I experienced the joy Schutz had promised to deliver. I'm grateful to him. Not even the offer of love could threaten me.

This was the transformation I underwent in the course of that fantasy trip. The force of the experience began to fade quickly, and now, writing two weeks later, I find that little remains. But I still have a vision of a possibility I had not been aware of—a simple, easy connection with my own feeling and, consequently, with others'.

I had great difficulty emerging from my body. I was pinned against my intestines, pregnant with myself. When I finally began to move and restored all the missing organs and repaired those that were damaged, I feared that all this work was temporary, that if I were to leave the heart would vanish, the stomach dry up, the intestines be exposed. Schutz asked if there was anyone who could help me get out. I said: "My daughter." So I invited my daughter to enter my body. She stood near my heart and said: "Come on out, Daddy," and led me out. I ran to a meadow on my chest. I ran through long grass, toward a gate, directly toward the sun. There I lay down and rested.

Occasionally, during my trip, I heard others crying, but I had lost track of the group. I opened my eyes. I had an initial sense of others as darts of candlelight about me. The room seemed to have shifted. It was pitch black outside. Everyone was very close to me—Reb, Daniel, Brigitte, Bill, Joan, Victor, Kate, Clark, Gary, Sheba. Sheba still wept. Brigitte directed us all to lie down and to reach out and touch one another. She turned out the lights and gave us various instructions designed to release us and finally we parted.

It was not easy leaving these people I had met only five days before. Time was distorted and we seemed to have lived years together. It was not easy leaving Big Sur. On the final morning, the entire workshop met to say good-by. Our group gathered in a tight circle, hugging and kissing, and I found myself hugging everyone, behaving like the idiots I had noticed on first arriving at Esalen. I hugged Rebel. I told him he was a great kid and that a few years from now he might not even recall his present trouble. I told him not to envy his peers. He was probably much better than they.

Schutz ended our last meeting by playing a record from *The Man of La Mancha,* "The Impossible Dream." We were at that point of sentiment where corny lyrics announced truths and we could be illuminated by the wisdom of clichés.

The condition of vulnerability is precious and very fragile. Events and people and old routines and old habits conspire to bring you down. But not all the way down. There is still the recollection of that tingling sense of being wide awake, located in the here and now, feeling freely and entirely, all constraints discarded. It remains a condition to be realized. It could change the way we live.

Writing Exercises in Expository Argument: Political Theory

Exposition is the process of defining, explaining, and interpreting ideas in writing. Argument makes use of all the components of exposition for the purpose of convincing or persuading the reader of the validity of the ideas under consideration. While the major intention of all forms of exposition is to clarify, argument goes a step further. Its chief end is to win support for its contentions through effective, coherent presentation. The techniques employed for the achievement of the goal of persuasion are analysis, formulation of logical proof, and ethical and emotional appeal.

The student is asked to write a number of paragraphs reflecting the varieties of political points of view which have been presented in the section on political theory. The rhetoric in these exercises should depend heavily on the tools of reason: the establishment of a hypothesis, the analysis of the proposition, and the formulation of proof.

EXERCISE 1

Present an argument for the limitation of individual liberty in a democratic society.

EXERCISE 2

Present an argument for the limitation of collective power in a democratic society.

EXERCISE 3

Present an argument for the need of a coalition of democratic leftists in present-day American society.

Discussion-Instruction: Psychology

This section concentrates on the new American trends in psychological theory and therapy and their origins in the theories of Jung and Freud.

In his essay on the group encounter at Esalen, Leo Litwak has said, "It could change the way we live," and so it has. We are living in an age of group-think. All around us we find evidences of a new outlook in psychology and psychiatry. The new methods and the new forms are collective. We find that the changing attitude is apparent in the formation of sensitivity training groups, in women's liberation consciousness-raising groups, in group therapy, and in encounter groups. With changing conditions and an increasing interest in the function of the mind, Americans have changed their attitudes toward their psychological needs and have come to think of their relations to their own minds in terms of their relationship to other individuals, to groups of people, and to society as a whole. This new consciousness is rooted in both the individual, or private, and the mass psychology of the past. These two psychologies—influenced principally and originally by the work of Freud and Jung and modified by the work of Harry Stack Sullivan, behaviorists such as B. F. Skinner, and more modern methodologists such as Carl Rogers and R. D. Laing—are moving psychological explorations in revolutionary new directions. In order to understand the origins of psychological methodology, we must know something of the theories of Freud and Jung, the similarities and differences between them, and the ways in which they have affected the society in which we live. By applying this knowledge to the new methods of group therapy, we may gain some insight into the new directions in which psychology may be moving.

EXERCISE 1

In his essay on childhood memories Freud speaks of "concealing memories," the reminiscences one retains in order to conceal the more profound and traumatic events of childhood which the adult cannot bear to recall. These concealing memories, or standard childhood reminiscences, resemble myths and legends and stand in direct opposition to the real, or concealed, memories which can be rediscovered only by analysis of the individual. On the basis of these statements would you say that Freud was interested primarily in (check one)

    1. collective memory.

    2. individual experience.

Answer: 2

EXERCISE 2

If Freud felt that the usual childhood reminiscences resemble myths, which of the following would he regard as concealing memories and which as concealed memories?

    1. early feelings of rejection by the mother

    2. the memory that mother went on a long trip

    3. hatred of father

    4. longing to be king

Answers: 1. concealed; 2. concealing; 3. concealed; 4. concealing

EXERCISE 3

In *I Never Promised You a Rose Garden,* Deborah Blau recalls black shapes or bands which she frequently sees before her eyes. She also recalls a white form receding from view. She cannot tell what these shapes mean but they sadden her and intensify her emotional suffering. If she can recall the images but not the event which they indicate, what is she experiencing?

    1. concealing memories

    2. concealed memories

Answer: 1

EXERCISE 4

By a careful probing into her past, her doctor is able to elicit the information that she was left in her barred crib while the nurse she loved went away. When Deborah understands this she is moving toward an understanding of which of the following?

    1. the general nature of rejection

    2. the sad condition of all human suffering

    3. the traumatic event (symbolizing loss of love) which she has concealed

---

Answer: 3

EXERCISE 5

After her rediscovery of the event which she associated with loss of love, Deborah refers to the black crib bars as mourning bands over her eyes. The mourning band is a societal symbol or image (visual depiction of an idea or feeling) of grief at loss of a loved one. Which of the following, then, does her rediscovery of the events and of their meaning help her to accomplish or to achieve?

1. an understanding of the cause of her particular sadness and consequently a better ability to deal with it

2. a feeling that she is less lonely because she shares a common sorrow with all humanity (i.e., the sorrow of loss)

3. a feeling that she is not really a rejected or unworthy person

4. the feeling that she is a prototype of all human suffering

Answers: 1; 2

EXERCISE 6

Deborah Blau's ability to recognize the origins of her sorrow helps her to know herself and thus to know something of others who have suffered or of all who wear mourning bands. Thus, she comes to know grief. Which of the following, then, can we say are true?

1. The understanding of the self helps one to reach out to others.

2. When one understands the self, one understands common human needs.

3. Human emotions are embodied in symbolic forms; when we have experienced emotions, we recognize the symbols of them.

4. We may know other people's particular experiences or memories the moment we know our own.

Answers: 1; 3

EXERCISE 7

Freudian analysis prods one to explore honestly one's past life in order to recover the experiential origins of emotional difficulties. Freudian analysis is individual, non-mythic, centered upon certain fundamental human problems which, in the course of the analysis, appear in forms peculiar to the patient under treatment. Thus one may say that the Freudian method is best used to (check the appropriate responses)

1. explore universal symbols.

2. understand the pattern of all human life.

3. gain insight into the nature of one's special problems.

4. strip away the symbols and concealing images and reveal the real self.

Answers: 3; 4

EXERCISE 8

Although Jung's theories share much with Freud's, Jung differed from Freud in placing special emphasis upon what he called the mythological character of "typical modes of apprehension" which appear as "primordial images." These primordial images common to most men he called "archetypes." According to this description which of the following may be considered an archetype?

1. the circle as a form of perfection or eternity

2. the sea as a mother

3. the attic as a place associated with punishment

Answers: 1; 2

EXERCISE 9

The archetypes in their purest forms are, according to Jung, found in primitive tribes but in both primitive societies and literate societies they are rationalized. Which of the archetypes listed above do the following rationalizations describe?

1. The head, a sphere, is the seat of reason, the most godly of human qualities; therefore, the head is the supreme portion of the body.

2. Life came first out of the water and moved to land, hence we may say that water is life-giving.

Answers: 1; 2

EXERCISE 10

These rationalizations of archetypes are sometimes found in the forms of myths. Match the archetypal image with the myth which embodies it.

1. Venus is born in a seashell and carried to shore

2. Aeneas leaves the world, enters the underworld, there learns secrets from his ancestor, and brings the knowledge back to earth

a. the sea as a mother

b. separation, initiation, and return; the great circle

c. the world as serpent

Answers: 1-a; 2-b

EXERCISE 11

Jung's interest in mythology originates in his belief that myths, since they embody archetypes, are evidences of the existence of what he called "the collective unconscious." The collective unconscious is the underlying consciousness common to all and composed of the unity of instinct (universal human responses) and archetypes (primordial images). Freud, on the other hand, is concerned with the responses of the individual unconscious. Below is a story followed by two interpretations. Basing your answers upon what you know of the differences between the Jungian and the Freudian orientations, label the interpretations either Jungian or Freudian.

Story

In my dream I saw myself as a large figure who left a walled city, full of castles and towers, and entered a forest. I knew that I could not return from the forest until I had caught a great white bear, a forest dweller who spoke many tongues of animals and of humans. After numerous encounters with forest monsters, hard elements, and dangerous paths, I met and captured the white bear and began my journey back to the court, leading the white bear by a chain. He revealed to me the ways of learning all the tongues, and I imparted the information to the inhabitants of the castle to which I was called upon my return.

Response

1. The hero-god separates himself from society in quest of the secrets of life, repeating the old legend of separation, initiation, and return.

2. My father left home when I was small, and I felt that I was abandoned in a dangerous world until I entered a play group where I gained self-confidence by teaching some of my playmates how to garden, a talent I learned after my father left.

Answers: 1. Jungian; 2. Freudian

EXERCISE 12

Which of the two, the Jungian or the Freudian orientations or methods, might be most useful or most influential in each of the following areas?

1. the study of literary themes

2. the study of the individual's relation to society

3. one's recognition of one's own heroic qualities

4. one's search for a personal and private past

Answers: 1. Jung; 2. Jung
(and Freud); 3. Jung; 4. Freud

EXERCISE 13

In the Esalen essay we find an example of one kind of group encounter designed to help individuals search for themselves with the help of other individuals who are also seeking to understand themselves. This kind of group encounter seems to focus upon (check the appropriate responses)

1. the Jungian notion of the collective unconscious.

2. the Freudian individual unconscious.

3. a combination of Jungian and Freudian ideas (i.e., the group or collective self helps the individual to know both the separateness and the community of the self).

Answers: 1; 2; 3

EXERCISE 14

In an increasingly collective society certain segments of the population in America are also turning inward upon themselves because they claim that they are alienated from their societies. If we are concerned with increasing our own self-awareness as well as furthering the recognition of our human relations to others in a world which seems to isolate us one from the other, we must apply a number of theories and techniques. Group therapy combines, among other theories, those of Jung and Freud. The first main heading below indicates Jungian ideas, the second, Freudian. Basing your answers upon what you have learned from Exercise 13, check the statements most indicative of (A) Jung's contributions to changing techniques in the modes of emotional learning, and (B) Freud's contributions to changing techniques in the modes of emotional learning.

(A)   Awareness of our personal self as a unit of a species

1. makes us feel less alone.

2. gives us a sense of individuality and worth.

3. makes us feel unique and therefore alien.

(B)   Awareness of our own special formulative experiences

1. makes us realize the common forces that shape us all.

2. makes us realize that no one else has had our experiences.

3. gives us a sense of individuality and worth.

Answers: (A) 1; 2; (B) 1; 2; 3

EXERCISE 15

Combining the two sets of topic headings and the two sets of answers in the preceding exercise, consider the future trends of psychiatry and psychology in America and explain the reasons for your answers. Below is a suggested list.

1. Psychology and psychiatry will deal more in group methods.

2. The period of treatment for people in emotional difficulties will be shorter than it was.

3. The emphasis will lie more on the individual's relation to other people than on his relation to his own past.

4. The emphasis will lie more on the individual's relation to himself and to his own past than it will on his relation to others.

5. The new emphasis on the individual's relation to others will help him to understand himself better.

DIVERSITY AND COMMUNITY

Ethnic Groups: Melting Pot or Mosaic?

In the last few years attention has been drawn to the needs and aspirations of a variety of ethnic groups which contribute significantly to the cultural life of many large American cities and some rural areas as well. Increased public awareness of minorities has been stimulated by proliferating coverage in newspapers and periodicals. The American Indians have dramatized their plight by occupying Alcatraz Island as a reminder of their property rights. The Mexican-American grape pickers have gained support for their "causa," the agricultural labor movement, from such prominent political figures as the late Senator Robert Kennedy and Oklahoma Senator Fred Harris. The Black Panthers have taken their cause to the penthouses of the "radical chic" New York elite and the campuses of Yale and Columbia Universities. Sociologist Oscar Lewis has traced and preserved the lives of Puerto Ricans in the "culture of poverty" with extraordinary fidelity, taping dialogues of a single family with members residing in a number of Puerto Rican and American cities. Within the last two years archeological "digs" on Long Island and in Brooklyn have unearthed remarkably sophisticated black slave communities which flourished during the nineteenth century. And just recently the Young Lords, a group of Spanish and Puerto Rican New Yorkers, took over Lincoln Hospital in the Bronx in support of the economic demands of the hospital workers. Following the take-over, a group of junior physicians calling themselves the Pediatric Collective ousted the head of pediatrics and replaced him with a doctor of more acceptable ethnic background.

An unexpected development in this flourishing movement of collective activism is the emergence of The Jewish Defense League, a militant society whose avowed purpose is the vigilant counteraction to anti-Semitic acts or statements wherever they originate. Ethnic sensitivity is also being expressed through the recently organized Italian-American Civil Rights League, whose purpose is the protection of Italians from harassment arising from public linking of Italian names with organized crime. An organization of prominent blacks has met with the Human Rights Commission of the United Nations and presented for their consideration a measure against racial genocide based on the concept of racial extermination originating in the post-World War II Nuremberg Trials.

The embattled ethnic groups are profoundly concerned about Black Power movements, "negritude" in the arts, socio-racial conflict, and domestic colonialism. These are the issues which have increasingly permeated the academic disciplines of literature, sociology, political science, and history. And these are the themes of a variety of new experiments in communication and the arts—in television programs devoted to "soul," radio lecture series dealing with black history, films dedicated to redeeming the maligned American Indian stereotype in the traditional Western film "classics," and the special museum shows dedicated to the art of particular ethnic urban communities. An entirely self-contained black theater which originated in the community and took shape in workshop studios, mobile units in Harlem, school auditoriums, churches, and local Y's has moved to off-Broadway and Broadway, literally preempting and overwhelming conventional theater by its enormous creativity and vitality. Its theme is almost entirely the black experience in America, but because its human values eclipse racial themes, such plays as Douglas Turner Ward's *Days of Absence* and LeRoi Jones' *Dutchman* have made a permanent contribution to American drama.

The study of ethnic groups in America must be seen as a new way of educating, of casting light on the previously obscured cultural elements of our population, the contributions they have made, and the repressions they have suffered. Ethnic studies point out the existing relationships within our society: between the Americanization of European immigrants and the learned racism which accompanies that process; between trade unionism and racial exclusion in the North; between the growth of suburban communities and the racist thinking which contributed to that phenomenon and hastened the decay of the cities; and between the two confronting intellectual communities, black and white, which have emerged as the "two nations" of the university.

There are two major types of spokesmen for the minority groups in America today. The one is fairly represented by James Baldwin, who has said: Negroes are Americans and their destiny is the country's destiny. The spokesman for the other group is Eldridge Cleaver, who has consistently maintained that blacks must have a destiny exclusive of the majority and that that destiny must be achieved only through collective separatism. Baldwin examines the individual black experience, and his conclusion is profoundly pessimistic. Observing that the black man has been robbed of his past, he sees him incapable of regaining his dignity independently of his American environment. Cleaver, following in the path of Marcus Garvey, envisions the use of directed power for the purpose of creating a discrete black nation within the boundaries of an inhospitable larger nation. Baldwin is a lone survivor; his ideas are considered decadent today. Cleaver is the voice of conscious mass cultural separatism and survival.

Increasingly the mood is both militant and collective. The slogans are "All Power to the People," "Indian Power," "Black Power," and "Viva la Causa." The expressed political attitude behind the public postures is a somewhat distorted Jeffersonianism. "When the laws no longer serve the people," declared Huey Newton on August 16, 1970, "it is the people's right and the people's duty to free themselves from the yoke of such laws." The young revolutionary intellectual, Angela Davis, assesses the present mood of her people as the "building of a collective spirit, getting away from this individualistic orientation towards personal involvement. . . . What people have to start doing is to build that collective spirit. To overcome that notion of bourgeois individuality which separates one person from the next and which defines the individual as someone who can assert himself at the expense of his neighbor, at the expense of his brother by destroying his brother." The new collectivism is apparent in the universal reference to the "brothers" and "sisters" within the minority movements.

The ethnic minorities remain the loneliest crowds in America. Cast adrift from the mainstream of American life, they can only look ahead, for their past yields no real strengths. Yet, given the instability of American governmental policies, even their future remains uncertain. Often, after wresting civil rights legislation from one sympathetic administration, they are threatened with the diminution of these same hard-won concessions by the next. Their own leaders increasingly are offering them only one option for survival: militance or abandonment. Ironically, many of their most aggressive leaders are incapable of carrying through their own militant reforms because they themselves are frequently in political and personal jeopardy. Eldridge Cleaver is in exile, Bobby Seale in jail, Stokely Carmichael in flight. Their former Northern ally, the white liberal, is now in disrepute in most black circles. The Southern white still applies the old yardstick: Give them an inch and they'll take an ell. The future of ethnic minorities in America is shadowy in spite of their recent gains through legislation, yet they present the most dramatic and dynamic struggle within our culture. At issue is not only the survival and prosperity of minority groups, but the emerging psycho-historic revelation of the American character as well.

Vine Deloria, Jr.

The War Between the Redskins and the Feds

If Secretary of the Interior Walter Hickel has any sense of history, he must have been impressed with his situation at the convention of the National Congress of American Indians held earlier this fall [1969] in Albuquerque, N.M. Not since George Armstrong Custer's sensitivity-training session on the banks of the Little Big Horn had so many angry Indians surrounded a representative of the United States Government with blood in their eyes. Of the estimated million Indians in the United States, the N.C.A.I. represents the reservation population of some 400,000. With spokesmen for the remaining urban and other Indian communities of the East (500,000 urban Indians and 100,000 scattered Eastern bands) attending the convention, Hickel was greeted by representatives of the entire Indian community, including Eskimos, Indians and Aleuts from his home state of Alaska.

All summer, tension had been building within the Indian community as the tribes fearfully awaited the pronouncement of Indian policy by the new Nixon Administration. During the 1968 Presidential campaign Nixon had promised that, if elected, he would not unilaterally sever Federal relations with the tribes, nor would he allow the tribes to be pressured to alter the relationship themselves. Indian leadership, recalling that Nixon had been Vice President during the Eisenhower Administration, when the hated policy of termination of Federal responsibilities for Indians had been forced on the unwary tribes, was alerted for any signs of change, and skeptical of the "New Federalism."

Hickel's performance in 1969 appeared to have justified Indian suspicions. In late July, at a Western Governors' Conference in Seattle, he characterized the relationship of the Federal Government as "overprotective" of Indian rights. With a foot-in-mouth aplomb so characteristic of some of Nixon's interchangeable Cabinet members, Hickel compounded this error by labeling the reservations as "crutches" by which Indians avoided their full responsibilities as citizens.

By late summer, the moccasin telegraph was buzzing with rumors that the new Secretary of the Interior was a "terminationist," and that a great battle over the very existence of the reservations was imminent. Indian reservations have a total land base of more than 52 billion acres, scattered in 26 states and providing a home for people of 315 different tribal groups. The life expectancy of a reservation Indian is 46 years, rising nearly a year each year under current programs. Although the average income is slightly over $1,500 per family annually, and the housing is generally substandard, the reservations are all that remain of the continent the Indians once owned, and they are determined to fight for every handful of dust that remains.

The National Traditionalist Movement, spearheaded by the Iroquois League, called for Hickel's removal from office. The Iroquois (the only Indian tribe to declare war on Germany in 1917) set a strong nationalistic tone to the resistance, which quickly sprang up in Indian country.

From the urban Indian centers on the West Coast, the third-world-oriented United Native Americans took up the battle cry. "IMPEACH HICKEL" bumper stickers blossomed beside "Red Power" and the multitude of "Custer" slogans on Indian cars. Petitions calling for Hickel's removal began to circulate on the Coast.

As the N.C.A.I. convention opened, there was considerable discussion by the delegates as to the length at which Indians should *stabilize* Hickel's hairline. This remark was an obvious reference to Hickel's conception of his role as trustee in defending the water rights of the Pyramid Lake Paiutes of Nevada. The Pyramid Lake tribe has a beautiful lake, the largest fresh-water lake in the state. For the major part of this century it has tried to insure that sufficient water is delivered to the lake to maintain its excellent cutthroat trout fishery and its flock of pelicans. But the Federal Government has continually refused to defend the tribe's water rights by allowing other users to take water which is rightfully owned by the Paiutes. Consequently, the lake has had a declining shoreline for most of the century, a condition that precludes development of the reservation for recreation purposes.

Hickel's solution, proposed after a meeting with Governors Reagan of California and Laxalt of Nevada, was to reduce the water level 152 feet, creating a mud flat of 40,000 acres and thus "stabilizing" the water level. It was the same logic used by the Army to destroy a Vietnamese village—"We had to destroy the village to save it." It naturally followed that the only way to save Pyramid Lake was to drain it.

With these remarks to his credit, it is a wonder that Hickel was the recipient of only sporadic boos and catcalls when he attempted to address the Indian convention. No one even speculated on the possibility of a canine ancestor in Hickel's immediate family tree. "Terminationist" is a much dirtier word in the Indian vocabulary.

Wally Hickel is not that bad a guy. He was genuinely puzzled by the reactions which his remarks had created in the Indian community. In his own mind he was simply searching for a new approach to a problem that he, as Secretary of the Interior, had a responsibility to resolve. But he had unexpectedly hit the one nerve which had been frayed raw by a century of abuse and betrayal: the treaty-trust relationship between Indians and the Federal Government.

Hickel's remarks at Seattle and on the water problems in Nevada prior to the meeting of the National Congress of American Indians fitted exactly into prior speeches and problems of other times and places which had resulted in policies and programs destructive of the reservation communities. He could not have said anything more inflammatory than that the Federal Government had been "overprotective" of Indian rights, implying that the Government would be less zealous in fulfilling its responsibilities during his tenure as Secretary of the Interior.

Had Hickel been thoroughly briefed on the sterling record his predecessors had achieved, it is doubtful that he would have made the "overprotective" statement. The Government has been overprotective of Indian rights only in the sense that John Dillinger "overprotected" banks by robbing them before other criminals showed up.

In 1908 the Supreme Court decided the case of *Winters v. United States* in which Indian water rights were given priority over any other rights on streams running through Indian reservations. It has been clear, therefore, for most of this century, that the Pyramid Lake Paiutes have first priority for sufficient water in the Truckee-Carson river system to stabilize their lake *at the level at which it stood when the reservation was established.* Yet Interior had watched as the Indian water went elsewhere and the lake declined precipitously each year.

In 1924 the Secretary of the Interior was authorized to construct the Coolidge Dam in Arizona. In the authorizing legislation it clearly stated that the project was "for the purpose, first, of providing water for the irrigation of lands allotted to Pima Indians on the Gila River Reservation, Arizona." The Federal Government delivered just about enough water for Ira Hayes, Pima Indian and Marine hero of Iwo Jima, to drown in. Never was there any good faith by the Government to help the Indians irrigate their lands. Consequently, the water made available by the project went to non-Indians residing off the reservation.

With water the crucial element in the development of Indian reservations, the concept of "overprotection" appears nonsensical in view of the fact that, attached to every major Interior Department appropriation bill is a little rider stating that no Federal funds can go to develop the water rights of the tribes in California, Oregon and Nevada. Indian reservations thus lie dormant and undeveloped in those states, while non-Indians have sufficient water to develop their own lands.

To add to the irony of the "overprotection" which Indian people supposedly receive is the fact that, when the United States has to deal with foreign nations, it presents a clean and pious front. In 1913 the case of the Cayuga Nation, member of the Iroquois League, came before the American-British Claims Arbitration. The British Government wanted just compensation from the United States under the provisions of the Peace of Utrecht for lands which the state of New York took from the Cayugas after the War of 1812.

In the appendix to the answer filed by the United States to the British complaint, the Government declared:

"Under that system the Indians residing within the United States are so far independent that they live under their own customs and not under the laws of the United States; that their rights upon the lands which they inhabit or hunt are secured to them by boundaries defined in amicable treaties between the United States and themselves; and that whenever those boundaries are varied, it is also by amicable and voluntary treaties, by which they receive from the United States ample compensation for every right they have to the lands ceded by them."

Traditionally, Indian tribes had been treated in this manner. They were early regarded as distinct and sovereign nations fully capable of entering into compacts, agreements and contracts with the United States. The Delaware Treaty of 1778, the earliest published treaty, spoke of "peace and friendship" which was necessary between the peoples of the United States and the tribe. It described the Delawares as being "dependent upon the (United States) for all articles of clothing, utensils and implements of war." It was fundamentally a trade agreement.

Until 1871 the tribes were treated as sovereign yet dependent domestic nations with whom the Federal Government was bound to treat for land cessions. In the treaties, the Government accepted the responsibility to protect the lands reserved by the tribes for their own use against encroachments by its own citizens. In that year, however, Congress decided that it would sign no more treaties with tribes. Instead, a policy emerged aimed at breaking up the tribal structures, even though the United States had promised in good faith that it would not interfere with traditional tribal customs and laws.

The shift in policy placed major emphasis on enticing, threatening, or deceiving individual Indians into forsaking their tribal relations. A comparable situation would exist if the Government refused to recognize General Motors as a corporation and insisted that it would become concerned with the individual stockholders, enticing them to sell their stock and liquidating the assets of the corporation, all the while wondering why General Motors was declining as an economic entity.

The tribes fought back. Asserting that the treaties were contracts between two parties, the tribe and the Federal Government, they often punished with death any leaders who signed away tribal rights. While fundamental logic supported the tribal position, overwhelming power and deceit by Government officials were able to carry the day. The treaties had been signed by nations, not an arbitrary conglomerate of individuals. Yet the official Federal policy was to assimilate individual Indians even if their rights as members of tribes had to be breached.

A major influence against the tribes was the ideology of the missionaries who were attempting to force their own ideas of culture on the captive audiences on the reservations. The missionaries believed that only by inculcating selfishness and the concept of private property into tribal society would individual Indians be able to become Christians and be saved.

Church pressure to individualize the tribes and dispose of the tribal land estate resulted in the passage of the Dawes Act in 1887. This act divided the reservations up into allotments of 160 acres, and each Indian was given a piece of land for farming. The remainder of the tribal holdings was declared "surplus" and opened to settlement by non-Indians.

Before allotment was forced on the tribes, there was no poverty on the reservations. The minority report issued against the policy mentioned the complete absence of pauperism among the Five Civilized Tribes of Oklahoma. It suggested that the Indian method of holding land for an entire community might be superior to the idea of non-Indian society, in that this method precluded a class of people that was perennially poor, while non-Indian society was plagued with poverty in its lower economic class.

The effect of individualizing the tribal estate was the creation of extreme poverty on many of the reservations. Individual Indians, unaccustomed to viewing land as a commodity, were easily swindled out of their allotments. Good farm land often went for a bottle of liquor, white trustees of individual Indian estates often mysteriously inherited their wards' property, and dying Indians were known to have mysteriously given their lands to churches before expiring. One Indian commissioner trod on eggshells during his term because a half-million-dollar Indian estate passed on to a missionary society instead of to the Indian heirs. Between 1887 and 1934 some 90 million acres of land left Indian ownership in a variety of ways. The actual circumstances in some cases have never seen the light of day.

Indians who sold their lands did not merge into white society and disappear. They simply moved onto their relatives' lands and remained within the tribal society. Thus, the land base was rapidly diminishing while the population continued to remain constant and, in some cases, grew spectacularly.

The situation had become so bad by 1926 that a massive study was authorized. It was called the Meriam Survey, and it pointed out that if the allotment process was not solved, the United States would soon have on its hands a landless, pauperized Indian population totally incapable of succeeding in American society.

In 1933, the New Deal Administration appointed John Collier as Indian Affairs Commissioner. He helped to write into law the basic charter of Indian rights called the Indian Reorganization Act. Indian tribes were given status as Federal corporations under this act, allotment was stopped and efforts were made to rebuild a land base for the Indian communities.

Tribal governments allocated a substantial portion of tribal income to purchase the allotments of individual Indians, thus holding in Indian hands the land that would have been lost forever. Tribes began their gradual revival of traditional ways, and were making excellent progress when World War II caused a dreadful reduction in domestic spending. Programs could not be funded until after the war.

In 1954 the chairmanship of the Indian Subcommittee of the Senate Interior Committee was taken over by Senator Arthur Watkins of Utah. Watkins was an arch-conservative who understood nothing of Indian treaties, was contemptuous of Indian people, and was determined to solve the "Indian problem" in his short tenure as chairman of the committee. He began a unilateral war against Indian communities that was known as "termination."

Watkins visualized himself as the Abraham Lincoln of the 20th century. Characterizing the reservations as havens of irresponsibility, and accepting the thesis that the Federal Government had been too protective of Indian rights, the Senator was determined to break the long-standing commitments of the United States to its Indian tribes—whether it was just or not.

"With the aim of 'equality before the law' in mind, our course should rightly be no other," Watkins announced. "Firm and constant consideration for those of Indian ancestry should lead us all to work diligently with all other Americans. Following in the footsteps of the Emancipation Proclamation of 94 years ago, I see the following words emblazoned in letters of fire above the heads of the Indians—THESE PEOPLE SHALL BE FREE."

If Watkins was determined to *free* the Indians, he was a generation too late. In 1924 the Indian Citizens Act was passed making all noncitizen Indians American citizens with full rights and privileges. The act further declared that the "granting of such citizenship shall not in any manner impair or otherwise affect the right of any Indians to tribal or other property."

The Indian Citizens Act thus gave full constitutional rights to individual Indians insofar as they were individuals. It specifically exempted any rights that individual Indians may have had in tribal property from its operation. The dual citizenship of Indian people was thus recognized.

But Watkins was convinced that holding an interest in tribal property in addition to holding citizenship was a handicap. Under this theory, everyone who benefited from a trust fund was automatically a second-class citizen.

A number of tribes fell victim to Watkins's crusade. The Menominees owned a forest in Wisconsin. They had a tribal sawmill and operated it to provide employment for tribal members, rather than to make a profit—although with their exemption from corporate taxation they often showed a profit. The tribe spent most of its income on social services, supporting its own hospital and providing its own law enforcement on the reservation. It was more genuinely a self-supporting community than many non-Indian communities near it.

Termination of Federal supervision meant an immediate tax bill of 55 per cent on the sawmill. To meet this, the saw mill had to be automated, thus throwing a substantial number of Indians out of work and onto the unemployment rolls. To meet the rising unemployment situation, the only industry, the sawmill, had to be taxed by the county. There was an immediate spiral downward in the capital structure of the tribe so that, in the years since the termination bill was passed, it has had to receive some $10-million in special state and Federal aid. The end is not yet in sight.

When the smoke had cleared, some 8,000 Indians had been deprived of rights their grandfathers had dearly purchased through land cessions. The Paiutes of Utah and Klamaths of Oregon were caught in a private trusteeship more restrictive than their original Federal trust relationship, from which they were to have been "freed." Fortunately, Texas made a tourist attraction out of the Alabama-Coushatta reservation in that state, thus preserving most of the tribal assets. The mixed-blood Utes of Utah formed their own organization and tried to remain together as a community. The Siletz and Grande Ronde Indians of Oregon, the California Indians, and the Catawbas of South Carolina simply vanished. Menominee County became the most depressed county in the nation.

In Watkins's mind, and in the mind of his successors on the Senate Interior Committee, the opportunity to remake American Indians into small businessmen was too much of a temptation. The termination policy continued to roll in spite of its catastrophic effects on the Indian communities.

Tribes refused to consider any programs, feeling that it was no use to build good houses when the reservation might be sold out from under them at any time. Development schemes to upgrade reservation resources were turned down by people with no apparent future. The progress which had been made by the tribes under the Indian Reorganization Act ground to a halt. Indian people spent a decade in limbo, hesitant to make any plans for fear they would come under attack by the irrational policy.

Watkins's rationale at the beginning had been that he was making the individual Indians first-class citizens, where they previously had been handicapped by maintaining their tribal relationships. It was the same reasoning that had led policy-makers in the last century to force allotment on the tribes and create the original poverty conditions on the reservations. When the termination legislation was finally drawn for the Menominees, the concluding phrase in section 10 of the bill was illuminating: "Nothing in this act shall affect the status of the members of the tribe as citizens of the United States"!

The argument of "freeing" the Indians was as phony as could be. The act did nothing but dissipate tribal capital and destroy the rights of Indian tribes to have their own communities. But termination fitted exactly into the integrationist-thought world of the period, and the expanding Civil Rights movement of the black community, which had been given impetus by the decision of *Brown v. Topeka Board of Education,* the famous school desegregation case of 1954. So it *seemed* the right thing to do.

Society has come a long way in its understanding of itself since 1954. The ensuing civil rights movement, which had shaken the foundations of society during the nineteen-fifties, changed abruptly into the black power movements of the late sixties. For half a decade we have been struggling to define the place of a group of people in American society and, as numerous reports have indicated, the divisions in the society have become more pronounced, the hatreds more violent and lasting.

Termination slowed down during the Kennedy-Johnson Administrations, but the basic Congressional directive has never been changed. Policy-makers in Congress and in the Interior Department continue to regard decisions made in haste in 1954 as imperatives which they must follow today. Only by a vigilant National Congress of American Indians watching the Washington scene day and night have Indian people been able to stop further implementation of this policy.

Walter Hickel, in his casual remarks, stirred up a hornet's nest of Indian concern. It did not seem possible to tribal leaders that the new Administration would return to a policy proven bankrupt when it was applied to their land holdings in 1887, again proven bankrupt in 1954 with the further dissipation of their remaining lands and resources, and completely out of tune with the social movements of today.

Indian tribes have been able, in spite of all pressures exerted against them, and the failure of the Federal Government to defend their rights, to maintain a capital in land and resources by which they can maintain their own communities. They have been able to keep tribal governments alive and functioning. In the War on Poverty, tribes provided services for all people within reservation boundaries, red or white, and many children received services that they would not have otherwise received because their counties did not want to sponsor programs under the Office of Economic Opportunity.

The record of Indian people as a recognized self-governing community is enlightening. The progress of the last decade is spectacular and sophisticated for a people with a national average of eight years of education. Indian people are now demanding control of education programs through the creation of Indian reservation school boards. They are certain they can do better than either the state or Federal education they have been given in the past. The variety of projects undertaken by Indian communities is staggering and encompasses everything from sawmills to ocean-going fishing vessels, motels to carpet factories.

American society has much to learn from Indian tribes. It may all be lost if another era of struggle over reservation existence is initiated. The black community, spearheaded by the demands for reparations by James Forman, is desperately seeking capital funds. Indian tribes already have capital in land and resources and have demonstrated how well it can be used.

Blacks and Mexicans are developing rural cooperatives in an effort to solve the poverty of their people in the rural areas. Indian tribes have already proven that rural corporations and cooperatives can and do work when undertaken by a united community.

Conservationists are pointing out the rapidly dwindling natural resources of the nation, the danger of total extinction of life unless strong conservation practices are begun at once. The Quinault and Lummi Indian tribes have already zoned their beaches to conserve their natural state, while the White Mountain Apaches have developed nearly 30 artificial lakes and maintain the best fishing and recreation areas in Arizona.

The power movements, the Amish situation in the Midwest, the desire of the Acadians in Louisiana to have French taught in schools, the conflict between the ethnic groups in the urban areas, all point toward new social concepts revolving around a number of ethnic and racial communities desiring to conduct their own affairs. Even the rising conservative trend in politics seeks power at the local level rather than continued direction from long distance.

Tribes have overcome enmities of the past. They were once far deeper and more bitter than in the current impasse between black and white. Unemployment is declining as tribal programs are committed to creating jobs, not simply making profits. Land is being renewed, beaches and rivers are being cleared and the reservations are becoming models of proper land use. Indian society is stabilizing itself to face the instantaneous electric world of today far better than are other segments of American society.

The Indian outrage at Hickel was a cry to society at large. "If you destroy us," it really said, "you will destroy your last chance to understand who you are, where you have been, and where you have to go next in order to survive as a people." One hopes Secretary Hickel and the Senators and Congressmen will hear this cry and understand.

Oscar Lewis

Simplicio: "I'd Rather Be in Puerto Rico"

I flew to New York on *la Eastern.* That was my first airplane trip. When I got on I was drunk. I'd shared a bottle of rum and several beers with Marcos and some of the boys at the airport. I had the seat to myself, so I lay down to rest. I fell asleep. I woke up when the plane was about to land. After it landed I got out, and there I was, lost. I didn't know where to go. I searched everywhere for one familiar face but I couldn't find anyone I knew.

About an hour later a man came up to me and asked, "Who are you?"

"I'm Simplicio."

"Felícita's brother?"

"Yes."

"I was looking for you," he said, putting his arm around my shoulder. He turned out to be my brother-in-law Edmundo, Felícita's husband. I had written so that they'd meet me at the airport. I'd sent a snapshot so they'd recognize me. "Come on, let's get your suitcase," Edmundo said. We got it and put it in the car. My brother-in-law had come with three other boys. As we drove down the streets, lined with tall buildings, I thought, "So many big buildings in this place, and this is where I'm going to live!"

We drove a hundred and fifty miles, to a place in the country in New Jersey. We stopped to eat at a restaurant because their house was too far away and we were hungry. I said, "I'll pay the bill," and paid out of fifteen dollars I had. They charged more than eight dollars, and then I had only seven left.

When we got to the house Felícita threw her arms around me. Then I said to her, "Here, take these five dollars and give them to Edmundo." That left me only two dollars.

My uncle Simón, *papá*'s brother, lived there too. They took me over to his house to meet him. He has always been good to me. I never met him until I came to the States, yet I address him familiarly as *tu,* never as *usted.* I feel closer to him than to my own father. I don't dare smoke in his presence, true, but we joke a lot. "If this one doesn't change, he won't live long," he said about me.

It was such a pretty, strange, different sort of place! After three days at my sister's house I got a job on a farm. I, who had never, never worked in the country before, got a job weeding around the *peach* trees with a tiny hoe. After the second day on that job I got so sunburned that the skin was peeling off my back. *Ave María!* I started to lose weight. I was paid nineteen dollars for the two days' work. I gave nine to Edmundo, sent five to Flora and kept the rest. My brother-in-law didn't like that. He expected me to turn my whole pay check over to him.

I started looking for another job. I didn't know much English but I did know a little. So I found a job packing tomatoes. I worked at both jobs at the same time, half a day in *el field* weeding *peaches* and half a day in *la packing.*[1] In all, I earned forty-nine dollars a week.

One day I decided to rest awhile. I was sunburned, sweaty and dead tired. To top everything off, *el boss,* who was Italian, came over and objected to my taking a break. He began to scold me, "I pay you a dollar an hour to work, see? Don't think things here are the way they are back in your country. You people come here because you're starving. You can't earn money back home—that's why you come here."

I stood up to him. "Listen, mister," I said, "I came here but it wasn't because I was starving back home, get it? I came from a country that's equal to this one, and American too."

"Where?" he asked.

"I'm a Puerto Rican," I answered, "and I have more right here than you do, because you're not American; you're not a citizen yet. But I'm an American and that's that. I can come and go as I please."

"Well, why did you come here?"

"I came to see the world, and because I thought there were good people here. There are good people too, good workers. And I know very well that he who doesn't work, doesn't eat."

Then he said, "Why don't you go back where you came from?"

"I go where I damn well please, do you hear?" I answered. I told him off because they didn't like Negroes there. Then I walked away.

Luckily the head of *la packing* had asked me if I wanted a *steady* job. I worked in a room upstairs dropping cans into the machine. It was an automatic machine, so I had to be responsible and not lose even a minute. It was hard work and my fingers were full of cuts, but I earned a lot of money.

Then I had that argument with Felícita over sending money to Flora, and she and Edmundo kicked me out. So I went to my uncle Simón's house. He had a three-story house all to himself. I slept downstairs on a little *caucho* they had. My aunt washed and ironed my clothes and fed me.

One day I went with Uncle Simón's wife to the house of a spiritist in New Jersey. But I waited outside for her. I never do go into those places. I've always felt like that. When I was about twelve they used to hold séances at my cousin Virginia's house. If I was there, I'd disappear the minute I knew they were going to have one of those.

The thing is, I don't believe in spiritism. Well, I do believe, only I never go to those places. I also believe that if you think of something it can come true. That has happened to me many times. Like one Christmas Eve my brother-in-law invited me

1. Packing house.

to a bar. I told him I wouldn't go, because if I did I'd get into a fight with some friends who worked where I did. I said to him, "I'm not going, there are some Puerto Ricans there." Finally I did go but I knew something was bound to happen to me there. Sure enough, a guy came and hit me on the back. I hit him, too, and we fought. I have a feeling about that. I'm superstitious.

I was very comfortable in my uncle's house. The only trouble is that he had two young daughters. They were my cousins, of course, but I didn't know them well enough to excuse their acting so familiarly with me. They would sit on my bed in their underclothes to talk to me. And at night they would come and lie down beside me and all that. I didn't like such carryings-on.

I never told Uncle Simón that this had anything to do with my leaving his house. What happened is that Edmundo sent for me. He was sick in the hospital, and he wanted me to move back into his house and take care of Felícita. After kicking me out like he did! But after all, Fela is my sister, so I went back. My uncle got huffy with me about that. But I explained to him that I wasn't the one who had gone to make up with Edmundo; Edmundo had come to me.

A week after I'd moved back with Felícita, Flora wrote. She announced that she, Soledad and Soledad's four children were coming up to the States. *Don* Camacho, who was Soledad's husband at that time, had paid all their fares.

That took me by surprise. *Don* Camacho did that because Soledad was dying to come to the States to see what it was like. She thought everything was *easy* up here. When they arrived—Flora, Soledad and the kids—I asked my sister right away, "*Muchacha,* how ever did you manage it?"

"Oh, it was easy," she said. "I wrote a letter saying things are good here and I signed it with your name. As soon as he read it, he gave me money for the fare."

I told her, "You shouldn't have done that. You should have known that if I didn't write such a letter it was because things are not good up here."

There were so many of us now, and Felícita's house was so small. There were fourteen people staying in the house at that time. Somehow we managed. When Felícita's husband came back from the hospital he didn't like it at all. And then, Felícita couldn't stand anything Soledad did. Finally Soledad found herself a husband. The trouble was that Fela was in love with the husband Soledad caught. Felícita was mad. Then Soledad said, "I have to make this arrangement because I can't stay here. I can't stand the way Felícita treats me any more." The boy she went with took her far away, about ninety miles from Felícita's house, way off at the end of nowhere. We didn't hear from her until sometime later.

I blame Edmundo, not Fela, for what happened. Someday I'll run into him somewhere and then we'll settle accounts. Want to know why I blame him? Because it's the man who gives the orders in his house and his wife has to obey him, right? And he didn't like Soledad. He said she was a tramp. So he made her life miserable until she had no choice but to take off with that man.

I stayed on with Flora. But the day Flora didn't prepare food for me, Felícita didn't either. So Felícita and I were on bad terms again. I didn't eat well or anything. When I got in from work and sat down in the front room, Edmundo was there, dog-faced and grim.

They moved into another house and we with them. It belonged to an American Jew who owned lots of houses. My uncle got me a job with the Jew but I never even got started on it because I got myself a job at *la packing* instead, at a dollar an hour. That was during the summer. At the beginning of the winter my sister kicked us out of her house. I had given her ten dollars and she objected; she wanted more. Well, that wasn't it, really. I'll tell you. You see, what happened is that Flora fell in love with a boy who worked at a hotel. I found a letter from him and I was going to kill her. I took a knife and cut all her clothes to pieces. She got scared and locked herself up in the bathroom. I tried to break in and get her. I didn't mean to kill her with the knife. I wanted to kill her with my bare hands, to strangle her. But then Felícita turned against me and that made me mad. I quarreled with her and said things. But then I went out, to forget.

When Edmundo got home Felícita told him what had happened. He began to talk. He said first we moved in with them and then we acted as if we were the owners of the house. I said to him, "Look here, I know I'm not the owner of this house and I don't have the right to give orders. But neither am I a hanger-on, because I'm Felícita's brother. Besides, I pay my way. The trouble with you is that you're greedy for money. You're a miser."

So without taking anything into account, he put us out in the street in winter. In the Christmas season. That's what he did. And Felícita didn't say a word.

Then I remembered that American Jew who owned a lot of houses. I went and knocked on his door. Another man would have told me that I wasn't any kin of his and had no call to go knocking on his door when I had *trouble.* But that man was like a father to me. I'm very fond of him, you know. People up here have been only too good to me. I can't complain.

When I called on him he opened the door. "What do you want, Simplicio? Come in."

"My sister kicked me out of her house."

"In this snow?"

"Yes."

"Why? Was there *trouble?*"

"No. It was all about money."

Then he told me, "All right. Stay here."

"I'm going back to get my wife tonight," I told him. I went to Flora and showed her the letter from her sweetheart. I told her, "*O.K.* Come with me now. As soon as I can, I'll take you back to your family."

That was on a Friday. Then the Jew gave me a job in his house, painting furniture and so on. He gave me a five-room place to live in, all furnished. There was a set of living-room furniture, bedroom furniture, rugs on the floors, washing machine, radio, TV, everything. On top of that he gave us all our food, and light, gas and water. He gave me all that for working for him. Besides, he paid me five dollars.

Then, through letters, we found out that Flora's sister was living in Breton, Pennsylvania. I said to Flora, "Let's go to your sister's house." This was on a Saturday. I had ten dollars with me. I didn't know the way to the railway station but we got there all right. I asked my two brothers-in-law to get me a job. Next day, Sunday,

I went back to my job with the old man and left Flora with her relatives. I told them to keep her.

I went on working with the old man and everything was going fine. I had to work hard, so I was always tired when I got home. The American gave me my dinner. Afterward I lay down to listen to the radio. I also amused myself doing exercises with some dumbbells the Jew had in his house. I missed Flora some, not very much. I lived about a month like that, with no problems and nothing to worry about.

Then a letter came from my brothers-in-law telling me that I had a job at a hospital in Pennsylvania. They said I could earn good money there. I told the Jew I had to visit my relatives and he took me to Pennsylvania himself. When we said good-bye there he told me, "Come back soon."

I said, "Yes. I'll be there the day after tomorrow." I said it because I didn't know how to take leave of him.

There was an empty apartment in Flora's brother's house. It belonged to a woman but she couldn't rent it because it was too old and run-down. So I slept up there and Flora slept down in her brother's place. We were separated like that for a while. But then Flora begged me to forgive her and we got together again. After all, she had never gone to bed with her sweetheart or anything like that. I warned her, though, "You did that to me, now I'm going to do worse." That's why I behave badly to her up here. She did what she did and now she has to pay for it, with interest.

I started on my job at the hospital waxing and polishing the floor with a machine. The work was easy, much easier than my job with the Jew, and I earned good money, fifty dollars a week. The only Puerto Ricans working there were Flora's brother and me. *El boss* was an American Negro and he was good to me. In him I had a real friend.

Then we shared an apartment with Flora's sister and her husband, and I paid half the rent and half the food bill. Occasionally I also gave them cash. Then—I don't know what happened, it was something to do with Flora, not with me—they kicked us out.

I waited until I got paid on Friday, and with the fifty dollars I had earned that week I went around town looking for a place to live. I found a five-room apartment, unfurnished, and had to leave the whole of my fifty dollars there. I moved in that very night, with our bed and our clothes.

I didn't have a cent left, so I went back to the hospital and asked the *boss* to lend me twenty dollars. He was very good to me, he gave it to me right away. I set ten dollars aside for the week's expenses, then used the rest to have the gas and electricity connected so we could cook. There we were, living in that enormous apartment without a stick of furniture to speak of! And paying twenty-five dollars a month rent, plus eight dollars for water and electricity.

Then my friend, the Negro, gave me a sofa, and a little old man who worked with me sold me a refrigerator for twenty dollars. I had to pay ten dollars down and ten more later on. But the refrigerator was worth every cent of it; it was a big one, and new. Everybody said I had been more than lucky. I could put forty dollars' worth of food in it and it would still look empty. Then a little old American woman offered to sell me her furniture, a sofa and two chairs, for twenty-five dollars. So I threw mine away and bought hers.

No Puerto Rican helped me at that time the way the Americans and the Italians did. They gave me a carpet and a set of furniture for the bedroom. A woman who lived downstairs gave me some things too. Yes, they helped me a lot. My friend, the Negro, came to visit me. For *las Christmas* he gave me money, meat, pork and lots of other things.

We could even fish there in Pennsylvania. But it wasn't like La Esmeralda. Up here you need a license. You go to a place and pay three-fifty. They ask you where you live, how much you weigh, what your color is and things like that. Then they give you a piece of paper and that's it. Except that you have to get a fishing rod. You can't just dangle the string from your hand. Luckily, the Jew for whom I used to work had a lot of fishing rods and I'd taken one with me.

On my free days we'd go fishing in the river. I did it to amuse myself. I didn't make any money from it. There, if you don't want the fish for yourself, you have to throw them back in. Nobody else will take them. I loved it. In summer we got up at five in the morning and spent the whole day at the river.

In winter we took our rifles and hunted wild ducks and geese. It's easy to get a rifle there, not like in Puerto Rico. All they ask is your name and address. Then you give them a snapshot of yourself, pay two-fifty, and you have your license. My rifle cost thirty-nine dollars.

I had a good life there. I couldn't keep dogs but I had some white mice. I trained them, and you should have seen how clever they were! When I got home from work I called them. They'd run and jump on me and begin to tickle me. If I told them, "Come on and take a bath," they got into the tub. I filled it and bathed with them. They took food from my hands too. They ate their fill and crawled into their cage to sleep. When I woke up in the morning they were already standing beside my bed, waiting for me to feed them. They grew up, big and beautiful. I wouldn't have gotten rid of them if it hadn't been for Flora. She doesn't like animals. She kept nagging me about them, saying they shit too much and dirtied up the place. And it's true their urine stank a lot. So one day I took them out to the woods and left them there.

I had been working there for eight months, earning a hundred and eighty dollars every fifteen days, plus *overtime,* when I got a letter from Puerto Rico from Edmundo, Felícita's husband. He asked me to send money for his fare back to the States. After having treated me the way he did! I told Flora, "O.K. Write and tell him I'll buy his ticket." After all, I had money to spare. I was going to send for him, but by all that's holy, I was going to drown him when he came. I would say to him one day, "Come on, let's go to the river." And then I'd do it. But it all came to nothing. Flora refused to write to him.

Then I sent for my *mamá*. I wanted her with me because I lacked for nothing here. It was like a holiday when she arrived. We went to get her at the airport in the American Negro's car. Fernanda already knew him through my letters. I had written that I had a friend who was very, very good to me. And that day we ate and all that, and he paid for everything.

Flora had a job taking care of two children, and she turned it over to my *mamá* to keep her busy and amused and so that she could earn some money. Fernanda used that money to buy *Christmas* presents for her grandchildren in Puerto Rico.

I had a spare bedroom and space for two beds in the parlor. So I told Soledad to come with her children and spend *Christmas* with us. So we all spent *Christmas* together.

I protected my *mamá* and took good care of her. I'd tell Flora to close the window against the cold in winter. Well, Fernanda would get up, still warm from the house heat, and would want to open the window and lean out. Then I'd tell her, "Nanda, that's bad. That's dangerous."

Fernanda fell in love with an old man whom I sometimes took to my house. I spoke to her about it. "Don't do that, Nanda. Look, people here aren't the same as in Puerto Rico. That man's Italian. Besides, he's married and has children."

"That's my business," she'd say, "not yours."

"Sure, it's your business, Nanda. I only advise you as a son. Don't fall for that man. You're up here with me, away from your husband. Don't let Héctor think that he was right when he said you came up here to chase an American Negro who was a friend of mine."

"Oh, don't bother me," she always said. "I only do this to amuse myself. There's nothing between that man and me."

But after about three months she got fed up with the States. For one thing, I went to drink at a *bar* once a week and she objected to that. And she hated the cold. But, *bendito,* what really made her go and decide never to come back was a fight I had with a boy. He fell and cut his face. After the fight each of us went to his own house. Up here the cops let you go home because they know who you are and where to find you. I didn't say a word about my trouble to the family.

The next day I went to work at the hospital as usual. In the afternoon the cops came and asked, "Are you Simplicio Ríos?"

"Yes."

"We're looking for you." And they snapped the handcuffs on me and took me to the police station. The first people I saw when I got there were Fernanda and Flora. The cops had been around to my house first. They handcuffed the boy and me. When Fernanda saw that, she had a fit of hysterics. They took us to the prison and shut both of us up in a cage. This was on a Friday. We spent the night there, and thank God, they took us to court on Saturday afternoon. The judge said we had to pay a total of one hundred and sixty-two dollars' fine. This boy and I got together and between us we managed to pay in full. So by two in the afternoon we were free.

When I got home Fernanda was crying. "You see what comes from keeping bad company? Now I'm really going back to Puerto Rico," she said. And she went. There was no holding her. She kept after me, "I want to go. Get me a ticket," until I gave in. I bought her a ticket and went to see her off at the airport.

Sometime after she got back to Puerto Rico she wrote that she had left Héctor. I asked her at once whether she wanted to come and live with me again but she said no. I knew she wanted to stay there because of the new husband she'd gotten. If she ever wants to come up, I'll send for her again.

After Fernanda left, Soledad had a nervous breakdown. She went crazy. She came to my house and asked me to take care of her little girls because she was sick and had to stay in the hospital. I said, "*O.K.,* leave them here."

I had the children three months, until she got well. I gave those children every-thing they needed, as if they had been in their own home. That's why I tell her that she should leave those girls with me. Because I took good care of them and saw to it that they behaved, and all that in spite of Flora who didn't want to take charge of them. She said they kicked up a rumpus in the house and got on her nerves. I said, "Never mind. I'll see to it that they behave properly. That's what relatives are for."

I couldn't go and see Soledad while she was sick. The hospital was too far away. When she got well she came to get the children.

I was doing all right until I got into trouble on the job. Some fellows gave me a shot of rum. They forced it on me, see? I didn't even want it. Then a man broke a bottle of oxygen and accused me of doing it. I insisted that it hadn't been me. They were a bunch of American Negroes but I tangled with them. I fought three of them at once. The *boss* walked in while we were at it and he suspended me from the job for four months.

I said to myself, "In four months I'll starve to death. And I can't stand to have to ask for money." I was fed up with the place, anyway. I still went fishing but I was bored all the same. It was a dull life. By five in the evening I had to be home in bed, because if I went out I never met anyone. There were no people around at night, nobody at all. There was nothing in the whole city but hospitals, graveyards and bars. And it was a problem to get into the bars because they don't like Negroes there either. Near my home, a few miles away, there was a place called Morristown. They wouldn't allow a Negro to set foot there. I've passed through in a car but I never got out. It's better not to stop if you want to avoid trouble. Imagine, they won't even sell gasoline to a Negro there. I never once saw a Negro in that town. They have them in a place apart, you see, living in a separate section with *buildings* for Negroes only.

There were churches too. But I don't go to church. I'm a Catholic, but Fer-nanda sent us to church because they served a snack for children at four-thirty every afternoon. That's why she sent me. There I learned some prayers on my own, Our Father, Hail Mary—but I never got to take my First Communion because they made no preparations at home for it. They didn't get me clothes for it or anything. So I skipped the class for four days at a time and went to the movies instead. When Fer-nanda found out, she scolded me. I did go to confession, but that was thirteen or fourteen years ago. I haven't been to church since.

In spite of the fact that I don't go to church, I always light candles for the saints. And I believe in God. I pray to him every day as I go down the street. But I'll tell you one thing, it's not good to go to church every day. I worship God in my heart. I go to church when I want to, because I feel like it. But this business of going every day or whenever the priest says you must, I'm against it. I'm a Catholic, of course, because that is the one religion I have known. And I know it was the first religion that ever existed. Most Protestants were baptized in the Catholic Church and changed later. Not that I blame them, every one has his creed and searches for God in his own way. But I can't agree with this business of forbidding people to smoke, drink or go to dances. And I don't like dancing and singing aloud in church and going into fits. I don't deny that if you have that religion you are unable to restrain yourself. But who knows? I might wind up in that church myself someday. Each of us has his own heart and his own way of thinking. But what I believe now, at this moment, is that it is a sort of fake religion. Who ever heard of not believing in the saints?

Although I'm not sure, sometimes I think God made Adam and Eve normal, like us. All human beings come from them, don't they? Then, where did those people with monkey faces and ostrich bodies come from? Another thing, Adam and Eve were white. So where did the Negroes come from, and the yellow people? Where did we Puerto Ricans come from? That idea is out of date. Because if each and every one of us is descended from Adam and Eve, how come there are so many different languages in the world? May God forgive me, but that somehow doesn't make much sense. A scientist once wrote a book that makes a lot more sense. He says that the world changed little by little. That we started out like the bugs and have changed step by step until the present. Now we are a little bit civilized but still not enough. So it may be that we, too, will go on changing—you know, evolving.

I like the saints and believe in them. I want them near me. But as for asking them for things, I only ask Saint Raymond and he helps me. I always ask him to give me health so that I can keep on working. I've never asked him to get me a job. That's something you have to get for yourself. Health is the most important thing of all.

And so, when they suspended me from the hospital, I commended myself to the saints and said to my wife, "Flora, we're going to New York." I had one regret on leaving. I knew I would miss my friend, the American Negro. He was like a father to me and he was my color, see? I was very, very fond of him.

I got Soledad's address, and without really knowing how to get there, I got on a train to New York. From there I took the subway at Thirty-fourth Street. That brought me to the Bronx, where Soledad used to live, but she had moved. Luckily, she had left her new address with some neighbors. After searching all over the place I found her house, but she wasn't there. I had to wait and wait until she came home. When she came, I told her what had happened to me. She said, "Stay here. I'll let you two have a room." So we did.

I went to a bar with Soledad's husband, Benedicto, and I liked it. After that I went every night. I was practically going broke. Then Benedicto sailed off on a ship. I got to thinking, and I said to Soledad, "What shall I do, Soledad? I guess I'd better go get my things in Pennsylvania and find myself a place to live." I looked until I found a place. I paid twenty-two dollars down, plus one dollar for the key. That was two weeks' rent. I paid it in advance, because my money was running out and I was afraid I wouldn't find a job. And if you at least have a place of your own, you're not too badly off.

After finding a place, I went to Pennsylvania to get my things. And you know, it's true that what's done in a year can be undone in an hour. The only things I brought here were the washing machine, the TV set, two lamps, the table and our clothes. I sold all the rest, for twenty-five dollars. And I left the apartment, after painting it and making it so pretty and fixing the bathroom. I left the refrigerator, bed, most of the furniture, new carpets for all the five rooms. I even had something to keep stuff in, a sort of desk, all made of glass. All of that I sold for twenty-five dollars so that I could come here to suffer.

When I finally got my bearings in New York I liked it better than Pennsylvania. It seemed different, see? There's more going on here, many big houses, lots of Puerto Ricans, all sorts of amusements. So I told Flora I was staying here, even though the job I have now is harder than the one in Pennsylvania. But that's not the important thing. Over there, that job was my only chance to work. If they had fired me, what could I have done? Here in New York, if they fire me I'll get another job right around the corner. The factory even gives me life insurance. That way, if something happens to me, my wife will be taken care of. She'll get ten thousand, maybe it's three thousand dollars. That will be some help.

I'm glad I'm a man. That way I don't have to bother with the monthly illness or getting pregnant or anything like that. Not that women are so bad off. They can make themselves pretty, and flirt and all that. And then, a woman doesn't have to go after a man. The man is the one who has to chase after the woman and give up his seat to her and so on. But even so, I'm grateful to have been born a man. Because that way I can work hard to get whatever I want and I can have fun, too, because a man, on account of being a man, can do anything he pleases.

If I fall for a woman, I let her see it. Right now I have one that I courted in our very house, right here in the Bronx. The woman I'm telling you about had moved into the same *building* where we lived. This was during the *Christmas* season and it was snowing. Flora's brother Sotero and I were downstairs. Then this girl came out and began to play in the snow. Her sister came out too. Sotero and I got into the game, Sotero with the other girl and I with mine—Leila she's called. Nothing came of it that day.

After that, both sisters came to call at my house. Then I looked at mine and fell in love with her. I asked Leila where she planned to spend Christmas Eve and said I was going to spend it with my relatives. She asked me if she could go, too. So we dressed up and went over to my cousin's through a heavy snowfall. On the way there I didn't say one word to her. After midnight we returned to my place and there we finally got to talking. Next day, everytime I looked at her, we both had to laugh. On New Year's Eve I kissed the girl on the stroke of midnight, the first kiss I ever gave her. After that we drank and drank until dawn.

Flora realized what was going on and didn't want me to go to Leila's house. But our *toilet* faced the door of her apartment, so I would sneak out through there. When I went to see her we would dance. Flora would call out to me, "Come home now, it's time to sleep."

"Not yet," I'd say. "In a minute." One day Flora came over and punched me. I merely said, "Come on, Flora, be quiet." Then I took her home, put her to bed and went back to Leila.

Sometime later Leila moved to Third Avenue. One night I was there with her when Flora and Soledad appeared. Leila was pregnant and Flora saw she was wearing a maternity dress. The two of them tangled then and there. I simply walked out on both of them, went home to change my shirt, and then out to a bar to drink. But even after that I kept on seeing Leila. Hell, I have a lot of shirts and pants at her house and she washes them for me. I change my clothes over there sometimes. She respects me and does everything I ask her to.

That's why I say that I'm the one who wears the pants at my house. I don't deny that Flora slaps my face and curses me out and all that. I say "yes, yes, yes" to everything. Let her waste her saliva and beat her brain, I do as I please. I go out, have a good time. Then I go home and go to bed without even saying hello to her.

I do my duty as a man of course. I support my family and make people respect my home. I mean, if someone comes around to my place and starts speaking dirty or cursing I say, "Listen, I'm the only one who has a right to speak like that in this house. I'm the one that pays for it." That I do. And to do that, one has to work.

My ambition is to get enough money to go back to Puerto Rico. Then I'd buy a bit of land and make a home of my own to give security to my children, although I have no children yet. And all because Flora won't go to see a doctor and find out if she can be cured and give me a child. Maybe they can't do anything about it now. I have an idea they did something to her at the hospital the last time she miscarried, to keep her from getting pregnant again. She got so sick, you see. I think that's why she's never gotten pregnant again since then, although we don't do anything to prevent it. I guess I'll have to go make myself some children with some other woman.

I've asked Flora to go to the hospital, because I'm young and would like to have children some day. She says she won't go because she's scared. Well, if she doesn't want to, I won't force her. But she has no right to complain if I try to have children with other women. If I should have a child, ah, I'd take it home with me. If Flora won't accept the child, I'll go to the other woman, the mother of my child.

Seriously, I really have thought that. When Leila got pregnant I felt so good because the child was mine. Leila was seven months gone when she lost the baby. They went to get me at my house about five times that night. But I thought it was a put-up job, see? I didn't believe a word they said. But then I thought it over. By six in the morning I was at her mother's house. And it was the truth. Leila had been taken to that hospital where women go to have babies.

I rushed over but they wouldn't let me in. They said come back that evening at seven. I was so desperately eager to get in that I went ahead of time, at four o'clock, with a big bag of grapes, apples and all sorts of fruit. They wouldn't let me in. I waited there until seven and then they let me in, but they wouldn't let me take the fruit.

Leila stayed in the hospital three days. The baby died. He was a boy. They took him to another hospital to preserve him in alcohol. I felt the baby's death deeply, deeply. And think of it, she miscarried because of me, because I'd scared her half to death. I hardly ever get mad at anybody. But when I do, I go wild. I throw whatever I can get hold of. It's all over in a minute. But in that minute I'm not in this world; I don't know what I'm doing.

This happened on a Thursday when I was over at Leila's. She says to me, "Let's go upstairs. They're having a small dance."

"No," I say, "let's not."

"Oh, come on."

"Well, *O.K.*" When we get there a little old man says to me, "I'm going to put on a record now, especially for your woman. I want to dance with her."

I said no. The old man punched me in the chest. I let it pass. We went back down to Leila's apartment and I locked the door.

About ten minutes later the old man knocks on the door, furious. He yells, "Come on out, you! I'm going to stick you like a codfish."[2] I opened at once. The old man was standing there with a steel knife in one hand and a small parrot-beaked blade in the other. "I came to get you," he says.

"Oh, forget it," I answered. He pushed on into the apartment. I went crazy. I grabbed a chair and smashed it over his head. I clobbered him. He's been covered with scars ever since. Well, that calmed him down, all right. Then his friends came and took him to the hospital. That was the night Leila lost the baby. She's never gotten pregnant again.

So, if I can't have children of my own, I'd like to keep Gabi, Felícita's son. If they give him to me for good, I'll take good care of him. But they'll have to give me a free hand to bring him up my way, according to my own ideas. I'll give him my name and teach and direct him as I think fit. I'll give him a good education. With me, he can feel he has a father. I'll give him everything he needs and take him places. I wouldn't want him to grow up as I did, with too much freedom. I'll give him freedom, but not absolute freedom. Let him be free, yes, but let him learn to respect me too.

I've had problems with some people here in the Bronx but not gang fights, or anything like that. One time, for instance, I got in between two of my friends who were fighting and one of them socked me over the lip. Another day a boy in a *bar* called me a queer. As far as I'm concerned that's the worst insult! Listen, if they call me *"cabrón"* I don't mind. Because *cabrón* means a man who likes to have a good time, who knows his way around and likes to dance and be gay and have women and more women. So it doesn't bother me in the least to be called *cabrón*. But I won't stand to have anybody call me a queer. Because a queer is a man who likes other men. You can imagine how I felt when that guy called me that. I told him not to call me that and he repeated it. "Oh, so you want to fight?" I said, and he answered, "Sure."

So we went outside. But he brought a friend of his along and they held me and hit me when I was helpless like that. They gave me a black eye and a swollen lip. Then the man who hit me ran away. I turned on the other one, the one who was holding me. "The other one escaped," I said, "but I'll be damned if you do." I socked him hard and broke his head. I'm even with that one now. And the other one is going to get his, too. I haven't seen him since, but I'm watching for him. If I'm sober when we meet, I'll get him. If you let someone make a fool of you, you're sunk. One has to be tough with a character like that.

Those things happen to me when I'm drinking. Truth to tell, I don't even know why I drink. I live my own life, see? I don't have any hard-drinking friends because I don't like that. What I like is going out alone and drinking by myself. I have many

---

2. Codfish are flattened out and piled up with a stake driven through them when they are put out to dry.

friends and I have my cousins, Chango and Tito, who are good guys and side with me. I could go with them if I wanted to. But I don't. I figure that my duty is not to go anywhere from Monday to Friday except to work and back to my home. Friday to Saturday, my entertainment is to drink and go places by myself or, at most, with one friend. Saturdays I'm out all night, calling on my sweethearts. There's a little American girl, Sandra, who's mad about me. She works with me. She's eighteen and a virgin. Know what she says to me? "Simplicio," she says, "we can't do anything now because I'm a virgin. But I'm going to marry another man so you can be with me afterward without getting blamed for anything." I say, "Gosh! Go ahead and do it," and I walk off.

I've had lots of things happen to me during these jaunts. Some places don't want you because you're a Negro. Once I went to a *bar* near *el Brooklyn Bridge* with a friend from New York. I'd been told that it was a place for whites. So I told my friend, "Wait outside for me. I want to see if they'll serve me." When I asked for a shot of whiskey *el bartender* said they didn't have it. So I say again, "Come on. Give me a shot of whiskey."

"We don't serve Negroes here."

"What did you say?" I asked and punched him in the face. When I struck out, all the glasses and stuff on the *bar* went crashing to the floor. The *bartender* cut me over the cheekbone. I had to beat it fast. If I'd stayed they would have killed me.

A lot of people here look down on a guy because of his color, see? But I don't know, sometimes it works the other way around. Because once I went with a white friend to a *bar* around here where they don't allow white men. That's not racial prejudice because I went in and they served me, but they refused to serve him because he's white. I don't understand it.

And there's something else. The only thing that has any value up here is money. You can't go out without money because nobody gives anybody anything. But nothing! In Puerto Rico, if you go to a cheap restaurant you can get a meal for thirty-five cents. And if you don't have that much, they'll give you the scrapings from the bottom of the pot or a dish of leftovers for fifteen cents. You can always get something, even if it's from the day before. But it's different here. If you're broke you starve. People are sour and talk rough, *"Hell, get out of here,"* without turning a hair. And if you accidentally bump into somebody, it gets you nowhere to say, *"I'm sorry."* If you bump into someone in Puerto Rico, you stop and say, "Excuse me. I didn't mean to do that." And you hold them so they won't trip saying, "I'm sorry, sir."

Nobody here bothers about things like that. Life is too hurried. You don't have time to do anything but work and eat. You walk along minding your business. And if you bump into the governor himself you just keep walking. Hell, in *el subway* they push you around and toss you about like a match stick.

The thing that shocks me most is, how can you act like a man up here—a gentleman, I mean—when women won't let you give up your seat for them? Not even the little ladies. No, not even the pregnant women. If you get up in a crowded *subway* and offer a woman your seat she'll just say, *"I'm sorry."*

If you give your seat to a woman in Puerto Rico, she sits down, and what's more, she's grateful to you and thanks you. In New York, if you do that, all you get is a rude answer. I say this because once I saw a little old lady and I said to her, *"Mrs., do you want to sit down?"* She snapped at me, *"I don't want to sit down."* I was so embarrassed. It seems that people here don't give up their seat even to a little old woman who hardly has strength to stand straight. But now I do the same thing. If I see a woman standing, it's just like seeing a man. I look the other way and keep my seat.

Yes, women here think they're men. You see them wearing pants and smoking in the street. They have no respect for their husbands; he goes his way and she hers. A man has no way of knowing what his wife's up to. He's away at work all day and his friends won't tell him what his wife is up to, the way they do in Puerto Rico.

And on top of everything else, women have more rights than men. If you hit your wife she can have you arrested. The law's on her side. So here, women are the ones who rule. It's not like in Puerto Rico, where the man gives the orders. And that's the way it should be. The man should rule his home and his wife has to respect him. If she doesn't, how can he make himself respected among men?

I have noticed that Americans are different from Puerto Ricans in everything, even in love. White Americans, I mean. Because here there are two races, and two kinds of love. A white American sees a girl passing by. He stops his car and calls out to her, *"Do you want a ride?"* And the girl climbs into the car. Then they introduce themselves to each other, kiss and drive on as if this were the most natural thing in the world. They drive around for a while, then they get off at the Park, to do whatever they're going to do. Afterward each goes his own way, as if nothing had happened.

Even with their own wives the Americans are different. Look, my *boss* has a beautiful wife. She's eighteen. Well, she goes to the factory and he acts as if nobody had come. When she leaves he says, *"See you at home."* Sometimes she calls him and asks how he's doing. He answers, *"All right. See you later, honey,"* and hangs up. Those things shocked me and made me mad at first. But then I realized everybody acted the same way and I got used to it.

Life is good here but I'd rather live in Puerto Rico. I like it better. It's so beautiful! But as long as I'm here in New York, my ambition is to make money. I'm going to enroll in night school and learn to speak English well. Then maybe someday I'll get my wish, to be in the *merchant marine.* That way I could work on a ship and get the money to go back to Puerto Rico and buy a house of my own, because you never do get to own one here. You pay and keep on paying, year in and year out, and you never do get to own it. No, what I want is a little cottage in Puerto Rico where I can keep hogs, chickens and all sorts of animals. A home. A place where I can look at the mountains.

If I'm able to build myself a house there, I'll take my *mamá* to live with me. I'll divide the house in two and keep her there. That would be a good life, living in the country in Puerto Rico with my wife and with everything that I own here, my TV set, the record player and all. And with the rest of my family near me. Every day I wake up with that hope. Although I have doubts, too, now and then. Sometimes I have a dream. I see myself leaving New York and going back to Puerto Rico. But when I get there I find myself friendless and alone. Nobody looks at me. No one seems to know me. I'm all dirty. And in my dream I think, "What am I doing here in Puerto Rico where nobody knows me anymore." Then I begin to cry. I feel, oh, I feel I sort of shouldn't be in Puerto Rico at all. That's when I always wake up and say, "It was only a dream, I'm still in New York."

Stokely Carmichael

Black Power: Its Need and Substance

"To carve out a place for itself in the politico-social order," V. O. Key, Jr. wrote in *Politics, Parties and Pressure Groups,* "a new group may have to fight for reorientation of many of the values of the old order" (p. 57). This is especially true when that group is composed of black people in the American society—a society that has for centuries deliberately and systematically excluded them from political participation. Black people in the United States must raise hard questions, questions which challenge the very nature of the society itself: its long-standing values, beliefs and institutions.

To do this, we must first redefine ourselves. Our basic need is to reclaim our history and our identity from what must be called cultural terrorism, from the depredation of self-justifying white guilt. We shall have to struggle for the right to create our own terms through which to define ourselves and our relationship to the society, and to have these terms recognized. This is the first necessity of a free people, and the first right that any oppressor must suspend.

In *Politics Among Nations,* Hans Morgenthau defined political power as "the psychological control over the minds of men" (p. 29). This control includes the attempt by the oppressor to have *his* definitions, *his* historical descriptions, *accepted* by the oppressed. This was true in Africa no less than in the United States. To black Africans, the word "Uhuru" means "freedom," but they had to fight the white colonizers for the right to use the term. The recorded history of this country's dealings with red and black men offers other examples. In the wars between the white settlers and the "Indians," a battle won by the Cavalry was described as a "victory." The "Indians'" triumphs, however, were "massacres." (The American colonists were not unaware of the need to define their acts in their own terms. They labeled their fight against England a "revolution"; the English attempted to demean it by calling it "insubordination" or "riotous.")

The historical period following Reconstruction in the South after the Civil War has been called by many historians the period of Redemption, implying that the bigoted southern slave societies were "redeemed" from the hands of "reckless and irresponsible" black rulers. Professor John Hope Franklin's *Reconstruction* or Dr. W. E. B. Dubois' *Black Reconstruction* should be sufficient to dispel inaccurate historical notions, but the larger society persists in its own self-serving accounts. Thus black people came to be depicted as "lazy," "apathetic," "dumb," "shiftless," "good-timers." Just as red men had to be recorded as "savages" to justify the white man's theft of their land, so black men had to be vilified in order to justify their continued oppression. Those who have the right to define are the masters of the situation. Lewis Carroll understood this:

> "When I use a word," Humpty Dumpty said in a rather scornful tone, "it means just what I choose it to mean—neither more nor less."
>
> "The question is," said Alice, "whether you can make words mean so many different things."
>
> "The question is," said Humpty Dumpty, "which is to be master—that's all."[1]

Today, the American educational system continues to reinforce the entrenched values of the society through the use of words. Few people in this country question that this is "the land of the free and the home of the brave." They have had these words drummed into them from childhood. Few people question that this is the "Great Society" or that this country is fighting "Communist aggression" around the world. We mouth these things over and over, and they become truisms not to be questioned. In a similar way, black people have been saddled with epithets.

"Integration" is another current example of a word which has been defined according to the way white Americans see it. To many of them, it means black men wanting to marry white daughters; it means "race mixing"—implying bed or dance partners. To black people, it has meant a way to improve their lives—economically and politically. But the predominant white definition has stuck in the minds of too many people.

Black people must redefine themselves, and only *they* can do that. Throughout this country, vast segments of the black communities are beginning to recognize the need to assert their own definitions, to reclaim their history, their culture; to create their own sense of community and togetherness. There is a growing resentment of the word "Negro," for example, because this term is the invention of our oppressor; it is *his* image of us that he describes. Many blacks are now calling themselves African-Americans, Afro-Americans or black people because that is *our* image of ourselves. When we begin to define our own image, the stereotypes—that is, lies—that our oppressor has developed will begin in the white community and end there. The black community will have a positive image of itself that *it* has created. This means we will no longer call ourselves lazy, apathetic, dumb, good-timers, shiftless, etc. Those are words used by white America to define us. If we accept these adjectives, as some of us have in the past, then we see ourselves only in a negative way, precisely the way white America wants us to see ourselves. Our incentive is broken and our will to fight is surrendered. From now on we shall view ourselves as African-Americans and as black people who are in fact energetic, determined, intelligent, beautiful and peace-loving.

There is a terminology and ethos peculiar to the black community of which black people are beginning to be no longer ashamed. Black communities are the only large segments of this society where people refer to each other as brother—soul-

1. Lewis Carroll, *Through the Looking Glass.* New York: Doubleday Books, Inc., p. 196.

brother, soul-sister. Some people may look upon this as *ersatz*, as make-believe, but it is not that. It is real. It is a growing sense of community. It is a growing realization that black Americans have a common bond not only among themselves, but with their African brothers. In *Black Man's Burden,* John O. Killens described his trip to ten African countries as follows:

> *Everywhere I went people called me brother. . . . "Welcome, American brother." It was a good feeling for me, to be in Africa. To walk in a land for the first time in your entire life knowing within yourself that your color would not be held against you. No black man ever knows this in America [p. 160].*

More and more black Americans are developing this feeling. They are becoming aware that they have a history which pre-dates their forced introduction to this country. African-American history means a long history beginning on the continent of Africa, a history not taught in the standard textbooks of this country. It is absolutely essential that black people know this history, that they know their roots, that they develop an awareness of their cultural heritage. Too long have they been kept in submission by being told that they had no culture, no manifest heritage, before they landed on the slave auction blocks in this country. If black people are to know themselves as a vibrant, valiant people, they must know their roots. And they will soon learn that the Hollywood image of man-eating cannibals waiting for, and waiting on, the Great White Hunter is a lie.

With redefinition will come a clearer notion of the role black Americans can play in this world. This role will emerge clearly out of the unique, common experiences of Afro-Asians. Killens concludes:

> *I believe furthermore that the American Negro can be the bridge between the West and Africa-Asia. We black Americans can serve as a bridge to mutual understanding. The one thing we black Americans have in common with the other colored peoples of the world is that we have all felt the cruel and ruthless heel of white supremacy. We have all been "niggerized" on one level or another. And all of us are determined to "deniggerize" the earth. To rid the world of "niggers" is the Black Man's Burden, human reconstruction is the grand objective [p. 176].*

Only when black people fully develop this sense of community, of themselves, can they begin to deal effectively with the problems of racism in *this* country. This is what we mean by a new consciousness; this is the vital first step.

The next step is what we shall call the process of political modernization—a process which must take place if the society is to be rid of racism. "Political modernization" includes many things, but we mean by it three major concepts: (1) questioning old values and institutions of the society; (2) searching for new and different forms of political structure to solve political and economic problems; and (3) broadening the base of political participation to include more people in the decision-making process. These notions (we shall take up each in turn) are central to our thinking throughout this book and to contemporary American history as a whole. As David Apter wrote in *The Politics of Modernization,* ". . . the struggle to modernize is what has given meaning to our generation. It tests our cherished institutions and our beliefs. . . . So compelling a force has it become that we are forced to ask new questions of our own institutions. Each country, whether modernized or modernizing, stands in both judgment and fear of the results. Our own society is no exception" (p. 2).

The values of this society support a racist system; we find it incongruous to ask black people to adopt and support most of those values. We also reject the assumption that the basic institutions of this society must be preserved. The goal of black people must *not* be to assimilate into middle-class America, for that class—as a whole—is without a viable conscience as regards humanity. The values of the middle class permit the perpetuation of the ravages of the black community. The values of that class are based on material aggrandizement, not the expansion of humanity. The values of that class ultimately support cloistered little closed societies tucked away neatly in tree-lined suburbia. The values of that class do *not* lead to the creation of an open society. That class *mouths* its preference for a free, competitive society, while at the same time forcefully and even viciously denying to black people as a group the opportunity to compete.

We are not unmindful of other descriptions of the social utility of the middle class. Banfield and Wilson, in *City Politics,* concluded:

> *The departure of the middle class from the central city is important in other ways. . . . The middle class supplies a social and political leavening in the life of a city. Middle-class people demand good schools and integrity in government. They support churches, lodges, parent-teacher associations, scout troops, better-housing committees, art galleries, and operas. It is the middle class, in short, that asserts a conception of the public interest. Now its activity is increasingly concentrated in the suburbs [p. 14].*

But this same middle class manifests a sense of superior group position in regard to race. This class wants "good government" *for themselves;* it wants good schools *for its children.* At the same time, many of its members sneak into the black community by day, exploit it, and take the money home to their middle-class communities at night to support their operas and art galleries and comfortable homes. When not actually robbing, they will fight off the handful of more affluent black people who seek to move in; when they approve or even seek token integration, it applies only to black people like themselves—as "white" as possible. *This class is the backbone of institutional racism in this country.*

Thus we reject the goal of assimilation into middle-class America because the values of that class are in themselves anti-humanist and because that class as a social force perpetuates racism. We must face the fact that, in the past, what we have called the movement has not really questioned the middle-class values and institutions of this country. If anything, it has accepted those values and institutions without fully realizing their racist nature. Reorientation means an emphasis on the dignity of man, not on the sanctity of property. It means the creation of a society where human misery and poverty are repugnant to that society, not an indication of laziness or lack of initiative. The creation of new values means the establishment of a society based, as Killens expresses it in *Black Man's Burden*, on "free people," not "free enterprise" (p.167). To do this means to modernize—*indeed, to civilize*—this country.

Supporting the old values are old political and economic structures; these must also be "modernized." We should at this point distinguish between "structures" and "system." By system, we have in mind the entire American complex of basic institutions, values, beliefs, etc. By structures, we mean the specific institutions (political parties, interest groups, bureaucratic administrations) which exist to conduct the business of that system. Obviously, the first is broader than the second. Also, the second assumes the legitimacy of the first. Our view is that, given the illegitimacy of the system, we cannot then proceed to transform that system with existing structures.

The two major political parties in this country have become non-viable entities for the legitimate representation of the real needs of masses—especially blacks—in this country. Walter Lippmann raised the same point in his syndicated column of December 8, 1966. He pointed out that the party system in the United States developed before our society became as technologically complex as it is now. He says that the ways in which men live and define themselves are changing radically. Old ideological issues, once the subject of passionate controversy, Lippmann argues, are of little interest today. He asks whether the great urban complexes—which are rapidly becoming the centers of black population in the U.S.—can be run with the same systems and ideas that derive from a time when America was a country of small villages and farms. While not addressing himself directly to the question of race, Lippmann raises a major question about our political institutions; and the crisis of race in America may be its major symptom.

Black people have seen the city planning commissions, the urban renewal commissions, the boards of education and the police departments fail to speak to their needs in a meaningful way. We must devise new structures, new institutions to replace those forms or to make them responsive. There is nothing sacred or inevitable about old institutions; the focus must be on people, not forms.

Existing structures and established ways of doing things have a way of perpetuating themselves and for this reason, the modernizing process will be difficult. Therefore, timidity in calling into question the boards of education or the police departments will not do. They must be challenged forcefully and clearly. If this means the creation of parallel community institutions, then that must be the solution. If this means that black parents must gain control over the operation of the schools in the black community, then that must be the solution. The search for new forms means the search for institutions that will, for once, make decisions in the interest of black people. It means, for example, a building inspection department that neither winks at violations of building codes by absentee slumlords nor imposes meaningless fines which permit them to continue their exploitation of the black community.

Essential to the modernization of structures is a broadened base of political participation. More and more people must become politically sensitive and active (we have already seen this happening in some areas of the South). People must no longer be tied, by small incentives or handouts, to a corrupting and corruptible white machine. Black people will choose their own leaders and hold those leaders responsible to *them*. A broadened base means an end to the condition described by James Wilson in *Negro Politics,* whereby "Negroes tended to be the objects rather than the subjects of civic action. Things are often done for, or about, or to, or because of Negroes, but they are less frequently done *by* Negroes" (p. 133). Broadening the base of political participation, then, has as much to do with the quality of black participation as with the quantity. We are fully aware that the black vote, especially in the North, has been pulled out of white pockets and "delivered" whenever it was in the interest of white politicians to do so. That vote must no longer be controllable by those who have neither the interests nor the demonstrated concern of black people in mind.

As the base broadens, as more and more black people become activated, they will perceive more clearly the special disadvantages heaped upon them as a group. They will perceive that the larger society is growing more affluent while the black society is retrogressing, as daily life and mounting statistics clearly show (see Chapters I and VIII). V. O. Key describes what often happens next, in *Politics, Parties and Pressure Groups:* "A factor of great significance in the setting off of political movements is an abrupt change for the worse in the status of one group relative to that of other groups in society. . . . A rapid change for the worse . . . in the relative status of any group . . . is likely to precipitate political action" (p. 24). Black people will become increasingly active as they notice that their retrogressive status exists in large measure because of values and institutions arraigned against them. They will begin to stress and strain and call the entire system into question. Political modernization will be in motion. We believe that it is now in motion. One form of that motion is Black Power.

The adoption of the concept of Black Power is one of the most legitimate and healthy developments in American politics and race relations in our time. The concept of Black Power speaks to all the needs mentioned in this chapter. It is a call for black people in this country to unite, to recognize their heritage, to build a sense of community. It is a call for black people to begin to define their own goals, to lead their own organizations and to support those organizations. It is a call to reject the racist institutions and values of this society.

The concept of Black Power rests on a fundamental premise: *Before a group can enter the open society, it must first close ranks.* By this we mean that group solidarity is necessary before a group can operate effectively from a bargaining position of strength in a pluralistic society. Traditionally, each new ethnic group in this society has found the route to social and political viability through the organization of its own institutions with which to represent its needs within the larger society. Studies in voting behavior specifically, and political behavior generally, have made it clear that politically the American pot has not melted. Italians vote for Rubino over

O'Brien; Irish for Murphy over Goldberg, etc. This phenomenon may seem distasteful to some, but it has been and remains today a central fact of the American political system. There are other examples of ways in which groups in the society have remembered their roots and used this effectively in the political arena. Theodore Sorensen describes the politics of foreign aid during the Kennedy Administration in his book *Kennedy:*

> *No powerful constituencies or interest groups backed foreign aid. The Marshall Plan at least had appealed to Americans who traced their roots to the Western European nations aided. But there were few voters who identified with India, Colombia or Tanganyika [p. 351].*

The extent to which black Americans can and do "trace their roots" to Africa, to that extent will they be able to be more effective on the political scene.

A white reporter set forth this point in other terms when he made the following observation about white Mississippi's manipulation of the anti-poverty program:

> *The war on poverty has been predicated on the notion that there is such a thing as a community which can be defined geographically and mobilized for a collective effort to help the poor. This theory has no relationship to reality in the deep South. In every Mississippi county there are two communities. Despite all the pious platitudes of the moderates on both sides, these two communities habitually see their interests in terms of conflict rather than cooperation. Only when the Negro community can muster enough political, economic and professional strength to compete on somewhat equal terms, will Negroes believe in the possibility of true cooperation and whites accept its necessity. En route to integration, the Negro community needs to develop a greater independence—a chance to run its own affairs and not cave in whenever "the man" barks—or so it seems to me, and to most of the knowledgeable people with whom I talked in Mississippi. To OEO, this judgment may sound like black nationalism. . . .[2]*

The point is obvious: black people must lead and run their own organizations. Only black people can convey the revolutionary idea—and it is a revolutionary idea—that black people are able to do things themselves. Only they can help create in the community an aroused and continuing black consciousness that will provide the basis for political strength. In the past, white allies have often furthered white supremacy without the whites involved realizing it, or even wanting to do so. Black people must come together and do things for themselves. They must achieve self-identity and self-determination in order to have their daily needs met.

Black Power means, for example, that in Lowndes County, Alabama, a black sheriff can end police brutality. A black tax assessor and tax collector and county board of revenue can lay, collect, and channel tax monies for the building of better

2. Christopher Jencks, "Accommodating Whites: A New Look at Mississippi," *The New Republic* (April 16, 1966).

roads and schools serving black people. In such areas as Lowndes, where black people have a majority, they will attempt to use power to exercise control. This is what they seek: control. When black people lack a majority, Black Power means proper representation and sharing of control. It means the creation of power bases, of strength, from which black people can press to change local or nation-wide patterns of oppression—instead of from weakness.

It does not mean *merely* putting black faces into office. Black visibility is not Black Power. Most of the black politicians around the country today are not examples of Black Power. The power must be that of a community, and emanate from there. The black politicians must start from there. The black politicians must stop being representatives of "downtown" machines, whatever the cost might be in terms of lost patronage and holiday handouts.

Black Power recognizes—it must recognize—the ethnic basis of American politics as well as the power-oriented nature of American politics. Black Power therefore calls for black people to consolidate behind their own, so that they can bargain from a position of strength. But while we endorse the *procedure* of group solidarity and identity for the purpose of attaining certain goals in the body politic, this does not mean that black people should strive for the same kind of rewards (i.e., end results) obtained by the white society. The ultimate values and goals are not domination or exploitation of other groups, but rather an effective share in the total power of the society.

Nevertheless, some observers have labeled those who advocate Black Power as racists; they have said that the call for self-identification and self-determination is "racism in reverse" or "black supremacy." This is a deliberate and absurd lie. There is no analogy—by any stretch of definition or imagination—between the advocates of Black Power and white racists. Racism is not merely exclusion on the basis of race but exclusion for the purpose of subjugating or maintaining subjugation. The goal of the racists is to keep black people on the bottom, arbitrarily and dictatorially, as they have done in this country for over three hundred years. The goal of black self-determination and black self-identity—Black Power—is full participation in the decision-making processes affecting the lives of black people, and recognition of the virtues in themselves as black people. The black people of this country have not lynched whites, bombed their churches, murdered their children and manipulated laws and institutions to maintain oppression. White racists have. Congressional laws, one after the other, have not been necessary to stop black people from oppressing others and denying others the full enjoyment of their rights. White racists have made such laws necessary. The goal of Black Power is positive and functional to a free and viable society. No white racist can make this claim.

A great deal of public attention and press space was devoted to the hysterical accusation of "black racism" when the call for Black Power was first sounded. A national committee of influential black churchmen affiliated with the National Council of Churches, despite their obvious respectability and responsibility, had to resort to a paid advertisement to articulate their position, while anyone yapping "black racism" made front-page news. In their statement, published in the *New York Times* of July 31, 1966, the churchmen said:

*We, an informal group of Negro churchmen in America, are deeply disturbed
about the crisis brought upon our country by historic distortions of important
human realities in the controversy about "black power." What we see shining
through the variety of rhetoric is not anything new but the same old problem
of power and race which has faced our beloved country since 1619.*

*. . . The conscience of black men is corrupted because having no power to
implement the demands of conscience, the concern for justice in the absence
of justice becomes a chaotic self-surrender. Powerlessness breeds a race of
beggars. We are faced with a situation where powerless conscience meets con-
scienceless power, threatening the very foundations of our Nation.*

*We deplore the overt violence of riots, but we feel it is more important to
focus on the real sources of these eruptions. These sources may be abetted
inside the Ghetto, but their basic cause lies in the silent and covert violence
which white middle class America inflicts upon the victims of the inner city.*

*. . . In short, the failure of American leaders to use American power to
create equal opportunity in life as well as law, this is the real problem and
not the anguished cry for black power.*

*. . . Without the capacity to participate with power, i.e., to have some orga-
nized political and economic strength to really influence people with whom
one interacts, integration is not meaningful.*

*. . . America has asked its Negro citizens to fight for opportunity as individ-
uals, whereas at certain points in our history what we have needed most has
been opportunity for the whole group, not just for selected and approved
Negroes.*

*. . . We must not apologize for the existence of this form of group power,
for we have been oppressed as a group and not as individuals. We will not
find our way out of that oppression until both we and America accept the
need for Negro Americans, as well as for Jews, Italians, Poles, and white
Anglo-Saxon Protestants, among others, to have and to wield group power.*

It is a commentary on the fundamentally racist nature of this society that the
concept of group strength for black people must be articulated—not to mention defended. No other group would submit to being led by others. Italians do not run the
Anti-Defamation League of B'nai B'rith. Irish do not chair Christopher Columbus
Societies. Yet when black people call for black-run and all-black organizations, they
are immediately classed in a category with the Ku Klux Klan. This is interesting and
ironic, but by no means surprising: the society does not expect black people to be able
to take care of their business, and there are many who prefer it precisely that way.

In the end, we cannot and shall not offer any guarantees that Black Power, if
achieved, would be non-racist. No one can predict human behavior. Social change
always has unanticipated consequences. If black racism is what the larger society
fears, we cannot help them. We can only state what we hope will be the result, given
the fact that the present situation is unacceptable and that we have no real alternative but to work for Black Power. The final truth is that the white society is not entitled to reassurances, even if it were possible to offer them.

We have outlined the meaning and goals of Black Power; we have also discussed one major thing which it is not. There are others of greater importance. The advocates of Black Power reject the old slogans and meaningless rhetoric of previous years in the civil rights struggle. The language of yesterday is indeed irrelevant: progress, non-violence, integration, fear of "white backlash," coalition. Let us look at the rhetoric and see why these terms must be set aside or redefined.

One of the tragedies of the struggle against racism is that up to this point there has been no national organization which could speak to the growing militancy of young black people in the urban ghettos and the black-belt South. There has been only a "civil rights" movement, whose tone of voice was adapted to an audience of middle-class whites. It served as a sort of buffer zone between that audience and angry young blacks. It claimed to speak for the needs of a community, but it did not speak in the tone of that community. None of its so-called leaders could go into a rioting community and be listened to. In a sense, the blame must be shared—along with the mass media—by those leaders for what happened in Watts, Harlem, Chicago, Cleveland and other places. Each time the black people in those cities saw Dr. Martin Luther King get slapped they became angry. When they saw little black girls bombed to death *in a church* and civil rights workers ambushed and murdered, they were angrier; and when nothing happened, they were steaming mad. We had nothing to offer that they could see, except to go out and be beaten again. We helped to build their frustration.

We had only the old language of love and suffering. And in most places—that is, from the liberals and middle class—we got back the old language of patience and progress. The civil rights leaders were saying to the country: "Look, you guys are supposed to be nice guys, and we are only going to do what we are supposed to do. Why do you beat us up? Why don't you give us what we ask? Why don't you straighten yourselves out?" For the masses of black people, this language resulted in virtually nothing. In fact, their objective day-to-day condition worsened. The unemployment rate among black people increased while that among whites declined. Housing conditions in the black communities deteriorated. Schools in the black ghettos continued to plod along on outmoded techniques, inadequate curricula, and with all too many tired and indifferent teachers. Meanwhile, the President picked up the refrain of "We Shall Overcome" while the Congress passed civil rights law after civil rights law, only to have them effectively nullified by deliberately weak enforcement. "Progress is being made," we were told.

Such language, along with admonitions to remain non-violent and fear the white backlash, convinced some that that course was the *only* course to follow. It misled some into believing that a black minority could bow its head and get whipped into a meaningful position of power. The very notion is absurd. The white society devised the language, adopted the rules and had the black community narcotized into believing that that language and those rules were, in fact, relevant. The black community was told time and again how *other* immigrants finally won *acceptance:* that is, by following the Protestant Ethic of Work and Achievement. They worked hard; therefore, they achieved. We were not told that it was by building Irish Power, Italian Power, Polish Power or Jewish Power that these groups got themselves together and operated from positions of strength. We were not told that "the American dream" wasn't designed for black people. That while today, to whites, the dream may *seem* to include black people, it cannot do so by the very nature of this nation's political and economic system, which imposes institutional racism on the black masses if not upon every individual black. A notable comment on that "dream" was made by Dr. Percy Julian, the black scientist and director of the Julian Research Institute in Chicago, a man for whom the dream seems to have come true. While not subscribing to "black power" as he understood it, Dr. Julian clearly understood the basis for it: "The false concept of basic Negro inferiority is one of the curses that still lingers. It is a problem created by the white man. Our children just no longer are going to accept the patience we were taught by our generation. We were taught a pretty little lie—excel and the whole world lies open before you. *I obeyed the injunction and found it to be wishful thinking."* (Authors' italics)[3]

A key phrase in our buffer-zone days was non-violence. For years it has been thought that black people would not literally fight for their lives. Why this has been so is not entirely clear; neither the larger society nor black people are noted for pas-sivity. The notion apparently stems from the years of marches and demonstrations and sit-ins where black people did not strike back and the violence always came from white mobs. There are many who still sincerely believe in that approach. From our viewpoint, rampaging white mobs and white night-riders must be made to understand that their days of free head-whipping are over. Black people should and must fight back. Nothing more quickly repels someone bent on destroying you than the unequiv-ocal message: "O.K., fool, make your move, and run the same risk I run—of dying."

When the concept of Black Power is set forth, many people immediately con-jure up notions of violence. The country's reaction to the Deacons for Defense and Justice, which originated in Louisiana, is instructive. Here is a group which realized that the "law" and law enforcement agencies would not protect people, so they had to do it themselves. If a nation fails to protect its citizens, then that nation cannot condemn those who take up the task themselves. The Deacons and all other blacks who resort to self-defense represent a simple answer to a simple question: what man would not defend his family and home from attack?

But this frightened some white people, because they knew that black people would now fight back. They knew that this was precisely what *they* would have long since done if *they* were subjected to the injustices and oppression heaped on blacks. Those of us who advocate Black Power are quite clear in our own minds that a "non-violent" approach to civil rights is an approach black people cannot afford and a luxury white people do not deserve. It is crystal clear to us—and it must become so with the white society—*that there can be no social order without social justice.* White people must be made to understand that they must stop messing with black people, or the blacks *will* fight back!

Next, we must deal with the term "integration." According to its advocates, social justice will be accomplished by "integrating the Negro into the mainstream institutions of the society from which he has been traditionally excluded." This

3. *New York Times* (April 30, 1967), p. 30.

concept is based on the assumption that there is nothing of value in the black community and that little of value could be created among black people. The thing to do is siphon off the "acceptable" black people into the surrounding middle-class white community.

The goals of integrationists are middle-class goals, articulated primarily by a small group of Negroes with middle-class aspirations or status. Their kind of integration has meant that a few blacks "make it," leaving the black community, sapping it of leadership potential and know-how. . . . Those token Negroes—absorbed into a white mass—are of no value to the remaining black masses. They become meaningless show-pieces for a conscience-soothed white society. Such people will state that they would prefer to be treated "only as individuals, not as Negroes"; that they "are not and should not be preoccupied with race." This is a totally unrealistic position. In the first place, black people have not suffered as individuals but as members of a group; therefore, their liberation lies in group action. This is why SNCC—and the concept of Black Power—affirms that helping *individual* black people to solve their problems on an *individual* basis does little to alleviate the mass of black people. Secondly, while color blindness *may* be a sound goal ultimately, we must realize that race is an overwhelming fact of life in this historical period. There is no black man in this country who can live "simply as a man." His blackness is an ever-present fact of this racist society, whether he recognizes it or not. It is unlikely that this or the next generation will witness the time when race will no longer be relevant in the conduct of public affairs and in public policy decision-making. To realize this and to attempt to deal with it does not make one a racist or overly preoccupied with race; it puts one in the forefront of a significant *struggle*. If there is no intense struggle today, there will be no meaningful results tomorrow.

"Integration" as a goal today speaks to the problem of blackness not only in an unrealistic way but also in a despicable way. It is based on complete acceptance of the fact that in order to have a decent house or education, black people must move into a white neighborhood or send their children to a white school. This reinforces, among both black and white, the idea that "white" is automatically superior and "black" is by definition inferior. For this reason, "integration" is a subterfuge for the maintenance of white supremacy. It allows the nation to focus on a handful of Southern black children who get into white schools at a great price, and to ignore the ninety-four percent who are left in unimproved all-black schools. Such situations will not change until black people become equal in a way that means something, and integration ceases to be a one-way street. Then integration does not mean draining skills and energies from the black ghetto into white neighborhoods. To sprinkle black children among white pupils in outlying schools is at best a stop-gap measure. The goal is not to take black children out of the black community and expose them to white middle-class values; the goal is to build and strengthen the black community.

"Integration" also means that black people must give up their identity, deny their heritage. We recall the conclusion of Killian and Grigg: "At the present time, integration as a solution to the race problem demands that the Negro foreswear his identity as a Negro." The fact is that integration, as traditionally articulated, would abolish the black community. The fact is that what must be abolished is not the black community, but the dependent colonial status that has been inflicted upon it.

The racial and cultural personality of the black community must be preserved and that community must win its freedom while preserving its cultural integrity. Integrity includes a pride—in the sense of self-acceptance, not chauvinism—in being black, in the historical attainments and contributions of black people. No person can be healthy, complete and mature if he must deny a part of himself; this is what "integration" has required thus far. This is the essential difference between integration as it is currently practiced and the concept of Black Power.

The idea of cultural integrity is so obvious that it seems almost simple-minded to spell things out at this length. Yet millions of Americans resist such truths when they are applied to black people. Again, that resistance is a comment on the fundamental racism in the society. Irish Catholics took care of their own first without a lot of apology for doing so, without any dubious language from timid leadership about guarding against "backlash." Everyone understood it to be a perfectly legitimate procedure. Of course, there would be "backlash." Organization begets counter-organization, but this was no reason to defer.

The so-called white backlash against black people is something else: the embedded traditions of institutional racism being brought into the open and calling forth overt manifestations of individual racism. In the summer of 1966, when the protest marches into Cicero, Illinois, began, the black people knew they were not allowed to live in Cicero and the white people knew it. When blacks began to demand the right to live in homes in that town, the whites simply reminded them of the status quo. Some people called this "backlash." It was, in fact, racism defending itself. In the black community, this is called "White folks showing their color." It is ludicrous to blame black people for what is simply an overt manifestation of white racism. Dr. Martin Luther King stated clearly that the protest marches were not the cause of the racism but merely exposed a long-term cancerous condition in the society.

We come now to the rhetoric of coalition as part of the traditional approach to ending racism: the concept of the civil rights movement as a kind of liaison between the powerful white community and a dependent black community. "Coalition" involves the whole question of how one approaches politics and political alliances. It is so basic to an understanding of Black Power that we will devote an entire chapter to the subject.

The Campus: From the Tower to the Barricade

The young John Milton, in an agony of decision making common to the seventeenth-century student, articulated the dilemma he faced at Cambridge in the pastoral elegy "Lycidas." He recalls the path he chose at the very outset of his career, the thorny road of study, duty, and reform. A Puritan and republican of deep conviction, he had turned his back with reluctance on the more attractive Cavalier way of life and its seductive enticement to "sport with Amaryllis in the shade" in an existence both carefree and self-indulgent, befitting the young and privileged scholar in a troubled political time. The American collegian of the 1920s would not have understood Milton's internal conflict. The Benchleys, Thurbers, and Perelmans, America's finest humorists of the era, have left a legacy of light-hearted prose set against the backdrop of the happiest and most irresponsible of all playgrounds, the American university. With nostalgia Benchley recalls the esoterica of his academic curriculum, the seminar in lace-making he chose because it freed him for the serious scheduling of poker parties and beer busts, and the mandatory three-day program which he chose (regardless of the courses which it encompassed) in order that he might be free from the ardors of Friday classes. Perelman fondly recalls the halcyon days at Brown University when he lay for days on end in a room which he had decorated to approximate a dahabeah on the Nile, daydreaming of Nita Naldi and Clara Bow. The tameness of literary fare dished out by the college of Thurber's memory may be judged by the model of intrigue and passion which he studied as an undergraduate: de Maupassant's short story "The Necklace," a piece which has long since passed into the bland anthologies compiled for elementary schools.

It is probable that F. Scott Fitzgerald would have been hard put to recognize the Dartmouth of 1970 from his own rollicking bibulous week in 1939 at the famed Winter Carnival. In those days a man could retire with a cozy girl and a bottle and abandon both responsibility and sobriety for the duration in an environment entirely hospitable to his pleasure. Today, the same young man, operating within a framework of even greater permissiveness, would be conscious of the fact that he was taking his pleasure in a school which has provided some of the most serious leadership in draft resistance in the nation, a school which houses forty trained draft counselors retained for the sole purpose of advising students of their rights and prerogatives in their opposition to United States military policy in Southeast Asia. About one hundred and twenty of two hundred and twenty-five graduating seniors at Dartmouth have filed as conscientious objectors, and although this figure is a little higher than the count on others of the nation's campuses, the situation at Dartmouth may serve as a model for a great many of the nation's universities. For a great many young men the act of conscientious objection was merely a culminating act of conscience, capping four years of activism on campus, marches on Washington, sit-ins, civil rights protests, "liberation" of university buildings, and door-to-door political canvassing in communities adjacent to their schools. The university, which had been written off as the "soft underbelly" of our civilization, has demonstrated that it has emerged from the ivory tower to become a proving ground for powerful political and social reforms as well as radical curricular and administrative change. Two cases in point are the primary victory of Eugene McCarthy in New Hampshire in 1968 and the restraint upon Columbia University in its proposed construction of a gymnasium which would have deprived the neighboring community of an existing playground.

Articulate young men such as Harvard's Steven Kelman, author of *Push Comes to Shove,* are invited to testify before congressional committees on campus unrest and are listened to with respect. The President appoints young collegians to advisory staff positions as liaison between college youth and the government. Students are increasingly exercising their collective power to change the communities in which they find themselves. The "Princeton Plan" is devised to permit students to rearrange class schedules in order that they may go out into the community to campaign for the political candidates of their choice. This accommodation of politically oriented students by college administrations is a far cry from Merrill Root's fearful outcry in the 1950s against the mildest stirrings of collective action on campus, an activity which he equated with ideological communism.

Another interesting phenomenon of the campus revolution is the radicalized professor. Staughton Lynd, Leslie Fiedler, and Noam Chomsky are a few of the prominent names among the many professors who have begun to man the barricades along with their students. Strongly influenced by Herbert Marcuse's five theses pointing to the probability of a revolution to correct the ills of contemporary society, these radicalized professors have begun to understand what their students are shouting about: the university's discouragement of the aspirations of blacks and the young and the people of the third world. They are willing to sacrifice their old elitist dreams for the fresh reality of faculty-power. Having been attacked by the student body as irrelevant and gutless, they have a choice: business as usual or militance. Therefore, in many instances, radicalized professors scrap the classical curriculum for contemporary sociological studies, ethnic literature, the "new journalism" of Norman Mailer and Tom Wolfe, and seminars "on the issues." Dispensing with registrar's requirements in the face of national crises such as the invasion of Cambodia or the Kent State killings, radicalized professors cancel classes, rescind examinations and papers, and abolish letter grades as relevant forms of protest and principled counter-measures to unpopular national policy. Their rationale is often a sincere wish to destroy the old sociocultural criteria for the university and replace them with new academic standards and procedures which will link the university to the real and emerging world.

To the left of the involved student and the radicalized professor is the most extreme element of all the university activists—the New Left. The "ultras" of the Students for a Democratic Society are not interested in the reconstruction of the university as a more positive influence on society. They see the university as the weakest link and thus the easiest target in the society which they deplore, and their goal is simply destruction of this vulnerable unit. In a system that is rotten, the only recourse is violence. In contradistinction to the campus liberals who see alternatives to the current national policy and are willing to dedicate their efforts to achieving specific goals, the New Left offers no alternative and sees no solution beyond the goal of demolition. It is made up of the students whose "collective political action," in the opinion of Sidney Hook, "is an invitation to educational disaster."

There is no doubt that the university is undergoing rapid, and, some say, dangerous change. Some think that it is headed back to the structure of the medieval university of Bologna, where it was accepted that the masters and administrative officers served entirely at the students' pleasure; and that we will see the time when students alone decide all matters of curriculum, hiring, and policy. Others see the advent of tougher administrative policies to counteract extremism and politicization, under such authoritative administrators as Hayakawa of San Francisco State and Van Hesburgh of Notre Dame. The middle road of responsibility and freedom is well expressed by Edward Etherington, former President of Wesleyan University, in his matriculation address of September 16, 1969:

> *I stand for responsible freedom, but not for license; for student government, but not for administrative or faculty default; for individuality, but not for indulgent self-interest; for a variety of life styles, but not for incivility in university life; for the rights of dissent, but not for the oppression of those who are not dissenters. Most of all, I stand convinced that we can have some influence in solving the grave problems of our times if we can—through agreement and consent—maintain a creative and honorable academic institution which we and others can respect.*

E. Merrill Root

What Is the Battle?

The colleges of America are the battlefield for the most crucial war in the modern world—a war never cold, always hot, a war that for centuries will determine the shape of things to come. It is man's timeless spiritual war to affirm the freedom of the individual, the dignity of the person, against the flattening pressures of the group. Walt Whitman knew this war:

> To thee, old Cause!
> Thou peerless, passionate, good cause!
> Thou stern, remorseless, sweet Idea!
> Deathless throughout the ages, races, lands!

The continuance of America's great tradition of liberty and of a freely expanding society depends upon the outcome.

This war for the mind in the colleges is one segment, though a major one, of the wider civil war that fissures the modern world. In the field of education the issues are most articulately stated, because here the combatants are men whose profession is to think and to expound. Here, if anywhere, the spiritual and intellectual war ought to be lifted out of the brute struggle of politics into the purer realm of balanced thought. Men of good will in the universities should be able to resolve the fighting in a dynamic equilibrium between community and individual.

What, specifically, is the war about? Who are the combatants? What are the issues? What is the present status of the opposed forces?

Let us turn to a remarkable contemporary document, written by one of the most candid of today's political "liberals." It is the article "Can the Liberals Rally?" by the Honorable Joseph S. Clark, Jr., former mayor of Philadelphia, published in *The Atlantic Monthly* for July 1953. In this article, the fact of the battle for the mind in American colleges is affirmed. It is explained by a "liberal" speaking for "liberals" in a magazine congenial to his thesis. Mayor Clark does a service by so freely speaking. He deserves praise for his courage and thanks for his candor. He writes:

> *To lay a ghost at the outset and to dismiss semantics, a liberal is here defined as one who believes in using* the full force of government *for the advancement of social, political, and economic justice at the municipal, state, national and international levels. . . . A liberal believes that government is a proper tool to use in the development of a society which attempts to carry Christian principles of conduct into practical effect. (Emphasis added.)*

He continues:

> *The philosophy of the reformers in the universities becomes the action platform of the liberal politicians of the next generation.*

And he openly affirms that American colleges fight as conscious partisans of the "liberal" viewpoint.

> *There is a vast potential reservoir of political leadership coming from the schools and universities. . . . Moreover, it is a potential leadership psychologically prepared to enlist under the liberal banner. Big business has not yet taken over American education. Adlai Stevenson has more supporters among the schoolteachers and college professors than Tom Dewey. It is significant that what used to be called "history" is now "social studies." Spiritually and economically youth is conditioned to respond to a liberal program of orderly policing of our society by government, subject to the popular will, in the interests of social justice. (Emphasis added.)*

So Mayor Clark lays the battle for the mind in American colleges on the table—flat and final as the show-down in poker. He affirms that the youth in our colleges and universities has been "psychologically prepared to enlist under the liberal banner." By such psychological "conditioning," youth has been led to accept the "orderly policing of our society by government." Mayor Clark believes that the "liberals" have already won the battle for the mind in our colleges, that the generations of students are already indoctrinated into accepting the action of *government*—"the full force of government"—as the chief or even sole agent of human advance.

Mayor Clark has the right to say this. And his right to say it is guaranteed by the Constitution of the United States—which was conceived and framed to *prevent* the "orderly policing of our society by government." But if he is correct in his facts —if state "liberalism" *has* won a virtual monopoly of place and voice in American colleges today, "conditioning" youth into a single pattern, then there is no genuine liberalism left in American colleges. For only one side has place and voice.

To see the situation from a different standpoint, let us take another contemporary authority, who clarifies still further the battle for the mind in American colleges. This eminent modern has observed the battle from the other side of the Atlantic—and of the argument. By pleasant coincidence, he is also named Clark. He is Professor Colin Clark, an Australian political economist now lecturing at Oxford University in England. In July 1953 he wrote a letter to *The Manchester Guardian Weekly,* in which he said:

> *What happened in the 1930's was that a substantial element among the university population and among authors and literary critics adopted Marxism. And what we are witnessing now is the complete discrediting of Marxism in all its forms—Bolshevik or Menshevik, extreme or moderate, academic or practical. And with this obstacle removed, the group who used to be called "the intellectuals" quite naturally resume their proper position in the national life [of England] as men who can influence, but not dominate, the public taste and the course of public affairs.*
>
> *This appears to be the happy development of events in Britain, but is far from true, alas, in the United States or the British Commonwealth countries,* where academic Marxism—or crypto-Marxism—is stronger than ever. *The almost unbearable tension in American academic and civil-service life at the present time springs from the intransigence of Senator McCarthy on the one hand,* but on the other hand from the widespread adherence, amongst the younger university men in America,[1] to the monstrous falsehood (and to the belief in a totalitarian state which it implies) that all human actions, political, cultural or religious, arise ultimately from economic causes. *(Emphasis added.)*

Professor Clark and Mayor Clark, two independent witnesses who differ diametrically in values but agree on fact, affirm that a battle for the mind is being waged in American colleges today. They agree on the issues and on the present status of the struggle.

What, then, of the nontotalitarian side that seldom finds place or voice on our campuses? What of that *radical individualism*, that *classic liberalism*, to which students are not "conditioned" and of whose existence they are hardly aware? I speak of that liberalism which proved its integrity in the age-old struggle against the power of the state; of that liberalism which Ortega y Gasset said seeks always to answer the

---

1. And the older university men. (Author.)

question: "Regardless of who exercises the public power, what should its limits be?" The answer, he said, is this: "Whether the public power is exercised by an autocrat or by the people, it cannot be absolute; the individual has rights which are over and above any interference by the state."[2]

Genuine liberalism, radical and intense, long ago found American voice. Emerson wrote:

> *Society everywhere is a conspiracy against the manhood of every one of its members. . . . Society never advances; society develops only as man improves. . . . The wise and just man will always feel that he imparts strength to the State, not receives security from it. . . . The first rule of economy is that every man shall maintain himself. The harvest will be better preserved and go farther laid up in each farmer's cornbarn and each woman's basket than if it were kept in national granaries. In like manner an amount of money will go farther if expended by each man or woman for their own wants and in the feeling that this is their all, than if expended by a great steward or National Commissioners of the Treasury. . . . In dealing with the State, we ought to remember that its institutions are not aboriginal, though they existed before we were born; that they are not superior to the citizen; that every one of them was once the act of a single man; every law and usage was a man's expedient to meet a particular case, that they were all imitable, all alterable, we may make as good, we may make better. . . . The wise know that foolish legislation is a rope of sand which perishes in the twisting; that the State must follow and not lead the character and progress of the citizen; and that the form of government which prevails is the expression of what cultivation exists in the population which permits it. . . . The less government we have the better; the fewer laws and the less confided power. The antidote to this abuse of formal government is the influence of private character, the growth of the individual. . . . In all my lectures, I have taught one doctrine, namely, infinitude of the private man.*

Robert Hutchins, in an article in *Look,* March 9, 1954, says that we must have "full, frank, free discussion," that we must have the presentation of "all sides of a problem." He says: "To omit one opinion is to offer tacit support to its opponent. If an issue is presented as though it were one—that is, as though there were only one side to it— this is not education; it is indoctrination." We should agree; and, on the basis of his definition of education and indoctrination, we must wonder why scarcely a whisper of Ortega y Gasset's or Emerson's type of liberalism is heard on most American campuses today. If it is not heard, we do not have all sides represented; we have indoctrination.

The battle for the mind in American colleges, then, is between two philosophies, two ways of life, two worlds. It is a battle between collectivism, that would reduce unique persons to efficient functions of a dominant mass; and individualism, that would exalt the status of the persons who freely constitute it. It is a conflict between state liberalism and classic liberalism.

2. *Invertebrate Spain,* W. W. Norton and Co., 1937, p. 125.

This leads to definition. The *American College Dictionary* defines collectivism as:

The socialist principle of control by the people collectively, or the state, of all means of production or economic activity.

And collectivism is bound to mean control over intellectual functions of society also, since those who stress economics tend to believe that economic determinism controls other aspects of human life, as philosophy and art.

Individualism, in the same dictionary, is defined as:

A social theory advocating the liberty, rights, or independent action of the individual.

By nature, therefore, individualism sees society as the means and the individual as the end. Man does not exist to serve society, as among the bees and the ants; society exists to serve unique, individual persons, each of whom is Unamuno's man of flesh and bone, each with the destiny of the single soul. How can a true liberal fail to see that he, by nature, belongs with man set free, with "the liberty, rights, or independent action of the individual"? A genuine liberal, to be a liberal, must be against mass and for man. The same dictionary says of the liberal that he is

. . . favorable to or in accord with the policy of leaving the individual as unrestricted as possible in the opportunities for self-expression or self-fulfillment.

No collectivist regime, whether fascism, Fabianism, or communism, can possibly be "favorable to or in accord with the policy of leaving the individual as unrestricted as possible." Instead, collectivism by its inherent nature and by its efficient practice regulates, prohibits, and compels. How, then, can the genuine liberal be favorable to or in accord with the theory or practice of collectivism?

The same dictionary defines liberty as:

. . . freedom from control, interference, obligation, restriction, hampering conditions, etc.; power or right of doing, thinking, speaking, etc., according to choice . . . freedom from captivity, confinement, or physical restraint. . . .[3]

And Webster's *New Collegiate Dictionary* says of liberty:

Individual liberty now generally involves freedom of the person in going and coming, equality before the courts, security of private property, freedom of opinion and its expression, and freedom of conscience.

Every one of the freedoms spoken of in either definition is curtailed even under the mildest regime of collectivism (Fabian socialism); every one of them is, under the

3. Harper and Brothers, Text Edition, 1948.

extreme collectivisms of fascism or communism, abolished. And all that we now possess of these glories of freedom has been won by the long struggle of true liberalism against the inertia of the mass and the power of the state.

Today our vision is easily clouded because most intellectuals have never faced the fact that all collectivisms, no matter how they differ in mood or means, are united in "the socialist principle of control by the people collectively, or the state." Fascism, Fabian socialism, communism are *collectivisms*. Fascism is anti-individualistic, anti-capitalistic national *socialism:* Mussolini loved to "dance on the putrefying corpse of liberty" and fashioned the dictatorial corporative state; Hitler spoke the soul of all collectivism thus: *"True idealism is nothing but subjecting the individual's interests and life to the community."*

Fascism, then, is the *collectivist* right—an intense, narrow form of collectivism, making the national state the end and arbiter. Communism is the collectivist left—an intense, wide form of collectivism, where (man's most terrible nightmare) the state is coincident with the world. Fabian socialism is the collectivist center—the least intense form of collectivism, seeking first national-social control and then world collectivism, through parliamentary politics and intellectual propaganda.

The three collectivisms differ in mood and means, but they are the same in purpose; with Hitler they all say: "True idealism is nothing but subjecting the individual's interests and life to the community." All are the antithesis of genuine liberalism.

Contemporary "liberalism" (as defined by Mayor Clark) is the ally of collectivism and a form of Fabian socialism. The "liberal" argues the primacy of economics and seeks the supremacy of the group as an aggregate of individuals. He argues that government is the chief or sole agent of advance. *Genuine* liberalism has always been the supreme enemy of this view: it has sought to release man from the restraints of the state, to crack the solidity of government, so that the energy of individual men, motivated by spontaneous aspiration, flows in a free fountain of creation.

The contemporary "liberal" does not merit the name: he is, and will hereafter be designated as, a *state* liberal, or a *total* liberal, or a *collectivist* liberal. The *true* liberal subordinates security to opportunity; he accepts struggle and danger as the price that a man must pay for being a free moral agent. He seeks, before all, to set man free from dictation by the group.

The terms right, center, left, to make any sense, must be qualified and identified as belonging *either* to the world of collectivism *or* to the world of individualism. Each is a separate and incommensurable world. To call the right of individualism "fascism," or the left of individualism "communism," or the center of collectivism (Fabian socialism) "liberalism" is sloppy thinking. The late Senator Taft was a man of the individualistic right, but he was as far from the brutalities of fascism as a man can go. Thoreau was of the individualistic left, but he said even of the mild collectivism of Brook Farm: "I had rather keep bachelor's hall in Hell than go to Heaven in company." Emerson was a liberal of the individualistic center, but he repudiated socialism and stressed the "infinitude of the private man."

What is suppressed today is *individualism*—its conservatives, its liberals, its radicals equally. What needs to be restored today, to proportionate place and voice, is *individualism*—its liberals and its radicals just as much as its "conservatives." The irony of the hour is that, to do this, "conservatism" (as the victim chosen by collectivists to be the villain of their purge) must be defended. But conservatism must be defended, because genuine liberalism and radicalism cannot again exist until conservative individualism wins its legitimate voice. Conservatism means a preserving or conserving of the timeless values—but it must go to the roots.

The *radical conservative* will uproot the weed, and root the wheat more firmly. The radical conservative sees truth as a destiny of reason, above mere utility; justice as a destiny of right, above pressure groups and utilitarian sanctions; beauty as a destiny of harmony and form, above the fashions of the hour.

The radical conservative has one more word. Whittaker Chambers says:

> It [communism] is not new. It is, in fact, man's second oldest faith. Its promise was whispered in the first days of the Creation under the Tree of the Knowledge of Good and Evil: "Ye shall be as gods." It is the great alternative faith of mankind. Like all great faiths, its force derives from a simple vision. Other ages have had great visions. They have always been different versions of the same vision: the vision of God and man's relationship to God. The Communist vision is the vision of Man without God.
>
> It is the vision of man's mind displacing God as the creative intelligence of the world. It is the vision of man's liberated mind, by the sole force of its rational intelligence, redirecting man's destiny and reorganizing man's life and the world. It is the vision of man, once more the central figure of the Creation, not because God made him in His image, but because man's mind makes him the most intelligent of the animals. Copernicus and his successors displaced man as the central fact of the universe by proving that the earth was not the central star of the universe. Communism restores man to his sovereignty by the simple method of denying God.[4]

Indeed, whenever man's arithmetic supposes God a cosmic zero, man by this act destroys the very arithmetic by which alone he adds up to man. If there is no eternal Reason within and yet beyond phenomena, reason is relativism, and truth the most convenient lie; if there is no meaning within and yet above the world, morality is reduced to manners, and right to the biggest battalions. Man becomes a shadow without a sun, lost in the nihilism of total shadow.

God, then, is a major issue in the battle for the mind.

So we come to our theme. We shall study the battle for the mind in American colleges—the conflict of collectivism and individualism, of state liberal and genuine liberal, of the "orderly policing of our society by government" and "the infinitude of the private man," of the "conditioning" of the generations into a single pattern.

The purpose of this study is *not* to suppress or destroy collectivism, or to deny its proportionate place. The purpose is to create the climate for a great debate, on

4. *Witness*, by Whittaker Chambers. Random House, 1952, pp. 9-10.

the plane of logic, fact, and reason, before the forum of the American people, between collectivism and individualism. The point is that *there is no debate today and cannot be any until individualism can freely and proportionately speak.* No debate can take place until the *extremes* of collectivism—supported by violence and propaganda—the twin extremes of fascism and communism, are repudiated. Most intellectuals have long since repudiated the extreme right of collectivism (fascism); they ought now to repudiate the extreme left of collectivism (communism). Until that is done, free debate cannot occur, for it will always be dominated by the Party that uses ideas only as tools of militant political will.

Once communism, as well as fascism, is repudiated by all free men, the great debate can begin. The American people, as audience and arbiters, can examine the evidence and hear the arguments between individualism and collectivism. But first, it is necessary that the impure issue of communism be dismissed, and democratic collectivism and democratic individualism be given equal freedom and proportion in the great debate. Above all, *individualism must again be allowed to speak.*

To clear the way, two illusions must be blown aside. First, we must cease to talk in abstractions: we must see *concretely.* Communists talk abstractly of "liquidating" their "class enemies"—which sounds as harmless as pouring cyanide on the pages of a telephone directory. But the poet or the plain man sees the concrete reality: he sees the pistol placed behind the right ear; he hears the muffled bang; he watches the gray cerebral matter spurt out of the shattered skull. When the Duke of Cornwall plants a foot on poor bound Gloucester's eyes to stamp them into the liquidation of bruised and broken plasm, Shakespeare does not set upon his tongue the glib lie of the abstract. Cornwall's words are: *"Out, vile jelly!"*

Professor Harold Laski in his last book said that *a man in a Soviet forced labor camp nevertheless knows that he is progressing through a tunnel toward the light.* Here is proof, in George Orwell's words, that "much of left-wing thought is a kind of playing with fire by people who don't even know that fire is hot." Professor Laski, in his socialistic ivory tower, saw the *abstract idea;* but the man (or woman) in the Soviet labor camp endures the *concrete fact* of slow starvation, of club and bayonet, of the frost-rimed logs with which he must fumble in the fifty-below-zero Siberian nights.

The second illusion to be transcended is the central superstition of our time —common to Hitler, Stalin, Mussolini, Bernard Shaw, and the state liberals—that we are on the crest of an irresistible "wave of the future"—inexorable, inevitable, fated. For free men, there is no "wave of the future"; there are only waves of circumstance in which men struggle. Men may, as it is fashionable to do, abandon choice and will, and drift till they drown; or they may strike out across the waves of circumstance. Every student and professor should become the Secret Sharer in Joseph Conrad's great story—"a free man, a proud swimmer, striking out for a new destiny."

Robert Benchley

What College Did to Me

My College Education was no haphazard affair. My courses were all selected with a very definite aim in view, with a serious purpose in mind—no classes before eleven in the morning or after two-thirty in the afternoon, and nothing on Saturday at all. That was my slogan. On that rock was my education built.

As what is known as the Classical Course involved practically no afternoon laboratory work, whereas in the Scientific Course a man's time was never his own until four p.m. anyway, I went in for the classics. But only such classics as allowed for a good sleep in the morning. A man has his health to think of. There is such a thing as being a studying fool.

In my days (I was a classmate of the founder of the college) a student could elect to take any courses in the catalogue, provided no two of his choices came at the same hour. The only things he was not supposed to mix were Scotch and gin. This was known as the Elective System. Now I understand that the boys have to have, during the four years, at least three courses beginning with the same letter. This probably makes it very awkward for those who like to get away of a Friday afternoon for the weekend.

Under the Elective System my schedule was somewhat as follows:

Mondays, Wednesdays, and Fridays at 11:00: Botany 2a (The History of Flowers and Their Meaning)

Tuesdays and Thursdays at 11:00: English 26 (The Social Life of the Minor Sixteenth Century Poets)

Mondays, Wednesdays, and Fridays at 12:00: Music 9 (History and Appreciation of the Clavichord)

Tuesdays and Thursdays at 12:00: German 12b (Early Minnesingers—Walter von Vogelweider, Ulric Glannsdorf, and Freimann von Stremhofen: Their Songs and Times)

Mondays, Wednesdays, and Fridays at 1:30: Fine Arts 6 (Doric Columns: Their Uses, History, and Various Heights)

Tuesdays and Thursdays at 1:30: French 1c (Exceptions to the verb *être*)

This was, of course, just one year's work. The next year I followed these courses up with supplementary courses in the history of lace-making, Russian taxation systems before Catharine the Great, North American glacial deposits, and Early Renaissance etchers.

This gave me a general idea of the progress of civilization and a certain practical knowledge which has stood me in good stead in thousands of ways since my graduation.

My system of studying was no less strict. In lecture courses I had my notebooks so arranged that one-half of the page could be devoted to drawings of five-pointed stars (exquisitely shaded), girls' heads, and tick-tack-toe. Some of the drawings in my economics notebook in the course on Early English Trade Winds were the finest things I have ever done. One of them was a whole tree (an oak) with every leaf in perfect detail. Several instructors commented on my work in this field.

These notes I would take home after the lecture, together with whatever supplementary reading the course called for. Notes and textbooks would then be placed on a table under a strong lamplight. Next came the sharpening of pencils, which would take perhaps fifteen minutes. I had some of the best sharpened pencils in college. These I placed on the table beside the notes and books.

At this point it was necessary to light a pipe, which involved going to the table where the tobacco was. As it so happened, on the same table was a poker hand, all dealt, lying in front of a vacant chair. Four other chairs were oddly enough occupied by students, also preparing to study. It therefore resolved itself into something of a seminar, or group conference, on the courses under discussion. For example, the first student would say:

"I can't open."

The second student would perhaps say the same thing.

The third student would say: "I'll open for fifty cents."

And the seminar would be on.

At the end of the seminar, I would go back to my desk, pile the notes and books on top of each other, put the light out, and go to bed, tired but happy in the realization that I had not only spent the evening busily but had helped put four of my friends through college.

An inventory of stock acquired at college discloses the following bits of culture and erudition which have nestled in my mind after all these years.

THINGS I LEARNED FRESHMAN YEAR

1. Charlemagne either died or was born or did something with the Holy Roman Empire in 800.

2. By placing one paper bag inside another paper bag you can carry home a milk shake in it.

3. There is a double l in the middle of "parallel."

4. Powder rubbed on the chin will take the place of a shave if the room isn't very light.

5. French nouns ending in "aison" are feminine.

6. Almost everything you need to know about a subject is in the encyclopedia.

7. A tasty sandwich can be made by spreading peanut butter on raisin bread.

8. A floating body displaces its own weight in the liquid in which it floats.

9. A sock with a hole in the toe can be worn inside out with comparative comfort.

10. The chances are against filling an inside straight.

11. There is a law in economics called *The Law of Diminishing Returns,* which means that after a certain margin is reached returns begin to diminish. This may not be correctly stated, but there *is* a law by that name.

12. You begin tuning a mandolin with A and tune the other strings from that.

SOPHOMORE YEAR

1. A good imitation of measles rash can be effected by stabbing the forearm with a stiff whisk-broom.

2. Queen Elizabeth was not above suspicion.

3. In Spanish you pronounce z like *th*.

4. Nine-tenths of the girls in a girls' college are not pretty.

5. You can sleep undetected in a lecture course by resting the head on the hand as if shading the eyes.

6. Weakness in drawing technique can be hidden by using a wash instead of black and white line.

7. Quite a respectable bun can be acquired by smoking three or four pipefuls of strong tobacco when you have no food in your stomach.

8. The ancient Phoenicians were really Jews, and got as far north as England where they operated tin mines.

9. You can get dressed much quicker in the morning if the night before when you are going to bed you take off your trousers and underdrawers at once, leaving the latter inside the former.

JUNIOR YEAR

1. Emerson left his pastorate because he had some argument about communion.

2. All women are untrustworthy.

3. Pushing your arms back as far as they will go fifty times each day increases your chest measurement.

4. Marcus Aurelius had a son who turned out to be a bad boy.

5. Eight hours of sleep are not necessary.

6. Heraclitus believed that fire was the basis of all life.

7. A good way to keep your trousers pressed is to hang them from the bureau drawer.

8. The chances are that you will never fill an inside straight.

9. The Republicans believe in a centralized government, the Democrats in a de-centralized one.

10. It is not necessarily effeminate to drink tea.

SENIOR YEAR

1. A dinner coat looks better than full dress.

2. There is as yet no law determining what constitutes trespass in an airplane.

3. Six hours of sleep are not necessary.

4. Bicarbonate of soda taken before retiring makes you feel better the next day.

5. You needn't be fully dressed if you wear a cap and gown to a nine-o'clock recitation.

6. Theater tickets may be charged.
7. Flowers may be charged.
8. May is the shortest month in the year.

The foregoing outline of my education is true enough in its way, and is what people like to think about a college course. It has become quite the cynical thing to admit laughingly that college did one no good. It is part of the American Credo that all that the college student learns is to catch punts and dance. I had to write something like that to satisfy the editors. As a matter of fact, I learned a great deal in college and have those four years to thank for whatever I know today.

(The above note was written to satisfy those of my instructors and financial backers who may read this. As a matter of fact, the original outline is true, and I had to look up the date about Charlemagne at that.)

Irving Kristol

What Business Is a University In?

The American nation today—especially the most educated part of it—seems to be even more confused than usual. On practically every campus of this country, learned professors are vociferously demanding the prohibition of cyclamates or DDT or whatever—while in the same breath arguing for the legalization of marijuana or hashish or whatever. Similarly, most professors and college administrators have concluded that they have neither the obligation nor the capacity to supervise the sexual habits or elevate the moral characters of their students—but they appear to have concluded simultaneously that they *do* have the obligation and capacity to solve our urban problems, conduct American foreign policy, reshape the American economy and perfect the American national character. They will abolish violence from American life—but they will stoically tolerate it on the campus rather than take "repressive" action. They will protect their students from air pollution—but not from venereal disease, drug addiction, pregnancy or psychedelic psychosis. Never has one had better cause to appreciate the cogency of William F. Buckley's observation that he would rather be governed by the first 2,000 names in the Boston telephone directory than by the Harvard faculty.

It is a familiar sociological phenomenon that, when an institution no longer knows what it is doing, it starts trying to do everything. The loss of genuine purpose is invariably accompanied by the lust for a dozen pseudo purposes. It would be a truly revolutionary event if the administration and faculty of one of our major universities were to meet in solemn conclave and then announce to the world: "Look, let's face it. We don't know what in hell to do with the money you give us or the young people you send us. Our traditional procedures and practices are obviously no longer relevant to the present situation. The reforms we have introduced in recent years seem not to have made much difference—except, perhaps, for the worse. We're not even sure whose fault it is: ours, the students' or the world's. But we are, at this moment in time, a losing proposition. We are therefore disbanding for a year and are going home to think things over."

One need not be a prophet to know that this scenario is a highly improbable one. What is more likely is that such a conclave would abolish all surviving parietal rules, all required courses and all grades—while declaring its intention of using its collective intelligence in order to save our cities. Should anyone chance to wonder aloud whether the university indeed possessed a "collective intelligence" suitable for this purpose, he would be dismissed as a frivolous heckler.

And yet, this very question, as to whether a university possesses something that can be called a "collective intelligence," and if it does what the range of such intelligence is, is really at the heart of the matter. For the idea of "corporate responsibility"—the idea that "the university" must act so as to solve our social problems—makes no sense without it.

Now, if I may somewhat simplify a complicated matter, an institution can be said to have a corporate responsibility to the extent that (a) its actions reflect the consent, active or passive, of the majority of its members; (b) it is organized in such a way as to make collective decisions and take collective actions, and (c) its decisions are, in some way and to some degree, a constraint upon its members. It follows that an individual, when he elects to join such an institution, accepts responsibility for its actions and decisions—accepts responsibility for them as a whole, and regardless of his disagreement with particular ones. Particular disagreements are inevitable, of course, but they are irrelevant to the question of general responsibility.

Is a university this kind of institution? I think one has to reply—yes, it is: but only to a trifling degree and only in a limited area. The degree has to do with the extent to which the university is something more than—or, if you prefer, less than—a community of scholars (more precisely, a community of teaching scholars).

The ideal of "a community of scholars" is still very much alive—at least the phrase is still used. No doubt the reality frequently falls far short of the ideal. But I believe that it is an authentic ideal, sincerely celebrated for the most part, and actually in existence here and there. What is puzzling, however, is that the very same people who say the university is a community of scholars will also assert that the university has a collective and corporate responsibility for rebuilding our cities, ending the war in Vietnam and solving our racial crisis. These two notions would appear to be—I should say they are—totally incompatible.

In a community of scholars, there may be *individual scholars* who wish—some because they sense that their expert knowledge would be useful, some others because their conception of the good citizen prescribes it, and still others because they are simply bored with their work—to get involved in public affairs. Such an action, by an individual scholar, poses no intellectual problem. It has always been assumed, since the birth of the university in the Middle Ages, that a scholar had a right *not* to get involved with worldly matters, if that was his choice. In the past century, the struggle for what was called "academic freedom"—a struggle that has been largely, if not entirely, successful—has given the scholar the positive right to get involved, if he does wish to. The number of scholars who have exercised this right, during this past decade, is larger than ever before in our history. I need only mention the names of Daniel Patrick Moynihan, John Kenneth Galbraith, Henry Kissinger, Arthur Burns, W. W. Rostow and Arthur Schlesinger.

But I do not see how a "community of scholars" can *collectively* and *institutionally* decide either to abstain from politics or to participate in politics in a particular fashion. That kind of decision-making is precisely what a "community of scholars" is incapable of, if it is to remain true to its self-definition. For, in order to make such decisions, it would have to become a *political community*—which is to say that *power* would be the focus of organization. A leadership would have to be instituted; modes of selecting this leadership would have to be established; formal channels of communication between leaders and members would have to be defined; a system of judicial restraint, constraints and punishments would have to be erected; an administrative hierarchy would be needed to carry out the decisions—and so on and so on.

We all know what such collectivities—whether they be in the public sector or the private, whether their intentions be philanthropic or mercenary—are like. They are *organizations*. And whatever the difficulties inherent in giving substance to the idea of a "community of scholars," I know of no one who ever argued that these difficulties could be overcome by transforming the academic community into an academic organization, and by converting scholars into organization men.

To be sure, there are many people these days—mainly younger people, both students and faculty—who criticize the very ideal of a "community of scholars" as being antiquated and, in the light of our present condition, even reactionary. These younger people are moved by an urgent sense of crisis—and this is to their credit, because the crisis we are living through is real enough and urgent enough. And it seems to them an act of flagrant irresponsibility for the intelligent and learned men in our universities not to be contributing to the solution of this crisis. An understandable sentiment—but, I fear, an invalid one, in that it is based on profound misconceptions of the nature of the social sciences and of the relationship between theory and practice in the realm of human affairs.

My meaning, stated bluntly, is this: There is no reason to think—there is not the slightest shred of evidence—that the organized, collective intelligence of professors has anything whatsoever to contribute to the solving of our social, economic, political or moral problems.

In this respect, the social sciences differ radically from the physical sciences. In the latter, the whole is very often greater than the sum of its parts—a team of scientists, organized for joint endeavor, is capable of achieving things that no single scientist, however brilliant, can hope to accomplish. (For instance, it can build an atom bomb.) I suspect that this analogy is in the minds of those who would have sociologists, economists, philosophers, historians, even professors of English unite for benign social purposes. But the analogy, for better or worse, is false. I know of

no organized enterprise in the social sciences—no research project, no experiment—
that has been notably creative. On the contrary: it is the work of individual scholars
that represents the major contributions, while the organized teams usually content
themselves with exploring the significance and implications of *his* work.

Governments and other political authorities, to be sure, when they consult
social scientists, always try to consult with a group rather than with an individual.
But this is for reasons political, not scientific; it is an effort to diffuse responsibility
rather than achieve truth. There is no reason whatsoever to think that the Council
of Economic Advisers, for instance, is more likely to be right, in its analysis and predictions, than any individual economist. And it is very easy to find many instances
where it has been wrong. Similarly, there is no reason to think that 10 criminologists,
or demographers, or housing experts, working together, are more likely to achieve a
correct understanding of a social problem than would one of them, working alone.
Indeed, anyone who has ever participated in a meeting of such experts has soon
realized that original creative thinking does not easily survive the press of conflicting
opinions.

Why the social sciences should differ from the physical sciences in this way, I
leave it to the philosophers of knowledge to explain. That they *do* differ is, I submit,
a fact. Yet, oddly enough, this is a fact that many social scientists themselves find
incredible. In college after college, in this country today, members of departments
of sociology, anthropology, economics, etc., are insisting that it is incumbent upon
them—not only as a possible moral obligation for the individual but as a necessary
political obligation for the group—to "get involved in solving our social problems."

Perhaps the explanation has something to do with the fact that the population
explosion in our universities has brought on to campus a great many professors who
have little interest in, or talent for, scholarship, but who simultaneously feel that
the mere possession of a Ph.D. gives them a title to political and moral authority
that society insufficiently respects. Perhaps there are other and truer explanations.
One wouldn't mind seeing *this* problem studied—though I wouldn't recommend
that anyone hold his breath until it is.

A second misconception involves the relation of social theory to political practice. It is not merely that conflicting *interests* make it difficult to act according to a
persuasive piece of social or economic analysis—though this is true enough, and certainly not unimportant. What is even more serious is that social problems usually
reflect conflicts of *values*—between different sections of the populations, of course,
but also *within* the hearts and minds of the majority of individuals who compose
the entire community.

The reason politics is such a difficult art is less that people are insufficiently
enlightened and more that it is in the nature of human beings to want incompatible
things at the same time. We want to diminish air pollution, but we are not willing to
stop driving automobiles. We want less noise in the skies, even as we fly on faster
jets. We want low-cost housing for poor people but, once we have seen it, we decide
that what we really need is *expensive* low-cost housing for poor people—with no increase in taxes, naturally. And so on, and on, and on—the catalogue is endless.

It is because our social problems are of this nature that the prime political virtue is, not theoretical rectitude, but practical sagacity (what the ancients used to call "prudence"). This is not an academic virtue; indeed, where it exists it can be an academic weakness. We want our social theorists to be bold and keen and unconstrained in the use they make of their imaginative and analytical powers. And it is precisely because we want this that we must look askance at the proposition that academic men ought, as a species, to get involved in the management of our society.

I have mentioned that there is a sense in which the university, as an institution, *does* have a corporate responsibility—but that this is so only to a trifling degree and in a limited area. No university is merely a "community of scholars." In order for such a community to exist and survive, it needs to be buttressed by an organizational component, by an administration which manages money and real estate and employees and relations with the world outside. Such organization and administration do indeed imply responsibilities. More precisely, they imply a responsibility—the responsibility to be reasonable with regard to the interests and sensibilities of other organizations and other people. And I don't think they imply anything more than that.

For example, a university that has a building program has the same responsibility as a business corporation or a government agency to see to it that injurious consequences to residents of the neighborhood are minimized if they cannot be entirely avoided. I do not think its responsibility is *more* than this. I certainly do not think that the university has the responsibility to create a "model" neighborhood or a "model" environment around it. For one thing, such a "model" reflects a man's personal values, not his academic knowledge. Nor can academic knowledge itself tell us how to translate a model into a reality—otherwise, philosophers would indeed have the divine right to be kings! Moreover, no one has given the university the authority to impose its notions of a "good" neighborhood or a "healthy" environment upon its environs. To assume such authority, therefore, would be an illicit usurpation of power. One might even call it "impudent," were that word still in good standing.

Similarly, the university has the obligation to invest its money to achieve the highest return, yet in such a way as not to offend the sensibilities of the academic community that resides within the university's organizational shell. If the members of this community feel it improper for such funds to be invested in, say, South African securities, then a reasonable administration will respect these sensibilities and avoid such investments.

On the other hand, an administration should pay no attention to those who insist that it select its investments mainly for the beneficent social consequences they will have. No one knows which investments have such consequences. After all, an investment in today's low-cost housing may mean an investment in tomorrow's outrageous slum—and the benevolent university might find itself in the position of actually being a malevolent "slumlord."

In addition, of course, there are acts of pure philanthropy that a well-heeled institution ought to perform out of a sense of *noblesse oblige.* It would be both nice and proper if Harvard established and supported a free private school in the slums of

Roxbury. On the other hand, I am appalled at suggestions that Harvard devote its resources to "solving the problems of ghetto education."

There are no grounds for thinking that Harvard's faculty members—even if they be in the School of Education—are any better at solving the problems of ghetto education than anyone else. (At the moment, indeed, the Harvard faculty would seem to have its hands full trying to solve the problems of Harvard education.) Yes, of course, there are individual scholars at Harvard who know a great deal about ghetto education. There are also scholars at Harvard who know a great deal about the sociology of the family, but that doesn't mean they'd necessarily make good marriage counselors. It only means their books ought to be read by marriage counselors.

Activities of the kind I have mentioned seem to me pretty much to exhaust the question of the university's corporate responsibilities to the community at large. There are, to be sure, a whole series of borderline cases. Should the university accept Government contracts for research? I see no way of giving an a priori answer to this question. If such contracts and such research fit into its educational program, I see no reason why a university shouldn't accept them—if it wants to. I don't see that it has any *obligation* to accept them. The Government can always get such research done outside the university, if it has to. And in this connection, I see no difference in principle in research for the Department of Agriculture and research for the Department of Defense. What counts is the way such research fits into the *educational* program of the university. It ought to go without saying that, if it has no relevance to education, then it has no place in the university.

The question—now agitating many minds—as to whether a university should take a position on the Vietnam war or some other controversial issue of the day strikes me as being simply beneath discussion. If critics of the Vietnam war can get an overwhelming majority of the faculty to sign an *ad hoc* statement in opposition to the war, why should they then insist that the university senate *officially* subscribe to such statement? Such official action only makes sense if it in some way binds the dissenting minority. Since it does nothing of the sort, its only meaning is the expectation that it might intimidate this minority into silence—through fear, through shame, through embarrassment. This is as neat a definition of McCarthyism as one can find. And, in truth, the present demand that the university, by a majority vote, take a stand on such political issues is nothing but an expression of McCarthyism from the Left. I repeat: it is *nothing but* that—no matter how many ingenious rationalizations are provided and no matter how self-righteous the proponents.

I do not wish to end on a negative note. I am aware that I have mainly been arguing what the responsibility of the university is not. Let me therefore propose a positive thought. The university does indeed have one major collective responsibility which it has been shamefully neglecting; this is its responsibility for education.

We are all of us aware that university education in the United States today is an utter shambles. We have all seen bright, young high-school graduates move on to our college campuses and, after only a relatively short period, display a feebler intellect, a less cultivated sensibility and a greater vulgarity of soul than either God or their parents bequeathed to them. I have a son who is now preparing to enter college and, frankly, I am heartsick at the thought that this young man—who may be a budding scholar—is going to have to live through four years at one of our institutions of higher learning. Other parents, I know, are similarly perplexed and distressed at the prospect of plunging their children into the psychedelic phantasmagoria of campus life, where the college chaplain is more likely to have faith in encounter therapy than in a mere deity.

Now, I know that this is a fearfully difficult situation. The university today must cope with a large, heterogeneous student body. It must confront a "counter-culture" that often renders young minds impervious to the very idea of education. It must take into account the proliferation of scientific, social-scientific and quasi-scientific disciplines, and of the decay of the traditional conception of a curriculum. It must satisfy the demands of high-minded students, professionally-minded students, vocationally-minded students and students who go to college with no ulterior—or even discernible—motive whatsoever.

All of this, and other things too, make for crisis and disarray. The faculty and administration of our universities cannot fairly be blamed for creating or provoking this crisis—though they often are so blamed, the human penchant for scapegoating being as powerful as it is. But they *can* be blamed for the pitiful inadequacy of their response. Why, one wonders, are practically all campus newspapers in the hands of the extreme left? Why are the student unions and student funds controlled by militant minorities? Why don't the administration and the faculty demand a student referendum on these matters—with compulsory voting, if that is needed to make student elections meaningful? The reason, I suspect, is that they fear the left would lose—and would then be even more troublesome than it is. So, fearful of democracy, they try bribery, with predictable results.

And where, one may ask, are the philosophies of education appropriate to our new condition? Where are even the intellectual controversies over the nature and function of higher education? Where are the bold definitions and redefinitions of the purpose of the curriculum? Where are the fine distinctions among the different kinds of education suitable for different kinds of students?

They are nowhere, so far as I can see, though scholars are supposed to be good at precisely this sort of thing. Instead, we have endless committee meetings that result in a mindless shuffling and reshuffling of bits and pieces of the educational structure—together with an amiable willingness to label *anything* as education if that will only buy some temporary peace on the campus.

The collective responsibility of the university is education. That is its original mission, that is its original purpose, that is the only thing it can claim expertise or authority for. To return to this original purpose, with renewed seriousness, would be an action at once radical and constructive.

Steven Kelman

Beyond New Leftism

American students created two momentous political events last year: the primary victory of Eugene McCarthy in New Hampshire, and the anti-war demonstrations in Chicago. Yet despite these two surges, the student movement, now almost a decade old, is in a state of internal disintegration and flux. This is true of both its moderate and militant wings. Indeed, the outward differences between the liberal students of the McCarthy crusade and those of the SDS-style New Left have tended to obscure the fact that in both movements the causes of confusion are similar.

It is one sign of the disintegration of liberalism as an ideology on the campus today that campus liberals have virtually abandoned any attempt to offer an alternative political analysis to that of the New Left. What drove a young activist last year into SDS rather than into the McCarthy movement was fundamentally a different perception of his role. Members of SDS view themselves as part of the wretched of the earth, whereas Young Democrats see themselves as future directors of the Bureau of Housing and Urban Development. When asked to justify their membership in the Young Democrats rather than in SDS, they will almost inevitably refer, not to any serious political differences, but to the possibility of being "more effective." Campus liberalism today is above all a movement for "respectable" students, future-oriented and careful about undertaking anything which might endanger their records or careers. Liberal college students could put out long hours and sleep on hard floors for "clean Gene," secure in the knowledge that they were signing their names to nothing that might eventually make its way to the FBI. In this respect the atmosphere of the early 1950's is still widely prevalent on campus.

Capitalizing on their opponents' weaknesses, SDS in turn constantly attacked the McCarthy movement last year for "working within the system" and for being simpleminded in its political analysis. In reply, the McCarthy people, instead of dissecting the terms foisted on them by SDS, baldly answered back that they were proud to be working within the system.

Now, when SDS members talk about "the system" they are referring to a political structure which they believe to be thoroughly undemocratic and elite-controlled. Thus, however much one may disagree with their premises about the nature of American society, the New Left's terrorist-confrontation approach at least has a certain primitive logical consistency, since by definition one cannot change a "totalitarian" system by any sort of democratic means. But when campus liberals adopt the SDS term "the system," the expression emerges bastardized, if not unrecognizable. Far from being a focus for social criticism, it exists as a vague presence alternately to be paid allegiance to or turned away from. For SDS "the system" simply is undemocratic; for liberals, America is democratic but its people, albeit democratically, are making the wrong decisions. The Harvard *Crimson*, for instance, reported last March that a volunteer at the end of the McCarthy campaign in New Hampshire had "lost his faith in the system." ("Losing one's faith" in something is the most frequent trauma of the liberal student activist.) Actually, he had lost his faith not in "the system" but in individual Americans, for it developed that he felt that the people he had come in contact with during the campaign were stupid. Such is the level of the crisis of campus liberalism.

Lacking strong intellectual moorings, the liberal, hesitant about committing himself to Marxism-Leninism, which is both dogmatic and a danger to his future, and yet continually frustrated by the difficulties of producing the changes in policies that he wants—especially an end to the war in Vietnam—is reduced to a proud fuzziness. In this state he is susceptible to the tactics and the ideology both of the Right and of the extreme Left. The most convincing argument which impels some liberal activists into radical movements like The Resistance goes something like: "We wrote letters, we marched, we petitioned, we worked for McCarthy. But the war still went on." I have heard this argument put forth literally tens of times, and *never* heard a liberal respond: "But did we ever convince a majority of Americans that our views are right?" The system in which these liberals so easily lose faith is democracy itself.[1]

Both campus liberalism and SDS-style radicalism today draw on similar social currents and intellectual modes in the university. Today's generation of student political activists, both liberals and radicals, has grown up in a climate of unprecedented social and political isolation from the American people. Radicals in the 30's usually came from families suffering directly from the same Depression which affected most other Americans. Thus the imperative, for example, to participate in trade-union organizing came not only from the Marxist liturgy but also from the facts of life. By contrast, the affluent middle-class position of most activists today has led to a merger of traditional middle-class prejudices against the "boobocracy" with the more sophisticated political notions of the elitist wing of the intellectual Left. While activist students lose their optimistic faith in American society as they grow up, they retain their hostility toward most non-middle-class whites. A sign, reading simply "Dumb Power," held by a heckler at a Wallace rally in Boston, indicates well the component of snobbism in student political consciousness. This was expressed in civil-rights activism in the South and in protests against the war in Vietnam, the two great student causes of the 60's, both of which offered the opportunity to compare one's beliefs favorably with those of ignorant rednecks or longshoremen.

Such attitudes toward "the people" are bound to produce a very insecure belief in democracy and democratic social change. The young may hold on to the ideology of democracy longer than they hold on to their faith in the American political

---

1. To be sure, some campus liberal activists developed their own stab-in-the-back legend—that the nomination was stolen from McCarthy despite the overwhelming popular support for his position. But the polls show that a majority of rank-and-file Democrats supported Humphrey. The primaries which McCarthy occasionally won attracted disproportionately upper-income voters—McCarthy's strongest voting bloc. Of McCarthy supporters, according to an election-eve CBS poll, 20 percent were planning to vote for Wallace and 31 percent were planning to vote for Nixon, which indicates that their anti-Johnson feelings hardly stemmed from a progressive direction. It is, however, through this disingenuous legend that some managed to reconcile their otherwise contemptuous attitudes toward the "masses" with their traditional belief in democracy. Many McCarthy supporters, to their credit, resisted this theory.

system, but an intellectual faith in democracy cannot survive forever in the face of a gut feeling that the people are consistently wrong.

Members of SDS extricate themselves from this dilemma by developing an alternative ideology. They postulate, paying the debt to their childhood, the fundamental goodness of people. In fact, they argue that if the people are informed of the facts, they will *always* make the decisions that SDS thinks they should make. If they appear never to make the right judgments, it must be because of manipulation and "false consciousness." To SDS, there can never be legitimate disagreements, only different levels of consciousness. In the short run, before the destruction of the system which fosters false consciousness, one need not be concerned about "bourgeois democratic" methods or "bourgeois civil liberties." (That SDS has resurrected these hoary terms is but another indication that, today, there is little "new" about the "New" Left.)

The liberal activist, however, unable to relate to any other forces in the society (except, perhaps, as a nostalgic nod to yesteryear, the Negroes) adopts the 1960's variant of the Puritan ethic, according to which political success is a function, not of winning mass support, but of hard work and "commitment." It was this doctrine which led to the massive outpouring of effort into the McCarthy campaign.

The elitist "liberalism" that often lurked under the innocent facade of some of McCarthy's followers—the converse of the elitist "radicalism" which dominates SDS—descends from the opportunistic liberalism of the 1950's. If one believes, with the new liberals, that the mass of the American people are inherently conservative, ignorant, and mesmerized by an alleged private affluence, one looks to the educated or to those, like the blacks, whose minority status has given them a unique existential experience, as the only agents for social change.

If, on the other hand, like SDS, one rejects the possibility of change coming from within American society, one turns romantically to Ho, Che, and the peasant masses of the Third World. It was just such a denial of the potential of an authentic, majoritarian movement of social change in America, a denial now shared by both groups of student elitists, that served as the intellectual pretext for so many ex-radicals and liberals to justify their participation in the "American celebration" during the Eisenhower years. It is all too possible that, if the war ends, the Nixon era may cause the elitism of the intelligentsia to show its other face—the self-satisfied and often conservative meliorism of the 1950's.

The simple fact for those concerned about social progress is that liberalism is in serious intellectual crisis, and this intellectual crisis relates directly to its political crisis. One can only hope for—and work toward—the development of a trend within the student movement that will reject the middle-class snobbery which has separated intellectual protests from the mundane and often inarticulate desires for change that are a part of the feelings of a majority of the American people. A principled commitment and willingness to defend democracy is viable in the long run only if combined with a political strategy that has realistic chances of obtaining majority support for the types of programs one wants. It is precisely the lack of such a strategy for gaining a democratic majority which has made sincere campus liberal activists so unfortunately subject to influence from elitism and anti-democratic New Left conceptions. The present contemptuous dismissal of the trade-union movement, a force without which any progressive majority is simply numerically impossible, is a good example of this loss of perspective.

One need not believe—as I do—that the labor movement is the major mass force for social progress in our society to recognize that during the past decade American Left intellectuals, following the lead of some of the most conservative interests in America, have underestimated the role of the labor movement in social change. While foundation officials, clergymen, and even businessmen are viewed as capable of being won to the cause through moral and intellectual appeals, trade-union officials are viewed as "fat cats" with vested interests and ingrained conservative prejudices. This view has allowed Nelson Rockefeller to appear as a spokesman for the "new politics," while making George Meany a leading symbol of reaction. But more importantly, it has led to a dismissal of any thoughtful discussion of the basic economic structure of the country as an obsolete vestige of the 30's. Unable to cope with the dichotomy of workers being left-wing on economic and social issues while less liberal on non-economic or foreign policy issues, many intellectuals dismiss them altogether.[2] When it was suggested to a leader of the Harvard Young Democrats who was active in the McCarthy campaign that the working class might be a fruitful ally in working for a more egalitarian society, he replied, quite sincerely, "Why do you pick the working class out of the clear blue sky? Why not housewives?"

The "new" student liberalism has accepted and propagated the opinion that union rank-and-file members are largely reactionaries and even "honkies." It has blamed rioting and crime in the Negro community on a generalized "white racism" or, more specifically, on the police, rather than on real-estate interests, low-wage employers, and political conservatives whose policies have been responsible for ghetto conditions in the first place. It permits those who went to high school in the suburbs or to prep school in New England to sneer "racist" at low-income urban whites who are rightly concerned with crime, living conditions, or keeping their jobs—and to cop out on the more difficult task of providing alternative answers to these problems from those presented by the Nixons and Wallaces. It leads student liberals frequently to make statements like, "The unions are *the* most reactionary force in this country," only to retreat embarrassedly when reminded of the role of corporate business.

If students who are drawn to the democratic framework still hope to accomplish anything of lasting value they will have to put forward not only alternative tactics to those of the New Left, but an alternative political philosophy and social morality as well. At present, however, the moral critique of the "new" student liberalism is radical, but its social analysis and political strategy are not.

2. In this respect, Seymour Martin Lipset's seminal essay, "Working-Class Authoritarianism," has been widely misinterpreted by many elitist liberals, who view it as "proof" of the reactionary nature of the working class. Lipset in fact argues from statistical evidence that the fact that workers are more left-wing than the middle class on political issues relating to economic and social affairs, while less tolerant and more likely to be prejudiced, arises from the same cause—the workers' disadvantaged position in society. The task of democratic Left groups, Lipset argues, is to counter, through stronger economic and social programs, the conservative attempt to appeal to prejudice.

Nevertheless, some significant beginnings have been made toward reestablishing a principled and intelligent democratic-Left current within the student movement. First, there are the youth workers from the Kennedy campaign—the insurgent movement within the Democratic party which had the most blue-collar and black support—who have formed the Kennedy Action Corps. Given the possibility of a 1972 Presidential bid by Edward Kennedy, this group may have something more than the memory of RFK to keep it alive. It could serve as a political bridge between the campuses and the "forgotten Americans."

Second, there is the New Democratic Coalition, an alliance of some of the younger leaders of both the Kennedy and McCarthy campaigns, which could be another center for democratic radicalism. Here, too, much depends on the way in which the group resolves the different approaches to domestic politics reflected in its leadership. Its Executive Committee, for example, includes Michael Harrington, national chairman of the Socialist party, and David Hoeh, leader of the McCarthy New Hampshire delegation to the Democratic Convention and subsequently an unsuccessful Congressional candidate.

Harrington is a major proponent of the "coalition" strategy for social progress. He calls for an alliance of Negroes, labor, the poor, and middle-class liberals and democratic radicals to press for massive federal social spending, democratic planning, and a democratic foreign policy. Harrington is also one of the most effective proponents of the view that middle-class liberals and radicals must develop a creative relationship with organized labor.

Hoeh, while no doubt sharing many of Harrington's ultimate goals, has a fundamentally different view on how to achieve them. He too favors working within the Democratic party. But in an article in the *New Republic* last October he indicated that he placed fundamental reliance on the liberal middle class, and that he included in his "new coalition," without the mildest reservation, what he called "giant business." The only part of the working class honored with admission was what he referred to as "progressive labor."

Third, as a result of the current confusion among liberal students and the Marxist-Leninist dogmatism of the New Left, democratic socialism, which many older Americans may think of as only one of the more appealing leftist doctrines of a completely bygone era, is now undergoing a campus revival. While it is true that democratic socialist ideas have influenced several youth organizations, their main vehicle of expression has been the Young People's Socialist League, the youth affiliate of the Socialist party of the late Norman Thomas. Three years ago YPSL was revived by a group of young people, many of whom were disaffected veterans of SDS. The mentors of YPSL have been Michael Harrington, Irving Howe, and other intellectuals grouped around the League for Industrial Democracy and *Dissent* magazine; trade unionists coming out of the socialist movement, among them Albert Shanker of the American Federation of Teachers and Walter Reuther of the UAW; and civil-rights activists like A. Philip Randolph, Bayard Rustin, and Tom Kahn.

The socialists have not been caught in the bind of some moderate opponents of the New Left, who appear to be pleading for gradualism and compromise as the alternatives to enthusiasm and radical change. In the explosive atmosphere which exists on many American campuses, pleas for gradualism have become synonymous with defense of the status quo. This is not an entirely invalid view, for as Harrington argues in *Toward a Democratic Left*, the new technology has created social conditions which require that man must either master technology, or be mastered by it. To procrastinate is to lend oneself to the worst. The real question is not whether there will be change, but what character the change will take. Will it develop into new forms of oppression, or will it be democratic and creative?

The student democratic socialists acknowledge the necessity for radical change, but they insist that this change—as well as the society they want to develop—be democratic. Hence their opposition to SDS, and the very different tactics which they have adopted. Their activities are directed toward overcoming the hostilities that prevent various disadvantaged groups from uniting around common concerns so as to be able to build a majoritarian coalition that can rebuild the Democratic party; and toward defending the ideals of free discussion and democracy. The Harvard chapter of YPSL, for example, of which the present author is a former chairman, has been involved in supporting striking Harvard printers and in organizing the boycott of California grapes in support of Cesar Chavez's farm workers' union. It issued a critique of "Economics 1," Harvard's largest course, which succeeded in bringing important changes to its reading list. Without sit-ins or confrontations, but merely by publicizing a document which even its opponents admitted was "well-researched and well-written," YPSL accomplished what no previous "student power" efforts for curriculum change ever had. On the issue of the status of military-training programs on campus, such as academic credit, YPSL called for a student referendum. SDS opposed the referendum, and demanded the unilateral right, through confrontation, to determine not only that ROTC be deprived of its special privileges, but furthermore, that it should be expelled from campus on the grounds that no student has the right to participate in it.

The turning point for YPSL at Harvard was the sit-in staged by SDS's psychodrama politics at its presence of a recruiter from the Dow Chemical Company on campus. The Dow Affair represented SDS's psychodrama politics at its worst. Originally SDS had voted against a sit-in. But a small group of members decided to ignore the majority's decision, sat in, and demanded that the Dow recruiter sign a statement saying that Dow would never come back to Harvard. At that point, the mass of SDS members, ever willing to subordinate political judgment to the excitement of getting in on the action—and above all never willing to be "out-radicalized" by others—joined in.

The sit-in, coming at a time of heightened opposition to the war and widespread frustration (the Young Democrats had endorsed a "Dump Johnson" drive, but the McCarthy movement had not yet been launched), was an electrifying event on campus. But support for the sit-in was surprisingly low, and of those outside SDS who joined it, many later became guilt-ridden and felt that, in a fit of emotion, they had let themselves be "had" into supporting a totalitarian position. Furthermore, and just as importantly, many students were annoyed by the abdication of student liberal leaders. The *Crimson* supported the sit-in, saying that Dow had no right to be on campus, and the Young Democrats, who were split, finally voted only a mild disapproval of the sit-in, after voting down a stronger condemnation.

At this point, YPSL, still relatively unknown on campus, came out with a statement and petition supporting "the rights of free speech and free recruitment on campus," and warning that on the precedent of SDS tactics, rightist students could also keep out those they disliked. At the same time the petition asked for clemency for the protestors and called upon the faculty to take a position on the war. University administrators, who were under great pressure from alumni and others to expel some of the leaders of the sit-in, based their case for leniency largely on this petition, which had over 1200 signatures. It was with this statement—which mixed a pro-civil liberties position with a strong anti-war stand—that YPSL established for itself an independent role on campus.

The modest successes of YPSL at Harvard and elsewhere indicate that there is an unexploited potential constituency on other campuses as well. Up to now, the mood has been set largely by SDS, whose politics offered an easy outlet for the alienated young in the form of such political gestures as yelling "pig," "liberating" a university building, or following Che's life style. Meanwhile, campus liberals, suspended uneasily between confrontations and careerism, have simply given up the fight. The lesson of the Dow Affair at Harvard seems to be that many students will seize upon a thoughtful alternative to the New Left's political actions once the opportunity is offered.

Indeed, despite the fact that their posture is less frenetic—and therefore less appealing—than that of New Leftists, democratic radicals may be heading for a brighter future than might at first glance appear. (It is interesting to note that at Harvard this year both SDS and campus liberalism are in a state of drastic decline, while YPSL is growing. SDS has been attracting about half the number of people to its meetings, as compared with the previous year, and the Young Democrats' membership is less than a third of what it was two years ago.) McCarthy's failure seems to have burned out many of the students who were all too briefly lit up by the message of his campaign. Many are reverting to "revolutionary pessimism"—radicalism about what needs to be done, but conservatism about the chances of accomplishing it. At the same time, SDS is threatened, not only by serious ideological divisions, especially with the Maoists, but, what is worse, by sociopaths like those who form the "Motherfucker" faction. This group has eliminated whatever political content might originally have existed in the New Left by denying the possibility of individual sanity in a corrupt society, and resorting to mental terrorism. "The future of our struggle is the future of crime in the streets," their leader has proclaimed. To protest the war, the "Motherfuckers" throw cow's blood and urine indiscriminately at passing cars. They disrupt SDS's own meetings, surely a case of the chickens coming home to roost. Those in the SDS leadership who are politically serious and committed, despair at the problem of such *enragés*. But, at least for the present, there is little they can do about it.

The experience of YPSL at Harvard indicates that the kind of approach offered by democratic socialists could find widespread acceptance among students who are capable of steering an intelligent course between protestors and politicos. This is the course that will have to be followed by any radical democratic movement that hopes to have a future in America, and those committed to building such a movement may yet find new and unexpected allies among the young.

The Young: Anomie in the Group

To an unprecedented degree, the young of this generation have dominated the scene as no previous generation has. Sociologists, educators, and psychologists find the behavior of this group fascinating and instructive of the climate of our times. Young people constitute a discrete and powerful market for the merchandising of goods; fashion boutiques have been created to reflect and serve their collective image. Canny entrepreneurs have fashioned large-scale entertainments and festivals to satisfy their cultural tastes, drawing mammoth audiences from their ranks. Nurtured from infancy by large doses of fantasy-freeing television programming, operating under a flexible code of sexual behavior, liberated from the restraints of chaperonage, and given full mobility by an affluent society, this generation of young people has traveled further, mingled more with the young of other cultures, and behaved with fewer restraints than any similarly constituted group in history. They have been defended for their unconventionality and idealism and vilified for their irresponsibility and wantonness. Paul Goodman, a champion of the young, has charged in *Growing Up Absurd* that young people in our automated world have been cheated of meaningful goals by a crass and obtuse society. Cartoonist Al Capp accuses them of softness and lack of moral fiber. Charles Reich, in a remarkable book about the "new consciousness" of the young entitled *The Greening of America,* applauds the courageous and unconventional young who are producing an "interdependent society that requires collective responsibility"; they are rejecting the old myths which have contributed to the mindless operation of the state and replacing them with human values.

The young of today are energetic and restless as the young of all generations have been, but in a different way and to a much greater degree. Television action series have instilled in them a craving for movement, and African culture has introduced them to the new excitement of uninhibited body motion. Beat literature and motorcycle films have glamorized the rootless migrations of the hobo-hero "on the road," stimulating a culture of hitchhike roaming. The clothing young people wear is fluid and suited to the free-form migratory life. Blue jeans, sandals, gypsy scarves, ponchos, and rucksacks are the fashion accoutrements of a nomadic existence. They are the indispensable paraphernalia for camping out, moving on, and functional service. They are also, in Reich's estimate, "the deliberate rejection of the neon colors and artificial, plastic-coated look of the affluent society." In addition, the unisex trend in hair and clothing contributes to the breaking down of formal barriers between people. It encourages an undifferentiated communion, manifested particularly in the rock festival congregations which have become notable for the shared experience of rhythmic music, fellowship, and, frequently, a drug-induced euphoria.

The lives of the young are beset with contradictions. They pride themselves on their united stand against the materialistic goals of their parents' generation, yet they themselves own a great variety of expensive goods necessary for the maintenance of their special life-style: tape recorders, phonographs, record collections, automobiles, motorcycles, surfing equipment, skiing apparatus. They wear the peace symbol as an intrinsic element of their costume, carry placards for peace, and make the peace sign as a kind of ritual benediction to each other. Ironically, however, it is those very young who often become violent in the defense of their pacifist causes. They truly yearn to "do their own thing" as a measure of their individual identity, but they travel in swarms, and create their own rigid, formulaic regimentation in speech patterns, behavior codes, clothing, and goals. Polish novelist Jerzy Kosinski, himself a product of a collective society, made some disconcerting observations in the editorial pages of the *New York Times* in October 1970:

> *Today, the attempt to define "Who am I?" is often replaced in each of our minds by the question, "Who do they want me to be?" Thus the knowledge we form of ourselves is nothing but a collective image which, like ubiquitous television, engulfs us. One image is interchangeable with another. But what about the self? I am convinced, and I see it manifested in almost every phase of modern living, from the corporate to the Woodstock ends of the spectrum, from the hardhat executive to the professional revolutionary, that we are a culture of the denial of the self.*

> *In its increasing collectivization, modern society offers every conceivable escape from the realization of self. Participation in the collective rites, such as mass-spectator sports, rock and pop festivals, is a stage in the loss of self, which has assiduously rubbed off from earliest childhood by the collective-conformist eraser. . . . The phrase "doing one's own thing" is really no more than a mockery uttered by people whose own thing is to be part of an amorphous supergang.*

The young have always been a vulnerable societal group, human beings in transition from fragile childhood to stable maturity. But in times past they were at least certain of their particular groove in the societal framework. They were half-formed adults who were in training for full-fledged membership in an adult world structure. Their adolescence was in effect a preparation for eventual inclusion. Now, however, for many the structure has been renamed "establishment," and it has become a dirty word. Rather than seek acceptance into so corrupt an institution, some of the young are contriving its ultimate dissolution. They choose to remain in limbo, on the fringe of a society which does not prompt them to exercise their best talents for its support because it does not represent a desirable goal. From this "out" position, they develop a new consciousness, which Reich calls "Consciousness III," the third of the broad types of awareness of society which characterize American social outlooks today. In *The Greening of America* Reich expresses enthusiasm for this new social point of departure:

> *The key to the Consciousness III commitment lies in the concept of full personal responsibility. . . . Consciousness III does not think much of fighting for change from the comfort of personal security and elegance. He feels that if he*

is to be true to himself he must respond with himself. If he is deeply commit-
ted, he may take a job teaching in a ghetto school, which offers neither prestige
nor comfort but offers the satisfaction of personal contact with ghetto children.
. . . It is this notion of full personal responsibility that makes the new genera-
tion, when it finds itself excluded from the decision-making process, demand
a part in that process.

Even the most ardent supporters of the young recognize that their youth is a
temporary commodity. They are politically powerless, their elected representatives
in a large measure wary of and even hostile toward their aspirations. They have set
in motion a cult of youth in this country which has produced an instability in the
conventional age-group hierarchy. Their elders in their early middle years, primarily
in the middle-to-upper socioeconomic bracket, have relinquished their rightful maturity in pursuit of the very youth culture which is so antagonistic toward them. In
so doing, they have deprived themselves of the authority necessary for the stable
guidance of their children. The young have responded with mistrust and resentment
of their elders, exacerbating the much publicized but very real generation gap.

The much vaunted "be-ins" and rock festivals, such as those which took place
in the Isle of Wight and Central Park, are in reality mass pilgrimages in which anxious
young people pursue that elusive commodity: love. This antirational, anticerebral,
largely inarticulate generation is not so much an exponent of love, as their song
lyrics might indicate, as a seeker of realization through love. The psychic energy
generated and released at the huge group encounters engenders a denial of self as
the individual willingly yields to the encompassing general outpouring of good will.
Love, the desirable end of a willing subjugation of the self, becomes a sacrament.
The spirit is released in the hallucinogenic ritual as the food or "joint" is passed
from hand to hand in symbolic sharing, and, finally, everyone beds down together
under the open sky. The catalyst is the inhibition-releasing, pulsing music played in
a primitive and bucolic setting. The question is whether the pastoral collective experience can free these young seekers from the "entrapments of collectivism," the TV
and the radio, "the great gray educational machine" which Mr. Kosinski so deplores.
Will the young succeed in creating the "new consciousness" which Professor Reich
sees as the hope of the future, or will they remain the "dead souls" which Mr. Kosinski sees all about him? Much depends not only upon the character and courage
of the young as they challenge the institutions of their society, but also upon the
flexibility of the institutions themselves as they are required to change to accommodate an impatient and irreverent generation.

Margaret Mead

The Future: Prefigurative Cultures and Unknown Children

Our present crisis has been variously attributed to the overwhelming rapidity of change, the collapse of the family, the decay of capitalism, the triumph of a soulless technology, and, in wholesale repudiation, to the final breakdown of the Establishment. Behind these attributions there is a more basic conflict between those for whom the present represents no more than an intensification of our existing cofigurative culture, in which peers are more than ever replacing parents as the significant models of behavior, and those who contend that we are in fact entering a totally new phase of cultural evolution.

Most commentators, in spite of their differences in viewpoint, still see the future essentially as an extension of the past. Teller can still speak of the outcome of a nuclear war as a state of destruction relatively no more drastic than the ravages wrought by Genghis Khan. Writing about the present crisis, moralists refer to the decay of religious systems in the past and historians point out that time and again civilization has survived the crumbling of empires.

Similarly, most commentators treat as no more than an extreme form of adolescent rebellion the repudiation of present and past by the dissident youth of every persuasion in every kind of society in the world. So Max Lerner can say "Every adolescent must pass through two crucial periods: one when he identifies with a model —a father, an older brother, a teacher—the second when he disassociates himself from his model, rebels against him, reasserts his own selfhood." There is little substantial difference between Lerner's view and that of David Riesman in his delineation of the autonomous man, who emerges from the present without too sharp a break with the past.

Perhaps the most extraordinary response to youthful rebellion has been that of Mao, who has attempted to turn the restive young against their parents as a way of preserving the momentum of the revolution made by the grandparent generation. Little as we understand the details of what has been going on in China, what we do know suggests a tremendous effort to transform the desire to destroy, which characterizes the attitudes of young activists all around the world, into an effective instrument for the preservation of the recently established Chinese Communist regime. If the Maoists succeed in this attempt, they will have the most dramatic use of the techniques of temporary cofiguration to bring about a return to a postfigurative culture of which we have any record. There are indications that the modern Chinese may treat such new Western technologies as electronics as parallel to processes of assimilation that have occurred many times in the long history of Chinese civilization—no more significant than a new form of metallurgy.

Theorists who emphasize the parallels between past and present in their interpretations of the generation gap ignore the irreversibility of the changes that have taken place since the beginning of the industrial revolution. This is especially striking in their handling of modern technological development, which they treat as comparable in its effects to the changes that occurred as one civilization in the past took over from another such techniques as agriculture, script, navigation, or the organization of labor and law.

It is, of course, possible to discuss both postfigurative and cofigurative cultures in terms of slow or rapid change without specifying the nature of the process. For example, when the children of agricultural and handicraft workers entered the first factories, this marked the beginning of an irreversible change. But the fact that accommodation to this new way of living was slow, since it was spread out over several generations, meant that the changes were not necessarily perceived to be more drastic than those experienced by the peoples who were incorporated by conquest into the Roman Empire. So also, when attention is focused on generation relationships and on the type of modeling through which a culture is transmitted, it is possible to treat as fully comparable a past situation, as when a formerly land-bound people learned the techniques of fishing, and a present situation, as when the children of emigrant Haitians learn computer programming.

It is only when one specifies the nature of the process that the contrast between past and present change becomes clear. One urgent problem, I believe, is the delineation of the nature of change in the modern world, including its speed and dimensions, so that we can better understand the distinctions that must be made between change in the past and that which is now ongoing.

The primary evidence that our present situation is unique, without any parallel in the past, is that the generation gap is world-wide. The particular events taking place in any country—China, England, Pakistan, Japan, the United States, New Guinea, or elsewhere—are not enough to explain the unrest that is stirring modern youth everywhere. Recent technological change or the handicaps imposed by its absence, revolution or the suppression of revolutionary activities, the crumbling of faith in ancient creeds or the attraction of new creeds—all these serve only as partial explanations of the particular forms taken by youth revolt in different countries. Undoubtedly, an upsurge of nationalism is more likely in a country like Japan, which is recovering from a recent defeat, or in countries that have newly broken away from their colonial past than it is, for example, in the United States. It is easier for the government of a country as isolated as China to order vast changes by edict than it is for the government of the Soviet Union, acting on a European stage, to subdue Czechoslovakian resistance. The breakdown of the family is more apparent in the West than in the East. The speed of change is more conspicuous and more consciously perceived in the least and in the most industrialized countries than it is in countries occupying an intermediate position. But all this is, in a sense, incidental when the focus of attention is on youthful dissidence, which is world-wide in its dimensions.

Concentration on particularities can only hinder the search for an explanatory principle. Instead, it is necessary to strip the occurrences in each country of their superficial, national, and immediately temporal aspects. The desire for a liberated form of communism in Czechoslovakia, the search for "racial" equality in the United States, the desire to liberate Japan from American military influence, the support given to excessive conservatism in Northern Ireland and Rhodesia or to the excesses of communism in Cuba—all these are particularistic forms. Youthful activism is common to them all.

   It was with the hope of turning anthropological analysis to this use that I tried
to describe the essential characteristics of the postfigurative model and some of the
forms taken by the cofigurative model under certain conditions of rapid change. It
is my belief that the delineation of these models, as we have come to understand
them through the study of older cultures, can help to clarify what is happening in the
contemporary world.

   The key question is this: What are the new conditions that have brought about
the revolt of youth right around the world?

   The first of these is the emergence of a world community. For the first time
human beings throughout the world, in their information about one another and responses to one another, have become a community that is united by shared knowledge and danger. We cannot say for certain now that at any period in the past there
was a single community made up of many small societies whose members were aware
of one another in such a way that consciousness of what differentiated one small society from another heightened the self-consciousness of each constituent group. But
as far as we know, no such single, interacting community has existed within archae-
ological time. The largest clusters of interacting human groups were fragments of a
still larger unknown whole. The greatest empires pushed their borders outward into
regions where there were peoples whose languages, customs and very appearance were
unknown. In the very partially charted world of the past the idea that all men were,
in the same sense, human beings was either unreal or a mystical belief. Men could
think about the fatherhood of God and the brotherhood of man and biologists could
argue the issue of monogenesis versus polygenesis; but what all men had in common
was a matter of continuing speculation and dispute.

   The events of the last twenty-five years changed this drastically. Exploration
has been complete enough to convince us that there are no humanoid types on the
planet except our own species. World-wide rapid air travel and globe-encircling television satellites have turned us into one community in which events taking place on
one side of the earth become immediately and simultaneously available to peoples
everywhere else. No artist or political censor has time to intervene and edit as a
leader is shot or a flag planted on the moon. The world is a community though it
still lacks as yet the forms of organization and the sanctions by which a political community can be governed.

   The nineteenth-century industrial revolution replaced the cruder forms of energy. The twentieth-century scientific revolution has made it possible to multiply
agricultural production manyfold but also drastically and dangerously to modify
the ecology of the entire planet and destroy all living things. Science has made possible, through the use of computers, a new concentration of intellectual efforts that
allows men to begin the exploration of the solar system, and opens the way to simu-
lations by means of which men, especially men working in organized groups, can
transcend earlier intellectual accomplishments.

   The revolution in the development of food resources is on a world-wide scale.
Up to the present, in many parts of the world, the medical revolution has so increased
the population that the major effect of increased, efficient food production has been
to stave off famine. But if we are able to bring the human population into a new bal-

ance, all of humanity can be, for the first time, well nourished. The medical revolution by reducing the pressure for population increase has begun, in turn, to release women from the age-old necessity of devoting themselves almost completely to reproductivity and, thus, will profoundly alter women's future and the future rearing of children.

Most importantly, these changes have taken place almost simultaneously—within the lifetime of one generation—and the impact of knowledge of the change is world-wide. Only yesterday, a New Guinea native's only contact with modern civilization may have been a trade knife that was passed from hand to hand into his village or an airplane seen in the sky; today, as soon as he enters the smallest frontier settlement, he meets the transistor radio. Until yesterday, the village dwellers everywhere were cut off from the urban life of their own country; today radio and television bring them sounds and sights of cities all over the world.

Men who are the carriers of vastly different cultural traditions are entering the present at the same point in time. It is as if, all around the world, men were converging on identical immigration posts, each with its identifying sign: "You are now about to enter the post-World War II world at Gate 1 (or Gate 23 or Gate 2003, etc.)." Whoever they are and wherever their particular point of entry may be, all men are equally immigrants into the new era—some come as refugees and some as castaways.

They are like the immigrants who came as pioneers to a new land, lacking all knowledge of what demands the new conditions of life would make upon them. Those who came later could take their peer groups as models. But among the first comers, the young adults had as models only their own tentative adaptations and innovations. Their past, the culture that had shaped their understanding—their thoughts, their feelings, and their conceptions of the world—was no sure guide to the present. And the elders among them, bound to the past, could provide no models for the future.

Today, everyone born and bred before World War II is such an immigrant in time—as his forebears were in space—struggling to grapple with the unfamiliar conditions of life in a new era. Like all immigrants and pioneers, these immigrants in time are the bearers of older cultures. The difference today is that they represent all the cultures of the world. And all of them, whether they are sophisticated French intellectuals or members of a remote New Guinea tribe, land-bound peasants in Haiti or nuclear physicists, have certain characteristics in common.

Whoever they are, these immigrants grew up under skies across which no satellite had ever flashed. Their perception of the past was an edited version of what had happened. Whether they were wholly dependent on oral memory, art, and drama or also had access to print and still photography and film, what they could know had been altered by the very act of preservation. Their perception of the immediate present was limited to what they could take in through their own eyes and ears and to the edited versions of other men's sensory experience and memories. Their conception of the future was essentially one in which change was incorporated into a deeper changelessness. The New Guinea native, entering the complex modern world, followed cultural models provided by Europeans and expected in some way to share their future. The industrialist or military planner, envisaging what a computer, not yet constructed, might make possible, treated it as another addition to the repertoire of inventions that have enhanced man's skills. It expanded what men could do, but did not change the future.

It is significant that mid-twentieth-century science fiction, written by young writers with little experience of human life, rang untrue to the sophisticated and experienced ear and was less interesting to most well-educated men than such myths as those of Icarus and Daedalus, which include men and gods as well as the mechanisms of flight. Most scientists shared the lack of prescience of other members of their generation and failed to share the dreams of modern science fiction writers.

When the first atom bomb was exploded at the end of World War II, only a few individuals realized that all humanity was entering a new age. And to this day the majority of those over twenty-five have failed to grasp emotionally, however well they may grasp intellectually, the difference between any war in which, no matter how terrible the casualties, mankind will survive, and one in which there will be no survivors. They continue to think that a war, fought with more lethal weapons, would just be a worse war; they still do not grasp the implications of scientific weapons of extinction. Even scientists, when they form committees, are apt to have as their goal not the total abolition of war, but the prevention of the particular kinds of warfare for which they themselves feel an uncomfortable special responsibility—such as the use of pesticides in Vietnam.

In this sense, then, of having moved into a present for which none of us was prepared by our understanding of the past, our interpretations of ongoing experience or our expectations about the future, all of us who grew up before World War II are pioneers, immigrants in time who have left behind our familiar worlds to live in a new age under conditions that are different from any we have known. Our thinking still binds us to the past—to the world as it existed in our childhood and youth. Born and bred before the electronic revolution, most of us do not realize what it means.

We still hold the seats of power and command the resources and the skills necessary to keep order and organize the kinds of societies we know about. We control the educational systems, the apprenticeship systems, the career ladders up which the young must climb, step by step. The elders in the advanced countries control the resources needed by the young and less advanced countries for their development. Nevertheless, we have passed the point of no return. We are committed to life in an unfamiliar setting; we are making do with what we know. We are building makeshift dwellings in old patterns with new and better understood materials.

The young generation, however, the articulate young rebels all around the world who are lashing out against the controls to which they are subjected, are like the first generation born into a new country. They are at home in this time. Satellites are familiar in their skies. They have never known a time when war did not threaten annihilation. Those who use computers do not anthropomorphize them; they know that they are programmed by human beings. When they are given the facts, they can understand immediately that continued pollution of the air and water and soil will soon make the planet uninhabitable and that it will be impossible to feed an indefinitely expanding world population. They can see that control of conception is feasible and necessary. As members of one species in an underdeveloped world community, they recognize that invidious distinctions based on race and caste are anachronisms. They insist on the vital necessity of some form of world order.

They live in a world in which events are presented to them in all their complex immediacy; they are no longer bound by the simplified linear sequences dictated by the printed word. In their eyes the killing of an enemy is not qualitatively different from the murder of a neighbor. They cannot reconcile our efforts to save our own children by every known means with our readiness to destroy the children of others with napalm. Old distinctions between peacetime and wartime, friend and foe, "my" group and "theirs"—the outsiders, the aliens—have lost their meaning. They know that the people of one nation alone cannot save their own children; each holds the responsibility for the others' children.

Although I have said *they know* these things, perhaps I should say that this is *how they feel.* Like the first generation born in a new country, they listen only half-comprehendingly to their parents' talk about the past. For as the children of pioneers had no access to the landscapes, memories of which could still move their parents to tears, the young today cannot share their parents' responses to events that deeply moved them in the past. But this is not all that separates the young from their elders. Watching, they can see that their elders are groping, that they are managing clumsily and often unsuccessfully the tasks imposed on them by the new conditions. They have no firsthand knowledge of the way their parents lived far across the seas, of how differently wood responded to tools, or land to hoe. They see that their elders are using means that are inappropriate, that their performance is poor, and the outcome very uncertain. The young do not know what must be done, but they feel that there must be a better way.

Just how they do feel was expressed in an essay by Shannon Dickson, a fifteen-year-old Texan boy:

> There is a mass confusion in the minds of my generation in trying to find a solution for ourselves and the world around us.
>
> We see the world as a huge rumble as it swiftly goes by with wars, poverty, prejudice, and the lack of understanding among people and nations.
>
> Then we stop and think: there must be a better way and we have to find it.
>
> We see the huge rat race of arguing people trying to beat their fellow man out. All of this builds up, causing unrest between nations and in the home. My generation is being used almost like a machine. We are to learn set standards, strive for better education so we can follow in our elders' footsteps. But why? If we are to be a generation of repetition, the situation will be worse. But how shall we change? We need a great deal of love for everyone, we need a universal understanding among people, we need to think of ourselves and to express our feelings, but that is not all. I have yet to discover what else we need, nor have I practiced these things as fully as I should. Because when I try I'm sneered at by my elders and those who do not hear, or look at it with a closed mind. Computers take the place of minds; electronics are taking over, only confusing things more.
>
> I admit we should follow some basic rules but first you should look at who is making the rules.

*Sometimes I walk down a deserted beach listening to the waves and birds
and I hear them forever calling and forever crying and sometimes we feel that
way but everyone goes on with his own little routines, afraid to stop and listen
for fear of cracking their nutshell.*

The answer is out there somewhere. We need to search for it.

They feel that there must be a better way and that they must find it.

Today, nowhere in the world are there elders who know what the children
know, no matter how remote and simple the societies are in which the children live.
In the past there were always some elders who knew more than any children in terms
of their experience of having grown up within a cultural system. Today there are
none. It is not only that parents are no longer guides, but that there are no guides,
whether one seeks them in one's own country or abroad. There are no elders who
know what those who have been reared within the last twenty years know about
the world into which they were born.

The elders are separated from them by the fact that they, too, are a strangely
isolated generation. No generation has ever known, experienced, and incorporated
such rapid changes, watched the sources of power, the means of communication,
the definition of humanity, the limits of their explorable universe, the certainties of
a known and limited world, the fundamental imperatives of life and death—all change
before their eyes. They know more about change than any generation has ever known
and so stand, over, against, and vastly alienated, from the young, who by the very nature of their position, have had to reject their elders' past.

Just as the early Americans had to teach themselves not to daydream of the
past but concentrate on the present, and so in turn taught their children not to day-
dream but to act, so today's elders have to treat their own past as incommunicable,
and teach their children, even in the midst of lamenting that it is so, not to ask, because they can never understand. We have to realize that no other generation will
ever experience what we have experienced. In this sense we must recognize that we
have no descendants, as our children have no forebears.

The elders are a strangely isolated generation. No other generation has ever
known, experienced, and struggled to incorporate such massive and rapid change—
has watched while the sources of energy, the means of communication, the certainties of a known world, the limits of the explorable universe, the definition of humanity, and the fundamental imperatives of life and death have changed before their
eyes. Adults today know more about change than any previous generation. So we
are set apart both from earlier generations and from the young who have rejected
the past and all that their elders are making of the present.

At this breaking point between two radically different and closely related
groups, both are inevitably very lonely, as we face each other knowing that they will
never experience what we have experienced, and that we can never experience what
they have experienced.

This sense of distance, this feeling of lacking a living connection with members
of the other generation, sometimes takes bizarre forms. In the summer of 1968 a
group of American clergy who were meeting in Uppsala talked with some of the

young American conscientious objectors who had taken refuge in Sweden, and in a written report they said: "We are persuaded that these are our children." They could not take their cultural paternity for granted, but had to persuade themselves that it was so—after long discussion. So incredible it seemed—to believe that any of their children could leave the United States, where, in the past, the persecuted of Europe had taken refuge. They spoke almost as if a process of blood typing had had to be introduced to prove their spiritual paternity.

In most discussions of the generation gap, the alienation of the young is emphasized, while the alienation of their elders may be wholly overlooked. What the commentators forget is that true communication is a dialogue and that both parties to the dialogue lack a vocabulary.

We are familiar with the problems of communication between speakers of two languages who have been reared in radically different cultures, one, for example, in China and the other in the United States. Not only language, but also the incommensurability of their experience prevents them from understanding each other. Yet a willingness to learn the other's language and to explore the premises of both cultures can open the way to conversation. It can be done, but it is not often done.

The problem becomes more difficult, because it is more subtle, when speakers from two different cultures share what is regarded as a common tongue, such as English for Americans and Englishmen, Spanish for Spaniards and Latin Americans. Then true communication becomes possible only when both realize that they speak not one, but two languages in which the "same" words have divergent, sometimes radically different meanings. Then, if they are willing to listen and to ask, they can begin to talk and talk with delight.

This is also the problem of the two generations. Once the fact of a deep, new, unprecedented world-wide generation gap is firmly established, in the minds of both the young and the old, communication can be established again. But as long as any adult thinks that he, like the parents and teachers of old, can become introspective, invoke his own youth to understand the youth before him, then he is lost.

But this is what most elders are still doing. The fact that they delegate authority —that the father sends his sons away to school to learn new ideas and the older scientist sends his pupils to other laboratories to work on newer problems—changes nothing. It only means that parents and teachers are continuing to use the mechanisms of cofiguration characteristic of a world in which parents, having given up the right to teach their own children, expect their children to learn from other adults and their more knowledgeable age mates. Even in science, where we have tried to build in the expectation of discovery and innovations, students learn from old models, and normal young scientists work to fill in blank spaces in accepted paradigms. In today's accelerating rate of scientific discovery, the old are outmoded rapidly and replaced by near peers, but still within a framework of authority.

In the deepest sense, now as in the past, the elders are still in control. And partly because they are in control, they do not realize that the conditions for beginning a new dialogue with the young do not yet exist.

Ironically, it is often those who were, as teachers, very close to former generations of students, who now feel that the generation gap cannot be bridged and that their devotion to teaching has been betrayed by the young who cannot learn in the old ways.

From one point of view the situation in which we now find ourselves can be described as a crisis in faith, in which men, having lost their faith not only in religion but also in political ideology and in science, feel they have been deprived of every kind of security. I believe this crisis in faith can be attributed, at least in part, to the fact that there are now no elders who know more than the young themselves about what the young are experiencing. C. H. Waddington has hypothesized that one component of human evolution and the capacity for choice is the ability of the human child to accept on authority from elders the criteria for right and wrong. The acceptance of the distinction between right and wrong by the child is a consequence of his dependence on parental figures who are trusted, feared, and loved, who hold the child's very life in their hands. But today the elders can no longer present with certainty moral imperatives to the young.

True, in many parts of the world the parental generation still lives by a postfigurative set of values. From parents in such cultures children may learn that there have been unquestioned absolutes, and this learning may carry over into later experience as an expectation that absolute values can and should be re-established. Nativistic cults, dogmatic religious and political movements flourish most vigorously at the point of recent breakdown of postfigurative cultures and least in those cultures in which orderly change is expected to occur within a set of stable values at higher levels of abstraction.

The older industrialized countries of the West have incorporated in their cultural assumptions the idea of change without revolution through the development of new social techniques to deal with the conditions brought about by economic change and technological advances. In these same countries, obsolescence tends to be treated as survival, loved or deprecated as the case may be. In England, the messenger who carried a dispatch case to France was retained long after the dispatches were sent by post; there, too, the pageantry of the throne exists side by side with the parliamentary government that has long superseded the throne as the source of power. In Sweden the most modern laws about sex behavior coexist with the most uncompromising orthodox religious support of an absolute morality.

Similarly, in the United States there is both a deep commitment to developmental change, which is interpreted as progress, and a continuing resort to absolutism, which takes many forms. There are the religious sects and minor political groups, the principal appeal of which is their dogmatism with regard to right and wrong. There are the Utopian communities that have been a constant feature of our social, political, and intellectual development. And there is the tacit acceptance of a color caste system that exists in violation of our declared belief in the fundamental equality of all men.

Elsewhere in the world where change has been rapid, abrupt and often violent, where the idea of orderly processes of change has not taken hold, there is a continuing possibility of sudden eruptions that may take the form of revolutions and counterrevolutions—as in most Latin American countries—or may bring about, in sudden reversal—even though in a new form—the re-establishment of an archaic orthodoxy in which nonbelievers may be persecuted, tortured, and burned alive. The young people, today, who turn themselves into living torches mirror in very complex ways both the attitudes of orthodox absolutism and reactions to it. They follow the example of Buddhists who responded to the dogmatisms of communism and reactive anticommunism with an extreme violation of their own permissive and unabsolute religious values. But their acts also represent, implicitly, the treatment accorded heretics and nonbelievers by any absolutist system that allows no appeal from its dogmas.

There are still parents who answer a child's questions—why must I go to bed? or eat my vegetables? or stop sucking my thumb? or learn to read?—with simple assertions: Because it is *right* to do so, because *God* says so, or because *I* say so. These parents are preparing the way for the re-establishment of postfigurative elements in the culture. But these elements will be far more rigid and intractable than in the past because they must be defended in a world in which conflicting points of view, rather than orthodoxies, are prevalent and accessible.

Most parents, however, are too uncertain to assert old dogmatisms. They do not know how to teach these children who are so different from what they themselves once were, and most children are unable to learn from parents and elders they will never resemble. In the past, in the United States, the children of immigrant parents pleaded with them not to speak their foreign language in public and not to wear their outlandish, foreign clothes. They knew the burning shame of being, at the same time, unable to repudiate their parents and unable to accept simply and naturally their way of speaking and doing things. But in time they learned to find new teachers as guides, to model their behavior on that of more adapted age mates, and to slip in, unnoticed, among a group whose parents were more bearable.

Today the dissident young discover very rapidly that this solution is no longer possible. The breach between themselves and their parents also exists between their friends and their friends' parents and between their friends and their teachers. There are no bearable answers in the old books or in the brightly colored, superficially livened-up new textbooks they are asked to study.

Some look abroad for models. They are attracted by Camus, who, in his conflict between his Algerian birth and his intellectual allegiance to France, expressed some of the conflict they feel; but he is dead. They try to adapt to their own purposes the words of an aging Marxist, Marcuse, or the writings of the existentialists. They develop cultist attitudes of desperate admiration for the heroes of other young revolutionary groups. White students ally themselves with the black separatists. Black students attempt to restructure the past in their struggle to restructure the present.

These young dissidents realize the critical need for immediate world action on problems that affect the whole world. What they want is, in some way, to begin all over again. The idea of orderly, developmental change is lost for this generation of young, who cannot take over the past from their elders, but can only repudiate what their elders are doing now. The past for them is a colossal, unintelligible failure and the future may hold nothing but the destruction of the planet. Caught between the two, they are ready to make way for something new by a kind of social bulldozing—like the bulldozing in which every tree and feature of the landscape is destroyed to make way for a new community. Awareness of the reality of the crisis (which is, in fact, perceived most accurately not by the young, but by their discerning and prophetic elders) and the sense the young have that their elders do not understand the modern world, because they do not understand the modern world, because they do not understand rebellion in which planned reformation of the present system is almost inconceivable.

Nevertheless those who have no power also have no routes to power except through those against whom they are rebelling. In the end, it was men who gave the vote to women; and it will be the House of Lords that votes to abolish the House of Lords, and those over eighteen who must agree if those under eighteen are to vote, as also, in the final analysis, nations will act to limit national sovereignty. Effective, rapid evolutionary change, in which no one is guillotined and no one is forced into exile, depends on the co-operation of a large number of those in power with the dispossessed who are seeking power. The innovating idea may come from others, but the initiative for successful action must come from those whose privileges, now regarded as obsolete, are about to be abolished.

There are those among the dissident young who recognize this. Significantly, they want their parents or those who represent their parents—deans and college presidents and editorial writers—to be on their side, to agree with them or at least to give them a blessing. Behind their demands is their hope that, even as they demonstrate against the college administration, the college president will come and talk with them—and bring his children. But there are also some who entertain no such hope.

I have spoken mainly about the most articulate young people, those who want to drop out of the whole system and those who want to take the system apart and start over. But the feeling that nothing out of the past is meaningful and workable is very much more pervasive. Among the less articulate it is expressed in such things as the refusal to learn at school, co-operate at work, or follow normal political paths. Perhaps most noncompliance is of this passive kind. But the periodic massing of students behind their more active peers suggests that even passive noncompliance is highly inflammable.

Resistance among the young is also expressed by an essentially uninvolved and exploitative compliance with rules that are regarded as meaningless. Perhaps those who take this stand are the most frightening. Going through the forms by which men were educated for generations, but which no longer serve to educate those who accept them, can only teach students to regard all social systems in terms of exploitation.

But whatever stand they take, none of the young, neither the most idealistic nor the most cynical, is untouched by the sense that there are no adults anywhere in the world from whom they can learn what the next steps should be.

These, in brief, are the conditions of our time. These are the two generations —pioneers in a new era and their children, who have as yet to find a way of communicating about the world in which both live, though their perceptions of it are so different. No one knows what the next steps should be. Recognizing that this is so is, I submit, the beginning of an answer.

For I believe we are on the verge of developing a new kind of culture, one that is as much a departure in style from cofigurative cultures, as the institutionalization of cofiguration in orderly—and disorderly—change was a departure from the post-figurative style. I call this new style *prefigurative,* because in this new culture it will be the child—and not the parent and grandparent that represents what is to come. Instead of the erect, white-haired elder who, in postfigurative cultures, stood for the past and the future in all their grandeur and continuity, the unborn child, already conceived but still in the womb, must become the symbol of what life will be like. This is a child whose sex and appearance and capabilities are unknown. This is a child who is a genius or suffers from some deep impairment, who will need imaginative, innovative, and dedicated adult care far beyond any we give today.

About the unborn child little can be known with certainty. We can tell with delicate instruments that supplement the ear that the child is alive, that its heart is beating. Other instruments, still more delicate, can give some clues as to the child's well-being. We can predict the approximate time when it will be born. We know that unless the mother is protected, nourished, and cared for, the child's chance for life will sink with her own; should she sicken and die, the child's life will also flicker out. But all else is promise.

No one can know in advance what the child will become—how swift his limbs will be, what will delight his eye, whether his tempo will be fast or slow, whether he will waken ready to cope with the world or only reach his best hours when the day people are tiring. No one can know how his mind will work—whether he will learn best from sight or sound or touch or movement. But knowing what we do not know and cannot predict, we can construct an environment in which a child, still unknown, can be safe and can grow and discover himself and the world.

In a safe and flexible environment there must be skilled care, anesthetics, oxygen, and blood on hand to protect the mother and the child in a difficult birth. There must be supportive care for the mother who becomes depressed or frightened. There must be artificial food for the infant who cannot be breast-fed. For the child who cannot sleep in the dark, there must be soft light. For the child who is sensitive to sound, there must be ways of muting noise.

As the child begins to reach out to people, he must be carried—held or propped or cradled—into company. As his eyes respond to color, there must be many colors, differing in hue, saturation, and brightness, for him to choose among. There must be many kinds of objects for him to classify, many rhythms and melodies to start him dancing. And as he begins to form an image of the world, he must have examples of the worlds other men have made and crayons and paints and clay so he can give form to the world of his own imagination.

Even so simple an enumeration of ways of meeting a child's needs makes us conscious of how much children have been bound to the ways of their forebears through love and dependence and trust. It also makes us conscious of how little flexibility there is in the child's dependence on adults as compared to the great flexibility that can be developed in the adult's succoring care. Without adult care, the infant will die in a few hours. Without adult care, the child will never learn to speak. Without the experience of trust, the child will never become a trusting member of society, who is able to love and care for others. The child is wholly dependent, and it is on this dependency that human culture has been built as, generation after generation for hundreds of thousands of years, adults have imposed on children, through their care for them, their vision of what life should be. Dependency has made conscience possible and, as both Julian Huxley and C. H. Waddington have argued so eloquently, ethics are not external to nature but are crucial to human evolution.

The continuity of culture and the incorporation of every innovation depended on the success of the postfigurative system by which the young were taught to replicate the lives of their ancestors. Then, as men learned to live in many different environments and as they traveled and traded with one another, contrasts among different postfigurative cultures began to provide the necessary conditions for change and for the development of cofigurative cultures in which people who had been reared to one form of commitment learned to adapt themselves to other forms but with the same absolute commitment.

Later, as the idea of change became embodied as a postfigurative element in many cultures, the young could learn from their elders that they should go beyond them—achieve more and do different things. But this beyond was always within the informed imagination of their elders; the son might be expected to cross the seas his father never crossed, study nuclear physics when his father had only an elementary school education, fly in the plane which his father watched from the ground. The peasant's son became a scholar; the poor man's son crossed the ocean his father had never seen; the teacher's son became a scientist.

Love and trust, based on dependency and answering care, made it possible for the individual who had been reared in one culture to move into another, transforming without destroying his earlier learning. It is seldom the first generation of voluntary immigrants and pioneers who cannot meet the demands of a new environment. Their previous learning carries them through. But unless they embody what is new postfiguratively, they cannot pass on to their children what they themselves had acquired through their own early training—the ability to learn from others the things their parents could not teach them.

Now, in a world in which there are no more knowledgeable others to whom parents can commit the children they themselves cannot teach, parents feel uncertain and helpless. Still believing that there should be answers, parents ask: How can we tell our children what is right? So some parents try to solve the problem by advising their children, very vaguely: You will have to figure that out for yourselves. And some parents ask: What are the others doing? But this resource of a cofigurative culture is becoming meaningless to parents who feel that the "others"—their children's age mates—are moving in ways that are unsafe for their own children to emulate and who find that they do not understand what their children figure out for themselves.

It is the adults who still believe that there is a safe and socially approved road to a kind of life they themselves have not experienced who react with the greatest anger and bitterness to the discovery that what they had hoped for no longer exists for their children. These are the parents, the trustees, the legislators, the columnists, and commentators who denounce most vocally what is happening in schools and colleges and universities in which they had placed their hopes for their children.

Today, as we are coming to understand better the circular processes through which culture is developed and transmitted, we recognize that man's most human characteristic is not his ability to learn, which he shares with many other species, but his ability to teach and store what others have developed and taught him. Learning, which is based on human dependency, is relatively simple. But human capacities for creating elaborate teachable systems, for understanding and utilizing the resources of the natural world, and for governing society and creating imaginary worlds, all these are very complex. In the past, men relied on the least elaborate part of the circular system, the dependent learning by children, for continuity of transmission and for the embodiment of the new. Now, with our greater understanding of the process, we must cultivate the most flexible and complex part of the system—the behavior of adults. We must, in fact, teach ourselves how to alter adult behavior so that we can give up postfigurative upbringing, with its tolerated cofigurative components, and discover prefigurative ways of teaching and learning that will keep the future open. We must create new models for adults who can teach their children not what to learn, but how to learn and not what they should be committed to, but the value of commitment.

Postfigurative cultures, which focused on the elders—those who had learned the most and were able to do the most with what they had learned—were essentially closed systems that continually replicated the past. We must now move toward the creation of open systems that focus on the future—and so on children, those whose capacities are least known and whose choices must be left open.

In doing this we explicitly recognize that the paths by which we came into the present can never be traversed again. The past is the road by which we have arrived where we are. Older forms of culture have provided us with the knowledge, the techniques, and the tools necessary for our contemporary civilization. Coming by different roads out of the past, all the peoples of the earth are now arriving in the new world community. No road into the present need be repudiated and no former way of life forgotten. But all these different pasts, our own and all others, must be treated as precursors.

It is significant how extremely difficult it has been even for the prophetic writers of science fiction to imagine and accept an unknown future. At the close of *Childhood's End,* Arthur Clarke wrote: "The stars are not for men."

Space operas picture the return of the last broken spaceship from imagined galactic societies to the "hall of the beginning" on Terra of Sol. In the *Midwich Cuckoos,* John Wyndham killed off the strange golden-eyed, perceptive children bred by earth women to visitors from outer space. The film, *2001: A Space Odyssey,* ended in failure. This deep unwillingness to have children go too far into the future suggests that the adult imagination, acting alone, remains fettered to the past.

So the freeing of men's imagination from the past depends, I believe, on the development of a new kind of communication with those who are most deeply involved with the future—the young who were born in the new world. That is, it depends on the direct participation of those who, up to now, have not had access to power and whose nature those in power cannot fully imagine. In the past, in cofigurational cultures, the elders were gradually cut off from limiting the future of their children. Now, as I see it, the development of prefigurational cultures will depend on the existence of a continuing dialogue in which the young, free to act on their own initiative, can lead their elders in the direction of the unknown. Then the older generation will have access to the new experiential knowledge, without which no meaningful plans can be made. It is only with the direct participation of the young, who have that knowledge, that we can build a viable future.

Instead of directing their rebellion toward the retrieval of a grandparental Utopian dream, as the Maoists seem to be doing with the young activists in China, we must learn together with the young how to take the next steps. Out of their new knowledge—new to the world and new to us—must come the questions to those who are already equipped by education and experience to search for answers.

Archibald Macleish wrote in *The Hamlet of A. Macleish,*

We have learned the answers, all the answers:
It is the question that we do not know.

His book was sent to me in 1928 while I was in the Admiralties, studying the Manus. At that time it seemed almost certain that the Manus, a people still proudly adapted to their stone-age culture, whose only experience of another kind of civilization was with the dehumanizing and degrading contact-culture, would eventually become poorly educated proletarians in a world they could neither understand nor influence.

Today, forty years later, the Manus people have skipped thousands of years and been able to take their destiny in their own hands, as they could not in the days when, locked within the stone age, they bullied and ravished the villages of their less aggressive neighbors. Today they are preparing their children for college, for law schools and medical schools, and transferring the leadership they once exercised, fitfully and with poor organization, in a tiny archipelago, as a tribe, into the wider world of a developing nation. And today, when the quotation came back to me, I phrased it differently because now we can say that we *do* know at least who must ask the questions if we, who have a long heritage of answers at our disposal, are to be able to answer them. The children, the young, must ask the questions that we would never think to ask, but enough trust must be re-established so that the elders will be permitted to work with them on the answers. As in a new country with makeshift shelters adapted hastily from out-of-date models, the children must be able to proclaim that they are cold and where the drafts are coming from. Father is still the man who has the skill and the strength to cut down the tree to build a different kind of house.

During the last few years, I have been exposed to something that I at first branded as a temptation. Young people sometimes turn to me, when we have been co-operating vividly in a goal we share, and say, "You belong to us." This I felt to be a temptation which must be resisted at all costs, especially in a country where youth, in every form, is a tempting refuge for the middle-aged and aging. So I used to reply, "No, I do not belong to your generation. You think I do because you are currently in favor of things that I have been working on for forty years. But that does not make me a member of your generation. And how do I know that you will not in fact, be opposing these very goals ten years from now?" But I think that this reply was another example of our insistence that the future will be like the past, that most people go through cycles of revolt and reaction, that experience in the past can be applied to the future. Because I made that assumption I failed to see that perhaps they may have been saying something different. I was reared, as they wish they had been, by a grandmother and parents who did not think they could set their children's feet on any given path. I was reared almost seven decades ahead of my time, as to-day's twenty-year-olds proclaim they will rear their children, leaving them free to grow, straight and tall, into a future that must be left open and free. It is in a sense as a tribute to such a childhood that I am able to insist that we can change into a prefigurative culture, consciously, delightedly, and industriously, rearing unknown children for an unknown world.

But to do this we, the peoples of the world, must relocate the future. For the West the future has lain ahead of us, sometimes only a few hours ahead, sometimes a thousand years ahead, but always ahead, not here yet, beyond our reach. For many Oceanic peoples, the future lies behind, not before. For the Balinese the future is like an exposed but undeveloped film, slowly unrolling, while men stand and wait for what will be revealed. It is seen catching up with them, a figure of speech that we, too, use when we speak of hearing time's relentless footsteps behind us.

If we are to build a prefigurative culture in which the past is instrumental rather than coercive, we must change the location of the future. Here again we can take a cue from the young who seem to want instant Utopias. They say: The Future Is Now. This seems unreasonable and impetuous, and in some of the demands they make it is unrealizable in concrete detail; but here again, I think they give us the way to reshape our thinking. We must place the future, like the unborn child in the womb of a woman, within a community of men, women, and children, among us, already here, already to be nourished and succored and protected, already in need of things for which, if they are not prepared before it is born, it will be too late. So, as the young say, The Future Is Now.

Tom Wolfe

The Pump House Gang

Our boys never hair out. The black panther has black feet. Black feet on the crum-bling black panther. Pan-thuh. Mee-dah. Pam Stacy, 16 years old, a cute girl here in La Jolla, California, with a pair of orange bell-bottom hip-huggers on, sits on a step about four steps down the stairway to the beach and she can see a pair of revolting black feet without lifting her head. So she says it out loud, "The black panther."

Somebody farther down the stairs, one of the boys with the *major* hair and khaki shorts, says, "The black feet of the black panther."

"Mee-dah," says another kid. This happens to be the cry of a, well, *underground* society known as the Mac Meda Destruction Company.

"The pan-thuh."

"The poon-thuh."

All these kids, seventeen of them, members of the Pump House crowd, are lollygagging around the stairs down to Windansea Beach, La Jolla, California, about 11 a.m., and they all look at the black feet, which are a woman's pair of black street shoes, out of which stick a pair of old veiny white ankles, which lead up like a senile cone to a fudge of tallowy, edematous flesh, her thighs, squeezing out of her bathing suit, with old faded yellow bruises on them, which she probably got from running eight feet to catch a bus or something. She is standing with her old work-a-hubby, who has on *san*dals: you know, a pair of navy-blue anklet socks and these sandals with big, wide, new-smelling tan straps going this way and that, *for keeps.* Man, they look like orthopedic sandals, if one can imagine that. Obviously, these people come from Tucson or Albuquerque or one of those hincty adobe towns. All these hincty, crumbling black feet come to La Jolla-by-the-sea from the adobe towns for the week-end. They even drive in cars all full of thermos bottles and mayonnaisey sandwiches and some kind of latticework wooden-back support for the old crock who drives and Venetian blinds on the back window.

"The black panther."

"Pan-thuh."

"Poon-thuh."

"Mee-dah."

Nobody says it to the two old crocks directly. God, they must be practically 50 years old. Naturally, they're carrying every piece of garbage imaginable: the folding aluminum chairs, the newspapers, the lending-library book with the clear plastic wrapper on it, the sunglasses, the sun ointment, about a vat of goo—

It is a Mexican standoff. In a Mexican standoff, both parties narrow their eyes and glare but nobody throws a punch. Of course, nobody in the Pump House crowd would ever even jostle these people or say anything right to them; they are too cool for that.

Everybody in the Pump House crowd looks over, even Tom Coman, who is a cool person. Tom Coman, 16 years old, got thrown out of his garage last night. He is sitting up on top of the railing, near the stairs, up over the beach, with his legs apart. Some nice long willowy girl in yellow slacks is standing on the sidewalk but leaning into him with her arms around his body, just resting. Neale Jones, 16, a boy with great lank perfect surfer's hair, is standing nearby with a Band-Aid on his upper lip, where the sun has burnt it raw. Little Vicki Ballard is up on the sidewalk. Her older sister, Liz, is down the stairs by the Pump House itself, a concrete block, 15 feet high, full of machinery for the La Jolla water system. Liz is wearing her great "Liz" styles, a hulking rabbit-fur vest and black-leather boots over her Levis, even though it is about 85 out here and the sun is plugged in up there like God's own dentist lamp and the Pacific is heaving in with some fair-to-middling surf. Kit Tilden is lollygagging around, and Tom Jones, Connie Carter, Roger Johnson, Sharon Sand-quist, Mary Beth White, Rupert Fellows, Glenn Jackson, Dan Watson from San Diego, they are all out here, and everybody takes a look at the panthers.

The old guy, one means, you know, he must be practically 50 years old, he says to his wife, "Come on, let's go farther up," and he takes her by her fat upper arm as if to wheel her around and aim her away from here.

But she says, "No! We have just as much right to be here as they do."

"That's *not the point—*"

"Are you going to—"

"*Mrs. Roberts,*" the work-a-hubby says, calling his own wife by her official married name, as if to say she took a vow once and his word is law, even if he is not testing it with the blond kids here—"farther up, *Mrs. Roberts.*"

They start to walk up the sidewalk, but one kid won't move his feet, and, oh, god, her work-a-hubby breaks into a terrible shaking Jello smile as she steps over them, as if to say, Excuse me, sir, I don't mean to make trouble, please, and don't you and your colleagues rise up and jump me, screaming *Gotcha—*

Mee-dah!

But exactly! This beach *is* verboten for people practically 50 years old. This is a segregated beach. They can look down on Windansea Beach and see nothing but lean tan kids. It is posted "no swimming" (for safety reasons), meaning surfing only. In effect, it is segregated by age. From Los Angeles on down the California coast, this is an era of age segregation. People have always tended to segregate themselves by age, teenagers hanging around with teenagers, old people with old people, like the old men who sit on the benches up near the Bronx Zoo and smoke black cigars. But before, age segregation has gone on within a larger community. Sooner or later during the day everybody has melted back into the old community network that embraces practically everyone, all ages.

But in California today surfers, not to mention rock 'n' roll kids and the hot-rodders or Hair Boys, named for their fanciful pompadours—all sorts of sets of kids—they don't merely hang around together. They establish whole little societies for themselves. In some cases they live with one another for months at a time. The "Sunset Strip" on Sunset Boulevard used to be a kind of Times Square for Holly-wood hot dogs of all ages, anyone who wanted to promenade in his version of the high life. Today "The Strip" is almost completely the preserve of kids from about 16 to 25. It is lined with go-go clubs. One of them, a place called It's Boss, is set up for people 16 to 25 and won't let in anybody over 25, and there are some terrible I'm-dying-a-thousand-deaths scenes when a girl comes up with her boyfriend and the guy at the door at It's Boss doesn't think she looks under 25 and tells her she will have to produce some identification proving she is young enough to come in here and live The Strip kind of life and—she's *had* it, because she can't get up the I.D. and nothing in the world is going to make a woman look stupider than to stand around trying to argue *I'm younger than I look, I'm younger than I look.* So she practically shrivels up like a Peruvian shrunken head in front of her boyfriend and he trundles her off, looking for some place you can get an old doll like this into.

One of the few remaining clubs for "older people," curiously, is the Playboy Club. There are apartment houses for people 20 to 30 only, such as the Sheri Plaza in Holly-wood and the E'Questre Inn in Burbank. There are whole suburban housing develop-ments, mostly private developments, where only people over 45 or 50 can buy a house. Whole towns, meantime, have become identified as "young": Venice, New-port Beach, Balboa—or "old": Pasadena, Riverside, Coronado Island.

Behind much of it—especially something like a whole nightclub district of a major city, "The Strip," going teenage—is, simply, money. World War II and the prosperity that followed pumped incredible amounts of money into the population, the white population at least, at every class level. All of a sudden here is an area with thousands of people from 16 to 25 who can get their hands on enough money to support a whole nightclub belt and to have the cars to get there and to set up auton-omous worlds of their own in a fairly posh resort community like La Jolla—

—Tom Coman's garage. Some old bastard took Tom Coman's garage away from him, and that means eight or nine surfers are out of a place to stay.

"I went by there this morning, you ought to see the guy," Tom Coman says. Yellow Stretch Pants doesn't move. She has him around the waist. "He was out there painting and he had this brush and about a thousand gallons of ammonia. He was really going to scrub me out of there."

"What did he do with the furniture?"

"I don't know. He threw it out."

"What are you going to do?"

"I don't know."

"Where are you going to stay?"

"I don't know. I'll stay on the beach. It wouldn't be the first time. I haven't had a place to stay for three years, so I'm not going to start worrying now."

Everybody thinks that over awhile. Yellow Stretch just hangs on and smiles. Tom Coman, 16 years old, piping fate again. One of the girls says, "You can stay at my place, Tom."

"Um. Who's got a cigarette?"

Pam Stacy says, "You can have these."

Tom Coman lights a cigarette and says, "Let's have a destructo." A destructo is what can happen in a garage after eight or 10 surfers are kicked out of it.

"Mee-dah!"

"Wouldn't that be bitchen?" says Tom Coman. Bitchen is a surfer's term that means "great," usually.

"Bitchen!"

"Mee-dah!"

It's incredible—that old guy out there trying to scour the whole surfing life out of that garage. He's a pathetic figure. His shoulders are hunched over and he's dousing and scrubbing away and the sun doesn't give him a tan, it gives him these ... *mottles* on the back of his neck. But never mind! The hell with destructo. One only has a destructo spontaneously, a Dionysian ... *bursting out,* like those holes through the wall during the Mac Meda Destruction Company Convention at Man-hattan Beach—Mee-dah!

Something will pan out. It's a magic economy—yes!—all up and down the coast from Los Angeles to Baja California kids can go to one of these beach towns and live the complete surfing life. They take off from home and get to the beach, and if they need a place to stay, well, somebody rents a garage for twenty bucks a month and everybody moves in, girls and boys. Furniture—it's like, one means, you know, one *appropriates* furniture from here and there. It's like the Volkswagen buses a lot of kids now use as beach wagons instead of woodies. Woodies are old station wagons, usually Fords, with wooden bodies, from back before 1953. One of the great things about a Volkswagen bus is that one can . . . *exchange* motors in about three minutes A good VW motor exchanger can go up to a parked Volkswagen, and a few ratchets of the old wrench here and it's up and out and he has a new motor. There must be a few nice old black panthers around wondering why their nice hubby-mommy VWs don't run so good anymore—but—then—they—are—probably—puzzled—about—a—lot of things. Yes.

Cash—it's practically in the air. Around the beach in La Jolla a guy can walk right out in the street and stand there, stop cars and make the candid move. Mister, I've got a quarter, how about 50 cents so I can get a *large* draft. Or, I need some after-ski boots. And the panthers give one a Jello smile and hand it over. Or a guy who knows how to do it can get $40 from a single night digging clams, and it's nice out there. Or he can go around and take up a collection for a keg party, a keg of beer. Man, anybody who won't kick in a quarter for a keg is a jerk. A couple of good keg collections—that's a trip to Hawaii, which is the surfer's version of a trip to Europe: there is a great surf and great everything there. Neale spent three weeks in Hawaii last year. He got $30 from a girl friend, he scrounged a little here and there and got $70 more and he headed off for Hawaii with $100.02, that being the exact plane fare, and borrowed 25 cents when he got there to . . . blast the place up. He spent the 25 cents in a photo booth, showed the photos to the people on the set of *Hawaii* and got a job in the movie. What's the big orgy about money? It's warm, nobody even wears shoes, nobody is starving.

All right, Mother gets worried about all this, but it is limited worry, as John Shine says. Mainly, Mother says, *Sayonara*, you all, and you head off for the beach.

The thing is, everybody, practically everybody, comes from a good family. Everyone has been . . . *reared well*, as they say. Everybody is very upper-middle, if you want to bring it down to that. It's just that this is a new order. Why hang around in the hubby-mommy household with everybody getting neurotic hang-ups with each other and slamming doors and saying, Why can't they have some privacy? Or, it doesn't mean anything that I have to work for a living, does it? It doesn't mean a thing to you. All of you just lie around here sitting in the big orange easy chair smoking cigarettes. I'd hate for you to have to smoke standing up, you'd probably get phlebitis from it—Listen to me, Sarah—

—why go through all that? It's a good life out here. Nobody is mugging everybody for money and affection. There are a lot of bright people out here, and there are a lot of interesting things. One night there was a toga party in a garage, and everybody dressed in sheets, like togas, boys and girls and they put on the appropriated television set to an old Deanna Durbin movie and turned off the sound and put on Rolling Stones records, and you should have seen Deanna Durbin opening her puckered kumquat mouth with Mick Jagger's voice bawling out, *I ain't got no satisfaction.* Of course, finally everybody started pulling the togas off each other, but that is another thing. And one time they had a keg party down on the beach in Mission Bay and the lights from the amusement park were reflected all over the water and that, the whole design of the thing, those nutty lights, that was part of the party. Liz put out the fire throwing a "sand potion" or something on it. One can laugh at Liz and her potions, her necromancy and everything; but there is a lot of thought going into it, a lot of, well, mysticism.

You can even laugh at mysticism if you want to, but there is a kid like Larry Alderson, who spent two years with a monk, and he learned a lot of stuff, and Artie Nelander is going to spend next summer with some Outer Mongolian tribe; he really means to do that. Maybe the "mysterioso" stuff is a lot of garbage, but still, it is interesting. The surfers around the Pump House use that word, mysterioso, quite a lot. It refers to the mystery of the Oh Mighty Hulking Pacific Ocean and everything. Sometimes a guy will stare at the surf and say, "Mysterioso." They keep telling the story of Bob Simmons' wipeout, and somebody will say "mysterioso."

Simmons was a fantastic surfer. He was fantastic even though he had a bad leg. He rode the really big waves. One day he got wiped out at Windansea. When a big wave overtakes a surfer, it drives him right to the bottom. The board came in but he never came up and they never found his body. Very mysterioso. The black panthers all talked about what happened to "the Simmons boy." But the mysterioso thing was how he could have died at all. If he had been one of the old pan-thuhs, hell, sure he could have got killed. But Simmons was, well, one's own age, he was the kind of guy who could have been in the Pump House gang, he was . . . *immune,* he was plugged into the whole pattern, he could feel the whole Oh Mighty Hulking Sea, he didn't have to think it out step by step. But he got wiped out and killed. Very mysterioso.

Immune! If one is in the Pump House gang and really keyed in to this whole thing, it's—well, one is . . . *immune,* one is not full of black pan-thuh panic. Two kids, a 14-year-old girl and a 16-year-old boy, go out to Windansea at dawn, in the middle of winter, cold as hell, and take on 12-foot waves all by themselves. The girl, Jackie Haddad, daughter of a certified public accountant, wrote a composition about it, just for herself, called "My Ultimate Journey":

"It was six o'clock in the morning, damp, foggy and cold. We could feel the bitter air biting at our cheeks. The night before, my friend Tommy and I had seen one of the greatest surf films, *Surf Classics.* The film had excited us so much we made up our minds to go surfing the following morning. That is what brought us down on the cold, wet, soggy sand of Windansea early on a December morning.

"We were the first surfers on the beach. The sets were rolling in at eight to 10, filled with occasional 12-footers. We waxed up and waited for a break in the waves. The break came, neither of us said a word, but instantly grabbed our boards and ran into the water. The paddle out was difficult, not being used to the freezing water.

"We barely made it over the first wave of the set, a large set. Suddenly Tommy put on a burst of speed and shot past me. He cleared the biggest wave of the set. It didn't hit me hard as I rolled under it. It dragged me almost 20 yards before exhausting its strength. I climbed on my board gasping for air. I paddled out to where Tommy was resting. He laughed at me for being wet already. I almost hit him but I began laughing, too. We rested a few minutes and then lined up our position with a well known spot on the shore.

"I took off first. I bottom-turned hard and started climbing up the wave. A radical cut-back caught me off balance and I fell, barely hanging onto my board. I recovered in time to see Tommy go straight over the falls on a 10-footer. His board shot nearly 30 feet in the air. Luckily, I could get it before the next set came in, so Tommy didn't have to make the long swim in. I pushed it to him and then laughed. All of a sudden Tommy yelled, 'Outside!'

"Both of us paddled furiously. We barely made it up to the last wave, it was a monster. In precision timing we wheeled around and I took off. I cut left in reverse stance, then cut back, driving hard toward the famous Windansea bowl. As I crouched, a huge wall of energy came down over me, covering me up. I moved toward the nose to gain more speed and shot out of the fast-flowing suction just in time to kick out as the wave closed out.

"As I turned around I saw Tommy make a beautiful drop-in, then the wave peaked and fell all at once. Miraculously he beat the suction. He cut back and did a spinner, which followed with a reverse kick-up.

"Our last wave was the biggest. When we got to shore, we rested, neither of us saying a word, but each lost in his own private world of thoughts. After we had rested, we began to walk home. We were about half way and the rain came pouring down. That night we both had bad colds, but we agreed it was worth having them after the thrill and satisfaction of an extra good day of surfing."

John Shine and Artie Nelander are out there right now. They are just "outside," about one fifth of a mile out from the shore, beyond where the waves start breaking. They are straddling their surfboards with their backs to the shore, looking out toward the horizon, waiting for a good set. Their backs look like some kind of salmon-colored porcelain shells, a couple of tiny shells bobbing up and down as the swells roll under them, staring out to sea like Phrygian sacristans looking for a sign.

John and Artie! They are—they are what one means when one talks about the surfing life. It's like, you know, one means, they have this life all of their own; it's like a glass-bottom boat, and it floats over the "real" world, or the square world or whatever one wants to call it. They are not exactly off in a world of their own, they are and they aren't. What it is, they float right through the real world, but it can't touch them. They do these things, like the time they went to Malibu, and there was this party in some guy's apartment, and there wasn't enough *legal* parking space for everybody, and so somebody went out and painted the red curbs white and everybody parked. Then the cops came. Everybody ran out. Artie and John took an airport bus to the Los Angeles Airport, just like they were going to take a plane, in khaki shorts and T-shirts with Mac Meda Destruction Company stenciled on them. Then they took a helicopter to Disneyland. At Disneyland crazy Ditch had his big raincoat on and a lot of flasks strapped onto his body underneath. Scotch, bourbon, all kinds of stuff. He had plastic tubes from the flasks sticking out of the flyfront of his raincoat and everybody was sipping whiskey through the tubes—

—Ooooo-eeee—Mee-dah! They chant this chant, Mee-dah, in a real fakey deep voice, and it *really bugs people.* They don't know what the hell it is. It is the cry of the Mac Meda Destruction Company. The Mac Meda Destruction Company is . . . an *underground* society that started in La Jolla about three years ago. Nobody can remember exactly how; they have arguments about it. Anyhow, it is mainly something to *bug* people with and organize huge beer orgies with. They have their own complete, bogus phone number in La Jolla. They have Mac Meda Destruction Company decals. They stick them on phone booths, on cars, any place. Some mommy-hubby will come out of the shopping plaza and walk up to his Mustang, which is supposed to make him a hell of a tiger now, and he'll see a sticker on the side of it saying, "Mac Meda Destruction Company," and for about two days or something he'll think the sky is going to fall in.

But the big thing is the parties, the "conventions." Anybody can join, any kid, anybody can come, as long as they've heard about it, and they can only hear about it by word of mouth. One was in the Sorrento Valley, in the gulches and arroyos, and the fuzz came, and so the older guys put the young ones and the basket cases, the ones just too stoned out of their gourds, into the tule grass, and the cops shined their searchlights and all they saw was tule grass, while the basket cases moaned scarlet and oozed on their bellies like reptiles and everybody else ran down the arroyos, yelling Mee-dah.

The last one was at Manhattan Beach, inside somebody's poor hulking house. The party got *very Dionysian* that night and somebody put a hole through one wall, and everybody else decided to see if they could make it bigger. Everybody was stoned out of their hulking gourds, and it got to be about 3:30 a.m. and everybody decided to go see the riots. These were the riots in Watts. The Los Angeles *Times* and the San Diego *Union* were all saying, WATTS NO-MAN'S LAND and STAY WAY FROM WATTS YOU GET YO' SE'F KILLED, but naturally nobody believed that. Watts was a blast, and the Pump House gang was immune to the trembling gourd panic rattles of the L. A. *Times* black pan-thuhs. Immune!

So John Shine, Artie Nelander and Jerry Sterncorb got in John's VW bus, known as the Hog of Steel, and they went to Watts. Gary Wickham and some other guys ran into an old man at a bar who said he owned a house in Watts and had been driven out by the drunk niggers. So they drove in a car to save the old guy's house from the drunk niggers. Artie and John had a tape recorder and decided they were going to make a record called "Random Sounds from the Watts Riots." They drove right into Watts in the Hog of Steel and there was blood on the streets and roofs blowing off the stores and all these apricot flames and drunk Negroes falling through the busted plate glass of the liquor stores. Artie got a nice recording of a lot of Negroes chanting "Burn, baby, burn." They all got out and talked to some Negro kids in a gang going into a furniture store, and the Negro kids didn't say Kill Whitey or Geed'um or any of that. They just said, Come on, man, it's a party and it's free. After they had been in there for about three hours talking to Negroes and watching drunks collapse in the liquor stores, some cop with a helmet on came roaring up and said, "Get the hell out of here, you kids, we cannot and will not provide protection."

Meantime, Gary Wickham and his friends drove in in a car with the old guy, and a car full of Negroes *did* stop them and say, Whitey, Geed'um, and all that stuff, but one of the guys in Gary's car just draped a pistol he had out the window and the colored guys drove off. Gary and everybody drove the old guy to his house and they all walked in and had a great raunchy time drinking beer and raising hell. A couple of Negroes, the old guy's neighbors, came over and told the old guy to cut out the racket. There were flames in the sky and ashes coming down with little rims of fire on them, like apricot crescents. The old guy got very cocky about all his "protection" and went out on the front porch about dawn and started yelling at some Negroes across the street, telling them "No more drunk niggers in Watts" and a lot of other unwise slogans. So Gary Wickham got up and everybody left. They were there about four hours altogether and when they drove out, they had to go through a National Guard checkpoint, and a lieutenant from the San Fernando Valley told them he could not and would not provide protection.

But exactly! Watts just happened to be what was going on at the time, as far as the netherworld of La Jolla surfing was concerned, and so one goes there and sees what is happening and comes back and tells everybody about it and laughs at the L.A. *Times.* That is what makes it so weird when all these black pan-thuhs come around to pick up "surfing styles," like the clothing manufacturers. They don't know what any of it means. It's like archaeologists discovering hieroglyphics or something, and they say, god, that's neat—Egypt!—but they don't know what the hell it is. They don't know anything about . . . *The Life.* It's great to think of a lot of old emphysematous pan-thuhs in the Garment District in New York City struggling in off the street against a gummy 15-mile-an-hour wind full of soot and coffee-brown snow and gasping in the elevator to clear their old nicotine-phlegm tubes on the way upstairs to make out the invoices on a lot of surfer stuff for 1966, the big nylon windbreakers with the wide, white horizontal competition stripes, nylon swimming trunks with competition stripes, bell-bottom slacks for girls, the big hairy sleeveless jackets, vests, the blue "tennies," meaning tennis shoes, and the . . . *look,* the Major Hair, all this long lank blond hair, the plain face kind of tanned and bleached out at the same time, but with big eyes. It all starts in a few places, a few strategic groups, the Pump House gang being one of them, and then it moves up the beach, to places like Newport Beach and as far up as Malibu.

Well, actually there is a kind of back-and-forth thing with some of the older guys, the old heroes of surfing, like Bruce Brown, John Severson, Hobie Alter and Phil Edwards. Bruce Brown will do one of those incredible surfing movies and he is out in the surf himself filming Phil Edwards coming down a 20-footer in Hawaii, and Phil has on a pair of nylon swimming trunks, which he has had made in Hawaii, because they dry out fast—and it is like a grapevine. Everybody's got to have a pair of nylon swimming trunks, and then the manufacturers move in, and everybody's making nylon swimming trunks, boxer trunk style, and pretty soon every kid in Utica, N.Y., is buying a pair of them, with the competition stripe and the whole thing, and they never heard of Phil Edwards. So it works back and forth—but so what? Phil Edwards is part of it. He may be an old guy, he is 28 years old, but he and Bruce Brown, who is even older, 30, and John Severson, 32, and Hobie Alter, 29, never haired out to the square world even though they make thousands. Hair refers to courage. A guy who "has a lot of hair" is courageous; a guy who "hairs out" is yellow.

Bruce Brown and Severson and Alter are known as the "surfing millionaires." They are not millionaires, actually, but they must be among the top businessmen south of Los Angeles. Brown grossed something around $500,000 in 1965 even before his movie *Endless Summer* became a hit nationally; and he has only about three people working for him. He goes out on a surfboard with a camera encased in a plastic shell and takes his own movies and edits them himself and goes around showing them himself and narrating them at places like the Santa Monica Civic Auditorium, where 24,000 came in eight days once, at $1.50 a person, and all he has to pay is for developing the film and hiring the hall. John Severson has the big surfing magazine, *Surfer*. Hobie Alter is the biggest surfboard manufacturer, all hand-made boards. He made 5,000 boards in 1965 at $140 a board. He also designed the "Hobie" skate boards and gets 25 cents for every one sold. He grossed between $900,000 and $1 million in 1964.

God, if only everybody could grow up like these guys and know that crossing the horror dividing line, 25 years old, won't be the end of everything. One means, keep on living *The Life* and not get sucked into the ticky-tacky life with some insurance salesman sitting forward in your stuffed chair on your wall-to-wall telling you that life is like a football game and you sit there and take that stuff. The hell with that! Bruce Brown has the money and *The Life*. He has a great house on a cliff about 60 feet above the beach at Dana Point. He is married and has two children, but it is not that hubby-mommy you're-breaking-my-gourd scene. His office is only two blocks from his house and he doesn't even have to go on the streets to get there. He gets on his Triumph scrambling motorcycle and cuts straight across a couple of vacant lots and one can see him . . . *bounding* to work over the vacant lots. The Triumph hits ruts and hummocks and things and Bruce Brown bounces into the air with the motor —*thragggggh*—moaning away, and when he gets to the curbing in front of his office, he just leans back and pulls up the front wheel and hops it and gets off and walks into the office barefooted. *Barefooted;* why not? He wears the same things now that he did when he was doing nothing but surfing. He has on a faded gray sweatshirt with the sleeves cut off just above the elbows and a pair of faded corduroys. His hair is the lightest corn yellow imaginable, towheaded, practically white, from the sun. Even his eyes seem to be bleached. He has a rain-barrel old-apple-tree Tom-Sawyer little-boy roughneck look about him, like Bobby Kennedy.

Sometimes he carries on his business right there at the house. He has a dugout room built into the side of the cliff, about 15 feet down from the level of the house. It is like a big pale green box set into the side of the cliff, and inside is a kind of upholstered bench or settee you can lie down on if you want to and look out at the Pacific. The surf is crashing like a maniac on the rocks down below. He has a telephone in there. Sometimes it will ring, and Bruce Brown says hello, and the surf is crashing away down below, roaring like mad, and the guy on the other end, maybe one of the TV networks calling from New York or some movie hair-out from Los Angeles, says:

"What is all that noise? It sounds like you're sitting out in the surf."

"That's right," says Bruce Brown, "I have my desk out on the beach now. It's nice out here."

The guy on the other end doesn't know what to think. He is another Mr. Efficiency who just got back from bloating his colon up at a three-hour executive lunch somewhere and now he is Mr.-Big-Time-Let's-Get-This-Show-on-the-Road.

"On the beach?"

"Yeah. It's cooler down here. And it's good for you, but it's not so great for the desk. You know what I have now? A warped leg."

"A warped leg?"

"Yeah, and this is an $800 desk."

Those nutball California kids—and he will still be muttering that five days after Bruce Brown delivers his film, on time, and Mr. Efficiency is still going through memo thickets or heaving his way into the bar car to Darien—in the very moment that Bruce Brown and Hobie Alter are both on their motorcycles out on the vacant lot in Dana Point. Hobie Alter left his surfboard plant about two in the afternoon because the wind was up and it would be good catamaranning and he wanted to go out and see how far he could tip his new catamaran without going over, and he did tip it over, about half a mile out in high swells and it was hell getting the thing right side up again. But he did, and he got back in time to go scrambling on the lot with Bruce Brown. They are out there, roaring over the ruts, bouncing up in the air, and every now and then they roar up the embankment so they can . . . fly, going up in the air about six feet off the ground as they come up off the embankment—*thraaagggggh*—all these people in the houses around there come to the door and look out. These two . . . nuts are at it again. Well, they can only fool around there for 20 minutes, because that is about how long it takes the cops to get there if anybody gets burned up enough and calls, and what efficient business magnate wants to get hauled off by the Dana Point cops for scrambling on his motorcycle in a vacant lot.

Bruce Brown has it figured out so no one in the whole rubber-bloated black pan-thuh world can trap him, though. He bought a forest in the Sierras. There is nothing on it but trees. His own wilds: no house, no nothing, just Bruce Brown's forest. Beautiful things happen up there. One day, right after he bought it, he was on the edge of his forest, where the road comes into it, and one of these big rancher king motheroos with the broad belly and the $70 lisle Safari shirt comes tooling up in a Pontiac convertible with a funnel of dust pouring out behind. He gravels it to a great flashy stop and yells:

"Hey! You!"

Of course, what he sees is some towheaded barefooted kid in a torn-off sweatshirt fooling around the edge of the road.

"Hey! You!"

"Yeah?" says Bruce Brown.

"Don't you know this is private property?"

"Yeah," says Bruce Brown.

"Well, then, why don't you get your ass off it?"

"Because it's mine, it's my private property," says Bruce Brown. "Now you get *yours* off it."

And Safari gets a few rays from that old apple-tree rain-barrel don't-cross-that-line look and doesn't say anything and roars off, slipping gravel, the dumb crumbling panthuh.

But . . . perfect! It is like, one means, you know, poetic justice for all the nights Bruce Brown slept out on the beach at San Onofre and such places in the old surfing days and would wake up with some old crock's black feet standing beside his head and some phlegmy black rubber voice saying:

"All right, kid, don't you know this is private property?"

And he would prop his head up and out there would be the Pacific Ocean, a kind of shadowy magenta-mauve, and one thing, *that* was nobody's private property—

But how many Bruce Browns can there be? There is a built-in trouble with age segregation. Eventually one *does* reach the horror age of 25, the horror dividing line. Surfing and the surfing life have been going big since 1958, and already there are kids who—well, who aren't kids anymore, they are pushing 30, and they are stagnating on the beach. Pretty soon the California littoral will be littered with these guys, stroked out on the beach like beached white whales, and girls, too, who can't give up the mystique, the mysterioso mystique, Oh Mighty Hulking Sea, who can't *conceive* of living any other life. It is pathetic when they are edged out of groups like the Pump House gang. Already there are some guys who hang around with the older crowd around the Shack who are stagnating on the beach. Some of the older guys, like Gary Wickham, who is 24, are still in *The Life,* they still have it, but even Gary Wickham will be 25 one day and then 26 and then. . . . and then even pan-thuh age. Is one really going to be pan-thuh age one day? Watch those black feet go. And Tom Coman still snuggles with Yellow Slacks, and Liz still roosts moodily in her rabbit fur at the bottom of the Pump House and Pam still sits on the steps contemplating the mysterioso mysteries of Pump House ascension and John and Artie still bob, tiny pink porcelain shells, way out there waiting for godsown bitchen *set,* and godsown sun is still turned on like a dentist's lamp and so far—

—the panthers scrape on up the sidewalk. They are at just about the point Leonard Anderson and Donna Blanchard got that day, December 6, 1964, when Leonard said, Pipe it, and fired two shots, one at her and one at himself. Leonard was 18 and Donna was 21—21!—god, for a girl in the Pump House gang that is almost the horror line right there. But it was all so mysterioso. Leonard was just lying down on the beach at the foot of the Pump House, near the stairs, just talking to John K. Weldon down there, and then Donna appeared at the top of the stairs and Leonard got up and went up the stairs to meet her, and they didn't say anything, they weren't *angry* over anything, they never had been, although the police said they had, they just turned and went a few feet down the sidewalk, away from the Pump House and—blam blam!—these two shots. Leonard fell dead on the sidewalk and Donna died that afternoon in Scripps Memorial Hospital. Nobody knew what to think. But one thing it seemed like—well, it seemed like Donna and Leonard thought they had lived *The Life* as far as it would go and now it was running out. All that was left to do was—but that is an *insane* idea. It can't be like that, *The Life* can't run out, people can't change all that much just because godsown chronometer runs on and the body packing starts deteriorating and the fudgy tallow shows up at the thighs where they squeeze out of the bathing suit—

Tom, boy! John, boy! Gary, boy! Neale, boy! Artie, boy! Pam, Liz, Vicki, Jackie Haddad! After all this—just a pair of bitchen black panther bunions inching down the sidewalk away from the old Pump House stairs?

Sara Davidson

Rock Style: Defying the American Dream

Electric sound rushes out of the Gray Manse in Lake Mahopac, New York, splitting the still, winter air. On week nights, carloads of teen-agers from sleepy towns in up-state Putnam County follow the road around the lake and park in the driveway, drinking beer and listening. Some of them get up the nerve to walk past the marble columns into the three-story mansion, and come bolting out, laughing and squealing details of the strange world inside.

The Gray Manse, once the summer estate of a marine welding executive, is home, rehearsal hall, and recreation center for Rhinoceros, a year-old rock group that consists of seven musicians, two equipment managers, a road manager, a rotating pool of young women, and a friend called Lan, a young man who makes clothes, cuts hair, and cooks. Two of the band members are rehearsing in the basement. The rest of the house, at five in the evening, is waking up and having breakfast. John Finley, a short, toothy figure with coarse blond hair that makes two or three waves before dropping to his shoulders, rides down the grand staircase in a moving chair. The rooms on the bottom floor are high-ceilinged, lavish period settings from the nineteenth century, like an antique suite at the Metropolitan Museum with all the velvet ropes down. John, in sky-blue pants and a purple and blue poncho, is swallowed up by the colors and textures: blue oriental carpets, gold-encrusted statues, stuffed elk, Victorian furniture, and candelabra.

On the upper floors, the rock group has been able to impose its own milieu—candles, frankincense, psychedelic posters, and Indian silks thrown over the fluted lampshades. There are stereo and television sets in every room, all playing at top volume. In the front bedroom, Alan Gerber, twenty-one, is lying on a pink silk spread listening to Thelonious Monk.

When John comes upstairs with a bowl of cereal and milk, he puts on a gospel record, *Run, Sinner, Run* by the Davis Sisters. "Nothing moves me as much as gospel music," he says.

Across the hall, Danny and Steve Weis, brothers, are watching *Land of the Giants* on television and listening to Judy Collins on the stereo. Danny, twenty, is the pivotal sexual force of the group. He is tall and haughty, with ice-blue eyes, a pouting mouth, and a head of long, flaxen hair that is layered, teased, permanent-waved, ratted, and sprayed until it has acquired the consistency of cat's fur. Steve, seventeen, is dark-haired and so thin—110 pounds on a six-foot, one-inch frame—that when he stands on stage in skin-tight black pants, he looks like a Vogue model photographed with a distorting lens.

A blast of organ sound rises from the basement, drowning out all the records and television sets. Michael Fonfara has turned his amplifier all the way up and is jamming on the keyboard in the high register. Danny says to his brother, "Let's go down and join him." Billy Mundi and Doug Hastings, who are married and don't live in the main house, have arrived, and the band is soon assembled.

Danny, on lead guitar, rips into a new song and moves around the room, pulling after him the red umbilical cord that ties him to the amplifier. He stands in front of Doug, and they stare into each other's eyes, moving and nodding in unison until —sync—they are playing in sync, not looking at each other's hands on the guitars, only the eyes. Danny turns to his brother, Steve, on bass guitar, pulling him into the rhythm—sync. Then he walks to Billy on the drums, catching his eyes and matching up with him. Then Michael on organ, Alan on piano, John singing at the microphone, until everyone in the room is pitching the same way, nodding at each other, and the air is steaming with this communion.

At this moment, which the musicians call "magic" or "holy," they experience intimations of transcendence of self. Alan describes it: "When we're really getting it together, playing, we're all at peace together. You're not even you anymore. You don't have to contend with the hangups that Alan has. All of a sudden, you're part of something that seven people are feeling. The music is crashing all around you, but you're at peace, in the center of it." Beyond the ear-bruising electric pounding is a state where, John says, "You cease to be. You're just a vessel, the instrument of your soul. The music is playing you." The group works for that transcendence every time they play. They reach it for moments, during certain songs, but the complete experience is rare. "When we play a set that has it throughout, everybody walks off like this," John folds his hands in prayer. "It makes us happier than anything in life."

Rhinoceros, a coalition of rock veterans who have served their time in different bands, is past the scuffling stage that young rock groups go through—playing at college dances, auditioning on off-nights at coffee houses, dragging demonstration tapes from record company to record company. With an album out on Elektra and a single, *Apricot Brandy,* which is 47 on the national charts with a red bullet meaning WATCH-IT, Rhinoceros·is able to demand enough money for performances to keep the ten-man entourage living high in Mahopac. They rehearse during the week, travel and play on weekends, and, if popularity grows, will make a new album every eight to nine months.

When the band rehearses until the early hours of the morning, the current groupies, who go by exotic names like Pandora, Nico, and Honey, have the run of the Gray Manse. They gather on the second-floor landing, trade scarves, blouses, hair rollers, and fish stories about the rock stars they have slept with. The groupies are part of a network of girls across the country who make a life of pursuing rock musicians. They live together, work on and off in discotheques and clubs, clothing stores and record companies, leaving the job for any musician who will take them home for a few days.

Honey claims to be the ex-girlfriend of Jimi Hendrix—the supreme phallic symbol of hard rock. She is telling the other girls, "Jim Morrison wants me to come live with him, and Mick Jagger is sending me a ticket to London. . . ." Pandora, a rougey blonde wearing a feather and sequin costume, has just been hired as a Play-boy bunny. Smiling, empty-eyed, she says, "They want me for centerfold."

The groupies dress each other up in see-through blouses, golden chains, and furs, and descend the stairs to the basement. No one in the band acknowledges their entrance. They leave after a half-hour and take a two-hour communal bath. Like a mini-harem, the girls amuse each other and stay apart from the band, until it's time to go to sleep. They raid the downstairs kitchen, find nothing but Wonder bread, cereal, giant jars of peanut butter and jelly, and king-size cartons of milk. Once in a while, someone in the house will make soup or a stew, but the normal daily diet is cereal and sandwiches. The girls settle for Puffed Rice with powdered sugar, and decide to explore the glassed-in sun porch of the mansion. Among the wicker and chintz furniture is an old Victrola with a cabinet full of 78 records. Honey takes one out, cranks up the machine, and places the heavy, cylindrical needle down. As the pounding of Rhinoceros rattles all the glass, George M. Cohan begins to sing in a scratchy, distant voice: "My girl May, she meets me every day, in fact we used to go to school together. . . ."

One of Howard Johnson's orange and blue installations comes into focus on the New Jersey Turnpike, halfway between New York and Philadelphia. Four of the Rhinoceros trek across the parking lot in their blazing colored silks, leathers, fringes, tassels, and flying hair. They are greeted by whistles and catcalls from a group of truck drivers. Alan turns to John, who is wearing a neon-orange T-shirt and suede vest, his blond curls bouncing and his eyes puffed up and pink from sleep. "You look like a depraved chick."

The band drives in two rented cars, collecting receipts at every tollbooth, gas station, and highway eatery. Danny Hannagan and Burt Schraeder, the equipment men, drive the instruments and amplifiers, together worth more than $10,000, in a rented Avis truck with giant Rhino posters on the sides. When they fly, they call a special airline service that packs the equipment and hustles it through terminals. Hopefully, the baggage, Danny, and Burt arrive at the concert hall several hours ahead of the group, so that when the band walks in, everything is set up to play.

In Philadelphia, the first car stops at a gas station for directions. Doug rolls down the window to talk to the attendants in the glassed office, but before he can open his mouth, one of the mechanics yells, "Naaaaaa," and gives them the finger with his grease-blackened hand. "Naaaaa, dirty punks, naaaaaa."

Every time it happens, the group is taken by surprise. "What's with that guy? Jee-sus. I wish we had a long stick with a boxing glove at the end of it, so we could just let him have it."

It is the hair, of course. The hair brands them—outsider, alien. There are two attitudes people take toward the band. One is a castrating, motherly kind of amusement: "Boys will be boys, aren't they cute in their little costumes." The chef at the Mahopac Diner where the band often eats keeps their picture on the counter, feeds them and clucks over their bony frames. The other attitude is more common: "Naaaaaa, ya dirty punk." John Finley was once waiting to pay the cashier in a Boston restaurant when a florid-faced Irishman turned on him: "You're obnoxious, you creep. Braahhh!" Never, except in hippie districts of big cities, do people look at the band members simply as other people. Rock musicians have built this moat between themselves and the rest of the world with a stylized look—shoulder-length hair is the chief ingredient—that represents a deeper, inner separation.

Playing rock is a means of living out a definition of the good life that defies the American dream: never have a steady job, keep crazy hours, get stoned, play music, draw constant attention, and, if you do all these things well, make lots of money. The band members look at ads in the magazines—see the gray-haired couple in the rowboat, the happy wife is handing her happy husband a worm for his fishing rod. If you squirrel away now for the future, you can retire at sixty and have a cottage on a lake. The reasoning behind this scene—years of working, saving, putting off, sacrificing—has no meaning to rock musicians, and to an increasing number of young people who listen with puzzlement to job recruiters on the campus, talking of pensions and sick pay and medical benefits. They know people their own age who have bypassed the corporation jobs and are living at the rainbow's end of the work ethic—the mansion on Lake Mahopac. If young people can live in Big Sur, or Florida, or the Catskills, without saving for forty years at the Dime Savings Bank, what does this mean to people who have gone the other way, postponed their desires, worked at dehumanizing jobs? It means, to some of them, that maybe what they did was all unnecessary. Is it surprising that the man in Boston is moved to rage when he sees John Finley with his long curls and wallet full of money?

None of the Rhinos, who range from seventeen to twenty-six, has ever had a regular job, nine to five, or even a part-time job. With the exception of Billy, who is an ex-Hell's Angel from East Los Angeles, they all come from middle-class families. Their fathers are insurance salesmen, engineers, shoe retailers, who made sure their sons didn't starve until they were making their living through rock. Billy was out on his own at eighteen. "It was either music or a white-collar job," Billy thought. So he started playing rock and studying music at UCLA.

Each Tuesday, the band members get $70 in cash. Their manager pays the rent on the house in Mahopac, which is $400 a month in the winter but jumps to $1,700 a month in the summer. The manager also pays for car rentals, musical equipment and maintenance, and expenses on the road. As the band's album, *Rhinoceros*, climbs up the charts, they can demand higher prices for live performances. But it is difficult for the album to catch on until the band moves around the country, stirring up interest. The two feed each other.

In the early stages, they are lucky to break even. If they earn $1,000 a night, the manager and booking agent each take 15 per cent off the top. After hotels, meals, and transportation costs, there is perhaps $100 to be split seven ways. Rhinoceros is beginning to command $2,000 to $3,000 a night. Blood, Sweat and Tears, whose album was number one in the country, could ask $7,000 to $10,000. Supergroups like the Doors can earn $50,000 including a percentage of the gate.

From inside the Rhino car, Philadelphia looks gray. The people on the streets seem bloodless. They look inside the Rhino car and their eyes pop, they do double-takes. At the Franklin Motor Inn, the boys pair off, two to a room. The television sets snap on instantly and stay on until the band checks out. Michael and Danny set up colored candles and start incense burning on charcoal.

At 8:00 P.M., after eating steaks and shrimp, both the consistency of rubber, in the motel restaurant, they drive to the Electric Factory. The place is a psychedelic barn with a circus theme—swings, slides, funny-house mirrors, Dayglo-painted benches, and a hot-dog stand. In the dressing room, John starts to write the set, deciding what numbers to play in what order. Everyone except John and Doug, who meditates for a half hour before playing, is stoned, pacing, anxious to get on stage. They file out past benches of teen-agers in shetland sweaters and respectable haircuts, tune up, and are on.

Danny's costume is a long, Western-style black leather jacket and a black bowler hat. With his pale skin and yellow-white hair sticking out in points from under the hat, he looks like a spook—one of those skeletons in top hat and tails that dance through children's cartoons. Danny bends at the knees, straight-backed, and starts the band into *Apricot Brandy.*

The sound of Rhinoceros is hard white rhythm 'n blues, with country, funk, and gospel influence. When the group first made recordings, John says, "We listened to the tapes and they sounded just like a rhinoceros. The bass and drums sounded lumbering and fat." He hits his fists on his knees. "Choonka, choonka, choonka! Like a big animal going through the mud." Rhinoceros never plays a song the same way twice; the performance varies with the group's emotions. On stage, Danny moves around to each player, yelling, "Oh yeah, go!" Alan pitches forward over the piano, and when he sings, his soft features pinch up around his aquiline nose, giving him the pained, sour look of an ascetic Jew. Doug, with his happy face and ringlets of brown hair, arches his body against the guitar. Michael plays the organ half-standing against a high stool. He wears pink goggles and an Indian mirror cloth shirt unbuttoned to show his olive skin. John directs the show, talking to the audience, banging on a cow-bell.

John is soaking when he comes off stage. He pulls off his shirt, and a blonde wearing a tweed skirt that barely covers her plump bottom starts massaging his shoulders. Girls are twittering about the dressing room, and a student from Temple University is interviewing the band with a cassette recorder.

During the second set, the band begins to feel magic rising. Everyone is synced together, drawing out songs with improvisations. At the end of a walloping chorus, Danny is jumping off the floor, guitar and all. John is bouncing like a dude, knees apart, head thrown back. The frenzy reaches the audience, making them wriggle and squirm. Song spills into song, until they arrive at *Monster.* It begins with strange, whirring noises and chords that build to a kind of electronic doomsday. John and Alan sway, their chins up, bodies dangling. Strobe lights flicker, faster and faster. When the music explodes, John is frozen in attitude, his head all the way back, his hands flayed apart in the air. It is as if he is suspended in a wind machine, at the still point, and the entire band is there.

It is snowing outside, at 1:30 A.M. The band hurries back to the hotel with a newly acquired flock of groupies. There is a lot of knocking on doors, tromping from room to room, smoking, drinking from a flask of Seagram's apricot brandy, and watching television until the last station in Philadelphia goes dark at 4:30 A.M. Many of the groupies encourage rock stars to add whipping to their sexual encounters. One groupie called Ruby, an emaciated blonde with hooded black eyes on a vacant moon-shaped face, gave a young musician two sleeping pills, and the next thing he knew, he was tied with scarves to the four corners of the bed. Ruby, in black boots and a leather dress, was hitting him, just enough to sting, with the edge of a belt. "I flashed on it," the musician said later. "I thought I'd take the trip, see what it was like." The next day he tied Ruby up, "and she seemed to dig it." That night he threw her out. "Groupies love to be treated like dirt."

Michael says, "Most of the girls Rhinoceros has been meeting lately are interested in getting into whipping. You know, you take off your belt and kind of tease them with it, and then you start doing it harder." John comments, "Whipping and bondage are symbols of the mental games that go on between us anyway—the possessiveness, the emotional sadism. There's some of that in all of us."

There is some of the groupie in almost every girl who watches a rock singer in leather pants and metal hardware, snapping his body and making a sound so loud it is very near pain. Only a small number, though, live out their desires to be possessed by rock artists. A San Francisco groupie made her compulsion explicit by having a gold ring put in her nose. The band members claim to dislike groupies, and pass them around like cigarettes. But groupies flourish in all the big cities because rock stars need them. They don't bring wives or girlfriends with them on the road, because, they say, "the chick and the band end up fighting for the guy's attention and loyalty."

In Philadelphia, Billy and Roger Di Fiori, the road manager, pass up the girls for a Roy Rogers movie and the wrestling matches. They sit in their room all day, flipping the dials and gabbing at each other in *Mad* magazine talk. Billy is twenty-six, the oldest in the band, and has taken on the role of ringmaster, group therapist, and policeman. He came to Rhinoceros from the Mothers of Invention, which was the last stop on a train of rock groups: Buffalo Springfield, Thor 'n Shield, The Elysium Senate, Skip 'n Flip, The Medallions, and Ross Dietrick and the Four Peppers. One of the top drummers in the industry (he once worked three months as a tympanist in the Los Angeles Philharmonic), he is in high demand as a studio musician. Most people are frightened when they first see Billy—a round, grizzly-haired figure with a big stomach and bird legs. During a month on the road, Billy never wore anything but a pair of purple and blue striped pants with calico patches, a T-shirt, and a green cap, which no one is allowed to touch. When he climbs on stage, the T-shirt rides up and the pants slip down, showing the cleavage of his behind.

But Billy is the only one of Rhinoceros who finished college—a B.A. in music from UCLA. He learned bass drum in high school, when he still had other interests, like riding with the Hell's Angels motorcycle gang. "I still have to get in a fight once in a while. When I joined this band they were afraid I'd either punch them in the mouth or light them on fire. I use that to keep them in line." Bill complains that Rhinoceros has the problems common to every band with teen-agers in it. "All the kids have the mentality of a sixteen-year-old. They left home to make good and impress their parents that they were doing something." Bill bawls out the band for yelling foul words in the hotel corridors, for belching into the microphones on stage, for setting off firecrackers in the parking lot, and for fighting over petty matters and ruining performances. "I'm willing to put as much time into this band as everybody else," he says. "But after it's all over, I want to go to Juilliard, to finish what I need for a master's degree so I can teach music in high school. I want to get my own band of men. I want to become the John Cage, Stravinsky, Beethoven, Wagner, and everybody else rolled into one for this era, for this time."

Among the thinkers of the band—Billy, Alan, and John—there is a conviction that rock is the primary musical expression of this time. Electricity, rockets, exploding neutrons, and instant communications caught up with popular music in the early 1950s, when gingerbread tunes like *How Much is that Doggie in the Window?* were bumped off the Hit Parade by *Sh-Boom* and Bill Haley and the Comets, whose *Rock Around the Clock* and *Shake, Rattle and Roll* cemented the phrase, "rock 'n roll." Rosemary Clooney, Eddie Fisher, and Teresa Brewer faded quickly, rock dug in, and in the early 1960s, the whole way of popular dancing changed. The Lindy, the symmetrical one, two, back step, that had held through the first decade of rock, suddenly fragmented into the twist, the frug, the monkey, the string of dances named after animals and primitive sounds in which there is no touching between partners, only spasmodic jerking.

Alan contrasts rock songs with the symphonies of Beethoven and Mozart. "In Beethoven's time, they had an hour to develop a work. Life wasn't so—snap snap." He pops his fingers. "The pace was more relaxed, and society was more ordered. Today, you have a three-minute song, it's fast and loud, it sounds like the world around us. You go up on top of a skyscraper and look down at the city and what do you feel? Cha-cha Bohnng! a-Bohnng-a, bam Bam! Tchong tchong! That's what you hear in rock."

Over the door to the Electric Factory, Ben Franklin, who started it all with his kite and key, looks down his cardboard nose through pre-hippie wire-frame glasses. Saturday night, John has written a set that Danny doesn't like. John wants to sing a number they haven't done in a while, "because if we really get it on, we'll kill the audience, and we'll get it on us too."

Danny says the song needs work. "Why can't we do *You're My Girl?*"

John says, "I'm sick of it."

"Look, man, I play a lot of songs I'm tired of."

"Yeah, but I'm the one that's gotta get the song on vocally."

Mike and Steve side with Danny. Doug and Alan are with John. Danny's face is twitching. "I can see everybody getting uptight. Let's stop it right here." He cuts the air with his hand.

John stomps out, slamming the door. Steve throws a cigarette pack after him. Outside, John is raging. He crumples the paper on which he wrote the set. He hurls a record against the wall and steams back in. "I don't know what to do. I don't know how to write the set."

Danny says, "It's your uptightness that's the root of the problem."

"Okay, I'm uptight. Leave me alone."

They are ten minutes late for the stage call. The scrubbed kids who paid three dollars to get into the Factory are talking and giggling in their seats. Danny goes back to the dressing room. "Are you ready?" John nods, weakly.

The set begins—the same songs as the night before, but they are dead. When it is over, the band walks off solemnly, straight back to the dressing room, no chatting or fooling with the chickies. The feeling between them is tangible, sexual, as between lovers who have seen a quarrel blow up over nothing and burn out, leaving them close and bittersweet.

Billy speaks first. "What went wrong is that we had a teen-age quarrel."

Danny sighs. "I just wanna forget about it." His stomach is knotted up and cramped, and he needs to get the paregoric out of the car.

"You shouldn't let John bug you," Billy says. "John digs bugging people, isn't that right?" John nods. Billy says, "When John gets uptight, let him tear his hair— when he does that, he's getting rid of it. He sits in here writing a song, or a poem, because that's what a set is, and you guys say you don't wanna play it. He's hurt, and I don't blame him. I'd be pissed too."

The door swings open. Two freckled boys wearing Western hats and kerchiefs announce, in little pubescent voices, "We're from the *Free Press*. Can we talk to you?" Half the band walks out, and the two boys sit down. "What are your names?" Silence. "I'm Alan." "I'm John." And then, this great grizzly man who has ridden with the Hell's Angels and groveled with the Mothers of Invention says, sweetly, "I'm Billy."

"Any good group that can stick together can make it." Paul Rothchild, a producer at Elektra Records, noticed in the fall of 1967 that a number of groups were breaking up and many others were having internal difficulties. He began wondering what would happen if he took one from this group, one from that, and put the best musicians together. Would it work?

Rothchild called every talented musician he knew and invited him to Los Angeles. His vision was of a supergroup of superstars, who would hammer a new approach to white rhythm 'n blues. He sent plane tickets to thirty, and on November 30, they began showing up at his house in Laurel Canyon. Alan Gerber flew out from Chicago. John Finley, who had recently quit Jon and Lee and the Checkmates, then the top group in Canada, walked into the white living room with its hardwood floor, fieldstone fireplace, and giant swimming pool visible in back, looked around at fifteen people he had never seen before and said to himself, "We're gonna be a group?" John sat in the most distant corner and didn't say a word. Neither did Doug Hastings, who had come down from Seattle where he was playing with the Daily Flash. Rothchild passed a guitar to a young man from Oklahoma and said, "Play." Alan recalls, "It was great. Then he passed it to another guy, and he was great too. I was so spaced out that when they passed it to me, I said, groovy, and sang my songs."

The boys stayed for several months at the Sandy Koufax Tropicana Motel, rehearsing at a rented theater. "We would jam in shifts," John said. "It was dog eat dog." Rothchild listened to the sessions, discouraged some people, brought in others, including Danny Weis and Jerry Penrod from the Iron Butterfly, Michael Fonfara from the Electric Flag, and Billy Mundi from the Mothers. By March, Rothchild decided the group was complete at seven members.

The name, Rhinoceros, came from Alan. It is his favorite animal. When the group played for the first time at the Kaleidoscope in Los Angeles, the sound was so loud and heavy that the name seemed natural. Two months later they went into the recording studio for eight days and made an album. Most rock groups spend close to a month in the studio, recording a few parts at a time and then dubbing voice and additional parts over that. The only way Rhinoceros wanted to record was live, all together, standing in a circle and playing into a cluster of mikes—one feeding back to them, the others recording.

Before the album was made, Elektra had spent $50,000 on the group, paying their room, board, and transportation, equipment rentals, rehearsal costs, and then buying out old contracts for three of them. The expense of making, promoting, and distributing the album raised the total to $80,000. By spring of this year, Rhinoceros had sold 100,000 albums. Not until they sell a quarter of a million will the band have written off its debt to Elektra and begin to earn money from the record.

In the fall of 1968, they decided to move to New York to build their reputation; there were more playing opportunities for the group there than in any other part of the country. The band lived in the cozily decaying Chelsea Hotel in New York for a few months, then found the house in Mahopac. About that time, Jerry, who was playing bass, started having fits of despair. One night in a town on Long Island, the band had a blowup before going on stage. When it was time to play, Jerry had disappeared. From information that has trickled back, the band says, Jerry "went straight—cut his hair, went back to art school in California, and moved back with his parents." Danny's brother, Steve, who had been working as equipment manager and had casually learned Jerry's parts, was asked to take his place.

If no one else quits, Rhinoceros will be an unusual case. Even the most successful groups have been unable to hold together beyond a few years: the Mamas and Papas, Cream, Big Brother and the Holding Company, the Lovin' Spoonful, Love, Traffic, the Byrds, the Buffalo Springfield. The list of casualties runs on, and the cause of death is almost always personal squabbles. Danny Weis quit the Iron Butterfly because of a fierce battle with the organist. "I can't even remember the reason now," Danny said. "Oh yes, he resented me playing leads more often than him." After that Danny gathered a group that was to be called Nirvana, but before they could get off the ground, Danny fought with the bass player and the group disintegrated. The musicians wander, forming new groups, or becoming studio musicians, producers, or single artists.

Jac Holzman, president of Elektra, whose production is 70 per cent rock, says it is difficult for a group to stay together more than a year after a record is released unless they see a steady increase in public acceptance. "The group hangs together by a string. It's one gigantic holding action until the miracle happens."

When success does come, it is a rare group that can stay on the road for more than three years. Holzman says, "Working on the road in dismal locations is demeaning, exhausting, and disheartening. Something has to be done to find better situations for musicians to play. Otherwise, no group can take the pressure of road performances."

Friday morning at eleven o'clock, when the band is due to leave Mahopac, is the time everyone decides to do laundry. Alan discovers another rip in the only pair of jeans he wears. "Lan, could you do a fast patch job? If I don't have my pants, I'll feel insecure."

Danny bounds up the stairs. "Cunnilingus, everyone."

"Cunnilingus," John calls from his room.

John has finished packing, and is staring out the window at the snowbound road. When John is feeling down, objects look ominous and distorted. He broods and wonders, "Why haven't I ever been able to make it with a chick?" John is twenty-four, and the longest relationship he has had with a girl lasted three weeks. He drives the sixty miles to New York with the band every Sunday to go to The Scene, a rock club where groupies hang out, but rarely brings the girls back to Mahopac. "I don't want to have to deal with them the next day." He raps his fists against the glass. "Why is it that I reject people? Why do I insist on feeling alone and being alone?"

John is not the only one in the group who is as they put it, "going through changes." Danny also has been forced to look at himself with some care. Since he joined his first rock group at twelve, Danny has always had to be the star. With Rhinoceros, the stress was on playing together, rather than separately to the fans. Danny was called down, and made to realize, he says, "that I'd been on an ego trip for eighteen years, and that I didn't really want to be the fancy lead guitar player whom all the chicks drooled over. When that happened, I stopped wearing all my satin clothes with lace and silks. I started listening to others in the band."

Danny, like the others, learned music when he was very young. His father, John Weis, was a country-western guitarist who played with Spade Cooley and Tex Williams. His mother sang, and the whole family played at churches and naval training bases around San Diego. Danny was an honor student at high school, but left home at seventeen when his group, the Iron Butterfly, was offered a chance to play at a club in Hollywood. "We got $40 a week and lived in a room above the club that had no bed, no heat, and smelled awful." He met a girl, twenty-five, who was a trapeze artist and stunt woman, moved in with her and got married at eighteen. The marriage ended two years later.

"Being married to a musician is tough on a chick," Danny says. "You sit at home every night by yourself while your husband is surrounded by chicks who throw themselves at him. I learned from being married that you have to get all the sex thing out of your system, because the music is so tied up with sex that it's a real struggle, even if you're married, not to go after it."

The language, the argot of rock is grounded in sexuality. The instrument is your "axe." What you play on it are "licks" and "chops." If two players get into competition, they "fight each other with their axes." A band gets on stage to "get it on," "put it together," "be together." If you "dig" something, you "flash on it," "turn on," "get into it." Something serious is "heavy," something relaxed is "laid back." A girl is never called a girl, she is always a "chick." The male is a "cat." They manage to express a fairly wide range of feelings with a vocabulary so narrow that when John tried to explain a subtle relationship, he stopped in frustration. "This is terrible. My grasp of English is slipping away."

The communication between band and audience is as physical as it is aural. Steve says, "I know certain lines on the guitar that, if I'm interested in a chick, I can look straight at her and do it to her. This one line starts high on the neck of the guitar and goes down to the lowest part, fast. It's like a slap in the crotch." When Mike works on the organ, he is thinking of making love. "The beat does it to me." And Danny says he gets so sexually and emotionally excited that, "I've come on stage lots of times, just from the music, and it's unbelievable. Sometimes I fall off the stage, and other times, I cry, right up there." Jimi Hendrix, feeling the same surges, set fire to his guitar. Jim Morrison of the Doors sang *Touch Me* and then is alleged to have exposed himself on a Florida stage.

After a set, the band waits for girls to approach them. "You've made the first move by playing. It's up to them to take you up on it." Steve knows musicians who by the time they were seventeen had more experience with sex, drugs, and drink than many men have in a lifetime. One started sniffing glue at eleven and, by fifteen, had tried marijuana, speed, LSD, barbiturates, mescaline, opium, hashish, and every kind of trip chemically possible in the drug culture. He had also had groupies in combinations of two and three. Steve's own father had died when the boy was fourteen, and Steve was shunted from school to school as a problem child. When he paid attention, he gave evidence of brilliant perception, but, he says, he was stoned almost every day he went to class. At sixteen, he convinced his mother to let him go to Hollywood to live with his brother Danny and his wife. Danny, then eighteen, became Steve's legal guardian.

All of the band members believe they will have to get out of the atmosphere of drugs and sex some day. Danny tried meditation with the Maharishi Mahesh Yogi, but found that "that way of life doesn't go with rock 'n roll." The boys' view of the future barely stretches beyond six months. When asked what he would like to be doing in ten years, Alan was silent. "Well . . . the most important thing for me is, I just wanna go off and live in the country, in the woods, and find peace with myself. I wanna write and play my music. And I won't be smoking dope. I'll be eating health foods." Doug, in his soft, composed voice, says, "It's impossible for me to say what I'll be doing when I'm forty. I think you can have a good life doing anything in the world, if you want it badly enough and don't cop out to your paranoias."

Danny says he will play guitar the rest of his life. He watched his father, who was "the best guitar player there was," become an insurance salesman to support his family. "It killed him. I saw him die from it. He wanted to play music and he had to sell insurance. I knew I could never do that. I said to myself, fuck it, I don't care if I starve. I'm gonna play music until I die."

Friday night in Schenectady, the marquee in front of the Holiday Inn says, "Happy Birthday Peggy." Watching television in his room, Danny picks up the electric guitar and tries to get Michael's attention. The guitar is barely audible when not plugged in, but after several minutes of crazy whirling runs, Mike turns his head away from *The High Chaparral* and drawls, "You're insaaaaaane."

When the guitar is plugged into an electric amplifier, it works like this: the musician plucks the strings, causing them to vibrate. The vibrations are picked up by a set of small magnets under the strings and sent as electric impulses through a cord to the amplifier. The amplifier magnifies the impulses, converts them back to musical sounds, and feeds them out a speaker. Each guitarist uses a separate amplifier, and will use two or three in a large hall to make the sound louder and fuller. Michael's Hammond organ needs a special Leslie organ amplifier and several mikes in front of it. Alan plays a Rocky Mountain Instruments electric piano which has its own amplifier. The vocal parts and drums are not amplified, but carried directly over a public-address system. Most bands amplify themselves up to the point of distortion. It is always different to hear a group live than to hear them on records, because the volume transforms the experience. Even between numbers, there is a constant electric buzz. "It's security," John says. "The louder you are, the more confident you feel, especially in a strange place."

Schenectady, a depressed industrial town in central New York, is not only strange but grim. The job is at the Aerodrome, a warehouse converted into a seedy psychedelic nightclub. Girls with troubled complexions, wearing cheap hairpieces and elephant pants, flail about by themselves on the dance floor. In the room that Rhinoceros must share with a local group called The Pumpkin, John begins to write the set. The band's repertoire is twenty-five songs, all but two of which are their own compositions. The lyrics are simplistic, juvenile, with the limited scope of 1950s rock—I love her, need her, miss her—but with none of the existential wit of the Beatles' simple songs. (But then, in their early years, when the Beatles were the age of Rhinoceros, their subject matter was not much more sophisticated: *"I Wanna Be Your Man," "I Want to Hold Your Hand," "I Saw Her Standing There," "All My Loving."*)

While all the members of Rhinoceros have agile minds, none of them reads anything at all. Four had extensive training in classical music. Michael taught piano at age twelve, and Alan was composing chamber music at Chicago Musical College when he quit to join the band. But they don't read. It's as if the print medium, with its even lines, is too confining and laborious. Danny says, "My mind is always going so fast I can't get into books or stories or anything." Neither do they have any awareness of politics. "We don't have any idea of making revolution," Danny says. "We just wanna make people feel good." The social commentary that seeps through their songs is instinctive, rather than conscious, as in John's *Top of the Ladder:*

> You read about it in the paper every day,
> Someone's always climbin' up that ladder,
>   and makin' a big scene.
> Now baby I know just what I need,
> I'll see you at the top—of the ladder![1]

The sets at the Aerodrome go well. John is ebullient when he comes off stage, but Alan is depressed. "This is the kind of place that makes me hate playing rock 'n

1. From "Top of the Ladder" by John Finley. Copyright © 1969 by Nina Music & Rhino Music. All rights reserved. Used by permission of Warner-Tamerlane Publishing Corp.

roll." Danny is sitting stone still. "It's weird out there." John says, "Maybe I was wrong. I felt great singing, but since I've been off stage . . ." He goes out to the bar, and a shrill-voiced girl says to him, "I'm not very pretty but I'm fun to watch," and starts twitching her pasty face. "Shit."

Boston is better from the start. "The whole thing feels special," Alan says, halfway along the Massachusetts Turnpike. No one in the band knows exactly how to get to Boston. On the itinerary handed them that morning, there are no directions, no time listed for sound checks or performance, and the hotel is misspelled, "Sheriton Boston." Even if they had directions, they would probably lose them. They lose everything—letters, tickets, keys, money, phone numbers. The Boston Pop Festival, the itinerary says, is at the Boston Armory. When they find the armory, it is boarded up and dark. The festival, they learn after driving around for several hours, is at the Boston Arena. No one in the car is worried or nervous. They are all soaring.

Danny describes the perfect gig: "A good gig is going there, being happy in the car, and feeling well healthwise. I usually ache all over, have a headache or a backache and very little energy, mainly because I don't exercise. All I do is sit, sleep, and eat. The next thing is getting real smashed before the gig, playing a magic set, meeting really pretty chicks and having a groovy thing at a Holiday Inn, or some other hotel that has good, hard double beds, so they're good for my back. That's a good gig."

For John, a good gig is building up emotional power over the audience. "To do that, you have to live the music, not perform it. If you sound sad, you have to feel sad and be sad. If the spirit and emotion is there, you can make people jump out of their seats, cry and scream. That's what gospel music does for me. That's how preachers earn their money. When I was playing with the Checkmates, we'd have so much power, I could touch people one hundred yards away, reach out with my hand and touch them with my soul, and they'd scream. One gig we did, there was a killing while we were on. I don't know what that means, but it happened. It was, well, curious."

The Sheraton Boston is riotous with fountains, suspended staircases, tropical plants, and Peggy Lee singing *Fever* over the Muzak. The band doesn't usually stay in hotels like this. They prefer motels that are easy to get in and out of. The first carload walk into the lobby in their freak clothes and hair falling to their shoulders, and the lobby turns, as if the hundred or so people milling about are one body.

Steve is the most conspicuous. He is all in black, with a black satin shirt open to the waist, a large silver and turquoise cross bumping against his concave chest, and black, crushed velvet pants. Over his pale face is a black desperado hat with a low crown and wide, curving brim. Alan is wearing a blue and green flowered satin shirt with puffed sleeves, a green suede vest, and his jeans with the leather patches. His silky brown hair hangs over his eyes, and together with his sideburns and moustache, completely dominates his appearance.

The hotel manager refuses to give the group rooms until they pay in advance. They try to eat dinner, and are turned away from all four restaurants in the hotel for lack of coat and tie. They drive to a restaurant called the Red Fez in Roxbury, frequented by shaggy students from Brandeis and Harvard. A waitress comes at them holding out her arms. "I'm sorry, we're closing." A sign in the window says, "Open until 3:00 A.M." It is long before 3:00. The waitress is glaring at Danny with his white, cat's fur hair and Steve in his black satins and desperado hat. "Yeah, we understand," John says. The band doesn't press trouble. They leave quickly. This is the dues they pay for living outside, for not keeping a foot in the other world. No one in the group owns a tie. "It comes down to which one you want more, your freedom or their approval," John says. "I enjoy dressing and being who I am. It means more to me than going in that restaurant. I don't need them. They're the cretins."

Giving up on dinner, they drive to the Boston Arena, an old roller rink, filled with mildewed air and dirt. "It looks terrible," Steve says, as they fight through a jam-up in the parking lot. The policeman at the gate doesn't believe they are Rhinoceros, and holds them aside until an official is summoned. The group still hasn't found out what time they're going to play, and it's too late now for a sound check. They are escorted to their dressing room, a musty green cell with a bank of toilets, showers, and dirty sinks, in which a dozen Cokes have been placed. "Aaaaggh, it's a latrine," Steve yells. It is 9:00 P.M., they are to play in thirty minutes, and half the band hasn't shown up. "Let's not get worked up over it," John says. "We'll just upset ourselves." The other carload walks in with ten minutes to go. They had been stopped in Connecticut for speeding, taken to the police station and arraigned, then had gotten lost on the way into Boston and driven right through the city and out for ten miles before they realized it.

Rhinoceros is third on the program, after Daddy Warbucks and the Grass Roots. They will be followed by the Caldwell-Winfield Blues Band and Canned Heat. The Arena, they discover, is an "echo bomb." The bleachers are half filled—about a thousand people huddled in coats against the drafts. The vast spaces in the building make it impersonal. With ticket prices $5 and $6.50, the audience is practically all white. High-school students are running down the aisles and talking above the music.

The whole band knows, though, that they're going to have a good time. In the first number, they throw back their heads, laugh and call to each other. Danny starts his rounds, moving up to John and getting into rhythm with him. Then he faces Steve, who nods his wilting head at Danny, "Mmmmmm, Yeah!" and then at Billy, in his green cap and dark granny glasses. John begins to lose himself in *Top of the Ladder*, jumping, skipping, snapping his body in half with the downbeat of the drums. When the song ends, he mops himself with a towel, then grabs the mike. "Hey, wanna catch some ass, wanna get it on?" Laughs, and a few jokers yell, "Yeah." John says, "Let's catch some ass," and Danny hits *Apricot Brandy*.

There are hearty boos when John says, "We've only got five minutes left. But we'd like to go out stomping." Everyone in the band except Billy stands up now and pounds the floor, Thwack! Thwack! clapping their hands and waving tambourines. They keep up a rhythm, two minutes, then Danny waves at Billy, "One, two, three, go!"

Through the song, *You're My Girl*, the band is jumping, waving their free arms, grabbing anything to shake—sticks, bells. Michael is playing the organ standing up, bouncing and yelling. The kids in the front rows are on their feet screaming. Even the policemen in front of the stage are nodding, their white caps moving, ever so slightly, up and down.

When the band finishes, dripping wet, people rush at them and grab their hands. They make their way to the dressing room, sigh and collapse.

Alan: "I had such a good time!"

Mike: "Oh, fuck, it was so good."

Steve: "We kiiiiiilled 'em!"

John: "It feels so great to crack a challenge like that. Those people didn't wanna move, and we made 'em wiggle asses. We really had to work at it."

They close the door, and sit together in the musty room with its urinal smell. Their bodies are limp, their eyes glazed, fixed on the ceiling. They smile, and blink, and every now and then make this sound, a soft, airy sigh, which is the beginning of a laugh: "Aaaaaaaaaahhh."

Albert Goldman

On and On Mick's Orgy Rolls

"Don't expect them to scream!" That was the tight-lipped warning passed to Mick Jagger on the now-legendary night, Nov. 8, 1969, when the Rolling Stones took the stage to bring back the good old days of rock 'n' roll to America. The place was the Los Angeles Forum, an 18,000-seat, color-coded, deep-freeze tank with the acoustics of an undampened bowling alley. The bill was black-heavy with people like B. B. King, the regnant blues belter, and Ike and Tina Turner, the belle and beau of the ball-'n'-sock-it circuit. Two hours of diathermy by these deep-fat fryers had put the packed house into a sweaty, happy mood, when suddenly the Forum's zeppelin searchlights switched off and through the murmurous hush of 18,000 craning minds, there sliced the hysterical cry, "THE ROLLING STONES!!!"

Wham! The stage explodes in blue-white incandescence. Out firks the manic form of Mick Jagger, a black forked radish, cinched with a wickedly studded belt and topped off with a towering red, white and blue Uncle Sam hat. After him chases Keith Richard, flame-colored, sequin-spangled, ear-ringed, brandishing a plastic see-through guitar. Then the other Stones: Bill Wyman, a red-clad executioner; Charlie Watts, a T-shirted construction worker, and the new guy, Mick Taylor, with his bright cotton shirt puffed at the sleeves in enormous mutton chops.

Boomeranging the Uncle Sam with one hand while collaring the mike with the other, Jagger screams "Hello!," springs into the air and slams down in a split, as the Stones start bashing out "Jumpin' Jack Flash." The audience, recoiling in audio-visual shock, not only screeeeeeeeeams, but starts climbing the furniture, dancing in the aisles and charging the unguarded stage. Tasting the crowd's warm, salty blood, Mick the Jagger goes mad, tears off his belt, flogs the stage floor, incites the mob to riot and offers himself as their superhuman sacrifice.

Up and up the fever chart zigzags, on and on the orgy rolls, until after two shows, eight hours, a couple of buckets of sweat and a million killing watts of electro-encephalic energy, apocalypse is attained. It's 5:30 in the morning—the Woodstock hour—and Jagger is jigging on the ruins of Western Civilization. He's into his final medley, with a dozen powerful amps screaming, "I Can't Get No Satisfaction." Suddenly, the Stones turn the corner into "Street Fighting Man," and the whole audience levitates. Every man, woman and love-child mounts his chair, raises his right arm over his head and makes his biggest, blackest, hardest fist! What a climax! What a gesture! What pure Nuremberg!

> Held a general's rank, rode a tank
> When the Blitzkrieg raged and the bodies stank!
> —The Rolling Stones
> "Sympathy for the Devil"[1]

Ja wohl! Mein friends, dot's right! Dot good ole rock 'n' role could warm the cockles of a storm trooper's heart. O.K. They don't give you a torch and an armband, like in the *real* old days, and send you down the Rhine to swing with the summer solstice. But you can still squeeze in hip by haunch with thousands of good kamerads; still fatten eyes, ears, soul on the Leader; still plotz out while he socks it to you in stop-time, and, best of all, boys and girls, you can get your rocks off, no, with that good old arm action that means—well, you know what it means.

No question about it, Der Führer would have been gassed out of his kugel by the scene at the Forum. The ultimate performer, Mario's Magician, the prophet who wrote in "Mein Kampf" about the little guy's desire to step out of his day job, where he feels he's a nothing, and become part of "a body of thousands and thousands of people with a like conviction." There, that shows you, Der Führer was so far ahead of his time that only now are the kids catching up with him and showing their fondness for the old freak by digging him under the sneaky guises of comedy and camp.

Still, young people today don't know half enough about Hitler. They've been brainwashed by those shrecky Hollywood movies made during the war years, when one Jewish actor after another took off the Hit as a lunatic and a murderer. (They say he even took dope! It wasn't dope, just a few pain killers.) Young people should only know that Der Führer was a self-proclaimed revolutionary and youth leader. He was the first great tribal shaman and magical minstrel. He was the first to mix the primitive with the futuristic, the first to get it all together, the lights, the sounds, the great clothes and gladiatorial salutes. Why, the guy even wore a maxi coat! O.K. He wasn't much to look at—though he was a terrific dancer! Still who ever offered a beauty prize to Peter Townshend, with that nose of his—or John Lennon with *his* thing? Energy is beauty, baby. Great dictators are **transfigured by zap!**

Actually, the idea that rock is Fascism spelled Fashion is as familiar as the fact that smoking causes cancer. The political parallel has been exploited in films like

1. From "Sympathy for the Devil" by Mick Jagger and Keith Richard. Copyright © 1968 Abkco Music Inc. Used by permission. All rights reserved. International Copyright secured.

"Privilege" and "Wild in the Streets," sermonized upon by Sunday journalists and, most recently, the Rock-Berlin Axis has been explored by the current generation's greatest masterpiece, The Who's rock opera, "Tommy." When the opera's deaf, dumb and blind hero, martyr of the older generation and messiah of the younger, throws off the shackles of his afflictions, he instantly becomes a teen tyrant who fetters his disciples with the same manacles of mind and sense once locked on him. True, the kids rebel finally and go hymning off into the rosy revolutionary dawn. But they leave behind them "Tommy's" minatory message: "Beware the victims and the martyrs; they shall become oppressors in their generations."

What no one has the courage to confess these days is the irresistible attractiveness of the Fascist ceremonial. Denied any real control over his political destiny, filled with hatred and rebelliousness against an old order that strikes him as cruel and corrupt, unrelieved by the satisfactions of work or religion, how else, one wonders, is modern man to right his psychic balance or satisfy the urgencies of his soul? The ethic of love, love, love, give, give, give, good, good, good is beautiful. When, however, has it justified itself as the rule of life? Everything we have learned from the masters of the modern mind testifies to the vanity of being better than you are. The current generation seems like an army of doppelgängers, chanting love and peace as they march to the most militant strains ever blared from the horns of war.

To take the Rolling Stones—in many senses the archetypal rock group—as instance: what a record they have compiled as impersonators of the Devil! Granted there is more evil in one tuning peg of Jimi Hendrix's guitar than in a million copies of "Their Satanic Majesties"; still, the fact remains that the Stones owe much of their success to what might be called the "will to evil." Commencing with such callow misdemeanors as "Let's Spend the Night Together" and escalating through the graver sins of "She Comes in Colors," "Street Fighting Man" and "Sympathy for the Devil," the boys have sneered and fleered and ground their heel into the face of middle-class respectability. They have testified, to the tune of millions of dollars, to the great contemporary longing to be bad.

What has emerged from their triumphal progress—which includes some notable drug busts and the sorry death of Brian Jones—is a public image of sado-homosexual-junkie-diabolic-sarcastic-nigger-evil unprecedented in the annals of pop culture. If the youth public that is so into peace and beatitude were not titillated out of its tepees by this specter of Sodom and gonorrhea, how could they possibly promote the Stones to their present position as the laureates of rock 'n' riot?

The irony—perhaps the vindication—of this strange history is that, in pursuing their evil courses, the Stones have attained to beauty. In their early years, they were little better than facsimile stampers, Xeroxing the work of their black betters, like Chuck Berry and Bo Diddley. In their naughty middle years, they achieved a not-so-fine art of caricature, becoming the musical equivalents of the cartoonist Crumb, reducing a plethora of pop images to a fistful of jeering grotesques. Commencing with their closest communion with sin, "Sympathy for the Devil," they suddenly shifted from a head music of ideas about other people's ideas to a genuine musical life flow. The rolling, roiling *moto perpetuo* of "Sympathy" showed that the Stones had a real musical body that answered to the rhythm of Mick Jagger's body, shaking and soliciting from the stage. Now, in their forthcoming album, "Let It Bleed," this movement toward musical and sensuous beauty reaches its culmination in a remarkable track that blazes a new trail for English rock.

The beauty part of the new record is not the expanded version of "You Can't Always Get What You Want," featuring a 60-voice boy's choir, or the new country version of "Honky Tonk Woman"—though those are good cuts for everyday consumption. The real Thanksgiving sound is offered on the first band, titled "Gimmie Shelter." An obsessively lovely specimen of tribal rock, this richly textured chant is rainmaking music. It dissolves the hardness of the Stones and transforms them into spirit voices singing high above the mazey figures on the dancing ground. The music takes no course, assumes no shape, reaches no climax; it simply repeats over an endless drone until it has soaked its way through your soul.

Half blue grass and half green gage, "Gimmie Shelter" is music to get stoned by. Taken as a counterpoint to the ranting rave-ups the Stones have been staging this past week as they roll toward Madison Square Garden, this cool, impersonal, self-absorbed incantation suggests the schizzy split dividing every contemporary head. It suggests what is actually the fact: that the same kids who are Sieg Heiling one night at some diabolic rally in Pandemonium may be lying the next night in their tents and sleeping bags passing the peace pipe from hand to hand as they watch the tribal fires flicker and go out.

. . . Or "A Whitewash of Jagger"?

"A crime without an instigator" is the way Altamont was described by Ralph J. Gleason, the West Coast critic who made the most exhaustive study of the ill-fated Rolling Stones festival last December. Certainly, none of the participants—including the Hell's Angels who rolled out from Oakland on their hogs to dig the sounds and drink the free beer—intended that Mick Jagger's "Christmas and Chanukah rite for American youth" should degenerate into an orgy of violence and madness, leaving in its wake four dead, hundreds injured, thousands freaked-out and the counter-culture riven to its base.

Yet to concede that accident and the irrational played a part in shaping this grisly sequence of events is not the same thing as saying that the Stones and Angels were wholly innocent of the blood spilt or the brains scattered. Nor should anyone think that the forces which erupted so murderously at Altamont were not lurking at many another rock concert, threatening to pass from the fence-breaking, cop-baiting stage over into something far more serious and regrettable. Altamont was the culmination of a long series of bad trips in the rock world, and its perfect matching of the most sinister figures in American and British pop culture, the Hell's Angels and the Rolling Stones, is one of those master strokes of history beyond the invention of any fiction writer or filmmaker.

Now we have a film, curiously titled "Gimme Shelter," which undertakes to tell the story of Altamont, but which really uses its brightly colored footage to white-wash the Rolling Stones, who must share some of the responsibility for the disaster and who also, as it happens, are the people who hired the filmmakers (the Maysles Brothers and Charlotte Zwerin) and controlled the rights to whatever film they produced. Viewed as a piece of special pleading on behalf of the Stones, the film is an ingenious bit of work. Three different techniques are employed to get the boss off the hook without sacrificing the enormous money-making potential in showing the Angels' brutal behavior toward the crowd or the crowning horror of Meredith Hunter's murder, an event enthusiastically described by a member of the Maysles Brothers' organization as "an 'In Cold Blood' that wasn't staged."

The first line of cop-out is to devote roughly half the film to the exemplary Rolling Stones concert at Madison Square Garden (and other cheery matters), providing thus the basis for Mick Jagger's astonished cry of disbelief, on the stage at Altamont, "All the other scenes were *cool!*" The effect of this editing is to persuade the viewer that Altamont was a bizarre and mysterious exception to that rule of nature which states that Rolling Stones concerts are invariably joyous and beautiful occasions.

What the film does not confront is the fact that all the other Stones concerts were given under entirely different conditions, with high admission prices screening out the heavy weirdos, tightly controlled indoor arenas holding the people under a lid, and unobtrusive, hippie-costumed bouncers tossing the teeny-boppers off the stage.

Jagger's mistake was melding ignorance with megalomania. He didn't have the faintest idea of what would happen when he summoned up 300,000 people in the middle of the California wasteland. He didn't know anything about the West Coast Angels, who are distinctly different from the Hyde Park variety. He assumed, undoubtedly, that if things got out of hand, he could do his Moses-dividing-the-Red-Sea bit and roll back the crowds by sheer force of personality. One of the film's few valid ironies is the image of a sadly deflated Jagger, standing onstage like a little boy in a Superman suit, vainly pleading with people who have lost interest in his music because they are fighting for their lives!

The film's second line of apology is to omit all mention of how it was that the Angels showed up at Altamont Racetrack charged with the unlikely responsibility of acting as Praetorian Guard for the Emperor Mick. The craziness of this idea has never been properly appreciated. People have said that the Angels performed similar peace-keeping functions in the past in the Bay area. This is absolutely false. The Angels did guard the power lines and run the lost-child service at the original Golden Gate Park Be-In; they also held many dances and affairs of their own promotion, but never, before Altamont, did they function anywhere as a police force.

The fact is that Jagger and the Angels were playing footsie for months before they mated so disastrously at Altamont. Delegations of Angels waited on the Prince of Darkness in London, English Angels sauntered around Hyde Park during the Stones's memorial concert for the dead Brian Jones. When Mick raised the question of his security at the beginning of the negotiations for the American free concert, Emmett Grogan, the original Digger, and Rock Scully, former manager of the Grateful Dead, suggested the Angels as bodyguards. "We'll have a hundred Hell's Angels on their hogs escort the Stones. . . . Nobody'll come near the Angels, man. They won't dare!" Can you imagine how irresistible this idea must have seemed to Mick?

After the concert was over, however, and the Angels had acted as Angels always act, Jagger and the Stones reacted with injured innocence. Ah, here it was again, the appalling American brutality against which they were warned! This after-the-fact moralizing emanating from such eminent moralists as the Rolling Stones—provides the filmmakers with their final escape hatch. Time after time we're offered the spectacle of the Stones watching the Altamont footage and reacting to it with suppressed sorrow and disbelief. What more evidence do we require of their basic goodness? Probably the most contrived footage in the whole film comes just after we see the black youth, Meredith Hunter, stabbed to death. "Where's the gun?" cries Jagger. Back the film footage rolls to show us the delicious moment again—this time in slow motion—with a commentary and context that suggest that if the Angel had not stabbed Hunter, Hunter might have aimed his gun at the stage and shot Mick Jagger!

The verité is that Meredith Hunter was a young man with no record of crime (as opposed to his assailant, Alan Passaro, who had already been jailed for dope-dealing and theft when he was arraigned for the murder). Though packing a protective pistol, a precaution adopted by many anxious blacks, Hunter was running away from the Angels' fists and leaded pool cues when suddenly he turned around, pulled out his weapon and came back toward his tormentors. At that moment, he was caught by Passaro, spun around in a typical street fighting man's maneuver and stabbed in the back. Numerous subsequent wounds by other knife-fighters plus who knows how many heavy-booted kicks and hand chops left Hunter a virtual corpse before the first medical attendant could reach him.

All this violence took place within the bright circle of light illuminating the performance area and before the cameras of the Maysles Brothers. (What is the legal status of people who photograph murders?) You couldn't find a closer parallel in any ritual murder in all the thousands of pages of "The Golden Bough." No wonder Jagger was shocked. He had been wiped out by the real thing. Evil—not the campy little trick he turns but knife-wielding, blood-spurting Evil—had come onstage and knocked the diabolic superstar into an Uncle Sam hat. (Incidentally, all this criminal activity went forward without intervention by the police because there were no police at Altamont, the Alameda County sheriff's office having decided—perhaps, as Ralph J. Gleason suggested in a lengthy article in Esquire, in accordance with a long-standing detente with the Hell's Angels—that their presence was not needed at a little free-for-all involving only 300,000 people hopelessly ill-provided with food, sanitation, medical succor or even a place to park.)

I must not end this review of "Gimme Shelter" without registering my enthusiastic praise for the cameramen who hung in there on that cold, weird night in the California desert, reeling in thousands of unforgettable feet showing the Angels, hulking, shaggy bison men in lynx fur hats and bloody insignia, solemnly striding about, meting out punishment to the masochistic fans who lunge like breeding salmon at the stage and its mincing occupant, Mick Jagger. As the bearded patriarchs scowl and their weighty staffs descend on naked bodies and defenseless heads, the thrill of a disciplinary ritual is felt throughout the theater. The most unruly generation in American history is demanding—and receiving—punishment by big father figures with ogre faces, beer bellies and the humorless promptness of dragons rising to the provocation of young, twerpy hippies.

Bravo, you measly brothers! You've captured on film the epic of a self-destructive generation. "Gimme Shelter" gives us the thrills that so many porno-oriented Danish flicks have failed to deliver. Who cares about truth when we can revel in the fantasies of cinema vérité? Up with Mick Jagger! Up with Angel Sonny Barger! Up with the fat, the naked, the pathetically flapping victims of the camera as carnal scourge!

The Alternate Family:
The Community and the Commune

We have built us a dome
On our beautiful plantation,
And we all have one home,
And one family relation.

The song of the Oneida Community, a nineteenth-century utopian settlement, echoes
the dreams and the hopes of the earlier Shakers and heralds the modern communitarian movement which we are witnessing in America today. The communes which
seem so threatening, so new, so revolutionary to many Americans today are, in fact,
neither new nor revolutionary. Their history is a long one and the commune dwellers themselves are acutely aware of the long history of their solution to the agony
of alienation. They trace their origins to varying sources. Some call themselves
descendants of the primitive Christians who, in the monastic communities of the
Augustinians and the Benedictines, lived according to a rule and practiced, by mutual
consent, group labor, group devotions, and the threefold ideal of poverty, chastity,
and obedience. Some consider their settlements fundamentally communist in origin
and point to their interest in abolishing powerful central government, monopolistic
tendencies, and social discriminations.

The communitarian tradition in America is a long one but it flourished best in
the 1840s, a period of the national history which we are, in many senses, repeating
today. Our age incorporates many of the ideals and methods of the American transcendentalists' world. Like the modern communitarians, the transcendentalists did
not hesitate to adopt religious, social, and political views from a vast international
store of ancient and contemporary systems of thought. From the East they learned
contemplation, a respect for the physical environment, and a nature mysticism born,
in part, of universal pantheism. From France, Russia, Germany, England, and Scotland they borrowed new concepts of social structure. William Ellery Channing knew
and admired the social philosophy of Charles Fourier who believed that the ideal
community was what he called a "phalanstère." This was a large cooperative organization consisting of separate family units with an avowed purpose to encourage both
collective production and personal individuality. Brook Farm was the best-known
American outgrowth of Fourierist ideals, but it was neither the first nor the last
utopian community to flourish in America.

Although Brook Farm encouraged those religious tendencies which we recognize as transcendental, it was founded with social rather than religious aims. The
earliest American communes were religious in origin. The most famous of these was
New Lebanon, an eighteenth-century Connecticut community founded by Mother
Anne Lee, a Shaker who, like her Puritan forebears, emigrated to America to escape
religious persecution in her native England. In her endeavor to establish a habitation
congenial to the Shakers, she felt compelled to found a settlement which would

shelter her and her followers from what the Shakers called "The World" or "The World's people." Like the early communitarian Christians, the Shakers practiced chastity and engaged in both economic and educational activities directed toward independence from a society hostile to their ideas. In this and other settlements the Shakers devoted their lives to "setting their house in order," both literally and figuratively. Their festivals were always rituals, their vision mystical.

For generations the Shakers were the most successful of all the communitarian sects, yet other religious communes survived and lent strength to the trend toward the exclusive and homogeneous village. The German Rappist colony of Harmony, the more enduring socioreligious colony of Amana founded by Christian Metz, the Russian Dukhobor colony which finally settled in Canada, are but a few of the communities of worshippers. One of the most successful single communities was the Oneida. There perfectionists gathered to engage in the collective production of silver and textiles which would support a haven for freedom of religious thought as well as specific communal institutions such as "complex marriage," a system which permitted any man and woman to cohabit freely with any other member of the commune. Morality and discipline were a community affair, administered through a technique known as "mutual criticism." In sessions similar to later group therapy meetings, the person at fault would appear before the entire community, who would state their opinions frankly, one after another, and offer constructive suggestions for the improvement of his character. In later years, after the practices of complex marriage and mutual criticism were done away with in the community's struggle to survive in a manner more acceptable to the mores of the "outside," the group still maintained its absolute collective attitude toward property and daily living. The new charter of 1879 included the following propositions:

> *We shall hold our property and business in common, as now.*
> *We shall live together in a common household and eat at*
> *a common table, as now.*

The modern commune dwellers see the outside world in much the same way as did their predecessors; like the prophet Isaiah they condemn society as a "sinful nation, a people laden with iniquity." Their very foundation is symptomatic of a rejection of the society they see about them and of a need to form what has been called an alternate society. A young woman living in a commune in New York City explained that need recently in an interview with the *New York Times:* "Basically the whole idea is an expanded family. In the city you're exposed constantly to the paranoia, the 9-to-5 hustle, dog eat dog. It's hard to come home after that and relate to people." The comparison between the lack of a satisfactory common goal in the ordinary life pattern and the cohesion of the commune, is reminiscent of Robert Owen's goal for the New Harmony commune in 1857: "Happiness cannot be obtained individually; it is useless to expect isolated happiness; all must partake of it or the few can never enjoy it."

Although current communes originated in agrarian settlements, principally in California and the West, urban communes have become more common as people

have banded together, in most cases merely to counteract the anonymity and loneliness of city life. In some instances mutuality of interest, such as women's liberation,
shared professional goals, political activism, or religious practice, provides the underlying basis for communal living; in others spiralling rentals and rising cost of living
are the major motives. All household goods are commonly shared as well as household expenses. There are indications that communal living has made some inroads
on marriage statistics within the last few years. Commune dwellers feel that their
life-style provides the companionship of marriage without the "dead-end" commitment it entails. In all communes most members have had some experience in sensitivity training or group encounters.

Most communes have no authority figures. Like the free society of Vaux,
founded in 1902, the present communitarian would agree that he "admits no other
discipline than that imposed upon himself by each conscious individual because he
knows that he should make his life conform to the logic of things as they are, under
the penalty of falling into worse disasters." Some of these "things as they are" are,
in the words of one young commune dweller, "warm, loving people," security,
spontaneity, and the ability to "flow more freely" toward other human beings.

In spite of the collective life-style which characterizes all communes, from the
hog farmers in New Mexico to the meditation colonies in Big Sur, the groups are
anarchic rather than socialist in nature since they adhere to faith in the individual
and the conviction that large-scale regimentation is at the root of the social evils
they are combating. Although in the popular imagination the word *commune* con-
jures up visions of free sex, drugs, orgies, and political anarchy, in actual fact many
commune residents are as bland in their sexual behavior as were Alcott and his band
of intellectual theoreticians at Fruitlands. The "brother" and "sister" relationship,
so popular as symbols of family closeness in deprived cultures which had very little
real family structure, has become a real basis for living in an idealized society. Until
the goal of self-sufficient life on a piece of land in a rural setting is achieved, the current mode of communal existence in the cities and small towns resembles nothing
so much as informal dormitory living, its members going about their business and
coming together in casual, not intimate, fashion. In most communes the very substructure of idealism upon which the society is founded precludes extreme or antisocial behavior. Unlike the earlier rural settlements, the majority of the new communes are neither self-supporting nor separated from the world. Work for livelihood
is done outside the commune, with the commune replacing the traditional family
residence.

Whatever the communal settlement—whether the meliorist Fruitlands, where
the ideal of perfection was seen as an organic extension of man's return to the purifying rituals of farming, or the orthodox "chavurah" of Jewish students studying at
M.I.T. and Harvard—the very nature of this recurrent phenomenon in American life
bespeaks an idealism in the native American character. Robert Owen is an excellent
spokesman for this visionary view. Convinced that the truth of his principles, expressed and made concrete in the New Harmony commune, would spread "from
Community to Community, from State to State, from Continent to Continent, fi-
ally overshadowing the whole earth, shedding light, fragrance and abundance, intelli-

gence and happiness upon the sons of man," he announced his ultimate goal: "to change (this country) from an ignorant, selfish system which shall gradually unite all interest into one, and remove all causes for contest between individuals."

Charles Lane and Bronson Alcott
Letter from Fruitlands

Dear Sir:

Having perused your several letters in the *Herald of Freedom,* and finding, moreover, a general invitation to correspondence from "persons who feel prepared to cooperate in the work of reform upon principles" akin to those you have set forth, I take this public means of communicating with one, who seems to be really desirous of aiding entire human regeneration.

After many years passed in admiration of a better order in human society, with a constant expectation that some beginning would shortly be made, and a continued reliance that some party would make it, the idea has gradually gained possession of my mind, that it is not right thus to linger for the leadings of other men, but that each should at once proceed to live out the proposed life to the utmost possible extent. Assured that the most potent hindrances to goodness abide in the Soul itself; next in the body; thirdly in the house and family; and in the fourth degree only in our neighbors, or in society at large; I have daily found less and less reason to complain of public institutions, or of the dilatoriness of reformers of genetic minds.

Animated by pure reform principles, or rather by pure creative spirit, I have not hesitated to withdraw as far and as fast as hopeful prudence dictated from the practices and principles of the Old World, and acting upon the conviction that whatever others might do, or leave undone, however others might fail in the realization of their ideal good, I, at least, should advance, I have accordingly arrived in that region where I perceive you theoretically, and I hope, actually dwell. I agree with you that it would be well to cross the ocean of Life from the narrow island of selfishness to the broad continent of universal Love at one dash; but the winds are not always propitious, and steam is only a recent invention. I cannot yet boast of a year's emancipation from old England. One free step leads to another; and the third must necessarily precede the fourth, as the second was before the third.

A. Bronson Alcott's visit to England last year opened to me some of the superior conditions for a pure life which this country offers compared to the land of my nativity and that of your ancestors. My love for purity and goodness was sufficiently strong it seems to loosen me from a position as regards pecuniary income, affectionate friends, and mental liberty, which millions there and thousands here might envy. It has happened however that of the many persons with whom Mr. Alcott hoped to act in conjunction and concert, not one is yet fully liberated by Providence to that end. So that instead of forming items in a large enterprise, we are left to be the principal actors in promoting an idea less in extent, but greater in intent, than any yet presented to our observation.

Our removal to this estate in humble confidence has drawn to us several practical coadjutors, and opened many inquiries by letter for a statement of our principles and modes of life. We cannot perhaps turn our replies to better account, than to transcribe some portions of them for your information, and we trust, for your sincere satisfaction.

You must be aware, however, that written words cannot do much towards the elucidation of principles comprehending all human relationships, and claiming an origin profound as man's inmost consciousness of the ever present Living Spirit. A dwelling together, a concert in soul, and a consorting in body, is a position needful to entire understanding, which we hope at no distant day to attain with yourself and many other sincere friends. We have not yet drawn out any preordained plan of daily operations, as we are impressed with the conviction that by a faithful reliance on the Spirit which actuates us, we are sure of attaining to clear revelations of daily practical duties as they are to be daily done by us. When the Spirit of Love and Wisdom abounds, literal forms are needless, irksome or hinderative; where the Spirit is lacking, no preconceived rules can compensate.

To us it appears not so much that improved circumstances are to meliorate mankind, as that improved men will originate the superior condition for themselves and others. Upon the Human Will, and not upon circumstances, as some philosophers assert, rests the function, power and duty, of generating a better social state. The human beings in whom the Eternal Spirit has ascended from low animal delights or mere human affections, to a state of spiritual chastity and intuition, are in themselves a divine atmosphere, they *are* superior circumstances and are constant in endeavoring to create, as well as to modify, all other conditions, so that these also shall more and more conduce to the like consciousness in others.

Hence our perseverance in efforts to attain simplicity in diet, plain garments, pure bathing, unsullied dwellings, open conduct, gentle behavior, kindly sympathies, serene minds. These, and several other particulars needful to the true end of man's residence on earth, may be designated the Family Life. Our Happiness, though not the direct object in human energy, may be accepted as the conformation of rectitude, and this is not otherwise attainable than in the Holy Family. The Family in its highest, divinest sense is therefore our true position, our sacred earthly destiny. It comprehends every divine, every human relation consistent with universal good, and all others it rejects, as it disdains all animal sensualities.

The evils of life are not so much social, or political, as personal, and a personal reform only can eradicate them.

Let the Family, furthermore, be viewed as the home of pure social affections, the school of expanding intelligence, the sphere of unbought art, the scene of joyous employment, and we feel in that single sentiment, a fulness of action, of life, of being, which no scientific social contrivance can ensure, nor selfish accident supply.

Family is not dependent upon numbers, nor upon skill, nor riches, but upon union in and with that spirit which alone can bless any enterprise whatever.

On this topic of Family association, it will not involve an entire agreement with the Shakers to say they are at least entitled to deeper consideration than they yet appear to have secured. There are many important acts in their career worthy of observation. It is perhaps most striking that the only really successful extensive Community of interest, spiritual and secular, in modern times was established by A Woman. Again, we witness in this people the bringing together of the two sexes in a new relation, or rather with a new idea of the old relation. This has led to results more harmonic than anyone seriously believes attainable for the human race, either in isolation or association, so long as divided, conflicting family arrangements are permitted. The great secular success of the Shakers; their order, cleanliness, intelligence and serenity are so eminent, that it is worthy of enquiry how far these are attribthe to an adherence to their peculiar doctrine.

As to Property, we discover not its just disposal either in individual or social tenures, but in its entire absorption into the New Spirit, which ever gives and never grasps.

While we write, negotiations are entertained for our removal to a place of less inconvenience, by friends who have long waited for some proof of a determination to act up to the idea they have cherished. Many, no doubt, are yet unprepared "to give up all and follow him" (the Spirit) who can importantly aid in the New Advent, and conscientiously accomplish the legal processes needful under the present circumstances. We do not recognize the purchase of land; but its redemption from the debasing state of *proprium,* or property, to divine uses, we clearly understand when those whom the world esteems as owners are found yielding their individual rights to the Supreme Owner. Looking at the subject practically in relation to a climate in which a costly shelter is necessary, and where a family with many children has to be provided for, the possibility of at once stepping boldly out of the toils into which the errors of our predecessors have cast us, is not so evident as it is desirable.

Trade we hope entirely to avoid at an early day. As a nursery for many evil propensities it is almost universally felt to be a most undesirable course. Such needful articles as we cannot yet raise by our own hand labor from the soil, thus redeemed from human ownership, we shall endeavor to obtain by friendly exchanges, and, as nearly as possible, without the intervention of money.

Of all the traffic in which civilized society is involved, that of human labor is perhaps the most detrimental. From the state of serfdom to the receipt of wages may be a step in human progress; but it is certainly full time for taking a new step out of the hiring system.

Our outward exertions are in the first instance directed to the soil, and as our ultimate aim is to furnish an instance of self-sustaining cultivation without the subjugation of either men or cattle, or the use of foul animal manures, we have at the outset to encounter struggles and oppositions somewhat formidable. Until the land is restored to its pristine fertility by the annual return of its own green crops, as sweet and animating manures, the human hand and simple implement cannot wholly supersede the employment of machinery and cattle. So long as cattle are used in agriculture, it is very evident that man will remain a slave, whether he be proprietor or hireling. The driving of cattle beyond their natural and pleasurable exertion; the waiting upon them as cook and chambermaid three parts of the year; the excessive labor of mowing, curing, and housing hay, and of collecting other fodder, and the large extra quantity of land needful to keep up this system, form a continuation of unfavorable circumstances which must depress the human affections so long as it continues, and overlay them by the injurious and extravagant development of the animal and bestial natures in man. It is calculated that if no animal food were consumed, one-fourth of the land now used would suffice for human sustenance. And the extensive tracts of country now appropriated to grazing, mowing, and other modes of animal provision, could be cultivated by and for intelligent and affectionate human neighbors. The sty and the stable too often secure more of the farmer's regard than he bestows on the garden and the children. No hope is there for humanity while Woman is withdrawn from the tender assiduities which adorn her and her household, to the servitudes of the dairy and the flesh pots. If the beasts were wholly absent from man's neighborhood, the human population might be at least four times as dense as it now is without raising the price of land. This would give to the country all the advantages of concentration without the vices which always spring up in the dense city.

Debauchery of both the earthly soil and the human body is the result of this cattle keeping. The land is scourged for crops to feed the animals, whose ordures are used under the erroneous supposition of restoring lost fertility; disease is thus infused into the human body; stimulants and medicines are resorted to for relief, which end in a precipitation of the original evil to a more disastrous depth. These misfortunes which affect not only the body, but by reaction rise to the sphere of the soul, would be avoided, or at least in part, by the disuse of animal food. Our diet is therefore strictly the pure and bloodless kind. No animal substances, neither flesh, butter, cheese, eggs, nor milk, pollute our table or corrupt our bodies, neither tea, coffee, molasses, nor rice, tempts us beyond the bounds of indigenous productions. Our sole beverage is pure fountain water. The native grains, fruits, herbs, and roots, dressed with the utmost cleanliness and regard to their purpose of edifying a healthful body, furnish the pleasantest refections and in the greatest variety requisite to the supply of the various organs. The field, the orchard, the garden, in their bounteous products of wheat, rye, barley, maize, oats, buckwheat, apples, pears, peaches, plums, cherries, currants, berries, potatoes, peas, beans, beets, carrots, melons, and other vines, yield an ample store for human nutrition, without dependence on foreign climes, or the degeneration of shipping and trade. The almost inexhaustible variety of the several stages and sorts of vegetable growth, and the several modes of preparation, are a full answer to the question which is often put by those who have never ventured into the region of a pure and chaste diet: "If you give up flesh meat, upon what then can you live?"

Our other domestic habits are in harmony with those of diet. We rise with early dawn, begin the day with cold bathing, succeeded by a music lesson, and then a chaste repast. Each one finds occupation until the meridian meal, when usually some interesting and deep-searching conversation gives rest to the body and development to the mind. Occupation, according to the season and the weather, engages us out of doors or within, until the evening meal,—when we again assemble in social communion, prolonged generally until sunset, when we resort to sweet repose for the next day's activity.

In these steps of reform we do not rely as much on scientific reasoning of physiological skill, as on the Spirit's dictates. The pure soul, by the law of its own nature, adopts a pure diet and cleanly customs; nor needs detailed instruction for daily conduct. On a revision of our proceedings it would seem, that if we were in the right course in our particular instance, the greater part of man's duty consists in leaving alone much that he is in the habit of doing. It is a fasting from the present activity, rather than an increased indulgence in it, which, with patient watchfulness tends to newness of life. "Shall I sip tea or coffee?" the inquiry may be. No; abstain from all ardent, as from alcoholic drinks. "Shall I consume pork, beef, or mutton?" Not if you value health or life. "Shall I stimulate with milk?" No. "Shall I warm my bathing water?" Not if cheerfulness is valuable. "Shall I clothe in many garments?" Not if purity is aimed at. "Shall I prolong my dark hours, consuming animal oil and losing bright daylight in the morning?" Not if a clear mind is an object. "Shall I teach my children the dogmas inflicted on myself, under the pretence that I am trans- mitting truth?" Nay, if you love them intrude not these between them and the Spirit of all Truth. "Shall I subjugate cattle?" "Shall I trade?" "Shall I claim property in any created thing?" "Shall I interest myself in politics?" To how many of these ques- tions could we ask them deeply enough, could they be heard as having relation to our eternal welfare, would the response be "Abstain"? Be not so active to do, as sin- cere to be. Being in preference to doing, is the great aim and this comes to us rather by a resigned willingness than a wilful activity;—which is indeed a check to all divine growth. Outward abstinence is a sign of inward fulness; and the only source of true progress is inward. We may occupy ourselves actively in human improvements;—but these unless inwardly well-impelled, never attain to, but rather hinder, divine progress in man. During the utterance of this narrative it has undergone a change in its per- sonal expression which might offend the hypercritical; but we feel assured that you will kindly accept it as unartful offering of both your friends in ceaseless aspiration.

Charles Lane,
A. Bronson Alcott.

Harvard, Mass.,
August, 1843.

Mark Holloway
Oneida

We have built us a dome
On our beautiful plantation,
And we all have one home,
And one family relation.
Oneida song.

American communities played a significant part in American history to the extent
to which they occupied themselves with problems that were vital to the nation. The
Pietists of the eighteenth century had been pioneers in the anti-slavery movement;
and their work was carried on in the nineteenth century by the Shakers, New Harmony, the pre-Fourierist and Fourierist Associations, and Oneida. New Harmony
and Brook Farm had revolutionised education; and the emancipation of women had
been achieved to some extent by all these groups, for they proved that women were
capable of fulfilling as wide a variety of administrative and occupational duties as
men. In the case of the Shakers this liberal attitude to the status of women was based
upon their peculiar concept of a bisexual God; it was also a policy dictated to some
extent, consciously or unconsciously, by celibacy, in which state the attempt of one
sex to dominate the other could only have proved disastrous. In most cases, however,
the liberal attitude to women was a logical consequence of the communistic attitude
towards property. The Puritans—those thrifty guardians of mercantile interests and
worldly goods—had proved to be the most domineering tyrants in the home, and the
most unrelenting martinets with regard to the least sexual irregularity. When the
power of the Calvinistic Church was challenged and in many cases overthrown by
eighteenth-century secularism, and again by revivalism, the puritanical attitude to
sex was also swept away. Humanist enlightenment prepared the way for Mary Woll-
stonecraft, Fanny Wright, and Margaret Fuller. Reason demanded, at the very least,
that women should be allowed to exercise their undoubted scholarly and intellectual
faculties. Revivalism, on the other hand, led to a complete revision of the attitude
towards the purely physical relationship of the sexes. The dances of the celibate
Shakers and "The Jerks" of those who attended the enormous camp meetings of the
frontier, were similar means of erotic sublimation, while Mormonism, with its licensed
polygamy, showed a preoccupation with sex while denying the purely intellectual
concept of feminine emancipation.

The Shakers, and most revivalists, had been content to permit the maximum
amount of licence that was compatible with absolute chastity. The complement of
this licence was a rigid system of taboo, which was observed with a ritualistic attention to detail. Such a discipline also existed, without the corresponding sublimatory
licence, at Oberlin Theological Seminary, of which the President was Charles Grandi-
son Finney, the famous revivalist. The students of both sexes who attended the Seminary prided themselves upon their ability to withstand all sexual temptation. But

since their spiritual muscles were in such fine trim, the desire to exercise them was correspondingly great. How could they be certain of their stamina and resistance— how, indeed, could they even keep in training—without regular practice in jumping the hurdles and leaping the ditches of sexual temptation? Some means must be found of arousing passion in order that it might be resisted—some means, of course, that would have the blessing of religious sanction.

What better method could be found than that ancient custom of taking "spiritual wives"—a tradition handed down from the Agapetæ of early Christian days? So, at any rate, thought Lucinia Umphreville, who had studied these matters under Finney. She proclaimed the doctrine in that part of New York State known as the Burnt Over Region—in which the fires of revivalism had flamed with an all-consuming thoroughness. Miss Umphreville stated that perfection could be derived from passionate love, provided the lovers lived together without indulging their carnal desires. Should they be so weak as to submit to temptation, the spiritual couples would prove that they were unworthy and ill-assorted. They would have to look for new partners, and go on experimenting and searching until the ideal partner was found. Umphrevillian Perfectionism, in fact, by making provision for lapses from grace, slyly admitted erotic possibilities by a side door. It was the very type of casuistical justification for which the Burnt Over Region had been waiting; and it was not long before a number of congregations devoted to the propagation of this form of Perfectionism, had sprung up in New England. They even possessed, in *The Battle Axe,* a newspaper devoted to their beliefs. In the middle 'thirties there appeared among these Perfectionists an earnest and eager young man who was to give the doctrine a revolutionary twist of his own by actually establishing a colony of Perfectionists who would openly practise a completely new system of sexual relations.

John Humphrey Noyes, unlike the founders of most religious communities, came of a well-established family. His father had represented Vermont in Congress, and his mother was a great-aunt of Rutherford Birchard Hayes, nineteenth President of the United States. Noyes was a born rebel, and was happily endowed with the temerity that such men require in order to achieve success. He was converted at a revival in 1831, at the age of twenty, having previously shown little interest in theology or, indeed, in the studies he had been pursuing at Dartmouth. Moving now to Andover and Yale Divinity Schools, he prepared to enter the ministry, but to enter it upon his own terms: "If you are to be a minister," said his father, "you must think and preach as the rest of the ministers do; if you get out of the traces, they will whip you in." "Never!" replied Noyes, "never will I be whipped by ministers or anybody else into views that do not commend themselves to my understanding as guided by the Bible and enlightened by the Spirit." This animated reply was a prophetic utterance, for Noyes very soon got out of the traces. His trouble was that he simply couldn't believe he was a sinner. Try as he might, he couldn't summon up any feelings of deep guilt or despair. Yet this very waywardness was itself a sin in the eyes of the orthodox; and Noyes, being unable to admit it, somehow had to devise a means of abolishing sin altogether. His solution to this problem was so astoundingly simple that it amounted to a stroke of genius. In the summer of 1833, while reading the last words of the Fourth Gospel, Noyes received a sudden illumination concerning Christ's

words, "If I will that he tarry till I come, what is that to thee?" "I knew," wrote
Noyes, "that the time appointed for the Second Advent was within one generation
from the time of Christ's personal ministry"—in A.D. 70, to be precise. The Second
Coming had taken place centuries ago—so long ago, in fact, that no record of the
event had been preserved. The sinners had been divided from the saved, and he that
sinned now, so Noyes preached, was of the devil. Noyes himself had the courage to
proclaim that he did not sin, and the grace to confess that Christ had absolved him.[1]
Thus, in coming to terms with an innate conviction that eternal damnation was an
unnecessary and troublesome doctrine, Noyes formulated a belief that differed from
those of former sectarian heresies only by its boldness and simplicity.

The implications of a Second Advent that has already taken place are bound
to be far-reaching. The Shakers and the Noyesian Perfectionists, both of whom
thought that they were living in a state of regeneration, believed that if they were
not quite in heaven itself, they were at least close enough to it to order their lives
upon heavenly conventions. One such convention for which Biblical authority existed
was the absence of marriage in Heaven—where "they neither marry nor are given in
marriage." The Shakers, who wanted to be celibate, used this text in order to justify
their desires: the followers of Noyes, who did not want celibacy, used the same text
to support a form of regulated promiscuity. In 1837 *The Battle Axe* published a
letter from Noyes explaining his conception of the sexual relations that ought to
exist between men and women. In his letter, he stated uncompromisingly that when
the will of God is done on earth as it is in Heaven "*there will be no marriage*. The
marriage supper of the Lamb is a feast at which *every dish is free to every guest.*
Exclusiveness, jealousy, quarrelling have no place there, for the same reason as that
which forbids a guest at a thanksgiving dinner to claim each his separate dish, and
quarrel with the rest for his rights. In a holy community, there is no more reason
why sexual intercourse should be restrained by law, than why eating and drinking
should be—and there is as little occasion for shame in the one case as in the other."

Here was boldness carried to lengths that had never before been approached.
All the subconscious sexual desires of the past ten or twenty years had at last found
a spokesman whom nothing could daunt, a tactician who drove straight through the
enemy's lines of defence armed only with an ingenious shield of his own devising.

Since Noyes had made his unlawful system of sexual intercourse depend upon
membership of a holy community, the next step was obviously to found one. In
1834 (after engaging in anti-slavery activity), Noyes had returned to his parental
home at Putney, Vermont. Here he began to give Bible classes, and to convert his
family to his views. Here he married Harriet Holton, granddaughter of a Lieutenant-
governor of the state; and began to publish *The Witness,* which was written, composed, type-set, printed, and mailed by the family. In 1839, the group was joined
by George Cragin—who had been a revivalist under Finney—and his family, and by
J. L. Skinner, who married one of Noyes's sisters. Others, including William Alfred
Hinds, also joined. So far there had been no formal organisation, but in 1840 the

---

1. This confession was made on 20th February 1834. The anniversaries of this date were observed at Putney and Oneida Communities.

Putney Association came into being—as a purely religious body, thus described in *The Witness:*

> *Our establishment, such as it is, exists in the midst of an ordinary village, and differs not in its relation to the community around from a manufacturing corporation or any other ordinary association. A few families of the same religious faith, without any formal scheme or written laws, have agreed to regard themselves as one family, and their relations to one another are regulated as far as possible by this idea. The special object of the association is not to make money, nor to exemplify the perfection of social life, but to support the publication of the gospel of salvation from sin, by papers, books, tracts, etc. Formal community of property is not regarded by us as obligatory on principle, but as expedient with reference to our present circumstances and objects. We are attempting no scientific experiments in political economy nor in social science, and beg to be excused from association in the public mind with those who are making such experiments. Our highest ambition is to be able to preach Christ without being burdensome to any, and to act out as far as possible the family spirit of the gospel. When we find a better way than our present plan to attain these objects we shall freely change our mode of living.*

They soon found "a better way than their present plan" of living, and in 1844 adopted communism, in which change Noyes had been influenced by the example of the Shakers. With 500 acres of fertile land, seven houses, a store, and a printing office, the little community established itself upon a sound basis, combining manual labour in the afternoons with reading, writing, debating, singing and prayer in the evenings. Hebrew, Greek, and Latin were taught; and on Sundays there were chapel meetings attended by "outsiders." The famous weekly meetings for mutual criticism also began here; and it was at Putney, also, that Noyes first formulated his ideas of Male Continence and Complex Marriage, which were adopted by the community in 1846.

These latter practices were more than the inquisitive neighbours were prepared to tolerate. In the following year the persecution of the community culminated in the indictment of Noyes on the grounds of adultery. Noyes, who was too sagacious to play the part of a useless martyr, and who by this time was regarded by his followers as the Moses of the new dispensation, destined to lead them to a Promised Land, hastily purchased that land in another state. This Canaan consisted of twenty-three acres, with a few buildings on it, at Oneida, an excellent site in the Burnt Over Region. In 1847, therefore, it was unanimously adopted by the forty or fifty members at Putney "that the Kingdom of God had come." *The Witness* ceased publication and Noyes went to Oneida to take over the new estate, where in March 1848 he was joined by the greater number of his followers, the removal being completed in the following year.

During the years at Putney, they had rejected Fourierism, but "drank copiously of the spirit of the *Harbinger* and of the Socialists; and have always acknowledged that they received a great impulse from Brook Farm. Thus the Oneida Community really issued from a conjunction between the Revivalism of Orthodoxy and the Socialism of Unitarianism. . . . In the fall of 1847, when Brook Farm was breaking up, the Putney Community was also breaking up, but in the agonies, not of death, but of birth."[2]

The birth of Oneida Community was preceded by the conceptions of Male Continence and Complex Marriage. Both systems, although given religious justification, were invented by Noyes in order to overcome the suffering which was then the common experience of women in childbirth. Mrs. Noyes had given birth to five babies in six years, and four of them had been stillborn. Her husband could see no religious reason for permitting such pain and disappointment; but, since he disapproved of contraceptives, he advocated the practice of "self-control," or *coitus reservatus*. At the same time Noyes the organiser, the lover of scientific method and order, was shocked by haphazard procreation, which often resulted in the birth of deformed or mentally deficient children. "We are opposed," he wrote in *Bible Communism,* "to random procreation, which is unavoidable in the marriage system. But we are in favour of intelligent, well-ordered procreation. The physiologists say that the race cannot be raised from ruin till propagation is made a matter of science; but they point out no way of making it so. Procreation is controlled and reduced to a science in the case of valuable domestic brutes; but marriage and fashion forbid any such system among human beings. We believe the time will come when involuntary and random propagation will cease, and when scientific combination will be applied to human generation as freely and successfully as it is to that of other animals. The way will be open for this when amativeness can have its proper gratification without drawing after it procreation as a necessary sequence. And at all events, we believe that good sense and benevolence will very soon sanction and enforce the rule that women shall bear children only when they choose. They have the principal burdens of breeding to bear, and they rather than men should have their choice of time and circumstances, at least till science takes charge of the business."

But "amativeness" was seldom satisfied by monogamy, which "gives to sexual appetite only a scanty and monotonous allowance, and so produces the natural vices of poverty, contraction of taste, and stinginess or jealousy. It makes no provision for the sexual appetite at the very time when that appetite is the strongest. By the custom of the world, marriage, in the average of cases, takes place at about the age of twenty-four; whereas puberty commences at the age of fourteen. For ten years, therefore, and that in the very flush of life, the sexual appetite is starved. This law of society bears hardest on females, because they have less opportunity of choosing their time of marriage than men."

The obvious remedy for these abuses was male continence combined with complete freedom of intercourse. Such a system would also remove that discrepancy between community of goods and private possession of persons that must always be obnoxious to a logical-minded individual like Noyes; for was it not absurd that man "should be allowed and required to love in all directions, and yet be forbidden to express love except in one direction?"

2. Noyes, p. 616.

Complex marriage meant, in theory, that any man and woman might freely co-habit within the limits of the community. In practice, however, there was less free-dom than might have been expected. The partners in this new form of relationship were obliged to obtain each other's consent, "not by private conversation or court-ship, but through the intervention of some third person or persons."[3] The exclusive attachment of two persons was regarded as selfish and "idolatrous" and was strongly discouraged. It was usually broken up by means of "mutual criticism"—and so were the innocent "partialities" of one child for another. While no one was obliged, under any circumstances, to receive the attentions of someone whom he or she did not like, the propagation of children was controlled by the elder members of the community. They advised that the young of one sex should be paired off with the aged of the other sex; and at one time twenty-four men and twenty women were specially selected in order to conduct a eugenic experiment designed "to produce the usual number of offspring to which people in the middle classes are able to afford judicious moral and spiritual care, with the advantage of a liberal education."[4]

On the whole the system was remarkably successful. Apart from a few sorrows due to the breaking-up of an exclusive attachment, the sexual relations of the mem-bers inspired them with a lively interest in each other, and Pierrepont Noyes—one of the sons of John Humphrey—believes "that the opportunity for romantic friendships also played a part in rendering life more colourful than elsewhere. Even elderly peo-ple, whose physical passions had burned low, preserved the fine essence of earlier associations."[5]

It is likely that Noyes's attention was first drawn towards the religious justifica-tion of Complex Marriage at Andover Theological Seminary, where Professor Moses Stuart taught that the description of the marriage relations in Rom. vii applied to carnal man before conversion, and was not a matter of Christian experience. Noyes certainly derived the idea of Mutual Criticism from Andover, where it was practised by the students in order to further their spiritual development.

At Oneida, Mutual Criticism was the medium of all discipline. Usually a mem-ber who was confronted with a moral problem or who was conscious of some form of guilt would request a criticism; but sometimes the treatment was administered as a corrective for unacknowledged delinquency; and it was even used, as psycho-analysis is now used, as a cure for physical ailments—apparently with a number of satisfactory results. The person to be criticised would sometimes appear before the entire society, but more often before a committee selected from those who knew him best. Each member would then state quite frankly the faults and merits of the person concerned, while he sat in silence. Any tendency to spitefulness or prejudice on the part of a member of the committee would be corrected by other members, and by the knowl-edge that such conduct would in itself call for criticism. At the end of the session, the chairman of the committee would usually sum up and offer such advice, reproof, or encouragement as seemed necessary. No ill-feeling was provoked in the "victim," who almost always emerged from the ordeal with a clear knowledge of how to repair

3. Nordhoff, p. 276.
4. Noyes, *Essay on Scientific Propagation*.
5. *My Father's House*, p. 131.

his faults or avoid the causes of his distress. Like other Oneida institutions, Mutual Criticism was an adaptation of similar customs that existed in various religious communities; but it was an improvement on most of them, since it was untainted with authoritarianism.

The accommodation at Oneida was primitive, consisting of two log-houses, a log-hut, and an old saw-mill; and the community suffered several years of hardship until they were joined by Sewell Newhouse, an inventor of steel traps. The community began the manufacture of these gadgets, and was saved from financial disaster; but they made no clear profit until 1857, and were still sleeping in garrets and out-houses twelve years after the foundation of Oneida. In this time, however, they had also produced travelling bags and satchels, preserved fruit, and silk—all of which commodities were made with such care and thoroughness that the community earned a wide reputation for skilled workmanship.

Meanwhile, they had bought more land and acquired more members. At the beginning of 1849 the membership had been eighty-seven; during that year it doubled; in 1851 there were 205; in 1875, 298; in 1878, 306. Not all of these members lived at Oneida, for in 1849 a small branch community had been started at Brooklyn, and others followed at Wallingford, Newark, Putney, Cambridge, and Manlius. In 1855 some of these branches were abandoned in favour of a policy of concentration at Oneida and Wallingford.

Most of the members were New England farmers and mechanics, but there were also lawyers, clergymen, merchants, physicians, and teachers. After the completion, in the early 'sixties, of the large brick Mansion House at Oneida, they all lived under one roof, except for two or three dozen mechanics who lived near the workshops that were situated about a mile away. (These factories were fitted with the latest labour-saving machinery, and turned out 300,000 traps, and silk-twist to the value of $20,000 a year.) Nearer to the Mansion House were offices, a school (with chemical laboratory and photographic apparatus), a carpenter's shop, barns, stables, laundry, and other necessary buildings.

The Mansion House itself was centrally heated throughout, and well supplied with baths and labour-saving kitchens. It contained several large halls, a visitor's parlour, a reading and reference library of 5,000 volumes, with all the leading newspapers and journals on file, two "family" or recreation rooms, and a large number of bedrooms. (The older members had separate bedrooms; the younger usually slept two in a room.) Also, above the dining-hall was the printing office of the *Oneida Circular*.

A firm believer in the power of the written word, Noyes had already published several journals before arriving at Oneida. He was, in fact, a prolific and energetic writer of books and pamphlets as well—most of them marked by a lucid and vigorous style. *The Berean*, published in 1847 at Putney, was an exposition of his religious views, even as *Bible Communism*, published in 1848 at Oneida, contained his social theories. The *Circular*, which superseded some earlier journals at Oneida, was a weekly paper, well produced, and well written, but distributed in a most unorthodox manner, as its own announcement will show:

The Circular *is sent to all applicants, whether they pay or not. It costs and is worth at least two dollars per volume. Those who want it and ought to have it are divisible into three classes, viz.: 1, those who can not afford to pay two dollars; 2, those who can afford to pay only two dollars; and, 3, those who can afford to pay more than two dollars. The first ought to have it free; the second ought to pay the cost of it; and the third ought to pay enough more than the cost to make up the deficiencies of the first. This is the law of Communism. We have no means of enforcing it, and no wish to do so, except by stating it and leaving it to the good sense of those concerned. We take the risk of offering the* Circular *to all without price; but free subscriptions will be received only from persons making application for themselves, either directly or by giving express authority to those who apply for them.*

At the time of Nordhoff's visit, 2,000 copies were printed weekly, at an annual loss of $600—which proves the importance that Noyes set upon propaganda. Propaganda, in fact, was even introduced into the advertisement columns of the *Circular,* in a somewhat facetious manner. A few examples will suffice:

TO BROKERS

WANTED—Any amount of SHARES OF SECOND-COMING STOCK, bearing the date A.D. 70, or thereabouts, will find a ready market and command a high premium at this office.
ROOMS TO LET in the "Many Mansions" that Christ has prepared for those that love him.
PATENT SIEVES. The series of sieves for CRITICISM having been thoroughly tested, are now offered to the public for general use. They are warranted to sift the tares from the wheat, and in all cases to discriminate between good and evil. A person, after having passed through this series, comes out free from the encumbrances of egotism, pride, etc., etc. All persons are invited to test them gratuitously.
GRAND FIRE ANNIHILATOR!—AN INVENTION for overcoming Evil with Good.
MEEK & LOWLY.

In spite of this rather tiresome evangelical playfulness, the Oneida Perfectionists were by no means narrow-minded. They encouraged freedom of enquiry and education, placed the works of Huxley, Darwin, and Herbert Spencer on their library shelves, and engaged in every form of art, amusement, and decorative embellishment that might bring them culture and happiness. They had an excellent orchestra; dances; plays; pantomimes, entertainers, and stereopticons for the children; chess, draughts, and card games; and frequent picnics. They encircled their home with a wide lawn, and surrounded the lawn with ornamental trees and shrubs. They owned summer resorts at Oneida Lake, twelve miles away, where they fished and hunted; and also at Short Beach, Connecticut, on Long Island Sound. Believing that "every man, woman and child should be surrounded with circumstances favouring the best development of heart, mind and body, and that no one should be excluded on account of age, sex or race, from engaging in any occupation for which he or she is adapted by nature or culture," they provided, either at Oneida or Wallingford, as many complementary occupations and amenities as possible. Oneida concentrated mainly on industry, although possessing large orchards and 100 head of cattle; Wallingford paid greater attention to farming and horticulture, although it owned two small factories—one for the production of silk and one at which spoons were made. Perfect community of interest existed between these two societies, and members moved freely to and from the one or the other. They made no definite rules with regard to the time of rising in the morning or the hours of work, but encountered very little shiftlessness. (Any tendency to laziness or lukewarmness was countered by the system of mutual criticism.) Their freedom in this respect, however, was purchased by the employment of a greater number of hired labourers per head than in any other communistic society. The two communities between them employed as many as 250—all of whom were well treated—saying that, although they expected that communism would at some time displace the hireling system, "in the meantime we propose to help our neighbours and ourselves by furnishing remunerative labour to those who are not prepared for Communism." In practice, however, the number of hired labourers never declined, and most of the members of the community lived the privileged lives of superintendents of departments. They also frequently changed their jobs—especially the more disagreeable ones—in order to avoid monotony. (For the same reason, they sometimes changed the order of their evening meetings, their amusements, and even the times of their meals.)

Their affairs were ordered by twenty-one standing committees and forty-eight administrative departments, which together covered every conceivable activity and interest from hair-cutting and dentistry to education and silk-manufacture. The heads of all departments formed a Business Board which met every Sunday morning. At this meeting, which was open to all members, the business of the past week was discussed, and a secretary took notes of the proposals and recommendations made for the following week. The secretary's report was then read out in the Sunday evening meeting and discussed; only those proposals which received general approval were carried out. Reports of all these meetings were exchanged between the two communities.

Accounts were sent in once a month by the heads of departments, and at an annual meeting of the Business Board the work for the year was carefully laid out, estimates having been sent in to the Finance Committee, which made the appropriate allocations of money. Any member of the community could submit projects, with an estimate of the costs involved, to this meeting, and nothing was decided without general consent. In appointing members to various occupations, their inclinations and abilities were both carefully considered; but the committee responsible for these appointments could vary the employments either to suit the individual or the needs of the community. Women served on these committees, and shared in all activities, on an equal footing with men.

Their book-keeping—in the charge of a young woman—was so carefully orga-
nised that they could tell at a glance the exact financial position of any department,
or of the entire community; they also kept a methodical inventory, which was revised
annually, of all their possessions; and the same love of systematic administration was
responsible for a board which revealed at a glance the whereabouts of every member
on any given day.

"The men," wrote Nordhoff, "dress as people in the world do, but plainly, each
one following his own fancy. The women wear a dress consisting of a bodice, loose
trousers, and a short skirt falling to just above the knee. Their hair is cut just below
the ears, and I noticed that the younger women usually gave it a curl. The dress is no
doubt extremely convenient: it admits of walking in mud or snow, and allows freedom of exercise; and it is entirely modest. But it was to my unaccustomed eyes totally and fatally lacking in grace and beauty." They had no peculiar mode of addressing each other; the men were called "mister" and the women "miss," with the exception of those who had been married before entering the society. "It was somewhat
startling to me," Nordhoff confessed, "to hear Miss —— speak about her baby."

As to the babies themselves, they were cared for by the mother until weaned,
when they were placed in the infants' department of the Children's House, which
occupied one wing of the Mansion. Here they were cared for from 8 a.m. to 5 p.m.
by nurses who worked half-day shifts. At about eighteen months the infants were promoted to another department, in which they stayed all day; and eventually at about
three years of age the children left their mothers even at night, and remained in the
Children's House until the age of thirteen or fourteen. During all this time parents
were free to visit their children and take them for walks, whenever they wished; nor
was the mother ever separated from her child for any considerable length of time,
but as soon as the infant had been weaned she gradually gave up all particular responsibility for its clothing, diet, and night-care, and began to resume her place in the industries of the community.

Children were allowed to sleep as long as they wished in the mornings, and
were encouraged to learn some trade or craft as well as their lessons in ordinary subjects. Before they began to take part in the industries of the community, promising
talent was given an opportunity to leave the community for the purpose of special
study or instruction. They sent several young men to Yale, where they took up professional studies—of medicine, law, engineering, and architecture. Others, of both
sexes, were sent to factories, in order to learn new techniques and acquire thorough
experience—for the community gained from their knowledge when these students
returned. The inventiveness, ingenuity, and practical skill in Oneida workshops, business, and administration were largely due to this link with the world. For instance,
when they began to manufacture silk, one of their students brought back a machine
as a pattern; the community then made all the machines it needed in its own foundry
and shops. Similarly, a young chemical student brought back the secrets of dyeing;
and, apart from these derived ideas, they invented improvements of their own, such
as a gadget to measure silk by the yard during winding, and another to test its
strength. Many labour-saving devices appeared in the Mansion itself, of which the
most interesting were the circular tables installed in the dining-hall. These, which

were designed to accommodate about a dozen people each, had a stationary rim, on which were set plates, saucers, cups, and cutlery, and at the centre a revolving disc on which the food was placed. By turning the disc, each person could help himself without troubling his neighbours.

Contact with the outside world, especially with its scientific theories, did not seduce the men and women who had followed Father Noyes through all the early trials of the community. The religious basis of their existence was very real to them, and for this reason alone Darwin, Spencer, Huxley, and Tyndall were safe enough on the library shelves. By 1870, however, a new generation had grown up at Oneida—a generation that had no emotional experience of Perfectionism. These young people might be taught that the basis of their unorthodox lives was a Biblical sanction, but they were too far removed from the stirring revivalism of the 'forties to appreciate the fact. Some of them, like one of the sons of the founder, were open agnostics, and a number secretly disapproved of what seemed to them to be an immoral mode of life. A subterranean disharmony began to appear, and came to the surface in 1876, when Noyes attempted to transfer the leadership of the community to his agnostic son, Dr. Theodore Noyes. The doctor's lack of religion was bad enough, but his policy of remaining aloof from the community, and his experiments with a system of thorough regimentation, were too much. Noyes, who had retired to Wallingford, was obliged to return and resume control; but factions had already been formed that were to prove disastrous. Certain dissatisfied members were ready to support those "outsiders" who had never ceased to attack the community on the grounds of immorality. So far, under the solidarity commanded by Noyes and by religious fervour, Oneida had survived all such attacks. Even the Presbyterian Synod of Central New York, which had appointed a committee of seven to investigate the activities of the community, had been unable to bring it to an end; and the fierce denunciations and campaigns of Professor Mears of Hamilton College would doubtless have suffered the same fate had it not been for dissension in the community itself. Noyes apparently had definite evidence that a number of his followers were prepared to support Mears, and with the same realism he had shown in leaving Putney he suddenly and secretly left Oneida on 23rd June 1876, after taking the advice of some trustworthy members. He established himself in Canadian territory, at Niagara Falls, and never returned to America. But he did not lose interest in the community, and kept constantly in touch with it, either by post or by receiving delegates who came to seek his advice. It seemed obvious that Oneida would be obliged to abandon its peculiar system of sexual relationship if it wished to survive; on 20th August 1879, therefore, Noyes sent the following list of propositions to the community:

> That we give up the practice of Complex Marriage, not as renouncing belief in the principles and prospective finality of that institution, but in deference to the public sentiment which is evidently rising against it;
>   That we place ourselves, not on the platform of the Shakers, on the one hand, nor of the world, on the other, but on Paul's platform which allows marriage but prefers celibacy.

If you accept these modifications the Community will consist of two distinct classes—the married and the celibates—both legitimate, but the last preferred.

What will remain of our Communism after these modifications may be defined thus:

We shall hold our property and businesses in common, as now;

We shall live together in a common household and eat at a common table, as now;

We shall have a common children's department, as now;

We shall have our daily evening meetings, and all of our present means of moral and spiritual improvement.

Surely, here is Communism enough to hold us together and inspire us with heroism for a new career.

These propositions were accepted by a full assembly at Oneida, and were quickly followed by a considerable number of marriages—that state being vastly more popular than the recommended celibacy—and an attempt was now made to settle down once more to community life. Complex marriage, however, had been so much a part of the communistic pattern, and the recent disturbance had been so profound that a commission was appointed in 1880 to consider the advisability of re-organising upon a joint-stock basis. The question was discussed carefully and peaceably, and after sixteen months of study and preparation communism was abandoned. On 1st January 1881 the joint-stock company called "Oneida Community, Limited" was set up without the loss of a single working-hour in any of the industries. The financial settlement, which was equitable, wise, and generous, included the free education of children up to the age of sixteen, when each of them received a bonus of $200 to give them a start in life. There were only half a dozen members sufficiently discontented with this arrangement to bring lawsuits—which they lost. On the other hand, there were a number of members so distressed by the abandonment of communism that they wished to set up a new community. They were, probably wisely, dissuaded from this project by Noyes.

Under the new system, members gradually began to leave the Mansion House, setting themselves up with their families in separate houses. A colony of twenty went to California; others to New York and Boston; while some fifty or more went to Niagara, where they found employment in the neighbourhood of their exiled leader.

Noyes lived on until 13th April 1886, sustained by the belief that Oneida had been planned by the heavenly powers, and still revered by the small colony of adherents who had followed him to Niagara. He was a man, wrote Goldwin Smith, "whose ability is written on his brow, on the pages of his vigorously written books, and on the work of his organising hands"; a man with an unusual degree of moral courage and a virile faith that was tempered by wise judgement and a wide outlook.

Noyes's sound judgement and businesslike ability—which were responsible for the most interesting and one of the most successful of native American communities— were not shared by the founder of the Icarians, who came from France in 1848, when the Perfectionists had just moved to Oneida.

Sara Davidson

Open Land: Getting Back
to the Communal Garden

Wheeler Ranch: free land—live-in, drop-in.
—Commune Directory

The front wheels drop and the car thuds down a wet, muddy ravine. Thick night fog, raining hard. The car squishes to a stop, front end buried in clay and the right rear wheel spinning. I get out and sink to my ankles. No flashlight. No waterproof gear. Utter blackness, except for the car's dulled lights under the dirt. I climb back in, but because of the 45-degree angle, I'm pitched forward against the dashboard. Turn on the radio. Only eight o'clock—a long wait until daylight. Am I anywhere near Wheeler Ranch? Haven't seen another car or a light anywhere on this road. I start honking the horn. Cows bellow back from what seems very close range. I imagine angry ranchers with shotguns. Tomorrow is Sunday—eight miles back to the nearest town, and nothing will be open. Is there an AAA out here? Good God, I'll pay anybody anything! If they'll just get me out of this.

  I had started north from San Francisco in late afternoon, having heard vague descriptions of a commune called Wheeler's that was much beloved by those who had passed through it. The commune had had trouble with local police, and no one was sure whether the buildings were still standing or who was there. At sunset, a storm came up, and rather than turn back, I continued slowly along narrow, unlit country roads, my headlights occasionally picking up messages like "Stop War," painted on the side of a barn, and "Drive slowly, no M.D. Around," on a fence post. When I reached the woodsy, frontier town I knew to be near Wheeler's, I stopped in a bar to ask directions. Heads turned. People froze, glasses in hand. A woman with an expressionless, milky face said, "Honey, there isn't any sign. You just go up the road six miles and there's a gate on the left. Then you have to drive a ways to git to it. From where I live, you can see their shacks and what have you. But you can't see anything from the road."
  After six miles, there was a gate and a sign, "Beware of cattle." I opened it and drove down to a fork, picked the left road, went around in a circle and came back to the fork, took the right and bumped against two logs in the road. I got out and moved them. Nothing could stop me now. Another fork. To the left the road was impassable—deep ruts and rocks; to the right, a barbed-wire fence. Raining harder, darker. This is enough. Get out of here fast. Try to turn the car around, struggling to see . . . then the sickening dip.
  I got into my sleeping bag and tried to find a comfortable position in the crazily tilted car. My mood swung between panic and forced calm. At about 5:00 a.m., I heard rustling noises, and could make out the silhouettes of six horses which walked around the car, snorting. An hour later, the rain let up, and a few feet from the car I found a crude sign with an arrow, "Wheeler's." I walked a mile, then another mile,

through rolling green hills, thinking, "If I can just get out of here." At last, around a bend were two tents and a sign, "Welcome, God, love." The first tent had a light burning inside, and turned out to be a greenhouse filled with boxes of seedlings. At the second tent, I pushed open the door and bells tinkled. Someone with streaked brown hair was curled in a real bed on two mattresses. There was linoleum on the floor, a small stove, a table, and books and clothes neatly arranged on shelves. The young man lifted his head and smiled. "Come in."

I was covered with mud, my hair was wild and my eyes red and twitching. "I tried to drive in last night, my car went down a ravine and got stuck in the mud, and I've been sleeping in it all night."

"Far out," he said.

"I was terrified."

The young man, who had gray eyes set close together and one gold earring, said, "Of what?"

"There were horses."

He laughed. "Far out. One of the horses walked into Nancy's house and made a hole in the floor. Now she just sweeps her dirt and garbage down the hole."

My throat was burning. "Could we make some coffee?"

He looked at me sideways. "I don't have any." He handed me a clump of green weeds. "Here's some yerba buena. You can make tea." I stared at the weeds.

"What's your name?" I asked.

"Shoshone."

"Mine's Sara."

"Far out."

He got dressed, watered the plants in the greenhouse, and started down a path into the bushes, motioning for me to follow. Every few feet, he would stop to pick yerba buena, listen to birds, watch a trio of pheasants take off, and admire trees that were recently planted—almond, Elberta peach, cherry, plum. They were all in blossom, but I was in no mood to appreciate them. After every ten minutes of walking, we would come to a clearing with a tent or wooden shack, wake up the people in their soggy sleeping bags and ask them to help push the car out. The dwellings at Wheeler's are straight out of Dogpatch—old boards nailed unevenly together, odd pieces of plastic strung across poles to make wobbly igloos, with round stovepipes poking out the side. Most have dirt floors, though the better ones have wood. In one tent, we found a young man who had shaved his head except for one stripe of hair down the center, like a Mohican. He grinned with his eyes closed. "In an hour or so, I might feel like helping you." We came to a crooked green shack with a peace sign on the door and the inside papered with paintings of Krishna. Nancy, a blond former social worker, was sleeping on the floor with her children, Gregory, eight, and Michelle, nine. Both have blond hair of the same length and it is impossible to tell at first which is the girl and which the boy. At communities like this, it is common for children to ask each other when they meet, "What are you?" Nancy said, "Don't waste your energy trying to push the car. Get Bill Wheeler to pull you out with his jeep. What's your hurry now? Sunday's the best day here. You've got to stay for the steam bath and the feast. There'll be lots of visitors." She yawned. "Lots of food, lots of dope. It never rains for the feast."

Shoshone and I walked back to the main road that cuts across the 320-acre ranch. The sun had burned through the fog, highlighting streaks of yellow wild flowers in the fields. Black Angus cows were grazing by the road. People in hillbilly clothes, with funny hats and sashes, were coming out of the bushes carrying musical instruments and sacks of rice and beans. About a mile from the front gate we came to the community garden, with a scarecrow made of rusty metal in the shape of a nude girl. Two children were chasing each other from row to row, shrieking with laughter, as their mother picked cabbage. A sign read, "Permit not required to settle here."

Bill Wheeler was working in his studio, an airy, wood-and-glass building with large skylights, set on a hill. When Bill bought the ranch in 1963, looking for a place to paint and live quietly, he built the studio for his family. Four years later, when he opened the land to anyone who wanted to settle there, the county condemned his studio as living quarters because it lacked the required amount of concrete under one side. Bill moved into a tent and used the studio for his painting and for community meetings.

Bill is a tall, lean man of thirty with an aristocratic forehead, straight nose, deep-set blue eyes, and a full beard and flowing hair streaked yellow by the sun. His voice is gentle with a constant hint of mirth, yet it projects, like his clear gaze, a strength, which is understood in this community as divine grace. Quiet, unhurried, he progresses with steady confidence toward a goal or solution of a problem. He is also a voluptuary who takes Rabelaisian delight in the community's lack of sexual inhibitions and in the sight of young girls walking nude through the grass. He lives at the center of the ranch with his third wife, Gay, twenty-two, and their infant daughter, Raspberry. His humor and self-assurance make it easy for those around him to submit to the hippie credo that "God will provide," because they know that what God does not, Bill Wheeler will.

Bill promises to rescue my car after he has chopped wood and started a fire for the steam bath. "Don't worry," a friend says, patting me on the back. "Bill's saved people who've given up hope, lost all confidence." A grizzly blond called Damian says, "Why don't you let me pull her out?" Bill says, "Damian, I love you, but I wouldn't trust you with any of my vehicles." Later, we pass Damian on the road, into which he is blissfully urinating. "Ha," Bill says, "the first time I met Damian he was peeing."

With the jeep and a chain, Bill pulls out the car in less than two minutes, and as it slides back onto secure road, I feel my tension drain away. Maybe I should stay for the feast. Maybe it really is beautiful here. I park the car at the county road, outside the first gate, and walk the three miles back to Wheeler's. The access road cuts across property owned by James G. Kelly, a breeder of show cattle and horses, who is enraged at the presence of up to a hundred itinerant hippies on the ranch adjacent to his. He has started court action to block Wheeler from using the access road, and his hired hands walk around with guns slung over their shoulders and their faces pinched with bilious hate.

On a bluff behind Wheeler's garden, the steam bath is set to go. Red-hot rocks are taken from the fire into a plastic tent that can be sealed on all sides. Shifts of eight or nine people undress and sit on the mud floor, letting out whoops, chanting and singing. Gallon wine jugs filled with water are poured on the rocks, and the tent fills up with steam so hot and thick that the children start coughing and no one can see anyone else. After a few minutes, they step out, covered with sweat, and wash off in a cold shower. The women shampoo their hair and soap up the children. The men dig out ticks from under the skin. Much gaiety and good-natured ogling, and then, as the last shift is coming out, a teen-age visitor carrying the underground *Berkeley Tribe* wanders in and stops, dumbfounded, staring with holy-fool eyes, his mouth open and drooling, at all that flesh and hair and sweat.

The garden, like a jigsaw puzzle whose pieces have floated together, presents the image of a nineteenth century tableau: women in long skirts and shawls, men in lace-up boots, coveralls, and patched jeans tied with pieces of rope, sitting on the grass playing banjos, guitars, lyres, wood flutes, dulcimers, and an accordian. In a field to the right are the community animals—chickens, cows, goats, donkeys, and horses. As far as the eye can see, there are no houses, no traffic, nothing but verdant hills, a stream, and the ocean with whitecaps rising in the distance. Nine-year-old Michelle is prancing about in a pink shawl and a floppy hat warbling, "It's time for the feast!" Nancy says, "The pickin's are sort of spare, because tomorrow is welfare day and everybody's broke." She carries from the outdoor wood stove pots of brown rice —plain, she says, "for the purists who are on Georges Ohsawa's ten-day brown-rice diet"—and rice with fruit and nuts for everyone else; beans, red and white; oranges and apples; yogurt; hash; pot; acid; mescaline. A girl says there are worms in the green apples. Another, with a studious voice and glasses, says, "That's cool, it means they were organically grown. I'd rather eat a worm than a chemical any day." They eat with their fingers from paper plates, and when the plates are gone, directly from the pot. A man in his forties with red-spotted cheeks asks me if I have any pills. "I'll take anything. I'm on acid now." I offer him aspirin. He swallows eight.

Everyone who lives at Wheeler's ranch is a vegetarian. By some strange inversion, they feel that by eating meat they are hastening their own death. Vegetarianism is, ironically, the aspect of their life-style that aggravates even the most liberal parents. ("What? You won't eat meat? That's ridiculous!") Bill Wheeler says that diet is "very very central to the revolution. It's a freeing process which people go through, from living on processed foods and eating gluttonous portions of meat and potatoes, to natural foods and a simple diet that is kinder to your body. A lot has to do with economics. It's much cheaper to live on grains and vegetables you can grow in your garden. When Gay and I moved here, we had to decide whether to raise animals to slaughter. Gay said she couldn't do it. Every Thanksgiving, there's a movement to raise money to buy turkeys, because some people think the holiday isn't complete without them. But an amazing thing happens when carrion is consumed. People are really greedy, and it's messy. The stench and the grease stay with us for days."

Gravy, roast beef, mashed potatoes, Parker House rolls, buttered peas—the weekly fare when Bill was growing up in Bridgeport, Connecticut. His father, a lawyer who speculated famously in real estate, told Bill he could do anything with his life as long as he got an education. So Bill, self-reliant, introspective, who loved the outdoors, went to Yale and studied painting. After graduating, he came to San Francisco to find a farmhouse where he could work. When he saw the 320-acre ranch which was then a sheep and Christmas tree farm, he felt, "I've got to have it. This is my land." He bought it with his inheritance, and still has enough money to live comfortably the rest of his life. "My parents would be shocked out of their gourds if they saw the land now," Bill says. "They died before I opened it."

The idea of open land, or free land, was introduced to Bill by Lou Gottlieb, a singer with the pop folk group, "The Limelighters," who, in 1962, bought a 32-acre piece of land called Morning Star about ten miles from Wheeler's Ranch. Gottlieb visits Wheeler's every Sunday for the feast; when I met him, he was walking barefoot with a pink blanket wrapped around him like a poncho and fastened with a giant safety pin. A man of soaring height with crow eyes and a dark, silky beard, he talks in sermonettes, rising on his toes with enthusiasm. Gottlieb and a friend, Ramon Sender, decided in 1966 to start a community at Morning Star with one governing precept: access to the land would be denied to no one. With no rules, no organization, they felt, hostilities would not arise, and people could be reborn by living in harmony with the earth. Gottlieb deeded the land to God, and, shortly, a woman sued God because her home had been struck by lightning. "Now that God owns property," her lawyer argued, "He can be sued for natural disasters." It was not until 1967, Gottlieb says, that hippies began to patronize open land.

"From the first, the land selected the people. Those who couldn't work hard didn't survive. When the land got crowded, people split. The vibrations of the land will always protect the community." Gottlieb points to the sky. "With open land, *He* is the casting director." What happens, I ask, if someone behaves violently or destructively? Gottlieb frowns. "There have been a few cases where we've had to ask people to go, but it's at terrible, terrible cost to everyone's soul that this is done. When the land begins to throw off people, everyone suffers." He shakes his body, as if he were the land, rejecting a germ. "Open land has no historical precedent. When you give free land, not free food or money, you pull the carpet out from under the capitalist system. Once a piece of land is freed, 'no trespassing' signs pop up all along the adjoining roads."

Bill Wheeler refers to his ranch as "the land," and talks about people who live on the land, babies that are born on the land, music played on the land. He "opened the land," as he phrases it, in the winter of 1967, after Sonoma County officials tried to close Morning Star by bulldozing trees and all the buildings except Gottlieb's house. Some Morning Star people moved to Wheeler's, but others traveled to New Mexico, where they founded Morning Star East on a mesa near Taos owned by another wealthy hippie. The Southwest, particularly northern New Mexico and Colorado, has more communes on open land than any other region. The communes there are all crowded, and Taos is becoming a Haight-Ashbury in the desert. More land continues to be opened in New Mexico, as well as in California, Oregon, and Washington. Gottlieb plans to buy land and deed it to God in Holland, Sweden, Mexico, and Spain. "We're fighting against the territorial imperative," he says. "The hippies should get the Nobel Prize for creating this simple idea. Why did no one think of it before the hippies? Because hippies don't work, so they have time to dream up truly creative ideas."

It was surprising to hear people refer to themselves as "hippies"; I thought the term had been rendered meaningless by overuse. Our culture has absorbed so much of the style of hip—clothes, hair, language, drugs, music—that it has obscured the substance of the movement with which people at Morning Star and Wheeler's still strongly identify. Being a hippie, to them, means dropping out completely, and finding another way to live, to support oneself physically and spiritually. It does not mean being a company freak, working nine to five in a straight job and roaming the East Village on weekends. It means saying no to competition, no to the work ethic, no to consumption of technology's products, no to political systems and games. Lou Gottlieb, who was once a Communist party member, says, "The entire Left is a dead end." The hippie alternative is to turn inward and reach backward for roots, simplicity, and the tribal experience. In the first bloom of the movement, people flowed into slums where housing would be cheap and many things could be obtained free—food scraps from restaurants, second-hand clothes, free clinics and services. But the slums proved inhospitable. The hippies did nothing to improve the dilapidated neighborhoods, and they were preyed upon by criminals, pushers, and the desperate. In late 1967, they began trekking to rural land where there would be few people and life would be hard. They took up what Ramon Sender calls "voluntary primitivism," building houses out of mud and trees, planting and harvesting crops by hand, rolling loose tobacco into cigarettes, grinding their own wheat, baking bread, canning vegetables, delivering their own babies, and educating their own children. They gave up electricity, the telephone, running water, gas stoves, even rock music, which, of all things, is supposed to be the cornerstone of hip culture. They started to sing and play their own music—folky and quiet.

Getting close to the earth meant conditioning their bodies to cold, discomfort, and strenuous exercise. At Wheeler's, people walk twenty miles a day, carrying water and wood, gardening, and visiting each other. Only four-wheel-drive vehicles can cross the ranch, and ultimately Bill wants all cars banned. "We would rather live without machines. And the fact that we have no good roads protects us from tourists. People are car-bound, even police. They would never come in here without their vehicles." Although it rains a good part of the year, most of the huts do not have stoves and are not waterproof. "Houses shouldn't be designed to keep out the weather," Bill says. "We want to get in touch with it." He installed six chemical toilets on the ranch to comply with county sanitation requirements, but, he says, "I wouldn't go in one of those toilets if you paid me. It's very important for us to be able to use the ground, because we are completing a cycle, returning to Mother Earth what she's given us." Garbage is also returned to the ground. Food scraps are buried in a compost pile of sawdust and hay until they decompose and mix with the soil. Paper is burned, and metal buried. But not everyone is conscientious; there are piles of trash on various parts of the ranch.

Because of the haphazard sanitation system, the water at Wheeler's is contaminated, and until people adjust to it, they suffer dysentery, just as tourists do who drink the water in Mexico. There are periodic waves of hepatitis, clap, crabs, scabies, and streptococcic throat infections. No one brushes his teeth more than once a week, and then they often use "organic toothpaste," made from eggplant cooked in tinfoil.

They are experimenting with herbs and Indian healing remedies to become free of manufactured medicinal drugs, but see no contradiction in continuing to swallow any mind-altering chemical they are offered. The delivery of babies on the land has become an important ritual. With friends, children, and animals keeping watch, chanting, and getting collectively stoned, women have given birth to babies they have named Morning Star, Psyche Joy, Covelo Vishnu God, Rainbow Canyon King, and Raspberry Sundown Hummingbird Wheeler.

The childbirth ritual and the weekly feasts are conscious attempts at what is called "retribalization." But Wheeler's Ranch, like many hippie settlements, has rejected communal living in favor of a loose community of individuals. People live alone or in monogamous units, cook for themselves, and build their own houses and sometimes gardens. "There should not be a main lodge, because you get too many people trying to live under one roof and it doesn't work," Bill says. As a result, there are cliques who eat together, share resources, and rarely mix with others on the ranch. There was one group marriage between two teen-age girls, a forty-year-old man, and two married couples, which ended when one of the husbands saw his wife with another man in the group, pulled a knife, and dragged her off, yelling, "Forget this shit. She belongs to me."

With couples, the double standard is an unwritten rule: the men can roam but the women must be faithful. There are many more men than women, and when a new girl arrives, she is pounced upon, claimed, and made the subject of wide gossip. Mary Cordelia Stevens, or Corky, a handsome eighteen-year-old from a Chicago suburb, hiked into the ranch one afternoon last October and sat down by the front gate to eat a can of Spam. The first young man who came by invited her to a party where everyone took TCP, a tranquilizer for horses. It was a strange trip—people rolling around the floor of the tipi, moaning, retching, laughing, hallucinating. Corky went home with one guy and stayed with him for three weeks, during which time she was almost constantly stoned. "You sort of have to be stoned to get through the first days here," she says. "Then you know the trip." Corky is a strapping, well-proportioned, large-boned girl with a milkmaid's face and long blond hair. She talks softly, with many giggles: "I love to go around naked. There's so much sexual energy here, it's great. Everybody's turned on to each other's bodies." Corky left the ranch to go home for Christmas and to officially drop out of Antioch College; she hitchhiked back, built her own house and chicken coop, learned to plant, do laundry in a tin tub with a washboard, and milk the cows. "I love dealing with things that are simple and direct."

Bill Wheeler admires Corky for making it on her own, which few of the women do. Bill is torn between his desire to be the benefactor-protector and his intolerance of people who aren't self-reliant. "I'm contemptuous of people who can't pull their own weight," he says. Yet he constantly worries about the welfare of others. He also feels conflict between wanting a tribe, indeed wanting to be chieftain, and wanting privacy. "Open land requires a leap of faith," he says, "but it's worth it, because it guarantees there will always be change, and stagnation is death." Because of the fluidity of the community, it is almost impossible for it to become economically self-sufficient. None of the communes have been able to live entirely off the land. Most are unwilling to go into cash crops or light industry because in an open community with no rules, there are not enough people who can be counted on to work regularly. The women with children receive welfare, some of the men collect unemployment and food stamps, and others get money from home. They spend very little—perhaps $600 a year per person. "We're not up here to make money," Bill says, "or to live like country squires."

When darkness falls, the ranch becomes eerily quiet and mobility stops. No one uses flashlights. Those who have lived there some time can feel their way along the paths by memory. Others stay in their huts, have dinner, go to sleep, and get up with the sun. Around 7:00 p.m., people gather at the barn with bottles for the late milking. During the week, the night milking is the main social event. Corky says, "It's the only time you know you're going to see people. Otherwise you could wander around for days and not see anyone." A girl from Holland and two boys have gathered mussels at a nearby beach during the day, and invite everyone to the tipi to eat them. We sit for some time in silence, watching the mussels steam open in a pot over the grate. A boy with glassy blue eyes whose lids seem weighted down starts to pick out the orange flesh with his dirt-caked hands and drops them in a pan greased with Spry. A mangy cat snaps every third mussel out of the pan. No one stops it. . . .

Nancy, in her shack about a mile from the tipi, is fixing a green stew of onions, cabbage, kale, leeks, and potatoes; she calls to three people who live nearby to come share it. Nancy has a seventeen-year-old, all-American-girl face—straight blond hair and pink cheeks—on a plump, saggy-stomached mother's body. She has been married twice, gone to graduate school, worked as a social worker and a prostitute, joined the Sexual Freedom League, and taken many overdoses of drugs. Her children have been on more acid trips than most adults at the ranch. "They get very quiet on acid," she says. "The experience is less staggering for kids than for adults, because acid returns you to the consciousness of childhood." Nancy says the children have not been sick since they moved to Wheeler's two years ago. "I can see divine guidance leading us here. This place has been touched by God." She had a vision of planting trees on the land, and ordered fifty of exotic variety, like strawberry guava, camelia, and loquat. Stirring the green stew, she smiles vacuously. "I feel anticipant of a very happy future."

With morning comes a hailstorm, and Bill Wheeler must go to court in Santa Rosa for trial on charges of assaulting a policeman when a squad came to the ranch looking for juvenile runaways and Army deserters. Bill, Gay, Gay's brother Peter, Nancy, Shoshone, and Corky spread out through the courthouse, peeling off mildewed clothes and piling them on benches. Peter, a gigantic, muscular fellow of twenty-three, rips his pants all the way up the back, and, like most people at Wheeler's, he is not wearing underwear. Gay changes Raspberry's diapers on the floor of the ladies' room. Nancy takes off her rain-soaked long johns and leaves them in one of the stalls.

It is a tedious day. Witnesses give conflicting testimony, but all corroborate that one of the officers struck Wheeler first, leading to a shoving, running, tackling, pot-throwing skirmish which also involved Peter. The defendants spend the night in a motel, going over testimony with their lawyer. Bill and Corky go to a supermarket to buy dinner, and wheel down the aisle checking labels for chemicals, opening jars to take a taste with the finger, uhmmm, laughing at the "obsolete consciousness" of the place. They buy greens, Roquefort dressing, peanut butter, organic honey, and two

Sara Lee cakes. The next morning, Nancy says she couldn't sleep with the radiator and all the trucks. Gay says, "I had a dream in which I saw death. It was a blond man with no facial hair, and he looked at me with this all-concealing expression." Bill, outside, staring at the Kodak blue swimming pool: "I dreamed last night that Gay and I got separated somehow and I was stuck with Raspberry." He shudders. "You know, I feel love for other people, but Gay is the only one I want to spend my life with."

The jury goes out at 3:00 p.m. and deliberates until 9:00. In the courtroom, a mottled group in pioneer clothes, mud-spattered and frizzy-wet, are chanting, "Om." The jury cannot agree on four counts, and finds Bill and Peter not guilty on three counts. The judge declares a mistrial. The county fathers are not finished, though. They are still attempting to close the access road to Wheeler's and to get an injunction to raze all buildings on the ranch as health hazards. Bill Wheeler is not worried, nor are his charges, climbing in the jeep and singing, "Any day now . . ." God will provide.

> We must do away with the absolutely specious notion that everybody has to earn a living. . . . We keep inventing jobs because of this false idea that everybody has to be employed at some kind of drudgery because, according to Malthusian-Darwinian theory, he must justify his right to exist. . . . The true business of people should be to . . . think about whatever it was they were thinking about before somebody came along and told them they had to earn a living.
>
> —R. Buckminster Fuller

Highway 101 ribboning down the coast: narcotic pastels, the smell of char-broiled hamburgers cooking, motels with artificial gas-flame fireplaces. Total sensory Muzak. California banks now print their checks in salmon and mauve colors with reproductions of the Golden Gate Bridge, the High Sierras, the Mojave Desert, and other panoramas. "Beautiful money," they call it. As I cross the San Rafael Bridge, which, because the clouds are low, seems to shoot straight into the sky and disappear, Radio KABL in San Francisco is playing "Shangri-la."

South of the city in Menlo Park, one of a chain of gracious suburbs languishing in industrial smoke, Stewart Brand created the *Whole Earth Catalog,* and now presides over the Whole Earth Truck Store and mystique. Brand, a thirty-year-old biologist who was a fringe member of Ken Kesey's Merry Pranksters, put out the first catalog in 1968 as a mail-order source book for people starting communes or alternate life-styles. The success of the catalog—it is selling a thousand copies a day—indicates it is answering needs that cut across age and philosophical gaps. One of these is the need to regain control over the environment, so that when the refrigerator breaks, or the electric power goes out, you don't have to stand around helplessly waiting for repairmen, middlemen, and technical "experts" to fix things at your expense. The *Whole Earth Catalog* lists books and tools that enable one to build furniture, fix cars, learn real-estate law, raise bees for honey, publish your own books, build houses out of foam, auto tops, or mud, and even bury your own dead so that the rites of passage are simple and meaningful. The *Catalog* also speaks to the need to break out of the inflationary cycle of higher earning and higher spending. It offers books such as *How to Get Out of the Rat Race and Live on $10 a Month* and *How to Live on Nothing,* and suggests *The Moonlighters' Manual* for people who want to earn subsistence money with minimum commitment of psyche.

Brand says, "I admit we encourage starting from scratch. We don't say it will be easy, but education comes from making mistakes. Take delivering babies at home. That's hazardous! We carry books that tell how hazardous it is. People have lost babies that way, but it won't hit the fan until we lose a few mothers. When it works, though, it's glorious." Brand, with oversized blue eyes and gaunt cheeks, breaks into infectious laughter as he describes his fantasies. "The city-country pull is behind everything going on now. An anthropologist Cherokee we know feels the cycle goes like this: a kid grows up, has talent, goes to the city to fulfill himself, becomes an ideologue, his personality deteriorates, and to recuperate, he goes back to the land." The impulse to return to the land and to form "intentional communities," or communes, is being felt in the sudden demand for publications like *The Green Revolution,* founded in the 1940s to promote rural revival, and *The Modern Utopian,* produced by "Alternatives! Foundation" in Sebastopol, California, which also runs a commune matching service.

Brand says there are few real alternative life-styles right now: "There's black pride, and the long-haired run for the hills. That's it. What we want are alternative economies and alternative political systems. Maybe alternative ecologies. You can't do this with six people." Brand points out that new social programs "are always parasitic, like newborn babies. They feed off the parent culture until they're strong enough to be self-sustaining." The communes in New Mexico, he says, can eventually develop their own economy by trading goods and services and paying in tokens, "like the casinos in Las Vegas. The climate is great for experiments now. There's no end of resources for promising ideas. But people had better hurry, because the avenues will start being closed off." He laughs, thrusting his chin up. "Things are getting weirder and weirder."

Roads across the upper Northwest are flat and ruler-straight, snowbound for long months, turning arid and dusty in the summer. At an empty crossing in a poor, wheat-growing county, the road suddenly dips and winds down to a valley filled with tall pines and primitive log cabins. The community hidden in this natural canyon is Freedom Farm, founded in 1963. It is one of the oldest communes to be started on open land. The residents—about twenty-four adults and almost as many children—are serious, straightforward people who, with calculated bluntness, say they are dropouts, social misfits, unable or unwilling to cope with the world "outside." The community has no rules, except that no one can be asked to leave. Because it predates the hippie movement, there is an absence of mystical claptrap and jargon like "far out." Only a few are vegetarians. Members do not want the location of the farm published for fear of being inundated with "psychedelic beggars."

I drove to the canyon in the morning and, having learned my lesson, left the car at the top and walked down the steep, icy road. The farm is divided into two parts— 80 acres at the north end of the canyon and 120 acres at the south. The families live

separately, as they do at Wheeler's, but their homes are more elaborate and solidly
built. The first house in the north end is a hexagonal log cabin built by Huw Williams,
who started the farm when he was nineteen. Huw is slight, soft-spoken, with a wispy
blond beard. His face and voice are expressionless, but when he speaks, he is likely to
say something startling, humorous, or indicative of deep feeling. When I arrived, he
was cutting out pieces of leather, wearing a green-and-brown lumberman's shirt and
a knife strapped to his waist. His wife, Sylvia, was nursing their youngest son, while
their two-year-old, Sennett, wearing nothing but a T-shirt, was playing on the floor
with a half-breed Norwegian elkhound. The cabin was snugly warm, but smelled
faintly of urine from Sennett peeing repeatedly on the rug. There was a cast-iron
stove, tables and benches built from logs, a crib, an old-fashioned cradle, and a large
bed raised off the floor for warmth and storage space. On the wall there was a calen-
dar opened to January, although it was March.

I asked Huw how the community had stayed together for seven years. He said,
deadpan, "The secret is not to try. We've got a lot of rugged individualists here, and
everyone is into a different thing. In reflection, it feels good that we survived. A lot
of us were from wealthy backgrounds, and the idea of giving it all up and living off
the land was a challenge." Huw grew up on a ranch 40 miles from the canyon. "I had
everything. When I was fourteen, I had my own car, a half-dozen cows, and $600 in
the bank." When he was fifteen, his house burned down and he saw his elaborate
collections—stamps, models, books—disappear. He vowed not to become attached to
possessions after that, and took to sleeping outdoors. He remembers being terrified
of violence, and idolized Gandhi, Christ, and Tolstoy. At seventeen, he became a
conscientious objector and began to work in draft resistance. While on a peace walk
from New Hampshire to Washington, D.C., he decided to drop out of the University
of Washington and start a nonviolent training center, a community where people
could live by sharing rather than competing. He persuaded his mother to give him
80 acres in the canyon for the project, rented a house, called the Hart House, and
advertised in peace papers for people to come and share it with him.

The first summer, more than fifty came and went and they all lived in the Hart
House. One of the visitors was Sylvia, a fair-skinned girl with long chestnut hair and
warm wistful eyes that hint of sadness. They were married, and Huw stopped talking
about a peace center and started studying intentional communities. He decided he
wanted a community that would be open to anyone, flexible, with no prescribed
rules to live by. Work would get done, Huw felt, because people would want to do
it to achieve certain ends. "It's a Western idea. You inspire people by giving them a
goal, making it seem important; then they'll do anything to get there." If people did
not want to work, Huw felt, forcing them would not be the answer.

The results were chaotic. "Emotional crises, fights over everything. A constant
battle to get things done. A typical scene would be for one guy to spend two hours
fixing a meal. He had to make three separate dishes—one for vegetarians, one for non-
vegetarians, and one for people who wouldn't eat government-surplus food. He would
put them on the table, everybody would grab, and if you stood back you got nothing.
When people live that close together, they become less sensitive, and manners go right
out the window. It was educational, but we knew it wasn't suitable for raising children."

The group pooled resources and bought another 120 acres two miles away. Huw and Sylvia built their own cabin and moved out of the Hart House; another couple followed. Then around 1966, the drug scene exploded and the farm was swamped with speed freaks, runaways, addicts, and crazies. A schism grew between the permanent people and the transients. The transients thought the permanents were uptight and stingy. The permanents said the transients were abusing the land. When most of the permanents had built their own cabins, they began talking about burning down the Hart House. I heard many versions of the incident. Some say a man, whom I shall call George, burned it. Some say everyone did it. Some said they watched and were against it but felt they should not stop it. Afterwards, most of the transients left, and the farm settled into its present pattern of individual families tending their own gardens, buying their own supplies, and raising their own animals. Each family has at least two vehicles—a car and a tractor, or a motorcycle or truck. Huw says, "We do our share of polluting."

The majority at Freedom live on welfare, unemployment compensation, and food stamps. A few take part-time jobs picking apples or wheat, one does free-lance writing, and some do crafts. Huw makes about $50 a month on his leather work, Ken Meister makes wall hangings, Rico and Pat sell jewelry to psychedelic shops, and Steve raises rabbits. Huw believes the farm could support itself by growing organic grains and selling them by mail order, but he hasn't been able to get enough cooperation to do this. "It's impossible to have both a commune, where everyone lives and works collectively, and free land, where anyone can settle," he says. "Some day we might have a commune on the land, but not everyone who lived on the land would have to join it."

The only communal rituals are Thanksgiving at the schoolhouse and the corn dance, held on the first full moon of May. Huw devised the corn dance from a Hopi Indian ceremony, and each year it gets wilder. Huw builds a drum, and at sundown everyone gathers on a hillside with food, wine, the children in costumes, animals, and musical instruments. They take turns beating the drum but must keep it beating until dawn. They roast potatoes, and sometimes a kid, a pig, or a turkey, get stoned, dance, howl, and drop to sleep. "But that's only once a year," one of the men says. "We could have one every month, and it would hold the community together." Not everyone wants this solidarity, however. Some are like hermits and have staked out corners of the canyon where they want to be left alone. The families who live nearby get together for dinners, chores, and baby-sitting. At the north end, the Williamses, the Swansons, and the Goldens pop in and out constantly. On the day I arrive, they are having a garden meeting at the Swansons' to decide what to order for spring planting.

The Swansons, who have three young children, moved into the canyon this year after buying, for $1,000, the two-story house a man called Steve had built for his own family. Steve had had a falling out with Huw and wanted to move to the south acres. The Swansons needed a place they could move into right away. The house has the best equipment at the farm, with a flush toilet (sectioned off by a blanket hung from the ceiling), running water, and electricity that drives a stove, refrigerator, and freezer. Jack Swanson, an outgoing, ruddy-faced man of thirty-five, with short hair and a moustache, works on a newspaper 150 miles away and commutes to the farm for weekends. His wife, Barbara, twenty-four, is the image of a Midwestern college girl: jeans cut off to Bermuda length, blouses with Peter Pan collars, and a daisy-printed scarf around her short brown hair. But it is quickly apparent that she is a strong-willed nonconformist. "I've always been a black sheep," she says. "I hate supermarkets—everything's been chemically preserved. You might as well be in a morgue." Barbara is gifted at baking, pickling, and canning, and wants to raise sheep to weave and dye the wool herself. She and Jack tried living in various cities, then a suburb, then a farm in Idaho, where they found they lacked the skills to make it work. "We were so ill-equipped by society to live off the earth," Jack says. "We thought about moving to Freedom Farm for three or four years, but when times were good, we put it off." Last year their third child was born with a lung disease which required months of hospitalization and left them deep in debt. Moving to the farm seemed a way out. "If we had stayed in the suburbs, we found we were spending everything we made, with rent and car payments, and could never pay off the debts. I had to make more and more just to stay even. The price was too high for what we wanted in life," Jack says. "Here, because I don't pay rent and because we can raise food ourselves, I don't have to make as much money. We get help in farming, and have good company. In two or three months, this house is all mine—no interest, no taxes. Outside it would cost me $20,000 and 8 per cent interest."

A rainstorm hits at midnight and by morning the snow has washed off the canyon walls, the stream has flooded over, and the roads are slushy mud ruts. Sylvia saddles two horses and we ride down to the south 120. There are seven cabins on the valley floor, and three hidden by trees on the cliff. Outside one of the houses, Steve is feeding his rabbits; the mute, wiggling animals are clustering around the cage doors. Steve breeds the rabbits to sell to a processor and hopes to earn $100 a month from the business. He also kills them to eat. "It's tough to do," he says, "but if people are going to eat meat, they should be willing to kill the animal." While Steve is building his new house, he has moved with his wife and four children into the cabin of a couple I shall call George and Liz Snow. George is a hefty, porcine man of thirty-nine, a drifter who earned a doctorate in statistics, headed an advertising agency, ran guns to Cuba, worked as a civil servant, a mason, a dishwasher, and rode the freights. He can calculate the angles of a geodesic dome and quote Boccaccio and Shakespeare. He has had three wives, and does not want his name known because "there are a lot of people I don't want to find me."

Steve, a hard-lived thirty-four, has a past that rivals George's for tumult: nine years as an Army engineer, AWOL, running a coffee house in El Paso, six months in a Mexican jail on a marijuana charge, working nine-to-five as chief engineer in a fire-alarm factory in New Haven, Connecticut, then cross-country to Spokane. Steve has great dynamism and charm that are both appealing and abrasive. His assertiveness inevitably led to friction in every situation, until, tired of bucking the system, he moved to the farm. "I liked the structure of this community," he says. "Up there, I can't get along with one out of a thousand people. Here I make it with one out of two." He adds, "We're in the business of survival while the world goes crazy. It's good to know how to build a fire, or a waterwheel, because if the world ends, you're there now."

Everyone at Freedom seems to share this sense of imminent doomsday. Huw says, "When the country is wiped out, electricity will stop coming through the wires, so you might as well do without it now. I don't believe you should use any machine you can't fix yourself." Steve says, "Technology can't feed all the world's people." Stash, a young man who lives alone at the farm, asks, "Am I going to start starving in twenty years?"

Steve: "Not if you have a plot to garden."

Stash: "What if the ravaging hordes come through?"

Steve: "Be prepared for the end, or get yourself a gun."

There is an impulse to dismiss this talk as a projection of people's sense of their own private doom, except for the fact that the fear is widespread. Stewart Brand writes in the *Whole Earth Catalog:* "One barometer of people's social-confidence level is the sales of books on survival. I can report that sales on *The Survival Book* are booming; it's one of our fastest moving items."

Several times a week, Steve, Stash, and Steve's daughter Laura, fourteen, drive to the small town nearby to buy groceries, visit a friend, and, if the hot water holds out, take showers. They stop at Joe's Bar for beer and hamburgers—40 cents "with all the trimmings." Laura, a graceful, quiet girl, walks across the deserted street to buy *Mad* magazine and look at rock record albums. There are three teen-agers at the farm—all girls—and all have tried running away to the city. One was arrested for shoplifting, another was picked up in a crash pad with seven men. Steve says, "We have just as much trouble with our kids as straight, middle-class parents do. I'd like to talk to people in other communities and find out how they handle their teen-agers. Maybe we could send ours there." Stash says, "Or bring teen-age boys here." The women at the farm have started to joke uneasily that their sons will become uptight businessmen and their daughters will be suburban housewives. The history of utopian communities in this country has been that the second generation leaves. It is easy to imagine commune-raised children having their first haute-cuisine meal, or sleeping in silk pajamas in a luxury hotel, or taking a jet plane. Are they not bound to be dazzled? Sylvia says, "Our way of life is an overreaction to something, and our kids will probably overreact to us. It's absurd. Kids run away from this, and all the runaways from the city come here."

In theory, the farm is an expanded family, and children can move around and live with different people or build houses of their own. In the summer, they take blankets and sleeping bags up in the cliffs to sleep in a noisy, laughing bunch. When I visited, all the children except one were staying in their parents' houses. Low-key tension seemed to be running through the community, with Steve and Huw Williams at opposite poles. Steve's wife, Ann, told me, "We don't go along with Huw's philosophy of anarchy. We don't think it works. You need some authority and discipline in any social situation." Huw says, "The thing about anarchy is that I'm willing to do a job myself, if I have to, rather than start imposing rules on others. Steve and George want things to be done efficiently with someone giving orders, like the Army."

At dinner when the sun goes down, Steve's and George's house throbs with good will and festivity. The cabin, like most at the farm, is not divided into separate rooms. All nine people—Steve, Ann, and their four children, the Snows and their baby—sleep on the upstairs level, while the downstairs serves as kitchen, dining and living room. "The teen-agers wish there were more privacy," Steve says, "but for us and the younger children, it feels really close." Most couples at the farm are untroubled about making love in front of the children. "We don't make a point of it," one man says, "but if they happen to see it, and it's done in love and with good vibrations, they won't be afraid or embarrassed."

While Ann and Liz cook hasenpfeffer, Steve's daughters, Laura and Karen, ten, improvise making gingerbread with vinegar and brown sugar as a substitute for molasses. A blue jay chatters in a cage hung from the ceiling. Geese honk outside, and five dogs chase each other around the room. Steve plays the guitar and sings. The hasenpfeffer is superb. The rabbits have been pickled for two days, cooked in red wine, herbs, and sour cream. There are large bowls of beets, potatoes, jello, and the gingerbread, which tastes perfect, with homemade apple sauce. Afterwards, we all get toothpicks. Liz, an uninhibited, roly-poly girl of twenty-three, is describing how she hitchhiked to the farm, met George, stayed, and got married. "I like it here," she says, pursing her lips, "because I can stand nude on my front porch and yell, fuck! Also, I think I like it here because I'm fat, and there aren't many mirrors around. Clothes don't matter, and people don't judge you by your appearance like they do out there." She adds, "I've always been different from others. I think most of the people here are misfits—they have problems in communicating, relating to one another." Ann says, "Communication is ridiculous. We've begun to feel gossip is much better. It gradually gets around to the person it's about, and that's okay. Most people here can't say things to each other's face."

I walk home—I'm staying in a vacant cabin—across a field, with the stars standing out in brilliant relief from the black sky. Lights flicker in the cabins sprinkled through the valley. Ken Meister is milking late in the barn. The fire is still going in my cabin; I add two logs, light the kerosene lamps, and climb under the blankets on the high bed. Stream water sweeps by the cabin in low whooshes, the fire sputters. The rhythm of the canyon, after a few days, seems to have entered my body. I fall asleep around ten, wake up at six, and can feel the time even though there are no clocks around. In the morning light, though, I find two dead mice on the floor, and must walk a mile to get water, then build a fire to heat it. It becomes clear why, in a community like this, the sex roles are so well-defined and satisfying. When men actually do heavy physical labor like chopping trees, baling hay, and digging irrigation ditches, it feels very fulfilling for the woman to tend the cabin, grind wheat, put up fruit, and sew or knit. Each depends on the other for basic needs—shelter, warmth, food. With no intermediaries, such as supermarkets and banks, there is a direct relationship between work and survival. It is thus possible, according to Huw, for even the most repetitive jobs such as washing dishes or sawing wood to be spiritually rewarding. "Sawing puts my head in a good place," he says. "It's like a yogic exercise."

In addition to his farming and leather work, Huw has assumed the job of teacher for the four children of school age. Huw believes school should be a free, anarchic experience, and that the students should set their own learning programs. Suddenly given this freedom, the children, who were accustomed to public school, said they wanted to play and ride the horses. Huw finally told them they must be at the school house every day for at least one hour. They float in and out, and Huw stays half the day. He walks home for lunch and passes Karen and another girl on the road. Karen taunts him, "Did you see the mess we made at the school?"

"Yes," Huw says.

"Did you see our note?"

Huw walks on, staring at the ground. "It makes me feel you don't have much respect for the tools or the school."

She laughs. "Course we don't have any respect!"

"Well, it's your school," Huw says softly.

Karen shouts, "You said it was your school the other day. You're an Indian giver."

Huw: "I never said it was my school. Your parents said that." Aside to me, he says, "They're getting better at arguing every day. Still not very good, though." I tell Huw they seem to enjoy tormenting him. "I know. I'm the only adult around here they can do that to without getting clobbered. It gives them a sense of power. It's ironic, because I keep saying they're mature and responsible, and their parents say they need strict authority and discipline. So who do they rebel against? Me. I'm going to call a school meeting tonight. Maybe we can talk some of this out."

In the afternoon I visit Rico and Pat, whose A-frame house is the most beautiful and imaginative at the farm. It has three levels—a basement, where they work on jewelry and have stored a year's supply of food; a kitchen-living-room floor; and a high sleeping porch reached by a ladder. The second story is carpeted, with harem-like cushions, furs, and wall hangings. There are low tables, one of which lifts to reveal a sunken white porcelain bathtub with running water heated by the wood stove. Rico, twenty-five, designed the house so efficiently that even in winter, when the temperature drops to 20 below zero, it is warm enough for him to lounge about wearing nothing but a black cape. Pat and Rico have talked about living with six adults in some form of group marriage, but, Pat says, "there's no one here we could really do it with. The sexual experiments that have gone on have been rather compulsive and desperate. Some of us think jealousy is innate." Rico says, "I think it's cultural." Pat says, "Hopefully our kids will be able to grow up without it. I think the children who are born here will really have a chance to develop freely. The older children who've come here recently are too far gone to appreciate the environment."

In the evening, ten parents and five children show up at the school, a one-room house built with eighteen sides, so that a geodesic dome can be constructed on top. The room has a furnace, bookshelves and work tables, rugs and cushions on the floor. Sylvia is sitting on a stool in the center nursing her son. Two boys in yellow pajamas are running in circles, squealing, "Ba-ba-ba!" Karen is drawing on the blackboard—of all things, a city skyscape. Rico is doing a yoga headstand. Steve and Huw begin arguing about whether the children should have to come to the school every day. Steve says, in a booming voice, "I think the whole canyon should be a learning community, a total educational environment. The kids can learn something from everyone. If you want to teach them, why don't you come to our house?" Huw, standing with a clipboard against his hip, says, "They have to come here to satisfy the county school superintendent. But it seems futile when they come in and say I'm not qualified to teach them. Where do they get that?''

Steve says, "From me. I don't think you're qualified." Huw: "Well I'm prepared to quit and give you the option of doing something else, or sending them to public school."

Steve says, "Don't quit. I know your motives are pure as the driven snow. . . ."

Huw says, "I'm doing it for myself as well, to prove I can do it. But it all fits together."

They reach an understanding without speaking further.

Steve then says, "I'd like to propose that we go door-to-door in this community and get everyone enthused about the school as a center for adult learning and cultural activity first, and for the kiddies second. Because when you turn on the adults, the kids will follow. The school building needs finishing—the dome should be built this summer. Unless there's more enthusiasm in this community, I'm not going to contribute a thing. But if we get everybody to boost this, by God I'll be the first one out to dig."

Huw says, "You don't think the people who took the time to come tonight is enough interest? I may be cynical, but I think the only way to get some of the others here would be to have pot and dope."

Steve: "Get them interested in the idea of guest speakers, musicians, from India, all over. We can build bunk dorms to accommodate them."

Huw: "Okay. I think we should get together every Sunday night to discuss ideas, hash things over. In the meantime, why don't we buy materials to finish the building?"

On the morning I leave, sunlight washes down the valley from a cloudless sky. Huw, in his green lumberman's shirt, rides with me to the top road. "My dream is to see this canyon filled with families who live here all the time, with lots of children." He continues in a lulling rhythm: "We could export some kind of food or product. The school is very important—it should be integrated in the whole community. Children from all over could come to work, learn, and live with different families. I'd like to have doctors here and a clinic where people could be healed naturally. Eventually there should be a ham radio system set up between all the communities in the country, and a blimp, so we could make field trips back and forth. I don't think one community is enough to meet our needs. We need a world culture."

Huw stands, with hands on hips, the weight set back on his heels—a small figure against the umber field. "Some day I'm going to inherit six hundred more acres down there, and it'll all be free. Land should be available for anybody to use like it was with the Indians." He smiles with the right corner of his mouth. "The Indians could no more understand owning land than they could owning the sky."

.   .   .

Last Halloween in Jemez, New Mexico, the squidlike "rock-drug-alternate-culture" underground gathered itself together to discuss what to do with the energy manifested at Woodstock. How can we use that power, they asked, and prevent it from being sickened and turned as it was at the Rolling Stones Free Concert in Altamont? The answer seemed to generate itself: buy land, throw away the deed, open it to anyone and call it Earth People's Park. Hold an earth-warming festival and ecological world's fair—all free. A nonprofit corporation was formed to collect money and handle legal problems. But there would be no authorities and no rules in Earth People's Park. Paul Krassner, Tom Law, Milan Melvin, Ken Kesey, Mama Cass Elliot, and the Hog Farm traveling communal circus led by Hugh Romney fanned out to sell the idea. They asked everyone who had been at Woodstock in body or spirit to contribute a dollar. At first, they talked of buying 20,000 acres in New Mexico or Colorado. In a few months, they were talking about 400,000 acres in many small pieces, all over the country. They flooded the media with promises of "a way out of the disaster of the cities, a viable alternative." Hugh Romney, calling himself Wavy Gravy, in an aviator suit, sheepskin vest, and a Donald Duck hat, spoke on television about simplicity, community, and harmony with the land. The cards, letters, and money poured in. Some were hand-printed, with bits of leaves and stardust in the creases, some were typed on business stationery. One, from a young man in La Grange, Illinois, seemed to touch all the chords:

> *Hello. Maybe we're not as alone as I thought. I am 24, my developed skills are as an advertising writer-producer-director. It seems such a waste. I have energy. I can simplify my life and I want to help. I am convinced that a new life-style, one which holds something spiritual as sacred, is necessary in this land. People can return to the slow and happy pace of life that they abandoned along with their understanding of brotherhood. Thank you for opening doors.*
>
> *P.S.—Please let me know what site you purchase so I can leave as soon as possible for it.*

The Environment: The Individual and the Community of Nature

In 1871 Mark Twain wrote, "It was in this Sacramento Valley, just referred to, that a deal of the most lucrative of the early gold mining was done, and you may still see, in places, its grassy slopes and levels torn and guttered and disfigured by the avaricious spoilers of fifteen and twenty years ago. You may see such disfigurements far and wide over California—and in some such places, where only meadows and forests are visible—not a living creature, not a house, no stick or stone or remnant of a ruin, and not a sound, not even a whisper to disturb the Sabbath stillness—you will find it hard to believe that there stood at one time a fiercely-flourishing little city." A century ago the archetypal pioneer was already bemoaning the loss of the "territory," the unexplored and untamed land of adventure. Nor was the pioneer the first American to record the progress of civilization and its accompanying ravages on the inexhaustible reaches of the natural environment. The transcendentalists had also decried the disappearance of majesty. Thoreau begged "to speak a word for Nature, for absolute freedom and wildness." Emerson warned that, if we are obsessed with the use of the natural world, "nature is debased."

These early protests against the spoliation of nature mark the first stages of a growing desire to conserve the wilderness. The conservation movement is one of the best indicators of economic and cultural development in America. That such a movement attracted few followers until the nineteenth century is not surprising, for only visible encroachment upon nature could evoke nostalgia and fear in the inhabitants of such a vast land. To the founders of our nation, struggling against threatening elements, the wilderness was the villain, and the notion that it should remain untouched was anathema to the Puritans. The Puritan ideology, while it might encompass an awe at the splendor of nature's marvels, was essentially hostile to wild nature. The wilderness was meant for taming. Once the hills were cleared of trees and the land cultivated, then the foundations of the New Jerusalem could be laid. This task was part of that famous "errand in the wilderness"—to subdue and reform the uncultivated land and the uncivilized "savage."

Other national and religious groups were moved to clear the land and to build cities because they saw in the land the raw material of personal wealth. Occasionally, the desire for gain was authorized by religious doctrine. The Calvinists, for example, maintained that economic success was one indication of that eternal salvation to which their lives on earth were dedicated. For them the great untilled lands seemed to cry out to be used. Settlers of every variety felt that if Europe was no longer a land of opportunity, if it no longer provided a yield of untouched waters and dense forests, they must seek a richer future in America. They punctuated the landscape with their hopes for a new and better life and their nostalgia for the old world they had left, comforting themselves by naming fragments of the inhospitable landscape Aberdeen, Essex, New Rochelle, and New Holland.

Still others came seeking adventure, and that adventure lay in taming a wild and giant continent. The American tradition of the tall tale is a memorial to the American nature hero whose feat lay in bringing nature to its knees. Paul Bunyan felled huge trees; Pecos Bill tamed wild horses; and the literary descendant of the epic hero, Natty Bumppo, saw the conquest of the forests and the prairies. Realizing that when the environment submitted and the prairies disappeared, he must die, he tried to stay this "victory," but he failed.

These movements and the people who represent them all share a boundless optimism. Each group acted on the belief that America was an inexhaustible mine of wealth, of adventure, of natural resources. In this land of opportunity, "profit" and "use" were bywords, and in the eyes of the pioneers, profit and use could only enhance both the people and the nation. For them, as for us, progress always meant the growth and diffusion of civilization.

If progress is the single word which summarizes the obsession and the history of America, then we must understand that exploitation is inherent in progress. Exploitation is part of the American heritage. The exploration of America is recorded in early chronicles which hold out the promise of a wealth waiting to be taken. In a *New York Times* article on September 19, 1970, Brooks Atkinson quoted a New England village parson, John Brereton: looking at the coast of Martha's Vineyard and marveling at the berries, fruits, herds of deer, schools of fish, and other natural resources, he decided that "in comparison whereof the most fertil part of England is (of itselfe) but barren." His wonder was only a harbinger of the dreams of later immigrants who were to see in the fertile soil and its fruits the promise of material comfort.

Instant wealth and thereby instant honor and aristocracy were available to those who succeeded in harvesting natural resource booms. There were gold rushes, copper rushes, silver rushes, land rushes, oil rushes, coal rushes, and each discovery of new natural wealth led to a consuming activity which drained the land.

To reach new territory, to ship produce, to carry supplies, Americans needed new and more efficient forms of overland transportation. The stage coach, traveling across the narrow paths and primitive roads, gave way to the railroads which "neighed like Boanerges." The building of railroads entailed the importation of vast numbers of workers to grade and blast the earth. More people moved across and into virgin lands; more timber was cut to lay ties and build houses. Great pits and strips were gouged out of iron-bearing land, and so the encroachment of the wilderness began. It heralded the beginnings of an urban civilization and the depletion of the wilderness, the inevitable concomitant of urbanism.

Now faced with the problems of overpopulation, industrialization, and consequent air, land, and sea pollution, we find it easy to descry the depredations of homesteaders, hunters, inventors, and industrialists upon our natural environment. Yet we forget that it was an enduring idealism which perpetuated the blind faith that the land, like Philomel's pitcher, could never be drained. The very pride and love and economic faith, the loss of which we now mourn, was inextricably bound to a belief in the lasting perfection of the land. Of course, these lofty sentiments only partly explain the rape of the American wilderness. Less idealistic forces were also at work.

Blind greed moved many who, struggling to win wealth or to amass more wealth, simply did not think of the land or the animals. Obsessed with their own ambitions, they took what they saw before them. Ignorance is the best excuse we can offer to justify or explain their behavior. How could they fear that they might ravage or destroy the land when they had before them no models of man-made deserts or records of animal species destroyed by humans?

Three trends in the American response to the natural environment war with one another—and always have done so. The first is the movement to cultivate the wilderness. This movement, characterized by the conviction that human intervention improves nature, was typical of the Puritans who wished to make an informal garden of the wilderness, and is typical today of ecological painters who dye streams in order to beautify them. The second is the effort to preserve nature, an effort first encouraged by the transcendentalists, who believed that in the grandeur of nature one might glimpse the divine. The modern counterpart is the national parks program—an effort to save the last remnants of nature for those whose eyes are starved for visual delights and whose tense nerves can find rest only in respite from the tensions of an urban society. The third is the movement toward progress—a progress which views nature as either a force hostile to human efforts or the raw material of a consumer economy. The land developers cited by Emerson held this view, and today's land developers, who regard the land as a waiting presence, would applaud Ronald Reagan's defense of felling virgin timber to build houses: "If you've seen one redwood, you've seen them all."

The evidence is before us. We can test the effects of our response to the environment: we know that the Aswan Dam has raised the temperature of the Mediterranean to levels dangerous to marine life, that the elimination of wildcats in the Grand Canyon has resulted in an overpopulation of deer which destroy the vegetation, that the dumping of industrial wastes into the Hudson River has made it unfit for drinking and swimming and smelling, that the proliferation of automobiles has contributed to a rising percentage of deaths from cancer. As Brooks Atkinson has said: "The destruction and contamination of America in three centuries includes too many aspects of life to be itemized—including the recent death of a charming seven-year-old boy from innocently breathing parathion in his father's tobacco field."

We face a difficult dilemma. The growth of civilization has always meant the growth of cities. The more wilderness, the less room for people. We praise progress and we value technology, which we equate with progress, but we cannot use our environment without changing it. Perhaps we are on the brink of choice: with the complete destruction of the natural environment imminent, we have come to treasure it more. We realize that the task of the next few generations will be to strike a balance between wealth, industry, and convenience on one hand, and the preservation of the spiritual resource of the "useless beauty of untouched nature" on the other.

Peter Carroll

from **Puritanism and the Wilderness**

Studies of Puritan intellectual history traditionally stress the Old World origins of
the New England mind. The writings of Samuel Eliot Morison, Perry Miller, and
Edmund S. Morgan, to name the most influential historians of Puritanism, attest to
the fecundity of this approach. As a transplanted culture, seventeenth-century New
England provides a valuable and convenient example of the tenacity of a priori concepts. Religion, the bench mark of all seventeenth-century thought, obviously was
transported to the New World in the minds of the first New England colonists. Moreover, the cluster of ideas which surrounded Puritan religion—the notion of the organic state, the belief in the just price, the mission to establish a city on a hill—also
reflects the European basis of New England's intellectual apparatus.

But in describing the geography of the Puritan mind, these studies tend to minimize, if not neglect, the importance of the New World in restructuring and redefin-
ing Puritan ideas. Placed in a radically new environment—the raw American wilderness
—Old World attitudes and concepts were forced to prove themselves anew. The novelty of the American situation impinged, at times subtly, at times brutally, at times
to no apparent effect, upon the founders of New England. This dialogue between the
European mind and the American environment can be analyzed in the context of
Puritan attitudes and responses to the wilderness. By using the wilderness as a focal
point, it is possible to assess the relative importance of the virgin forest as a condi-
tioner of Old World thought in America.

The Puritans had developed specific views of the wilderness situation prior to
their migration to Massachusetts Bay. Derived largely from Biblical metaphors, these
concepts provided New Englanders with elaborate rhetorical devices with which they
could judge their own experiences. Disregarding inherent contradictions, the colonists
identified the New England forest with the Biblical wilderness and employed traditional Christian language to articulate their life in America. The notion of the wilderness as a refuge from worldly corruption, for example, moved the settlers of New
England to stress the advantages of sanctuary in justifying their departure from the
degeneracy of England. In other contexts, the Puritans interpreted the wilderness as
the place of religious insight, and therefore could challenge ecclesiastical deviation
both in America and in Europe. Furthermore, as the children of Israel, they translated
their hardships in the New World as God's testing of his chosen people—a necessary
prelude to everlasting salvation. The continued use of these metaphors illustrates the
Puritans' remarkable ability to apply preconceived ideas to the experientially different world of New England.

These continuities, however, comprise only one aspect (though indeed an important one) of the Puritans' view of the New World. While the colonists interpreted
the American wilderness with traditional metaphors, in effect, the physical realities
of the New World challenged the symbolic wilderness of the Bible. The modifications
wrought by this interaction can be examined in the realm of Puritan social theory.

Within the matrix of Puritan social thought lay two logically antithetical versions of the mission to New England. First, the founders of Massachusetts Bay intended to erect a city on a hill, a unified, organic society bound internally by Christian love. Modelled, in theory, on the medieval town, such a city would enclose the the entire population within the confines of strong walls. In insisting upon social cohesion, the leaders of New England expected the commonwealth to function without reference to the areas outside the community.

Beneath the ideal of a collective society, however, lay the seeds of its destruction, the paradoxical element within Puritan social theory. In defending their migration to the New World, the colonists emphasized the importance of settling uncultivated areas. According to Genesis, they argued, the Lord had commanded the sons of Adam to subdue the earth and, they concluded with self-assurance, God undoubtedly had included the American continent in this commission. The Puritans' endorsement of the subjugation of wild lands, however, provided enterprising settlers with an effective rationalization for expanding beyond the organic community intended by the founding fathers. In time, the colonists celebrated the process of transforming the wilderness despite the evident dangers to the collective society. The resulting tension emerged to govern the Puritans' comprehension of the wilderness condition.

Throughout the seventeenth century, neither idea established hegemony over the other. Instead, both versions of the wilderness community—the cohesive and the expansive—flourished simultaneously. Despite the obvious contradictions, Puritan leaders praised both virtues and argued for both causes. While they blessed the subjugation of the forest because it fulfilled a divine commandment, the ministers urged the settlers to resist the forces of frontier expansion. This failure to resolve the paradox between cohesion and dispersal resulted in an abdication of social leadership. As the colonial authorities wavered within the balance, New England society lacked a clearly defined direction in adjusting to the wilderness in the seventeenth century. In the area of social theory, therefore, traditional solutions proved unworkable in the American environment.

The Puritans' inability to produce a suitable theory of society during the seventeenth century reveals the importance of the wilderness in the development of New England thought. Although traditional metaphors and symbols facilitated the process of adaptation in the early years of settlement, such language failed to satisfy the needs of a new society in America. By raising questions and posing challenges, the wilderness forced the Puritans to come to grips with their unique environment and altered considerably their understanding of the wilderness condition and the nature of a colonial society.

In March 1629, Charles I abruptly dismissed a rancorous Parliament and embarked on an era of personal rule. For Puritans throughout England, the royal decision signaled the defeat of the forces of reformation. Nervous about the future of their country, many of these disenchanted men now began to consider the possibility of departing from their native land to erect a godly commonwealth in America. As they projected their hopes to the lands beyond the Atlantic Ocean, the vision of the New World captivated their imaginations and excited their minds. Influenced by promotional literature and inner expectations rather than by concrete experience, the Puritan colonizers articulated their notions of America in ambiguous language. The wilderness continent meant different things to different people, and Puritan views of America ranged from a paradise to a wasteland.

Separating the vision from the reality lay the Atlantic Ocean. This vast sea played a dual role in the formation of New England society. It led the colonists into new realms of experience and, at the same time, sealed them off from the familiar world of the English countryside. Thus as a channel and as a barrier the Atlantic influenced the colonial mind from the beginning of settlement and figured prominently in the Puritans' quest for identity in New England.

The European vision of America, nevertheless, provided limited preparation for the initial contacts with the virgin continent. When confronted by the wilderness, the Puritans' ambiguous notions of the New World produced contradictory responses. Those who expected a veritable Eden lamented the absence of milk and honey in Massachusetts; others who anticipated barren soil lauded the ability of the land to sustain agricultural undertakings. Moreover, a lack of understanding of New England geography resulted in disproportionate statements about the American situation. Only after continued contact with the wilderness did the colonists restrain their tendency to generalize from singular experiences.

Although the wilderness environment often repudiated the Old World image of America, the varied responses among Puritans to the wilderness reveals the importance of understanding the European mind as an antecedent of New England thought. The differences between Puritan views of the wilderness in England and in America illuminate both the continuities of Old World thought and the modifications wrought by the New World within the minds of the settlers of Massachusetts Bay. As they assessed the lands of New England, the Puritan colonists relied upon traditional images as well as their experiences in the wilderness.

Two generations after the settlement of New England, Puritan historians extolled the courage of their patriarchs, the men who first established beachheads upon the virgin continent. William Hubbard, whose *General History of New England* won the endorsement of the Massachusetts General Court in 1682, recounted the single-minded commitment of John Winthrop, "that honorable and worthy gentleman," who guided the Great Migration of 1630. At "a solemn feast" shortly before his last farewell, Governor Winthrop, "finding his bowels yearn within him," broke into "a flood of tears" which "set them all a weeping." But despite the distress at losing dear friends forever, this passionate outburst failed to dampen their spirits "as to think of breaking off their purpose so far carried on."[1] Cotton Mather, writing nearly three decades after Hubbard, was similarly struck by the resolution of the founding fathers. It was, he felt, "a strange work of God" which inspired diverse men "to secede into

---

1. William Hubbard, "A General History of New-England from the Discovery to 1680," reprinted in *Collections of the Massachusetts Historical Society*, second ser., V-VI (1848), V, 125. (Hereafter cited as *Colls. M.H.S.*); *Records of the Governor and Company of the Massachusetts Bay in New England*, ed. by Nathaniel B. Shurtleff, 5 vols. (Boston, 1853-54), V, 378. (Hereafter cited as *Recs. of Mass. Bay.*)

a wilderness, they knew not where, and suffer in that wilderness, they knew not what."[2]

The Puritans, despite this ignorance of their destination, were strikingly confident about their adventure. Assured that they were transporting the Protestant Reformation to a new citadel in America, they projected their optimism onto the unknown soil of New England. Although a paucity of sources compels the contemporary historian to rely for analysis upon the expectations of a few influential men, it is nevertheless apparent that most of the passengers who crowded aboard the ships bound for Massachusetts agreed with John Winthrop that America was "the good land."[3] To be sure, this statement meant different things to different people. Conditioned by Biblical metaphors and promotional literature, the Puritans viewed the wilderness from a variety of perspectives. For some, New England signified the New Canaan; others anticipated a barren wasteland; some regarded America as a land of spiritual darkness; and an important segment of the ministry lauded the New World as a refuge. But regardless of these paradoxical assessments, a sense of self-assurance pervaded the entire mission.[4]

Probably the most influential theme in bulwarking Puritan optimism on the eve of migration was the idea of New England as the promised land. John Cotton, then minister of the Boston congregation in Lincolnshire, journeyed to Southampton to bid farewell to the Winthrop fleet and preached on the text, "Moreover I will appoint a place for my people Israell, and I will plant them, that they may dwell in a place of their owne, and move no more."[5] He assured the departing colonizers that God selects a specific country in which to plant His people. They shall have "firme and durable possession" there, and the Lord will not uproot them if they continue to propagate their religion.[6] In a similar tone, John Winthrop parried the words of the less optimistic. In answer to the objection that "many speak ill of this Countrye [New England], of the barrennesse etc. of it," Winthrop retorted, "so did the Spyes of the lande of Canaan."[7]

The origin of the paradisaical motif lay not only in Biblical exegesis, but also in the promotional tracts designed to attract settlers to New England. While similar advertisements attempted to promote other colonial endeavors during the seventeenth century, these writings excited the imagination of the Puritan colonizers.[8] In

2. Cotton Mather, *Magnalia Christi Americana; Or, The Ecclesiastical History of New-England,* 2 vols. (Hartford, 1855), I, 240 (first published in 1702).
3. John Winthrop, "A Modell of Christian Charity," *Colls. M.H.S.,* third ser., VII (1838), 48. It is possible to deduce the optimism about America among the rank-and-file migrants from their initial antipathy to the American forest. . . .
4. For a summary of the various Christian ideas about the Wilderness, see George Hunston Williams, *Wilderness and Paradise in Christian Thought* (New York, 1962).
5. II Samuel 7:10. Biblical citations throughout this study refer to the King James version.
6. John Cotton, "Gods Promise to His Plantation," in *Old South Leaflets,* III (Boston, n.d.), 4–5, 14.
7. "General Conclusions and Particular Considerations: Early Draft" [1629], *Winthrop Papers,* 5 vols. (Boston, 1929–), II, 127.
8. For a discussion of some of these non-Puritan promotionalists, see Robert Ralston Cawley, *The Voyagers and Elizabethan Drama* (Boston, 1938), pp. 290–91.

depicting the New World as the terrestrial paradise, this literature portrayed New England in iridescent colors and acclaimed the lusciousness of the land.

John Smith wrote one of the earliest of these brochures in 1616 in which he praised the fecundity of the American soil and its capacity to produce "any grain, fruits or seeds you will sow or plant." He favorably compared the soil with that of England and assured readers that "all good provisions for man's sustenance may with . . . facility be had, by a little extraordinary labor." And although Smith was sufficiently realistic to state that the plenty of New England was seasonable, he nevertheless added, "worthy is that person to starve that here cannot live, if he have sense, strength and health." The natural blessings of America, he continued, are so plentiful "that a hundred men may, in one hour or two, make their provisions for a day." John White, whose promotional undertakings were published shortly after the embarkation of the 1630 expedition, also stressed the beneficence of the American forest. Using an economic argument in favor of the colonization of New England, White described the natural abundance and variety of fish and furs, timber and vines. He also praised the salubriousness of the climate there ("No Countrey yeelds a more propitious ayre for our temper, then New-England. . . .") and suggested the availability of plenty. White brushed aside all testimony to the contrary and concluded that the soil could produce sufficient quantities of food.[9] Even more immediate than these pamphlets in bolstering the spirits of the Winthrop group were the optimistic letters sent back to England by Francis Higginson of Salem who arrived in New England in 1629. These reports, which circulated among the Puritan colonizers, extolled the beauty and plenty of New England.[10]

Although the Puritans were usually confident about the physical attributes of New England, they had serious doubts about its spiritual state. For beneath the florid plenty of the New World, the Puritan settlers saw the Devil lurking in the wilderness. In an age dominated by theological presuppositions, it was evident to them that America lacked all the blessings of Christianity. To many, the savage state of the wilderness signified Satanic power; they were convinced that America, the land of spiritual darkness, was the realm of the Antichrist. The inhabitants of that world, the Indians, were believed to be trapped in "the snare of the Divell." John White considered these people to be "men transformed into beasts," the very "bond-slaves of Sathan."[11] Because the importation of true religion into this doctrinally barren ground would threaten the Devil's kingdom, the Puritans were prepared to meet with strong Satanic opposition in America. The Devil, they felt, would muster all his power to prevent the incursion of Christianity into the wilderness. Satan would rely upon the reprobates of the world—the English episcopacy as well as the Indian—as instruments of his malice.

9. John Smith, "A Description of New England . . ." [1616], reprinted in *Colls. M.H.S.*, third ser., VI, 112, 115–16, 121; John White, "The Planter's Plea or the grounds of plantations examined and usuall objections answered" [1630], reprinted in *Proceedings of the Massachusetts Historical Society*, LXII (1929), 384–85, 386, 388–89. (Hereafter cited as *Proc. M.H.S.*)
10. John Winthrop to His Wife, October 9, 1629, Margaret Winthrop to Her Husband [October 13, 1629], *Winthrop Papers*, II, 157–58. . . .
11. "Sir John Eliot's Copy of the New England Tracts" [1629], *Winthrop Papers*, II, 145; White, "Planter's Plea," 394–95.

Thus Francis Higginson urged the settlers to come quickly before Satanic efforts effectively delayed the migration by prohibiting egress from England.[12]

Instead of making the Puritans wary of entering the New World, these religious assumptions merely strengthened their desire to erect the true church in the wilderness. New England, wrote John White, "is destitute of all helpes, and meanes, by which the people might come out of the snare of Satan." This situation then led him to extol the historical transit of religion from east to west. And John Winthrop observed that the settlement of New England would be "a service to the church of great consequens by carringe the gospell into those parts to raise a bulworke against the kingdom of antichrist."[13] Nearly every defender of colonization in the seventeenth century proclaimed the advantages of exporting Christianity to America. Regardless of doctrinal variations, such appeals reflected and highlighted the theological premises of contemporaneous society, the need to interpret all behavior in religious terms. For the Puritans, the logic of this position became a prime justification for the establishment of a colony in New England.[14]

The planting of religion in Massachusetts, however, meant more than simply importing good Christians into the wilderness; it also denoted the desire to convert the Indians from their sinful state. To be sure, other exponents of colonization frequently employed similar rhetoric to justify their settlements.[15] But there is no reason to doubt the sincerity of the promoters of New England. Recent scholarship confirms the idea that the Puritans did not regard the Indians as a race apart, but merely as man in the state of sin.[16] That was, nevertheless, an unenviable situation, and the Puritans articulated a desire to alter the spiritual orientation of the natives. Over a year before the sailing of the Winthrop fleet, Mathew Cradock, then Governor of the New England Company, expressed sorrow at the low level of spiritual development among the Indians and urged the people of New England to strengthen their efforts "to bringe [the natives] out of that woeful state and condition they now are in." John White similarly exhorted the colonists to treat the Indians mercifully and supported the erection of churches among them. Although the natives appeared to be in the clutches of Satan and "live without God in this present world," their situation was not necessarily permanent, for the Puritans could raise them "unto a forme of Piety and godlinesse." John Cotton's valedictory address at Southampton also re-

12. Francis Higginson, "Some brief Collections out of a letter that Mr. Higginson sent to . . . Leicester" [1629], reprinted in Alexander Young, comp., *Chronicles of the First Planters of the Colony of Massachusetts Bay* (Boston, 1846), p. 260. . . .
13. White, "Planter's Plea," 388, 377; "General Observations for the Plantation of New England" [1629], *Winthrop Papers*, II, 111.
14. Several historians have noted that the seventeenth-century promotionalists stressed the need to advance the cause of Christianity through colonization; see, for example, Louis B. Wright, *Religion and Empire: The Alliance between Piety and Commerce in English Expansion, 1558–1625* (Chapel Hill, 1943), p. 155 and Cawley, *The Voyagers*, pp. 299–300. J. H. Parry, in *The Age of Reconnaissance* (New York, 1963), p. 232, writes, "Every colonizing company in every European country . . . claimed the spreading of the Gospel among its leading motives."
15. See, Wright, *Religion and Empire*, pp. 5–6 and Perry Miller, "Religion and Society in the Early Literature of Virginia," *Errand Into the Wilderness* (Cambridge, [Mass.], 1956), p. 101.
16. For the best examination of the Puritan idea of the Indian, see Alden T. Vaughan, *New England Frontier: Puritans and Indians, 1620–1675* (Boston, 1965).

flected this concern for the Indians' salvation and advocated the conversion of the heathen.[17]

Besides the absence of appropriate religious institutions, the American wilderness also lacked the garments of civilization. Many Puritans viewed "the good land" simply as vacant soil. This idea was reinforced by the knowledge of the plague which decimated the Indian population in New England shortly before the arrival of the Pilgrims in 1620. The sparsity of Indian inhabitants in Massachusetts not only enabled the Puritans to justify the settlement of that area, but also provided them with a rationalization for claiming title to the surrounding lands. John Cotton interpreted the Indian epidemic as a sign from God that He would have the English settle there. When the Lord chooses to transplant His people, preached Cotton, "hee makes a Countrey though not altogether void of inhabitants, yet voyd in that place where they reside." John White endorsed this view and added that men have "a cleare and sufficient warrant from the mouth of God" for "replenishing wast and voyd Countries."[18] Thus the idea of America as a wasteland did little to diminish the Puritans' optimistic attitude toward the wilderness.

The belief that America was vacant soil also served as a convenient justification for the Puritans' claim to the Indian lands. John Cotton argued that "hee that taketh possession" of vacant lands, "and bestoweth culture and husbandry upon it," has an unimpeachable claim to that land. John Winthrop bolstered this position by citing Genesis 1:28 wherein the Lord gave man a general commission to "encrease and multiply and replenish the earth and subdue it." This is especially true, he added, since England is overpopulated and abundant land "lyes waste" elsewhere. Supporting these colonizing endeavors, John White appealed to God's command that men replenish and subdue the earth. This task, he maintained, binds Adam's posterity "as long as the earth yeelds empty places to be replenished." Moreover, he concluded, as a result of the Indian epidemic in New England, "there is no person left to lay claime to the soyle which they possessed." Winthrop also argued that the Indians' claim to the American wastes was extremely tenuous because "they inclose noe Land, neither have [they] any setled habytation, nor any tame Cattle to improve the Land by." The natives, he maintained, "ramble over much land without title or property." And if "the whole earthe is the Lordes garden," he asked, why should we contend for living space while other places equally "fruitfull and convenient for the use of man . . . lye waste without any improvement"?[19]

The idea of the wilderness as a wasteland which had to be cultivated and improved led logically to the notion that America, if not the New Eden, was, at least, a potential paradise. Such a view of the wilderness was the most realistic, because it implicitly anticipated a struggle in transforming the waste places into habitable grounds. In reply to the objection that New England would offer a lean subsistence,

17. Mathew Cradock to John Endecott [?], February 16, 1628/29, *Recs. of Mass. Bay,* I, 384; White, "Planter's Plea," 394–95, 376; Cotton, "Gods Promise," 14–15.
18. Cotton, "Gods Promise," 5–6; White, "Planter's Plea," 376.
19. Cotton, "Gods Promise," 6; John Winthrop to–[1629], *Winthrop Papers,* II, 123; White, "Planter's Plea," 376, 371–72, 385–86; "Reasons To Be Considered, And Objections With Answers" [1629], *Winthrop Papers,* II, 140–41; "General Observations," 113, 115.

Winthrop insisted that "whatsoever we stand in need of is treasured up in the earthe by the Creator, and is to be fetched thence by the sweatt of our browes." Another version of the belief that the wilderness, if not a land of plenty, at least possessed the potentiality of abundance can be seen in proposals to exploit what natural wealth existed in New England. Among these possibilities were the husbandry of livestock, fishing, fur trading, salt manufacture, and vine planting. The implementation of such a program, it would seem, was to be no easy task. John White, in a rare moment of moderation, confessed that "there is nothing to bee expected in New-England but competency to live on at best, and that must be purchased with hard labour." Even as they huddled in the ships about to leave for Massachusetts, the settlers forecasted "manifold necessities and tribulations" in the wilderness.[20]

But instead of cooling their ardor for New England, the Puritans translated their expected hardships into blessings. White claimed that countries with "riche soile" where men could live in ease were the source of social evil. "Piety and godlinesse," he wrote, emerge in places like New England "which may yeeld sufficiency" only "with hard labour and industry." Entering upon uncultivated lands inspires frugality and invention. Such efforts provide "a naturall remedy against covetousnesse, fraud, and violence" because "every man may enjoy enough without wrong or injury to his neighbor." John Winthrop assumed a similar stance in rejecting the charge that he was brought up "amonge boockes" and would therefore suffer greatly in "a barbarous place where [there] is no learnynge and lesse cyvillytie." "It may be," reasoned Winthrop, that "God will by this meanes bring us to repent of our former Intemperance." The same motives moved the Lord to carry "the Isralites into the wildernesse and made them forgette the fleshpotts of Egipt."[21] Winthrop, in this manner, glossed over the anticipated difficulties of settling the raw continent.

In his emphasis upon the need to be liberated from the "fleshpotts" of the world he knew best, Winthrop implicitly suggested that "the good land" was also a sanctuary. This idea of America as a refuge clarifies the haste and compulsory nature of the migration of 1630. It implies that the Winthrop fleet sailed not only *to* New England, but also *away* from old England.[22] What then had occurred at home to compel the Puritans to flee into the remote wilderness?

It must be remembered that the Puritan vision, like that of most seventeenth-century men, focussed sharply upon religion and God. Everything in this world had theological ramifications, and nothing possessed meaning aside from God. Thus the Puritans believed that political, social, and economic affairs reflected, in some way, the mind of God. When the Lord smiled upon a nation, He blessed that people with political stability, social security, and economic well-being; when God frowned upon

20. "Objections Answered: First Draft" [1629], "Sir John Eliot's Copy," "The Humble Petition," April 1630, *Winthrop Papers*, II, 136, 146–47, 233; White, "Planter's Plea," 390–91.
21. White, "Planter's Plea," 390–91, 373; Robert Ryece to John Winthrop, August 12, 1629, "Reasons To Be Considered," *Winthrop Papers*, II, 105–106, 144.
22. Edmund S. Morgan suggested the significance of New England as a refuge for Governor Winthrop in *The Puritan Dilemma: The Story of John Winthrop* (Boston, 1958). It appears, however, that this idea was also extremely influential among other Puritan intellectuals. Michael Walzer places the concept within the context of intellectual alienation; see, *The Revolution of the Saints: A Study in the Origins of Radical Politics* (Cambridge, Mass., 1965), pp. 142–43.

a land, He permitted these blessings to be dissipated. The Puritans articulated the sense of God's grace upon a country with the metaphor of the "Hedge," a protective wall which surrounded a people and assured them that the Lord would not forsake that nation. John Preston, a staunch defender of English Puritanism, described God's special protectiveness for His people with the metaphor of the wall. And John Cotton, viewing the Hedge as "some defence set about church or commonwealth, whether counsel, laws, or guard of military men," remarked that "the breaking of a hedge" violates this protective shell and threatens the safety of the entire nation.[23]

The nature of English society in the 1620s led many Puritans to believe that a shattering of this Hedge was imminent. Time and again the Puritans lamented the evils of the age and feared that the worst was yet to come. Early in 1622 John Winthrop wrote of "the present evill tymes" and predicted a dismal future. "The Lord looke mercifully upon this sinfull lande," he continued, "and turne us to him by some repentence, otherwise we may feare it hath seene the best dayes." Such words were repeated so frequently that "the evill of the tymes" became a cliché. In 1623 Winthrop admitted that the sins "of the whole land doe call for judgementes rather then blessinges," and he placed his hopes in the manifold mercies of the Lord. For a time, he even expressed interest in a plantation in Ireland as a means of escaping from the sinfulness of English society. But in 1624 the political wheel turned, and it appeared that England might reform itself. In that year Prince Charles's efforts to marry a Spanish princess appeared futile, and the Duke of Buckingham seemed amenable to the summoning of Parliament. By 1626, however, the wheel had turned again, and the Winthrop correspondence became cluttered with regrets at "the dangers and discouragementes of these declininge tymes."[24] As the decade drew to a close, cries of anguish reverberated through the land. "Consider the present time of the Church," intoned John Preston shortly before his death in 1628, "consider how soone the times may come upon us, when we shal be put to it; for now things are *in praecipito;* hastening downe to the bottome of the hill." John Wilson, later pastor of the Boston church in New England, lamented the evils of the age with an equally poignant sense of frustration. "What hope is left us," he implored, but the mercy of the Lord.[25]

Wilson's faith in the Lord was not unfounded. For at this moment of peril, the Almighty God, in His infinite mercy, provided a wilderness sanctuary for His people. If the Lord would turn his face from the English and punish that nation with His wrath, He would seek to preserve His children from the impending storm. Francis Higginson bade farewell to England on this theme. According to New England tradi-

23. John Preston, *The New Covenant, or the Saints Portion* . . . (London, 1629), p. 43; John Cotton, "A Brief Exposition Upon Ecclesiastes," reprinted in *Nichol's Series of Commentaries* (Edinburgh, 1868), II, Part II, 108, 109.
24. John Winthrop to Thomas Fones, January 29, 1621[/22]; John Winthrop to John Winthrop, Jr., August 6, 1622; Forth Winthrop to John Winthrop, Jr., April 17, 1623; John Winthrop to John Winthrop, Jr., April 20, 1623; John Winthrop to His Wife, September 27, 1623; John Winthrop to John Winthrop, Jr., March 7, 1623[/24]; John Winthrop to John Winthrop, Jr., December 18, 1626; *Winthrop Papers,* I, 268, 271, 279, 281, 286, 311, 337. For a description of the social problems of the 1620s, see Carl Bridenbaugh, *Vexed and Troubled Englishmen: 1590–1642* (New York, 1968), *passim.*
25. John Preston, *Life Eternall* . . . , fourth ed. (London, 1634), Part I, 87; John Wilson to John Winthrop, February 3, 1628 [N.S.], *Winthrop Papers,* II, 57–58.

tion, Higginson foresaw the calamities with which God would chasten the mother land and composed a sermon on the text, "When you see Jerusalem compassed with armies, then flee to the mountains."[26] Preaching to a large congregation in Leicester, he warned his audience of its provoking sins and the likelihood of divine chastisement. New England, he felt, was a haven for the chosen people during the coming time of troubles. At this time, John Winthrop's thoughts were also being channeled in this direction. Writing to his wife, he criticized the evils of the time and observed that "the increasinge of our sinnes gives us so great cause to looke for some heavye Scquorge [sic] and Judgment to be comminge upon us." God "hath admonished, threatened, corrected, and astonished us," he continued, "yet we growe worse and worse." Referring to the setbacks to Protestantism on the European continent, the success of the forces of Counter-Reformation in France, Denmark, and Germany, Winthrop bemoaned England's failure to take heed and reform itself. This hardheartedness, he asserted, would inevitably attract the Lord's wrath. "I am veryly perswaded," he wrote, "God will bringe some heavye Affliction upon this lande, and that speedylye." Yet despite these impending horrors, Winthrop did not conclude with despair. Optimistically he added, "If the Lord seeth it wilbe good for us, he will provide a shelter and a hidinge place for us and ours."[27]

The theme of the wilderness as a refuge became increasingly important in Winthrop's justification of the migration of 1630. Citing appropriate Biblical passages, he argued that members of the church "may be of better use to their mother Churche heere in tyme then those whom she shall kepe in her bosome."[28] The true church, he maintained, "hath noe place lefte to flie into but the wildernesse." Stressing the catastrophes which had befallen European Protestantism elsewhere, Winthrop asserted that the Lord probably selected New England as a sanctuary for those He wished to save. English Puritans should learn from the tragedies elsewhere "to avoyde the plague when it is foreseene, and not to tarrye, as they did, till it overtake us."[29]

Winthrop's reasoning won the support of other Puritans. One correspondent, Robert Ryece, agreed that "it is juste to seeke refuge for saftye, especially where safest hope maye be founde." Echoing Winthrop's sentiments, Ryece praised the wonders of divine providence "that hathe reysed this newe plantation, for so comfortable a refuge." And citing the evils of the age, he concurred that it is better "to seeke to dye . . . in the wyldernes" than to remain besmirched in a land of sin.[30] The great William Ames, a leading English Puritan, defended the Winthrop migration along similar lines. Although he opposed the removal of communicants from church society as a violation of the sacred covenant, he asserted that under certain circumstances such departures were lawful and necessary. For example, he proceeded, "if a man cannot continue his communion, without a communication of their sinnes," or "if there be any eminent danger of being seduced," it was then appropriate for

---

26. Luke 21:20, 21. The discussion of Francis Higginson is based upon Mather, *Magnalia*, I, 361–62. Although Mather's interpretation of the refuge idea is frequently distorted, his narrative regarding Higginson is probably accurate since the *Magnalia* won the endorsement of Higginson's son, John, who at the age of thirteen accompanied his father to New England.
27. John Winthrop to His Wife, May 15, 1629, *Winthrop Papers*, II, 91–92.
28. Revelation 12. "General Conclusions and Particular Considerations," 125.
29. "Reasons To Be Considered," 138–39; "General Observations," 111, 116.
30. Robert Ryece to John Winthrop [1629], *Winthrop Papers*, II, 128–30.

the true Christian to withdraw. Thus the need to avoid culpability for other people's crimes authorized the quest for safer lands.[31]

John Cotton agreed with Ames's appraisal of the situation in his farewell address to the Winthrop group. He emphasized the importance of evading calamities, "when some grievous sinnes overspread a Country." "A wise man," he suggested, who "foreseeth a plague . . . [may] hide himselfe from it." John White approached this problem from a slightly different perspective. Since his tract was obviously designed for widespread public consumption, he had to justify the departure of so many men at a time of social crisis. After dismissing the allegation that the departure would weaken England, White then denied that "this withdrawing of our selves in time of so great hazard betrayes weaknesse of heart." Unlike the founders of Plymouth Colony, the settlers of Massachusetts Bay never embraced a Separatist theology which involved the total repudiation of English society because of the religious deviations within the Church of England. The establishment of a colony in New England therefore did not absolve the Puritans from their temporal obligations to live in the world of sin. To those who might suggest that the Puritans were withdrawing from all worldly corruption, White replied that New England would not be beyond the scope of divine punishment if she too lapsed into sin. He thereby protected the Puritan refugees from the logic of their hasty retreat.[32]

The belief that America was a haven from inevitable catastrophe in England continued to influence important Puritan preachers to migrate to safer shores. To be sure, there was no unanimity among Puritans that the storm would break. Some, like James Hopkins, were reluctant to leave their homes. In a letter to Winthrop, he declared, "if our peace be continued . . . we hold our selves tied heere, and dare not breake loose till god sett us loose." But many felt that safety demanded that they depart at once. Shortly after the silencing of John Cotton by the Laudian episcopacy, an anonymous writer expressed fear that such policies would threaten the safety of the nation. These perils are greater than any "Arme of flesh," for they provoke "the Lord our Shield . . . to Depart from us." Such warnings apparently influenced Cotton, for he later claimed to have solicited the advice of "the chefe of our people," "the men of God greatly revered for their piety and saintly wisdom," before deciding to embark for New England. These men urged Cotton "to withdraw . . . from the present storme" and continue his ministry in America.[33]

Thomas Hooker, a ship-mate of Cotton's during the voyage to New England, repudiated his native land for similar reasons. In the farewell address to his English congregation, Hooker preached on the danger of God's desertion of England. He

31. William Ames, *Conscience with the Power and Cases thereof* . . . (London, 1643), Book V, 141. For a discussion of the relationship between Ames and the Massachusetts Bay Company, see Keith L. Sprunger, "William Ames and the Settlement of Massachusetts Bay," *New England Quarterly,* XXXIX (1966), 66–79.
32. Cotton, "Gods Promise," 9; White, "Planter's Plea," 405.
33. James Hopkins to John Winthrop, February 25, 1632 [/33], *Winthrop Papers,* III, 106; —to [John Cotton] [c. 1633], John Cotton Mss., Prince Collection, Boston Public Library; "Mr. Cotton's letter, giving the Reasons of his and Mr. Hooker's Removal to New-England," December 3, 1634, reprinted in [Thomas Hutchinson, comp.], *A Collection of Original Papers Relative to the History of the Colony of Massachusetts-Bay* (Boston, 1769), p. 56; John Cotton, "An Apologetical Preface," in John Norton, *The Answer to . . . Appolonius . . .* [1648], ed. and tr. by Douglas Horton (Cambridge, Mass., 1958), pp. 10–11.

warned that the Lord was "taking down the wals" of his protection by permitting the foundation stones, magistrates and ministers, to withdraw. God was uprooting the Hedge of grace which formerly had assured England of a semblance of domestic tranquillity. With his eye on the Continent, where Protestant "Churches [are] made heaps of stones," Hooker suggested that England was surely headed for a similar fate. "All things," he remarked, "are ripe for ruin," and "when God departs all miseries come."[34]

Other Puritan divines were equally impressed by the need to flee England before the Lord unleashed the worst of His fury. Thomas Shepard, who, with Hooker and Cotton, was destined to play a prominent role in the shaping of the New England Way, responded as they did to the English situation. In his autobiography written in the mid-1640s, Shepard alleged that the departure of Cotton and Hooker had a great impact upon him. "I saw the harts of most of the godly . . . bent that way and I did thinke I should feele many miseries if I stayd behind." But even before his decision to migrate to New England, Shepard had attacked the sinfulness of the age in which he lived. "Consider the approaching times," he wrote, "I doe beleeve the Lord at this day is coming . . . to teare and rend from you your choysest blessings, peace and plenty." Such a catharsis was necessary, he asserted, because "our age grows full, and proud, and wanton." The Lord, he maintained, would punish "this God-glutted, Christ-glutted, Gospel-glutted age" with "sore afflictions of famine, war, bloud, mortality, deaths of Gods precious servants especially." Such a catalog of horror persuaded Shepard to seek sanctuary in America. In a farewell letter to a friend, he prayed that the Lord would carry him "to that good land, and those glorious ordinances" of Christ. In this missive, he restated his loathing for England's degeneracy and expressed hope that the recipient would be "preserved from national sins, which shortly [will] bring national and most heavy plagues."[35]

Richard Mather, who later became the bulwark of the Dorchester church in New England, drafted an elaborate defense of his proposed departure from England in which he too proclaimed the dangers of remaining in a sinful land. Entitled "Arguments tending to prove the Removing from *Old England* to *New* . . . to be not onely lawful, but also necessary . . . ," the tract condemned the duplicity of English society and endorsed the desirability of flight. By remaining in corrupt places, wrote Mather, "We do endanger our selves to be corrupted." Declaring that such inertia "is a Tempting of God," Mather reminded himself that it was a Christian duty to flee from a place which proscribed God's ordinances. Like Shepard, Mather listed the provoking sins of the age and interpreted them as precursors of divine punishment. "To remove from a place where are fearful signs of Desolation," he concluded, "to a place where one may have well-grounded hope of preservation, and of Gods protection, is necessary to them that are free." And Mather had no doubt that New England was such a

34. Thomas Hooker, *The Danger of Desertion or A Farewell Sermon of Mr. Thomas Hooker* . . . (London, 1641), pp. 4, 5, 11. Hooker apparently preached in a similar manner while in self-exile on the Continent; see, "The Examination of Mrs. Ann Hutchinson at the court at Newtown," reprinted in Thomas Hutchinson, *The History of the Colony and Province of Massachusetts-Bay*, ed. by Lawrence Shaw Mayo, 3 vols. (Cambridge, Mass., 1936), II, 385.
35. [Thomas Shepard], "The Autobiography of Thomas Shepard," *Publications of the Colonial Society of Massachusetts*, XXVII (1932), 375; Thomas Shepard, *The Sound Beleever, Or A Treatise of Evangelicall Conversion* (London, 1653), pp. 139–40, 251–52; Thomas Shepard, "Some Select Cases Resolved," reprinted in *Three Valuable Pieces* (Boston, 1747), p. 53.

place.[36] A less influential Puritan, Michael Metcalfe, bade farewell to his native land with similar language. In a public letter to his parishioners, he condemned England for its sins. Urging repentance and reformation, he warned that the Almighty "is about to try his people in the furnace of affliction."[37]

But for Metcalfe, as for the other Puritans, the New England wilderness afforded a haven from that wrath. Although the Lord might uproot His Hedge and bring suffering upon England, "the good land" beyond the sea remained as a refuge for His chosen people. The men and women who migrated to New England applied a variety of attributes to that land. And although they possessed scant knowledge of America, they did not venture forth in complete ignorance; their imaginations had already filled the void.

Ralph Waldo Emerson

Ode

Inscribed to W. H. Channing

Though loath to grieve
The evil time's sole patriot,
I cannot leave
My honied thought
For the priest's cant,
Or statesman's rant.

If I refuse
My study for their politique,
Which at the best is trick,
The angry Muse
Puts confusion in my brain.

But who is he that prates
Of the culture of mankind,
Of better arts and life?
Go, blindworm, go,
Behold the famous States
Harrying Mexico
With rifle and with knife!

36. Richard Mather's essay is printed in [Increase Mather], *The Life and Death of . . . Richard Mather* (Cambridge, Mass., 1670), pp. 12–18.

37. Michael Metcalfe "To all the true professors of Christs gospel within the city of Norwich," January 13, 1636 [/37], printed in *New England Historical and Genealogical Register,* XVI (1862), 281–83. (Hereafter cited as *N.E.H.G.R.*) Metcalfe later became schoolmaster of Dedham, Massachusetts.

Or who, with accent bolder,
Dare praise the freedom-loving mountaineer?
I found by thee, O rushing Contoocook!
And in thy valleys, Agiochook!
The jackals of the negro-holder.

The God who made New Hampshire
Taunted the lofty land
With little men;
Small bat and wren
House in the oak:
If earth-fire cleave
The upheaved land, and bury the folk,
The southern crocodile would grieve.
Virtue palters; Right is hence;
Freedom praised, but hid;
Funeral eloquence
Rattles the coffin-lid.

What boots thy zeal,
O glowing friend,
That would indignant rend
The northland from the south?
Wherefore? to what good end?
Boston Bay and Bunker Hill
Would serve things still;
Things are of the snake.

The horseman serves the horse,
The neatherd serves the neat,
The merchant serves the purse,
The eater serves his meat;
'T is the day of the chattel,
Web to weave, and corn to grind;
Things are in the saddle,
And ride mankind.

There are two laws discrete,
Not reconciled—
Law for man, and law for thing;
The last builds town and fleet,
But it runs wild,
And doth the man unking.

'T is fit the forest fall,
The steep be graded,
The mountain tunnelled,

The sand shaded,
The orchard planted,
The glebe tilled,
The prairie granted,
The steamer built.

Let man serve law for man;
Live for friendship, live for love,
For truth's and harmony's behoof;
The state may follow how it can,
As Olympus follows Jove.

    Yet do not I implore
The wrinkled shopman to my sounding woods,
Nor bid the unwilling senator
Ask votes of thrushes in the solitudes.
Every one to his chosen work;
Foolish hands may mix and mar;
Wise and sure the issues are.
Round they roll till dark is light,
Sex to sex, and even to odd;
The over-god
Who marries Right to Might,
Who peoples, unpeoples,
He who exterminates
Races by stronger races,
Black by white faces,
Knows to bring honey
Out of the lion;
Grafts gentlest scion
On pirate and Turk.

The Cossack eats Poland,
Like stolen fruit;
Her last noble is ruined,
Her last poet mute:
Straight, into double band
The victors divide;
Half for freedom strike and stand;
The astonished Muse finds thousands at her side.

Forebearance

Hast thou named all the birds without a gun?
Loved the wood-rose, and left it on its stalk?
At rich men's tables eaten bread and pulse?
Unarmed, faced danger with a heart of trust?
And loved so well a high behavior,
In man or maid, that thou from speech refrained,
Nobility more nobly to repay?
O, be my friend, and teach me to be thine!

Hamatreya

Bulkeley, Hunt, Willard, Hosmer, Meriam, Flint
Possessed the land which rendered to their toil
Hay, corn, roots, hemp, flax, apples, wool and wood.
Each of these landlords walked amidst his farm,
Saying, " 'Tis mine, my children's and my name's.
How sweet the west wind sounds in my own trees!
How graceful climb those shadows on my hill!
I fancy these pure waters and the flags
Know me, as does my dog: we sympathize;
And, I affirm, my actions smack of the soil."

Where are these men? Asleep beneath their grounds:
And strangers, fond as they, their furrows plough.
Earth laughs in flowers, to see her boastful boys
Earth-proud, proud of the earth which is not theirs;
Who steer the plough, but cannot steer their feet
Clear of the grave.
They added ridge to valley, brook to pond,
And sighed for all that bounded their domain;
"This suits me for a pasture; that's my park;
We must have clay, lime, gravel, granite-ledge,
And misty lowland, where to go for peat.
The land is well,—lies fairly to the south.
'Tis good, when you have crossed the sea and back,
To find the sitfast acres where you left them."
Ah! the hot owner sees not Death, who adds
Him to his land, a lump of mould the more.
Hear what the Earth says:—

EARTH-SONG

"Mine and yours;
Mine, not yours.
Earth endures;
Stars abide—
Shine down in the old sea;
Old are the shores;
But where are the old men?
I who have seen much,
Such have I never seen.

"The lawyer's deed
Ran sure,
In tail,
To them, and to their heirs
Who shall succeed,
Without fail,
Forevermore.

"Here is the land,
Shaggy with wood,
With its old valley,
Mound and flood.
But the heritors?—
Fled like the flood's foam.
The lawyer, and the laws,
And the kingdom,
Clean swept herefrom.

"They called me theirs,
Who so controlled me;
Yet every one
Wished to stay, and is gone.
How am I theirs,
If they cannot hold me,
But I hold them?"

When I heard the Earth-song
I was no longer brave;
My avarice cooled
Like lust in the chill of the grave.

Joseph Wood Krutch
The Human Surplus

While those whose chief concern is to "maintain prosperity" rejoice in the prospect of limitless human fertility, there are others who fear that the bumper crop of babies is already a surplus, and in a recent popular article Arnold Toynbee put the stamp of his prestige upon two familiar propositions. Like nearly everybody else he believes that another world war would destroy civilization. And like a great many, at least, he believes also that if a major war is avoided overpopulation will soon threaten the very civilization that has been saved. Too few people are going to be left if we have a major war; too many will soon crowd the earth if we do not. And that seems to constitute as neat a pair of horns as any upon which the poor puzzled man of good will was ever tossed.

A cynic might suggest that the conclusion is obvious: what we need are wars of precisely the right size. Perhaps if "progress" had stopped with TNT and Napalm they would have conveniently taken the place of those famines, pestilences, and diseases of infancy which once supplied the natural checks. Unfortunately, perhaps, "progress" did not stop there, and any world government powerful enough and wise enough to prevent war on a global scale will have to make other arrangements for the prevention of overpopulation.

When the population got too dense for comfort in any given region it might, for instance, license sportsmen from neighboring countries to thin it out. This would furnish healthy recreation for the hunters and if a bag limit based on an accurate estimation of population density was set, that density would soon be reduced to an optimum. Thus the necessary elimination of the socially undesirable could become a source of innocent merriment for the others. The method is now commonly employed by the game managers of some public lands and some of them say it works very well.

Any squeamishness which might be felt at first would no doubt be soon conquered. One of Shaw's characters remarks that all biological necessities soon become respectable and a great many sober social scientists seem to agree that "moral" and "immoral" have no meaning except in the context of the social needs of a community. How then could they object a priori to a plan which would provide a sportsman's equivalent of war?

Unfortunately, those of us who have never been able to mature a genuinely realistic view of things and who still have a lingering, irrational reluctance to break the taboos of our tribe find this logical solution of the problem somewhat less than satisfactory even though we are not prepared to come up with a glib one that is.

Once, of course, we just said "birth control" and let it go at that. We were sure that if the birth of a child were not something which happened but something which was willed, then there would never be any more children than could be properly fed and housed. Obviously, however, it does not work out that way, and it is plain enough by now that, for whatever mysterious reasons, the birth rate does not necessarily fall when methods of controlling it are available.

In the United States the birth rate is said to be approximately the same as that in India, where the "planned parenthood" movement is just getting under way. In Ireland, on the other hand, where the laws against the dissemination of information concerning contraception are fanatically stringent, the birth rate has fallen so low that the very existence of the Irish race in Ireland seems threatened. How accurate these figures are I do not know; but the trends are unmistakable and it is obvious that both those who hoped for salvation and those who feared race suicide, wildly overestimated the effect which birth control would have.

Does it seem quite safe to say that we in America will face the problem when we come to it and that we quite properly refuse to worry about the possibility of too many people when it looks rather more likely that there won't be any at all? Too many (and there are already too many in a great many places) is certainly one cause of those very wars which threaten to leave too few. We could, of course, put the whole question up to Time and Nature, but it is one of the distinguishing peculiarities of the human mind that it is often not well pleased with the summary solutions which Time and Nature do supply in their own rough-and-ready fashion to this and other problems.

No one can say that the problem itself has gone unrecognized. It has recently been discussed in a number of very able books like Sears' *Deserts on the March,* Cook's *Human Fertility,* Sir Charles Galton Darwin's *The Next Million Years,* and Harrison Brown's *The Challenge of Man's Future.* Facts and statistics are readily available. Moreover, and with almost monotonous regularity, general surveys of our probable future say substantially what Toynbee said in his popular article. Yet only a minority of those accustomed to consider the state of the world seem actually to take the situation very seriously and it is frequently disregarded even when it is obviously relevant.

According to the calculations sponsored by the United Nations, world population increased from 1,810 million in 1920 to 2,734 million in 1956; is now increasing at the rate of forty-four million per year; and promises to continue to accelerate. In the undeveloped countries the falling death rate accompanied by an increasing birth rate is especially striking. In Ceylon, for instance, though it is already a densely populated country, the aid given by the World Health Organization is partly responsible for a decline in the death rate from 20.3 to 11 per thousand within ten years. Here the birth rate remained nearly stationary, but in Puerto Rico the death rate in 1955 was 7.2 while the birth rate had risen to 35.

What the effect of aid from the outside can be when it helps more people to stay alive without lowering the rate at which babies are born is illustrated by Sir Charles Galton Darwin in his *The Next Million Years:*

> *Not long ago the [Indian] province of Sind was mainly desert; the ground was quite fertile but there was no rainfall. A great engineering undertaking, the Sukkur barrage, has spread the waters of the Indus over a very wide area, and turned much of the desert into a garden. According to universally accepted*

standards this was a great benefit to the world for it made possible the adequate feeding of a people previously on the verge of starvation. But things did not work out like that, for after a few years the effect was only to have a large number of people on the verge of starvation instead of a small number.

No system of world government can possibly prevent wars of aggression if population pressures become intolerable. No scheme for sharing the wealth can mean much if there are more people than there is wealth to be shared.

What, to take a minor example, is the use of talking about "saving our National Parks" when it is perfectly obvious that there is no possibility of saving them if everything they contain, even the mere space they occupy, has become desperately needed?

The economists may tell us that only by a continuously increasing rate of population growth can prosperity be maintained, but the time must come when there is simply no room for any more people and long before that time arrives the problems created by overcrowding will be insoluble in any fashion compatible with an even moderately good life.

In many areas that time has already come, and there is even in America today hardly a plan to make human life safer or better either politically or socially which can be more than a temporary expedient unless somehow or other the mere number of men upon this earth keeps within reasonable limits. None of the major "world problems" is solvable on the assumption that population growth will continue at the present rate. On the other hand, a great many of them would not exist at all if, at the present moment, the population in many trouble spots were not too large for the physical or technical resources of the areas in question. Can there be any doubt that even in the United States, which is still, comparatively speaking, uncrowded, the rate at which the population is growing makes it very difficult to solve problems which would not otherwise be too difficult? Is it not, for example, the near impossibility of keeping up with growing needs which prevents us from remedying the much discussed inadequacies, physical and intellectual, of the educational system?

Why is it that most people still avert their eyes from this most fundamental of all world problems while they strive desperately for temporary amelioration? The very fact that no ready solution is available—not even a purely theoretical formulation which disregards all practical difficulties—is a partial explanation. But there never will be a radical solution unless the need for it is recognized, and the thesis here is (1) that the need is not adequately recognized and (2) that the reason is psychological as well as practical.

The most important practical problems have already been alluded to. On the one hand, prosperity as we know and worship it depends upon ever expanding consumption. Unless the "bumper crop of babies" grows larger and larger every year, not even the concept of "psychological obsolescence" plus the ever increasing demands of national defense can enable us to get rid of the goods we must produce if we are to continue to find employment for the men who operate machines whose productivity per man-hour continues to increase. On the hand, should we find some way out of this dilemma we would still face the fact that if the population of other countries continued to increase we would almost certainly find ourselves someday invaded by hordes all the more expendable because their own territories could no longer support them.

Some realization of these stubborn facts reinforces a general unwillingness to contemplate the problems being created. But something else quite deep in human nature and quite independent of rational argument complicates the situation still further.

Even those who have read the books and accept the figures resist the logical conclusion because that conclusion outrages certain convictions which have roots so deep that they penetrate into animal instinct itself. "Increase and multiply" was a natural if not a divine injunction many millions of years before Genesis was written. The impulse to multiply as rapidly and as profusely as possible is built into the living organism. No animal before man ever opposed to that instinct any prudential considerations relative to either the parents or the offspring. To reproduce as multitudinously as possible and to let nature deal as she may with the surplus seems to have been the rule almost without exception. And man himself responds to the ancient imperative far more readily than to any which has been formulated during the very brief period since the ancient injunction was even tentatively qualified.

The chamber of commerce booster who takes it for granted that his community is "progressive" just to the extent that it is getting bigger, who assumes that all villages ought to become towns, that all towns ought to become cities, and that the splendor of a city is measured by the urgency of its traffic problem has become a figure of fun to the intellectual. But his premises are more ancient than theirs. When he cuts down the majestic elms which lined the village street to make way for the super highway and calls this "progress" his language may be vulgar but his instinct is of ancient lineage. And his premises are less different than some would like to think from the premises of those whose hearts rise at the thought that either their nation or some whole community of nations is "flourishing"—and who include as a necessary part of such flourishing getting bigger and more numerous.

In the days when it was still supposed that to make the techniques of birth control accessible would automatically reduce the birth rate, we used to laugh at the Catholic Church, which was accused of wanting more souls for heaven, at no matter what cost. But that its revulsion was far deeper than any theological apology for it is proved by the fact that most left-wing sociologists also refuse to consider population a problem and seem as eager to have more citizens for the proletarian utopia as the religious ever were to send more to their traditional heaven. In Latin countries they used to say, "God never sends a child without sending a loaf at the same time." Left-wingers have translated that dubious folk saying into an equally dubious sociological doctrine: technology always keeps pace with the needs of a growing population—or at least it would if the machinations of capitalist villains didn't prevent it from doing so.

Yet space, at least, would give out finally in the technologically most perfect world and there is no evidence that automatic checks operate soon enough anywhere "under the present system." The population continues to rise both in the United States where there is still abundance and in Puerto Rico where there is not. We are assured by what ought to be competent authority that even here our agricultural surpluses are certain to become deficiencies before long. And though it is all very well to talk about bringing the whole world up to our own level of plenty and comfort, verifiable figures demonstrate, as Harrison Brown has pointed out, that even the present populations of India and China alone could consume raw materials in excess of the world's present output. That output cannot possibly be extended indefinitely. There is a limit to the earth's resources and to our ability to exploit them. But there seems no limit to human fertility.

Such are the facts that only a few are willing to face, and they were not faced in most reviews of Harrison Brown's book because the reviewers, almost without exception, stressed what the author had to say about the problem of caring for an admittedly runaway population while paying little or no attention to his final conclusion, which was that these problems may be ultimately unsolvable. The plain truth seems to be, not only that we do not know what could be done to check the immoderate proliferation of the human species but also, what is worse, that we do not yet want to do anything about it; that we prefer to cling to the instinctive conviction that the more of us there are, the better. And we seem determined to continue to do so until one of three things happens: until war or pestilence wipes most of us out; until starvation removes a considerable though perhaps lesser number; or until, thanks to a technology which has advanced as rapidly as the most exuberant prophets predict that it will, we are literally living on top of one another in a world so intolerably crowded that even movement is almost impossible and we remain fixed to the supply lines of our cubicles like aphids on a rosebush.

One English engineer has seriously and happily predicted such a situation in a jaunty book called *What's the World Coming To?*, in which he cheerfully envisages apartment houses from which the inhabitants will seldom need to issue forth because nourishment will be piped in and social life will be conducted almost exclusively by way of private television sets. Nor is this vision as merely fantastic as one might suppose. Harrison Brown, drawing upon his astonishing mastery of geophysical data, expresses the belief that the earth could support in some fashion even the prodigious population with which it seems to be threatened—say fifty billion—under certain conditions; that it could support a hundred billion under certain other conditions; even two hundred billion under still others. And since demographers calculate that it will require several centuries at the present rate of increase to produce a population of even fifty billion, Mr. Brown seems to be giving us considerable leeway. But what are the conditions which would have to prevail?

Mr. Brown presumes not only the most successful imaginable technological advance but also, to provide for even the lowest of his three figures, the devotion of every foot of ground to immediately productive purposes. To double that figure we should have to depend almost exclusively upon tank-grown algae for food. To double it again we should have also to limit caloric requirements by severely restricting all movement not necessary to production.

Is it, then, any wonder that Brown should conclude by expressing his amazement that "A substantial fraction of humanity today is acting as though it were engaged in a contest to test nature's willingness to support humanity," and were determined not to rest content "until the earth is covered completely and to a considerable depth with a writhing mass of human beings much as a dead cow is covered with a pulsating mass of maggots."

At the present moment some men not only vaguely accept such a future but are actively and joyously preparing it. From time to time scientific journals report the progress of experiments in growing algae in sewage tanks and the process is now said to be practicable. Others, possessed of still bolder imaginations, expect even more of technology—as was recently illustrated in a statement by C. F. Kettering, of General Motors: "Despite today's farm surpluses, the human race must someday become independent of plant life . . . and that will be accomplished within the next fifty years." To Mr. Kettering, in other words, sewage-grown algae represented an unworthy compromise because it accepts as necessary the intervention of a natural process. When science has solved the mystery of photosynthesis it will have freed man from dependence upon any living thing other than himself. And when that day comes no inch of the earth's surface will have to be wasted upon any other form of life, plant or animal. All will be snuffed out and the globe covered with buildings as high as we care to make them.

In such a world the automobile will have of necessity disappeared, but Mr. Kettering no doubt consoled himself with the assurance that by then industrialists will be sufficiently busy with products not yet invented. And please notice that he said, not merely that the human race will, or could, or even should, become independent of plant life. He said that it "must" and he seemed to say it without regret. We cannot control population and, so he seemed to imply, there is no reason why we should want to.

Surely it is time to ask, not whether such a world as Mr. Brown describes with horror and Mr. Kettering seemed to contemplate with complacency, is possible, but also whether or not we want it. And if the answer is "no," then we should face the fact that unless we control population something like it is what we shall get—unless, that is to say, we get war, or famine, or pestilence first. One or all of them will be the penalty of our failure to develop a technology adequate to support an immoderate population. Mr. Kettering's world will be the reward—if reward is what we still insist upon calling it—of success!

If we really want a solution to the problem we may or may not find it. If we do not want a solution we certainly shall not. Yet it cannot, I think, be said that at the present moment most Americans, most Europeans, or most Asians do want it. And if the reason for that astounding fact really is that we are still too firmly in the grip of an instinct subhuman, subanthropoid, and submammalian, then we shall perhaps get nowhere until we realize that if we follow it blindly and indiscriminately we shall have to submit to one or another of nature's unpleasant methods of dealing with her surpluses.

Paul Ehrlich
Eco-Catastrophe!

The end of the ocean came late in the summer of 1979, and it came even more rapidly than the biologists had expected. There had been signs for more than a decade, commencing with the discovery in 1968 that DDT slows down photosynthesis in marine plant life. It was announced in a short paper in the technical journal, Science, but to ecologists it smacked of doomsday. They knew that all life in the sea depends on photosynthesis, the chemical process by which green plants bind the sun's energy and make it available to living things. And they knew that DDT and similar chlorinated hydrocarbons had polluted the entire surface of the earth, including the sea.

But that was only the first of many signs. There had been the final gasp of the whaling industry in 1973, and the end of the Peruvian anchovy fishery in 1975. Indeed, a score of other fisheries had disappeared quietly from over-exploitation and various eco-catastrophes by 1977. The term "eco-catastrophe" was coined by a California ecologist in 1969 to describe the most spectacular of man's attacks on the systems which sustain his life. He drew his inspiration from the Santa Barbara offshore oil disaster of that year, and from the news which spread among naturalists that virtually all of the Golden State's seashore bird life was doomed because of chlorinated hydrocarbon interference with its reproduction. Eco-catastrophes in the sea became increasingly common in the early 1970's. Mysterious "blooms" of previously rare microorganisms began to appear in offshore waters. Red tides—killer outbreaks of a minute single-celled plant—returned to the Florida Gulf coast and were sometimes accompanied by tides of other exotic hues.

It was clear by 1975 that the entire ecology of the ocean was changing. A few types of phytoplankton were becoming resistant to chlorinated hydrocarbons and were gaining the upper hand. Changes in the phytoplankton community led inevitably to changes in the community of zooplankton, the tiny animals which eat the phytoplankton. These changes were passed on up the chains of life in the ocean to the herring, plaice, cod and tuna. As the diversity of life in the ocean diminished, its stability also decreased.

Other changes had taken place by 1975. Most ocean fishes that returned to fresh water to breed, like the salmon, had become extinct, their breeding streams so dammed up and polluted that their powerful homing instinct only resulted in suicide. Many fishes and shellfishes that bred in restricted areas along the coasts followed them as onshore pollution escalated.

By 1977 the annual yield of fish from the sea was down to 30 million metric tons, less than one-half the per capita catch of a decade earlier. This helped malnutrition to escalate sharply in a world where an estimated 50 million people per year were already dying of starvation. The United Nations attempted to get all chlorinated hydrocarbon insecticides banned on a worldwide basis, but the move was defeated by the United States. This opposition was generated primarily by the American petrochemical industry, operating hand in glove with its subsidiary, the United States Department of Agriculture. Together they persuaded the government to oppose the U.N. move—which was not difficult since most Americans believed that Russia and China were more in need of fish products than was the United States. The United Nations also attempted to get fishing nations to adopt strict and enforced catch limits to preserve dwindling stocks. This move was blocked by Russia, who, with the most modern electronic equipment, was in the best position to glean what was left in the sea. It was, curiously, on the very day in 1977 when the Soviet Union announced its refusal that another ominous article appeared in Science. It announced that incident solar radiation had been so reduced by worldwide air pollution that serious effects on the world's vegetation could be expected.

Apparently it was a combination of ecosystem destabilization, sunlight reduction, and a rapid escalation in chlorinated hydrocarbon pollution from massive Thanodrin applications which triggered the ultimate catastrophe. Seventeen huge Soviet-financed Thanodrin plants were operating in underdeveloped countries by 1978. They had been part of a massive Russian "aid offensive" designed to fill the gap caused by the collapse of America's ballyhooed "Green Revolution."

It became apparent in the early '70s that the "Green Revolution" was more talk than substance. Distribution of high yield "miracle" grain seeds had caused temporary local spurts in agricultural production. Simultaneously, excellent weather had produced record harvests. The combination permitted bureaucrats, especially in the United States Department of Agriculture and the Agency for International Development (AID), to reverse their previous pessimism and indulge in an outburst of optimistic propaganda about staving off famine. They raved about the approaching transformation of agriculture in the underdeveloped countries (UDCs). The reason for the propaganda reversal was never made clear. Most historians agree that a combination of utter ignorance of ecology, a desire to justify past errors, and pressure from agro-industry (which was eager to sell pesticides, fertilizers, and farm machinery to the UDCs and agencies helping the UDCs) was behind the campaign. Whatever the motivation, the results were clear. Many concerned people, lacking the expertise to see through the Green Revolution drivel, relaxed. The population-food crisis was "solved."

But reality was not long in showing itself. Local famine persisted in northern India even after good weather brought an end to the ghastly Bihar famine of the mid-'60s. East Pakistan was next, followed by a resurgence of general famine in northern India. Other foci of famine rapidly developed in Indonesia, the Philippines, Malawi, the Congo, Egypt, Colombia, Ecuador, Honduras, the Dominican Republic, and Mexico.

Everywhere hard realities destroyed the illusion of the Green Revolution. Yields dropped as the progressive farmers who had first accepted the new seeds found that their higher yields brought lower prices—effective demand (hunger plus cash) was not sufficient in poor countries to keep prices up. Less progressive farmers, observing this, refused to make the extra effort required to cultivate the "miracle" grains. Transport systems proved inadequate to bring the necessary fertilizer to the fields where the new and extremely fertilizer-sensitive grains were being grown. The same systems were also inadequate to move produce to markets. Fertilizer plants were not built fast enough, and most of the underdeveloped countries could not scrape together funds to purchase supplies, even on concessional terms. Finally, the inevitable happened, and pests began to reduce yields in even the most carefully cultivated fields. Among the first were the famous "miracle rats" which invaded Philippine "miracle rice" fields early in 1969. They were quickly followed by many insects and viruses, thriving on the relatively pest-susceptible new grains, encouraged by the vast and dense plantings, and rapidly acquiring resistance to the chemicals used against them. As chaos spread until even the most obtuse agriculturists and economists realized that the Green Revolution had turned brown, the Russians stepped in.

In retrospect it seems incredible that the Russians, with the American mistakes known to them, could launch an even more incompetent program of aid to the underdeveloped world. Indeed, in the early 1970's there were cynics in the United States who claimed that outdoing the stupidity of American foreign aid would be physically impossible. Those critics were, however, obviously unaware that the Russians had been busily destroying their own environment for many years. The virtual disappearance of sturgeon from Russian rivers caused a great shortage of caviar by 1970. A standard joke among Russian scientists at that time was that they had created an artificial caviar which was indistinguishable from the real thing—except by taste. At any rate the Soviet Union, observing with interest the progressive deterioration of relations between the UDCs and the United States, came up with a solution. It had recently developed what it claimed was the ideal insecticide, a highly lethal chlorinated hydrocarbon complexed with a special agent for penetrating the external skeletal armor of insects. Announcing that the new pesticide, called Thanodrin, would truly produce a Green Revolution, the Soviets entered into negotiations with various UDCs for the construction of massive Thanodrin factories. The USSR would bear all the costs; all it wanted in return were certain trade and military concessions.

It is interesting now, with the perspective of years, to examine in some detail the reasons why the UDCs welcomed the Thanodrin plan with such open arms. Government officials in these countries ignored the protests of their own scientists that Thanodrin would not solve the problems which plagued them. The governments now knew that the basic cause of their problems was overpopulation, and that these problems had been exacerbated by the dullness, daydreaming, and cupidity endemic to all governments. They knew that only population control and limited development aimed primarily at agriculture could have spared them the horrors they now faced. They knew it, but they were not about to admit it. How much easier it was simply to accuse the Americans of failing to give them proper aid; how much simpler to accept the Russian panacea.

And then there was the general worsening of relations between the United States and the UDCs. Many things had contributed to this. The situation in America in the first half of the 1970's deserves our close scrutiny. Being more dependent on imports for raw materials than the Soviet Union, the United States had, in the early 1970's, adopted more and more heavy-handed policies in order to insure continuing supplies. Military adventures in Asia and Latin America had further lessened the international credibility of the United States as a great defender of freedom—an image which had begun to deteriorate rapidly during the pointless and fruitless Viet-Nam conflict. At home, acceptance of the carefully manufactured image lessened dramatically, as even the more romantic and chauvinistic citizens began to understand the role of the military and the industrial system in what John Kenneth Galbraith had aptly named "The New Industrial State."

At home in the USA the early '70s were traumatic times. Racial violence grew and the habitability of the cities diminished, as nothing substantial was done to ameliorate either racial inequities or urban blight. Welfare rolls grew as automation and general technological progress forced more and more people into the category of "unemployable." Simultaneously a taxpayers' revolt occurred. Although there was not enough money to build the schools, roads, water systems, sewage systems, jails, hospitals, urban transit lines, and all the other amenities needed to support a burgeoning population, Americans refused to tax themselves more heavily. Starting in Youngstown, Ohio in 1969 and followed closely by Richmond, California, community after community was forced to close its schools or curtail educational operations for lack of funds. Water supplies, already marginal in quality and quantity in many places by 1970, deteriorated quickly. Water rationing occurred in 1723 municipalities in the summer of 1974, and hepatitis and epidemic dysentery rates climbed about 500 per cent between 1970-1974.

Air pollution continued to be the most obvious manifestation of environmental deterioration. It was, by 1972, quite literally in the eyes of all Americans. The year 1973 saw not only the New York and Los Angeles smog disasters, but also the publication of the Surgeon General's massive report on air pollution and health. The public had been partially prepared for the worst by the publicity given to the U.N. pollution conference held in 1972. Deaths in the late '60s caused by smog were well known to scientists, but the public had ignored them because they mostly involved the early demise of the old and sick rather than people dropping dead on the freeways. But suddenly our citizens were faced with nearly 200,000 corpses and massive documentation that they could be the next to die from respiratory disease. They were not ready for that scale of disaster. After all, the U.N. conference had not predicted that accumulated air pollution would make the planet uninhabitable until almost 1990. The population was terrorized as TV screens became filled with scenes of horror from the disaster areas. Especially vivid was NBC's coverage of hundreds of unattended people choking out their lives outside of New York's hospitals. Terms like nitrogen oxide, acute bronchitis and cardiac arrest began to have real meaning for most Americans.

The ultimate horror was the announcement that chlorinated hydrocarbons were now a major constituent of air pollution in all American cities. Autopsies of smog disaster victims revealed an average chlorinated hydrocarbon load in fatty tissue equivalent to 26 parts per million of DDT. In October, 1973, the Department of Health, Education and Welfare announced studies which showed unequivocally that increasing death rates from hypertension, cirrhosis of the liver, liver cancer and a series of other diseases had resulted from the chlorinated hydrocarbon load. They estimated that Americans born since 1946 (when DDT usage began) now had a life expectancy of only 49 years, and predicted that if current patterns continued, this expectancy would reach 42 years by 1980, when it might level out. Plunging insurance stocks triggered a stock market panic. The president of . . . a major pesticide producer went on television to "publicly eat a teaspoonful of DDT" (it was really powdered milk) and announce that HEW had been infiltrated by Communists. Other giants of the petro-chemical industry, attempting to dispute the indisputable evidence, launched a massive pressure campaign on Congress to force HEW to "get out of agriculture's business." They were aided by the agro-chemical journals, which had decades of experience in misleading the public about the benefits and dangers of pesticides. But by now the public realized that it had been duped. The Nobel Prize for medicine and physiology was given to Drs. J. L. Radomski and W. B. Deichmann, who in the late 1960's had pioneered in the documentation of the long-term lethal effects of chlorinated hydrocarbons. A Presidential Commission with unimpeachable credentials directly accused the agro-chemical complex of "condemning many millions of Americans to an early death." The year 1973 was the year in which Americans finally came to understand the direct threat to their existence posed by environmental deterioration.

And 1973 was also the year in which most people finally comprehended the indirect threat. Even the president of Union Oil Company and several other industrialists publicly stated their concern over the reduction of bird populations which had resulted from pollution by DDT and other chlorinated hydrocarbons. Insect populations boomed because they were resistant to most pesticides and had been freed, by the incompetent use of those pesticides, from most of their natural enemies. Rodents swarmed over crops, multiplying rapidly in the absence of predatory birds. The effect of pests on the wheat crop was especially disastrous in the summer of 1973, since that was also the year of the great drought. Most of us can remember the shock which greeted the announcement by atmospheric physicists that the shift of the jet stream which had caused the drought was probably permanent. It signalled the birth of the Midwestern desert. Man's air-polluting activities had by then caused gross changes in climatic patterns. The news, of course, played hell with commodity and stock markets. Food prices skyrocketed, as savings were poured into hoarded canned goods. Official assurances that food supplies would remain ample fell on deaf ears, and even the government showed signs of nervousness when California migrant field workers went out on strike again in protest against the continued use of pesticides by growers. The strike burgeoned into farm burning and riots. The workers, calling themselves "The Walking Dead," demanded immediate compensation for their shortened lives, and crash research programs to attempt to lengthen them.

It was in the same speech in which President Edward Kennedy, after much delay, finally declared a national emergency and called out the National Guard to harvest California's crops, that the first mention of population control was made. Kennedy pointed out that the United States would no longer be able to offer any food aid to other nations and was likely to suffer food shortages herself. He suggested that, in view of the manifest failure of the Green Revolution, the only hope of the UDCs lay in population control. His statement, you will recall, created an uproar in the underdeveloped countries. Newspaper editorials accused the United States of wishing to prevent small countries from becoming large nations and thus threatening American hegemony. Politicians asserted that President Kennedy was a "creature of the giant drug combine" that wished to shove its pills down every woman's throat.

Among Americans, religious opposition to population control was very slight. Industry in general also backed the idea. Increasing poverty in the UDCs was both destroying markets and threatening supplies of raw materials. The seriousness of the raw material situation had been brought home during the Congressional Hard Resources hearings in 1971. The exposure of the ignorance of the cornucopian economists had been quite a spectacle—a spectacle brought into virtually every American's home in living color. Few would forget the distinguished geologist from the University of California who suggested that economists be legally required to learn at least the most elementary facts of geology. Fewer still would forget that an equally distinquished Harvard economist added that they might be required to learn some economics, too. The overall message was clear: America's resource situation was bad and bound to get worse. The hearings had led to a bill requiring the Departments of State, Interior, and Commerce to set up a joint resource procurement council with the express purpose of "insuring that proper consideration of American resource needs be an integral part of American foreign policy."

Suddenly the United States discovered that it had a national consensus: population control was the only possible salvation of the underdeveloped world. But that same consensus led to heated debate. How could the UDCs be persuaded to limit their populations, and should not the United States lead the way by limiting its own? Members of the intellectual community wanted America to set an example. They pointed out that the United States was in the midst of a new baby boom: her birth rate, well over 20 per thousand per year, and her growth rate of over one per cent per annum were among the very highest of the developed countries. They detailed the deterioration of the American physical and psychic environments, the growing health threats, the impending food shortages, and the insufficiency of funds for desperately needed public works. They contended that the nation was clearly unable or unwilling to properly care for the people it already had. What possible reason could there be, they queried, for adding any more? Besides, who would listen to requests by the United States for population control when that nation did not control her own profligate reproduction?

Those who opposed population controls for the U.S. were equally vociferous. The military-industrial complex, with its all-too-human mixture of ignorance and avarice, still saw strength and prosperity in numbers. Baby food magnates, already worried by the growing nitrate pollution of their products, saw their market disappearing. Steel manufacturers saw a decrease in aggregate demand and slippage for that holy of holies, the Gross National Product. And military men saw, in the growing population-food-environment crisis, a serious threat to their carefully nurtured Cold War. In the end, of course, economic arguments held sway, and the "inalienable right of every American couple to determine the size of its family," a freedom invented for the occasion in the early '70s, was not compromised.

The population control bill, which was passed by Congress early in 1974, was quite a document, nevertheless. On the domestic front, it authorized an increase from 100 to 150 million dollars in funds for "family planning" activities. This was made possible by a general feeling in the country that the growing army on welfare needed family planning. But the gist of the bill was a series of measures designed to impress the need for population control on the UDCs. All American aid to countries with overpopulation problems was required by law to consist in part of population control assistance. In order to receive any assistance each nation was required not only to accept the population control aid, but also to match it according to a complex formula. "Overpopulation" itself was defined by a formula based on U.N. statistics, and the UDCs were required not only to accept aid, but also to show progress in reducing birth rates. Every five years the status of the aid program for each nation was to be re-evaluated.

The reaction to the announcement of this program dwarfed the response to President Kennedy's speech. A coalition of UDCs attempted to get the U.N. General Assembly to condemn the United States as a "genetic aggressor." Most damaging of all to the American cause was the famous "25 Indians and a dog" speech by Mr. Shankarnarayan, Indian Ambassador to the U.N. Shankarnarayan pointed out that for several decades the United States, with less than six per cent of the people of the world had consumed roughly 50 per cent of the raw materials used every year. He described vividly America's contribution to worldwide environmental deterioration, and he scathingly denounced the miserly record of United States foreign aid as "unworthy of a fourth-rate power, let alone the most powerful nation on earth."

It was the climax of his speech, however, which most historians claim once and for all destroyed the image of the United States. Shankarnarayan informed the assembly that the average American family dog was fed more animal protein per week than the average Indian got in a month. "How do you justify taking fish from protein-starved Peruvians and feeding them to your animals?" he asked. "I contend," he concluded, "that the birth of an American baby is a greater disaster for the world than that of 25 Indian babies." When the applause had died away, Mr. Sorensen, the American representative, made a speech which said essentially that "other countries look after their own self-interest, too." When the vote came, the United States was condemned.

This condemnation set the tone of U.S.-UDC relations at the time the Russian Thanodrin proposal was made. The proposal seemed to offer the masses in the UDCs an opportunity to save themselves and humiliate the United States at the same time; and in human affairs, as we all know, biological realities could never interfere with such an opportunity. The scientists were silenced, the politicians said yes, the Thanodrin plants were built, and the results were what any beginning ecology student could have predicted. At first Thanodrin seemed to offer excellent control of many pests. True, there was a rash of human fatalities from improper use of the lethal chemical, but, as Russian technical advisors were prone to note, these were more than compensated for by increased yields. Thanodrin use skyrocketed throughout the underdeveloped world. The Mikoyan design group developed a dependable, cheap agricultural aircraft which the Soviets donated to the effort in large numbers. MIG sprayers became even more common in UDCs than MIG interceptors.

Then the troubles began. Insect strains with cuticles resistant to Thanodrin penetration began to appear. And as streams, rivers, fish culture ponds and onshore waters became rich in Thanodrin, more fisheries began to disappear. Bird populations were decimated. The sequence of events was standard for broadcast use of a synthetic pesticide: great success at first, followed by removal of natural enemies and development of resistance by the pest. Populations of crop-eating insects in areas treated with Thanodrin made steady comebacks and soon became more abundant than ever. Yields plunged, while farmers in their desperation increased the Thanodrin dose and shortened the time between treatments. Death from Thanodrin poisoning became common. The first violent incident occurred in the Canete Valley of Peru, where farmers had suffered a similar chlorinated hydrocarbon disaster in the mid-'50s. A Russian advisor serving as an agricultural pilot was assaulted and killed by a mob of enraged farmers in January, 1978. Trouble spread rapidly during 1978, especially after the word got out that two years earlier Russia herself had banned the use of Thanodrin at home because of its serious effects on ecological systems. Suddenly Russia, and not the United States, was the *bête noir* in the UDCs. "Thanodrin parties" became epidemic, with farmers, in their ignorance, dumping carloads of Thanodrin concentrate into the sea. Russian advisors fled, and four of the Thanodrin plants were leveled to the ground. Destruction of the plants in Rio and Calcutta led to hundreds of thousands of gallons of Thanodrin concentrate being dumped directly into the sea.

Mr. Shankarnarayan again rose to address the U.N., but this time it was Mr. Potemkin, representative of the Soviet Union, who was on the hot seat. Mr. Potemkin heard his nation described as the greatest mass killer of all time as Shankarnarayan predicted at least 30 million deaths from crop failures due to overdependence on Thanodrin. Russia was accused of "chemical aggression," and the General Assembly, after a weak reply by Potemkin, passed a vote of censure.

It was in January, 1979, that huge blooms of a previously unknown variety of diatom were reported off the coast of Peru. The blooms were accompanied by a massive die-off of sea life and of the pathetic remainder of the birds which had once feasted on the anchovies of the area. Almost immediately another huge bloom was reported in the Indian ocean, centering around the Seychelles, and then a third in the South Atlantic off the African coast. Both of these were accompanied by spectacular die-offs of marine animals. Even more ominous were growing reports of fish and bird kills at oceanic points where there were no spectacular blooms. Biologists were soon able to explain the phenomena: the diatom had evolved an enzyme which broke down Thanodrin; that enzyme also produced a breakdown product which interfered with the transmission of nerve impulses, and was therefore lethal to animals. Unfortunately, the biologists could suggest no way of repressing the poisonous diatom bloom in time. By September, 1979, all important animal life in the sea was extinct. Large areas of coastline had to be evacuated, as windrows of dead fish created a monumental stench.

But stench was the least of man's problems. Japan and China were faced with almost instant starvation from a total loss of the seafood on which they were so dependent. Both blamed Russia for their situation and demanded immediate mass shipments of food. Russia had none to send. On October 13, Chinese armies attacked Russia on a broad front. . . .

A pretty grim scenario. Unfortunately, we're a long way into it already. Everything mentioned as happening before 1970 has actually occurred; much of the rest is based on projections of trends already appearing. Evidence that pesticides have long-term lethal effects on human beings has started to accumulate, and recently Robert Finch, Secretary of the Department of Health, Education and Welfare expressed his extreme apprehension about the pesticide situation. Simultaneously the petrochemical industry continues its unconscionable poison-peddling. For instance, Shell Chemical has been carrying on a high-pressure campaign to sell the insecticide Azodrin to farmers as a killer of cotton pests. They continue their program even though they know that Azodrin is not only ineffective, but often *increases* the pest density. They've covered themselves nicely in an advertisement which states, "Even if an overpowering migration [sic] develops, the flexibility of Azodrin lets you regain control fast. Just increase the dosage according to label recommendations." It's a great game—get people to apply the poison and kill the natural enemies of the pests. Then blame the increased pests on "migration" and sell even more pesticide!

Right now fisheries are being wiped out by over-exploitation, made easy by modern electronic equipment. The companies producing the equipment know this. They even boast in advertising that only their equipment will keep fishermen in business until the final kill. Profits must obviously be maximized in the short run. Indeed, Western society is in the process of completing the rape and murder of the planet for economic gain. And, sadly, most of the rest of the world is eager for the opportunity to emulate our behavior. But the underdeveloped peoples will be denied that opportunity—the days of plunder are drawing inexorably to a close.

Most of the people who are going to die in the greatest cataclysm in the history of man have already been born. More than three and a half billion people already populate our moribund globe, and about half of them are hungry. Some 10 to 20 million will starve to death *this year.* In spite of this, the population of the earth will increase by 70 million souls in 1969. For mankind has artificially lowered the death rate of the human population, while in general birth rates have remained high. With the input side of the population system in high gear and the output side slowed down, our fragile planet has filled with people at an incredible rate. It took several million years for the population to reach a total of two billion people in 1930, while a *second two billion will have been added by 1975!* By that time some experts feel that food shortages will have escalated the present level of world hunger and starvation into famines of unbelievable proportions. Other experts, more optimistic, think the ultimate food-population collision will not occur until the decade of the 1980's. Of course more massive famine may be avoided if other events cause a prior rise in the human death rate.

Both worldwide plague and thermonuclear war are made more probable as population growth continues. These, along with famine, make up the trio of potential "death rate solutions" to the population problem—solutions in which the birth rate-death rate imbalance is redressed by a rise in the death rate rather than by a lowering of the birth rate. Make no mistake about it, *the imbalance will be redressed.* The shape of the population growth curve is one familiar to the biologist. It is the outbreak part of an outbreak-crash sequence. A population grows rapidly in the presence of abundant resources, finally runs out of food or some other necessity, and crashes to a low level or extinction. Man is not only running out of food, he is also destroying the life support systems of the Spaceship Earth. The situation was recently summarized very succinctly: "It is the top of the ninth inning. Man, always a threat at the plate, has been hitting Nature hard. It is important to remember, however, that NATURE BATS LAST."

Writing Exercises in Diction and Ideas: Ethnic Groups

Nearly all language means something more than it seems to mean. Words possess or suggest connotative or associative values over and beyond their literal or denotative meaning. This extra dimension derives from the emotional overtones intrinsic to the subject matter itself and is colored by the point of view and personality of the writer or speaker. The slogan "Never Again!" (the battle cry of the Jewish Defense League) is heavily charged with an implicit reference to past atrocities and with a militant warning about the future. Beyond the simple diction of the phrase is the syntactical imperative of command which is rendered more powerful through its monitory negative structure.

The articles in this section reflect the emotional attitudes of ethnic minorities in this country and their responses toward inequity. In some cases, the slogans of collective power are called into use; in others, conventional diction is employed for the purpose of reasonable solutions to existing injustices. In still other instances, the untutored language of a particular disadvantaged group is taped and reproduced for the purpose of presenting an authentic ethnic portrait. The student is asked now to read and evaluate the varieties of diction employed by the writers of the preceding essays, and to judge the particular contribution, either emotional or intellectual, made by the various writers to the cause of the ethnic minorities they represent.

EXERCISE 1

Stokely Carmichael assigns a negative connotation to the word "integration." How does he accomplish this end?

EXERCISE 2

What is the semantic connotation of the word "freeing" with respect to government practice toward American Indians?

EXERCISE 3

Discuss the psychological effects of the collective power slogans. What virtues do they represent? What potential dangers can they hold?

EXERCISE 4

Describe the impact of Simplicio's diction in the depiction of his personal plight in

"I'd Rather Be in Puerto Rico." Then compare it with Stokely Carmichael's diction as he serves as spokesman for the black community. Choose those phrases from the essays which have the greatest emotional power and those which best convey ideas. ideas.

Discussion-Instruction: The Environment

The purpose of this discussion section is to establish the relations between ecology, philosophy, and history.

EXERCISE 1

In the selections from Joseph Wood Krutch's *Human Nature and the Human Condition,* Peter Carroll's *Puritanism and the Wilderness,* and Ralph Waldo Emerson's poetry, you have been exposed to three different attitudes toward the natural environment. The historical background of each piece contributes to the orientation of each writer. Below is a description of the Puritan idea of nature, the transcendentalist idea of nature, and the contemporary or modern idea of nature. Match the letter preceding each description with the statement from each work (labeled a, b, c) which seems to reflect the philosophy appearing in the description.

1. The Puritans saw the wilderness both as the Church's haven from the sinful world and the dwelling place of the devil. It was a land to be civilized and planted with seed and spirit by men of God.

2. The transcendentalists, America's romantics, saw all of nature as a repository and microcosm of the divine spirit animating the universe. Those who sought to trammel nature were blasphemers.

3. Modern ecologists take both a romantic and a practical view of nature. Their love of its beauty, tempered by their scientific knowledge and talent for economic and social forecast, prompts them to descry our encroachments upon nature for practical as well as aesthetic reasons.

a. "Earth endures; stars abide."

b. "What is the use of talking about saving our national parks when it is perfectly obvious that the space they occupy is needed."

c. "Encrease and multiply and replenish the earth and subdue it."

Answers: 1–c; 2–a; 3–b

EXERCISE 2

Of these three approaches, two may be said to be religious and philosophical and one economic.

       1. is _____ .

       2. is _____ .

       3. is _____ .

Answers: 1 and 2, religious
and philosophical;
3, economic

EXERCISE 3

The Puritan view is clearly biblical but it differs markedly from the spiritual attitude of the transcendentalists, for the Puritan and the transcendentalist held different concepts of humanity's place in the universe. The modern concept is perhaps most unlike either of the others. The Puritans felt that their errand in the wilderness was to people it with the godly; the transcendentalists thought that they could witness divinity in untouched nature; the modern, more pragmatic ecologists consider humans intruders in the environment and think that they will destroy the terrestial host upon which they feed. Label each of the diagrams below either "Puritan" or "transcendental" or "modern ecological." (The circle symbolizes spirit, the square symbolizes nature, and the face, of course, symbolizes human beings.)

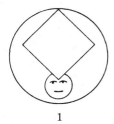
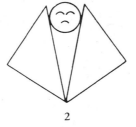
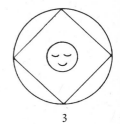

          1   2   3

Answers: 1. transcendental;
2. modern ecological; 3. Puritan

EXERCISE 4

Consider the diagrams in the preceding exercise and what they reveal about the nature of the Puritan, transcendental, and modern ecological attitudes toward the interrelations of humans, nature, and spirit. Label each of the statements about the above diagrams 1) Puritan, 2) transcendental, or 3) modern ecological.

1. The wilderness is but a part of life's hazards and temptations. Real life is the life after death, an eternity which will survive human life and the physical world.

2. The individual is an insignificant fragment in a giant physical universe.

3. The physical world is spirit writ large. This spirit resides beyond the world of human beings and nature but both humans and nature partake of that spirit.

Answers: 1. Puritan; 2. modern ecological; 3. transcendental

EXERCISE 5

Considering their attitudes, do you think the Puritans would react positively or negatively toward each of the following acts?

1. cutting down a redwood tree to build a house

2. leaving a city or town to enjoy the wilderness

3. flooding the Glen Canyon by building a dam

Answers: 1. positively; 2. negatively; 3. positively

EXERCISE 6

Match the correct response (a, b, or c) to each numbered statement to show how the transcendentalists would react to each statement.

1. the building of the new preplanned cities

2. the outdoor commune

3. the heating of the Mediterranean by the Aswan Dam

a. Man is losing his touch with divinity or the spirit of the universe.

b. In living nature we can catch glimpses of the nature of spirit.

c. Artificiality is disharmony with natural law.

Answers: 1–c; 2–b; 3–a

EXERCISE 7

How might the Puritan, the transcendentalist, and the modern ecologist react to the use of the sea as a dumping ground for atomic wastes? Match the numbers and the letters.

1. Subdue nature for God's purposes, not for ours.

2. Nature is the repository for spirit alone and should not be corrupted.

3. We have not yet considered the side effects of interference with nature and we may, without realizing what we are doing, destroy the natural world and ourselves with it.

a. Puritan

b. modern ecologist

c. transcendentalist

Answers: 1–a; 2–c; 3–b

EXERCISE 8

Considering the preceding exercises, would the Puritan, transcendentalist, or modern ecologist have the greatest stake in preserving the largest and most untouched wilderness area? Explain why.

EXERCISE 9

Compare the three statements below in light of the preceding exercises and discuss the attitudes toward, the reasons for, and the direction of the development of ecology from the Puritans to the modern ecologists.

The Puritans, the earliest of our American naturalists, saw corruption in the unredeemed Church of England and rebelled against the Act of Conformity which required a man to swear fealty to the Church of England. In an age of navigational explorations and expanding empire, they fled first to Holland and then to the wilderness of America. Neither especially young nor of especially humble origins, they established a religion of the saved or the "elect" in which the aristocrats of the church were those who had grace, a grace sometimes manifested by economic success in this world.

The transcendentalists were, in the main, unitarian young people who turned against the rational notions of their "cold Calvinist" fathers, as Perry Miller called them. To counter the rational and Calvinist views of their fathers, they rejected the profiteering and materialist values of their society and sought instead a close contact with nature. Many of them became absorbed in oriental philosophy, which seemed an embodiment of union with nature and a great natural spirit.

The modern ecologists live in an age of industrialism, an age in which scientific information for testing the effects of pollution on the environment, of atomic explosions in the atmosphere, etc., is steadily increasing. Some are hikers, some biologists, some naturalists. The ecological movement is not exclusive to the young, but it is much in favor with the young. All ecologists today are increasingly aware of the growing population density and the decreasing amount of "open land."

The Expression of the Self: Literature and the Arts

Fiction: A Tongue in Literature

The collective trend in American history is reflected in the earliest patterns of life in the nation, from the Commonwealth of the Pilgrims and the Mormon Colony at Salt Lake City to Bronson Alcott's Fruitlands, the Fourierist Association of Brook Farm, and the contemporary communes designed to re-create the cooperative life of early Christian settlements. The nineteenth century in particular was a fertile ground for a certain kind of collectivist ideology, a unique attitude inherited from eighteen-century Federalism. Nineteenth-century political philosophy was a blend of confidence in the individual state and support for a strong federal government. The philosophical climate, expressed through its most articulate spokesmen, Emerson and Channing, was both optimistic and melioristic, trusting in man's individual ability and in society's general expansion and progress. There was still frontier to be conquered and a new President in Washington who represented the emergence of the worker in national politics. Drawing his support from the working classes, Andrew Jackson opened the gates to populist politics and extended the franchise to the mass of American people previously denied the vote. Himself the candidate of a coalition made up of southern and western farmers and eastern workmen who were just beginning to organize, Jackson was to estimate the significance of the newly emerging power groups in American society in his Farewell Address of 1837: ". . . these classes of society [the agricultural, the mechanical, and the laboring classes] form the great body of the people of the United States; they are the bone and sinew of the country. . . ."

The nineteenth-century writers whose work most closely reflected Jackson's confidence in the concerted action of the American people were William Cullen Bryant, John Greenleaf Whittier, and Walt Whitman. Even James Fenimore Cooper, who most disliked the leveling tendency of American social life, in the main subscribed to the Jacksonian democratic principle. Melville, whose foreground figures were often "isolates," exalted the bulk of ordinary men welded together in a vigorous union in their conquest of the sea. Ishmael, the wanderer in *Moby Dick,* finds his humanity only when he forms an allegiance with his fellowmen. It is Melville's device to reduce his world to the dimensions of a ship, with his characters locked into each other's lives for the purpose of creating a tight working community. Ahab's sworn pledges to his seamen massed around him and the passing of the brimming flagon as token of their common cause, first to the harpooners, then to the mates, and finally to the ordinary seamen, attests to the vitality of the charged group in pursuit of a shared goal.

The social climate of the nineteenth century was marked by the proliferation of unions of people all working together for the good of groups or for the perpetuation of sectional ideologies. Abolitionists, secessionists, unionists, and transcendentalists all formed powerful organizations during the same brief span of time. Concurrently, the Industrial Revolution made it possible for the middle and lower classes to achieve a collective power long denied them. Industrialization gave birth to a variety of collective doctrines such as industrial bargaining, government regulation, and cooperative management. The visible symbols of an industrial mass-oriented society —the railroad, the machine, the factory, and the big city—were all to proliferate during this period, bringing people together into close communities through improved communications.

What then of the individual in this era of encroaching anonymity? The inevitable consequence of large population clusters around factories and of participation in an expanding commerce was the gradual disintegration of the individual. The struggle of the independent spirit obliged to contend with the authority of the community and the mores of the masses constitutes one of the central themes of nineteenth-century fiction. Nathaniel Hawthorne's fictional characters are isolated souls who recognize the accepted standards of conduct required by their society, but are unable and often unwilling to abide by them. In addition, they suffer the loss of Eden because they are burdened with the heritage of an early Puritan ethic. The insidious and punitive substructure of this pessimistic creed is guilt arising from the conviction that each soul is predestined for certain salvation or irrevocable damnation, and is helpless to subvert damnation through the agency of good works or prayer. Thus, the tormented focal figure struggling with his own soul in an inhospitable moral climate is also contending with the solid force of a forbidding society, metaphorically composed of the Puritans of Hester Prynne's Salem, the conventional congregation of "The Minister's Black Veil," and the insulated citizens who live at the foot of Mt. Graylock in "Ethan Brand." It is necessary to remember that although Hawthorne makes most frequent use of a seventeenth-century Puritan New England setting as a backdrop for his portraits of alienation and guilt, it is the nineteenth century and its problems which engage him primarily.

The ultimate weakening and final disappearance of Calvinist doctrine coincided with the real success of American enterprise in the latter portion of the nineteenth century. At the same time a stronger and stronger federal government reduced the value of the individual as a force in the body politic. The twentieth century brought with it a departure from the democratic ideal, that vision of the federation of individual men of excellence or unique inherited skills. It is a faceless mass which emerges from John Steinbeck's *Grapes of Wrath,* an assortment of archetypes, their own personalities diminished in favor of a group momentum or thrust for the common good. Economic survival is the motive of the thirties, a period of agrarian and urban depression. The process of industrialization has reached an advanced stage and depersonalization ensues as machine replaces man, as small town is swallowed by big city. A bleak naturalism replaces the alternating idealism and pessimism of the nineteenth century, as John Dos Passos and John Steinbeck replace Hawthorne and Melville as painters of the American portrait. The canvas is now extended beyond Hawthorne's regionalism and Melville's microcosmic ocean to the whole of the American landscape. Its masses of anonymous people are now caught in the dehumanizing dust bowls of its rural outposts or in the industrial machines of its sprawling cities. The struggling individual soul literally submerges in the vast bulk of humanity bent on its corporate survival. As the individual goes under, the type appears: Ma Joad, the Earth Mother; John Casey, the Savior; and Rose of Sharon, the Fertility Goddess. Along with these rural types come all the lower- and middle-class victims of urban American capitalism in Dos Passos' *U.S.A.,* a documentary novel of American exploitation. The central issue is now social justice for the masses and a firm belief, in Steinbeck's own words, that "what people do is right to do." The people in this case are the poor, and their heroes are the proletarian truck drivers who eat mammoth slabs of pie in the roadside diners and buy candy canes for the children of the brutalized poor. The novel is now a social tract, with "man," not "a man," as its undifferentiated hero. The enemy is the materialism which corrupts the potentially good; and ironically, the hero is big government, which, when it is kindly disposed, serves as the benevolent agency of liberation. The government camp in *The Grapes of Wrath* where the Joads find temporary haven demonstrates the idea that people can live decently if sponsored by an open-handed government. Other heroic forces of the era are the labor unions, the WPA, the Farm Security Administration, and the Federal Resettlement Administration, all founded on the conviction that the beleaguered lower echelons of commercial and agricultural society are the people worth saving.

It was perhaps this very concept of mass welfare coupled with the hardening materialism of American society and the rapid disappearance of sustaining religious structures that produced the quest novel of the fifties and sixties. The individual, forgotten for a decade or more, re-emerges, in search of self, of soul, of God. Since Christianity has lost its impetus as an organized religious apparatus for salvation, the young seekers in many of J. D. Salinger's stories resume the exploration of Eastern spiritualism begun earlier by Emerson and Whitman in their search for serenity of soul. The lone American in the middle years of the twentieth century is seen as rootless and unassimilated. Saul Bellow paints a portrait of a middle-aged man named Herzog in the crucial years of his life, and John Updike gives us a vivid study of a basketball hero whose tragedy as an adult resides in his having been frozen in a perpetual adolescence. The book is *Rabbit Run,* and its hero may be seen as a metaphor for America's growing pains and as a type of the many varieties of troubled young Holden Caulfields who will dominate contemporary fiction. Finally, the three splinter societies of American life, the Jewish, the Negro, and the Beat, present the special cases of the alienated in American society. Bernard Malamud's *The Assistant,* James Baldwin's *Another Country,* and Jack Kerouac's *On the Road* provide first-hand insights into the minds of the uprooted, the deracinated, and the embittered. Thus this current period in American literature may be seen as a vehicle for the neoromantic, the idealistic, and the visionary. The current stamp is alienation; one hopes that it will be succeeded by affirmation.

Nathaniel Hawthorne
Ethan Brand

A Chapter from an Abortive Romance
Bartram the lime-burner, a rough, heavy-looking man, begrimed with charcoal, sat
watching his kiln, at nightfall, while his little son played at building houses with the
scattered fragments of marble, when, on the hillside below them, they heard a roar
of laughter, not mirthful, but slow, and even solemn, like a wind shaking the boughs
of the forest.

"Father, what is that?" asked the little boy, leaving his play, and pressing be-
twixt his father's knees.

"Oh, some drunken man, I suppose," answered the lime-burner; "some merry
fellow from the bar-room in the village, who dared not laugh loud enough within
doors lest he should blow the roof of the house off. So here he is, shaking his jolly
sides at the foot of Graylock."

"But, father," said the child, more sensitive than the obtuse, middle-aged clown,
"he does not laugh like a man that is glad. So the noise frightens me!"

"Don't be a fool, child!" cried his father, gruffly. "You will never make a man,
I do believe; there is too much of your mother in you. I have known the rustling of
a leaf startle you. Hark! Here comes the merry fellow now. You shall see that there
is no harm in him."

Bartram and his little son, while they were talking thus, sat watching the same
lime-kiln that had been the scene of Ethan Brand's solitary and meditative life, before
he began his search for the Unpardonable Sin. Many years, as we have seen, had now
elapsed, since that portentous night when the IDEA was first developed. The kiln,
however, on the mountain-side, stood unimpaired, and was in nothing changed since
he had thrown his dark thoughts into the intense glow of its furnace, and melted
them, as it were, into the one thought that took possession of his life. It was a rude,
round, tower-like structure about twenty feet high, heavily built of rough stones,
and with a hillock of earth heaped about the larger part of its circumference; so that
the blocks and fragments of marble might be drawn by cart-loads, and thrown in at
the top. There was an opening at the bottom of the tower, like an oven-mouth, but
large enough to admit a man in a stooping posture, and provided with a massive iron
door. With the smoke and jets of flame issuing from the chinks and crevices of this
door, which seemed to give admittance into the hill-side, it resembled nothing so
much as the private entrance to the infernal regions, which the shepherds of the
Delectable Mountains were accustomed to show to pilgrims.

There are many such lime-kilns in that tract of country, for the purpose of
burning the white marble which composes a large part of the substance of the hills.
Some of them, built years ago, and long deserted, with weeds growing in the vacant
round of the interior, which is open to the sky, and grass and wildflowers rooting
themselves into the chinks of the stones, look already like relics of antiquity, and
may yet be overspread with the lichens of centuries to come. Others, where the

lime-burner still feeds his daily and night-long fire, afford points of interest to the wanderer among the hills, who seats himself on a log of wood or a fragment of marble, to hold a chat with the solitary man. It is a lonesome, and, when the character is inclined to thought, may be an intensely thoughtful occupation; as it proved in the case of Ethan Brand, who had mused to such strange purpose, in days gone by, while the fire in this very kiln was burning.

The man who now watched the fire was of a different order, and troubled himself with no thoughts save the very few that were requisite to his business. At frequent intervals, he flung back the clashing weight of the iron door, and, turning his face from the insufferable glare, thrust in huge logs of oak, or stirred the immense brands with a long pole. Within the furnace were seen the curling and riotous flames, and the burning marble, almost molten with the intensity of heat; while without, the reflection of the fire quivered on the dark intricacy of the surrounding forest, and showed in the foreground a bright and ruddy little picture of the hut, the spring beside its door, the athletic and coal-begrimed figure of the lime-burner, and the half-frightened child, shrinking into the protection of his father's shadow. And when, again, the iron door was closed, then reappeared the tender light of the half-full moon, which vainly strove to trace out the indistinct shapes of the neighboring mountains; and, in the upper sky, there was a flitting congregation of clouds, still faintly tinged with the rosy sunset, though thus far down into the valley the sunshine had vanished long and long ago.

The little boy now crept still closer to his father, as footsteps were heard ascending the hillside, and a human form thrust aside the bushes that clustered beneath the trees.

"Halloo! who is it?" cried the lime-burner, vexed at his son's timidity, yet half infected by it. "Come forward, and show yourself, like a man, or I'll fling this chunk of marble at your head!"

"You offer me a rough welcome," said a gloomy voice, as the unknown man drew nigh. "Yet I neither claim nor desire a kinder one, even at my own fireside."

To obtain a distincter view, Bartram threw open the iron door of the kiln, whence immediately issued a gush of fierce light, that smote full upon the stranger's face and figure. To a careless eye there appeared nothing very remarkable in his aspect, which was that of a man in a coarse, brown, country-made suit of clothes, tall and thin, with the staff and heavy shoes of a wayfarer. As he advanced, he fixed his eyes—which were very bright—intently upon the brightness of the furnace, as if he beheld, or expected to behold, some object worthy of note within it.

"Good evening, stranger," said the lime-burner; "whence come you, so late in the day?"

"I come from my search," answered the wayfarer; "for, at last, it is finished."

"Drunk!—or crazy!" muttered Bartram to himself. "I shall have trouble with the fellow. The sooner I drive him away, the better."

The little boy, all in a tremble, whispered to his father, and begged him to shut the door of the kiln, so that there might not be so much light; for that there was something in the man's face which he was afraid to look at, yet could not look away from. And, indeed, even the lime-burner's dull and torpid sense began to be impressed by an indescribable something in that thin, rugged, thoughtful visage, with the grizzled hair hanging wildly about it, and those deeply sunken eyes, which gleamed like fires within the entrance of a mysterious cavern. But, as he closed the door, the stranger turned towards him, and spoke in a quiet, familiar way, that made Bartram feel as if he were a sane and sensible man, after all.

"Your task draws to an end, I see," said he. "This marble has already been burning three days. A few hours more will convert the stone to lime."

"Why, who are you?" exclaimed the lime-burner. "You seem as well acquainted with my business as I am myself."

"And well I may be," said the stranger; "for I followed the same craft many a long year, and here, too, on this very spot. But you are a new-comer in these parts. Did you never hear of Ethan Brand?"

"The man that went in search of the Unpardonable Sin?" asked Bartram, with a laugh.

"The same," answered the stranger. "He has found what he sought, and therefore he comes back again."

"What! then you are Ethan Brand himself?" cried the lime-burner, in amazement. "I am a new-comer here, as you say, and they call it eighteen years since you left the foot of Graylock. But, I can tell you, the good folks still talk about Ethan Brand, in the village yonder, and what a strange errand took him away from his lime-kiln. Well, and so you have found the Unpardonable Sin?"

"Even so!" said the stranger, calmly.

"If the question is a fair one," proceeded Bartram, "where might it be?"

Ethan Brand laid his finger on his own heart.

"Here!" replied he.

And then, without mirth in his countenance, but as if moved by an involuntary recognition of the infinite absurdity of seeking throughout the world for what was the closest of all things to himself, and looking into every heart, save his own, for what was hidden in no other breast, he broke into a laugh of scorn. It was the same slow, heavy laugh, that had almost appalled the lime-burner when it heralded the wayfarer's approach.

The solitary mountain-side was made dismal by it. Laughter, when out of place, mistimed, or bursting forth from a disordered state of feeling, may be the most terrible modulation of the human voice. The laughter of one asleep, even if it be a little child,—the madman's laugh,—the wild, screaming laugh of a born idiot,—are sounds that we sometimes tremble to hear, and would always willingly forget. Poets have imagined no utterance of fiends or hobgoblins so fearfully appropriate as a laugh. And even the obtuse lime-burner felt his nerves shaken, as this strange man looked inward at his own heart, and burst into laughter that rolled away into the night, and was indistinctly reverberated among the hills.

"Joe," said he to his little son, "scamper down to the tavern in the village, and tell the jolly fellows there that Ethan Brand has come back, and that he has found the Unpardonable Sin!"

The boy darted away on his errand, to which Ethan Brand made no objection, nor seemed hardly to notice it. He sat on a log of wood, looking steadfastly at the iron door of the kiln. When the child was out of sight, and his swift and light foot-steps ceased to be heard treading first on the fallen leaves and then on the rocky mountain-path, the lime-burner began to regret his departure. He felt that the little fellow's presence had been a barrier between his guest and himself, and that he must now deal, heart to heart, with a man who, on his own confession, had committed the one only crime for which Heaven could afford no mercy. That crime, in its indistinct blackness, seemed to overshadow him. The lime-burner's own sins rose up within him, and made his memory riotous with a throng of evil shapes that asserted their kindred with the Master Sin, whatever it might be, which it was within the scope of man's cor-rupted nature to conceive and cherish. They were all of one family; they went to and fro between his breast and Ethan Brand's, and carried dark greetings from one to the other.

Then Bartram remembered the stories which had grown traditionary in refer-ence to this strange man, who had come upon him like a shadow of the night, and was making himself at home in his old place, after so long absence that the dead peo-ple, dead and buried for years, would have had more right to be at home, in any famil-iar spot, than he. Ethan Brand, it was said, had conversed with Satan himself in the lurid blaze of this very kiln. The legend had been matter of mirth heretofore, but looked grisly now. According to this tale, before Ethan Brand departed on his search, he had been accustomed to evoke a fiend from the hot furnace of the lime-kiln, night after night, in order to confer with him about the Unpardonable Sin; the man and the fiend each laboring to frame the image of some mode of guilt which could neither be atoned for nor forgiven. And, with the first gleam of light upon the mountain-top, the fiend crept in at the iron door, there to abide the intensest element of fire, until again summoned forth to share in the dreadful task of extending man's possible guilt beyond the scope of Heaven's else infinite mercy.

While the lime-burner was struggling with the horror of these thoughts, Ethan Brand rose from the log, and flung open the door of the kiln. The action was in such accordance with the idea in Bartram's mind, that he almost expected to see the Evil One issue forth, red-hot, from the raging furnace.

"Hold! hold!" cried he, with a tremulous attempt to laugh; for he was ashamed of his fears, although they overmastered him. "Don't, for mercy's sake, bring out your Devil now!"

"Man!" sternly replied Ethan Brand, "what need have I of the Devil? I have left him behind me, on my track. It is with such halfway sinners as you that he busies himself. Fear not, because I open the door. I do but act by old custom, and am going to trim your fire, like a lime-burner, as I was once."

He stirred the vast coals, thrust in more wood, and bent forward to gaze into the hollow prison-house of the fire, regardless of the fierce glow that reddened upon his face. The lime-burner sat watching him, and half suspected this strange guest of a purpose, if not to evoke a fiend, at least to plunge bodily into the flames, and thus vanish from the sight of man. Ethan Brand, however, drew quietly back, and closed the door of the kiln.

"I have looked," said he, "into many a human heart that was seven times hotter with sinful passions than yonder furnace is with fire. But I found not there what I sought. No, not the Unpardonable Sin!"

"What is the Unpardonable Sin?" asked the lime-burner; and then he shrank from his companion, trembling lest his question should be answered.

"It is a sin that grew within my own breast," replied Ethan Brand, standing erect, with a pride that distinguishes all enthusiasts of his stamp. "A sin that grew nowhere else! The sin of an intellect that triumphed over the sense of brotherhood with man and reverence for God, and sacrificed everything to its own mighty claims! The only sin that deserves a recompense of immortal agony! Freely, were it to do again, would I incur the guilt. Unshrinkingly I accept the retribution!"

"The man's head is turned," muttered the lime-burner to himself. "He may be a sinner like the rest of us,—nothing more likely,—but, I'll be sworn, he is a madman too."

Nevertheless, he felt uncomfortable at his situation, alone with Ethan Brand on the wild mountain-side, and was right glad to hear the rough murmur of tongues, and the footsteps of what seemed a pretty numerous party, stumbling over the stones and rustling through the underbrush. Soon appeared the whole lazy regiment that was wont to infest the village tavern, comprehending three or four individuals who had drunk flip beside the bar-room fire through all the winters, and smoked their pipes beneath the stoop through all the summers, since Ethan Brand's departure. Laughing boisterously, and mingling all their voices together in unceremonious talk, they now burst into the moonshine and narrow streaks of firelight that illuminated the open space before the lime-kiln. Bartram set the door ajar again, flooding the spot with light, that the whole company might get a fair view of Ethan Brand, and he of them.

There, among other old acquaintances, was a once ubiquitous man, now almost extinct, but whom we were formerly sure to encounter at the hotel of every thriving village throughout the country. It was the stage-agent. The present specimen of the genus was a wilted and smoke-dried man, wrinkled and red-nosed, in a smartly cut, brown, bob-tailed coat, with brass buttons, who, for a length of time unknown, had kept his desk and corner in the bar-room, and was still puffing what seemed to be the same cigar that he had lighted twenty years before. He had great fame as a dry joker, though, perhaps, less on account of any intrinsic humor than from a certain flavor of brandy-toddy and tobacco-smoke, which impregnated all his ideas and expressions, as well as his person. Another well-remembered, though strangely altered, face was that of Lawyer Giles, as people still called him in courtesy; an elderly ragamuffin, in his soiled shirt-sleeves and tow-cloth trousers. This poor fellow had been an attorney, in what he called his better days, a sharp practitioner, and in great vogue among the village litigants; but flip, and sling, and toddy, and cocktails, imbibed at all hours, morning, noon, and night, had caused him to slide from intellectual to various kinds and degrees of bodily labor, till at last, to adopt his own phrase, he slid into a soap-vat. In other words, Giles was now a soap-boiler, in a small way. He had come to be but the fragment of a human being, a part of one foot having been chopped off by an axe, and an entire hand torn away by the devilish grip of a steam-engine. Yet, though the corporeal hand was gone, a spiritual member remained; for, stretching forth the stump, Giles steadfastly averred that he felt an invisible thumb and fingers with as vivid a sensation as before the real ones were amputated. A maimed and miserable wretch he was; but one, nevertheless, whom the world could not trample on, and had no right to scorn, either in this or any previous stage of his misfortunes, since he had still kept up the courage and spirit of a man, asked nothing in charity, and with his one hand—and that the left one—fought a stern battle against want and hostile circumstances.

Among the throng, too, came another personage, who, with certain points of similarity to Lawyer Giles, had many more of difference. It was the village doctor; a man of some fifty years, whom, at an earlier period of his life, we introduced as paying a professional visit to Ethan Brand during the latter's supposed insanity. He was now a purple-visaged, rude, and brutal, yet half-gentlemanly figure, with something wild, ruined, and desperate in his talk, and in all the details of his gesture and manners. Brandy possessed this man like an evil spirit, and made him as surly and savage as a wild beast, and as miserable as a lost soul; but there was supposed to be in him such wonderful skill, such native gifts of healing, beyond any which medical science could impart, that society caught hold of him, and would not let him sink out of its reach. So, swaying to and fro upon his horse, and grumbling thick accents at the bedside, he visited all the sick-chambers for miles about among the mountain towns, and sometimes raised a dying man, as it were, by miracle, or quite as often, no doubt, sent his patient to a grave that was dug many a year too soon. The doctor had an everlasting pipe in his mouth, and, as somebody said, in allusion to his habit of swearing, it was always alight with hell-fire.

These three worthies pressed forward, and greeted Ethan Brand each after his own fashion, earnestly inviting him to partake of the contents of a certain black bottle, in which, as they averred, he would find something far better worth seeking for than the Unpardonable Sin. No mind, which has wrought itself by intense and solitary meditation into a high state of enthusiasm, can endure the kind of contact with low and vulgar modes of thought and feeling to which Ethan Brand was now subjected. It made him doubt—and, strange to say, it was a painful doubt—whether he had indeed found the Unpardonable Sin, and found it within himself. The whole question on which he had exhausted life, and more than life, looked like a delusion.

"Leave me," he said bitterly, "ye brute beasts, that have made yourselves so, shrivelling up your souls with fiery liquors! I have done with you. Years and years ago, I groped into your hearts, and found nothing there for my purpose. Get ye gone!"

"Why, you uncivil scoundrel," cried the fierce doctor, "is that the way you respond to the kindness of your best friends? Then let me tell you the truth. You have no more found the Unpardonable Sin than yonder boy Joe has. You are but a crazy fellow,—I told you so twenty years ago,—neither better nor worse than a crazy fellow, and the fit companion of old Humphrey, here!"

He pointed to an old man, shabbily dressed, with long white hair, thin visage, and unsteady eyes. For some years past this aged person had been wandering about among the hills, inquiring of all travellers whom he met for his daughter. The girl, it seemed, had gone off with a company of circus-performers; and occasionally tidings of her came to the village, and fine stories were told of her glittering appearance as she rode on horseback in the ring, or performed marvellous feats on the tight-rope.

The white-haired father now approached Ethan Brand, and gazed unsteadily into his face.

"They tell me you have been all over the earth," said he, wringing his hands with earnestness. "You must have seen my daughter, for she makes a grand figure in the world, and everybody goes to see her. Did she send any word to her old father, or say when she was coming back?"

Ethan Brand's eye quailed beneath the old man's. That daughter, from whom he so earnestly desired a word of greeting, was the Esther of our tale, the very girl whom, with such cold and remorseless purpose, Ethan Brand had made the subject of a psychological experiment, and wasted, absorbed, and perhaps annihilated her soul, in the process.

"Yes," murmured he, turning away from the hoary wanderer; "it is no delusion. There is an Unpardonable Sin!"

While these things were passing, a merry scene was going forward in the area of cheerful light, beside the spring and before the door of the hut. A number of the youth of the village, young men and girls, had hurried up the hillside, impelled by curiosity to see Ethan Brand, the hero of so many a legend familiar to their childhood. Finding nothing, however, very remarkable in his aspect,—nothing but a sunburnt wayfarer, in plain garb and dusty shoes, who sat looking into the fire as if he fancied pictures among the coals,—these young people speedily grew tired of observing him. As it happened, there was other amusement at hand. An old German Jew, travelling with a diorama on his back, was passing down the mountain-road towards the village just as the party turned aside from it, and, in hopes of eking out the profits of the day, the showman had kept them company to the lime-kiln.

"Come, old Dutchman," cried one of the young men, "let us see your pictures, if you can swear they are worth looking at!"

"Oh, yes, Captain," answered the Jew,—whether as a matter of courtesy or craft, he styled everybody Captain,—"I shall show you, indeed, some very superb pictures!"

So, placing his box in a proper position, he invited the young men and girls to look through the glass orifices of the machine, and proceeded to exhibit a series of the most outrageous scratchings and daubings, as specimens of the fine arts, that ever an itinerant showman had the face to impose upon his circle of spectators. The pictures were worn out, moreover, tattered, full of cracks and wrinkles, dingy with tobacco-smoke, and otherwise in a most pitiable condition. Some purported to be cities, public edifices, and ruined castles in Europe; others represented Napoleon's battles and Nelson's sea-fights; and in the midst of these would be seen a gigantic, brown, hairy hand,—which might have been mistaken for the Hand of Destiny, though, in truth, it was only the showman's,—pointing its forefinger to various scenes of the conflict, while its owner gave historical illustrations. When, with much merriment at its abominable deficiency of merit, the exhibition was concluded, the German bade little Joe put his head into the box. Viewed through the magnifying-glasses, the boy's round, rosy visage assumed the strangest imaginable aspect of an immense Titanic child, the mouth grinning broadly, and the eyes and every other feature overflowing with fun at the joke. Suddenly, however, that merry face turned pale, and its expression changed to horror, for this easily impressed and excitable child had become sensible that the eye of Ethan Brand was fixed upon him through the glass.

"You make the little man to be afraid, Captain," said the German Jew, turning up the dark and strong outline of his visage, from his stooping posture. "But look again, and, by chance, I shall cause you to see somewhat that is very fine, upon my word!"

Ethan Brand gazed into the box for an instant, and then starting back, looked fixedly at the German. What had he seen? Nothing, apparently; for a curious youth, who had peeped in almost at the same moment, beheld only a vacant space of canvas.

"I remember you now," muttered Ethan Brand to the showman.

"Ah, Captain," whispered the Jew of Nuremberg, with a dark smile, "I find it to be a heavy matter in my show-box,—this Unpardonable Sin! By my faith, Captain, it has wearied my shoulders, this long day, to carry it over the mountain."

"Peace," answered Ethan Brand, sternly, "or get thee into the furnace yonder!"

The Jew's exhibition had scarcely concluded, when a great, elderly dog—who seemed to be his own master, as no person in the company laid claim to him—saw fit to render himself the object of public notice. Hitherto, he had shown himself a very quiet, well-disposed old dog, going round from one to another, and, by way of being sociable, offering his rough head to be patted by any kindly hand that would take so much trouble. But now, all of a sudden, this grave and venerable quadruped, of his own mere motion, and without the slightest suggestion from anybody else, began to run round after his tail, which, to heighten the absurdity of the proceeding, was a great deal shorter than it should have been. Never was seen such headlong eagerness in pursuit of an object that could not possibly be attained; never was heard such a tremendous outbreak of growling, snarling, barking, and snapping,—as if one end of the ridiculous brute's body were at deadly and most unforgivable enmity with the other. Faster and faster, round about went the cur; and faster and still faster fled the unapproachable brevity of his tail; and louder and fiercer grew his yells of rage and animosity; until, utterly exhausted, and as far from the goal as ever, the foolish old dog ceased his performance as suddenly as he had begun it. The next moment he was as mild, quiet, sensible, and respectable in his deportment, as when he first scraped acquaintance with the company.

As may be supposed, the exhibition was greeted with universal laughter, clapping of hands, and shouts of encore, to which the canine performer responded by wagging all that there was to wag of his tail, but appeared totally unable to repeat his very successful effort to amuse the spectators.

Meanwhile, Ethan Brand had resumed his seat upon the log, and moved, it might be, by a perception of some remote analogy between his own case and that of this self-pursuing cur, he broke into the awful laugh, which, more than any other token, expressed the condition of his inward being. From that moment, the merriment of the party was at an end; they stood aghast, dreading lest the inauspicious sound should be reverberated around the horizon, and that mountain would thunder it to mountain, and so the horror be prolonged upon their ears. Then, whispering one to another that it was late,—that the moon was almost down,—that the August night was growing chill,—they hurried homewards, leaving the lime-burner and little Joe to deal as they might with their unwelcome guest. Save for these three human beings, the open space on the hillside was a solitude, set in a vast gloom of forest.

Beyond that darksome verge, the firelight glimmered on the stately trunks and almost black foliage of pines, intermixed with the lighter verdure of sapling oaks, maples, and poplars, while here and there lay the gigantic corpses of dead trees, decaying on the leaf-strewn soil. And it seemed to little Joe—a timorous and imaginative child—that the silent forest was holding its breath until some fearful thing should happen.

Ethan Brand thrust more wood into the fire, and closed the door of the kiln; then looking over his shoulder at the lime-burner and his son, he bade, rather than advised, them to retire to rest.

"For myself, I cannot sleep," said he. "I have matters that it concerns me to meditate upon. I will watch the fire, as I used to do in the old time."

"And call the Devil out of the furnace to keep you company, I suppose," muttered Bartram, who had been making intimate acquaintance with the black bottle above mentioned. "But watch, if you like, and call as many devils as you like! For my part, I shall be all the better for a snooze. Come, Joe!"

As the boy followed his father into the hut, he looked back at the wayfarer, and the tears came into his eyes, for his tender spirit had an intuition of the bleak and terrible loneliness in which this man had enveloped himself.

When they had gone, Ethan Brand sat listening to the crackling of the kindled wood, and looking at the little spirts of fire that issued through the chinks of the door. These trifles, however, once so familiar, had but the slightest hold of his attention, while deep within his mind he was reviewing the gradual but marvellous change that had been wrought upon him by the search to which he had devoted himself. He remembered how the night dew had fallen upon him,—how the dark forest had whispered to him,—how the stars had gleamed upon him,—a simple and loving man, watching his fire in the years gone by, and ever musing as it burned. He remembered with what tenderness, with what love and sympathy for mankind, and what pity for human guilt and woe, he had first begun to contemplate those ideas which afterwards became the inspiration of his life; with what reverence he had then looked into the heart of man, viewing it as a temple originally divine, and, however desecrated, still to be held sacred by a brother; with what awful fear he had deprecated the success of his pursuit, and prayed that the Unpardonable Sin might never be revealed to him. Then ensued that vast intellectual development, which, in its progress, disturbed the counterpoise between his mind and heart. The idea that possessed his life had operated as a means of education; it had gone on cultivating his powers to the highest point of which they were susceptible; it had raised him from the level of an unlettered laborer to stand on a starlit eminence, whither the philosophers of the earth, laden with the lore of universities, might vainly strive to clamber after him. So much for the intellect! But where was the heart? That, indeed, had withered,—had contracted,—had hardened,—had perished! It had ceased to partake of the universal throb. He had lost his hold of the magnetic chain of humanity. He was no longer a brother-man, opening the chambers or the dungeons of our common nature by the key of holy sympathy, which gave him a right to share in all its secrets; he was now a cold observer, looking on mankind as the subject of his experiment, and, at length, converting man and woman to be his puppets, and pulling the wires that moved them to such degrees of crime as were demanded for his study.

Thus Ethan Brand became a fiend. He began to be so from the moment that his moral nature had ceased to keep the pace of improvement with his intellect. And now, as his highest effort and inevitable development,—as the bright and gorgeous flower, and rich, delicious fruit of his life's labor,—he had produced the Unpardonable Sin!

"What more have I to seek? what more to achieve?" said Ethan Brand to himself. "My task is done, and well done!"

Starting from the log with a certain alacrity in his gait and ascending the hillock of earth that was raised against the stone circumference of the lime-kiln, he thus reached the top of the structure. It was a space of perhaps ten feet across, from edge to edge, presenting a view of the upper surface of the immense mass of broken marble with which the kiln was heaped. All these innumerable blocks and fragments of marble were red-hot and vividly on fire, sending up great spouts of blue flame, which quivered aloft and danced madly, as within a magic circle, and sank and rose again, with continual and multitudinous activity. As the lonely man bent forward over this terrible body of fire, the blasting heat smote up against his person with a breath that, it might be supposed, would have scorched and shrivelled him up in a moment.

Ethan Brand stood erect, and raised his arms on high. The blue flames played upon his face, and imparted the wild and ghastly light which alone could have suited its expression; it was that of a fiend on the verge of plunging into his gulf of intensest torment.

"O Mother Earth," cried he, "who art no more my Mother, and into whose bosom this frame shall never be resolved! O mankind, whose brotherhood I have cast off, and trampled thy great heart beneath my feet! O stars of heaven, that shone on me of old, as if to light me onward and upward!—farewell all, and forever. Come, deadly element of Fire,—henceforth my familiar frame! Embrace me, as I do thee!"

That night the sound of a fearful peal of laughter rolled heavily through the sleep of the lime-burner and his little son; dim shapes of horror and anguish haunted their dreams, and seemed still present in the rude hovel, when they opened their eyes to the daylight.

"Up, boy, up!" cried the lime-burner, staring about him. "Thank Heaven, the night is gone, at last; and rather than pass such another, I would watch my lime-kiln, wide awake, for a twelvemonth. This Ethan Brand, with his humbug of an Unpardonable Sin, has done me no such mighty favor, in taking my place!"

He issued from the hut, followed by little Joe, who kept fast hold of his father's hand. The early sunshine was already pouring its gold upon the mountain-tops, and though the valleys were still in shadow, they smiled cheerfully in the promise of the bright day that was hastening onward. The village, completely shut in by hills, which swelled away gently about it, looked as if it had rested peacefully in the hollow of the great hand of Providence. Every dwelling was distinctly visible; the little spires of the two churches pointed upwards, and caught a foreglimmering of brightness from the sun-gilt skies upon their gilded weathercocks. The tavern was astir, and the figure of the old, smoke-dried stage-agent, cigar in mouth, was seen beneath the stoop. Old Graylock was glorified with a golden cloud upon his head. Scattered likewise over the breasts of the surrounding mountains, there were heaps of hoary mist, in fantastic shapes, some of them far down into the valley, others high up towards the summits, and still others, of the same family of mist or cloud, hovering in the gold radiance of the upper atmosphere. Stepping from one to another of the clouds that rested on the hills, and thence to the loftier brotherhood that sailed in air, it seemed almost as if a mortal man might thus ascend into the heavenly regions. Earth was so mingled with sky that it was a day-dream to look at it.

To supply that charm of the familiar and homely, which Nature so readily adopts into a scene like this, the stage coach was rattling down the mountain-road, and the driver sounded his horn, while Echo caught up the notes, and intertwined them into a rich and varied and elaborate harmony, of which the original performer could lay claim to little share. The great hills played a concert among themselves, each contributing a strain of airy sweetness.

Little Joe's face brightened at once.

"Dear father," cried he, skipping cheerily to and fro, "that strange man is gone, and the sky and the mountains all seem glad of it!"

"Yes," growled the lime-burner, with an oath, "but he has let the fire go down, and no thanks to him if five hundred bushels of lime are not spoiled. If I catch the fellow hereabouts again, I shall feel like tossing him into the furnace!"

With his long pole in his hand, he ascended to the top of the kiln. After a moment's pause, he called to his son.

"Come up here, Joe!" said he.

So little Joe ran up the hillock, and stood by his father's side. The marble was all burnt into perfect, snow-white lime. But on its surface, in the midst of the circle, —snow-white too, and thoroughly converted into lime,—lay a human skeleton, in the attitude of a person who, after long toil, lies down to long repose. Within the ribs—strange to say—was the shape of a human heart.

"Was the fellow's heart made of marble?" cried Bartram, in some perplexity at this phenomenon. "At any rate, it is burnt into what looks like special good lime; and, taking all the bones together, my kiln is half a bushel the richer for him."

So saying, the rude lime-burner lifted his pole, and, letting it fall upon the skeleton, the relics of Ethan Brand were crumbled into fragments.

Herman Melville

Knights and Squires

The chief mate of the Pequod was Starbuck, a native of Nantucket, and a Quaker by descent. He was a long, earnest man, and though born on an icy coast, seemed well adapted to endure hot latitudes, his flesh being hard as twice-baked biscuit. Transported to the Indies, his live blood would not spoil like bottled ale. He must have been born in some time of general drought and famine, or upon one of those fast days for which his state is famous. Only some thirty arid summers had he seen; those summers had dried up all his physical superfluousness. But this, his thinness, so to speak, seemed no more the token of wasting anxieties and cares, than it seemed the indication of any bodily blight. It was merely the condensation of the man. He was by no means ill-looking; quite the contrary. His pure tight skin was an excellent fit; and closely wrapped up in it, and embalmed with inner health and strength, like a revivified Egyptian, this Starbuck seemed prepared to endure for long ages to come, and to endure always, as now; for be it Polar snow or torrid sun, like a patent chronometer, his interior vitality was warranted to do well in all climates. Looking into his eyes, you seemed to see there the yet lingering images of those thousand-fold perils he had calmly confronted through life. A staid, steadfast man, whose life for the most part was a telling pantomime of action, and not a tame chapter of sounds. Yet, for all his hardy sobriety and fortitude, there were certain qualities in him which at times affected, and in some cases seemed well nigh to overbalance all the rest. Uncommonly conscientious for a seaman, and endued with a deep natural reverence, the wild watery loneliness of his life did therefore strongly incline him to superstition; but to that sort of superstition, which in some organizations seems rather to spring, somehow, from intelligence than from ignorance. Outward portents and inward presentiments were his. And if at times these things bent the welded iron of his soul, much more did his far-away domestic memories of his young Cape wife and child, tend to bend him still more from the original ruggedness of his nature, and open him still further to those latent influences which, in some honest-hearted men, restrain the gush of dare-devil daring, so often evinced by others in the more perilous vicissitudes of the fishery. "I will have no man in my boat," said Starbuck, "who is not afraid of a whale." By this, he seemed to mean, not only that the most reliable and useful courage was that which arises from the fair estimation of the encountered peril, but that an utterly fearless man is a far more dangerous comrade than a coward.

"Aye, aye," said Stubb, the second mate, "Starbuck, there, is as careful a man as you'll find anywhere in this fishery." But we shall ere long see what that word "careful" precisely means when used by a man like Stubb, or almost any other whale hunter.

Starbuck was no crusader after perils; in him courage was not a sentiment; but a thing simply useful to him, and always at hand upon all mortally practical occasions. Besides, he thought, perhaps, that in this business of whaling, courage was one of the great staple outfits of the ship, like her beef and her bread, and not to be foolishly wasted. Wherefore he had no fancy for lowering for whales after sun-down; nor for persisting in fighting a fish that too much persisted in fighting him. For, thought Starbuck, I am here in this critical ocean to kill whales for my living, and not to be killed by them for theirs; and that hundreds of men had been so killed Starbuck well knew. What doom was his own father's? Where, in the bottomless deeps, could he find the torn limbs of his brother?

With memories like these in him, and, moreover, given to a certain superstitiousness, as has been said; the courage of this Starbuck, which could, nevertheless, still flourish, must indeed have been extreme. But it was not in reasonable nature that a man so organized, and with such terrible experiences and remembrances as he had; it was not in nature that these things should fail in latently engendering an element in him, which, under suitable circumstances, would break out from its confinement, and burn all his courage up. And brave as he might be, it was that sort of bravery chiefly, visible in some intrepid men, which, while generally abiding firm in the conflict with seas, or winds, or whales, or any of the ordinary irrational horrors of the world, yet cannot withstand those more terrific, because more spiritual terrors, which sometimes menace you from the concentrating brow of an enraged and mighty man.

But were the coming narrative to reveal, in any instance, the complete abasement of poor Starbuck's fortitude, scarce might I have the heart to write it; for it is a thing most sorrowful, nay shocking, to expose the fall of valor in the soul. Men may seem detestable as joint stock-companies and nations; knaves, fools, and murderers there may be; men may have mean and meagre faces; but man, in the ideal, is so noble and so sparkling, such a grand and glowing creature, that over any ignominious blemish in him all his fellows should run to throw their costliest robes. That immaculate manliness we feel within ourselves, so far within us, that it remains intact though all the outer character seem gone; bleeds with keenest anguish at the undraped spectacle of a valor-ruined man. Nor can piety itself, at such a shameful sight, completely stifle her upbraidings against the permitting stars. But this august dignity I treat of, is not the dignity of kings and robes, but that abounding dignity which has no robed investiture. Thou shalt see it shining in the arm that wields a pick or drives a spike; that democratic dignity which, on all hands, radiates without end from God; Himself! The great God absolute! The centre and circumference of all democracy! His omnipresence, our divine equality!

If, then, to meanest mariners, and renegades and castaways, I shall hereafter ascribe high qualities, though dark; weave round them tragic graces; if even the most mournful, perchance the most abased, among them all, shall at times lift himself to the exalted mounts; if I shall touch that workman's arm with some ethereal light; if I shall spread a rainbow over his disastrous set of sun; then against all mortal critics bear me out in it, thou just Spirit of Equality, which hast spread one royal mantle of humanity over all my kind! Bear me out in it, thou great democratic God! who didst not refuse to the swart convict, Bunyan, the pale, poetic pearl; Thou who didst clothe with doubly hammered leaves of finest gold, the stumped and paupered arm of old Cervantes; Thou who didst pick up Andrew Jackson from the pebbles; who didst hurl him upon a war-horse; who didst thunder him higher than a throne! Thou who, in all Thy mighty, earthly marchings, ever cullest Thy selectest champions from the kingly commons; bear me out in it, O God!

Stubb was the second mate. He was a native of Cape Cod; and hence, according to local usage, was called a Cape-Cod-man. A happy-go-lucky; neither craven nor valiant; taking perils as they came with an indifferent air; and while engaged in the most imminent crisis of the chase, toiling away, calm and collected as a journeyman joiner engaged for the year. Good-humored, easy, and careless, he presided over his whale-boat as if the most deadly encounter were but a dinner, and his crew all invited guests. He was as particular about the comfortable arrangements of his part of the boat, as an old stage-driver is about the snugness of his box. When close to the whale, in the very death-lock of the fight, he handled his unpitying lance coolly and off-handedly, as a whistling tinker his hammer. He would hum over his old rigadig tunes while flank and flank with the most exasperated monster. Long usage had, for this Stubb, converted the jaws of death into an easy chair. What he thought of death itself, there is no telling. Whether he ever thought of it at all, might be a question; but, if he ever did chance to cast his mind that way after a comfortable dinner, no doubt, like a good sailor, he took it to be a sort of call of the watch to tumble aloft, and bestir themselves there, about something which he would find out when he obeyed the order, and not sooner.

What, perhaps, with other things, made Stubb such an easy-going, unfearing man, so cheerily trudging off with the burden of life in a world full of grave peddlers, all bowed to the ground with their packs; what helped to bring about that almost impious good-humor of his; that thing must have been his pipe. For, like his nose, his short, black little pipe was one of the regular features of his face. You would almost as soon have expected him to turn out of his bunk without his nose as without his pipe. He kept a whole row of pipes there ready loaded, stuck in a rack, within easy reach of his hand; and, whenever he turned in, he smoked them all out in succession, lighting one from the other to the end of the chapter; then loading them again to be in readiness anew. For, when Stubb dressed, instead of first putting his legs into his trowsers, he put his pipe into his mouth.

I say this continual smoking must have been one cause, at least, of his peculiar disposition; for every one knows that this earthly air, whether ashore or afloat, is terribly infected with the nameless miseries of the numberless mortals who have died exhaling it; and as in time of the cholera, some people go about with a camphorated handkerchief to their mouths; so, likewise, against all mortal tribulations, Stubb's tobacco smoke might have operated as a sort of disinfecting agent.

The third mate was Flask, a native of Tisbury, in Martha's Vineyard. A short, stout, ruddy young fellow, very pugnacious concerning whales, who somehow seemed to think that the great Leviathans had personally and hereditarily affronted him; and therefore it was a sort of point of honor with him, to destroy them whenever encountered. So utterly lost was he to all sense of reverence for the many marvels of their majestic bulk and mystic ways; and so dead to anything like an apprehension of any possible danger from encountering them; that in his poor opinion, the wondrous whale was but a species of magnified mouse, or at least water-rat, requiring only a little circumvention and some small application of time and trouble in order to kill and boil. This ignorant, unconscious fearlessness of his made him a little waggish in the matter of whales; he followed these fish for the fun of it; and a three years' voyage round Cape Horn was only a jolly joke that lasted that length of time. As a carpenter's nails are divided into wrought nails and cut nails; so mankind may be similarly divided. Little Flask was one of the wrought ones; made to clinch tight and last long. They called him King-Post on board of the Pequod; because, in form, he could be well likened to the short, square timber known by that name in Arctic whalers; and which by the means of many radiating side timbers inserted into it, serves to brace the ship against the icy concussions of those battering seas.

Now these three mates—Starbuck, Stubb, and Flask, were momentous men. They it was who by universal prescription commanded three of the Pequod's boats as headsmen. In that grand order of battle in which Captain Ahab would probably marshal his forces to descend on the whales, these three headsmen were as captains of companies. Or, being armed with their long keen whaling spears, they were as a picked trio of lancers; even as the harpooneers were flingers of javelins.

And since in this famous fishery, each mate or headsman, like a Gothic Knight of old, is always accompanied by his boat-steerer or harpooneer, who in certain conjunctures provides him with a fresh lance, when the former one has been badly twisted, or elbowed in the assault; and moreover, as there generally subsists between the two, a close intimacy and friendliness; it is therefore but meet, that in this place we set down who the Pequod's harpooneers were, and to what headsmen each of them belonged.

First of all was Queequeg, whom Starbuck, the chief mate, had selected for his squire. But Queequeg is already known.

Next was Tashtego, an unmixed Indian from Gay Head, the most westerly promontory of Martha's Vineyard, where there still exists the last remnant of a village of red men, which has long supplied the neighboring island of Nantucket with many of her most daring harpooneers. In the fishery, they usually go by the generic name of Gay-Headers. Tashtego's long, lean, sable hair, his high cheek bones, and black rounding eyes—for an Indian, Oriental in their largeness, but Antarctic in their glittering expression—all this sufficiently proclaimed him an inheritor of the unvitiated blood of those proud warrior hunters, who, in quest of the great New England moose, had scoured, bow in hand, the aboriginal forests of the main. But no longer snuffing in the trail of the wild beasts of the woodland, Tashtego now hunted in the wake of the great whales of the sea; the unerring harpoon of the son fitly replacing the infallible arrow of the sires. To look at the tawny brawn of his lithe snaky limbs, you would almost have credited the superstitions of some of the earlier Puritans, and half believed this wild Indian to be a son of the Prince of the Powers of the Air. Tashtego was Stubb the second mate's squire.

Third among the harpooneers was Daggoo, a gigantic, coal-black negro-savage, with a lion-like tread—an Ahasuerus to behold. Suspended from his ears were two golden hoops, so large that the sailors called them ring-bolts, and would talk of securing the top-sail halyards to them. In his youth Daggoo had voluntarily shipped on board of a whaler, lying in a lonely bay on his native coast. And never having been anywhere in the world but in Africa, Nantucket, and the pagan harbors most frequented by whalemen; and having now led for many years the bold life of the fishery in the ships of owners uncommonly heedful of what manner of men they shipped; Daggoo retained all his barbaric virtues, and erect as a giraffe, moved about the decks in all the pomp of six feet five in his socks. There was a corporeal humility in looking up at him; and a white man standing before him seemed a white flag come to beg truce of a fortress. Curious to tell, this imperial negro, Ahasuerus Daggoo, was the Squire of little Flask, who looked like a chess-man beside him. As for the residue of the Pequod's company, be it said, that at the present day not one in two of the many thousand men before the mast employed in the American whale fishery, are Americans born, though pretty nearly all the officers are. Herein it is the same with the American whale fishery as with the American army and military and merchant navies, and the engineering forces employed in the construction of the American Canals and Railroads. The same, I say, because in all these cases the native American liberally provides the brains, the rest of the world as generously supplying the muscles. No small number of these whaling seamen belong to the Azores, where the outward bound Nantucket whalers frequently touch to augment their crews from the hardy peasants of those rocky shores. In like manner, the Greenland whalers sailing out of Hull or London, put in at the Shetland Islands, to receive the full complement of their crew. Upon the passage homewards, they drop them there again. How it is, there is no telling, but Islanders seem to make the best whalemen. They were nearly all Islanders in the Pequod, *Isolatoes* too, I call such, not acknowledging the common continent of men, but each *Isolato* living on a separate continent of his own. Yet now, federated along one keel, what a set these Isolatoes were! An Anacharsis Clootz deputation from all the isles of the sea, and all the ends of the earth, accompanying Old Ahab in the Pequod to lay the world's grievances before that bar from which not very many of them ever come back. Black Little Pip—he never did—oh, no! he went before. Poor Alabama boy! On the grim Pequod's forecastle, ye shall ere long see him, beating his tambourine; prelusive of the eternal time, when sent for, to the great quarter-deck on high, he was bid strike in with angels, and beat his tambourine in glory; called a coward here, hailed a hero there!

John Steinbeck

from **The Grapes of Wrath**

To the red country and part of the gray country of Oklahoma, the last rains came gently, and they did not cut the scarred earth. The plows crossed and recrossed the rivulet marks. The last rains lifted the corn quickly and scattered weed colonies and grass along the sides of the roads so that the gray country and the dark red country began to disappear under a green cover. In the last part of May the sky grew pale and the clouds that had hung in high puffs for so long in the spring were dissipated. The sun flared down on the growing corn day after day until a line of brown spread along the edge of each green bayonet. The clouds appeared, and went away, and in a while they did not try any more. The weeds grew darker green to protect themselves, and they did not spread any more. The surface of the earth crusted, a thin hard crust, and as the sky became pale, so the earth became pale, pink in the red country and white in the gray country.

In the water-cut gullies the earth dusted down in dry little streams. Gophers and ant lions started small avalanches. And as the sharp sun struck day after day, the leaves of the young corn became less stiff and erect; they bent in a curve at first, and then, as the central ribs of strength grew weak, each leaf tilted downward. Then it was June, and the sun shone more fiercely. The brown lines on the corn leaves widened and moved in on the central ribs. The weeds frayed and edged back toward their roots. The air was thin and the sky more pale; and every day the earth paled.

In the roads where the teams moved, where the wheels milled the ground and the hooves of the horses beat the ground, the dirt crust broke and the dust formed. Every moving thing lifted the dust into the air: a walking man lifted a thin layer as high as his waist, and a wagon lifted the dust as high as the fence tops, and an automobile boiled a cloud behind it. The dust was long in settling back again.

When June was half gone, the big clouds moved up out of Texas and the Gulf, high heavy clouds, rain-heads. The men in the fields looked up at the clouds and sniffed at them and held wet fingers up to sense the wind. And the horses were nervous while the clouds were up. The rain-heads dropped a little spattering and hurried on to some other country. Behind them the sky was pale again and the sun flared. In the dust there were drop craters where the rain had fallen, and there were clean splashes on the corn, and that was all.

A gentle wind followed the rain clouds, driving them on northward, a wind that softly clashed the drying corn. A day went by and the wind increased, steady, unbroken by gusts. The dust from the roads fluffed up and spread out and fell on the weeds beside the fields, and fell into the fields a little way. Now the wind grew strong and hard and it worked at the rain crust in the corn fields. Little by little the sky was darkened by the mixing dust, and the wind felt over the earth, loosened the dust, and carried it away. The wind grew stronger. The rain crust broke and the dust lifted up out of the fields and drove gray plumes into the air like sluggish smoke. The corn threshed in the wind and made a dry, rushing sound. The finest dust did not settle back to earth now, but disappeared into the darkening sky.

The wind grew stronger, whisked under stones, carried up straws and old leaves, and even little clods, marking its course as it sailed across the fields. The air and the sky darkened and through them the sun shone redly, and there was a raw sting in the air. During a night the wind raced faster over the land, dug cunningly among the rootlets of the corn, and the corn fought the wind with its weakened leaves until the roots were freed by the prying wind and then each stalk settled wearily sideways toward the earth and pointed the direction of the wind.

The dawn came, but no day. In the gray sky a red sun appeared, a dim red circle that gave a little light, like dusk; and as that day advanced, the dusk slipped back toward darkness, and the wind cried and whimpered over the fallen corn.

Men and women huddled in their houses, and they tied handkerchiefs over their noses when they went out, and wore goggles to protect their eyes.

When the night came again it was black night, for the stars could not pierce the dust to get down, and the window lights could not even spread beyond their own yards. Now the dust was evenly mixed with the air, an emulsion of dust and air. Houses were shut tight, and cloth wedged around doors and windows, but the dust came in so thinly that it could not be seen in the air, and it settled like pollen on the chairs and tables, on the dishes. The people brushed it from their shoulders. Little lines of dust lay at the door sills.

In the middle of that night the wind passed on and left the land quiet. The dust-filled air muffled sound more completely than fog does. The people, lying in their beds, heard the wind stop. They awakened when the rushing wind was gone. They lay quietly and listened deep into the stillness. Then the roosters crowed, and their voices were muffled, and the people stirred restlessly in their beds and wanted the morning. They knew it would take a long time for the dust to settle out of the air. In the morning the dust hung like fog, and the sun was as red as ripe new blood. All day the dust sifted down from the sky, and the next day it sifted down. An even blanket covered the earth. It settled on the corn, piled up on the tops of the fence posts, piled up on the wires; it settled on roofs, blanketed the weeds and trees.

The people came out of their houses and smelled the hot stinging air and covered their noses from it. And the children came out of the houses, but they did not run or shout as they would have done after a rain. Men stood by their fences and looked at the ruined corn, drying fast now, only a little green showing through the film of dust. The men were silent and they did not move often. And the women came out of the houses to stand beside their men—to feel whether this time the men would break. The women studied the men's faces secretly, for the corn could go, as long as something else remained. The children stood near by, drawing figures in the dust with bare toes, and the children sent exploring senses out to see whether men and women would break. The children peeked at the faces of the men and women, and then drew careful lines in the dust with their toes. Horses came to the watering troughs and nuzzled the water to clear the surface dust. After a while the faces of the watching men lost their bemused perplexity and became hard and angry and resistant. Then the women knew that they were safe and that there was no break. Then they asked, What'll we do? And the men replied, I don't know. But it was all right. The women knew it was all right, and the watching children knew it was all right. · Women and children knew deep in themselves that no misfortune was too great to bear if their men were whole. The women went into the houses to their work, and the children began to play, but cautiously at first. As the day went forward the sun became less red. It flared down on the dust-blanketed land. The men sat in the doorways of their houses; their hands were busy with sticks and little rocks. The men sat still—thinking—figuring.

.   .   .

The cars of the migrant people crawled out of the side roads onto the great cross-country highway, and they took the migrant way to the West. In the daylight they scuttled like bugs to the westward; and as the dark caught them, they clustered like bugs near to shelter and to water. And because they were lonely and perplexed, because they had all come from a place of sadness and worry and defeat, and because they were all going to a new mysterious place, they huddled together; they talked together; they shared their lives, their food, and the things they hoped for in the new country. Thus it might be that one family camped near a spring, and another camped for the spring and for company, and a third because two families had pioneered the place and found it good. And when the sun went down, perhaps twenty families and twenty cars were there.

In the evening a strange thing happened: the twenty families became one family, the children were the children of all. The loss of home became one loss, and the golden time in the West was one dream. And it might be that a sick child threw despair into the hearts of twenty families, of a hundred people; that a birth there in a tent kept a hundred people quiet and awestruck through the night and filled a hundred people with the birth-joy in the morning. A family which the night before had been lost and fearful might search its goods to find a present for a new baby. In the evening, sitting about the fires, the twenty were one. They grew to be units of the camps, units of the evenings and the nights. A guitar unwrapped from a blanket and tuned—and the songs, which were all of the people, were sung in the nights. Men sang the words, and women hummed the tunes.

Every night a world created, complete with furniture—friends made and enemies established; a world complete with braggarts and with cowards, with quiet men, with humble men, with kindly men. Every night relationships that make a world, established; and every morning the world torn down like a circus.

At first the families were timid in the building and tumbling worlds, but gradually the technique of building worlds became their technique. Then leaders emerged, then laws were made, then codes came into being. And as the worlds moved westward they were more complete and better furnished, for their builders were more experienced in building them.

The families learned what rights must be observed—the right of privacy in the tent; the right to keep the past black hidden in the heart; the right to talk and to listen; the right to refuse help or to accept, to offer help or to decline it; the right of son to court and daughter to be courted; the right of the hungry to be fed; the rights of the pregnant and the sick to transcend all other rights.

And the families learned, although no one told them, what rights are monstrous and must be destroyed: the right to intrude upon privacy, the right to be noisy while the camp slept, the right of seduction or rape, the right of adultery and theft and murder. These rights were crushed, because the little worlds could not exist for even a night with such rights alive.

And as the worlds moved westward, rules became laws, although no one told the families. It is unlawful to foul near the camp; it is unlawful in any way to foul the drinking water; it is unlawful to eat good rich food near one who is hungry, unless he is asked to share.

And with the laws, the punishments—and there were only two—a quick and murderous fight or ostracism; and ostracism was the worst. For if one broke the laws his name and face went with him, and he had no place in any world, no matter where created.

In the worlds, social conduct became fixed and rigid, so that a man must say "Good morning" when asked for it, so that a man might have a willing girl if he stayed with her, if he fathered her children and protected them. But a man might not have one girl one night and another the next, for this would endanger the worlds.

The families moved westward, and the technique of building the worlds improved so that the people could be safe in their worlds; and the form was so fixed that a family acting in the rules knew it was safe in the rules.

There grew up government in the worlds, with leaders, with elders. A man who was wise found that his wisdom was needed in every camp; a man who was a fool could not change his folly with his world. And a kind of insurance developed in these nights. A man with food fed a hungry man, and thus insured himself against hunger.

And when a baby died a pile of silver coins grew at the door flap, for a baby must be well buried, since it has had nothing else of life. An old man may be left in a potter's field, but not a baby.

A certain physical pattern is needed for the building of a world—water, a river bank, a stream, a spring, or even a faucet unguarded. And there is needed enough flat land to pitch the tents, a little brush or wood to build the fires. If there is a garbage dump not too far off, all the better; for there can be found equipment—stove tops, a curved fender to shelter the fire, and cans to cook in and to eat from.

And the worlds were built in the evening. The people, moving in from the highways, made them with their tents and their hearts and their brains.

In the morning the tents came down, the canvas was folded, the tent poles tied along the running board, the beds put in place on the cars, the pots in their places. And as the families moved westward, the technique of building up a home in the evening and tearing it down with the morning light became fixed; so that the folded tent was packed in one place, the cooking pots counted in their box. And as the cars moved westward, each member of the family grew into his proper place, grew into his duties; so that each member, old and young, had his place in the car; so that in the weary, hot evenings, when the cars pulled into the camping places, each member had his duty and went to it without instruction: children to gather wood, to carry water; men to pitch the tents and bring down the beds; women to cook the supper and to watch while the family fed. And this was done without command. The families, which had been units of which the boundaries were a house at night, a farm by day, changed their boundaries. In the long hot light, they were silent in the cars moving slowly westward; but at night they integrated with any group they found.

Thus they changed their social life—changed as in the whole universe only man can change. They were not farm men any more, but migrant men. And the thought, the planning, the long staring silence that had gone out to the fields, went now to the roads, to the distance, to the West. That man whose mind had been bound with acres lived with narrow concrete miles. And his thought and his worry were not any more with rainfall, with wind and dust, with the thrust of the crops. Eyes watched the tires, ears listened to the clattering motors, and minds struggled with oil, with gasoline, with the thinning rubber between air and road. Then a broken gear was tragedy. Then water in the evening was the yearning, and food over the fire. Then health to go on was the need and strength to go on, and spirit to go on. The wills thrust westward ahead of them, and fears that had once apprehended drought or flood now lingered with anything that might stop the westward crawling.

The camps became fixed—each a short day's journey from the last.

And on the road the panic overcame some of the families, so that they drove night and day, stopped to sleep in the cars, and drove on to the West, flying from the road, flying from movement. And these lusted so greatly to be settled that they set their faces into the West and drove toward it, forcing the clashing engines over the roads.

But most of the families changed and grew quickly into the new life. And when the sun went down—

Time to look out for a place to stop.

And—there's some tents ahead.

The car pulled off the road and stopped, and because others were there first, certain courtesies were necessary. And the man, the leader of the family, leaned from the car.

Can we pull up here an' sleep?

Why, sure, be proud to have you. What State you from?

Come all the way from Arkansas.

They's Arkansas people down that fourth tent.

That so?

And the great question, How's the water?

Well, she don't taste so good, but they's plenty.

Well, thank ya.

No thanks to me.

But the courtesies had to be. The car lumbered over the ground to the end tent, and stopped. Then down from the car the weary people climbed, and stretched stiff bodies. Then the new tent sprang up; the children went for water and the older boys cut brush or wood. The fires started and supper was put on to boil or to fry. Early comers moved over and States were exchanged, and friends and sometimes relatives discovered.

Oklahoma, huh? What county?

Cherokee.

Why, I got folks there. Know the Allens? They's Allens all over Cherokee. Know the Willises?

Why, sure.

And a new unit was formed. The dusk came, but before the dark was down the new family was of the camp. A word had been passed with every family. They were known people—good people.

I knowed the Allens all my life. Simon Allen, ol' Simon, had trouble with his first wife. She was part Cherokee. Purty as—as a black colt.

Sure, an' young Simon, he married a Rudolph, didn' he? That's what I thought. They went to live in Enid an' done well—real well.

Only Allen that ever done well. Got a garage.

When the water was carried and the wood cut, the children walked shyly, cautiously among the tents. And they made elaborate acquaintanceship gestures. A boy stopped near another boy and studied a stone, picked it up, examined it closely, spat on it, and rubbed it clean and inspected it until he forced the other to demand, What you got there?

And casually, Nothin'. Jus' a rock.

Well, what you lookin' at it like that for?

Thought I seen gold in it.

How'd you know? Gold ain't gold, it's black in a rock.

Sure, ever'body knows that.

I bet it's fool's gold, an' you figgered it was gold.

That ain't so, 'cause Pa, he's foun' lots a gold an' he tol' me how to look.

How'd you like to pick up a big ol' piece a gold?

Sa-a-ay! I'd git the bigges' old son-a-bitchin' piece a candy you ever seen.

I ain't let to swear, but I do, anyways.

Me too. Le's go to the spring.

And young girls found each other and boasted shyly of their popularity and their prospects. The women worked over the fire, hurrying to get food to the stomachs of the family—pork if there was money in plenty, pork and potatoes and onions. Dutch-oven biscuits or cornbread, and plenty of gravy to go over it. Side-meat or chops and a can of boiled tea, black and bitter. Fried dough in drippings if money was slim, dough fried crisp and brown and the drippings poured over it.

Those families which were very rich or very foolish with their money ate canned beans and canned peaches and packaged bread and bakery cake; but they ate secretly, in their tents, for it would not have been good to eat such fine things openly. Even so, children eating their fried dough smelled the warming beans and were unhappy about it.

When supper was over and the dishes dipped and wiped, the dark had come, and then the men squatted down to talk.

And they talked of the land behind them. I don' know what it's coming to, they said. The country's spoilt.

It'll come back though, on'y we won't be there.

Maybe, they thought, maybe we sinned some way we didn't know about.

Fella says to me, gov'ment fella, an' he says, she's gullied up on ya. Gov'ment fella. He says, if ya plowed 'cross the contour, she won't gully. Never did have no chance to try her. An' the new super' ain't plowin' 'cross the contour. Runnin' a furrow four miles long that ain't stoppin' or goin' aroun' Jesus Christ Hisself.

And they spoke softly of their homes: They was a little cool-house under the win'mill. Use' ta keep milk in there ta cream up, an' watermelons. Go in there midday when she was hotter'n a heifer, an' she'd be jus' as cool, as cool as you'd want. Cut open a melon in there an' she'd hurt your mouth, she was so cool. Water drippin' down from the tank.

They spoke of their tragedies: Had a brother Charley, hair as yella as corn, an' him a growed man. Played the 'cordeen nice too. He was harrowin' one day an' he went up to clear his lines. Well, a rattlesnake buzzed an' them horses bolted an' the harrow went over Charley, an' the points dug into his guts an' his stomach, an' they pulled his face off an'—God Almighty!

They spoke of the future: Wonder what it's like out there?

Well, the pitchers sure do look nice. I seen one where it's hot an' fine, an' walnut trees an' berries; an' right behind, close as a mule's ass to his withers, they's a tall up mountain covered with snow. That was a pretty thing to see.

If we can get work it'll be fine. Won't have no cold in the winter. Kids won't freeze on the way to school. I'm gonna take care my kids don't miss no more school. I can read good, but it ain't no pleasure to me like with a fella that's used to it.

And perhaps a man brought out his guitar to the front of his tent. And he sat on a box to play, and everyone in the camp moved slowly in toward him, drawn in toward him. Many men can chord a guitar, but perhaps this man was a picker. There you have something—the deep chords beating, beating, while the melody runs on the strings like little footsteps. Heavy hard fingers marching on the frets. The man played and the people moved slowly in on him until the circle was closed and tight, and then he sang "Ten-Cent Cotton and Forty-Cent Meat." And the circle sang softly with him. And he sang "Why Do You Cut Your Hair, Girls?" And the circle sang. He wailed the song, "I'm Leaving Old Texas," that eerie song that was sung before the Spaniards came, only the words were Indian then.

And now the group was welded to one thing, one unit, so that in the dark the eyes of the people were inward, and their minds played in other times, and their sadness was like rest, like sleep. He sang the "McAlester Blues" and then, to make up for it to the older people, he sang "Jesus Calls Me to His Side." The children drowsed with the music and went into the tents to sleep, and the singing came into their dreams.

And after a while the man with the guitar stood up and yawned. Good night, folks, he said.

And they murmured, Good night to you.

And each wished he could pick a guitar, because it is a gracious thing. Then the people went to their beds, and the camp was quiet. And the owls coasted overhead, and the coyotes gabbled in the distance, and into the camp skunks walked, looking for bits of food—waddling, arrogant skunks, afraid of nothing.

The night passed, and with the first streak of dawn the women came out of the tents, built up the fires, and put the coffee to boil. And the men came out and talked softly in the dawn.

When you cross the Colorado river, there's the desert, they say. Look out for the desert. See you don't get hung up. Take plenty water, case you get hung up.

I'm gonna take her at night.

Me too. She'll cut the living Jesus outa you.

The families ate quickly, and the dishes were dipped and wiped. The tents came down. There was a rush to go. And when the sun arose, the camping place was vacant, only a little litter left by the people. And the camping place was ready for a new world in a new night.

But along the highway the cars of the migrant people crawled out like bugs, and the narrow concrete miles stretched ahead.

.   .   .

The moving, questing people were migrants now. Those families which had lived on a little piece of land, who had lived and died on forty acres, had eaten or starved on the produce of forty acres, had now the whole West to rove in. And they scampered about, looking for work; and the highways were streams of people, and the ditch banks were lines of people. Behind them more were coming. The great highways streamed with moving people. There in the Middle- and Southwest had lived a simple agrarian folk who had not changed with industry, who had not farmed with machines or known the power and danger of machines in private hands. They had not grown up in the paradoxes of industry. Their senses were still sharp to the ridiculousness of the industrial life.

And then suddenly the machines pushed them out and they swarmed on the highways. The movement changed them; the highways, the camps along the road, the fear of hunger and the hunger itself, changed them. The children without dinner changed them, the endless moving changed them. They were migrants. And the hostility changed them, welded them, united them—hostility that made the little towns group and arm as though to repel an invader, squads with pick handles, clerks and storekeepers with shotguns, guarding the world against their own people.

In the West there was panic when the migrants multiplied on the highways. Men of property were terrified for their property. Men who had never been hungry saw the eyes of the hungry. Men who had never wanted anything very much saw the flare of want in the eyes of the migrants. And the men of the towns and of the soft suburban country gathered to defend themselves; and they reassured themselves that they were good and the invaders bad, as a man must do before he fights. They said, These goddamned Okies are dirty and ignorant. They're degenerate, sexual maniacs. These goddamned Okies are thieves. They'll steal anything. They've got no sense of property rights.

And the latter was true, for how can a man without property know the ache of ownership? And the defending people said, They bring disease, they're filthy. We can't have them in the schools. They're strangers. How'd you like to have your sister go out with one of 'em?

The local people whipped themselves into a mold of cruelty. Then they formed units, squads, and armed them—armed them with clubs, with gas, with guns. We own the country. We can't let these Okies get out of hand. And the men who were armed did not own the land, but they thought they did. And the clerks who drilled at night owned nothing, and the little storekeepers possessed only a drawerful of debts. But even a debt is something, even a job is something. The clerk thought, I get fifteen dollars a week. S'pose a goddamn Okie would work for twelve? And the little storekeeper thought, How could I compete with a debtless man?

And the migrants streamed in on the highways and their hunger was in their eyes, and their need was in their eyes. They had no argument, no system, nothing but their numbers and their needs. When there was work for a man, ten men fought for it—fought with a low wage. If that fella'll work for thirty cents, I'll work for twenty-five.

If he'll take twenty-five, I'll do it for twenty.

No, me, I'm hungry. I'll work for fifteen. I'll work for food. The kids. You ought to see them. Little boils, like, comin' out, an' they can't run aroun'. Give 'em some windfall fruit, an' they bloated up. Me. I'll work for a little piece of meat.

And this was good, for wages went down and prices stayed up. The great owners were glad and they sent out more handbills to bring more people in. And wages went down and prices stayed up. And pretty soon now we'll have serfs again.

And now the great owners and the companies invented a new method. A great owner bought a cannery. And when the peaches and the pears were ripe he cut the price of fruit below the cost of raising it. And as cannery owner he paid himself a low price for the fruit and kept the price of canned goods up and took his profit. And the little farmers who owned no canneries lost their farms, and they were taken by the great owners, the banks, and the companies who also owned the canneries. As time went on, there were fewer farms. The little farmers moved into town for a while and exhausted their credit, exhausted their friends, their relatives. And then they too went on the highways. And the roads were crowded with men ravenous for work, murderous for work.

And the companies, the banks worked at their own doom and they did not know it. The fields were fruitful, and starving men moved on the roads. The granaries were full and the children of the poor grew up rachitic, and the pustules of pellagra swelled on their sides. The great companies did not know that the line between hunger and anger is a thin line. And money that might have gone to wages went for gas, for guns, for agents and spies, for blacklists, for drilling. On the highways the people moved like ants and searched for work, for food. And the anger began to ferment.

Jean Stafford

The Interior Castle

Pansy Vanneman, injured in an automobile accident, often woke up before dawn when the night noises of the hospital still came, in hushed hurry, through her half-open door. By day, when the nurses talked audibly with the internes, laughed without inhibition, and took no pains to soften their footsteps on the resounding composition floors, the routine of the hospital seemed as bland and commonplace as that of a bank or a factory. But in the dark hours, the whispering and the quickly stilled clatter of glasses and basins, the moans of patients whose morphine was wearing off, the soft squeak of a stretcher as it rolled past on its way from the emergency ward—these suggested agony and death. Thus, on the first morning, Pansy had faltered to consciousness long before daylight and found herself in a ward from every bed of which, it seemed to her, came the bewildered protest of someone about to die. A caged light burned on the floor beside the bed next to hers. Her neighbor was dying and a priest was administering Extreme Unction. He was stout and elderly and he suffered from asthma so that the struggle of his breathing, so close to her, was the basic pattern and all the other sounds were superimposed upon it. Two middle-aged men in overcoats knelt on the floor beside the high bed. In a foreign tongue, the half-gone woman babbled against the hissing and sighing of the Latin prayers. She played with her rosary as if it were a toy: she tried, and failed, to put it into her mouth.

Pansy felt horror, but she felt no pity. An hour or so later, when the white ceiling lights were turned on and everything—faces, counterpanes, and the hands that groped upon them—was transformed into a uniform gray sordor, the woman was wheeled away in her bed to die somewhere else, in privacy. Pansy did not quite take this in, although she stared for a long time at the new, empty bed that had replaced the other.

The next morning, when she again woke up before the light, this time in a private room, she recalled the woman with such sorrow that she might have been a friend. Simultaneously, she mourned the driver of the taxicab in which she had been injured, for he had died at about noon the day before. She had been told this as she lay on a stretcher in the corridor, waiting to be taken to the x-ray room; an interne, passing by, had paused and smiled down at her and had said, 'Your cab-driver is dead. You were lucky.'

Six weeks after the accident, she woke one morning just as daylight was showing on the windows as a murky smear. It was a minute or two before she realized why she was so reluctant to be awake, why her uneasiness amounted almost to alarm. Then she remembered that her nose was to be operated on today. She lay straight and motionless under the seersucker counterpane. Her blood-red eyes in her darned face stared through the window and saw a frozen river and leafless elm trees and a grizzled esplanade where dogs danced on the ends of leashes, their bundled-up owners stumbling after them, half blind with sleepiness and cold. Warm as the hospital room was, it did not prevent Pansy from knowing, as keenly as though she were one of the walkers, how very cold it was outside. Each twig of a nearby tree was stark. Cold red brick buildings nudged the low-lying sky which was pale and inert like a punctured sac.

In six weeks, the scene had varied little: there was promise in the skies neither of sun nor of snow; no red sunsets marked these days. The trees could neither die nor leaf out again. Pansy could not remember another season in her life so constant, when the very minutes themselves were suffused with the winter pallor as they dropped from the moon-faced clock in the corridor. Likewise, her room accomplished no alterations from day to day. On the glass-topped bureau stood two potted plants telegraphed by faraway well-wishers. They did not fade, and if a leaf turned brown and fell, it soon was replaced; so did the blossoms renew themselves. The roots, like the skies and like the bare trees, seemed zealously determined to maintain a status quo. The bedside table, covered every day with a clean white towel, though the one removed was always immaculate, was furnished sparsely with a water glass, a bent drinking tube, a sweating pitcher, and a stack of paper handkerchiefs. There were a few letters in the drawer, a hairbrush, a pencil, and some postal cards on which, from time to time, she wrote brief messages to relatives and friends: 'Dr. Nash says that my reflexes are shipshape (*sic*) and Dr. Rivers says the frontal fracture has all but healed and that the occipital is coming along nicely. Dr. Nicholas, the nose doctor, promises to operate as soon as Dr. Rivers gives him the go-ahead sign (*sic*).'

The bed itself was never rumpled. Once fretful and now convalescent, Miss Vannemann might have been expected to toss or to turn the pillows or to unmoor the counterpane; but hour after hour and day after day she lay at full length and would not even suffer the nurses to raise the head-piece of the adjustable bed. So perfect and stubborn was her body's immobility that it was as if the room and the landscape, mortified by the ice, were extensions of herself. Her resolute quiescence and her disinclination to talk, the one seeming somehow to proceed from the other, resembled, so the nurses said, a final coma. And they observed, in pitying indignation, that she might as *well* be dead for all the interest she took in life. Amongst themselves they scolded her for what they thought a moral weakness: an automobile accident, no matter how serious, was not reason enough for anyone to give up the will to live or to be happy. She had not—to come down bluntly to the facts—had the decency to be grateful that it was the driver of the cab and not she who had died. (And how dreadfully the man had died!) She was twenty-five years old and she came from a distant city. These were really the only facts known about her. Evidently she had not been here long, for she had no visitors, a lack which was at first sadly moving to the nurses but which became to them a source of unreasonable annoyance: had anyone the right to live so one-dimensionally? It was impossible to laugh at her, for she said nothing absurd; her demands could not be complained of because they did not exist; she could not be hated for a sharp tongue nor for a supercilious one; she could not be admired for bravery or for wit or for interest in her fellow creatures. She was believed to be a frightful snob.

Pansy, for her part, took a secret and mischievous pleasure in the bewilderment of her attendants and the more they courted her with offers of magazines, cross-word puzzles, and a radio which she could rent from the hospital, the farther she retired from them into herself and into the world which she had created in her long hours here and which no one could even penetrate nor imagine. Sometimes she did not even answer the nurses' questions; as they rubbed her back with alcohol and steadily discoursed, she was as remote from them as if she were miles away. She did not think that she lived on a higher plane than that of the nurses and the doctors but that she lived on a different one and that at this particular time—this time of exploration and habituation—she had no extra strength to spend on making herself known to them. All she had been before and all the memories she might have brought out to disturb the monotony of, say, the morning bath, and all that the past meant to the future when she would leave the hospital, were of no present consequence to her. Not even in her thoughts did she employ more than a minimum of memory. And when she did remember, it was in flat pictures, rigorously independent of one another: she saw her thin, poetic mother who grew thinner and more poetic in her canvas deck-chair at Saranac reading *Lalla Rookh*. She saw herself in an inappropriate pink hat drinking iced tea in a garden so oppressive with the smell of phlox that the tea itself tasted of it. She recalled an afternoon in autumn in Vermont when she had heard three dogs' voices in the north woods and she could tell, by the characteristic minor key struck three times at intervals, like bells from several churches, that they had treed something; the eastern sky was pink and the trees on the horizon looked like some eccentric vascular system meticulously drawn on colored paper.

What Pansy thought of all the time was her own brain. Not only the brain as the seat of consciousness, but the physical organ itself which she envisaged, romantically, now as a jewel, now as a flower, now as a light in a glass, now as an envelope of rosy vellum containing other envelopes, one within the other, diminishing infinitely. It was always pink and always fragile, always deeply interior and invaluable. She believed that she had reached the innermost chamber of knowledge and that perhaps her knowledge was the same as the saint's achievement of pure love. It was only convention, she thought, that made one say 'sacred heart' and not 'sacred brain.'

Often, but never articulately, the color pink troubled her and the picture of herself in the wrong hat hung steadfastly before her mind's eye. None of the other girls had worn hats and since autumn had come early that year, they were dressed in green and rusty brown and dark yellow. Poor Pansy wore a white eyelet frock with a lacing of black ribbon around the square neck. When she came through the arch, overhung with bittersweet, and saw that they had not yet heard her, she almost turned back, but Mr. Oliver was there and she was in love with him. She was in love with him though he was ten years older than she and had never shown any interest in her beyond asking her once, quite fatuously but in an intimate voice, if the yodeling of the little boy who peddled clams did not make her wish to visit Switzerland. Actually, there was more to this question than met the eye, for some days later Pansy learned that Mr. Oliver, who was immensely rich, kept an apartment in Geneva. In the garden that day, he spoke to her only once. He said, 'My dear, you look exactly like something out of Katherine Mansfield,' and immediately turned and within her hearing asked Beatrice Sherburne to dine with him that night at the Country Club. Afterward, Pansy went down to the sea and threw the beautiful hat onto the full tide and saw it vanish in the wake of a trawler. Thereafter, when she heard the clam boy coming down the road, she locked the door and when the knocking had stopped and her mother called down from her chaise longue, 'Who was it, dearie?' she replied, 'A salesman.'

It was only the fact that the hat had been pink that worried her. The rest of the memory was trivial, for she knew that she could never again love anything as ecstatically as she loved the spirit of Pansy Vanneman, enclosed within her head.

But her study was not without distraction, and she fought two adversaries: pain and Dr. Nicholas. Against Dr. Nicholas, she defended herself valorously and in fear; but pain, the pain, that is, that was independent of his instruments, she sometimes forced upon herself adventurously like a child scaring himself in a graveyard.

Dr. Nicholas greatly admired her crushed and splintered nose which he daily probed and peered at, exclaiming that he had never seen anything like it. His shapely hands ached for their knives; he was impatient with the skull-fracture man's cautious delay. He spoke of 'our' nose and said 'we' would be a new person when we could breathe again. His own nose, the trademark of his profession, was magnificent. Not even his own brilliant surgery could have improved upon it nor could a first-rate sculptor have duplicated its direct downward line which permitted only the least curvature inward toward the end; nor the delicately rounded lateral declivities; nor the thin-walled, perfectly matched nostrils. Miss Vanneman did not doubt his humaneness nor his talent—he was a celebrated man—but she questioned whether he had imagination. Immediately beyond the prongs of his speculum lay her treasure whose price he, no more than the nurses, could estimate. She believed he could not destroy it, but she feared that he might maim it: might leave a scratch on one of the brilliant facets of the jewel, bruise a petal of the flower, smudge the glass where the light burned, blot the envelopes, and that then she would die or would go mad. While she did not question that in either eventuality her brain would after a time redeem its original impeccability, she did not quite yet wish to enter upon either kind of eternity, for she was not certain that she could carry with her her knowledge as well as its receptacle.

Blunderer that he was, Dr. Nicholas was an honorable enemy, not like the demon, pain, which skulked in a thousand guises within her head, and which often she recklessly willed to attack her and then drove back in terror. After the rout, sweat streamed from her face and soaked the neck of the coarse hospital shirt. To be sure, it came usually of its own accord, running like a wild fire through all the convolutions to fill with flame the small sockets and ravines and then, at last, to withdraw, leaving behind a throbbing and an echo. On these occasions, she was as helpless as a tree in a wind. But at the other times when, by closing her eyes and rolling up the eyeballs in such a way that she fancied she looked directly on the place where her brain was, the pain woke sluggishly and came toward her at a snail's pace. Then, bit by bit, it gained speed. Sometimes it faltered back, subsided altogether, and then it rushed like a tidal wave driven by a hurricane, lashing and roaring until she lifted her hands from the counterpane, crushed her broken teeth into her swollen lip, stared in panic at the soothing walls with her ruby eyes, stretched out her legs until she felt their bones must snap. Each cove, each narrow inlet, every living bay was flooded and the frail brain, a little hat-shaped boat, was washed from its mooring and set adrift. The skull was as vast as the world and the brain was as small as a seashell.

Then came calm weather and the safe journey home. She kept vigil for a while, though, and did not close her eyes, but gazing pacifically at the trees, conceived of the pain as the guardian of her treasure who would not let her see it; that was why she was handled so savagely whenever she turned her eyes inward. Once this watch was interrupted: by chance she looked into the corridor and saw a shaggy mop slink past the door, followed by a senile porter. A pair of ancient eyes, as rheumy as an old dog's, stared uncritically in at her and the toothless mouth formed a brutish word. She was so surprised that she immediately closed her eyes to shut out the shape of the word and the pain dug up the unmapped regions of her head with mattocks, ludicrously huge. It was the familiar pain, but this time, even as she endured it, she observed with detachment that its effect upon her was less than that of its contents, the by-products, for example, of temporal confusion and the bizarre misapplication of the style of one sensation to another. At the moment, for example, although her brain reiterated to her that *it* was being assailed, she was stroking her right wrist with her left hand as though to assuage the ache, long since dispelled, of the sprain in the joint. Some minutes after she had opened her eyes and left off soothing her wrist, she lay rigid experiencing the sequel to the pain, an ideal terror. For, as before on several occasions, she was overwhelmed with the knowledge that the pain had been consummated in the vessel of her mind and for the moment the vessel was unbeautiful: she thought, quailing, of those plastic folds as palpable as the fingers of locked hands containing in their very cells, their fissures, their repulsive hemispheres, the mind, the soul, the inscrutable intelligence.

The porter, then, like the pink hat and like her mother and the hounds' voices, loitered with her.

Dr. Nicholas came at nine o'clock to prepare her for the operation. With him came an entourage of white-frocked acolytes, and one of them wheeled in a wagon on which lay knives and scissors and pincers, cans of swabs and gauze. In the midst of these was a bowl of liquid whose rich purple color made it seem strange like the brew of an alchemist.

'All set?' he asked her, smiling. 'A little nervous, what? I don't blame you. I've often said I'd rather lose an arm than have a submucuous resection.' Pansy thought for a moment he was going to touch his nose. His approach to her was roundabout. He moved through the yellow light shed by the globe in the ceiling which gave his forehead a liquid gloss; he paused by the bureau and touched a blossom of the cyclamen; he looked out the window and said, to no one and to all, 'I couldn't start my car this morning. Came in a cab.' Then he came forward. As he came, he removed a speculum from the pocket of his short-sleeved coat and like a cat, inquiring of the nature of a surface with its paws, he put out his hand toward her and drew it back, gently murmuring, 'You must not be afraid, my dear. There is no danger, you know. Do you think for a minute I would operate if there were?'

Dr. Nicholas, young, brilliant, and handsome, was an aristocrat, a husband, a father, a clubman, a Christian, a kind counselor, and a trustee of his school alumni association. Like many of the medical profession, even those whose speciality was centered on the organ of the basest sense, he interested himself in the psychology of his patients: in several instances, for example, he had found that severe attacks of sinusitis were coincident with emotional crises. Miss Vanneman more than ordinarily captured his fancy since her skull had been fractured and her behavior throughout had been so extraordinary that he felt he was observing at first hand some of the results of shock, that incommensurable element, which frequently were too subtle to see. There was, for example, the matter of her complete passivity during a lumbar puncture, reports of which were written down in her history and were enlarged upon for him by Dr. Rivers' interne who had been in charge. Except for a tremor in her throat and a deepening of pallor, there were no signs at all that she was aware of what was happening to her. She made no sound, did not close her eyes nor clench her fists. She had had several punctures; her only reaction had been to the very first one, the morning after she had been brought in. When the interne explained to her that he was going to drain off cerebro-spinal fluid which was pressing against her brain, she exclaimed, 'My God!' but it was not an exclamation of fear. The young man had been unable to name what it was he had heard in her voice; he could only say that it had not been fear as he had observed it in other patients.

He wondered about her. There was no way of guessing whether she had always had a nature of so tolerant and undemanding a complexion. It gave him a melancholy pleasure to think that before her accident she had been high-spirited and loquacious; he was moved to think that perhaps she had been a beauty and that when she had first seen her face in the looking glass she had lost all joy in herself. It was very difficult to tell what the face had been, for it was so bruised and swollen, so hacked-up and lopsided. The black stitches the length of the nose, across the saddle, across the cheekbone, showed that there would be unsightly scars. He had ventured once to give her the name of a plastic surgeon but she had only replied with a vague, refusing smile. He had hoisted a manly shoulder and said, 'You're the doctor.'

Much as he pondered, coming to no conclusions, about what went on inside that pitiable skull, he was, of course, far more interested in the nose, deranged so badly that it would require his topmost skill to restore its functions to it. He would be obliged not only to make a submucuous resection, a simple run-of-the-mill operation, but to remove the vomer, always a delicate task but further complicated in this case by the proximity of the bone to the frontal fracture line which conceivably was not entirely closed. If it were not and he operated too soon and if a cold germ then found its way into the opening, the patient would be carried off by meningitis in the twinkling of an eye. He wondered if she knew in what potential danger she lay; he desired to assure her that he had brought his craft to its nearest perfection and that she had nothing to fear of him, but feeling that she was perhaps both ignorant and unimaginative and that such consolation would create a fear rather than dispel one, he held his tongue and came nearer to the bed.

Watching him, Pansy could already feel the prongs of his pliers opening her nostrils for the insertion of his fine probers. The pain he caused her with his instruments was of a different kind from that she felt unaided: it was a naked, clean, and vivid pain which made her faint and ill and made her wish to die. Once she had fainted as he ruthlessly explored and after she was brought around, he continued until he had finished his investigation. The memory of this outrage had afterwards several times made her cry.

This morning she looked at him and listened to him with hatred. Fixing her eyes upon the middle of his high, protuberant brow, she imagined the clutter behind it and she despised its obtuse imperfection, the reason's oblique comprehension of itself. In his bland unawareness, this nobody, this nose-bigot, was about to play with fire and she wished him ill.

He said, 'I can't blame you. No, I expect you're not looking forward to our little party. But I expect you'll be glad to be able to breathe again.'

He stationed his lieutenants. The interne stood opposite him on the left side of the bed. The surgical nurse wheeled the wagon within easy reach of his hands and stood beside it. Another nurse stood at the foot of the bed. A third drew the shades at the windows and attached the blinding light which shone down on the patient hotly, and then she left the room, softly closing the door. Pansy stared at the silver ribbon tied in a great bow round the green crepe paper of one of the flower pots. It made her realize for the first time that one of the days she had lain here had been Christmas, but she had no time to consider this strange and thrilling fact, for Dr. Nicholas was genially explaining his anaesthetic. He would soak packs of gauze in the purple fluid, a cocaine solution, and he would place them then in her nostrils, leaving them there for an hour. He warned her that the packing would be disagreeable (he did not say 'painful') but that it would be well worth a few minutes of discomfort not to be in the least sick after the operation. He asked her if she were ready and when she nodded her head, he adjusted the mirror on his forehead and began.

At the first touch of his speculum, Pansy's fingers mechanically bent to the palms of her hands and she stiffened. He said, 'A pack, Miss Kennedy,' and Pansy closed her eyes. There was a rush of plunging pain as he drove the sodden gobbet of gauze high up into her nose and something bitter burned in her throat so that she retched. The doctor paused a moment and the surgical nurse wiped her mouth. He returned to her with another pack, pushing it with his bodkin doggedly until it lodged against the first. Stop! Stop! cried all her nerves, wailing along the surface of her skin. The coats that covered them were torn off and they shuddered like naked people screaming. Stop! Stop! But Dr. Nicholas did not hear. Time and again he came back with a fresh pack and did not pause at all until one nostril was finished. She opened her eyes and saw him wipe the sweat off his forehead and saw the dark interne bending over her, fascinated. Miss Kennedy bathed her temples in ice water and Dr. Nicholas said, 'There. It won't be much longer. I'll tell them to send you some coffee, though I'm afraid you won't be able to taste it. Ever drink coffee with chicory in it? I have no use for it.'

She snatched at his irrelevancy and, though she had never tasted chicory, she said severely, 'I love it.'

Dr. Nicholas chuckled. 'De gustibus. Ready? A pack, Miss Kennedy.'

The second nostril was harder to pack since the other side was now distended and the passage was anyhow much narrower, as narrow, he had once remarked, as that in the nose of an infant. In such pain as passed all language and even the farthest fetched analogies, she turned her eyes inward thinking that under the obscuring cloak of the surgeon's pain, she could see her brain without the knowledge of its keeper. But Dr. Nicholas and his aides would give her no peace. They surrounded her with their murmuring and their foot-shuffling and the rustling of their starched uniforms, and her eyelids continually flew back in embarrassment and mistrust. She was claimed entirely by this present, meaningless pain and suddenly and sharply, she forgot what she had meant to do. She was aware of nothing but her ascent to the summit of something; what it was she did not know, whether it was a tower or a peak or Jacob's ladder. Now she was an abstract word, now she was a theorem of geometry, now she was a kite flying, a top spinning, a prism flashing, a kaleidoscope turning.

But none of the others in the room could see inside and when the surgeon was finished, the nurse at the foot of the bed said, 'Now you must take a look in the mirror. It's simply too comical.' And they all laughed intimately like old, fast friends. She smiled politely and looked at her reflection: over the gruesomely fattened snout, her scarlet eyes stared in fixed reproach upon the upturned lips, gray with bruises. But even in its smile of betrayal, the mouth itself was puzzled: it reminded her that something had been left behind, but she could not recall what it was. She was hollowed out and was as dry as a white bone.

They strapped her ankles to the operating table and put leather nooses round her wrists. Over her head was a mirror with a thousand facets in which she saw a thousand travesties of her face. At her right side was the table, shrouded in white, where lay the glittering blades of the many knives, thrusting out fitful rays of light. All the cloth was frosty; everything was white or silver and as cold as snow. Dr. Nicholas, a tall snowman with silver eyes and silver finger-nails, came into the room soundlessly for he walked on layers and layers of snow which deadened his footsteps; behind him came the interne, a smaller snowman, less impressively proportioned. At the foot of the table, a snow figure put her frozen hands upon Pansy's helpless feet. The doctor plucked the packs from the cold, numb nose. His laugh was like a cry on a bitter, still night: 'I will show you now,' he called across the expanse of snow, 'that you can feel nothing.' The pincers bit at nothing, snapped at the air and cracked a nerveless icicle. Pansy called back and heard her own voice echo: 'I feel nothing.'

Here the walls were gray, not tan. Suddenly the face of the nurse at the foot of the table broke apart and Pansy first thought it was in grief. But it was a smile and she said, 'Did you enjoy your coffee?' Down the gray corridors of the maze, the words rippled, ran like mice, birds, broken beads: Did you enjoy your coffee? your coffee? your coffee? Similarly once in another room that also had gray walls, the same voice had said, 'Shall I give her some whiskey?' She was overcome with gratitude that this young woman (how pretty she was with her white hair and her white face and her china-blue eyes!) had been with her that first night and was with her now.

In the great stillness of the winter, the operation began. The knives carved snow. Pansy was happy. She had been given a hypodermic just before they came to fetch her and she would have gone to sleep had she not enjoyed so much this trickery of Dr. Nicholas' whom now she tenderly loved.

There was a clock in the operating room and from time to time she looked at it. An hour passed. The snowman's face was melting; drops of water hung from his fine nose, but his silver eyes were as bright as ever. Her love was returned, she knew: he loved her nose exactly as she loved his knives. She looked at her face in the domed mirror and saw how the blood had streaked her lily-white cheeks and had stained her shroud. She returned to the private song: Did you enjoy your coffee? your coffee?

At the half-hour, a murmur, sanguine and slumbrous, came to her and only when she had repeated the words twice did they engrave their meaning upon her. Dr. Nicholas said, 'Stand back now, nurse. I'm at this girl's brain and I don't want my elbow jogged.' Instantly Pansy was alive. Her strapped ankles arched angrily; her wrists strained against their bracelets. She jerked her head and she felt the pain flare; she had made the knife slip.

'Be still!' cried the surgeon. 'Be quiet, please!'

He had made her remember what it was she had lost when he had rammed his gauze into her nose: she bustled like a housewife to shut the door. She thought, I must hurry before the robbers come. It would be like the time Mother left the cellar door open and the robber came and took, of all things, the terrarium.

Dr. Nicholas was whispering to her. He said, in the voice of a lover, 'If you can stand it five minutes more, I can perform the second operation now and you won't have to go through this again. What do you say?'

She did not reply. It took her several seconds to remember why it was her mother had set such store by the terrarium and then it came to her that the bishop's widow had brought her an herb from Palestine to put in it.

The interne said, 'You don't want to have your nose packed again, do you?'

The surgical nurse said, 'She's a good patient, isn't she, sir?'

'Never had a better,' replied Dr. Nicholas. 'But don't call me "sir." You must be a Canadian to call me "sir." '

The nurse at the foot of the bed said, 'I'll order some more coffee for you.'

'How about it, Miss Vannman?' said the doctor. 'Shall I go ahead?'

She debated. Once she had finally fled the hospital and fled Dr. Nicholas, nothing could compel her to come back. Still, she knew that the time would come when she could no longer live in seclusion, she must go into the world again and must be equipped to live in it; she banally acknowledged that she must be able to breathe. And finally, though the world to which she would return remained unreal, she gave the surgeon her permission.

He had now to penetrate regions that were not anaesthetized and this he told her frankly, but he said that there was no danger at all. He apologized for the slip of the tongue he had made: in point of fact, he had not been near her brain, it was only a figure of speech. He began. The knives ground and carved and curried and scoured the wounds they made; the scissors clipped hard gristle and the scalpels chipped off bone. It was as if a tangle of tiny nerves were being cut dexterously, one by one; the pain writhed spirally and came to her who was a pink bird and sat on the top of a cone. The pain was a pyramid made of a diamond; it was an intense light; it was the hottest fire, the coldest chill, the highest peak, the fastest force, the furthest reach, the newest time. It possessed nothing of her but its one infinitesimal scene: beyond the screen as thin as gossamer, the brain trembled for its life, hearing the knives hunting like wolves outside, sniffing and snapping. Mercy! Mercy! cried the scalped nerves.

At last, miraculously, she turned her eyes inward tranquilly. Dr. Nicholas had said, 'The worst is over. I am going to work on the floor of your nose,' and at his signal she closed her eyes and this time and this time alone, she saw her brain lying in a shell-pink satin case. It was a pink pearl, no bigger than a needle's eye, but it was so beautiful and so pure that its smallness made no difference. Anyhow, as she watched, it grew. It grew larger and larger until it was an enormous bubble that contained the surgeon and the whole room within its rosy luster. In a long ago summer, she had often been absorbed by the spectacle of flocks of yellow birds that visited a cedar tree and she remembered that everything that summer had been some shade of yellow. One year of childhood, her mother had frequently taken her to have tea with an aged schoolmistress upon whose mantelpiece there was a herd of ivory elephants; that had been the white year. There was a green spring when early in April she had seen a grass snake on a boulder, but the very summer that followed was violet, for vetch took her mother's garden. She saw a swatch of blue tulle lying in a raffia basket on the front porch of Uncle Marion's brown house. Never before had the world been pink, whatever else it had been. Or had it been, one other time? She could not be sure and she did not care. Of one thing she was certain: never had the world enclosed her before and never had the quiet been so smooth.

For only a moment the busybodies left her to her ecstasy and then, impatient and gossiping, they forced their way inside, slashed at her resisting trance with questions and congratulations, with statements of fact and jokes. 'Later,' she said to them dumbly. 'Later on, perhaps. I am busy now.' But their voices would not go away. They touched her, too, washing her face with cloths so cold they stung, stroking her wrists with firm, antiseptic fingers. The surgeon, squeezing her arm with avuncular pride, said, 'Good girl,' as if she were a bright dog that had retrieved a bone. Her silent mind abused him: 'You are a thief,' it said, 'you are a heartless vagabond and you should be put to death.' But he was leaving, adjusting his coat with an air of vainglory, and the interne, abject with admiration, followed him from the operating room smiling like a silly boy.

Shortly after they took her back to her room, the weather changed, not for the better. Momentarily the sun emerged from its concealing murk, but in a few minutes the snow came with a wind that promised a blizzard. There was great pain, but since it could not serve her, she rejected it and she lay as if in a hammock in a pause of bitterness. She closed her eyes, shutting herself up within her treasureless head.

Poetry: The Voice of Fable

"For every atom belonging to me as good belongs to you," intoned Walt Whitman in a great burst of populist song in 1855. Prior to this explosion of democratic impulse and camaraderie, there was little in American poetry to forecast Whitman's indiscriminate embrace of all humanity. Eighteenth-century poetry consisted almost entirely of the imitative epics of the Connecticut Wits—its subject matter American manners and morals, its tone alternately monitory and wryly humorous, and its orientation entirely aristocratic. Earlier, in the seventeenth century, the handful of Puritans who wrote verse did little more than poeticize the Testaments in a celebration of God's handiwork and fundamentalist Christian doctrine. With God as the measure of all things, it was incumbent on every person, in poet Michael Wigglesworth's words, to "pay his own." Puritan poetry taught religious morality in every mnemonic line, with the avowed purpose of revealing the inner life for inspection. That this end could be accomplished with some aesthetic merit and considerable grace is evident in the charming poetic introspections of Anne Bradstreet as well as the fiery metaphysical conceits of Edward Taylor.

The privacy and individualism of the Puritan poets was reaffirmed more than a century later in the poetry of Emily Dickinson, the nineteenth-century exponent of the inner life. "The soul selects her own society," she insists, "then shuts the door." Her poems are crammed with the vocabulary of Calvinist doctrine, although Puritanism had long vanished as a creed. Words such as "grace," "salvation," "destiny," and "Calvary" abound. The plain language of the Puritans is the stuff of which her economical poems are fashioned. Hers are the meditations of Bradstreet and Taylor adapted through a "kitchen" vocabulary to suit a more secularized, though intensely mystical and private conception of the universe. Nowhere in her poetry does the reader discern the democratic thrust, the Whitmanian awareness of the expanded population of her century, or of the industrial revolution which was altering the provincial quality of even the smallest towns in America. Her discourse with nature, which is the substance of the great majority of her poems, is in the singular. She addresses the single robin, the one daffodil, the lone blade of grass, "a sphere of simple green." There is little recognition of the simple plurality of nature's inevitable processes. Living and dying are for her lonely and exclusive experiences, devoid of such consolation as Bryant's "Thanatopsis" offers through the democratic implications of death and general immortality. For Dickinson there is no such vision. Not for a moment does the "I" shift to encompass the "we."

For the heroic epic which expresses the common aspirations of the American people and presents a testament of that faith which produced them, we must turn to *Leaves of Grass*. Because Whitman himself was "of the people" by birth, education, and temperament, his was the one authentic voice of the broad "democratic vistas" of the mid-nineteenth century. A prophet who announced himself as the "poet of equality," he saw his specific mission to be the creation of a native literature which had its roots in the American popular experience. This literature was to reflect with accuracy the dignity of each human being, high born or of humble origin, and the mingling of all in an egalitarian whole. The structure and language of his poetry was the concrete fulfillment of Alexis de Tocqueville's predictions that the inevitable process of democratization would affect the very language of a democratized society. Whitman experimented with language to express the vigorous and expansive life style of the "en masse" society which he saw emerging from a powerful, pulsing race of plain people. The primary motive forces in Whitman's poetry were energies heretofore without representation in American poetry: an overwhelming humanitarian love and a mystical absorption in the democratic process.

Whitman's idealization of the democratic mass in America was perpetuated in the twentieth century in the poetry of Carl Sandburg and Vachel Lindsay, and, in small measure, Edgar Lee Masters. Having made American writers aware of the many national and racial strains in the energetic American population, Whitman set into motion a romantic hymning of democratic destiny. Sandburg narrowed Whitman's vast encomiums to a celebration of the crude vigor of America's raw industrial cities, in poems which appeared in *Chicago Poems* in 1916 and later in *The People, Yes.* The broader rhythms of American life—the multiple origins of familiar prairie, remote jungle, and noisy cities—were the sources of Vachel Lindsay's poetry. In anticipation of the folk songs and popular ballads that were to sweep America in the 1930s, Lindsay created a unique poetry-elocution art form of a powerful and authentic nature, if of limited merit. His poetry, together with Sandburg's epics of the cities and Masters' lower-keyed profiles of rural personalities in *The Spoon River Anthology*, kept alive the tradition of democratic confidence which Whitman had set into motion.

For the most part, however, American poetry continues to be a personal outlet for the expression of the sacred self in an increasingly public and ruthlessly self-obliterating environment. In the twentieth century, Whitman's confidence in the undifferentiated American populace has dwindled. The restless migration and increasing industrialization which Whitman saw as heralds of an expanding and prosperous American democracy have stripped the glory from the idealized masses and revealed them as the faceless herd which Emerson had so fearfully foreseen. The search for the soul is on again with an overt anxiety not seen before. The Whitman who grappled all people to his broad compassionate bosom has been replaced by Robert Lowell, descendant of Puritans, who cries out, in "The Turkish Women," his soul's anguish. It is a natural, if extreme, extension of the agonies of T. S. Eliot's Prufrock and Ezra Pound's Mauberley, somewhat earlier lost souls—the former impotent, the latter embittered beyond salvation by a society which did not fulfill its democratic promise.

"I write about realms of the spirit," said Robert Frost, who returned to the rural setting of New England for the backdrop against which he was to investigate the universal dilemna of the soul. In Frost's poetry the realms of the spirit incorporate all the personal choices a person must make in a lifetime. These include the roads one must take, the walls one must construct, the home one must maintain, the toppled stones one must reset, the duties one owes to other individuals. Although his personal responsibilities are clear, his tone is far removed from Whitman's melioristic nineteenth-century optimism. "There's no connection man can reason out between his just deserts and what he gets," Frost's Job complains in *The Masque of Reason.* Edwin Arlington Robinson's Richard Corey would agree with him as would Eliot's Prufrock, who thinks he would have been better off as a lower organism that as a man.

What were the factors in American life which caused the transition from Whitman's warm reaching out to his fellow human being to Lowell's standing him off? In Eliot's estimate, it is the sterility of modern society; in Pound's, it is the crassness and materialism of a civilization which undervalues cultural traditions. In Allen Ginsberg's opinion, the true horror is located in a catalogue of the details of routine existence:

> hundreds of radiators all at once for Eureka,
> crates of Hawaiian underwear.[1]

The ironic element of Ginsberg's litany of woes is in his extensive use of the catalogue, a parody of Whitman's device for celebrating the far-reaching and varied human and material aspects of the democratic landscape. In Ginsberg's Beat poetry, it becomes an effective and conscious parody. Those glorious, burgeoning democratic types sketched in Whitman's Americana have deteriorated into the Sweeneys, Burbanks, Prufrocks, Cheevys, and Mauberleys, an effete or bestial lot of incompetents. They are like E. E. Cummings' Uncle Sol, the "sad sack" who succeeds only in dying and "starting a worm farm" after a life of tragicomic ineptitude. "The United States themselves are essentially the greatest poem," wrote Whitman in the Preface to the *Leaves of Grass* in 1855. A century later Lowell sees these same United States peopled with "Flabby, bald, lobotomized" failures "Tamed by *Miltown*" in "the tranquilized *Fifties.*" In imitation of Milton's lonely Satan, he cries, "I myself am hell; /nobody's here."[2] The poets' vision today is of a land indifferent to their message and often to their very existence.

1. From "In the Baggage Room at Greyhound" from *Howl and Other Poems* by Allen Ginsberg. Copyright 1956, 1959 by Allen Ginsberg. Reprinted by permission of City Lights Books.
2. From *Life Studies* by Robert Lowell, copyright 1956, 1959 by Robert Lowell, published by Farrar, Straus, & Giroux, Inc. Quotations are from, in order of appearance, line 48 of "Memories of West Street and Lepke," line 1 of "Man and Wife," line 12 of "Memories of West Street and Lepke," and lines 35–36 of "Skunk Hour." Reprinted by permission of Farrar, Straus, & Giroux, Inc.

Walt Whitman
from **Song of Myself**

44

It is time to explain myself—let us stand up.

What is known I strip away,
I launch all men and women forward with me into the Unknown.

The clock indicates the moment—but what does eternity indicate?

We have thus far exhausted trillions of winters and summers,
There are trillions ahead, and trillions ahead of them.

Births have brought us richness and variety,
And other births will bring us richness and variety.

I do not call one greater and one smaller,
That which fills its period and place is equal to any.

Were mankind murderous or jealous upon you, my brother, my sister?
I am sorry for you, they are not murderous or jealous upon me,
All has been gentle with me, I keep no account with lamentation,
(What have I to do with lamentation?)

I am an acme of things accomplish'd, and I an encloser of things to be.

My feet strike an apex of the apices of the stairs,
On every step bunches of ages, and larger bunches between the steps,
All below duly travel'd, and still I mount and mount.

Rise after rise bow the phantoms behind me,
Afar down I see the huge first Nothing, I know I was even there.
I waited unseen and always, and slept through the lethargic mist,
And took my time, and took no hurt from the fetid carbon.

Long I was hugg'd close—long and long.

Immense have been the preparations for me,
Faithful and friendly the arms that have help'd me.

Cycles ferried my cradle, rowing and rowing like cheerful boatmen,
For room to me stars kept aside in their own rings,
They sent influences to look after what was to hold me.

Before I was born out of my mother generations guided me,
My embryo has never been torpid, nothing could overlay it.

For it the nebula cohered to an orb,
The long slow strata piled to rest it on,
Vast vegetables gave it sustenance,
Monstrous sauroids transported it in their mouths and deposited it with care.

All forces have been steadily employ'd to complete and delight me.
Now on this spot I stand with my robust soul.

45

O span of youth! ever-push'd elasticity.
O manhood, balanced, florid and full.

My lovers suffocate me,
Crowding my lips, thick in the pores of my skin,
Jostling me through streets and public halls, coming naked to me at night,
Crying by day *Ahoy!* from the rocks of the river, swinging and chirping over
   my head,
Calling my name from flower-beds, vines, tangled underbrush,
Lighting on every moment of my life,
Bussing my body with soft balsamic busses,
Noiselessly passing handfuls out of their hearts and giving them to be mine.

Old age superbly rising! O welcome, ineffable grace of dying days!
Every condition promulges not only itself, it promulges what grows after and
   out of itself,
And the dark hush promulges as much as any.

I open my scuttle at night and see the far-sprinkled systems,
And all I see multiplied as high as I can cipher edge but the rim of the farther
   systems.

Wider and wider they spread, expanding, always expanding,
Outward and outward and forever outward.

My sun has his sun and round him obediently wheels,
He joins with his partners a group of superior circuit,
And greater sets follow, making specks of the greatest inside them.

There is no stoppage and never can be stoppage,
If I, you, and the worlds, and all beneath or upon their surfaces, were this
   moment reduced back to a pallid float, it would not avail in the long run,
We should surely bring up again where we now stand,
And surely go as much farther, and then farther and farther.

A few quadrillions of eras, a few octillions of cubic leagues, do not hazard the
   span or make it impatient,
They are but parts, any thing is but a part.

See ever so far, there is limitless space outside of that,
Count ever so much, there is limitless time around that.

My rendezvous is appointed, it is certain,
The Lord will be there and wait till I come on perfect terms,
The great Camerado, the lover true for whom I pine will be there.

46

I know I have the best of time and space, and was never measured and never
    will be measured.

I tramp a perpetual journey, (come listen all!)
My signs are a rain-proof coat, good shoes, and a staff cut from the woods,
No friend of mine takes his ease in my chair,
I have no chair, no church, no philosophy,
I lead no man to a dinner-table, library, exchange,
But each man and each woman of you I lead upon a knoll,
My left hand hooking you around the waist,
My right hand pointing to landscapes of continents and the public road.

Not I, not any one else can travel that road for you,
You must travel it for yourself.

It is not far, it is within reach,
Perhaps you have been on it since you were born and did not know,
Perhaps it is everywhere on water and on land.

Shoulder your duds dear son, and I will mine, and let us hasten forth,
Wonderful cities and free nations we shall fetch as we go.

If you tire, give me both burdens, and rest the chuff of your hand on my hip,
And in due time you shall repay the same service to me,
For after we start we never lie by again.

This day before dawn I ascended a hill and look'd at the crowded heaven,
And I said to my spirit *When we become the enfolders of those orbs, and the
    pleasure and knowledge of every thing in them, shall we be fill'd and
    satisfied then?*
And my spirit said *No, we but level that lift to pass and continue beyond.*

You are also asking me questions and I hear you,
I answer that I cannot answer, you must find out for yourself.

Sit a while dear son,
Here are biscuits to eat and here is milk to drink,
But as soon as you sleep and renew yourself in sweet clothes, I kiss you with
    a good-by kiss and open the gate for your egress hence.

Long enough have you dream'd contemptible dreams,
Now I wash the gum from your eyes,
You must habit yourself to the dazzle of the light and of every moment of
    your life.

Long have you timidly waded holding a plank by the shore,
Now I will you to be a bold swimmer,
To jump off in the midst of the sea, rise again, nod to me, shout, and laughingly
    dash with your hair.

47

I am the teacher of athletes,
He that by me spreads a wider breast than my own proves the width of my own,
He most honors my style who learns under it to destroy the teacher.

The boy I love, the same becomes a man not through derived power, but in
    his own right,
Wicked rather than virtuous out of conformity or fear,
Fond of his sweetheart, relishing well his steak,
Unrequited love or a slight cutting him worse than sharp steel cuts,
First-rate to ride, to fight, to hit the bull's eye, to sail a skiff, to sing a song,
    or play on the banjo,
Preferring scars and the beard and faces pitted with small-pox over all latherers,
And those well-tann'd to those that keep out of the sun.

I teach straying from me, yet who can stray from me?
I follow you whoever you are from the present hour,
My words itch at your ears till you understand them.

I do not say these things for a dollar or to fill up the time while I wait for a
    boat,
(It is you talking just as much as myself, I act as the tongue of you,
Tied in your mouth, in mine it begins to be loosen'd.)

I swear I will never again mention love or death inside a house,
And I swear I will never translate myself at all, only to him or her who privately
    stays with me in the open air.

If you would understand me go to the heights or water-shore,
The nearest gnat is an explanation, and a drop or motion of waves a key,
The maul, the oar, the hand-saw, second my words.

No shutter'd room or school can commune with me,
But roughs and little children better than they.

The young mechanic is closest to me, he knows me well,
The woodman that takes his axe and jug with him shall take me with him
    all day,

The farm-boy ploughing in the field feels good at the sound of my voice,
In vessels that sail my words sail, I go with fishermen and seamen and love
    them.

The soldier camp'd or upon the march is mine,
On the night ere the pending battle many seek me, and I do not fail them,
On that solemn night (it may be their last) those that know me seek me.

My face rubs to the hunter's face when he lies down alone in his blanket,
The driver thinking of me does not mind the jolt of his wagon,
The young mother and old mother comprehend me,
The girl and the wife rest the needle a moment and forget where they are,
They and all would resume what I have told them.

48

I have said that the soul is not more than the body,
And I have said that the body is not more than the soul,
And nothing, not God, is greater to one than one's self is,
And whoever walks a furlong without sympathy walks to his own funeral drest
    in his shroud,
And I or you pocketless of a dime may purchase the pick of the earth,
And to glance with an eye or slow a bean in its pod confounds the learning
    of all times,
And there is no trade or employment but the young man following it may
    become a hero,
And there is no object so soft but it makes a hub for the wheel'd universe,
And I say to any man or woman, let your soul stand cool and composed before
    a million universes.

And I say to mankind, Be not curious about God,
For I who am curious about each am not curious about God,
(No array of terms can say how much I am at peace about God and about
    death.)

I hear and behold God in every object, yet understand God not in the least,
Nor do I understand who there can be more wonderful than myself.

Why should I wish to see God better than this day?
I see something of God each hour of the twenty-four, and each moment then,
In the faces of men and women I see God, and in my own face in the glass,
I find letters from God dropt in the street, and every one is sign'd by God's
    name,
And I leave them where they are, for I know that wheresoe'er I go,
Others will punctually come for ever and ever.

49

And as to you Death, and you bitter hug of mortality, it is idle to try to alarm
    me.

To his work without flinching the accoucheur comes,
I see the elder-hand pressing receiving supporting,
I recline by the sills of the exquisite flexible doors,
And mark the outlet, and mark the relief and escape.

And as to you Corpse I think you are good manure, but that does not offend
    me,
I smell the white roses sweet-scented and growing,
I reach to the leafy lips, I reach to the polish'd breasts of melons.

And as to you Life I reckon you are the leavings of many deaths,
(No doubt I have died myself ten thousand times before.)

I hear you whispering there O stars of heaven,
O suns—O grass of graves—O perpetual transfers and promotions,
If you do not say any thing how can I say any thing?

Of the turbid pool that lies in the autumn forest,
Of the moon that descends the steeps of the soughing twilight,
Toss, sparkles of day and dusk—toss on the black stems that decay in the muck,
Toss to the moaning gibberish of the dry limbs.

I ascend from the moon, I ascend from the night,
I perceive that the ghastly glimmer is noonday sunbeams reflected,
And debouch to the steady and central from the offspring great or small.

50

There is that in me—I do not know what it is—but I know it is in me.

Wrench'd and sweaty—calm and cool then my body becomes,
I sleep—I sleep long.

I do not know it—it is without name—it is a word unsaid,
It is not in any dictionary, utterance, symbol.

Something it swings on more than the earth I swing on,
To it the creation is the friend whose embracing awakes me.

Perhaps I might tell more. Outlines! I plead for my brothers and sisters.

Do you see O my brothers and sisters?
It is not chaos or death—it is form, union, plan—it is eternal life—it is Happiness.

51

The past and present wilt—I have fill'd them, emptied them,
And proceed to fill my next fold of the future.

Listener up there! what have you to confide to me?
Look in my face while I snuff the sidle of evening,
(Talk honestly, no one else hears you, and I stay only a minute longer.)

Do I contradict myself?
Very well then I contradict myself,
(I am large, I contain multitudes.)

I concentrate toward them that are nigh, I wait on the door-slab.

Who has done his day's work? who will soonest be through with his supper?
Who wishes to walk with me?

Will you speak before I am gone? will you prove already too late?

52

The spotted hawk swoops by and accuses me, he complains of my gab and my
    loitering.

I too am not a bit tamed, I too am untranslatable,
I sound my barbaric yawp over the roofs of the world.

The last scud of day holds back for me,
It flings my likeness after the rest and true as any on the shadow'd wilds,
It coaxes me to the vapor and the dusk.

I depart as air, I shake my white locks at the runaway sun,
I effuse my flesh in eddies, and drift it in lacy jags.

I bequeath myself to the dirt to grow from the grass I love,
If you want me again look for me under your boot-soles.

You will hardly know who I am or what I mean,
But I shall be good health to you nevertheless,
And filter and fibre your blood.

Failing to fetch me at first keep encouraged,
Missing me one place search another,
I stop somewhere waiting for you.

Emily Dickinson

The Soul Selects Her Own Society

The soul selects her own society,
Then shuts the door;
On her divine majority
Obtrude no more.

Unmoved, she notes the chariot's pausing
At her low gate;
Unmoved, an emperor is kneeling
Upon her mat.

I've known her from an ample nation
Choose one;
Then close the valves of her attention
Like stone.

I'm Nobody! Who Are You?

I'm nobody! Who are you?
Are you nobody, too?
Then there's a pair of us—don't tell!
They'd banish us, you know.

How dreary to be somebody!
How public, like a frog
To tell your name the livelong day
To an admiring bog!

Much Madness Is Divinest Sense

Much madness is divinest sense
To a discerning eye;
Much sense the starkest madness.
'Tis the majority
In this, as all, prevails.
Assent, and you are sane;
Demur,—you're straightway dangerous,
And handled with a chain.

Edwin Arlington Robinson

Flammonde

The man Flammonde, from God knows where,
With firm address and foreign air,
With news of nations in his talk
And something royal in his walk,
With glint of iron in his eyes,
But never doubt, nor yet surprise,
Appeared, and stayed, and held his head
As one by kings accredited.

Erect, with his alert repose
About him, and about his clothes,
He pictured all tradition hears
Of what we owe to fifty years.
His cleansing heritage of taste
Paraded neither want nor waste;
And what he needed for his fee
To live, he borrowed graciously.

He never told us what he was,
Or what mischance, or other cause,
Had banished him from better days
To play the Prince of Castaways.
Meanwhile he played surpassing well
A part, for most, unplayable;
In fine, one pauses, half afraid
To say for certain that he played.

For that, one may as well forego
Conviction as to yes or no;
Nor can I say just how intense
Would then have been the difference
To several, who, having striven
In vain to get what he was given,
Would see the stranger taken on
By friends not easy to be won.

Moreover, many a malcontent
He soothed and found munificent;
His courtesy beguiled and foiled
Suspicion that his years were soiled;
His mien distinguished any crowd,
His credit strengthened when he bowed;

And women, young and old, were fond
Of looking at the man Flammonde.

There was a woman in our town
On whom the fashion was to frown;
But while our talk renewed the tinge
Of a long-faded scarlet fringe,
The man Flammonde saw none of that,
And what he saw we wondered at—
That none of us, in her distress,
Could hide or find our littleness.

There was a boy that all agreed
Had shut within him the rare seed
Of learning. We could understand,
But none of us could lift a hand.
The man Flammonde appraised the youth,
And told a few of us the truth;
And thereby, for a little gold,
A flowered future was unrolled.

There were two citizens who fought
For years and years, and over nought;
They made life awkward for their friends,
And shortened their own dividends.
The man Flammonde said what was wrong
Should be made right; nor was it long
Before they were again in line,
And had each other in to dine.

And these I mention are but four
Of many out of many more.
So much for them. But what of him—
So firm in every look and limb?
What small satanic sort of kink
Was in his brain? What broken link
Withheld him from the destinies
That came so near to being his?

What was he, when we came to sift
His meaning, and to note the drift
Of incommunicable ways
That make us ponder while we praise?
Why was it that his charm revealed
Somehow the surface of a shield?
What was it that we never caught?
What was he, and what was he not?

How much it was of him we met
We cannot ever know; nor yet
Shall all he gave us quite atone
For what was his, and his alone;
Nor need we now, since he knew best,
Nourish an ethical unrest:
Rarely at once will nature give
The power to be Flammonde and live.

We cannot know how much we learn
From those who never will return,
Until a flash of unforeseen
Remembrance falls on what has been.
We've each a darkening hill to climb;
And this is why, from time to time
In Tilbury Town, we looked beyond
Horizons for the man Flammonde.

Mr. Flood's Party

Old Eben Flood, climbing alone one night
Over the hill between the town below
And the forsaken upland hermitage
That held as much as he should ever know
On earth again of home, paused warily.
The road was his with not a native near;
And Eben, having leisure, said aloud,
For no man else in Tilbury Town to hear:

"Well, Mr. Flood, we have the harvest moon
Again, and we may not have many more;
The bird is on the wing, the poet says,
And you and I have said it here before.
Drink to the bird." He raised up to the light
The jug that he had gone so far to fill,
And answered huskily: "Well, Mr. Flood,
Since you propose it, I believe I will."

Alone, as if enduring to the end
A valiant armor of scarred hopes outworn,
He stood there in the middle of the road

Like Roland's ghost winding a silent horn.
Below him, in the town among the trees,
Where friends of other days had honored him,
A phantom salutation of the dead
Rang thinly till old Eben's eyes were dim.

Then, as a mother lays her sleeping child
Down tenderly, fearing it may awake,
He set the jug down slowly at his feet
With trembling care, knowing that most things break;
And only when assured that on firm earth
It stood, as the uncertain lives of men
Assuredly did not, he paced away,
And with his hand extended paused again:

"Well, Mr. Flood, we have not met like this
In a long time; and many a change has come
To both of us, I fear, since last it was
We had a drop together. Welcome home!"
Convivially returning with himself,
Again he raised the jug up to the light;
And with an acquiescent quaver said:
"Well, Mr. Flood, if you insist, I might.

"Only a very little, Mr. Flood—
For auld lang syne. No more, sir; that will do."
So, for the time, apparently it did,
And Eben evidently thought so too;
For soon amid the silver loneliness
Of night he lifted up his voice and sang,
Secure, with only two moons listening,
Until the whole harmonious landscape rang—

"For auld lang syne." The weary throat gave out,
The last word wavered, and the song was done.
He raised again the jug regretfully
And shook his head, and was again alone.
There was not much that was ahead of him,
And there was nothing in the town below—
Where strangers would have shut the many doors
That many friends had opened long ago.

Robert Frost
Desert Places

Snow falling and night falling fast, oh, fast
In a field I looked into going past,
And the ground almost covered smooth in snow,
But a few weeds and stubble showing last.

The woods around it have it—it is theirs.
All animals are smothered in their lairs.
I am too absent-spirited to count;
The loneliness includes me unawares.

And lonely as it is, that loneliness
Will be more lonely ere it will be less—
A blanker whiteness of benighted snow
With no expression, nothing to express.

They cannot scare me with their empty spaces
Between stars—on stars where no human race is.
I have it in me so much nearer home
To scare myself with my own desert places.

T. S. Eliot
The Hollow Men

A penny for the Old Guy

I

We are the hollow men
We are the stuffed men
Leaning together
Headpiece filled with straw. Alas!
Our dried voices, when
We whisper together
Are quiet and meaningless
As wind in dry grass
Or rats' feet over broken glass
In our dry cellar

Shape without form, shade without colour,
Paralysed force, gesture without motion;

   Those who have crossed
With direct eyes, to death's other Kingdom
Remember us—if at all—not as lost
Violent souls, but only
As the hollow men
The stuffed men.

II

Eyes I dare not meet in dreams
In death's dream kingdom
These do not appear:
There, the eyes are
Sunlight on a broken column
There, is a tree swinging
And voices are
In the wind's singing
More distant and more solemn
Than a fading star.

   Let me be no nearer
In death's dream kingdom
Let me also wear
Such deliberate disguises
Rat's coat, crowskin, crossed staves
In a field
Behaving as the wind behaves
No nearer—

   Not that final meeting
In the twilight kingdom

III

This is the dead land
This is cactus land
Here the stone images
Are raised, here they receive
The supplication of a dead man's hand
Under the twinkle of a fading star.

Is it like this
In death's other kingdom
Waking alone
At the hour when we are
Trembling with tenderness
Lips that would kiss
Form prayers to broken stone.

IV

The eyes are not here
There are no eyes here
In this valley of dying stars
In this hollow valley
This broken jaw of our lost kingdoms

In this last of meeting places
We grope together
And avoid speech
Gathered on this beach of the tumid river

Sightless, unless
The eyes reappear
As the perpetual star
Multifoliate rose
Of death's twilight kingdom
The hope only
Of empty men.

V

Here we go round the prickly pear
Prickly pear prickly pear
Here we go round the prickly pear
At five o'clock in the morning.

Between the idea
And the reality
Between the motion
And the act
Falls the Shadow

For Thine is the Kingdom

Between the conception
And the creation
Between the emotion
And the response
Falls the Shadow

                                                            Life is very long

Between the desire
And the spasm
Between the potency
And the existence
Between the essence
And the descent
Falls the Shadow

                                                    For Thine is the Kingdom

For Thine is
Life is
For Thine is the

This is the way the world ends
This is the way the world ends
This is the way the world ends
Not with a bang but a whimper.

Richard Wilbur

Mind

Mind in its purest play is like some bat
That beats about in caverns all alone,
Contriving by a kind of senseless wit
Not to conclude against a wall of stone.

It has no need to falter or explore;
Darkly it knows what obstacles are there,
And so may weave and flitter, dip and soar
In perfect courses through the blackest air.

And has this simile a like perfection?
The mind is like a bat. Precisely. Save
That in the very happiest intellection
A graceful error may correct the cave.

The Arts: Sight and Insight

For the first time in the history of America, music, painting, sculpture, and poetry have assumed such a major role in the formation of popular attitudes that their influence has been noted by politicians and sociologists. The decade of the seventies has been marked by numerous proclamations that the message of the drug culture is broadcast most effectively by the lyrics and the tempi of acid rock. So-called psychedelic painting and movies like *The Yellow Submarine* have carried to young and old, to the highbrow and the lowbrow, the specialized insights and ideals of community, mute understanding, and economic equality.

The social and political effects of the content of art are perhaps more apparent than is the equally interesting fact that art is no longer the province of the educated few. Mass communications media, economic prosperity contributing to the growth of leisure time, and the proliferation of advertising material have all played their parts in a popular art explosion. More Americans than ever before are familiar with some forms of painting and sculpture. Buses and food packages wear Peter Max designs. Giant Campbell soup cans, originating in Andy Warhol's studio, have been transformed into coffee mugs which are sold in novelty shops and supermarkets. Children's books frequently subordinate text to artful visual effects which are no longer illustrations but art-for-art's sake graphics. Even etchings, engravings, and lithographs by old masters, formerly the domain of the erudite few, are so widely sought that art syndicates have been formed to invest in the growing art market.

In the past decade we have witnessed the growth and diffusion of a popular art intended both to attract and to criticize a mass culture. The calculated appeal to the untutored response is one form of collectivism in American art. Group participation in the production of a work of art is another powerful form of collectivism in art. This latter collectivism is apparent today in action painting, in moviemaking, and even in the age-old collaboration painting. Yet, collective appeal and collective production are neither exclusive to nor original with this decade or this nation. In every age and in every culture we find both individual and collective artistic traditions.

The Parthenon frieze was probably conceived and overseen by one man—Phidias— and executed by many artisans. The statue of Hermes holding the infant Dionysus was undoubtedly conceived and executed by Praxiteles alone. The carvings on the Romanesque cathedrals of Europe were formerly considered group productions, but we now realize that individual stonecarvers, like Gislebertus of Autun, were solely responsible for at least some of the carvings, while others seem to have been completed by assistants. Perhaps the best-known dichotomies between individual and group effort are to be found in the productions of the Renaissance workshops. Masters and teachers like Leonardo da Vinci and Rubens often painted part of a picture and directed their students in completing the work.

The tradition of collaborative art is long in the history of the world but short in our national history. This is perhaps because the American obsession with materials and objects has resulted in a high valuation of the jack-of-all-trades, the artist-artisan, the creator-craftsman. For this reason, we are more familiar with the individual and even the eccentric artist than we are with the workshop of the arts. In order to understand the currents in contemporary American art, we must recognize both the continuing tradition of individual artistry and the newer collective trend.

This latter trend was initiated in the administration of Franklin Delano Roosevelt. His Works Projects Administration, whose labors extended from road building to mural painting, sponsored an art which was often conceived and produced by more than one artist and directed by popular tastes. The mural in the St. Louis Post Office, executed under the aegis of the W.P.A., depicted groups of people participating in the historic events of Missouri River life. It was the work of two artists, Mitchell Siporin and Edward Millman. Its theme, typical of W.P.A. art, is the history of the people. Inherent in the art of this period is the effort to create, to record, and to prophesy the history of the American people, American architecture, and machinery in terms comprehensible and attractive to both the general populace and the painter. In the sense that the art was concerned with the nation, it was also collective. Nowhere is the collective spirit of the period better expressed than it is in the words of the regionalist painter, Thomas Hart Benton, who said: "I abandoned once and for all my little world of art for art's sake and entered into a world which, though always around me I had not seen. This was the world of America."

Yet the populist art which we see so boldly proclaimed in the social paintings of the W.P.A. did not originate in the twentieth century. The nineteenth century is not devoid of painters who wished to speak to a large audience. Some succeeded; the desire to apotheosize and freeze forever the archetypes of American culture is clearly communicated in the work of Frederic Remington (1861–1909) who depicted scenes of western life. His paintings and sculpture portray the hunt, the life of the cowboy, and the struggle between the cowboy and the Indian. Characterized by a vitality and an energy which are perceptible to the most untrained observer, the figures in his paintings are epic versions of the human and animal types of the West raised to their highest power, and they are by now imprinted on the minds of Americans, be they elders or children, educated or uneducated.

The most obvious contemporary counterpart of this popular art is pop art. Though pop art is often more satirical than Remington's art, it too seeks to raise to the highest magnitude images of common life. Thus the ordinary becomes heroic and, more to the point, the populace becomes aware of the humor, the horror, the beauty, and the banality of the materials that make, surround, and entrap our society. Andy Warhol created giant soup cans; Claes Oldenberg created a pie case filled with hyperrealistic plastic pies; and Robert Indiana painted targets with stars, symbols of the carnival aspect of America, with all its animation and bold gaudiness.

Running counter to the popular tradition in art is the continuum of private and personal vision. In every age there were inimitable geniuses who were both solitary and highly individualistic. Theirs was an art which David Riesman might have defined as "inner directed," for though this art attempts to communicate to its viewers, it depicts an internal world of the artist's mind, a world and images which the popular mind does not see and often considers peculiar when it meets them on canvas. The works of Albert P. Ryder (1847–1917), an American romantic painter of the nineteenth century, present an apocalyptic vision of life. Their dark and luminous colors, their mists and often indistinct images reveal a mystical attitude toward painting as well as toward nature. The world of his painting was within his own mind, and he imposed upon nature the highly personal imprint of the eccentric genius. Nature is transformed, for it is the source, not the finished product of his forms and his atmosphere.

In the contemporary strain, Loren MacIver (1909–   ) is an equally personal artist whose painterly sensibility can be compared to the poetic sensibility of Emily Dickinson. In many of her works the minute is all-encompassing. On a giant canvas a small puddle becomes the world; its leaves, its twigs become the forests of the world. She does not attempt to make the strange into the commonplace, but to transform small familiar objects into universal images. Her private vision and personal need have been equally recognized by other American painters like Georgia O'Keefe, who said: "I decided I was a very stupid fool not to at least paint as I wanted to and say what I wanted to when I painted as that seemed to be the only thing I could do that didn't concern anybody but myself."

It is always easier to predict the direction of popular art than that of personal vision. Although not immune to the influences of social and historical forces, the private visionary is less a recorder than an introspectionist. Yet in all of the American artists we have mentioned, whether they are looking outward or within, we find common qualities which mark them as American. Remington, Ryder, and Indiana share an energy, a sense of motion, that is apparent in Remington's subjects and compositions, in Indiana's glittering color, in Ryder's brush strokes. In MacIver's heroic microcosms we see a concern for objects and materials endemic to American art. These concerns have always distinguished American art, set it apart, and revealed the culture from which it springs. Today's art audience in America is larger than ever, and the increased public exposure to visual media may help to sensitize Americans to those artistic qualities which mark their history and constitute their unique heritage.

The Race Track or Death on a Pale Horse by Albert Pinkham Ryder. The Cleveland Museum of Art, purchase from the J. H. Wade Fund.

James Chillman, Jr.

from **Frederic Remington, Artist of the Old West**

About two years before the death of Frederic Remington, the critic Perriton Maxwell said this of him: "It is a matter of self-congratulation that in ringing down the final curtain on the great Wild West drama, the relentless course of empire has left us at least one auditor with skill and enthusiasm and courage enough to perpetuate on canvas and in enduring bronze the most inspiring phases of its colorful existence." Yet Remington was no native of the plains. He was born in New York state and as a boy the only indications of his future career were a love of the outdoors and a love for drawing. When, upon the death of his father, he set out for the West to seek fortune and adventure, his sketch book was always with him. In it he drew what he saw. The sketches, at first crude, then of greater technical skill, were always records of observed fact. By them we begin to understand why, in his limited field, he stands so far above his numerous imitators.

It is not difficult to understand the great popularity of Remington's works or to account for the praise lavishly given by many fellow artists and critics. His own words furnish the answer. "I paint for boys," he said, "boys from ten to seventy." The romantic adventure about which every boy dreams was made visible in accurately painted scenes done by a master storyteller. Almost without exception the high praise that is given Remington is directed at his power to tell a story, the authenticity of his depicted facts and his ability to draw accurately.

It is just as easy to understand his adverse critics who see in his storytelling and factual painting a definite limit to creative imagination and expression. Remington is dismissed as only an illustrator and his works as only illustrations. As such, to these critics, the works seem hardly worth the time necessary for examination. Frederic Remington was an illustrator, of that there is no doubt, but that his paintings are only illustrations is a more open question.

The thoughtful layman may well ask, "Just what is wrong with illustration?" or "Why is it considered less worthy than any other art forms?" If it is less worthy, then how can we account for the interest in Remington's work which has grown rather than diminished? Is it to be explained only by the glib statement that the great popularity of a work of art is almost a sure sign of its lack of high merit, or could it be that certain elements in Remington's works give them more lasting, more artistically important qualities which the layman senses but cannot explain?

The term "illustration" in itself should carry no derogatory meaning. After all Giotto and Masaccio were illustrators, as were Rembrandt and Hogarth. Illustration plays a necessary part in art expression, but it so happens that illustration by its very nature turns the attention of the spectator away from the work of art itself to the incident or thing which the work of art explains or records. The stronger the illustration the more is the interest of the spectator focused upon the subject or story. The painting or piece of sculpture becomes simply the means by which a fact or series of facts is explained. It places these facts in visible form so that they may be readily grasped and understood and by this very quality keeps the interest of the spectator upon the facts represented. No wonder it has been said that one picture is worth a thousand words.

However, it is quite evident to most people that a painting or a piece of sculpture by the arrangement of its forms or colors can express a thought, suggest a quality, even evoke a strong emotional response in the spectator irrespective of any subject or story that may be involved. In some cases the subject has so little relevance that it is abandoned completely. Forms and colors, like notes in music, can be used to suggest or to create a definite world without the need of depicting it literally.

But most of us, being what we are, respond most quickly to forms that we know or can recognize or at least can readily imagine. To us the strength of an artist does not lie in his ability to abandon the visible world, but in his ability to intensify its significance by selecting and choosing those forms which are most relevant to the thought or feeling to be expressed.

This sense of the relevant, of the significant, in general and in detail, was strongly developed in Frederic Remington and perhaps this sense, more than any other quality, makes his work an authoritative statement, one of the necessary factors of all great art.

Remington's formal art education was so brief that he might well be called a self-taught artist. It is true that he studied at the Yale Art School under J. Alden Weir. He did not like academic restrictions but he did like football. Professor Weir is said to have remarked that "Remington was a queer-looking art student as he frequently had his face and legs bandaged." Later after achieving some success with his pen-and-ink studies we find him going to the Art Students League in New York for additional training as if to correct certain technical deficiencies and develop his knowledge of other media. But by far the greater part of his technical development came from self-study and the personal observation of the methods of his contemporaries. His technical methods were never bound by the conventional art school practice of his day, but though they were unorthodox, nevertheless they were sound.

He was, or soon became, familiar with most art mediums: pen, crayon, watercolor and oil, but his desire to paint seriously did not appear until he was thirty. His interest in sculpture came even later in his life, but he brought to his modelling and casting an enthusiasm which quickly developed great technical skill.

His technical progress in each art medium he used followed the same general pattern, which was similar to the method by which he collected the material forming the background necessary to the creation of a work of art. This method was not new—it was the old one of collecting as many facts as possible about as many things as possible by means of innumerable notes, written and sketched. It seems to be used most in times when the intellectual curiosity of both artist and public is directed objectively at the natural world and usually produces a work of art in which the literary content or "story" is given importance.

Leonardo da Vinci followed this method so completely that his notes, perhaps, are more valuable than his more finished works. In some ways the same thing might be said of Remington. In his sketch notes we meet Remington the realist, Remington the analyst, the Remington whose keen observation could pick easily the most important out of a group of facts. His final work was seldom done on the spot but at a later time after all of the facts were noted and revaluated. Remington was not one to take his easel to the subject, rather he brought the subject to the easel. It is not surprising then to realize that most of his major paintings of the West were actually painted in his studio in the East.

That these pictures have the feeling of being painted on the spot is due to the fact that his notes and sketches were not done from hearsay evidence but were made by close contact with each subject and rich acquaintance with its background. It is true that Remington painted many events which he could not have seen and some which happened before he was born, such as his painting called the "Drawing of a Black Bean," now in the collection of the Museum of Fine Arts of Houston, and the watercolor of "Custer's Last Stand" in the same museum. Remington was a boy of fifteen at the time of the massacre, but later he was with the United States Army of the West, and knew it well, as is amply attested in his illustrations for *Personal Recollections of General Miles,* and his *Frontier Sketches.*

Pen, crayon and water color lend themselves to note-taking. Remington's love for, and use of, the quick sketch in pencil or ink can be followed throughout his career. These sketches, some complete and some fragmentary, are the most interesting and revealing of his works and no understanding of his complete genius can be had without a careful consideration of them. But he was not content to depend upon his notes and sketches completely. His love of accuracy filled his studio with cowboy trappings. Indian costumes, ornaments, tools and weapons, objects of all sorts from many places served as source material for his work.

Largely because he had so many commissions as an illustrator, his first works in oil were usually in monochrome. To rich blacks, greys and whites were sometimes added tones of ochre or touches of brilliant reds, but always limited and restrained in amount. Many of these oils basically in black and white are among his strongest and most dramatic paintings. One of these, "The Infantry Square"[1] and also recorded as "The Battle," is not only an early oil but one of his most forceful works, strong and compact in composition, brilliant in technical execution.

It is evident that the use of monochrome was to facilitate reproduction in a day when color processes were both expensive and experimental, yet Remington finds in this relatively limited use of color one of his most powerful tools. In fact, when he does begin to use a full-color palette his oils give the feeling of a drawing carefully done, then lightly washed with color. His water colors are of the same nature. For all their charm and skillful execution they are essentially water-color drawings rather than water-color paintings.

Fundamentally, Remington is not a colorist; in fact he seems uninterested in color either as a resource in composition or to heighten emotional content. He uses it only as a help to factual representation. Perhaps it was this that made him aware of the Impressionists and their use of color to aid the solutions of the problems of light and luminosity. The "Pointillists," or broken-color Impressionists, seem to interest him most. These masters of light and air seem to suggest to him how the bright sunshine and luminous shadows of the Western spaces could be better painted. He experiments with their methods by breaking his purple shadows into touches of clear

1. *Harper's Monthly,* Sept., 1893.

blue and red, he softens his precise draughtsmanlike outlines by brush strokes that cross rather than follow them, but never does he adopt this technique of Impressionism completely.

As his interest grows in the possibilities of the oil medium his brushwork becomes bolder and the pigments thicker and richer in application. The character of his color changes from that of the tinted black-and-white to that of a more complete color expression. However, color to enhance the telling of a story can be quite different from color as a basic element of design, and indicates to what qualities we must look to find Remington the artist.

His sculpture, as well, loses as much as it gains by the insistence on factual accuracy. It can be seen that in character the sculpture is really nothing but his painting given an actual rather than a suggested third dimension. It is pictorial rather than sculptural and its great virtue—the vivid suggestion of life and action—is often marred by persistent emphasis on literal detail. A coiled lariat of bronzed wire, a bridle with reins and thin metal ribbons, a "ten-gallon" hat waving in the air, tend to destroy rather than to build a unified effect. Yet in spite of aesthetic faults there is no technical fumbling; the medium of bronze is used with understanding and competence. It is easy to understand why he seldom if ever worked in wood or stone. The designs he created were possible only in cast metal. As a sculptor he seemed to think in bronze, or rather he thought first of his subject and then of the medium in which to fashion it. Bronze was the only answer.

This is quite a different viewpoint from that which creates an appropriate subject for metal and still different from the one which allows the material itself to dictate the subject or at least the manner in which the subject is treated. With Remington it was always the subject, the story, first.

This is just as true of his painting. His great interest in that world which he saw and experienced led him to create an adequate means to express it. His own words tell us how his need of expression developed his art vocabulary. "Without knowing exactly how to do it," he says, "I began to try to record some facts around me and the more I looked the more the panorama unfolded."

These words give us the clue to his rapid technical development. His technique was always sufficient to the needs of the story, but it was the story that mattered. Living through an age which saw the development of subjective painting, he remained impersonally objective. His rôle was that of the reporter, not the commentator. He seemed unconcerned with the significance of the incident which he portrayed or with its meaning as a symptom of a general condition in the march of events. This is well illustrated by one of his most popular and best-known paintings, "The Fight for the Waterhole." Remington is an interested spectator of the episode, of how the persons concerned would appear under the particular conditions. He is neither for nor against the defenders. The effect on history, if this and other waterholes are won or lost, does not trouble him. He recounts the story and the reader may draw his own conclusions. He is a historian only in so far as he records events; the evaluation of their importance is left to others.

If morals are to be drawn from Remington's records the reader must draw them from the facts spread before his eyes. Rarely in his paintings does he seem to protest against evils or injustices, imagined or real, though he would have had opportunity, generously supplied, to collect material for such protests both from his life in the West and in Cuba during the Spanish American War. He does not dwell often on pain or tragedy. One of the few exceptions in his major works is the painting usually called "The Transgressor."[2] This deals with the horrible end of a small Mexican who, it seems, offended the Apaches, for which he was hung head downward over a cliff, suspended by one foot only. Even here the tale is told impersonally.

Remington espouses no cause, indulges in no social comments, nor is he interested in his personal reactions to the events he records. The manner in which he might be affected by his experiences is never shown in the character of his painting. Remington the man and Remington the artist can be seen more clearly by reading between the lines than by the lines themselves.

One of the most common approaches to art, certainly among occidental peoples, is the interest in factual knowledge; and to painting the interest in factual representation. Apelles received the plaudits of Athens when horses whinnied with delight on seeing his paintings of them, and Remington is acclaimed for his accurate recording of the things he sees. It was not the finished technique of his early pen sketches which started him on his way, for the brevity of his art training was all too apparent, but what got him his early commissions was the interest of the public in any fact that seemed authentic about the American Indian and the great West.

This interest in factual knowledge and representation was Remington's own approach, not only to the mastery of his technical means, but to the attainment of his artistic ends—the pictorial record, the pictorial reconstruction of a vanishing world. So intent was he on this vanishing world and so intent have been his adherents upon this past epoch in American history that the brilliance of his art is all but lost in the brilliance of his storytelling.

Some people tell stories so well that their method of telling becomes identified with themselves, and finally they are identified with their stories. This was Remington; his personality becomes absorbed by the personality of the story. We accept the content of his picture as fact, so he insists that, in so far as possible, this accepted fact be correct. For this alone his paintings become invaluable documents. This accuracy of detail is one of the reasons for the great popularity of his works, a popularity so great that it has caused many forgeries. Strangely enough the detection of these forgeries is often made by means of the factual accuracy of the originals.

If there is one weakness in Remington's storytelling it is not his love for accurate fact but his incurable romanticism. The romance of the Pioneer West, the romance of war, the romance and thrill of adventure, all are told, but the heartbreak, the suffering, the sting of defeat seldom appear. In his painting "The Emigrants" can be seen one of the tragic incidents in the conquering of the West, but with all the accuracy of fact, precision of detail and the simulated action, the spectator is sure that the hard-riding Indian is never going to stab the young pioneer, or if he does the youth will recover and the West will be won. Here perhaps is another reason for the popularity of Remington's work. Most Americans, too, are incurable romantics, at least in what they like in art.

2. "Tio Juan Hanging There Dead," *Harper's Monthly*, Feb., 1893.

In his paintings Remington is a romantic storyteller, in his sketches a realist in search of facts. Add these together and one sees why he has been acclaimed the great chronicler of a vanished epoch. Yet Remington is more than the teller of well-told tales; he is more than the careful collector of interesting and valuable data.

Thousands of years ago the cave men of Western Europe began to make records of the things they saw which were of vital importance to their lives. They did this by modelling, then drawing, then engraving the images of the animals which they hunted for food and clothing. Finally they painted, ceremoniously, the images of these animals on the walls of the dim interiors of their caves. By this time they had left the factual record far behind and reached the point of a great pictorial convention. As the earlier works amaze us by their precise recording of facts, so the later paintings astound us by the great economy of means by which effects are obtained and ideas communicated. The particular fact has been transformed into a universal truth. A bison is painted charging down the wall. It no longer is a certain bison; it becomes a pictorial symbol for all bison. The subject has been so well understood that its form, its action, its very nature is made visible by the most rigid economy of lines and color masses and a selection of only the facts essential to complete comprehension.

If Remington's work is closely examined, an almost parallel progression can be seen in his relatively short lifetime as an artist. First literal and exacting in his search for fact, Remington like the ancient engraver showed the legs of a running animal in positions that the average eye does not observe but which are verified by the slow-motion picture. He gradually developed the surety of touch and the economy of means which leads to a clear, concise and direct pictorial statement. Perhaps this is what Remington meant when he asked to be remembered as one who "knew the horse." Of all of his records, of all of his stories, the story of the horse is told the best.

If it is possible to point to the quality that makes Remington stand ahead of his followers and imitators or to that which causes him to be called "the foremost American painter in his chosen field," it will not be Remington the illustrator to whom we will look, nor to Remington the pictorial historian, but to Remington the artist. The difference lies not in technique, for able as he was he was no more talented than many others, but in his power of selection and his sense of the significant. He was able to select and to use only those forms which would emphasize the fundamental meaning of the story—seen romantically or not—and aid in its simple, honest and direct telling.

Perhaps this is why Frederic Remington and his art have become to the people of the United States symbols of that vanished world of romance and adventure which ever lives in their hearts.

John I. H. Baur
Loren MacIver

Loren MacIver speaks sparingly of herself and only a little less so of her work. Her mobile face with its wide, sensitive mouth is distressed at direct questions. "You know," she says, as if revealing the most confidential information. "I don't remember." Perhaps this is quite literally true, for few people live more spontaneously in the present or find such pleasure in the small, immediate circumstances of life. A mechanical mouse that dances, a stone that looks like a loaf of bread, a flower, a leaf, a decorated Swiss lollipop delight her and are the principal furnishings of her studio —otherwise immaculately bare except for her easel, a table, some straight chairs and an immense grand piano.

MacIver's pleasure in unexpected things is as infectious as a child's and it sometimes seems as if she deliberately sought to preserve a child-like innocence in both her paintings and her relations with the world. No one, talking with her or looking at her work, can doubt that this innocence is genuine, but it seems far from child-like in its essence—rather a mature, poetic wisdom that guards its secrets well. So her early life remains shadowy, perhaps because she prefers to keep it thus, perhaps because to her, as to the very young, it is truly remote and obscure in its chronology. She was born in New York City on February 2, 1909, the daughter of Charles Augustus Paul Newman and Julia (MacIver) Newman. Her mother, of Scotch-Irish descent, kept her maiden name, which Loren also adopted.

As far back as she can remember MacIver painted—casually and unselfconsciously, which is to say, like most small children. A few memories return to her—of inventing alphabets before she could write, of painting a derby hat with a sense of awe at its imposing blackness. When she was ten her parents, who seem to have encouraged, or at least not opposed, her painting, permitted her to enter Saturday classes at the Art Students League—the only formal art instruction she has had. Even that can scarcely be called formal since she spent most of her time wandering from one studio to another and recalls none of her teachers, only a kind of wonder at the variety of things that could be done from the model.

She left the League after a year but continued to paint in the spare time that her education at public school and two high schools permitted. Through her reticence there emerges an indistinct picture of a child possessed by an extraordinary imagination which she scarcely understood, although it was already shaping her future career. One indication was her early passion for the theater, a love which has never waned and which led her at this time to design imaginary sets for Tennyson's *Idylls of the King* and for a one-act fantasy by Dunsany, *The Glittering Gate*. But perhaps the clearest evidence is simply the fact that she continued to paint, freely and intuitively, at a time when almost every promising child artist either abandons painting or tries to conform to the pictorial admirations of high school—chiefly slick magazine illustration. MacIver never went through such a stage. Miraculously, she seems to have followed an unbroken line of development from childhood to maturity keeping intact her sense of wonder at the world's visual delights and her unconventional ways of recreating them on canvas. There has never been a period in her life when she would not have enjoyed painting a derby hat simply "because it was so black."

MacIver realizes, if it is pointed out to her, that such a consistent development through the normally fickle 'teens is exceptional, but she is quite unable to explain it. "Perhaps," she says, "it is because I never thought of painting as a career. I cannot tell you how casual it was. I never intended to be a painter. I just liked to paint." Even today she works in much the same spirit, unhampered by esthetic theory or artistic allegiances, painting essentially because she just likes to.

When she was twenty MacIver married the poet Lloyd Frankenberg, whom she had known in high school. Their first home was over a bakery at the corner of Eleventh and Bleeker Streets. For a year or two before, she had been painting in the studios of various friends but the first work that she has preserved, such as the unconventional portrait of her husband called *Sleep,* was done here in 1929, the year of her marriage. Since then they have moved often, though always within the limits of Greenwich Village, where MacIver's slim figure in faded blue jeans, looking a good deal like a small cowboy's, is now familiar.

In 1931 they discovered Cape Cod where they spent their summers for ten years. Since neither poets nor painters are likely to be affluent in youth, there must have been difficult times, of which neither speaks. Their home on the Cape, at North Truro, was a shack which they built entirely of driftwood collected on the beach. When nearby supplies ran out they gathered more at distant points, formed it into rafts and, picking an auspicious wind and tide, floated these down to their site. On the ocean side of the Cape it was not easy. With MacIver harnessed to the raft by a tow rope and Lloyd Frankenberg precariously poling to keep it off shore, they managed to amass enough supplies for a reasonably weathertight cabin. Heated by a wood stove, this was their only home during the winter of 1932. There was then no road near them and food had to be brought in by knapsack over a trail through the scrub pine. They did not try to winter there again but the shack remained their summer home until about 1940 when the war temporarily prevented its use. Recently they sold it.

Something of the bleakness and exhilaration of that early year on the Cape appears in MacIver's *Winter Dunes,* a seagull's eye view of their house and the tall figure of Lloyd Frankenberg striding along the beach. While the artist's technical skill and sense of design were still only partially developed, many of the essential elements in her mature style are already perceptible. Large among these is her fantasy, her easy re-entry into the world of children. Here the naive drawing of the figure and the device of painting her whole local world—house, sea, husband and distant village—in one vastly compressed scheme are obvious borrowings from child art. They give the picture its fresh, ingenuous feeling tempered, however, by the more sophisticated handling of the landscape, which is painted with a decorative, oriental touch. The combination effectively rescues the canvas from oversweetness, a pitfall that MacIver occasionally skirts by a more perilous margin, as in her earlier *Alice.*

Three paintings done on the Cape a year later, in 1933, show a marked change of approach. All are more soberly treated, more conventionally designed, less fantastical. It is as if she felt a need to discipline her imagination and perfect her technique through a closer study of nature. There was no essential sacrifice; the fragile mood, the delicacy of feeling were maintained, perhaps even strengthened. The chief difference was a new seriousness of purpose. Two of the trio, *Tern Eggs* and *Beach Plum Landscape,* forecast MacIver's recurrent interest in nature, seen both large and small. The former, especially, is significant because it is perhaps the first picture in which she invests quite ordinary objects with an aura of wonder and tenderness—a distinctive quality in much of her later work. Here it is achieved partly by the color but more by the arrangement, which suggests two precious stones mounted in a circlet of minor jewels. Two years later she achieved, in *Witchbowls,* a similar transformation of fishermen's glass net floats, collected on the beach, into a design of mysteriously glowing lights.

The third picture of 1933, *Douglas Roach,* is evidence of MacIver's early ability to portray people who interest her with an uncanny inwardness. This is not at all the same as capturing individual character, in the way that Eakins did, but rather a heightening of the mystery of personality, an expression of the indefinable spirit that shines fitfully behind humanity's "muddy vesture of decay." While she is unpredictable in her choice of sitters, one always senses a bond of humor, admiration or affection illuminating the portraits. Roach, for instance, was a Negro friend on the Cape, and a man of varied talents. As a part time wrestler, he achieved a degree of fame for his bright yellow trunks with a brilliant rising sun emblazoned on the seat. As a gardener, he called himself "the most promising man on the Cape," since he generally forgot to turn up when hired. Wearing the bright stocking cap in which she painted him, he was a frequent visitor at the shack where he came to bake cakes, a favorite avocation though not always a successful one since he refused to follow recipes. As a man of principles, he died of wounds received in the Spanish Civil War. It is quixotic, contradictory people like Roach and like her later clown friends whom MacIver paints best.

In the early 1930's the artist and her husband moved into a studio in an old house on Macdougal Street, owned by a Mr. Strunsky. The house facade, painted half transparently to reveal the interior of the rooms, is the subject of her *Strunsky House,* done in 1935. Here again MacIver turned in a new direction that contains many of the stylistic innovations which she was to carry further in her mature work. Chief of these is the flat, compartmented design, which reappears in several later cityscapes and in the *Votive Light* series. There is nothing geometrical in this structure; no lines ever meet at an exact right angle and all the boxes and squares are slightly askew as if to avoid any implication that life is orderly. Nevertheless, the sequence and rhythm of rectangles build a half-abstract pattern of great beauty while, in this instance at least, they serve the further purpose of suggesting the multiple relations of life in a city, the mystery of all the strange rooms surrounding the one brightly lit studio which was their home.

Here, too, MacIver began to experiment with soft color areas which blend and sometimes "bleed" into each other. These are partly a pictorial enrichment but they also seem intended to obscure the clear relation of forms and heighten the atmosphere of gentle mystery which pervades so much of her work. And finally, *Strunsky House* is notable because it is one of the first paintings in which the artist devised symbols to identify otherwise puzzling shapes. Her method, which she has used frequently since, is to reduce a familiar object to the fewest lines possible, devoid of all modeling, so that it is quite hard to "read" but, once deciphered, takes on symbolic meaning, a bottle marking one compartment as studio, a standing lamp as someone's more luxurious home and so forth.

Such clues are necessary because MacIver's paintings are never solely abstract or solely pictorial in conception. They always have a poetic motivation which depends as much on subject as on esthetic content. The artist prefers the formal arrangement to speak first, impressing the eye with the sheer beauty of color and design. For this reason the objects must not be recognized too easily. But they must be read eventually or the painting achieves only half its meaning. Her cryptic symbols are one means to this end.

From 1936 to 1939, MacIver was on the Federal Art Project of the WPA. This was a happy and productive time, marked by her first public recognition. Emily Francis had hung her work in group shows at Contemporary Arts from 1933 or 1934, and a few collectors, including Miss Louise Crane and Alfred Barr, had bought paintings at this time or slightly later. In 1935 the Museum of Modern Art purchased her picture, *The Shack,* the first to enter a public collection, but it was not until 1938, three years later, that she had her first one-man exhibition at Marian Willard's East River Gallery.

In 1939 Miss Louise Crane lent MacIver and her husband a little "Conch" house which she owned at Key West, Florida, and there they spent that winter and a good deal of the following year. As always, the new experience found immediate, if oblique, reflection in MacIver's art. She did not paint the Keys themselves but she painted the bright flowers on Ashe Street in a decorative, abstract design that made amusing use of the gaudy polka dot patterns with which local taste adorned the beer cans and other odd containers in which the flowers grew. She also enlarged quite faithfully on canvas the beautiful zigzag pattern of a tent olive shell, which they bought at a local shop. (In spite of its misleading name this is a sea shell, about three inches long, with a luminous brown surface patterned all over with "tents.") Neither of these pictures seems entirely successful, *Ashe Street Blooms* because it relies rather heavily on a conventional kind of decorative abstraction; *Off a Tent Olive Shell* because it relies equally on a natural pattern, insufficiently translated into terms of painting. Both were experiments which she did not pursue further.

On the other hand, *Moonlight,* a nocturnal vision of the interior of their Conch house, has a full measure of MacIver's delicate magic. The distortions, though remotely related to Picasso, flow naturally from the artist's urgent need to communicate the moon's transforming power, its necromancy in changing a familiar scene into a mysterious world where old relations vanish and strange ones take their place. The picture is perhaps her closest approach to expressionism, though of a very personal kind. Like the other Key West canvases it is somewhat apart from the main line of her development.

It is difficult to determine the exact moment at which an artist reaches his full powers. In MacIver's case the year 1940 and the painting *Hopscotch* make a reasonable claim to be the starting point of her artistic maturity. She was back in New York after her Key West experience and seems to have brought to the city a fresh eye and a clearer awareness of her own direction.

Hopscotch is, in many ways, one of her most remarkable accomplishments. The flat, fantastic pattern, somewhat resembling a prehistoric monster consuming numbered chalk squares, is both puzzling and beautiful. As in much of MacIver's best work, one senses first the handsome design and only gradually perceives the poetic motivation. The hopscotch lines are the clue. They lead to a realization that this is pavement, then to the further awareness that this is blistered pavement, not the odd creature of one's first impression. Yet something of that early image lingers, and the mystery of the painting's ultimate meaning grows rather than diminishes. The fragile child's game lying lightly beside the decay of solid asphalt suggests multiple interpretations which are elusive because they are essentially visual, not literary. MacIver achieves here a truly pictorial poetry wrought by a most difficult balance between suggestive design and a concrete image of utmost realism.

A very different picture of the same year, evidence that she was still experimenting, is *The Poet,* a symbolic portrait of Lloyd Frankenberg. Clad in a toga of soft red and blue, his head turns miraculously into the neck of a bottle, from which small bouquets of flowers—budding poems—issue. Such paintings have led several critics to group MacIver with the surrealists, but in this case it seems juster to see a gravely fanciful tribute to her gifted husband. Indeed none of MacIver's work shows more than a tenuous link to the dark probings of orthodox surrealism, and she has never been tempted by that movement's automatism.

While MacIver has occasionally returned to nature for her subjects, the city has been her principal theme from 1940 to the present. Unlike the New York realists, who painted its picturesque aspects, and even more unlike the futurists, who tried to capture its modernity, MacIver's attitude is oblique, poetic, filled with wonder at its beauty and a child-like delight in its small miracles.

Sometimes, though rarely, the artist paints a panoramic portrait of New York, like *The City* of 1941. Here, as in some of her early work, is a youthful world, full of odd little figures, more dolls than people, and a great store of amusing detail. Everything has a kind of story-telling significance. The shop windows can be identified, again through her use of symbols; the blocky pyramids, for instance, are cans and indicate grocery stores. Even the color has this sort of meaning, the darker bands behind the carts and trucks representing the darker color of the streets. Yet it was a subtle eye and a sophisticated hand that fitted all this incredible detail together, like the pieces of an immensely complicated puzzle, to make a flat design that vibrates with a pictorial life of its own.

For the most part, however, MacIver's paintings of the city contain no people and are focused on small, inanimate objects in which she has found an unexpected beauty that often carries with it poetic implications, as in *Hopscotch.* "Quite simple things can lead to discovery," she once wrote in a much-quoted statement for the Museum of Modern Art's *Fourteen Americans* exhibition catalogue. "This is what I would like to do with painting: starting with simple things, to lead the eye by various manipulations of colors, objects and tensions toward a transformation and a reward . . .

"My wish is to make something permanent out of the transitory, by means at once dramatic and colloquial. Certain moments have the gift of revealing the past and foretelling the future. It is these moments that I hope to catch."

Perhaps the key word here is "transformation." In a series of canvases done between 1940 and 1948, MacIver has changed an ashcan, a pushcart, church votive lights, a gas stove, a studio skylight and a battered window shade into images which reward the beholder with a sense of the forgotten beauty in commonplace things. To do this she has used many different means, varying her style widely to fit the mood of each subject. In *Ashcan* and *Skylight* the design is quite abstract, almost geometrical were it not for the irregular color patches of the clinkers which glow like a bouquet in the former, and the ghostly wash which waves behind the rigid grillwork of the latter. At the other extreme are *Fiery Rings* (the stove) and *Window Shade,* which are painted with a meticulous realism. Yet how far from realistic they are in effect. The shade's luminous button glows hypnotically within the rectangular composition and its light is echoed in the bright scratches that mount like the tracks of a mysterious bird.

Somewhere between these stylistic poles are *Pushcart* and the various votive light pictures. The former is dark and rich, more opulent in its alternation of blacks with glowing color than anything the artist had done before. The design is quite abstract, made entirely of stripes, circles, triangles and the simplified ovals of the fruit, its severity relieved only by the long undulating silhouette of the load. Yet every form is recognizable, none entirely arbitrary. Even the kaleidoscopic pattern of reds, purples, blues and greens behind the wheels is, MacIver explains, the colored wrappings from the fruit which the peddlers push between the spokes when business is brisk. Thus, like so much of her work, it has a secondary and warmly human meaning: this has been a good day for the pushcart man.

The several *Votive Lights*—in red, green and blue versions—are also flat, semi-abstract designs, softened here by the flicker of the candles, MacIver's "symbols of constancy." Yet again they are intimately related to the actual votive lights which she has observed near the altars of Catholic churches, even to their ranked arrangement in tin frames and their three colors, which have symbolic meaning in church ritual. For the artist, too, each of these colors gives a quite distinct feeling. It was for this reason primarily that she undertook her different versions.

Comparing these three groups of paintings, which overlap in date, it becomes apparent that MacIver's widely ranging style is dictated not by an esthetic program but by the varied nature of her subjects and her constant aim to reveal both the visual beauty and the human significance of her material in terms best suited to it. Critics have seen influences in her work of artists as far apart as Odilon Redon and Paul Klee. Certainly she is well aware of the great art of past and present and, like virtually every living painter, has felt its impact in a general way. But she quite rightly denies that anyone has been her model or has exerted a decisive influence on her, a fact which seems amply corroborated by her very flexible and personal style.

In the same years (1940–48) that MacIver was painting these canvases of the city, she also turned occasionally to nature. She has an abiding delight in flowers and often renders them quite simply and realistically, as in her *Mountain Laurel,* which has no overtones beyond its own drift-like beauty. At other times her imagination embroiders poetic concepts on natural themes. Her *Fall of Snow* enlarges the flakes to crystals, sees them shining bright with color against the sky and melting silently into the city's lilac darkness below. The spring buds in *Tree* are like candles tipping the branches. Many of these subjects were observed in the city and gain a special poignance by contrast with the surrounding concrete and steel. Her *Tree* was actually a low bush behind an iron fence near 61 Perry Street, which has been her home since 1942. But in the painting both railing and shrub have grown in strength and become a subtle opposition of forces. Similarly, in *Puddle,* the fallen twig of a Ginkgo tree lies like a frail skeleton in a rain pool cradled by the cracked city pavement.

How MacIver conceives these memorable images is a question she finds difficult to answer. In some cases they are the result of many experiences which gradually build up and enrich each other until they demand pictorial expression. Thus she has long loved pushcarts and old window shades and no one of either was the fuse that ignited those pictures. More often, however, a single, specific sight moves her with sudden force; the tree was a real one, the Ginkgo leaves in the rain compelled her to stop and make a sketch of the way a dark stain spread around them on the pavement. This does not mean that the painting which grows from such an experience is related only to the initial revelation; it still draws on other recollections which alter and nourish it. But it may explain why certain of MacIver's canvases have so immediate and urgent an impact, still preserving through their mutations the excitement of the artist's first conception.

Ever since she was a child MacIver has loved the circus and especially clowns. At about this time she made the acquaintance of two who were the inspiration for several of her most notable pictures. *Jimmy Savo* is certainly one of the best in MacIver's gallery of intimate portraits. The eloquent hands, the wistful face with its wide, almost feminine mouth (very much like MacIver's own) are in subtle contrast to the gaping collar, the fringe of hair and battered hat. This is the kind of opposition, sensitive and understated, that MacIver achieved in *Tree* and *Hopscotch,* and it makes the picture much more than a likeness. Indeed it was painted from a quick sketch done at a night club where Savo was appearing, aided only by a pose of about an hour at the studio when nearly finished. Like many of her best portraits it has an introspective quality emphasized by the slightly blurred features and the wide, unseeing eyes.

In the same year, 1944, MacIver painted an equally moving portrait of *Jimmy Savo's Shoes,* immensely long in relation to his slight form and so expressive that they seem to evoke his complete personality. She enjoys telling how she rushed them home in a taxi between performances, since they were his only pair, and of the great variety of things she found stuffing the toes. "Really, dear," said Savo when she mentioned it to him, "I haven't been in there recently myself."

The other clown whom MacIver admires greatly is Emmett Kelly at the Ringling Brothers and Barnum & Bailey Circus. Like Savo, he posed only briefly for his portrait, this time backstage with a giraffe peering over the canvas dressing room wall and dropping shreds of hay on her as she worked. But the monumental likeness which resulted is certainly one of the fine American portraits of our day. Kelly's principal departure from conventional clown makeup, *The New Yorker* once reported, "was his facial arrangement, which revolved around an expression so bedraggled and hopeless as to wring sympathy from a Hottentot. The line between horror and humor," it added, "is immeasurably thin and mysterious." It is this expression and this delicate balance which the artist has succeeded in transferring to canvas. The tattered clothes and the slash of a mouth weigh precisely against the sad eyes, again blurred and sightless, and the dispirited sag of the whole figure to the left. Withal, a certain bigness, vast simplicity and tender warmth make it a memorable image.

In one of his most famous acts Kelly sits in the center ring of the huge arena entirely alone—dwarfed, pathetic and ridiculous. This is the moment MacIver chose for her other Kelly painting, called *Circus*. Here, however, the figure is shadowy and of secondary importance. The artist's interest seems more deeply engaged in the whole scene and in the variety of puzzling shapes which she can devise from circus gear. Two particularly baffling ones are the eerie face at the lower right and the odd machine at the lower left. The former, she explains, is a disembodied sample of clown makeup, the latter a bobbing duck cart used by the clowns.

MacIver's material success grew rapidly during this period. In 1940 Pierre Matisse became her dealer and has given her a series of one-man exhibitions. In 1941 the Museum of Modern Art commissioned her to do the "sets" for four Coffee Concerts in the auditorium. These were drawn in pastel on black paper, then made into colored slides and projected on a screen behind the performers. The designs were linear, bright in color and made a strikingly effective use of Voodoo symbols, gay South American motifs and the like.

As MacIver's reputation grew she received a number of commercial commissions. Illustrations for an article in *Town and Country* in 1945 led to two cover designs for the same magazine and later a cover for *Fortune*. She has also done several book jackets, a poster for the National Foundation for Infantile Paralysis and some six Christmas cards. She has designed a "Hopscotch" rug (on which the game can actually be played), the title page for a limited edition of Robert Frost's *Steeple Bush* and a series of window backdrops on musical themes for Bergdorf Goodman. Her most ambitious projects have been two mural commissions, one for the S.S. *Argentina* in 1947; the other, four panels for American Export Line ships, done the following year. The latter are supremely deft and gay—quite without the graver implications of her easel painting. Bottles, toys, marine forms, tropical flora and fauna are scattered lightly over the long narrow canvases. Everything either floats or swims or sways and the apparently casual designs are knowingly handled to create a rhythmical motion as animated as dancing waves.

In 1948 MacIver, with her husband, made her first trip to Europe. They spent about two weeks in Paris, going to the circus, galleries and museums, where the artist distributed her admiration impartially, claiming no favorites among the old masters. From Paris they went, via Provence and Antibes, to Italy for about a month. There they stayed principally at Rome, Naples, Florence and Venice with shorter visits to the hill towns and a call on Jimmy Savo and his wife Tina, whose father had given her a small castle (because as a girl she had always wanted to live in one). The last leg of their trip took them to London, Ireland and Scotland.

MacIver did no painting in Europe but she stored up a great many impressions by means of the quick sketches which she habitually uses to fix an idea. Quite accurately she calls these "scrawls"—a few pencil lines which do no more than indicate the placing of the main masses and the principal lines of motion. Sometimes they are filled in with crayon or watercolor. More often she uses rapidly pencilled color notes.

In 1949, the year after her return, MacIver painted furiously, turning out more and larger canvases than she had ever done in a like period. These were mostly the fruit of her trip: *Cathedral, Coal and Wood, Paris, The Fratellini, Venice, Naples Aquarium* and, in 1950, *Dublin and Environs*. The European experience not only stimulated her activity; it also affected her in other ways. As a group these pictures are not only bigger in size but seem bolder in conception and design, more varied in color, more self-assured and perhaps less sensitive than her earlier work—at least less the "shy, tiptoe art," to borrow James Soby's apt phrase, of paintings like *Hopscotch* and *Window Shade*. MacIver later returned partially to her earlier direction, but for the moment she gave herself completely to the vivid impressions of a traveller in a foreign land.

Many of these big canvases are extremely handsome in color and design. The sweeping panorama of *Venice* with its multi-hued sail in the foreground, its iridescent water and its buildings rising from the sea like a shining vision, is perhaps the most sensuously beautiful picture she has ever painted. *Cathedral,* inspired by a visit to Chartres, plays the rich colors of stained glass against mossy gray stone in an abstract design that suggests the vertiginous feeling of looking upward at its soaring height. In *Naples Aquarium* there is a new luminosity, achieved partly by the contrast of the dark setting with the brilliant sea anemones, partly by her use of color which "bleeds" slightly along the strange creatures' edges, as if they were actually glowing.

Clowns have always drawn MacIver like a magnet and in Paris she and Lloyd Frankenberg spent many evenings at the Cirque Medrano, which is the setting for *The Fratellini*. It was "a little red plush place," explaining the pervading color of the picture. While she has not attempted to characterize the two great clowns as profoundly as Savo or Kelly, she has adroitly suggested their stage personalities by painting François ("the elegant type") as a delicately posed triangle, Albert ("the coarse type") as a loosely flapping apparition with the sequin on his eyelid glowing as magically as the button in *Window Shade*.

Most of this group are rather realistic, or at least quite easily deciphered, but in one of her last European paintings, MacIver returned to a more abstract and symbolic style. *Dublin and Environs* requires study and even some help from the artist before one can identify the dominant cross as stone walls, the streak of green as the color of fields (also needed, she explains, to pull against the sway of the cross), the bottle as "Paddy's Whisky," the shapes at the lower right as "fish or maybe potatoes." The numerous circles grew from the prevalence of that form in Irish architecture and other arts, including the cakes with mushroom decorations which fascinated her.

Since the European pictures MacIver has returned to her old themes, often carrying into them, however, the richness and opulent color of *Venice* and *Cathedral*. It is as if her eye now yearned for purely visual beauty more than for the wistful or poignant contrasts that she sought before. The minutiae of the city that have recently appealed to her have not been battered window shades and cracked pavements, but the rainbow hues of an oil slick, the fiery lights reflected from raindrops on a fire escape or on the windshield of a taxi. In her new pursuit she has gained a technical skill in capturing effects of sparkle and iridescence, which is at times almost incredible.

Oil Slick, the first of two pictures on that theme, introduces a new technical device which the artist has found useful in other recent paintings. The dark center, from which the oil spreads, is glazed to a rich transparency. But the jagged rings of bright color that spread out from it are painted very drily and have a surface almost like pastel. The center, she explains, is a thing you can stare at fixedly but the iridescence is best seen with a light glance, obliquely, in passing. Nevertheless she did not use the same method in the second picture, *Oil Splatters and Leaves,* which is glazed throughout and hence somewhat richer. The two differ in other ways. The former has a half symbolic feeling, perhaps because of the monumental way in which it spreads its enlarged design across the whole canvas. The latter is more decorative in its undulating rhythm, more poetic in its juxtaposition of leaves and stains.

No one but a Japanese artist has painted rain so successfully as MacIver. In the picture titled after a line of poetry by E. E. Cummings, *"the streets turn young with rain,"* it falls with the impetuous freshness of a spring shower. In her two *Fire Escape* paintings it slants through the night with a rush of falling water that is almost audible. The simple rectangular design of the latter recalls earlier work, like *Window Shade,* but here it is illuminated not by a single glowing button but by a whole string of jewel-like drops reflecting with various brilliance the light from the studio hall. Rain reflections are carried even further in *Taxi,* certainly one of her most imaginative works. The lower three-fourths of the canvas are blue darkness, empty except for a pale glow from the side window and the curling smoke of two cigarettes. But the streaming windshield is like a display of fireworks, an iridescent blaze of yellows, greens, reds and blues from refracted lamps and neon signs.

MacIver's growing interest in luminous color, in glowing and sparkling light, is apparent in many other subjects beside her city themes. In this respect, *Circus* of 1950 makes an illuminating contrast to *Circus* of 1947. No clown, indeed no recognizable figure appears in the later picture, which is scarcely more than two circles of brightly colored specks, a little difficult to interpret until one realizes that these are spotlights trained on the distant audience and picking out their multi-hued costumes.

In her recent nature subjects, too, a similar interest is evident. No longer are her trees and flowers in conflict with the city; MacIver has gone to the country to find them in their more luxuriant state and has painted them with quite unreal luminosity. Her *Hyacinth Bulbs* gleam phosphorescently against their dark background, which was not intended, the artist says, to represent night so much as to suggest, by contrast, the sudden speed with which the flowers emerge from their rock-like sheaths. The lily-of-the-valley in *Early* shines like the hyacinth bulbs, and the red maws of the young robins radiate a red glow into the darkness around them. Only in *Bamboo,* a glimpse of spring foliage seen through the slatted window shade of her bedroom, has she returned to city-bound nature, but even here the feeling is gently lyrical, a study in harmony rather than contrasts.

MacIver has continued to paint occasional portraits. Among these her likeness of their poet friend, E. E. Cummings, stands out as a sensitive *tour de force.* Cummings posed for her twice but she was not satisfied with the result and did the present version without a sitter. Here the figure is drawn entirely in pencil over the partly wet paint of the background, so that some of the lines are lightly incised in the pigment. Around the delicately drawn head and hand she has pencilled fragmentary quotations from his poems, which set the mood for the whole picture. "Spring is like a perhaps hand (which comes carefully out of Nowhere) arranging" is like Cummings' own disembodied hand, while MacIver's surface of cool greens, yellow-greens and pinks is an echo of "the sky was can dy lu/minous edible . . ." Like many of her recent things, this one is painted rather thinly over a dark ground, which gives a surprising richness to the pale hues on top.

One of the last canvases to leave MacIver's easel is a new panorama of the city at night which seems to combine the best qualities of both her early and late work. Below a frieze of shadowy, darkened skyscrapers she has drawn a long line of characteristic symbols: a leaf, a key, a neon lobster sign, a shoe, a hat. Isolated in the right foreground, a strange, caterpillar-like object casts a pale yellow glow into the surrounding darkness. It turns out to be the kiosk of the Christopher Street subway station, and the pattern of glowing colored glass at the left comes from the same source. In its sensitive restraint and its cryptic symbols of absent humanity, *New York* has all MacIver's old poetic feeling; in its luminosity, its boldly unconventional design and its immense technical skill it is beyond anything she could have done before.

Also fresh from her easel, indeed still unfinished when this was written, is an extraordinarily different picture called *Les Baux*, her romantic reconstruction of the wild village of that name cut into the bauxite cliffs near Nîmes in southern France. Once a headquarters of Provençal poetry, site of a medieval court of love, it is now a ghostly village of caves and rocks which felt to the artist like moonlight, even on a summer afternoon. To capture its strange unreality she has painted an abstract image of fantastic crystalline forms and great shafts of light, rich in shifting colors despite the predominantly blue tonality. Except for its luminous opulence it marks a departure from anything she has yet attempted.

Looking at *Les Baux* and *New York,* so completely unlike in spite of the fact that they were done within a few months of each other, one is struck again by Mac-Iver's absolute indifference to established styles and movements. Her persistent search for a visual beauty wedded inseparably to the mood of each changing subject continues to create unpredictable solutions as endlessly fresh and perceiving as her own poetic eye. In terms of that search her artistic development has been supremely consistent, for her images enter ever more deeply into one's consciousness, dissolving the film of stale custom and bestowing a new awareness of the world's bright miracles.

Richard S. Field

from **Jasper Johns: Prints 1960-1970**

Coat Hanger is the archetypical example of the artist's unexpected use of a common object. A decade ago it was impossible to "see" this image as anything but a portrait of a coat hanger. To accept such a lowly subject became merely a matter of extending one's tolerance—as it has since the Dutch began genre painting or Daumier and Degas went into the streets for their subjects. Just as acceptable were Leo Steinberg's sympathetic feelings of emptiness, loss, abandonment, or dehumanization in this common object. We are indeed free to associate on the meaning of the coat hanger—that it is empty, that like much of Johns's work, it seems to lack some human presence—but that is to become concerned with any image of a coat hanger and not specifically this one. For example, the same "content" could then be attributed to *Coat Hanger II*, but it would not serve to differentiate our experience of the artist's changing activity.

Criticism today has despaired of such sentimentalism and would rather examine the impersonal manipulations of the language of art. It is just that the coat hanger is such a well-known object that makes it effective—not as an overlooked object of beauty, but as a unit of discrete length, scale, and feel. By his new use of the coat hanger, Johns demonstrates some fundamentals of how we organize vision in looking at works of art. What seems to be a coat hanger resisting all explanation turns out to be an object that modifies the entire work of art. It transforms or translates the orderly but totally suspended surface of strokes into a "background"—or into a context. The measurability of the hanger imparts scale to and establishes our distance from the picture plane; it also gives a sense of scale and limited space to the background. Further ambiguity results from the similar graphic vocabulary used for both hanger and ground; yet the hanger is total illusion, the ground total drawing. The spectator historically and instantaneously shifts his attention from object as subject, to object as unit of scale and space, to object as pure abstract drawing.

In the second state, *Coat Hanger II,* the hanger is changed to a reserved white shape and is not nearly so illusionistically rendered as before. The background, too, is treated more broadly. In spite of the fact that the hanger is thrown into greater pictorial relief against the dark gray, it is simultaneously a more integral part of the ground because of the drawing procedure. The painting, *Coat Hanger* of 1959, does not possess this ambiguity but stresses the interaction between "real" hanger (an actual wire hanger is hung on a knob that projects from the canvas) and "real" painting. The absence of all tangible space in the lithographs naturally leads to new solutions to problems first posed in painting.

The two states (in classical printmaking terms) of *Coat Hanger* are the first manifestations of Johns's discovery of a medium in which he can "have his cake and eat it too." He can transform an image and preserve the original, and the original may even bear traces of having been transformed. To paraphrase the artist's own words, the image may not only be changed, but it can remember itself and remember itself being changed.

Flag I, II, and *III* combine more explicitly the transformations of the *Coat Hanger.* Each image is changed through the technique involved—wash, crayon, and scraping; each print is modulated by the size and color of the paper as well as the tone of the printing ink. The process is practically an illustration in printmaking of Johns's own prescription:

> *Take an object.*
> *Do something to it.*
> *Do something else to it.*
> *"   "   "   "   "*

Take a canvas.
Put a mark on it.
Put another mark on it.
    "   "   "   "   "

Johns, 1965, p. 192

Flag I is built up of dense black tusche strokes. The organization of this activity only reflects the flag pattern; even the stars are hard to pick out. Because Johns started with a two-dimensional idea, he discovered the possibility of working away from rather than toward an image. The second state, *Flag II,* is deliberately amorphous. Many spaces have been filled in, the values of figure and ground have been pulled together, and larger margins float the image in an atmosphere of uncertainty: the observer must seek to decipher the image. *Flag III* is once more printed in a darker tone on a white ground, but the gray ink is shot with white scratchings which parallel the rhythms of the stripes. The ground of the paper appears to weave in and out of the image, changing our focus one more time. These variations pose the formal problem of maintaining the sense of the picture plane while increasing the pictorial activity. This successive intensification of graphic activity from state to state anticipates the change that occurred in the group of lithographs Johns undertook in 1962.

If the works of 1960 are confined to draftsmanship and seem to be reworkings of drawings, *Painting with Two Balls I* indicates by its title a total departure. It is called "Painting" precisely because the drawing which serves as the intermediary is so titled (it in turn is based on a painting of 1960). Johns has now turned to transforming paintings into lithographs. Accordingly, his techniques are adjusted and expanded. No subsequent works on stone return to the simplicity of 1960 with the single and significant exception of the *Alphabet* of 1968–69, a lithograph essentially in black crayon.

In *Painting with Two Balls I,* color makes its first appearance; with it, there is also the suggestion of a painterly surface achieved through the overlapping brushed-on tusche (in *Flag I* the strokes were experienced rather separately). Over other areas the flat side of the crayon creates tonal planes. For all these painterly qualities, the lithograph differs fundamentally from its prototype in oil, setting up a tension within the artist's own work. After all, the illusion of a painting (i.e., the lithograph) is quite different from the experience of the original painting. In the oil version, the space opened by the balls is finite and tangible compared to the indefinite space of the opening depicted in the lithograph. The painting, with its tactile surface, keeps limiting the viewer's perceptions of depth and projection, while the lithograph, in spite of the spectator's awareness of the flatness of the paper, exploits the ambiguities of unlimited space.

This transformation, a property of lithography, compresses plasticity and expands illusion. Changes that occur when a painting is "repeated" on stone may be ascribed to the interaction of the idea and the medium. For example, the flatness of the paper in both drawing and lithograph may have suggested the addition of the scribbled lines; or, conversely, the need to control the space may have necessitated the addition of the lines! They convey a richer pictorialism and serve to set off the action of the balls which divide two of the three color sections. It is this representation which justifies the application of the title "Painting" to the lithograph. The same word appears in the painted version as well as on the stone itself, and even proves its validity by being partially "painted over."

When the lithograph itself is transformed, as in the monochromatic *Painting with Two Balls II,* the tension between works within the artist's *oeuvre* is carried to another level. Although this version is more unified and mysterious than the previous ones, the changes nevertheless call into question the observer's sensibility. For more often than not, he feels indifferent to such changes. If a monochrome had been transformed into a color image, his attitude might be different. In that case there would be an increase in emotional content. Perhaps the change to monochrome, which Johns favors, reflects a cooling off of content, providing a greater opportunity for spectator participation.

The same test of indifference may be felt in the lithographs *False Start I* and *II.* Johns points out something of this by labeling the colors indifferently, and doubly so: not only is a red patch labeled BLUE, but the word BLUE might be colored yellow. The double contradiction is employed only in the center where pictorial action in a Cubist or Abstract Expressionist canvas is the greatest. False expectations (a "false start") are created by the use of a stencil whose style is inextricably associated with "contents" (the content of a labeled crate is transferred to the "content" of a work of art). Somehow these contradictions do not disturb. At first they are not seen, and when perceived they are accepted as two or three separate systems of perceptions. It does not matter if the word BLUE is stenciled in yellow; the word "glass" does not have to be made out of glass to be meaningful in a given context. More shocking is the realization that the label BLUE does not truthfully reveal the nature of the red beneath. It speaks only about itself, and like the coat hanger, has very definite formal purposes, namely, those of scale and plane. We do not feel compelled or even able to bridge the gap between the communications systems of labels and paint strokes. We are led to understand that art produces its own field of acceptance and that we are all too ready to believe—or to refuse to question—the ingredients of a work of art.

Device of 1962 also derives from a drawing and a painting. On the highest metaphorical plane this image, and even *False Start,* could be viewed as an attempt to order an unorganized or chthonic chaos. If in these works, order is suggested although not fully achieved, they represent Johns's continued efforts to transform the "limitless arena" of Abstract Expressionist space into something conceptually controlled and measurable.

The textures of the lithograph were determined by chance physical and chemical reactions as the ink lay on the stone. But the device pictured in this work is apparently responsible for the semicircles in the same way that the two balls may be credited for the apparent wedge in *Painting with Two Balls.* In the paintings these were literal facts, but the lithographs are sharp reminders that real effects are not caused by illusionistic devices. Toby Mussman has commented about the implied opposition of concept and object:

> *A circle can never be drawn as perfectly true as the conceptual one, as the one which is defined mathematically by πr, Jasper Johns played out [this] paradox*

when he made a circle absurd (concrete) in Device Circle *by painting it literally within its definition.*

                                                        In Battcock, 1968, p. 248

As a further irony, the words inscribed on the stone take on an illusionistic field of their own, for they describe something that at best happened only in the preparation of the stone, but surely not in the inking or printing of it. *Hand* of 1963 poses a more deceptive treatment of a similar situation. The action of the hands was produced by smearing the stone, not by imprinting moving hands slippery with oil or soap! Johns has remarked that he is fascinated by the discrete separation of actions entailed in printmaking: *Hand* illustrates how this separation of actions may produce effects which tend to blur their original orderliness. By contrasting the observer's experience with pictorial devices, Johns is constantly questioning the nature of art and how its language works.

Red, Yellow, Blue is a lithograph of 1962–63, modestly printed in black and white (with a gray line); it may well be an allegory, more direct than heretofore, on the activity of the artist. The surface shows the workings of the painter's brush and ends with the brush painting itself. Like many paintings and several prints of the early Sixties, *Red, Yellow, Blue* is organized into three horizontal bands corresponding to the three primary colors of both art and reality. We experience these bands as planar divisions, as compositional devices rather than color, but as the figure of speech would have it, our perception of each band is "colored" by what we associate with it, namely, the words. Johns includes the horizontal and vertical, which are fundamental to easel painting; the brush, which is the perpetrator of illusion; and the three colors, which are the tools of painting itself. The vertical division also acts as a folding axis along which the mirrored letters are arranged. Johns is "using" color, bending it in fact, as Rosalind Krauss has pointed out, in a totally new manner. Yet it could refer, among other things, to the traditional view of art as a reflecting medium in which an objective situation is fixed on canvas. Not only is the reflection of the letters imperfect, but the slight tendency to read the delineation as a possible fold flaws the picture plane. It is amazing to discover so much allusionistic richness in so simple and so offhand a work.

Virtually all the lithographs of 1962 deal with and question certain kinds of activity. For example, the "drawing" that spreads across the "painted" surface of *Painting with Two Balls I* and *II* is wedged asunder by the two balls. These actions are a wry parody of the sexual and egotistical aspects of action painting (Abstract Expressionism); as well, they are Johns's own act of puncturing the illusionism of that kind of painting. The splashy effects of *False Start* are similarly challenged and controlled by a kind of false information which somehow mocks the spectator's willingness to swallow any kind of conceit so long as it is done in the name of art. *Device* and *Hand* carry the illusion of action even further but simultaneously imply a sense of control and order. *Red, Yellow, Blue* adds a modest compendium of materials and devices to the language of art.

The labels RED, YELLOW, and BLUE in the 1963 lithograph, *Hatteras,* have become partially obscured by the large "device circle," now created by the imprint of the artist's own hand and arm rather than drawn by a stick. Something new, already announced by *Hand* and the diminutive *Red, Yellow, Blue,* is entering Johns's work at this point, namely, a willingness to broaden his content to include both personal and historical references.

Allusion and contrast abound in *Hatteras:* Vitruvius' and Leonardo's theories of proportion are compared to the ruler which provides tangible measurement at the lithograph's bottom edge; Hart Crane's poem, *The Bridge,* is the known "inspiration" for Johns's own painting *Periscope,* the prototype for *Hatteras;* and the luminous circle with a revolving hand seems to evoke the Cape Hatteras lighthouse as well as Johns's lithograph, *Device.* There are cross-references between various kinds of measurements, such as the form of the circle and the cycle of the spectrum (red, yellow, blue). Similarly the illusion of movement in the circle is paraphrased by the illusion of color. Other traces of the artist's personal feelings or memories occur in the metamorphosed "footprint" (Frank O'Hara?) and in his own "handwriting," scribbles of crayon and tusche meandering from the right edge. But both are denied in some way —the footprint is only an abstract form while the scribbles are measured by the scale of the ruler which proceeds in the same right-to-left direction. Then there are layers of obscuring: an implied process such as the arc of the circle smudges or hides the letters; the tusche dissolves the crayon at the lower right. Yet, in typical Johns fashion, these activities, taking place on such disparate levels of meaning and vision, are all locked onto the essentially flat surface of the lithograph.

Target with Four Faces (1955) by Jasper Johns. Encaustic on newspaper on canvas, 26 x 26″; surmounted by 4 plaster faces in a wooden frame 3 3/4 x 26″ with hinged front. Collection, The Museum of Modern Art, New York. Gift of Mr. and Mrs. Robert C. Scull.

Oliver W. Larkin

American Self-Portrait

Ten years after their first visit to Middletown the Lynds re-examined it. To be sure, the motion-picture palaces were bigger now but their offerings had not changed; the citizen was still afraid of sharp thinking, still relied on "reluctant adaptation" to new forces. Yet fifty-nine out of a hundred Middletowners voted the New Deal in 1936; Federal funds built a swimming pool and a park there, and an Art Building to house the local collections; and something like a local school of painting was to be discerned in the community.

The arts were finding deeper roots in native soil when Holger Cahill reviewed a year of Federal Art in 1936. Nearly four hundred and fifty murals had been completed for schools, armories, post offices, city halls, prisons, and hospitals; in twenty-five states the Index of American Design was in action; half a million Southerners had visited nineteen community art centers, and many were enrolled in classes where painting, sculpture, and the handicrafts were taught. Beyond statistics Cahill saw the beginning of the end of that aloofness between artist and community which had plagued the nation's culture; his essay and the exhibition at the Museum of Modern Art were entitled "New Horizons in American Art."

The painter viewed those horizons for the most part not as a tourist in search of a picturesque motive but as an artist born and bred into the ways of a region. Sheldon Cheney remarked that one had to travel far in the nineteen thirties to understand American paintings; and at the close of the decade Roland McKinney covered three million square miles to find representative work for the San Francisco Fair, while a network of regional juries sifted twenty-five thousand local offerings for the rival exhibition in New York, a procedure which the *Times* criticized as "dangerously democratic." The American scene was being portrayed in terms evasively academic and starkly modern; in terms of nature alone or nature as the focus of man's work and recreation; in the print, the small panel, and the enormous mural, in modest pride and in nationalistic swagger.

A tour through the American scene, in other words, was a journey through more than half a century of painting methods. Neat and close-mouthed were Paul Sample's maple sugar scenes from Vermont with spare tree branches against snow and fresh colors he had learned from Jonas Lie. "Superclarity" was the word for Luigi Lucioni when he painted the brilliant greens of those same pastures and woods in summer in all their sharpness of detail; the Connecticut anecdotes of Lauren Ford were garrulous in the manner of Gothic illuminations. Thomas W. Nason and John J. Lankes described the New England countryside in superb woodcuts.

The great red barns of the Illinois wheat country and the mounds of yellow grain were painted with a metallic prettiness by Dale Nichols against skies which were too blue, while Aaron Bohrod more sensitively explored Chicago suburbs where a woman waited for a train. With rude dynamics and a bold brush, Joe Jones of St. Louis recorded the work rhythms of wheat farmers. As the traveler drove through the green-yellow fields of Minnesota, with red silos, golden haystacks, and white farms scattered over the rolling earth under vast and thunder-heavy skies, it seemed as though nature were imitating the water colors of Adolf Dehn.

There was something of Dehn's breadth in the landscape of John Steuart Curry, whose father had been a stockman in Dunavant and whose *Baptism in Kansas* was one of the first experiments of the new regionalism. Curry in 1928 grouped Signorelli nudes around a circular bathing pool; a few months later, the pool became a wooden tank and the figures inside it a Baptist preacher and a country girl. From that moment, although he was to paint circus acrobats and the epic of John Brown, he was best known for canvases interpreting, as he said, the struggle of man with nature—line storms, floods, and tornadoes. That struggle took place in a fertile country whose hills and farms Curry rendered with more sympathetic warmth than firm underlying form. He could design with occasional strength, as he did in *Roadworkers' Camp* of 1929 (Univ. of Neb., Lincoln), but his *Mother and Father* of that year had less vitality than Ralph Earl's portrait of the colonial Ellsworths, which it oddly resembled with its two figures seated beside a window from which barn, silo, and windmill were to be seen.

The Southwest demanded a more muscular treatment, and received it in Boardman Robinson's lithographs of Colorado and in those of Adolf Dehn. An impeccable craftsmanship modeled the flanks of New Mexico hills in Peter Hurd's paintings and·drew the cowboys raising dust in rodeos under a glittering June sky; Ward Lockwood, on the other hand, could find nothing more personal than a variant of Marin's symbols for the shapes of earth which one saw so clearly at far distances in the atmosphere of this country. Perhaps Orozco suggested to Jerry Bywaters how the shapes of cactus could be made to writhe against Texas cliffs, and there was more than a hint of Maxfield Parrish in Maynard Dixon's desert scenes in southern Nevada, Arizona, and California, the pink-orange lights and intense blue shadows of his naked lava ridges no more incredible than reality itself but seen with an eye for the obvious. Alexandre Hogue painted the Texas panhandle, the dunes ridged by the dry wind where starving cattle left their tracks, the abandoned windmill, the sand heaped on railway tracks, the whole anatomy of the Dust Bowl exposed with a surgeon's scalpel.

The camera challenged the brush in this western record; and what painter could match the desolation of Paul Strand's photograph of a ghost town, *Red River,* in 1930, or in the next year his *Ranchos de Taos Church* whose adobe planes had been molded by Indian hands before the sunlight and shadow added their subtle interplay with volumes? Strand believed with Thoreau that "you cannot say more than you see," and Strand's vision penetrated the picturesque to disclose the mind and the life of those who fashioned the terraced pueblos and the mining towns of the Southwest.

The great desert skies with clouds piling up in them were photographed by Ansel Adams, and his study of Laguna Pueblo and of an old woman at Coyote in New Mexico were "straight" photography at its most brilliant and most lucid. Before Edward Weston made his series at Oceano, California, in the thirties, his camera work in Mexico had been a significant part of the Renaissance there; into his *Death Valley* went rhythms of incredible beauty which wind had sculptured in sand; and Weston's eye discovered the very pattern of desolation in a few white scratches and blisters on the side of an automobile abandoned on the Mojave Desert.

Artists in the South could face realities or sentimentalize them. In the untidy suburbs of Washington Nicolai Cicovsky found red cliffs, a glimpse of the Potomac, and a brick carrier, and painted them with harsh and lively simplifications. The most prominent object in Lamar Dodd's view of Athens, Georgia, was a railway embankment cutting like a knife across its foreground. Alexander Brook's *Family Unit* was a Negro group standing before their small cabin with its enclosing fence, a quiet canvas of low browns and grays brushed with unsentimental simplicity. Both strength and spontaneity were in the studies which Arnold Blanch made in the swamps of the Carolina low country and the Georgia jungle, loose juxtapositions of Negro shacks with brackish yellow streams, the rusty brown earth, the barbed wire fence, and the spindly black children whose poverty had shocked this artist from Minnesota. For Hobson Pittman the deep South with its high-ceilinged plantation houses was a dream in vague colors and evanescent forms where moonlight shone through translucent walls and the wraiths of ante bellum ladies sat in the ghosts of rocking chairs.

Among the most conspicuous of the painters of the American scene were Thomas Benton and Grant Wood. They owed their prominence in part to Thomas Craven, who called the former the "foremost exponent of the multifarious operations of American life"; the latter, Copley's superior in design and in subtlety of characterization. Benton of Missouri, truculent and vocal, had little in common with the plodding and unpretentious man from Cedar Rapids, Iowa; yet both artists had sown wild oats in Montparnasse: Benton's synchromist moments produced bulging half-abstract nudes, and Iowa neighbors were puzzled for a time with Wood's effort to translate music into concentric circles of bright color.

Both men renounced these earlier indiscretions. Before the Federation of Arts in 1932 Benton declared that "no American art can come to those who do not live an American life, who do not have an American psychology, and who cannot find in America justification of their lives." In a pamphlet of 1935 Grant Wood more temperately argued that each section of the land had a personality of its own, that there was less temptation in the country regions for art to imitate art; without being dogmatic or sentimental, Wood recommended the common-sense utilization by the artist of those native materials which he knew best.

Benton's Americans, "living an American life," were to be seen on walls and in easel paintings. His Negro preachers and gamblers, cowboys and dancing Indians, racketeers, crooners, and strip teasers writhed and pranced in panels whose unity was a unity of the emphatic: the repeated serpentine contour, the balancing of one vortex of energy against another, the strident color oppositions, the modeling which emphasized bulging muscles, the elongated figures which looked like people seen from the side on motion-picture screens. His smoke plumes, saloon fronts, overalls, and flivvers all seemed to be made of the same material, and this man who despised formula had found a means of wrenching the observer from one episode to another which was itself a formula.

Grant Wood never tried, as Benton did, to sketch the nation as a whole. From Iowa towns and countryside came his *American Gothic* (Chicago Art Inst.) and *Dinner for Threshers*. The spongelike trees of his landscape he had borrowed from his mother's china plates; the patient procedure of building a glassy-smooth paint structure with layers of glaze he owed to his study of Dutch and Flemish primitives. If his faces looked rather stony and his rounded hills monotonous and hard, Iowans explained that these qualities were indigenous ones in a country where a hen's shadow at noon fell sharp as a cut silhouette on the barnyard. If *Dinner for Threshers* recalled *Last Suppers,* the row of backs with crossed suspenders was nonetheless a local phenomenon. And the satire of his *Daughters of Revolution* became effective through the painter's refusal to be more than mildly resentful.

The artists who drew the American city at full length in these years did not share Benton's scorn for it as a "coffin for living thinking." To Ralston Crawford the engineering of its bridges offered new sensations of movement and perspective to be distilled in a few thrusting dark shapes and austere patterns; to Louis Lozowick the clustered stacks of Manhattan were knife-edged and rich in detail as they stood against storm clouds in his lithographs. Francis Speight painted train yards in winter, and Burchfield made use of his dark palette to convey the monumentality of a drawbridge.

Ernest Fiene was occupied for several years with his series of eighteen city paintings; they were movements of a well-orchestrated suite; and although one of them was called *Nocturne* it suggested Copland rather than Chopin. Fiene knew his Manhattan as thoroughly as Daumier knew his Paris and he painted its demolitions, its sudden exposure of bedroom wallpaper, the forlorn masses of its half-dismantled buildings. His bold colors and hard contours clothed his affection for the play of weather and season over the skyscrapers, the white isolation of Washington's statue under the arc lamps in Union Square.

The city, however, is the people, as Henry Churchill reminds us, and most of the city paintings swarmed with them. As a visitor to Wilson, North Carolina, Lawrence Beall Smith found humor in Negro children lounging in their best dresses before a rundown brick corner store; as a man who intimately knew southern towns, Robert Gwathmey massed the roofs of Negro cottages to form dense walls of segregation and placed the same children in his dark and narrow spaces. In the North the city painters were now harsh and now indulgent: Louis Guglielmi carved an opening in a brick wall to show a relief client being bulldozed by an official, while a man and his wife bleakly pushed their groceries home in a gocart; out of "small truths" and an affection for familiar places Louis Bouché painted his *Barber Shop* with its tin ceiling, tiled floor, and polished white cuspidors; out of his distaste for false Bohemia, Paul Cadmus made his Greenwich Village cafeteria as meticulous as a Crivelli in its cruel itemizations of drunks and blowsy women. In *Billiards at Julian's,* Joseph de Martini made much of the brilliant green table under garish light, as Van Gogh had done at Arles (Boston Mus. Fine Arts).

"Well-bred people are no fun to paint," said Reginald Marsh, and they were conspicuously absent from his canvases. He had tried many subjects and many media; he had been a pupil of Sloan and a parlor socialist, a cartoonist and a scene designer, an illustrator of *The New Yorker* and a technical experimentalist with Kenneth Miller and Thomas Benton. Now he had his own way of manipulating tempera, a medium which had built the closed forms and clean depths of Italian painting. In the relatively simple spaces of his *High Yaller* he modeled coherently, but the line of derelicts in his *Holy Name Mission* was a dingy mass of undistinguishable shapes. Plump bathers tossed in air or massed crowds before a Coney Island sideshow called for a baroque master's skill with a complex interlocking movement. Too often the dynamism of Marsh failed to "jell," his whirling merry-go-rounds stalled, and his massed sunbathers became a lumpy swarm of breasts, rumps, and legs. Into the browns and grays of his palette seemed to have gone the body sweat and the coal dust of New York, and out of that veil emerged the powder-white bellies of his nightclub dancers, the letters of street signs, and the faces of his blonde dolls and unshaven bums.

In the medium of photography and with the support of the New York City Federal Art Project, Berenice Abbott made her extraordinary portrait of the New York boroughs for the Museum of the City of New York. Many of her prints were reproduced in *Changing New York* in 1939 with the incisive commentaries of Elizabeth McCausland. Here was the lumpy statue of De Peyster at Bowling Green, which Miss Abbott opposed to the clean dark shadows of skyscrapers, and the stacked Napoleonic masonry of the old Post Office against the Gothic filigree of the Woolworth Tower. The icy dignity of the eighties was in her houses at Fifth Avenue and Eighth Street; in *Warehouse* she made superb use of the line of paint which separated a brick wall into two bands, and the pattern of half-opened shutters throwing knifelike shadows along its front as counterpoint to the huge painted coffee advertisement.

"These States are the amplest poem," Whitman once wrote, and their amplitude inspired the mural artists in the New Deal years, who now possessed hundreds of walls where there had been only a few before. Here and there the decorous platitudes of Puvis de Chavannes and Blashfield found their imitators: Harry Louis Freund designed lunettes at Clinton, Missouri, where the nymphs of Puvis had become farmers and his classic hedges were transformed into stands of grain. But beyond these evasions in time were the great Renaissance solutions which had recently inspired the Mexicans— the solidities of Giotto, the stately grace of Ghirlandaio, the poised bodies of Piero della Francesca in their defined spaces, the controlled tumult of Michelangelo's hurtling bodies.

The American could not learn in a day what these masters knew of size and monumentality, of volume and weight on the large vertical painting plane. Much of his work was done in the studio for buildings long since completed, not on the scaffold as the structure itself took shape, reminding him constantly of its color, scale, and proportions, modifying his scheme, and suggesting bolder interpretations. Under these circumstances it was inevitable that America's mural renaissance should have a "middle layer of mediocrity," as E. M. Benson conceded, with too great a reliance on illustrative excitements.

One could date the new murals from 1930, when Benton summarized native activities at the New School for Social Research in New York, and Boardman Robinson produced ten panels on the history of commerce for the Kaufmann Department Store in Pittsburgh. The unity of Benton's walls was a unity of feverish action and intense color, nervous linear contours and harsh oppositions of scale. Their loose separate energies were held in equilibrium by means of moldings which half separated one episode from another, a device which resembled the make-up of a page in the *Police Gazette*. Robinson's forceful tones were achieved with automobile paint; his Carthaginians, Venetians, and Dutchmen, his Englishmen in China, and his American slave traders and clipper ships were modeled in semiabstract planes and edges, their monumentality purchased at some cost of the flow and freedom of his first drawings. The Kaufmann murals had a certain rigidity and crampedness but testified to Robinson's search for first principles and his rejection of the pretty posture and the tactfully empty space.

A few years later the Mexican example bore fruit in murals of genuine monumentality, many of them executed in true fresco. Among the best of these were Edgar Britton's series in the Lane Technical High School of Chicago, the harvesters of Karl Kelpe in the Hawthorne School at Oak Park, Illinois. William C. Palmer narrated *The Development of Medicine* on the walls of Queens County General Hospital with the explicitness of Rivera at Detroit; and Charles Alston's panels on primitive and modern medicine in the cramped lobby of the Harlem Hospital were solidly painted in clean quiet tones. In the Evander Childs High School, New York, James Michael Newell's five episodes, *Evolution of Western Civilization,* owed much to Rivera.

It was the Missouri River which suggested to Mitchell Siporin and Edward Millman the panoramic design of their mural for the St. Louis Post Office, nearly three thousand feet of wall space which required three years for its completion. The green banks and the blue river connected a series of group episodes painted in terse forms and earthy colors: Indians, French fur traders, Dred Scott, Thomas Hart Benton, Carl Schurz, and Mark Twain. In Washington George Biddle used the skeletonized architecture and the cross-sectioned walls of Giotto to describe the lives of tenement people for the Department of Justice. At New London, Connecticut, Thomas La Farge solved a difficult problem by adapting whaling episodes to spaces which were long and narrow.

Too often a horror of the conventional vacuum caused artists to compress their volumes into hot and overcrowded designs, as Umberto Romano did in the post office at Springfield, Massachusetts; at the opposite extreme a baroque looseness weakened Palmer's episodes of western travelers slaughtered by Indians and highwaymen, and Joe Jones's vigorous *Threshing* for the Charleston, Missouri, Post Office seemed indifferent to its surroundings. There was more coherence and monumental force in Curry's Topeka mural of John Brown, with the free-soilers and the proslavery men facing each other beside him, the westward moving pioneers in a more distant plane, the far tornado and forest fire, and below Brown's feet on the "dark and bloody ground" the bodies of the northern and the southern soldier. One could only regret the indecisive modeling and the smothered color of *The Tragic Prelude,* whose realization called for the fierce clarity of Orozco.

Philip Evergood was among those who knew that a mural was not an enlarged picture and that it need not state its case with cold formality. *The Story of Richmond Hill* had a triple theme: the benefactor who planned this garden community, the country pleasures of Richmond Hill, and the harsh city life from which it offered a release. On the right side were the rigid horizontals and verticals of steel and cement, the confined spaces of life in the shadow of the Elevated; on the left, the free relaxed motion of men and women under the open sky; mediating between these and resolving their antithesis, the founders of the community. Two doors—a dingy broken one on the right and a clean white one on the left — were familiar objects which became fresh symbols. There was antithesis of color too: the Richmond Hillers danced among vigorous greens, clean blues, yellows, and bright vermilions; in the city streets men went quietly to work among dark blues, metallic grays, and somber browns. Evergood's wall orchestrated work and play, a young gaiety and a tired maturity, a dream and a reality.

Less explicit in content but often sturdier in design were murals which preferred semiabstract to descriptive forms, and symbol to narrative. The *Electrical Research* of Henry Billings was composed of retorts and test tubes, and Eric Mose arbitrarily assembled parts of automobiles, airplanes, and locomotives for his decoration at the Samuel Gompers High School in New York. At the Newark Airport, Arshile Gorky proved that his abstract shapes and ingenious rhythms could be as entertaining on a large as on a small scale. One of the finest achievements of the period was Philip Guston's group *Maintaining America's Skills,* with its interlocking themes and the clean smoothness of its painted forms seen in silhouette against the concave entrance wall of the WPA Building at the New York World's Fair.

The painter of these years could sing the raucous present or he could remind his fellow citizens of a past which soon would disappear, discovering new subjects on Main Streets where the history of the country's architecture could still be read. The bristling mansards of Edward Hopper became an American staple with their malapropisms exposed to the glare of hot sunlight. His *Adams's House* at Gloucester was the ubiquitous clapboarded white box behind its picket fence, a bracketed cornice over its front door, a hydrant on the sidewalk, and a tipsy telephone pole with sagging wires behind which lay the town. In *The City* he contrasted a monotonous brick block with a mansarded survivor of the 1870's.

Hopper could provide moments of amused nostalgia but not always establish more permanent integrations; Burchfield struck a deeper note. On a page of *Hello, Towns!* Sherwood Anderson wrote that houses had faces which smiled or frowned; there were proud ones with a keep-off-the-grass expression and darkly secretive ones where one heard no laughter and no singing. Burchfield and Anderson were natives of the same part of northern Ohio; the former knew the decayed verandas of "Winesburg," the shambling unpainted farmhouses on side roads off Trunion Pike, and the monstrous brick mansions of the bankers on Buckeye Street. His *House by a Railroad* was as swiftly brushed in water color as Hopper's Gloucester scene and had the same elements—house front, sidewalk, and pole—yet managed to convey more connotations of bleakness, of autumn rain and wind. With a rank garden, rotting boards, and sagging branches, Burchfield painted the end of life for old people in rocking chairs under ragged pines; he conveyed the warmth of Indian summer, the soggy bleakness of a mining town whose houses descended a long, slush-bordered street. Once he had pictured houses which were the monsters of a child's imagining, and something of that empathy persisted in the naturalism of his mature years.

Comparing these painted records of American survivals with those of Walker Evans, the photographer, one asks whether the camera did not more insistently remind one of past ugliness and its human overtones. Evans recorded an ungainly soldiers' monument, hard white against a spider web of wires; the gingerbread squalor of a Birmingham boardinghouse; a Louisiana plantation rotting in the sun behind an uprooted tree; the same lumbering cast-iron façades which Hopper painted in *Williamsburg Bridge* and Burchfield in *Promenade* but with every least ugliness exposed by sharp light; the same Alabama country store one found in Benton but more dismally weathered by rain, more relentlessly baked by the sun.

Relics of another sort were meanwhile being studied by hundreds of artists in thirty-one states and preserved in the form of amazingly accurate drawings and water colors for the Index of American Design. Here in something like twenty thousand plates was proof that thousands of nameless Yankees had wrought superbly in wood and iron, silver and wool: the gaudy crispness of carved circus wagons and cigar-store Indians, the reticence of samplers, the slim perfection of Shaker cupboards, the prancing silhouette of the farmer's weather vane, and the florid tulips of the Pennsylvania potter.

The Index reminded Americans of a people's art in the past but also fostered their interest in contemporary work which preserved that tradition. A hod carrier named Mike O'Brien won a first prize at Denver in 1935 for a landscape painted on the remnants of a cardboard box, and Richmond gave the first show a Virginia Negro had ever received to Leslie Bolling, who carved small genre pieces in wood. Max Schallinger of Baltimore assembled his odd wooden figures in groups with ingenious mechanisms to make them gesture, pivot, and play harps; the same carved creatures navigated a delightful vessel which he contrived from the fragments of a real ship discovered on a beach.

When the Negro Horace Pippin was "discovered" in 1937, one compared the naïve fervor of his Biblical scenes with that of Edward Hicks, and praised the incredibly rich pattern, the monumentality of design in his flower pieces and interiors. But "primitive" was an inadequate word for this veteran of the first World War who worked all day and far into the night on a canvas, his injured right hand gripped by his left to steady the meticulous brush. There was a grave eloquence in his three tributes to John Brown which no other version of that much-painted subject could equal, and a searing intensity which was the projection of a sure intelligence and a noble depth of feeling.

In 1939 the Museum of Modern Art showed sixteen self-taught painters whom Sidney Janis had collected. Among them was Morris Hirshfield, whose shapes resembled the cut patterns of the coat factory where he worked, and who used a comb to paint a lion's mane. One saw Patrick J. Sullivan devising strange imagery to make people think: in *Man's Procrastinating Pastime* a forest stood for the unconscious mind, and its fallen trees and branches meant major and minor sins. A cabinetmaker named Bernard Freuchtben who had lost his business in the depression and whose wife had left him gave poignant form to his misfortune in *Lonely Man on a Lonely Road.*

Ten years after the crash of 1929 could one doubt that in painting, sculpture, and the graphic arts, as in the TVA, the country had reclaimed and put to work her vast creative resources? In the Palace of Fine Arts at San Francisco were four hundred works gathered from every region; at the New York Fair Holger Cahill directed the exhibition of more than a thousand entries, *American Art Today.* With all this evidence before him the citizen could attempt to answer Edward Alden Jewell's question, "Have We an American Art?" The labels on the frames in these exhibitions reminded one from how many foreign lands the artists or their parents had come and how many young talents like that of the Negro Jacob Lawrence had found instruction and encouragement during this decade; they proved that the history of native art could not be written in terms of the eastern seaboard. If any common denominator emerged it was a fresh consciousness of the American environment and a greater emphasis on factual content than on form.

The extreme nationalist argued that we had an art whose character distinguished it from that of other peoples, and he often spent more words in advertising this product than in improving its quality. Jewell's question could be more profitably answered if phrased in a different way: "To what degree had the experience of a people found forms to express its deeper meanings?" Was it enough that the "stubborn provincial" had exchanged the brandy fumes of Montparnasse for the smell of western earth and manure if he could penetrate no deeper into native soil? Was his provincialism as healthy in the modern world as that of fifteenth-century Florence? Artists like Benton had made what Craven called a "swift and fearless plunge into life," but had they not landed in rather shallow water? Could John Curry give the grandeur to his *John Brown* which Michelangelo gave to his *Moses,* in a community which celebrated Brown as a hero but half feared him as a demagogue and a radical?

For that matter, were the faces of patient travelers waiting for buses in American cities essentially different from those of Romans and Parisians? Was not Curry's "struggle of man against nature" much the same wherever there were farmers, and the Irving Place "Burlecue" of Marsh very much like the Folies-Bergère? The artists of the American scene had discovered one truth: that healthy art springs from its own soil and is nourished by its own climate. There was another truth: that the deeper art penetrates, the closer it comes not to what makes peoples different but to what they have in common. There was an obvious antithesis of South and North in America, of city and country, of farm and tenement, of wide and congested spaces, of naïveté and sophistication. Men who concentrated upon these often ignored the deeper contrasts and conflicts in the nation's life. To deal with these latter was the task of the so-called "social conscience" artists.

Writing Exercises in Descriptive Prose: The Arts

Albert P. Ryder is considered an eccentric and a romantic painter; Jasper Johns, a pop art painter of the new mainstream. Referring to the reproductions of the Ryder and Johns paintings (see pp. 355 and 378), examine the artists' subject matter, composition (or placement of the forms and shapes in relation to one another and the ground upon which they are painted), use of light and shadow, and visible brushstrokes. Read the discussion of the technical vocabulary of art criticism below, observe the two reproductions carefully, recall the critical material included in the monograph on Jasper Johns, and then write a descriptive essay of at least four paragraphs, following this outline:

PARAGRAPH 1

Describe form, light, composition, and conception (or central theme) in the Ryder painting.

PARAGRAPH 2

Describe form, light, composition, and conception in the Johns painting.[1]

PARAGRAPH 3

Compare the two different paintings with special attention to each artist's treatment of his subject matter.

PARAGRAPH 4

Explain what type of comment upon the world you feel each of the two artists was interested in making when he used the techniques and emphasized the subject matter you have observed in each of the paintings. (This paragraph will contain your conclusions.)

THE VOCABULARY OF ART CRITICISM

Each art and discipline has a specialized vocabulary which reflects the primary con-

1. Although the monograph on Johns dealt with his graphic works, the discussion of subject matter, themes, composition, and choice of forms is equally applicable to "Target with Four Faces."

cerns of its practitioners and students. The subsequent questions and comments will aid you in making acute observations of the paintings and in using the vocabulary peculiar to art and art criticism.

Is the painting *massive* (composed of masses or blocks of shapes) or *linear* (formed principally by the use of lines or outlines)? Is the painting marked by a *sharp contrast* of light and shadow, a *slight contrast* of light and shadow, or *no contrast* of light and shadow? Is the painting *curvilinear* (composed principally of curves), *angular* (composed of angles), or *rectilinear* (composed principally of straight lines)? What is the *focal point* of the painting (the point on which the painter forces the eye of the observer to focus)?

When you are writing this exercise keep in mind the fact that a painting is a projection of three dimensional objects onto a flat surface, so it is never the objects or scene represented; it is a planar portrayal of the objects or the scene. It is, in other words, a painting. Remember, when you criticize or analyze a painting, the story about the painter Henri Matisse. Showing a portrait of a woman to a female client, Matisse inquired how she liked the picture. The woman replied that the painting seemed all wrong because, she said, "That woman's arm is too long." "Madam," the painter replied, "that is not a woman, that is a painting."

Discussion-Instruction: Fiction

The symbolism of the group and the individual in literature and history are examined in this section. Each of the selections you have just read has been chosen for its merit as a literary illustration of individualism or collectivism. Since the passages are literary, we may assume that the author must use specifically literary techniques to convey and clarify his attitudes toward the individual and the mass. Hence, one of the best ways to understand individualism and collectivism as they appear in prose fiction is to examine the literary tools available to the author. Such elements as figures of speech, choices or the details of character and setting, and selective individual vocabulary not only mark the individual author but also indicate the period in which he writes and the ideas he espouses.

EXERCISE 1

An important element in figurative language is the *symbol*. Below is a group of symbols which appear in the material you have just read. Beside each symbol is an explanation of its meaning or meanings (what it represents in the story). Basing your answer upon the symbols and their explanations, select one or more definitions from the list which follows. Indicate your choice(s) by writing the appropriate number or numbers after the statement "A symbol is."

Knights and Squires = Epic master-servant relationship
The Pink Pearl   = Pansy's brain, her interior world
The Furnace   = The purifying force, Hell
The Caravan of Cars = The new technology of democracy on the move, western expansion

A symbol is:

1. a concrete image or expression which is used to express an abstract concept.

2. a word which always has more than one meaning.

3. a difficult or deliberately obscure reference.

4. a specific mark, token, or sign of a feeling, a state of being, or an idea.

Answers: 1; 4

EXERCISE 2

The symbols in these works are often related to the isolation or group association of the individual. In the chapter from *The Grapes of Wrath*, for example, the car represents one family and the caravan represents the whole society of migrant families. If, in the diagram below, the large circle represents the mass and the small circle represents the individual, choose the explanation which best suits each diagram by matching the letter of the diagram with the definition which explains the diagram. *Example:*

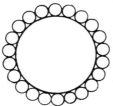

1. The massive identity of society is eclipsed by the separate identities of the numerous individuals who compose it.

2. Society is composed of numerous individuals.

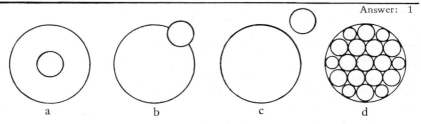

Answer: 1

a   b   c   d

1. The individual is central to and representative of his society so that he and his society are identical.

2. Society is an aggregate of individuals, a whole within which individuals preserve their separate identities.

3. The individual is totally outside of his milieu; he is isolated from the mass.

4. The individual partakes of and depends upon some of the qualities of his society but he lives just on the fringe of that society.

Answers: 1–a;   2–d;   3–c;   4–b

EXERCISE 3

Which of the social relationships of the following characters is best represented by which of the diagrams?

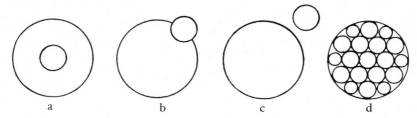

a   b   c   d

1. Starbuck and Queequeg

2. Pansy

3. The Joads

4. Ethan Brand

Answers: 1–d; 2–b; 3–a; 4–c

EXERCISE 4

Which of the diagrams best epitomizes each of the explanations below?

1. The collectivist view is that which sees society as the principal actor and force. The needs and desires and even the character of the individual are secondary and subjugated to those of the group either for the good of the group or for the good of the individuals.

2. The individualist view sees the group or society as a backdrop for and nourisher of the drives and needs of the exceptional man who may, in the course of working out a special destiny, find that he must live in isolation from his fellowman.

Answers: 1–a, d; 2–b, c

EXERCISE 5

In the passages below, symbols of individualism and collectivism are underlined. Match each symbol with the definition in the previous exercise which best defines it.

1. Pansy Vanneman, injured in an automobile accident, often woke up before dawn when *the night noises of the hospital* still came, in hushed hurry, through her half-open door.

2. A great elderly dog . . . began to run after his tail. . . . Faster and faster, round about went the cur; and faster and faster *fled the unapproachable brevity of his tail.*

3. The loss of home became *one loss,* and the golden time in the West was one dream.

4. Man may seem detestable as *joint stock-companies* and nations; but *man, in the ideal,* is so noble and sparkling, such a grand and glowing creature, that over any ignominious blemish in them *all men should run to throw their costliest robes.*

Answers: 1–1; 2–2; 3–1; 4–1, 2

EXERCISE 6

For the creation and reinforcement of themes, authors use various literary techniques available to them. They may, for example, use external details, such as the occupation of the character or the setting to clarify the philosophical position. You will note that the Joads were *migrant laborers* (a), the knights and squires *partners in a whaling vessel* (b), Pansy a *helpless patient* (c), and Ethan Brand a *lime burner* (d).

Below are statements which may characterize these occupations. Write the letter of the occupation beside the statement which best describes its qualities:

1. Bound by old codes, proud of their skills, highly individual yet extremely dependent upon their fellow workers for the opportunity to exercise their individual skills.

2. They are merely custodians of the natural forces. They live upon the natural environment and the product of their trade is the result of the destruction of this environment.

3. One of a great mass of people who consume the products of a culture. Only a few ever become either sufficiently independent or sufficiently alienated to reject the culture which surrounds them and seek further for new ideas.

4. An army of people seemingly undifferentiated by skill or occupation or even place of birth, they depend upon each other and upon massive social needs.

Answers: 1–b; 2–d; 3–c; 4–a

EXERCISE 7

Below are the settings of the stories. Match each with the list of characteristics which best describe it.

1. The ship

2. The hospital

3. The dusty highway

4. The mountainside lime kiln

a. Anonymous, undifferentiated, seemingly without end or beginning. People are swallowed up by it.

b. An entity, distinguished from its milieu by its unnaturalness, it functions to separate parts from the whole.

c. A structure designed to separate a group of people into individual units.

d. A whole composed of many highly specialized parts, each constructed to work with each other.

Answers: 1–c; 2–d; 3–b; 4–a

EXERCISE 8

Consider the relation between the character the author portrays and the setting in which he depicts this character. Below is a quality necessary to each occupation. Match it with the setting in which it would best flourish (and does in the stories).

1. Exploration of new states of existence

2. Overabsorption in mordid thoughts

3. Cooperation for common safety

4. Movement means loss of occupation and sense of self

a. Lonely mountainside

b. Shipboard

c. Hospital

d. Dusty highway

Answers: 1–a; 2–c; 3–b; 4–d

EXERCISE 9

As you can see from the preceding exercises, the authors not only use various literary techniques such as symbolism and the choice of discriminating details as emblems of individualism and collectivism, they also describe subtle variations in the types of individualism and collectivism with which they are concerned. We can become more aware of these differences and of the author's concerns by closely examining the language which each author uses. Consider each of the italicized words below. Which are individualist and which collective?

The sin of an *intellect* that triumphed over the sense of *brotherhood* with man.

It was always pink and always *fragile*, always deeply *interior* and invaluable.

A sick child threw despair into the *hearts of twenty families*.

I call such not acknowledging the *common continent of men,* but each *Isolato* living on a *separate continent* of his own. Yet now, *federated* along *one keel,* what a *set* these *Isolatoes* were.

Answers:	
Collective	*Individual*
Brotherhood	Intellect
Hearts of twenty families	Fragile
	Interior
Common continent of men	A sick child
	Isolato
Federated	Separate continent
One keel	
Set	Isolatoes

EXERCISE 10

Think about the negative or positive attributes of each individual and each collective term. Now let us examine some of the words in greater detail. Answer each question with the context of the word in mind. The questions are based on the quotations in Exercise 9.

1. Is brotherhood negative or positive in the first statement? How then does Hawthorne see intellect?

2. Is interior[ity] a desirable quality in the second sentence? If it is desirable, how is Stafford's individual to relate to mankind in the aggregate?

3. Is the phrase "a sick child" suggestive of sad isolation or comforting association? If it is suggestive of "sad isolation," what are the social and familial relations between a sick child and twenty families?

4. Does Melville imply more approval of "the common continent of men" or of the "separate continent" of isolatoes? If each man is an isolato, what part or role can he play in the common continent of men?

EXERCISE 11

Authors are not merely eternal men of literature; they are historical figures who live in time as do their characters. Often, as in these selections, the authors show the influence of political, philosophical, or religious ideas current during their lives. Below are four statements from the period of each author. Match the statement with the work in the fiction section which seems to embody the ideas expressed in the statement.

1. "To come in touch with the inner workings" of one's being, to achieve non-intellectual enlightenment—what Zen Buddhists call Satori, "is to be in a state of pure consciousness."

   "One Hand Clapping," Gwynn and Blotner

2. "One government can collect and avail itself of the talents and experience of the ablest men, in whatever part of the union they may be found. It can move on uniform principles of policy. It can harmonize, assimilate, and protect the several parts and members and extend the benefit of its foresight and precautions to each. In the formation of treaties it will regard the interest of the whole, and the particular interests of the parts as connected with that of the whole."

   The Fourth Federalist Paper, John Jay

3. "I see one-third of a nation ill-housed, ill-clad, ill-nourished. It is not in despair that I paint for you this picture. I paint it for you in hope, because the nation, seeing and understanding the injustice of it, proposes to paint it out. We are determined to make every American citizen the subject of his country's interest and concern, and we will never regard any faithful, law-abiding group within our borders as superfluous."

   The Fireside Chats, Franklin Delano Roosevelt

4. "The universe is the externalization of the soul. Since everything in nature answers to a moral power, if any phenomenon remains brute and dark it is because the corresponding faculty in the observer is not yet active."

   "The Poet," Ralph Waldo Emerson

Answers: 1⁻ "The Interior Castle";

2⁻ *Moby Dick;*

3⁻ *The Grapes of Wrath;*

4⁻ "Ethan Brand"

EXERCISE 12

The statements in Exercise 11 reflect political, social, religious, and philosophical ideas which influenced the authors of the selections you have read. The first is a statement about the mystical search for psychic self-awareness through a union with the forces of the universe. Zen is now popular as a religious philosophy in this country.

The second statement is from the Federalist papers. This is John Jay's discussion of democratic federalism, an eighteenth-century government philosophy which dealt with the relation of the parts of the nation to the nation as a whole and with individual political rights and their relation to general social and national concerns.

The third statement is from Franklin Roosevelt's Fireside Speeches. Under Roosevelt's administration a new social awareness was manifested in governmental policies like the New Deal, which proposed remedies for the socioeconomic problems of the masses of individual Americans suffering from poverty and unemployment.

The fourth statement is from Emerson's "The Poet." Although it was written in the nineteenth century, it partakes of the Puritan philosophical position that human beings and the universe are both manifestations of the spiritual forces or of the soul. According to this concept of the universe every physical and external form is but a token or symbol of the spiritual and internal divine force.

Basing your answers on this information, match the characters below with the adjectives which best describe the nature of their individualism or collectivism:

1. Knights and squires
2. Pansy
3. Ethan Brand
4. Tom Joad

a. Mystical and psychic
b. Economic and social
c. Structural and social
d. Moral and Religious

Answers: 1–c; 2–a; 3–d; 4–b

EXERCISE 13

Now consider and discuss the reasons why each type of individualism and collectivism portrayed in the literary selections is appropriate to its period and try to answer the following questions:

1. Are the contemporary selections more or less concerned with the subjugation of the individual to the social or religious one-ness?

2. Is Pansy or Ethan Brand more of a lonely eccentric?

3. What do your answers to Exercise 12 tell you about the nature of twentieth-century American individualism?

4. What do they tell you about collectivism in the twentieth century?

The Research Paper: Suggested Topics

The final exercise in this collection is the research paper. Since all research begins with a question and ends—hopefully—with an answer, the underlying inquiry in the topics suggested here ought to reflect the individual or collective philosophy intrinsic to each investigation. It has been apparent throughout this study that the general focus has been upon the social and cultural aspects of the individual and the collective in American life throughout the cycles of its history. The fictionalized portrayal of the solitary person in confrontation with societal forces has been demonstrated along with the highly personal approach to depiction in art. In certain areas of experience, as in ethnic activism, the trend is increasingly collective in our time, whereas in religion the inner life is still very much the province of the individual despite the increasing frequency of participatory services such as folk masses. In consideration of these trends we present a number of final suggestions for a research paper, culminating in a last exercise which brings together for the student's consideration two of the units in this anthology. Our purpose is to demonstrate the interdependence of various expressions of American life, its literature growing out of powerful philosophical stimuli, its art an organic outgrowth of its economic and religious substructures. We offer a number of examples of this linkage; enterprising students may construct their own.

SAMPLE TOPICS FOR RESEARCH

1. The Impact of the New Left on American Political Life

Suggested Readings

Herbert Marcuse, *Reason and Revolution*
Kenneth Keniston, *Young Radicals*
Steven Kelman, *Push Comes to Shove*
Norman Mailer, *The White Negro*
Abby Hoffman, *Revolution for the Hell of It*
Edgar Friedenberg, *The Dignity of the Young and Other Atavisms*
Jerry Rubin, *Do It!*

2. The New Marriage Between Eastern Mysticism and Christianity in American Religion

Suggested Readings

Alan Watts, *The Way of Zen*
Alan Watts, *Psychotherapy East and West*
Jack Kerouac, *Satori in Paris*
J. D. Salinger, *Franny and Zooey*

3. The Relation of Individual Revelation to the Congregational Movement in America

Suggested Readings

Thomas Hooker, "The Preparing of the Heart to Receive Christ."
A Confession of Faith from the Boston Synod (1679–1680)
A Platform of Church Discipline from the Cambridge Synod (1646)
John Woolman, *Journals* (1755–1758)
C. B., "Visit to the Shakers," *American Life in the 1840's*, edited by Carl Bode
The Autobiography of Peter Cartwright, edited by W. P. Strickland

4. The Disaffected Young and the Growth of the Communal Movement

Suggested Readings

Theodore Roszak, *The Making of a Counter Culture*
John W. Aldridge, *In the Country of the Young*
Arthur Morgan, *The Small Community*
Clare Huchet Bishop, *All Things Common*
Martin Buber, *Paths in Utopia*
Aldous Huxley, *Island*

5. Two Visions of America: Walt Whitman's *Song of Myself* and Jean-Claude Van
    Itallie's *America Hurrah!*

Suggested Readings

The entire Whitman poem and the text of the play will serve as the primary reading
sources. Additional insights may be gained from the readings below.

Supplements to the Nineteenth-century Whitman Vision

Carl Sandburg, *The People, Yes*
Ralph Waldo Emerson, *Self-Reliance, The Oversoul*

St. Jean de Crèvecoeur, *Letters from an American Farmer*
Alexis de Tocqueville, *Democracy in America*

Supplements to the Twentieth-century Van Itallie Vision

Edward Albee, *The American Dream*
Eugene O'Neill, *The Hairy Ape*
Norman Mailer, *An American Dream*
LeRoi Jones, *Dutchman*